HERITAGE OF MUSIC

VOLUME III
THE NINETEENTH-
CENTURY LEGACY

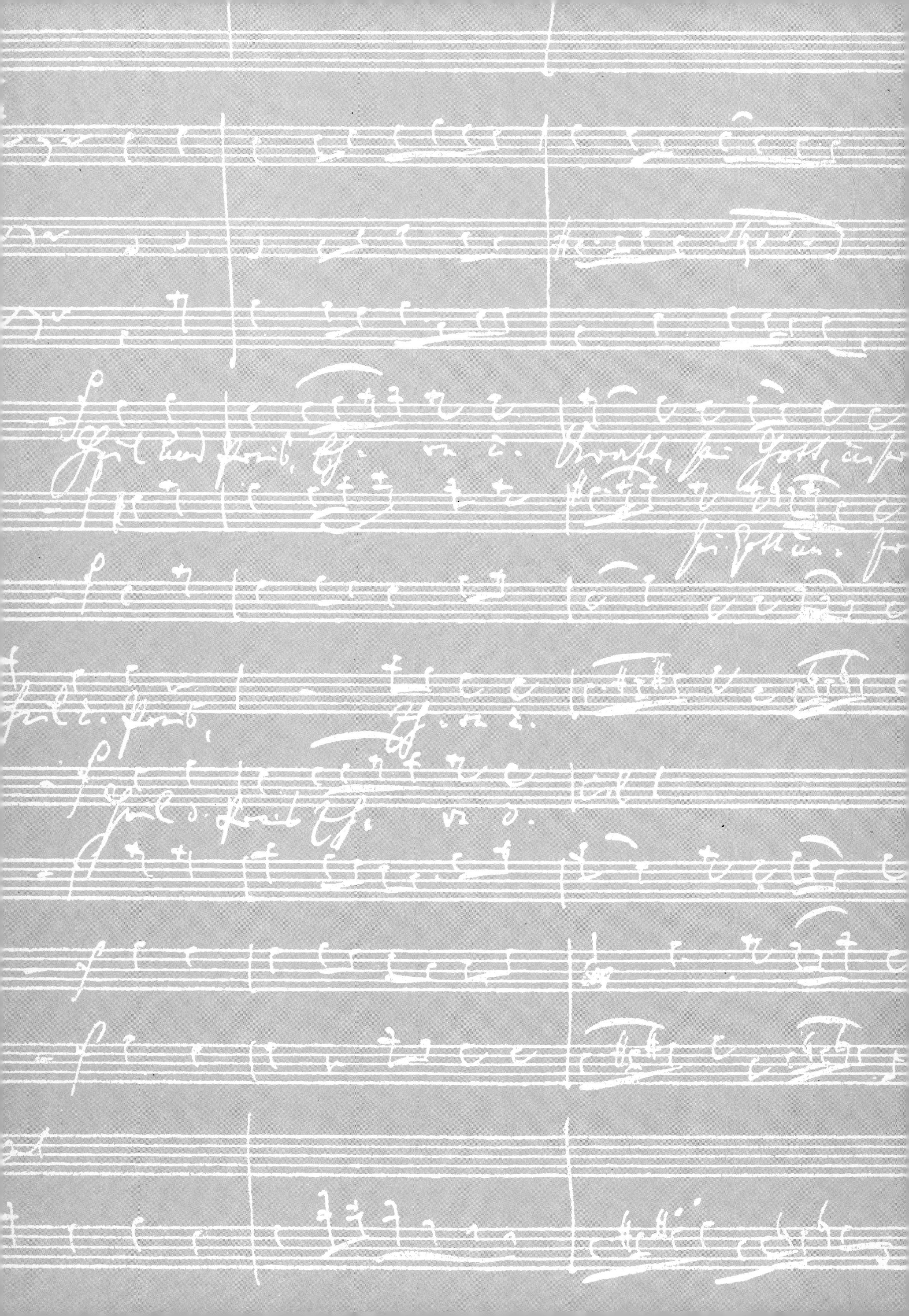

HERITAGE OF MUSIC

EDITED BY
MICHAEL RAEBURN AND ALAN KENDALL

VOLUME III
THE NINETEENTH-CENTURY LEGACY

CONSULTANT EDITORS
MARTIN COOPER AND HEINZ BECKER

OXFORD · NEW YORK
OXFORD UNIVERSITY PRESS
1989

Oxford University Press, Walton Street, Oxford OX2 6DP

Oxford   New York   Toronto
Delhi   Bombay   Calcutta   Madras   Karachi
Petaling Jaya   Singapore   Hong Kong   Tokyo
Nairobi   Dar es Salaam   Cape Town
Melbourne   Auckland

and associated companies in
Berlin   Ibadan

Oxford is a trade mark of Oxford University Press

Published in the United States
by Oxford University Press

British Library Cataloguing in Publication Data
Heritage of music.
   1. Music—History and criticism   I. Raeburn, Michael,
1940-   .II. Kendall, Alan, 1939-
   780'.903   ML193
ISBN 0–19–520493–X (set)
      0–19–505372–9 (vol.3)

Library of Congress Cataloguing in Publication Data
Main entry under title:
Heritage of music.
   Includes index.
   Contents: 1. Classical music and its origins —
2. Romantic music — 3. Legacy of nineteenth-century
music — [etc.]
   1. Music—History and criticism.   I. Raeburn, Michael,
1940-   . II. Kendall, Alan, 1939-
ML160.H527   1988   780'.9   85-21429
ISBN 0–19–520493–X (set)
      0–19–505372–9 (vol.3)

Produced by Heritage of Music Ltd
Design and art direction: David Warner
Picture research: Julia Engelhardt, Charlotte Mosley,
Robert Turnbull
Translation from German: Alexander Lieven
Color origination: Scala, Florence

Printed in Hong Kong

CONTENTS

NATIONAL STYLES IN THE NINETEENTH CENTURY: FRANCE AND RUSSIA

MARTIN COOPER

Opposite: Musicians in the Orchestra, painted in 1868 by Edgar Degas.

At the turning point of the nineteenth century, in 1850, Germany was unquestionably the leading musical country of Europe, Italy still maintaining its operatic primacy but otherwise negligible. The German scene itself was dominated during the 1860s and 1870s by the figures of Wagner and Brahms, whose musical divergences of taste and opinion were dramatized by their over-zealous disciples as a kind of war in which music-lovers felt bound to support one or other of the two parties. Yet behind the figure of Wagner himself, the conscious champion of the 'new,' were two others from whom he had learned much – the Frenchman Berlioz and the cosmopolitan Liszt, born a citizen of the old Austro-Hungarian Empire in what is now Hungary, but German-speaking and primarily German in both education and culture.

At the age of twelve Liszt went to Paris, as an infant prodigy, and during the next two decades developed a new French personality; and this in its turn was further extended and modified by long periods spent in Switzerland and Italy and by the recital tours which took him all over Europe and to Russia. Although his close concern with Hungarian culture came comparatively late (his knowledge of the language was never more than rudimentary), Liszt's instinctive understanding of Latin culture, his sympathetic acquaintance with the Slavonic world and his loose, marginal adherence to the German musical tradition gave him a uniquely cosmopolitan musical character. It was to him, therefore, that young composers often turned in those countries where the desire for liberation from German musical domination took on nationalistic forms. There is hardly one leading figure in any of these nationalist movements who was not deeply indebted to Liszt in one way or another. In some case that debt was purely musical, but in others it was also personal, Liszt not only championing their music but actually performing it, or having it performed at Weimar, where he conducted the Court Theater from 1848 to 1861.

Liszt's own musical innovations appealed to the younger generation of composers. His development of the 'symphonic poem' out of the Viennese classical symphony – a purely musical form until Beethoven's Sixth and Ninth Symphonies – introduced a strong literary element which enabled nationalistically minded composers to link their music to historical characters or events, as Liszt himself had done in his *Mazeppa* and *Hunnenschlacht*. In matters of musical form, too, he suggested new possibilities, developing the idea of 'cyclic' form from a hint in Schubert and his own instinct as an improviser of genius. In his orchestral works of the 1850s he brought into the concert hall the enriched harmonic palette of Wagner's operas and the vastly extended range of orchestral color discovered by Berlioz. Furthermore, the accident of his birth in a border district of Central Europe gave him an instinctive understanding of the varieties of folksong and a sympathy with those composers who wished both to extend their musical vocabulary and to assert the musical individuality of their national tradition by making use of folk music.

A typical instance of Liszt's generous interest is that of the Norwegian Grieg. In 1868, when Grieg was twenty-five, his application for a grant to study and travel abroad was warmly supported by Liszt, on the strength of Grieg's earlier Violin Sonata. Three years later Grieg called on Liszt in Rome to show him his new Piano Concerto, which Liszt played through at sight and praised enthusiastically. If as he grew older Liszt expressed his admiration rather too easily, it was still a valuable encouragement for young composers, neither German nor Austrian by birth, to achieve this link with one of the leading figures of the European musical establishment. At what a disadvantage such men must have felt themselves in their youth is suggested by remarks made by Igor Stravinsky in extreme old age, after his adoption of serial technique. He came, he says, from two 'minor musical cultures – the Russian and the French' and he goes on, as though defending himself: 'I know that I relate only from an angle to the German stem (Bach, Haydn, Mozart, Beethoven, Schubert, Brahms, Wagner, Mahler, Schoenberg) . . . but an angle may be an advantage.'

That Stravinsky, born in 1885, could still at eighty feel the weight of the German tradition as oppressive gives an indication of what must have been felt by the composers who had first dared to break away from that tradition a hundred years earlier. Two facts suggest that there was more than a chance, circumstantial affinity between the two 'minor musical cultures.' On the one hand there is the influence exerted by

Opposite
Top left: Cover to Bizet's own piano and vocal arrangement of his opera *Les Pêcheurs de perles.*

Top right: A wickedly funny cartoon version of the plot of Massenet's opera *Thaïs*, first produced in Paris in 1894.

Bottom: Backstage at the Paris Opéra, 1844. This was the theater in rue Peletier which burned down in 1873.

Above: Engraving of a scene from the first production of Gounod's *Faust* at the Théâtre Lyrique, Paris, in 1859.

Right: Henri Fantin-Latour's lithograph *The Commemoration*, 1875, in which the artist paid homage to Berlioz. Fantin admired Berlioz as the first Romantic and for his inspiration of Wagner: 'without question, Berlioz it was who first discovered the need to combine modern music with drama.'

Russian music on a whole generation of French composers, notably Debussy. On the other there is Stravinsky's own occupation of the leading role among French composers during most of the thirty years of his neo-classical period, from 1923 to 1953.

· France ·

During the two hundred years from 1650 to 1850 French music was dominated for long periods by a succession of foreign composers – Lully, Gluck, Cherubini, Rossini, Meyerbeer. These names alone reveal the disproportionate importance attached to opera during this time and the neglect of symphonic and chamber music in the very years when the Viennese 'classical' composers and their 'Romantic' German followers were creating what is still the greater part of the symphonic and chamber music repertory. It is significant that France's only major composer during the middle years of the nineteenth century, Hector Berlioz, was ill at ease with both symphonic and operatic conventions and most individual in the handling of large choral and orchestral masses. He, however, formed no school and initiated no movement among French composers, who have always regarded his music as in some way alien. It was a very different composer from Berlioz, one who lacked Berlioz's personality but commanded a technical facility that he never possessed, who led the movement away from the exclusive cultivation of opera by French composers.

Camille Saint-Saëns was born in 1835 and lived until 1921. He was a child prodigy gifted with quite exceptional aptitudes and facility, both as a performer and composer. His early symphonies and concertos reveal a close acquaintance with the works of Beethoven, Mozart, Weber and Mendelssohn, but they are already marked by a professional skill unmatched in France since the days of Rameau. He had met Liszt while still a boy and admired Liszt's music as well as his piano-playing, so that it was not surprising that during the 1870s he wrote four symphonic poems in imitation of those written by Liszt twenty years earlier. One of these, *Danse macabre*, has survived in the repertory, as have several of the concertos (five for piano, three for violin and two for cello) which Saint-Saëns wrote between 1870 and 1900. In many of these pieces an easy and skilful handling of classical forms is combined with improbable features (such as the reminiscences of both Bach and Offenbach in the Second Piano Concerto), which suggests a superficial 'personality' rather than a strong musical character in the composer. His penchant for the facile, elegant drawing-room music of the day found expression in a large number of small occasional pieces but sometimes appears also in more ambitious works, such as the slow movement of the Third Violin Concerto. The only one of Saint-Saëns's operas to achieve a major success was *Samson et Dalila*, performed by Liszt at Weimar in 1877; and his correct handling of traditional symphonic forms assured his works of performances elsewhere in Germany, a compliment which was paid to no other French contemporary except Berlioz.

None of Saint-Saëns's dozen other operas had a comparable success, and the important composer in the operatic world was Charles Gounod, almost twenty years Saint-Saëns's senior. It was Gounod who first protested against the cardboard splendors of Meyerbeer's 'grand' operas, which were mostly historical pageants that relied on spectacle and virtuosity for their appeal and contained little or no delineation of character. Gounod's finest operas (*Faust, Mireille,* and *Roméo et Juliette*) were conceived on an altogether less imposing scale and included scenes of intimate personal feeling and pathos, the sincerity of which is not prejudiced by their often naïvely sentimental character. Gounod was also an enthusiastic choral conductor and composer, the founder of the Royal Choral Society during his long stay in London as a refugee from the Franco-Prussian War. When he eventually returned to Paris, he found that he had lost the place which he had previously held in French musical life, and particularly in the operatic world. Already

123. PARIS — Place du Théâtre Français et Avenue de l'Opéra. C. L. C.

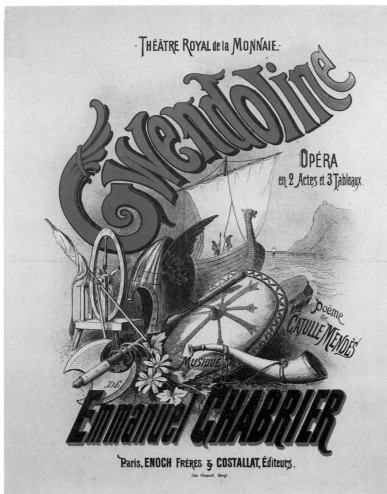

during the 1860s Georges Bizet, his junior by twenty years, had produced two promising operas, *Les Pêcheurs de perles* and *La Jolie Fille de Perth*; and in 1875 these successes were crowned by his *Carmen*, the eventual triumph of which Bizet did not live to see, although it had already reached its thirty-third performance on the night that he died, a few weeks after the première.

What Bizet would have achieved had he lived to be more than thirty-seven it is, of course, impossible to say; but the Symphony in C, written when he was a student, showed purely musical endowments – a sense of structure, style, balance, vitality of ideas and attention to detail – which, though not wasted in the opera house, yet pointed beyond it. Even occasional works, like the theater music for Alphonse Daudet's *L'Arlésienne* and *Jeux d'enfants* for piano duet, display the economy, the clarity of purpose and the imagination of a master. These gifts were all united in *Carmen* with an ability to evoke atmosphere, to sum up a dramatic position in a single number (the quintet in Act II, for instance, or the card scene in Act III) and finally to invent melody with an immediate appeal, almost all that is needed in fact to become a successful, if not necessarily a great, operatic composer. All that Bizet still lacked was a mature personality, self-confidence and the strength of mind to refuse easy solutions. His early death must be reckoned as the greatest loss sustained by French music during the nineteenth century, and while Jules Massenet might take his place, he could never hope to equal him. Massenet's *Manon* is a wholly delightful, well-made opera, whose music perfectly recreates the atmosphere of the Parisian *demi-*

Far left: The Place du Théâtre Français, looking towards the new Paris Opéra, soon after its completion in 1875.

Left: St Geneviève watching over sleeping Paris – one of the paintings Pierre Puvis de Chavannes produced in 1898 for the Panthéon, the French national shrine. Its qualities of classical symbolism and restraint are also conveyed in much French music of the period.

Opposite bottom: Poster for the first production (1886) of *Gwendoline* by Emmanuel Chabrier (1841-94), inspired by his love for Wagnerian music-drama.

Below: Vincent d'Indy (1851-1931) was another devoted French Wagnerian, but gave more time to reviving old music and the folksongs and dances of his native land.

monde of the eighteenth century, diversified with some dark romantic touches and well-calculated scenes of pathos. Less successful, but still musically rewarding within their unpretentious limits, were his *Werther, Thaïs* and *Thérèse*; but these were still in the future.

The war with Prussia, which brought the Second Empire down, and the subsequent experience of the Paris Commune changed the mood of the French people and made them take stock of their values – the 'values' so mercilessly mocked in Offenbach's operettas. Defeat brought a new sense of patriotism, and it was this that prompted the foundation in 1871 of the Société Nationale de Musique with its motto 'Ars Gallica' (French Art). Many of the young composers who were to make their names during the following thirty years enrolled under this banner. Yet the most important group in French music for the next twenty years gathered round the figure of a little-known Franco-Belgian organist, César Franck, whose organ class at the Conservatoire became a center of disaffection with the formal, opera-based teaching to be found in composition classes. The young composers who became his pupils ('la bande à Franck,' as they came to be called), were attracted by the idealism which marked both the man and his music. While Conservatoire students were trained to write the sort of operas the public demanded, Franck's pupils were initiated into the world of the great German classics and these included Wagner, whose name was still a bugbear at the Conservatoire. They were expected to write symphonies and chamber music rather than operas, and their approach was expected to be marked by a high seriousness.

Franck himself, who had started his musical career as an infant prodigy pianist, and then became a church organist, blossomed late as a composer, his creative gift developed by the atmosphere of personal affection and admiration of the pupils who had played an increasing part in his life since before the 1870 war. One of the earliest of these, Henri Duparc, was to become a great song-writer, and another, Vincent d'Indy, was a prolific composer, though best remembered today as a major influence on French musical life through his direction of the Schola Cantorum. This educational institution, founded in 1894, was devoted not only to teaching but also to performing early music, then unknown in France (Palestrina, Monteverdi, the Bach Passions, Marc-Antoine Charpentier), and investigating the folk music of the French provinces.

Franck, who died in 1890, wrote the best of his music during the 1880s – a symphony, a piano concerto (*Variations symphoniques*), a violin sonata, a string quartet, a piano quintet and two grandiose works for the piano, *Prélude, choral et fugue* and *Prélude, aria et final*. The titles of these last works are a reminder that Franck was to his death an organist by profession, and much admired by Liszt in that capacity. In fact the harmonic richness that

marks all his mature music is for the most part based on the chromatically moving bass lines that fall naturally under the feet of an improvising organist. If this feature can sometimes give Franck's works a certain saccharine flavor, the musical invention and constructive power shown particularly in the *Variations symphoniques* and the Violin Sonata, and to a lesser degree in the Symphony, raise Franck head and shoulders above the general run of French composers of the 1880s; and his music

imprinted an indelible character on that of his pupils, including Ernest Chausson and the Belgian Guillaume Lekeu, who died at the age of twenty-four. In the case of Chausson, however, best remembered now for his songs and a single symphony, an even stronger musical personality than that of his teacher threatened his musical independence of mind – namely Richard Wagner.

•The influence of Wagner •

Wagner's influence made itself felt in French literature before it had anything more than a superficial effect on French music. A *Revue Wagnérienne* was founded in 1885 to acquaint the French public with Wagner's literary and philosophical principles, and although it ran for only two years, contributors included Villiers de l'Isle Adam and Stéphane Mallarmé. The third number even included an attack on the composers who were 'content to learn from the music of Wagner without bothering to understand his philosophical and aesthetic theories.' As early as 1879 Wagner had expressed his views on the correct development of music in France; this was in an interview with a French journalist to whom he spoke with admiration of French epic and French folksongs. It was in effect an appeal to musical nationalism, and the only composer who followed Wagner's advice in this matter was Vincent d'Indy, who

Left: Edouard Lalo (1823-92). His opera *Le Roi d'Ys* (1888) owes something to Wagner with its story based on legend and myth. But his best-known work today, the *Symphonie espagnole* (1875) for violin and orchestra, represents the Spanish branch of his own family tree and was first performed by the Spanish violinist Pablo de Sarasate.

Below: The Wagnerian craze in France was reaching its peak when *La Vie Parisienne* published this cartoon in 1887, contrasting 'Wagnériennes' in France and in Germany.

collected the folksongs of his native countryside, the Vivarais, and used them in a number of compositions. Bayreuth, on the other hand, was a place of pilgrimage for almost all the young composers of the day, not only Franck's pupils, including d'Indy, Chausson and Lekeu (who fainted after the *Tristan* prelude), but also other more independent characters. Emmanuel Chabrier, an original musical wit who came to composition comparatively late, developed a double personality – one wholly French, which found expression in his songs, piano pieces and the opera *Le Roi malgré lui*, the other a dedicated Wagnerian, composer of the saga-like *Gwendoline*. Another independent, Edouard Lalo, earned a reputation for being a Wagnerian simply because he made more extended use of the brass, and cultivated a fuller and robuster scheme of orchestral sonorities than had been usual among French composers. His opera *Le Roi d'Ys* satisfied one of Wagner's demands by being based on a Breton legend, but the *Symphonie espagnole* by which he is remembered today owes more to Saint-Saëns than to Wagner.

Although Gabriel Fauré paid the obligatory visit to Bayreuth, the experience left hardly any mark on his music. Educated at an institute for training church musicians, he too began his career as a church organist, and the personal style which he gradually developed always carried the imprint of his early acquaintance with the modes of Gregorian plainchant. Fauré is the most quintessentially French of all the composers who flourished in the second half of the nineteenth century. He cultivated almost exclusively the smaller musical forms – songs, chamber and piano music – and even the Requiem, by which he is best known outside France, is on a modest scale and significantly omits the Dies Irae, with its obligatory thunderings and lightnings. His piano music owes something to both Schumann and Chopin, and his musical personality resembles Chopin's in that both transcended the salon style and infused the conventional nocturne, barcarolle and impromptu of the drawing room with a richness of invention and a harmonic interest which remove their works from the category of salon music.

Fauré's two piano quartets and his First Violin Sonata stand head and shoulders above any French chamber music of the period except Franck's. Among the hundred songs that he wrote during a long life the settings of Verlaine written in the early 1890s stand out as perfectly capturing a poet's mood and as flawless transpositions of this mood into musical terms. Before the appearance of Debussy, Fauré and Duparc had raised the French *mélodie* to a position in which, without challenging the German *Lied*, it was still possible to speak of the two in the same breath and to compare their very different qualities. Fauré's art, which became more austere and even intellectual in the later years when he was all but completely deaf, never changed its fundamental nature. The strong classical element asserted itself

more clearly, but was not in itself new; and the innovatory character of his harmony earned him the disapproval of such conservative composers as Ambroise Thomas (remembered now only for his opera *Mignon*).

It has often been said that Fauré's music, like some local wines, cannot be exported; and it is certainly true that his songs not only resist translation but also demand the French style of singing, which is more text-conscious and often nearer recitation than any other vocal school. If we look for some parallel to his music in the other arts, we might consider the paintings of Chardin and occasionally, in his more exalted 'classical' moments perhaps, Poussin. Fauré possessed the traditional French qualities with which we are generally most familiar in their literature – clarity, poise, moderation, balance and a persistent vein of that 'common' sense which belongs more characteristically to prose-writers than to poets. The twentieth century has seen an apparent revolt against this ideal among French artists and writers as well as composers, and perhaps Fauré, and after him Ravel, were to be among its last representatives. Paul Claudel summed up this uniquely French characteristic when he said that 'the names of the great French poets, the great creators, are not Malherbe or Despreaux, or Voltaire, or even Racine, but Rabelais, Pascal, Bossuet, Saint-Simon, Chateaubriand, Honoré de Balzac, Michelet.'

• Russia •

The only indigenous music in Russia until the late eighteenth century was either ecclesiastical or folk music, much of which was itself rooted in the Church. The Italian opera introduced to the Court in 1731 took firm root and was directed for the next two hundred years by a series of visiting Italian composers, who

Right: Henri Duparc (1848-1933), whose small group of songs or *mélodies*, while influenced by Wagnerian harmony, are among the finest by any French composer. An incurable nervous disease wrecked his life after 1885, though he did not die until 1933.

Below: This anti-Wagnerian pamphlet, published anonymously in 1886, expresses a reaction to the current wave of adulation for Wagner then sweeping through France.

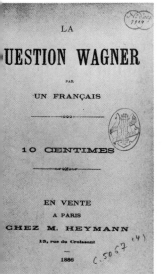

LA
UESTION WAGNER
PAR
UN FRANÇAIS

10 CENTIMES

EN VENTE
A PARIS
CHEZ M. HEYMANN
15, rue du Croissant
1886

included Galuppi, Traetta, Paisiello, Sarti and Cimarosa. Italian-trained composers composed operas on Russian subjects, and Catherine the Great's taste for French *opéra comique* introduced a further foreign element, which was strengthened by the presence of Boïeldieu in Russia between 1803 and 1810. Napoleon's invasion and defeat led to a great strengthening of Russian national consciousness, and this found expression in the operas of Alexei Verstovsky, an amateur pupil of Field and Steibelt. In his most successful opera, *Askold's*

house-serfs and nannies and the rituals of the Orthodox Church. The style of Glinka's operas was basically Italian, but with many French features, some Viennese dance music and a melodic style which combined in a wholly individual way the material of Russian folksong with formal characteristics borrowed from Donizetti and Rossini. Glinka's second opera, *Ruslan and Lyudmila* (1842), was musically richer and even more heterogeneous in character than his first. His *Kamarinskaya*, an orchestral fantasy on two Russian folksongs,

Left: A painting of Glinka (seated, far right) with friends at Ketchanovka, a country estate near St Petersburg, where he worked on *Ruslan and Lyudmila* during the summer of 1838.

Below: Young man with a guitar, an anonymous portrait from the 1830s, but one reflecting Russian interest in Spanish music. Glinka loved Spain, and while he was there even tried to learn flamenco dancing, but he confessed that the castanets defeated him.

Tomb, it was Verstovsky's declared intention 'to put into European form the character of Russian national music.' In fact this shamelessly direct imitation of Weber's *Der Freischütz*, which includes gypsy tunes, polonaises, a Rusalka ballad, unaccompanied male choruses, a witch and a comic coward, formed a kind of operatic bran-tub in which Russian composers were to dip for the next half-century.

Askold's Tomb, however, was soon to be quite overshadowed by the work of another basically amateur composer, Mikhail Glinka, who completed what little musical education he had with some lessons in Berlin on his way home from a long tour of Italian opera houses. Glinka's *A Life for the Tsar* (1838) accurately reflected the superficial cosmopolitanism of Russian polite society, whose members conversed in French, were waited on by English grooms, had their children were brought up by German tutors and French governesses, traveled extensively in Western Europe and were chiefly linked to Russia by sentimental memories of country childhoods and long summer holidays, the stories and songs of peasants,

Above: This painting by Grigory Soroka of N. Milukov's study, executed in 1844, is remarkable for its wholly Russian atmosphere, a quality writers and musicians were also trying to bring to their work.

Left: Poster for a concert of Glinka's music, with the composer at the piano, given in Paris in April 1845, on which occasion he also spent some time with Berlioz. The next month he had moved on to Spain, where he remained for two years.

proved a model for what Russian composers were to regard as one of their chief genres for the next half-century, while his songs initiated a mainly lyrical vein which, for all its affinities with the French *chanson* or Italian *canzona*, continued to inspire Russian composers for the next two generations.

Between the first performance of *Ruslan and Lyudmila* and the appearance of works by the next generation there is a gap of almost thirty years, during which the only Russian composer of interest was Alexander Dargomyzhsky, whose opera *Rusalka* appeared in 1856, a year in which the first Russian musical journal was published. When Wagner visited Russia in 1863, he found that his early music had already been publicized by an enthusiastic admirer who was himself a composer of opera, Alexander Serov, whose *Judith* and *Rogneda* were in fact closer to Meyerbeer than to Wagner.

Historically of far greater importance to the future of music in Russia, Berlioz paid two visits, the first in 1847 and the second in 1867, when he was already mortally ill. Despite this, the impression made by his music on a number

15

Above:
The St Petersburg
Conservatory, founded
by Anton Rubinstein in
1862. Balakirev formed
his own Free School of
Music in the city the
same year. The two men
held opposite views
about the course
Russian music should
follow.

Right: A lithograph
of 1846 by A. A. Agin
showing poster carriers
announcing the
publication of his
illustrations for Nikolai
Gogol's novel *Dead
Souls* (1842). As later
Russian writers revered
Gogol as their father
figure, so later Russian
composers regarded
Glinka.

of music-lovers, still untrained but of extra-ordinary artistic gifts, was enormous. They practiced widely different professions – Modest Musorgsky and César Cui were young officers, Nikolai Rimsky-Korsakov was a naval cadet, Alexander Borodin an extremely promising chemist, and they met at the house of a protégé of Glinka's, Mily Balakirev, a brilliant pianist and a powerful and eccentric personality. The common ideal which united the members of the group was that of a genuinely Russian music, largely independent of the evolution of the art in Western Europe and of the German symphonic ideal, but sympathetic towards the new fusion of music and literature achieved by Liszt in his symphonic poems and in the 'Faust' and 'Dante' Symphonies.

These musical nationalists were fortunate in having a powerful and enthusiastic champion in the critic Vladimir Stasov, and it was he who in 1868 laughingly nicknamed the Balakirev group 'the mighty handful' (*moguchaya kuchka*). During the next twenty-five years they produced between them a whole repertory of operas and symphonic poems, often based on Russian themes and employing Slavonic folk melodies, which effectively crossed the frontier and made a powerful impression in Western Europe.

Not all of the five were equally gifted or equally productive. Cui, half-French and half-Lithuanian by birth, was better known as a critic than a composer. Musorgsky, the most original of the group, was to die aged only forty-two in 1881, and although Balakirev himself lived until 1910, his output was considerably diminished by illness, both mental and physical. Borodin could only spare limited time for composition from a full scientific and educational career; and it was only Rimsky-Korsakov who became a wholly professional full-time musician and whose oeuvre included fourteen operas as well as numerous orchestral works when he died in 1908.

The St Petersburg Nationalists, however, were by no means unopposed in their ideas for the future of Russian music. Politics and social life in Russia during the second half of the nineteenth century were split between two factions – the conservative Slavophils in love with an idealized picture of the Slavonic past and the 'Westernizers', who included the great majority of the intelligentsia and saw Russia's only hope to lie in the assimilation of western ideas and ideals, including industrial development and eventually some parliamentary form of government. There were, of course, many gradations of these opinions, but the division was unmistakable, and it was roughly paralleled by a similar diversity of opinion among members of the musical world. The Nationalist composers of the 'mighty handful' corresponded roughly to the Slavophils and, by an odd contradiction, were centered in the newer northern capital of St Petersburg, while the 'westernizing' musicians were centered in Moscow.

As in all cases of this kind, the hostility between the two parties found its most spectacular expression in the field of education. Russia owes her first serious musical institutions to two brothers, Anton and Nikolai Rubinstein, both born in the 1830s of a German Jewish family. While Anton was a prolific composer and was to become one of the greatest pianists of the century, Nikolai – though also a pianist – was most remarkable for his work as an educator. It was he who, in 1859, founded in Moscow the Russian Musical Society, and five years later the Moscow Conservatory, of which he remained head until his death in 1881, while his brother Anton founded the St Petersburg Conservatory in 1862. The Rubinstein brothers formed the core of the opposition to Balakirev and his group, and it was Nikolai's pupils at the Moscow Conservatory whose western-style musical training enabled them to produce works whose professionalism showed up well against the often eccentric and patchy brilliance of the young Nationalist composers of St Petersburg. By far the most remarkable of these Moscow-trained composers was Peter Tchaikovsky, who was followed in the next generation by three great pianist-composers – Sergei Rachmaninov, Nikolai Medtner and Alexander Skriabin. And it was significant of Tchaikovsky's altogether greater technical scope and wider musical vision that by the time of his death in 1893 the antagonism between Nationalists and Westernizers had lost its old bitterness, and indeed much of its meaning, thanks to Tchaikovsky's own ability to unite the best of both parties' ideals in works which were both unmistakably Russian and yet of international significance.

• St Petersburg •

Before examining Tchaikovsky's music in more detail let us first return to the composers of the 'mighty handful' in St Petersburg. Balakirev's Free School of Music, founded in 1862, provided the platform for a number of his own and his followers' works, as well as promoting the contemporary western composers whom he particularly admired – Liszt, Berlioz and Schumann. During the first five years of the Free School the concerts included three overtures by Balakirev himself, Rimsky-Korsakov's First Symphony and his *Overture on Russian themes*, a choral work by Musorgsky, and works by Dargomyzhsky, Glinka and Cui. The essential Russian character of the Nationalist composers' music was by no means uniform. The study of existing Russian folksong and the incorporation of actual songs, or melodies based on such songs, was the largest single factor, but the idea was expanded to include not only other Slavonic folk music (Czech and Serb, for instance) but also the exotic oriental world which Russian imperialism had explored in the Near and Middle East. So that beside purely Russian-based works such as Rimsky-Korsakov's operas *May Night* and *Christmas Eve* (both founded on Gogol) or *Snowmaiden* are found other compositions, his symphony *Antar*, the symphonic suite *Sheherazade* and such operas as *Sadko* and *The Golden Cockerel*, in all of which oriental motifs play an

Left: Nikolai Rubinstein (1835-81), founder of the Moscow Conservatory in 1864. His most illustrious student was Tchaikovsky, though he deeply upset the composer with his severe criticism of the now famous First Piano Concerto.

Right. Nikolai's brother, Anton. In addition to his work as director of the St Petersburg Conservatory, Anton Rubinstein (1829-94) was himself a celebrated pianist and composer.

Above: A Russian print of 1852, *The Singing Teacher*. The affected pose of the young lady and her teacher and the peasant earthiness of the other two figures make an amusing comment on the extremes of nineteenth-century Russian life and culture.

Below: Alexander Pushkin (1799-1837), painted in 1827 by Orest Kiprinsky. Nearly every Russian composer was inspired by Pushkin's plays, stories and poems.

Songs and Dances of Death, as well as influencing the prosody of his masterpiece, *Boris Godunov*. This opera, based on a Pushkin play, consists essentially of historical vignettes, unforgettably vivid and economical scenes of court and popular life centering round the usurper Tsar Boris and the Russian people locked, as it seems for ever, in the agonies of a love-hate relationship with their rulers. The originality of Musorgsky's music, especially in matters of harmony and instrumentation, is unquestioned; but long before his death his alcoholism was so acute that it is often difficult to be sure of his final intentions. Both he and Borodin left unfinished works and were generously served by Rimsky-Korsakov, too zealous in his 'emendations' of Musorgsky, but providing an interim version of *Boris* acceptable to opera houses in the West and only partially superseded by a return to Musorgsky's own text.

Although the symphony was not so popular with the Nationalists as the symphonic poem, both Balakirev and Borodin wrote successful essays in the older form. In the smaller forms Borodin wrote two string quartets, the second of which is a fascinating example of French elegance crossed with exotic oriental material; and Balakirev composed a large quantity of mostly virtuoso piano music in conventional forms such as nocturne, scherzo, waltz, but also at the end of his life an interesting sonata. These forms, however, with the whole apparatus of traditional academic instruction and composition, were cultivated primarily by the conservatives of the Moscow Conservatory; and after Rubinstein this meant Tchaikovsky.

important part. Balakirev too wrote an orientally inspired tone-poem, *Thamar*, perhaps his finest work, while the virtuoso *Islamey* is the best known of his piano pieces. Similarly, Borodin took as the subject of his epic opera *Prince Igor* the conflict between medieval Russians and a neighboring Tartar tribe, whose dances form a central point of interest in the drama. Glinka too had pointed the way to this interest in exotic music with his chorus of Persian slaves and the music of the oriental Prince Ratmir in *Ruslan and Lyudmila*.

It was not Glinka so much as Dargomyzhsky, however, who suggested another very different method of giving music a profoundly Russian character by molding its rhythms and inflections on those of Russian speech. Dargomyzhsky had been dead for three years when his opera *The Stone Guest* was first performed – an integral setting of Pushkin's Don Juan poem in a recitative style only occasionally relieved by formal song. This was already known to Musorgsky, who found in it striking confirmation of ideas which he had himself been putting into practice in a number of songs, vignettes of Russian characters. His attempt to set Gogol's *The Marriage* in the same way as Dargomyzhsky had set Pushkin was never completed, but this 'realistic' Russian speech-song proved marvellously effective in *The Nursery* songs and in his two great cycles *Sunless* and

Tchaikovsky left a large and varied body of work, a high proportion of which has remained in the European repertory. Two of his eleven operas, three of his six symphonies, three concertos (including the Theme and Variations for Cello and Orchestra), his three ballets and some half dozen orchestral works – overtures, fantasias etc. – one of three string quartets, a piano trio and a string sextet represent a legacy hardly equalled in size or variety by any composer except the great German classics.

Tchaikovsky was a great melodist and a great master of the orchestra, and these two qualities go far to explain the lasting popularity of his music, especially that of his three ballets, in which the suggestion and evocation of scenery and atmosphere are combined with rhythmic grace and energy. The operas, like the last three symphonies, are essentially revelations of the composer's own personality, in which extreme emotional sensibility and physical vitality alternate with a Byronic sense of guilt, leading to despair and an indulgent self-pity. It is this very human combination of personal characteristics that Tchaikovsky projects, with the greatest eloquence and forcefulness, in these works. In both operas and symphonies there are many diversions – dance-movements, genre-scenes, marches and formal *divertissements* – and in all of these, as in the ballets, Tchaikovsky was deeply influenced by French models. He was a great admirer of Gounod, Bizet and Massenet, and it is hard to believe that he could have brought about such a revolution in ballet music without the example of Delibes's *Coppélia* and *Sylvia*. It must be remembered that both his First Piano Concerto and his Violin Concerto were rejected as unplayable when they were first written, revealing the fact that each demands a slightly new kind of virtuosity from the soloist. This display of virtuosity is often associated with a gypsy element, as in the finale of the Violin Concerto; and gypsy songs and gypsy music were associated in the Russian mind with bursting the bonds of convention

and allowing free rein to primitive instincts, nights of drinking and love-making such as St Petersburg citizens associated with the gypsy nightclubs on the islands in the Neva. Thus it was that Tchaikovsky's music combined a European polish and craftsmanship with the actual experiences of Russian life, not with mythical and historical splendors like those conjured up by Musorgsky's *St John's Night on the Bare Mountain*, Rimsky-Korsakov's *Tsar Saltan* or Borodin's *Prince Igor*.

If it was Tchaikovsky whose music in fact achieved most of the goals of the Nationalist composers, it was the young Glazunov who represented the eventual fusion of the two parties. Born in 1865, he studied for a time with Rimsky-Korsakov and soon achieved a technical fluency and a craftsmanship comparable to those of the young Saint-Saëns. Like Saint-

Right: Portrait of Vladimir Stasov (1824-1906) by Ilya Repin. Stasov championed both the large group of artists called the Itinerants, of which Repin was a leading member, and the nationalist composers, who aimed to bring out the Russian heart and soul in their paintings and music. He coined the phrase 'mighty handful' for Balakirev and his group of five.

Right: Cossacks Writing a Mocking Letter to the Turkish Sultan, painted in 1880 by Repin. It was vivid paintings like this that helped to fire the imagination of Balakirev, Borodin and Rimsky-Korsakov for Asiatic and oriental themes.

Saëns, too, his music showed more skill than personality after his early successes. One of these, the tone-poem *Stenka Razin*, had its first performance on an occasion when the new Russian music of the day was introduced to a Paris audience. This was in June 1889, when Rimsky-Korsakov conducted two concerts of Russian music at the Paris Universal Exhibition. The programs, well chosen for their representative character, fascinated a gener-

ation of French composers, in whose works this music was to resound at intervals during the next quarter of a century.

Anatol Lyadov, ten years older than Glazunov, was a pupil of Rimsky-Korsakov at the St Petersburg Conservatory and the composer of symphonic poems characteristically based on Russian fairytales and legends, as well as a number of attractive piano pieces. If the curse of alcoholism, which had destroyed Musorgsky, was to darken Glazunov's life and work, Lyadov suffered from a constitutional idleness, which restricted his composing to mostly small, unambitious forms.

The trio of composer-pianists who carried the traditions of the Moscow School into the twentieth century was led by Rachmaninov, much of whose orchestral music (two symphonies, three operas, two cantatas, church music, as well as the four piano concertos) remains in the repertory and represents the clearest and most conservative development of the cosmopolitan Russian vein explored by Tchaikovsky. In Rachmaninov's music the confessional, self-revealing strain is again present, but is colored by a nostalgia, a sense of frustration and despair which assumes the dimensions of a world view. In fact his Second Piano Concerto, written in 1901, was conceived during a nervous breakdown, and he is better represented by the robuster and more interesting Third Concerto, the Second Symphony, the cantatas *The Bells* and *Spring* and the *Rhapsody on a theme of Paganini* for piano and orchestra, which were composed almost a quarter of a century later, after the Revolution, when the composer left Russia and settled in America.

Born only a year earlier than Rachmaninov, in 1872, Alexander Skriabin died twenty-eight years before him; but in his short life Skriabin achieved a musical individuality unique of its kind. Apart from an early and uncharacteristic piano concerto, he is chiefly remembered today

Right: Portrait of Fyodor Chaliapin (1873-1938) by Valentin Serov (another of the Itinerants). The world-famous Russian bass did much to promote the music of his country. His performance in the title-role of Musorgsky's *Boris Godunov* set the standard for all others.

Right: This picture of a troupe of Russian peasant musicians, the 'Rozhichniki' (horn-band players), in Paris in 1892 indicates the growing interest abroad in Russian music towards the end of the nineteenth century. Only a few years later, the Diaghilev Russian Ballet would take Paris and western Europe by storm.

and the note of abstract musical idealism in his work has an unmistakably nineteenth-century ring.

It would be wrong not to mention the name of Sergei Taneyev in any review of Russian music during the second half of the last century. That he was a great pianist is suggested by the fact that, when he made his début at the age of nineteen, in 1875, playing Brahms's D minor Piano Concerto at a concert of the Russian Musical Society, Tchaikovsky, with whom Taneyev studied composition, commented on 'his maturity of intellect, his self-control and the calm, objective style of his interpretation.' During the following years Taneyev played his master's piano concerto, and within three years the master-pupil relationship had been reversed. Tchaikovsky submitted a new work to Taneyev with the words: 'I beg you not to be afraid of over-severity. I want just those stinging criticisms from you. So long as you give me the truth, what does it matter whether it is favorable or not?'

Taneyev, in fact, occupied with the Moscow composers of his day a position not unlike that which Balakirev occupied with the young composers who looked to him less for the purely technical criticism that Taneyev also gave, but rather for his expositions of musical aesthetics. Taneyev became a legend of musical erudition, but his music has never established itself in the repertory even in his own country, with the exception of a few songs. His operatic trilogy *Oresteia* earned him respect but not popularity, and perhaps the best of his music is to be found among his chamber works, which include six string quartets.

Left: Alexander Skriabin (1872-1915), perhaps the least nationalistic of all Russian composers. A fellow student of Rachmaninov at the Moscow Conservatory, he progressed from a piano style close to that of Chopin to a highly original idiom, colored by his interest in theosophy and the occult.

for his piano music – including ten sonatas – and for three orchestral works written between 1900 and 1910, *The Divine Poem, Poem of Ecstasy* and *Prometheus*. His early piano music, though already marked by a personal harmonic character, is often very close to Chopin; but from the Fourth Sonata (1903) onwards his style became increasingly individual under the influence of the mystical beliefs he borrowed and adapted from the 'theosophy' of Madame Blavatsky and the apocalyptic ideas and images of the Russian symbolist poets. The language of these later sonatas and of the rite-like orchestral works of these years is based on a chord consisting of superimposed fourths, which yields an idiom both as individual and as restricted as Debussy's whole-tone scale. Skriabin spent much of his later life in western Europe and was influenced by Debussy in his rejection of the conception of music as a continuous, logically developed discourse and in his preference for short, cell-like motifs and rhythms, patches of color and dynamic gestures arranged in patterns which have their visual counterpart in the work of his compatriot and contemporary Vasily Kandinsky.

Nikolai Medtner, as his name suggests, came of German stock, and his deep affinity with the German classical tradition is reflected in his sober, thoroughly professional music. Medtner remained a passionately convinced musical conservative to the end of his life, and although many of the piano pieces and songs which make up the greater part of his output are unquestionably Russian in inspiration and character, the affinity with Brahms is also obviously strong,

Left: The Russian choreographer and dancer Mikhail Fokine (1880-1942), as he appeared in his own version of the Polovtsian Dances from Borodin's opera *Prince Igor.*

FRANZ LISZT

HAMISH MILNE

The concept of the artist as hero was central to the Romantic ideal. By the time Beethoven's Herculean labors came to an end in 1827 the days were forever gone when a young Mozart could get his backside kicked for his *lèse-majesté* or the aging Haydn blink in bemused delight on receiving the respect and acclaim from the London gentry that was no more than his due. Not that patronage was dead – far from it; nor was the Romantic movement militantly republican in its aspirations. It has been unkindly said of Liszt that he had no desire to overturn the social hierarchy, merely to revise the seating arrangements. Romantic composers set up heroes from their own kind, from Goethe and Beethoven to Shakespeare, Dante, Michelangelo and Homer, men who transcended social conditions and reached Parnassus on the wings of their art. But the world at large demanded flesh-and-blood heroes and Liszt was the man of the hour, the embodiment of Romanticism in all its magnificence and folly, a superman who rubbed shoulders with kings and princes and whose very glance had women swooning at his feet. His music was a compendium of the Romantic muse, embracing a good measure of the divine madness of Berlioz, the aristocratic poetry of Chopin, the suave urbanity of Mendelssohn and the passionate introspection of Schumann. Where he was lacking, he could simulate with the conviction of a consummate actor or dazzle with a pyrotechnical brilliance that none could rival.

Thus a legend was born and grew until it all but buried the composer who, it could be argued, did as much to influence the course of music as any other single man. In his early maturity he took up the challenge posed by Beethoven's late works and finally, in his own words, 'hurled his lance far into the future' with the prophetic experiments of his old age. His output was so immense that it hardly seems to admit time for his other careers as pianist, conductor, teacher and promoter, let alone his exploits as lover, traveler and *bon viveur*.

The grand personality, the international celebrity was almost unknown in music before Liszt. Handel and Haydn (in his old age) had their hours of glory, to be sure, but the history of music had largely been written hitherto by diligent employees who composed to support modest expectations of security and to fulfill the requirements of privileged and enclosed local communities; that they infused their humdrum tasks with genius is in one sense a coincidental benefit to posterity. Liszt's arrival on the scene was preceded by a growing acceptance of 'art for art's sake' and coincided with the development of the railway (which made long-distance travel practical and bearable) and also with the birth of a mass audience whose thirst for superstars has lasted to this day.

A man who once boasted an ambition to own three hundred cravats cannot be said to have resisted the pitfalls of pride and avarice which attend the objects of hero worship, and yet the craving for solitude and ascetic simplicity, which first afflicted him in his teens, gradually gained ascendancy and dominated his old age. Perhaps only now, in our more liberal and psychologically oriented age, are the baffling contradictions of his character (fuel to his champions and detractors alike) susceptible to reconciliation and understanding. What is one to make of a man who neglected his own children abominably, yet supported his fellow musicians with matchless kindness and selfless generosity, and taught long hours without ever accepting payment? At the age of seventeen he experienced unquenchable longings to 'live the life of the saints and perhaps die the death of martyrs,' and eventually, in his fifties, he took minor orders; but his love-life was anything but saintly and, at times, blatantly promiscuous.

Similar contradictions abound in the music. Much of it has been castigated for glorifying the meretricious and pandering to the lowest tastes of the gallery, but he composed a large body of church music which has virtually no audience by reason of its unrelieved austerity. Devotional and sensual qualities are to be found side by side in many of his instrumental works. Some of his finest creations are undeniably marred by passages of bombast and commonplace grandiloquence, while some of his weakest have moments of intense beauty and inspiration.

For one man to be so disproportionately endowed with such diverse and prodigious gifts without exemption from his fair share of human weakness and folly laid him readily open to suspicion and hostility. However, it fitted admirably with his destiny as standard-bearer to Romanticism, which recognized no limitations of its power to transmute feeling and experience into art.

·The young prodigy·

Franz (Ferenc) Liszt was born on 22 October 1811, in the Hungarian village of Doborján, then more widely known by its German name of Raiding. The legend-builders portentously recall that 1811 was the Year of the Comet (which is true) and hint darkly at illegitimate aristocratic – alternatively gypsy – blood in the boy's veins (which is untrue). His father, Adám Liszt, was employed as a steward on the vast Esterházy estates and, in a secondary capacity as amateur cellist, had come into contact there with both Haydn and Hummel.

Liszt's extraordinary gifts seem to have revealed themselves almost from the moment he first clambered on to the piano stool at the age of five or six, and his father was quick to realize what transformation of the family fortunes might be wrought by the child's nimble fingers. Accordingly, in 1820 he presented the boy before an assemblage of Hungarian magnates at one of the Esterházy palaces and, as a result, secured a subscription fund of 600 Gulden a year towards Franz's musical education.

The family then moved to Vienna and, since Franz's academic education had been virtually abandoned, it was fortunate that Carl Czerny then took over as his piano teacher and instilled at a crucial age the discipline that had been so sadly lacking in Adám Liszt's haphazard tuition. Liszt later acknowledged that the foundations of his legendary technique had been laid during this two-year period. It is just possible that the boy Liszt met Schubert in Vienna, but the more widely propagated story of Beethoven mounting the stage to kiss the prodigy after a dazzling performance was almost certainly invented.

At the end of 1823, the Liszts moved to Paris and, when Franz was refused entry to the Conservatoire by the director Cherubini's enforcement of a rule barring all foreigners, he was launched on a full-time career as a child pianist. For five years he was paraded like a circus monkey for the delectation of high society in France, England and Switzerland, handsomely swelling the family's fortune in the process.

Some sort of revulsion against this relentless exploitation, against a success that was positively humiliating in its ease of acquisition, was predictable, but the violence of Liszt's reaction went far deeper than a conventional act of adolescent rebellion. The circus was winding up in any case, for in August 1827 Adám Liszt died in Boulogne, allegedly with this prophetic warning to his son on his lips: 'Je crains pour toi les femmes.' His wife had long since lost the taste for adventure and returned to her family in Austria, but now she hastened to her son's side and they set up home in the rue Montholon in Paris. Franz succumbed to deep depression, experiencing feelings of self-disgust and a longing to enter the church which almost amounted to religious mania. Music had turned sour on him, 'vilified and degraded to the level of a more or less profitable handicraft.' Thus, at the ripe old age of sixteen, he retired from public life, took up teaching and read voraciously in an attempt to recoup some of the education that had been sacrificed on the altar of Mammon.

Left: Adám Liszt (1776-1827). He was a friend of Hummel, who had succeeded Haydn in 1790 as director of music at Esterháza, and was a competent performer on most musical instruments. He gave piano lessons to his six-year-old son, who within two years could play the most difficult works.

Right: The young Liszt. Czerny, who gave Liszt lessons in 1821, wrote that he 'had no notion of fingering . . . and flung his fingers all over the keys' – but seemed to play the piano by instinct.

Below: Liszt receives the legendary kiss from Beethoven at his farewell concert in Vienna.

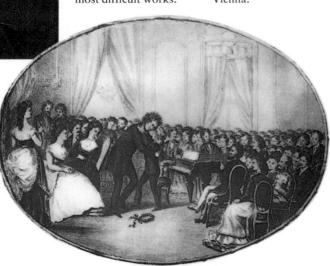

Within months, his father's deathbed forebodings were realized when Liszt fell deeply in love with one of his pupils, the sixteen-year-old daughter of a government minister. The affair with Caroline de Saint-Cricq was the first of many but, perhaps for that very reason, a deep and enduring passion (he left her a ring in his will) and almost certainly the most innocent. So when, upon discovering a music lesson still in progress in the small hours, the Count de Saint-Cricq threw him out, Liszt withdrew into a further decline so complete that he was presumed dead and an obituary notice appeared in a Paris newspaper.

It was two years before Liszt fully recovered from this nervous collapse but when he did emerge, eighteen years old and handsome as Adonis, he mingled confidently with Parisian society who well remembered 'le petit Lits.' In the course of the next decade he struck up acquaintance with most of the great figures of Parisian artistic life, Hugo, Balzac, de Musset, Heine, de Vigny and Delacroix among them. He formed an enduring friendship with Berlioz and got to know Chopin well, although their relationship was never as close and later deteriorated into estrangement. However, for Liszt the searing revelatory musical experience of the 1830s was the demonic virtuosity of the Italian violinist Niccolò Paganini. Liszt was mesmerized, and staggered away from the encounter determined to force himself to the limit to achieve comparable mastery of his own instrument. He locked himself away and practised up to fourteen hours a day. His *Clochette Fantasy* of 1832, based on a theme by Paganini,

relentlessly demands the near-impossible of the pianist and his instrument, and a new age of transcendental pianism had dawned.

It was not surprising that it was a woman who temporarily deflected him from this obsession. He was introduced to the Countess Marie d'Agoult towards the end of 1832 and their liaison, at once improbable and characteristic of the post-revolutionary Parisian entanglement of society and bohemia, lasted fitfully for the next ten years. Marie d'Agoult was twenty-eight at the time of their meeting (Liszt was twenty-two) and married to an undistinguished politician, fourteen years her senior, by whom she had borne two children. She seems to have been the decisive partner when, in 1835, she abandoned her family and fled to Switzerland, where the first of her three children by Liszt was born. Liszt, who had been undergoing one of his recurrent religious crises, was surprisingly amenable to the idea of abandoning his gregarious existence in Paris for teaching in Geneva and whole-hearted indulgence in grand romantic passion. The couple read to one another the works of the Olympians Dante and Petrarch, intermingled with apostles of Romanticism like Byron and Schiller, and in the years 1835 to 1839 they traveled widely in Switzerland and Italy, alone or in the company of like-minded free thinkers, bored aristocrats or genuine bohemian intellectuals like George Sand, whose relationship with Liszt became intense but (almost certainly) remained platonic.

Liszt's unfettered intellectual and emotional curiosity fed voraciously on all manner of stimuli

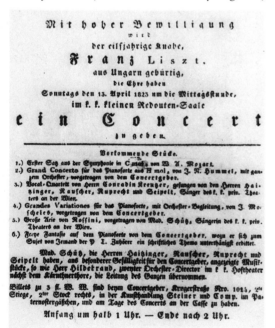

Above: It was decided that Liszt had learned all that Vienna could offer and that he should go and display his talents in Paris. This poster for his farewell concert on 13 April 1823 gives a

program of music by Mozart, Hummel and Moscheles. After another concert in Budapest he began a triumphant European tour to be hailed as a reincarnation of Mozart.

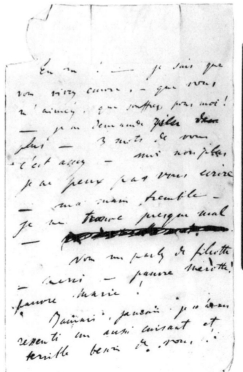

Above: A passionate letter written in May 1836 to Marie d'Agoult in which Liszt speaks

of the 'filiotte' – their daughter Blandine, who had been born in December 1835.

Above: Liszt in 1836, at the start of his romantic 'years of pilgrimage' in Switzerland and Italy with Marie d'Agoult. He wrote in the Geneva hotel register: 'born on Parnassus, coming from Doubt, going to Truth.'

Left: Title-page of *Orage* from *Années de pèlerinage*. This, the fifth of the first set of descriptive piano pieces, a depiction of a mountain storm, was conceived when Liszt was in Switzerland with Marie d'Agoult, who wrote that the works were inspired by the beauty of their surroundings. They were not revised and published until 1855.

Below: Costume designs for the one-act operetta *Don Sanche* which Liszt wrote in 1824-5 in Paris under his teacher Paer. A lavish production was given at the Académie Royale – the Paris Opéra – with Adolphe Nourrit in the title-role. The opera, given just before Liszt's fourteenth birthday, was well received, even by the formidable Cherubini.

from Saint-Simonisme to proletarianism, none of which he truly assimilated or evaluated but which usually found some reflection in his music, either immediately or in later years. Probably the most durable and pervasive influence was that of an eccentric mystic, the Abbé Lammenais, who struck deep into the vein of asceticism that was never far below the surface of Liszt's flamboyant exterior.

Marie had little chance of containing Liszt once he had satisfied this urge for seclusion and introspection. Initially, her infatuation was probably the realization of the fantasies of a rich, bored and neglected woman, and it ultimately foundered on a hopeless and destructive desire to keep for herself a lover whose very attraction depended to a large extent on his public charisma. For Liszt, the world was there to be conquered, and his pianistic triumphs provoked a violent jealousy in Marie that would have been fatal even if it had not been inflamed by his sexual infidelities.

Summer vacations spent at Nonnenwerth, an island retreat on the Rhine between Cologne and Coblenz, patched up their crumbling relationship for a while, but finally they parted on acrimonious terms in 1844. Two years later, the embittered Marie published *Nélida*, a rancorous account of their affair thinly disguised as a novel.

Above: The three children of Liszt and Marie d'Agoult. Blandine, probably the reason for their elopement, died in childbirth at the age of twenty-seven. Cosima, named after Lake Como, was born in Italy in 1837, and Daniel in Rome in 1839.

Above right: Countess Marie d'Agoult, who was married to an equerry at the French Court when she met Liszt. George Sand described her as 'straight as a candle, white as a holy wafer,' but she was more beautiful, vivacious and intelligent than this implies. Liszt's success in discounting the veracity of Marie's bitter biographical novel *Nélida* made a true assessment of his character more difficult for many years.

Although *Nélida* was damaging to Liszt, his notoriety as a Don Juan stemmed not so much from his protracted liaisons with Marie or Princess Carolyne Sayn-Wittgenstein (which had they been regularized by marriage would have attracted little comment) as from the profusion and catholicity of his casual affairs, which to this day arouse amazement, envy or censure according to temperament. In spite of his almost irresistible appeal to women, he was not notably fastidious or judicious in his choice, nor did he learn from his mistakes. A highly embarrassing and professionally damaging entanglement with the dancer-actress Lola Montez in the early 1840s did not prevent him (in his sixties) from entering upon a near-disastrous affair with a lunatic exhibitionist, the self-styled 'Cossack Countess' Olga Janina.

• The great virtuoso •

Liszt's rift with Marie d'Agoult took its first serious turn in 1839, and that year also marked the start of his assault on the concert halls of Europe, from which he emerged undisputed (to this day) as 'the greatest pianist who ever lived.' His reputation in Paris was already secure – he had returned from exile in 1836 to put paid to the rival claims of the upstart Thalberg. But now his target was the entire continent and, from 1839 to 1847, he blazed a triumphant path from Vienna to Madrid, from Ireland to the more remote regions of Russia.

After six concerts before an adoring public in Vienna, he went on to the homeland where he had not set foot since childhood. In these years leading up to Kossuth's uprising, Hungary felt a crying need for national heroes and Liszt seemed heaven-sent to fulfill it. Although he could not even speak Hungarian, Liszt donned his patriotic cloak with his customary theatrical flair and was fêted wherever he went, whipping up a frenzy of nationalistic fervor with his dashing arrangement of the *Rákóczy March*. The crowds cheered with hysteria and the nobility presented him with a sword of honor – a source of malicious delight to the Parisian cartoonists. He hardly deserved such adulation on political or cultural grounds and, perhaps in recognition of this, he started to compose the *Magyar Dállok*, later recast as the *Hungarian Rhapsodies*. His sources could hardly have been more corrupt, for the gypsy bands that he took to be representative of Hungarian folk music were, in fact, purveyors of popular tunes by dilettante composers, albeit in a highly sophisticated and idiosyncratic style. Not that this really detracts from the allure and garish brilliance of the *Hungarian Rhapsodies*, but it did consolidate a misconception of Hungarian folk art which persisted until the time of Bartók and Kodály.

Just how Liszt played, how he cast his spell, must remain forever a matter for conjecture, an insoluble enigma. That his technique, when he was at the peak of his form, was truly transcendental seems beyond argument, as is the fact that he swept away the classical style that had been perpetuated by men like Hummel and Moscheles. His approach to the piano was orchestral – 'ten fingers have the power to reproduce the harmonies which are created by hundreds of performers' – and a sober judge, Sir Charles Hallé, swore that his transcription of Berlioz's *Symphonie fantastique* was even more electrifying than the orchestral original. Yet for all that, it must have been his artistic and interpretative qualities, what Berlioz called his 'sensibilité divinatoire,' that left perceptive and experienced musicians groping tongue-tied for metaphors. Alexander Siloti, one of Liszt's last pupils, confessed himself utterly at a loss when asked to describe or demonstrate the 'unimaginable effect' of his master's playing on even the most inadequate instrument. Heine, always quick with an acid comment on Liszt the man, surrendered totally to Liszt the pianist: 'the piano vanishes and – music appears.' Nevertheless one cannot, even here, escape the violent subjective responses provoked by his personality and life-style. Mendelssohn, Chopin and Schumann all recorded their spellbound enchantment with his playing but later voiced puritanical, even spiteful reservations over his vulgarity and showmanship, which may have offended their social values as much as their artistic ones. Joachim deplored Liszt's habit of tinkering with the letter of the score, adding embellishments and improvising countermelodies and so on, but how does one reconcile this with Berlioz's account of a performance of Beethoven's mighty 'Hammerklavier' Sonata – 'not a note was left out, not a note added (I followed, score in hand).'

It must be conceded that many of Liszt's audiences lacked musical sophistication and discernment based on comparative experience, and surrendered to a totally novel phenomenon.

He was, however, conscious of his responsibility as an artist not only to move and entertain his audience, but also to educate. Works by J. S. Bach and Schubert or the late sonatas of Beethoven were included alongside rabble-rousers like the *Grand galop chromatique*. His dazzling paraphrases and transcriptions not only re-created the glamour and excitement of the opera house but also introduced the symphonies of Beethoven to many who would otherwise never have heard them.

Liszt's reception was nowhere more tumultuous than in Russia, yet it was here, on his third visit in 1847, that he abruptly rang down the curtain on his career as a traveling virtuoso. This same tour was also the start of his liaison with Princess Carolyne Sayn-Wittgenstein, his mistress for the next fifteen years and his friend and confidante until his death. Liszt first met the Princess after a charity concert in Kiev

Liszt's extravagant behavior made him an ideal target for the caricaturists of the day. The Viennese cartoon (*below*) satirizes his social climbing and lionization by the Viennese aristocracy: 'How Franz Liszt has to serve himself up at a dinner in Vienna.' The French one (*bottom left*) is one of the many gibes at the sword presented to a virtuoso who had been known to smash the fragile pianos of his day: 'In spite of his sword, Liszt has vanquished only sixteenth notes and slain only pianos.'

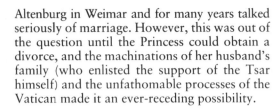

FRANZ LISZT

Below left: In 1840, having established his reputation as a pianist throughout Europe, Liszt was greeted in Hungary as a national hero and presented with a symbolic sword of honor. A Hungarian court saber with a Damascus blade, this was inlaid on each side with gold arabesques, while the curved hilt, of black bone and silver-gilt, was set with precious stones.

Below right: Liszt in Hungarian national costume in 1839. In 1838 he had given several concerts to aid the Hungarian victims of the Danube floods; and this generosity had increased his popularity in Hungary. There was some talk of him being given a Hungarian title, although this came to nothing. His vanity and desire for aristocratic society were now making him appear rather ridiculous in some quarters and were taken up with considerable delight by the Paris press in particular.

in February and their relationship took root during the months he spent on her estate at Woronince in the Ukraine towards the end of the year. Their affair was the target of ribald comment from its inception and, on the face of it, there was a bizarre incongruity in this alliance between the Don Juan figure of Liszt and the awkward, pious and unbendingly earnest Carolyne. She was neither beautiful nor elegant and passed her time consuming the heaviest and most indigestible literary diet imaginable – when, that is, she was not writing her own monumental tracts. She appealed to the deeper and (certainly by his reckoning) better side of Liszt's nature that was seldom on public display. George Sand was prompted to observe that he was 'gnawed by a secret wound,' which provoked his recurring religious crises and depressions and which now lay behind his decision to renounce his glittering stardom as pianist *ne plus ultra* and devote himself to composing and the furtherance of the art of music.

Some such idea must have been in his mind as early as 1842 when he had signed a provisional contract to oversee the music at the ducal court of Weimar, a decidedly unromantic regression to the role of Kapellmeister, although the agreement was naturally couched in terms infinitely more respectful than any offered to Bach or Haydn. The salary was (for him) derisory, but he had amassed a modest fortune during his years as a virtuoso and money certainly played no part in his decision. He now saw the post as a stable base from which to pursue his new objectives, and he applied himself to it far more vigorously and comprehensively than can have been originally envisaged. There is little doubt that he intended to make Carolyne a full partner in this new life, and in 1848 they set up house together at the

Altenburg in Weimar and for many years talked seriously of marriage. However, this was out of the question until the Princess could obtain a divorce, and the machinations of her husband's family (who enlisted the support of the Tsar himself) and the unfathomable processes of the Vatican made it an ever-receding possibility.

• Kapellmeister at Weimar •

The years 1848 to 1861 at Weimar were the most productive of Liszt's life. In both spheres – as musical director and composer – his objective was twofold: to learn and to achieve. In order to establish a center where modern music could flourish and be heard he had to master the art of conducting (at which he was a novice), and in order to achieve fulfillment and maturity as a composer he had to master the craft of orchestration.

The orchestra at Weimar was a modest one, better suited to the classical repertoire than the more opulent demands of Romantic music. Liszt managed to coax a harp and an extra pair of trombones out of the exchequer and set about his task with true evangelical fervor. But it was not his intention to erect an ivory tower for experimental music alone, and his operatic ventures included important revivals of operas by Gluck, Mozart, Beethoven and Schubert while, in the concert hall, he presented Handel's oratorios *Messiah* and *Samson* as well as symphonies by Mozart and Haydn. In the field of modern music, however, his zeal and perseverance were even more remarkable, and his championship of progressive composers eventually led to open hostility between the Weimar camp (the so-called 'New German School') and the Leipzig-Dresden stronghold of academics, who took up their pens in support of the more traditional stance of Mendelssohn, Schumann and (later) Brahms.

Liszt was not above making humorous jibes at the 'Leipzigerisch' conservatives, but, to his credit, he held aloof from the destructive partisanship of his acolytes and was big enough to see merit wherever he found it and, even more endearingly, to honor old friendships in the face of surly ingratitude. Schumann and Liszt had shared a cordial mutual respect in the early years of their acquaintance (Schumann dedicated his *Fantasy*, op.17, to Liszt) but, for a variety of reasons, Schumann had retracted the rare warmth he had shown in the early 1840s. His literary brainchild *Die Neue Zeitschrift für Musik*, once the mouthpiece of his own *Davidsbund*, had come under new editorial control in 1844 and now, to Schumann's chagrin, openly sided with the Weimar group. In addition, his wife Clara strongly disapproved of Liszt's lifestyle and possibly also felt a few pangs of jealousy at the furor aroused by his playing, which seldom, if ever, attended her own admirable but infinitely more sedate performances. Notwithstanding this alienation, Liszt devotedly mounted productions of Schumann's most

Right: An Evening at Liszt's by Joseph Danhauser, an idealized vision of Liszt playing to an entourage of friends. From left to right: Alexandre Dumas; Victor Hugo; George Sand, seated, in her male attire; Paganini and Rossini standing together; Liszt at the piano with Marie d'Agoult at his feet. The portrait behind is of Byron, the bust of Beethoven.

Below: Liszt's daughter, Cosima Wagner, an oil sketch by Franz von Lenbach. Cosima married her father's favorite pupil Hans von Bülow in 1857. When she left him to live with Wagner in 1867 Liszt was divided in his loyalties and sided with his pupil; this caused a rift with Cosima which never really healed. After the death of Wagner, Cosima devoted herself to his music and the organization of the festival at Bayreuth, which she directed from 1883 until 1908, remaining a rather autocratic figurehead until her death in 1930.

Left: Lola Montez, an Irish courtesan with whom Liszt had one of the many liaisons which precipitated the break with Marie d'Agoult. Marie wrote: 'I will be your mistress, but I will not be one of your mistresses.' Lola caused a particular furor when she pursued Liszt to a formal reception where she danced on the table.

Far right: A caricature sculpture of Liszt with his sword by Dantan the younger.

Right: A watercolor of Liszt by Zwecker. The dichotomy of Liszt's personality – the flamboyant, philandering showman and the spiritual abbé – were hard to reconcile.

impractical works, including the opera *Geno-veva*, the quasi-dramatic oratorio *Scenes from Faust* and Byron's melodrama *Manfred*.

Berlioz was another to profit handsomely from Liszt's longstanding friendship and admiration, which dated from the 1830s when Liszt had made his sensational transcriptions of the *Symphonie fantastique* and *Harold in Italy*. At Weimar he mounted Berlioz's opera *Benvenuto Cellini*, which had lain unheard since the fiasco of its Paris première in 1838, and presented two 'Berlioz Weeks' at which the composer was invited to conduct several of his major orchestral works.

Even these mammoth entrepreneurial feats were as little compared to those Liszt was prepared to undertake on Wagner's behalf. Their friendship was one of the most extraordinary and rewarding in the history of music, documented in a fascinating and voluminous correspondence. Wagner was an unrepentant egotist; Liszt, by this time, an idealist. Their first meeting in the early 1840s had been unmomentous and unfruitful but, since then, Liszt had heard *Rienzi* and *The Flying Dutchman* and was prepared to stake all on his conviction that Wagner was the supreme prophet of the music of the future, submerging his own artistic ambitions in the interest of what he openly considered a superior genius. Performances of *The Flying Dutchman*, *Tannhäuser* and *Lohengrin* (the première) were given at Weimar under Liszt's direction, but his friendship and support went further than even these massive undertakings, fraught though they were with every conceivable obstacle. Liszt sheltered Wagner from the police after his involvement in the 1848 Dresden uprising, he acceded as far as possible to Wagner's incessant requests for money and generally put up with the intolerable aspects of Wagner's character with the benevolence of a family chaplain.

After Liszt left Weimar, in a state of deep dejection, he lost the stomach for Wagner's endless importunities, but worse was yet to come. In 1857, Liszt's daughter Cosima had married Hans von Bülow, a favorite pupil and, like his teacher, an ardent Wagnerian, but by the mid-1860s she had become Wagner's mistress and, in 1867, gave birth to his child. Liszt's anger and horror may seem hypocritical in view of his own entanglements in the past (Cosima herself was the child of a similarly adulterous liaison), but the psychological barriers to acceptance were enmeshed in the interior conflicts of his personality. Not only did

he share the idealized hopes of any father for his daughter, but his relationships with Wagner and von Bülow, brotherly and paternal respectively, made any reconciliation a betrayal of one or the other. Furthermore, he must have been aware that Wagner, musical Messiah or no, lacked the attributes of a suitable husband and father to a spectacular degree. He opted unhesitatingly for von Bülow, assured him of his enduring friendship and did not speak to Wagner for five years. Reconciliation did not come until 1872, by which time Cosima had divorced von Bülow and married Wagner.

Liszt did not confine his attention to Titans like Wagner, Berlioz and Schumann. Eager young pianists and composers flocked to Weimar, which became the Mecca of the 'New German School,' and Liszt took numerous pupils and assistants under his wing, teaching the pianists free of charge and arranging performances of the works of his young protégés. Joachim Raff, Peter Cornelius, Karl Klindworth, Hans von Bülow and Edvard Lassen (who took over as director after Liszt's departure) all have a tenuous foothold in musical

Right: In 1863, while in retreat at the Oratory of the Madonna del Rosario, Liszt was given the unusual honor of a visit from Pope Pius IX. The Pope asked Liszt to improvise for him and was much moved by the experience. During his stay at the monastery Liszt worked on the *Deux Légendes* of St Francis of Assisi and St Francis of Paola.

Above: Silhouette of Abbé Liszt in Rome in 1870. From 1863 he spent several periods in retreat there; his longing for the religious life had returned, and he eventually took minor orders in 1865.

Right: Performance of the 'Gran' Mass in the church of Saint-Eustache, Paris, in 1861. Berlioz, who was no longer in total sympathy with the music of Liszt, was to have reviewed the Mass for the *Débats*, but he persuaded his friend Joseph d'Ortigue to do so instead. A few days later Berlioz walked out of a concert while one of Liszt's symphonic poems was being played. The 'Gran' Mass had its first performance at Gran, or Esztergom, in Hungary.

history, but the two most talented were probably Carl Tausig and Julius Reubke, both struck down by disease before reaching full maturity. Tausig, by temperament wild to the point of delinquency, wrought mayhem at the Altenburg during the two years he lived there as a student but was forgiven all for the sake of his *mains de bronze*, as Liszt called them. Reubke died of tuberculosis at the age of only twenty-four, but not before he had composed two monumental sonatas (for piano and for organ) in which a really powerful and exciting personality penetrates the unashamedly Lisztian idiom.

It is the scarcely credible but clearly demonstrable truth that, during his years as musical director, Liszt composed a quantity of music that alone would have kept many composers busy for a lifetime. In fact, most of the music by which he is well known today was either composed or reshaped into its definitive version between 1847 and 1860. The precise chronology of his music has always been hard to establish and will remain so because of his practice of constant revision. The final versions of the first two volumes of *Années de pèlerinage* and the six *Paganini Studies*, for instance, were among the first tasks undertaken by Liszt at Weimar, but they have their origin and inspiration in the events and experiences of the 1830s – his travels with Marie d'Agoult in the first case and the playing of Paganini in the second. The twelve *Transcendental Studies*, completed in 1851 and published the following year, can be traced back to a collection of modestly Czerny-like Exercises composed at the age of fifteen, and they are actually a simplification of an appallingly difficult intermediate version of 1838. The Piano Concerto in E flat was some twenty-five years

in gestation but, in the form we know it today, received its first performance (with Liszt as soloist under Berlioz's direction) during the second of the two 'Berlioz Weeks' he arranged at Weimar in 1855.

Liszt's most self-conscious contribution to the 'music of the future' was the series of twelve symphonic poems composed between 1848 and 1857 (an austere pendant, *From the Cradle to the Grave*, was Liszt's last orchestral work in 1882). Here he was brought face to face with his inexperience and ineptitude in orchestration, and he openly sought the help and advice of his young academically-trained assistants, August Conradi and Joachim Raff. He was grateful for their advice but later capitalized on the insights gained from conducting and revised the scoring in accordance with his own intentions.

No work by Liszt has entirely escaped controversy, but two works of the Weimar period are generally accepted as his masterpieces, the 'Faust' Symphony and the Piano Sonata

in B minor. Two other large-scale works, the 'Dante' Symphony and the Fantasy and Fugue *Ad Nos* for organ, rank not far behind them, while the 'Gran' Mass and Psalm XIII are landmarks in the field of religious music, to which he was increasingly drawn.

Sadly, from Liszt's point of view, the whole bold enterprise ended in frustration and disillusion. He had hoped to build on the town's inheritance from Goethe and Schiller and extend its cultural tradition into an Eldorado in which Court, theater and university (at nearby Jena) would combine to create an artistic environment free from intrigue, censorship and 'the quarrelsome formulae of our pseudo-classicists, who busy themselves crying out that art is dead, is dead . . .' – and he had sacrificed much to achieve that end. The Grand Duchess Maria Paulowna, who paid Liszt's salary from her own purse, was a passionate music-lover, as was the Grand Duke, but the Crown Prince Carl Alexander, who succeeded to the title in 1853 was more interested in the theater. There was further opposition at Court from those who mistrusted Liszt on account of his championship of the fugitive Wagner, and disquiet among the more staid citizens over his flagrant cohabitation with Princess Carolyne. Liszt's very success in establishing a 'New German School' at Weimar was not entirely to his advantage, for many of its inhabitants had more natural sympathy with the Leipzig-Dresden axis and were not at all pleased at the odium attracted to their city in some quarters of the press through its association with the 'music of the future.'

By 1857, Liszt confessed himself 'mortally sad and tired' and withdrew more and more into the Altenburg, avoiding anyone not directly concerned with music. His relationship with Court officials became increasingly strained, and breaking-point was reached in 1858 when his production of *The Barber of Bagdad*, by his pupil Peter Cornelius, was received with undisguised hostility. Liszt gave up and resigned his post. He remained at the Altenburg for a further two years, taking an occasional part in the town's musical life, but it was indecision that detained him; his official commitments were over. His troubles multiplied; his son Daniel died at the age of twenty and Carolyne's relentless pursuit of a divorce went round in nightmarish circles. He sank into depression and, reviewing his life, saw nothing but failure. He had turned his back on a life of success, luxury and pleasure, but to what avail? 'In the dozen years I have stayed at Weimar,' he wrote, 'I have been sustained by a feeling not lacking in nobility – the honor, dignity and great character of a woman to be protected against infamous persecutions, and, beyond that, a grand idea – the renewal of music by its intimate alliance to poetry, a freer and, so to speak, more appropriate development to the spirit of our times.' Several works reflect his somber frame of mind – the funeral oration *Les Morts*, the melodrama *Der traurige Mönch* and various religious choral pieces.

• Abbé Liszt •

In May 1860, Carolyne set out for Rome to do battle with the Vatican over her divorce. Her absence raised Liszt's spirits somewhat, and the following year he traveled to Paris for a convivial reunion with old friends. However, two meetings with Marie d'Agoult (whose presence there had been the principal reason for his prolonged absence from the city) were awkward and painful. A successful summer festival at Weimar, which did much to assuage his bitterness, was scarcely over when he heard from Carolyne that she had triumphed. The wedding

was fixed for 22 October, Liszt's fiftieth birthday. He now closed down the Altenburg for good and arrived in Rome a few days before the ceremony. At the very last minute, the Pope revoked the annulment on technical grounds and the marriage never took place. Perhaps Carolyne took the papal interdict as some sort of providential intervention, for she now accepted what she already knew in her heart – that if Liszt went to the altar with her now, it would be only to fulfill a duty – and they never spoke of marriage again. For the next five years he traveled intermittently but generally led a fairly reclusive life, renewing and deepening his acquaintance with the music of Palestrina, Victoria and Lassus and working steadily on two colossal oratorios, *Christus* and *The Legend of Saint Elizabeth*. A number of fine piano compositions also date from his Roman period, such as the richly evocative impressions of the fountains and cypresses of the Villa d'Este at Tivoli, where he lived for a while, and the two powerful *Légendes*, which balance his devotional and theatrical tendencies to unusually telling effect.

In 1865 Liszt astounded the world by taking minor orders in the church, and became 'the

Above: Liszt playing at the Villa Wahnfried, the home of the Wagners at Bayreuth. Wagner, with an open score on his knee, sits just left of center; Cosima is on the left with her arm around their son Siegfried.

Abbé Liszt' to the ribald amusement of former fellow socialites. 'Mephistopheles in abbé's garb' was Gregorovius's epithet, which does not seem inapt when we read Liszt's own account of a day divided between the Catechism of Perseverance and a piano transcription of 'Indian jugglery' from Meyerbeer's *L'Africaine*. No doubt his decision had its origins in the religious longings of his youth, in his hero-worship of the Abbé Lammenais, but, more than anything, it was probably a gesture of resignation, the old theatrical flair now put at the service of life's disillusionment.

In 1869 he was coaxed out of his semi-retirement by an invitation from the Grand Duke himself to return to Weimar, where the refurbished Hofgärtnerei was put at his disposal. Liszt's name had not lost its magic and the house was soon filled with adoring pupils. Moritz Rosenthal, Eugen d'Albert and Emil Sauer were among the young keyboard giants who attended these classes along with countless wealthy, often talentless, amateurs who jostled to secure a place in Europe's most fashionable pianistic finishing school. Its heady atmosphere is charmingly, if somewhat breathlessly captured in *Music Study in Germany*, a collection of letters by a young American student, Amy Fay. Liszt had no formal obligations during this second reign at Weimar, but he missed no opportunity to conduct, and

Above: Tivoli – Les Jardins de la Villa d'Este by Corot. In 1869 some rooms were made available to Liszt at the Villa d'Este outside Rome. Here he stayed several times over the following years while he was in the city. He longed for the peace and seclusion it offered, but once there missed the social lionizing he loved. The final volume of the *Années de pèlerinage* includes three pieces inspired by the gardens of the villa.

Right: Title-page of the oratorio *The Legend of St Elizabeth* (1862). The greater part of the work was composed at Altenburg – inspired by the neighboring Wartburg Castle and the frescoes of Moritz von Schwind, the German Romantic painter.

Left: Liszt and St Elizabeth, a caricature by Ruhl. In 1860 Liszt completed his oratorio on the story of St Elizabeth of Hungary, born in 1207, who was taken to Wartburg Castle to be married. Her acts of charity were derided by her husband, but he was converted by a miracle in which a basket of bread for the poor was transformed into roses. Moved by her example he went on the crusade of 1227 and died, whereupon Elizabeth was expelled from the castle and lived a life of charity and poverty.

added Wagner's *Die Meistersinger* and his own *Christus* to his formidable list of credits.

The newly established Royal Academy of Music in Budapest was next to call on his services, in 1870. Liszt owed a debt to Hungary for, despite his fervent proclamations of patriotism during his triumphant tour in 1839-40, he had lain low during the bloody revolution of 1848-9, and his only contribution to the cause came after the event in the form of the stirring elegies *Funérailles* and *Héroïde funèbre*. For him it was enough for 'Art to throw her ennobling veil over the tombs of the brave.' Friends like Heine and Princes Belgiojoso disagreed and bitterly reproached him for his evasive inertia. This dereliction may have been in his mind when he shouldered an additional burden as president of the new Academy and undertook to teach there for three months of each year. Thus began his *vie trifurquée*, as he called it, an endless triangle of journeys

Left: Raphael's *St Cecilia*: 'I do not know by what strange magic this picture presents itself with a double appeal to my inner eye: it is a fascinating expression of the human form, of everything in it which is noblest and most ideal, a wonder of grace, purity and harmony . . . it appears as a perfect and marvellous symbol of the art to which we devote our lives.' (Liszt)

Above: Liszt's patron saint, Francis of Paola – evoked in one of his *Deux Légendes* of 1866 – in a painting by Doré dedicated to Liszt and said to have hung in his study at Weimar. It depicts the story of the saint, who, too poor to pay for the ferry across the Straits of Messina, was bidden by the boatman: 'If he is a saint, let him walk!' – which he did.

between Rome, Weimar and Budapest. In his last years his travels became even more frenetic – to England, France, Austria, Belgium and Holland – and it was on a train journey to Bayreuth to hear *Parsifal* that he developed a racking cough which turned into pneumonia. He died on 31 July 1886 and was buried in Bayreuth, the shrine of his revered friend Richard Wagner, a not unseemly resting place for a man who could call nowhere home.

Liszt's artistic ego never fully recovered from the collapse of his great Weimar dream. He felt misunderstood and was tormented by doubts over his personal artistic achievement, though never over the path he had chosen. 'I can wait; meanwhile, my shoulders are broad,' he said, as his works were greeted with hostility or incomprehension, and he resigned himself to a lonely vigil, continuing to 'blacken manuscript paper' with laconic and prophetic fragments without regard to their impact or even much concern whether they were heard at all.

In his outward dealings with students and fellow musicians he showed little bitterness, only an occasional trace of cynicism when conversation turned to himself, and he continued to lavish advice and encouragement on rising composers such as Borodin and Grieg in his later years. His inner restlessness was rarely on public view and it is only through occasional outbursts in letters to his closest confidants that we learn of his tormenting memories of the 'banal and lying embraces of my mistresses' or of his vision of death as 'a deliverance from an unwilling yoke, the consequence of original sin.' While awaiting this deliverance (without too much impatience, it seems) he continued to rise to his desk at four in the morning, 'hurling his lance far into the future' without ever satisfying his unquenchable 'need to be *someone* to somebody.'

His was indeed 'music of the future,' and Debussy, Ravel, Bartók and Messiaen are but a few of the twentieth-century masters who acknowledged that he was *someone* to them.

• The man and his music •

The temptation to draw false conclusions about a composer's work from a superficial knowledge of the facts of his life is a pitfall generally to be avoided, for the composer's inner world has, it seems, no essential correlation with the external circumstances of his day-to-day life. Yet with Liszt it is scarcely possible to understand either the man or the music without some knowledge of both. The startling transformation of the dandy of the 1830s into the haunted abbé of the 1870s is not simply to be explained by the disappointments of Weimar, for its seeds were certainly sown in his childhood or adolescence. As early as 1834 (when the influence of Abbé Lammenais was at its strongest), he composed a group of piano pieces, the *Harmonies poétiques et religieuses* (not to be confused with a later collection published under the

same title) and the *Apparitions* which defy all accepted contemporary conventions in their harmonic boldness and their quest for the unfettered expression of emotional extremes. The 'Harmonies' suspends tonality for long periods by treating the diminished seventh chord (on which it starts and finishes) as its home base, and metrical irregularity adds to the feeling of improvisatory spontaneity. The expression marks alone ('avec un profond sentiment d'ennui,' 'avec violence,' 'soave con amore,' 'disperato,' etc.) denote an adventurous spirit already probing music's untapped poetic and dramatic resources. So the extraordinary harmonic radicalism of his old age should be seen not as a senile aberration, but as the culmination of a lifelong inclination to circumvent predictable harmonic patterns by means of whole-tone progressions, augmented and diminished intervals and other devices which became commonplace in the early years of the twentieth century. *Lyon* – a rousing tribute to the workers' uprising in that city – is another little-known early piece which exploits these harmonic ambiguities, and its cadences strain

Left: Princess Carolyne von Sayn-Wittgenstein, whom Liszt met in Russia in 1847 – rather unkindly described by Theodor von Bernhardi as 'small, dark, ugly, sickly but very clever . . . and ambitious for him [Liszt].' Certainly in the twelve years of their close liaison she encouraged him to settle down and work to an extent he had not done earlier. Liszt seems to have been truly attached to her and to have admired her as a cultivated and religious woman. The historian Gregorovius said of the Princess: 'Her whole being repels me but she has a sparkling wit.'

the bonds of tonal inevitability by approaching the home tonic from the most distant point via a compressed series of short cuts. This gives the music a bold virility and flamboyance which becomes an unmistakably Lisztian handprint (for example, the well-known opening measures of the Piano Concerto no.1 in E flat).

Liszt's early reputation was not built on these esoteric experimental works but on his pianism and its dazzling reflection in the numerous arrangements he made from works by other composers. It was a natural part of composing to him, and he continued the practice long after he retired from the concert platform. The accumulated legacy of some two hundred piano transcriptions ranges from Palestrina

Above: The Court Concert by Schams and Lafitte: Liszt playing at a concert for charity before the Emperor (and King of Hungary) Franz Joseph and many of the Hungarian nobility at the Municipal Concert Hall of Pest. This was one of the few occasions on which Liszt played publicly at this time, although those who did hear him play at private gatherings or to his pupils thought that his playing was finer even than in his days as a virtuoso.

Above right: Fancy-dress ball of the Männergesangsverein in Vienna in 1880; among the costumes can be seen those of Liszt, Offenbach and Wagner.

and Bach, through the classics to the music of his younger contemporaries. They are usually divided into two categories – the *partitions de piano* where his aim is a scrupulous and more or less objective realization of the composer's intentions in the new medium, and the operatic fantasies or paraphrases where he gives his imagination and subjective responses freer rein and Liszt the composer takes over from the arranger. Additionally, a great many song transcriptions occupy (and, to some extent, overlap) the middle ground between these two categories. They include numerous arrangements of well-known *Lieder* by Schubert and Schumann, and his setting of Beethoven's *Adelaide* is typical of his ambivalent approach to the genre. The opening Larghetto follows Beethoven's plan exactly, although sumptuously laid out for the instrument from the point of view of sonority and linear balance, and the concluding Allegro again gives strict priority to Beethoven's simple exultation. Between the two, however, Liszt interpolates a lengthy and elaborate cadenza in which he gives heady expression to his personal responses.

Liszt did not invent the concert transcription: Bach, with his numerous arrangements of his own and others' music, was his most illustrious, though by no means earliest predecessor. But, through his unique insights into the suggestive resources of his instrument, Liszt was certainly the first to vanquish 'the poverty and unrelieved vacuity' of conventional piano reductions which, he said, 'betrayed rather than conveyed Beethoven's or Mozart's thoughts.' He modestly likened his craft to that of the 'intelligent engraver, the conscientious translator' in seeking to transfer to the piano 'not only the grand outlines of Beethoven's compositions but also all those numerous fine details and smaller traits that so powerfully contribute to the completeness of the whole.'

The ingenious acoustic deceptions, manipulative devices and textural perspectives he devised to this end left their mark not only on future transcribers like Busoni and Godowsky but also on all composers of piano music.

The operatic paraphrases or *Réminiscences* are another matter. Here Liszt conjures, with uncanny *legerdemain* and imaginative vitality, the opulent splendor and excitement (and, sometimes, the absurd vanity) of grand opera from an instrument that had hitherto ventured little further than trite variations on popular arias. *Norma*, *Don Giovanni*, *La Juive* and *Les Huguenots* are among the most extravagant and exciting of these forays, and offer a resumé of vocal and dramatic highlights in glittering pianistic array. An excerpt like 'Im stillen Herd' from *Die Meistersinger*, on the other hand, is more of an introspective musing on a captivating moment, whereas in the *Faust Waltz*, Gounod's decorous tunes are infused with a malevolent *diablerie* that is entirely Lisztian.

Liszt's obsession with his instrument – 'All my desires, all my dreams, my joys and sorrows are there' – was also the primary stimulus for the *Paganini Studies* (themselves transcriptions) and the *Douze Etudes d'exécution transcendante*. Romantic dreams are given more poetic expression in the first two volumes of *Années de pèlerinage* which record his impressions of travels in Switzerland and Italy with Marie d'Agoult. The Swiss collection consists predominantly of evocations of nature such as the sparkling *Au bord d'une source* and the mighty *Orage*, which opens with a dissonant clangor (a progression to be found in the youthful 'Malédiction' Concerto and the symphonic poem *Prometheus*) that typifies the steely spine which distinguishes these pieces from the more effeminate effusions of minor Romantic miniaturists. The second book, *Italie*, is concerned

Right and below: Pieces from the *Années de pèlerinage. Deuxième année: Italie* (1858). Most of these piano solos were inspired by particular works of art that Liszt encountered, and by his reading of Dante and Petrarch in the happy days of his stay in Italy with Marie d'Agoult. The *Petrarch Sonnets* (*right*) Liszt had set to music as songs in 1838-9 and later transcribed for the *Années de pèlerinage*. The seventh piece (*below*) was the *Fantaisie quasi sonata après une lecture du Dante*, written two years after his 'Dante' Symphony of 1856.

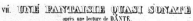

Above and opposite: Some of the works of art that so impressed Liszt in Italy, and that were to color his interpretation of music. He was particularly moved by the richness of the Renaissance period and became more convinced of the essential unity of all art. *The Triumph of Death* (*above*), a fresco in the Campo Santo in Pisa, inspired the idea of his *Totentanz*.

not so different as one might think from the 'Eroica' Symphony and the Requiem. Dante has found his pictorial expression in Orcagna and Michelangelo. One day no doubt he will find his musical expression in the Beethoven of the future.'

This was the artistic credo that was to govern the creation of the symphonic poems and his masterpieces the 'Faust' Symphony and the Piano Sonata in B minor, and, if the miniatures from the *Années de pèlerinage* are essentially of the same genre as Schumann's *Waldscenen* or other *Charakterstücke*, the two more substantial works from the collection, *Vallée d'Obermann* and *Après une lecture du Dante* (commonly, the 'Dante' Sonata) are already prototypes for the large-scale compositions of the 1850s. The principal objection of the avant-gardists to the classical forms perpetuated by Mendelssohn and Schumann was the degree of repetition necessitated by the demands of structural symmetry. Such formulae, they felt, impeded the dramatic narrative and were at odds with the spontaneous expression of personal feeling which was the new criterion of artistic vitality. Very early in his career, Liszt fixed upon his own solution by evolving a process of constant metamorphosis of themes whereby a melody or thematic idea could change its character (and often its rhythmic and harmonic characteristics) according to the expressive and emotional exigencies of the dramatic action. He did not abandon classical forms but gave them a new fluidity and freedom, which had far-reaching effects on subsequent generations. The 'Dante' Sonata exemplifies this process together with several other Lisztian trademarks: a theatrical 'fire and brimstone' view of hell alongside a chaste, modal religiosity, opulent *bel canto* melodies, sensuous love music, sardonic *diablerie* and grandiose climaxes are all there, presented with exultant virtuosity and uncanny powers of orchestral suggestion. The overall key pattern is roughly in accordance

with art rather than nature, and its celebration of Raphael, Michelangelo, Petrarch and Dante is a passionate manifesto for the ideology set forth in a letter written from Italy in 1839: 'Art revealed itself before my eyes in all its splendor; its universality and unity were disclosed to me. Each day brought home to me more and more the hidden connections uniting works of genius. Raphael and Michelangelo gave me a better understanding of Mozart and Beethoven. Giovanni da Pisa, Fra Beato and Francia explained to me Allegri, Marcello, Palestrina. Titian and Rossini appeared to me like two heavenly bodies shining with the same light. The Colosseum and the Campo Santo are

Above right: The Annunciation by Fra Beato Angelico. Liszt named Fra Angelico as one of the painters who revealed to him the music of the Italian Renaissance.

Right: Michelangelo's statue of Lorenzo de' Medici from his tomb in the Cappella Medici, which inspired *Il Penseroso*, the second piece of *Années de pèlerinage: Deuxième année.*

with the accepted norms of sonata principle, but the distinction between thematic groups and the divisions of exposition, development and recapitulation are no longer clearly defined. There is, to be sure, a certain amount of harmonic mystification as the fiercely declamatory introduction (undoubtedly illustrative of Dante's most famous lines, 'Lasciate ogni speranza Voi ch'entrate') proceeds through a series of tritones and obscure keys before establishing the home base of D minor, but this is itself a renewal of the slow introductions of classical symphonies, chromatically distorted to heighten the dramatic effect. The principle of Liszt's thematic transformation can be illustrated perfectly by tracing the progress of the main theme, a shuddering chromatic figure initially symbolizing the wailing of the damned, but later serving eloquently as the love music of Paolo and Francesca. Its ingenious diatonic expansion in the succeeding passage is a device more readily associated with Bartók than high Romanticism.

Such an idea was not totally new, for Berlioz had done something similar with the *idée fixe* which threads its way through the *Symphonie fantastique*. Schubert also had experimented along these lines in his 'Wanderer' Fantasy, a four-movememt work based on a single theme. Liszt knew Schubert's work well (he arranged it for piano and orchestra) and the 'cyclic' sonata form of his Piano Concerto in E flat can probably be traced back to this source. The flaws in many of Liszt's larger works hinge on their failure to mold convincing climaxes from fundamentally unsuitable material. The Ballade in B minor, for instance, opens impressively with a somber incantation of Byronic gloom which, when transmuted in B major as the piece approaches its climax, becomes tinged with sentimentality from whence it degenerates into grandiloquent bathos. A similar fate threatens the exquisite opening phrases of the Second Piano Concerto in A when enlisted into a triumphal march which only an exceptionally heroic performance can rescue from embarrassment. Such heroics could be taken for granted in Liszt's own performances but, at such moments, the posturings of lesser virtuosi can often aggravate their inherent banality where a great one can sweep past in triumph.

The symphonic poems, despite their totally serious intent, sometimes fall prey to this weakness. Their apotheotic climaxes can seem more declarations of intent than creative achievement. *Festklänge* (composed in 1853 as a decidedly premature celebration of his forthcoming nuptials), *Mazeppa* and *Les Préludes* all have moments of hollow bombast which are disconcerting in a composer of genius, but the elevated lyrical poetry of *Orpheus* brings reassurance, and there are passages to treasure in *Hamlet* and *Héroïde funèbre*.

• Liszt's greatest works •

Any suspicion that Liszt lacked the sustained inspiration for the large canvas is totally dispelled by two masterpieces, the Piano Sonata in B minor and the 'Faust' Symphony. The Sonata has been aptly described as Liszt's autobiography and, indeed, the many and various idiosyncrasies and contradictions of his genius, his very *id* in fact, seem to tumble from this unique and embracing work. Historically it is of the greatest importance because it brought renewal to a form which had actually regressed since Beethoven forced asunder the constraints it had hitherto implied. Liszt gathers together the traditional sonata movements into a single massive edifice, incorporating a fully fledged slow movement into its development section and admitting sufficient literal recapitulation to give stability to the structure. His mutation of themes matches their mercurially changing roles, now defiant, now heroic, pathetic or venomous, with unerring aptness, and the juxtaposition of unfettered recitative and high rhetoric with remorselessly driven sections in *tempo giusto* suggests a wild freedom restrained by an iron will. The virtuoso pianism becomes an additional creative element, and the ethereal conclusion (an inspired afterthought to replace the entirely unworthy bombast of the original ending) has a mystical aura that is as awe-inspiring as it is original.

The three movements of the 'Faust' Symphony overtly represent Faust, Gretchen and Mephistopheles, but are so powerfully drawn as to suggest irresistibly the forces and ideals of Liszt's own personality. The metamorphosis of themes here serves a specific as well as general artistic end. The themes of the 'Faust' movement, which wondrously convey his self-doubt, passions, amorous abandon or defiance are savagely distorted to represent Mephistopheles in an unusually precise analogy of Goethe's concept of evil as the spirit of negation. The central Gretchen movement evokes a virginal serenity and ecstasy rarely attained, and its

strains are recalled with telling effect in the elevated choral epilogue. Even the orchestration, Liszt's acknowledged Achilles heel, reaches a high level of attainment in the 'Faust' Symphony, and the allocation of Gretchen's theme to an oboe accompanied by a solo viola, and its subsequent elaboration by four solo violins, are touches of imaginative delicacy that any composer might envy.

Liszt's fascination with the sinister, sardonic and satanic was shared by several Romantic artists. The harsh, clanking *Totentanz*, for piano and orchestra, and the *Mephisto Waltzes* are further examples of his evocative powers in the darker regions of experience and imagination. The *Mephisto Waltz* no.1, which exists in equally brilliant versions for piano and for orchestra, is one of his most perfect achievements. Lenau's poem, *Der Tanz in der Dorfschenke*, on which it is based, relates how Mephisto seizes a violin at a village dance and plays such wild intoxicating music that one of the girls succumbs to Faust's seduction. Liszt's symphonic poem ostensibly adopts the traditional ternary structure of a country dance, but bends it to the narrative of the poem with a skill that is positively devilish in itself. The sinister, pulsating undercurrent to the tuning of the violin, the snatches of sardonic laughter and, above all, the grafting of the melodic contours of the voluptuous seduction music on to the stamping rhythms of the rustic dance in a thrillingly orgiastic climax are a supreme realization of Liszt's avowed aim of a 'closer alliance' of music and poetry.

It is characteristic of Liszt that he should see no incongruity in conceiving the flagrantly sensuous *Mephisto Waltz* no.1 at a time when he was increasingly preoccupied with religious choral music. Indeed sensuous and dramatic qualities are found side by side with devotional simplicity in two important works of the Weimar period, the 'Gran' Mass and Psalm XIII, which both employ full-scale orchestral forces in addition to choir and soloists. His two grandest oratorios pose the same paradox. *The Legend of Saint Elizabeth* is decidedly dramatic, even operatic in its highly charged recitatives and *scenas*, despite its liberal use of plainchant and other church sources; and although *Christus* is rather more static, it contains many Wagnerian cross-currents, especially in the agonized chromaticism of its moving third part, 'Passion and Resurrection'. However, the *Missa Choralis* of 1865 is of an unrelieved austerity and seems a conscious reversion to the purity of sixteenth-century church music, a little-publicized side of Liszt's art which had revealed itself as early as 1849 in a Mass composed for male voices. Liszt's ambivalent approach to religious music, oscillating between starkness and the heady, perfumed religiosity of *Parsifal*, is epitomized by *Via Crucis*, for voices and organ, in which bare modal unisons alternate with interludes of sparse but anguished chromaticism, which at times breaks free of all tonal implications and approaches the language of Schoenbergian expressionism.

Above: Cartoon of Liszt, *The Abbé* by Spy, dated May 1886, from the English magazine *Vanity Fair*. In this year Liszt visited London, Antwerp, Paris and Luxemburg for concerts in celebration of his seventy-fifth year. Concerts were given all over Europe in his honor. In April, in London, where this cartoon was made, he attended a performance of his *St Elizabeth* oratorio.

The late piano pieces were long dismissed as incoherent experiments, a record of disintegrating ideals or, at best, sketches for an indeterminate project. There is a bitterness in this music that is not ingratiating, nor is its harshness mitigated by coloring, or even light and shade. Pieces like the bleak *Nuages gris* or the inconclusive *En rêve* must remain enigmatic, but the barbaric splendor of *Csardas macabre* or *Unstern!* has much to tell us in the light of our experience of Bartók and Stravinsky.

No composer made a deeper impact on the music of others. Liszt's symphonic poems determined the format and much of the language of the tone-poems of Strauss, Tchaikovsky and Smetana and his *Les Jeux d'eaux à la Villa d'Este* resounds through much of Debussy, Ravel and even Messiaen. Mahler, Bartók, Schoenberg – the list begins to read like a roll-call of twentieth-century masters, such was the extent of Liszt's influence.

Of all great composers, Liszt was perhaps the most deeply flawed. But he was much more than a composer, and a *Hungarian Rhapsody* or a *Transcendental Study* reveals but a single facet of his greatness. The whole man is only to be found in a handful of masterpieces and, while his stature as a composer will continue to arouse controversy, it is a mean disposition that will deny him his status as one of music's greatest heroes.

Left: Study of Liszt by the French photographer Nadar.

Below: The funeral of Franz Liszt in Bayreuth 4 August 1886 (after a photograph). Liszt had traveled to Bayreuth for the Wagner festival in July, but was not invited to stay at Wahnfried with Cosima, who was much involved in the organization of the festival. He developed a fever and seems to have spent some days in his lodgings without proper care. He died on 31 July. Cosima was criticized by his friends and pupils for what they saw as a lack of respect for her father, particularly in not carrying out his wishes for his burial: he did not receive the last rites of the Church, nor was he given a Requiem Mass.

Before leaving vocal music and passing on to the compositions of Liszt's last years, attention should be drawn to his songs, a medium in which he conducted some of his boldest experiments from his earliest years. Some, admittedly, are tritely sentimental, others hollowly melodramatic, while others inflict curious wounds on foreign languages ('Kennst DU das Land' says Liszt's setting of 1842, subtly corrected in his revision of 1860). There are several, though, that anticipate the fragrant subtleties of the French *mélodie* ('Comment, disaient-ils') or the most sophisticated *tessitura* of Richard Strauss ('Ich möchte hingehen' – which also unambiguously anticipates the opening phrase of *Tristan und Isolde*), and his search for musical evocations of poetic moods leads to some curious aphorisms and unresolved cadences.

Unresolved dissonance is but one of the areas in which Liszt's late works anticipate twentieth-century music. An extreme example is the motet *Ossa arida*, for male voices and organ, in which all the notes of the diatonic scale are sounded simultaneously. His frequent use of tritones and of chords built of fourths and fifths in place of conventional triadic harmonies, his blurring of the distinction between major and minor and his use of medieval church modes and whole-tone scales, the deliberate primitivism of his bare unisons and unaccompanied melody, his ambiguous tonality, even atonality – all these phenomena which became the currency of twentieth-century composers in their retreat from the inflated Romantic ego are to be found in Liszt.

PETER ILYICH TCHAIKOVSKY

PAUL GRIFFITHS

Peter Ilyich Tchaikovsky was born on 7 May 1840 in Kamsko-Votkinsk, a mining town in the district of Vyatka. His father was chief inspector of the mines, his mother a woman of Huguenot descent and neurotic disposition. He spent his early childhood in the company of two older and two younger children; then in 1850, six years after the birth of her last child, his mother gave birth to twins, Anatol and Modest, of whom Modest in particular was to loom large in the composer's later life. For the moment, this was a happy time. Between the age of four and eight he had the attention of a French governess who taught him French and German, but her departure was a sore blow, exacerbated two years later, in 1850, when he was sent away from home to law school in St Petersburg. There he encountered homosexual practices that drew out or confirmed his own inclinations.

In 1854 his mother died suddenly of cholera. Until this time music seems to have been for him no more than it would have been for any child of his time and class: he had taken piano lessons; he had been much impressed by the family's musical box. But now, in the immediate wake of his mother's death, he began to compose, and so was established the practice of writing music as an emotional outlet.

His first composition was a waltz for the piano, written while the motherless family was spending the summer of 1854 at Oranienbaum on the Gulf of Finland. He also toyed with the idea of writing an opera, for which his training so far would surely not have fitted him. In 1855 he started lessons with a good piano teacher, Rudolf Kündinger, and in 1856 he met an affected Italian singing teacher, Luigi Piccioli, under whose influence he wrote an empty song in the Italian manner, 'Mezza-notte': this, privately printed in 1860, was his first published work. It was not a promising début, and it is hard to know if Tchaikovsky yet thought of himself as a serious composer.

By 1863, however, he had made his decision: he was twenty-three. Since leaving law school in 1859 he had lived a double life, working at the Ministry of Justice and attending regular classes in music, latterly at the St Petersburg Conservatory. Now he entered this establishment definitively as a student and stayed there for two and a half years. During this period, under the tutelage of Anton Rubinstein, the Conservatory's director, he composed little of note except for an unkempt overture, *The Storm* (1864), based on the recent play by Ostrovsky that some sixty years later would be made into an opera by Janáček as *Kátya Kabanová*. His graduation exercise, performed in January 1866, was a cantata setting Schiller's *Ode to Joy*, which though severely criticized in the press earned him a silver medal.

He had little need of it, for even before graduating he had been offered, and had accepted, a teaching post in Moscow, at the institution that during the course of 1866 was to be established as the Moscow Conservatory. The director here was Nikolai Rubinstein, brother of Anton, a man more receptive to new ideas, especially to those concerning nationalist music that were circulating in the group around Balakirev in St Petersburg. Encouraged by him, Tchaikovsky embarked on his First Symphony, in G minor, which was finished and revised by the end of 1866, though later revised again in 1874: such reconsideration became typical of Tchaikovsky, who was always prey to the criticism of others or to his own self-doubts. However this may be, the Symphony is a touching picture of Tchaikovsky's personality emerging from a generalized atmosphere of Mendelssohn and Schumann. Its subtitle, 'Winter daydreams,' suggests the Romantic mood, and the element of autobiography is not vitiated by the use of folk-style themes in three of the four movements: only the scherzo, which is placed third, is free of them.

Tchaikovsky's next major undertaking was his first opera. Again he turned to a play by Ostrovsky, *The Voyevoda*, and completed the composition between March 1867 and the summer of 1868, when he was visiting Paris. The piece was staged at the Bolshoi Theater the following February, but it was a failure, and Tchaikovsky later destroyed it, though not before he had incorporated much of the music in another opera, *The Oprichnik* (1870-2), and in his ballet *Swan Lake* (1875-6). Meanwhile he had loved, or thought he loved, and lost an opera singer, Désirée Artôt. He even announced his engagement to her, but it may well be that he was misinterpreting what was only on her part coquettish enjoyment of a young man's admiration. Other contacts of this period went deeper. In 1867 he met Berlioz, who had already been a wild influence on *The Storm*,

Above: The Tchaikovsky family in 1848. Mother and father, Alexander and Ilya, are seated. Zinaida and Nikolai stand between them. Alexandra (Sasha) and Ippolit are in front. Eight-year-old Peter stands on the far left of the picture. The twins, Modest and Anatol, were born two years later.

Right: The house where Peter was born, in the industrial town of Kamsko-Votkinsk, close to the Ural Mountains. His father was a mining inspector.

and the next year he made the acquaintance of Balakirev and his circle, among whom were Musorgsky, Borodin and Rimsky-Korsakov.

Balakirev criticized the young Tchaikovsky's symphonic fantasia, *Fate* (1868), and then had a close hand in shaping his next orchestral piece, the fantasy overture *Romeo and Juliet*. He composed this in October-November 1869, then revised it the next summer in response to Balakirev's adverse comments, and so created his first major work. The subject of fate's tragic intervention in romantic love was one that appealed to him very stongly; the strength of the appeal is obvious in the love music that swells so passionately in the orchestra. But at the same time, the demands of an overture form, requiring development and recapitulation, gave him the necessary distance from which to view his material objectively. He also remained at a distance from the Balakirev group, for though Balakirev was instrumental in the reworking of *Romeo and Juliet*, Tchaikovsky was a Conservatory-trained musician, and one who had already shown, in his First Symphony, his leanings towards the West. He retained an interest in Russian folksong – he used a Ukrainian song in the popular slow movement of his First String Quartet (1871) – but he was never an ardent nationalist.

Ukrainian melodies appear once again in his Second Symphony, in C minor, nicknamed for that reason 'Little Russian.' This was written in 1872 but, once more, substantially revised in 1879-80, so that the final version dates from after the Fourth Symphony. That may account for the effectiveness of the first movement, virtually replaced at the revision. The slow movement was rescued from the bridal march of another abandoned opera, *Undine* (1869). Following his symphony Tchaikovsky chose another Shakespeare subject for his symphonic fantasia *The Tempest* (1873), but found this play less conducive to symphonic treatment.

Next came another opera, Tchaikovsky's fourth after *The Voyevoda*, *Undine* and *The Oprichnik*. It was, for the first time, a fantastic comedy, based on a Gogol story: *Vakula the Smith*, refashioned in 1885 as *The Slippers*. As in the preceding symphony, Ukrainian folksong is here too a potent source of melody, but the opera draws just as freely on the fund of magical and picturesque elements that Glinka had devised for his operas *Ruslan and Lyudmila* and *A Life for the Tsar*. Composed in the summer of 1874, the work seems to have released a lyrical flow that spread beyond it, for within the next year Tchaikovsky had written three sets of six songs each, choosing his texts chiefly from tender Romantic Russian lyrics, though making one oriental excursion in 'The Canary' and including one strong ballad in 'The Corals.'

• Years of inspiration •

The important works that followed *Vakula* were, however, mostly orchestral, and they came in a flood: the First Piano Concerto (1874-5), the Third Symphony (1875-6), *Swan Lake* (1875-6), the symphonic fantasia *Fran-*

Right: The composer in 1862, the year he entered the newly opened St Petersburg Conservatory, while still working at the Ministry of Justice.

Far right: Désirée Artôt (1835-1907), the Belgian singer with whom Tchaikovsky was briefly infatuated when she appeared in Moscow with a visiting Italian opera company in 1868. The following year she married the Spanish baritone Padilla, who was also a member of the company.

cesca da Rimini (1876), the *Variations on a Rococo Theme* for cello and orchestra (also 1876), the Fourth Symphony (1877-8) and the Violin Concerto (1878). No other period in Tchaikovsky's life was so richly filled with masterpieces, and the achievement becomes all the more remarkable considering that while working on his Fourth Symphony Tchaikovsky also wrote his opera *Eugene Onegin*. Yet the explanation is quite straightforward. He was writing more because he was experiencing more; increasingly tormented by sexual guilt, he was moving towards a point of crisis that would eventually find him rushing headlong into marriage in 1877. And he poured into his music the sublimated passion and the tragic sense of oppression he felt.

To some extent the First Piano Concerto, in B flat minor, is a bridge between this period of hectic emotional turmoil and the earlier nationalist phase, for once more it makes use of Ukrainian themes (in the outer movements). However, its arresting opening melody is Tchaikovsky's own, and though this powerful subject (in the relative major, D flat) never returns, it makes an effective start to a concerto of great splendor and prowess, and it also chimes with an important subject in the finale, so that the whole work is contained within an imposing frame. But within this frame the music is as much confessional as heroic: the quick waltz in the middle of the slow movement is said to have been based on a song that Mlle Artôt used to sing, and so there may be some autobiographical message hidden here. All in all, the concerto – which was Tchaikovsky's first work for a solo instrument and orchestra – makes a splendid culmination to the tendency, since Beethoven, for such works to be dramatic displays of rivalry between soloist and orchestra.

It was not, however, received as such by its intended first soloist. Tchaikovsky played it through to his superior Nikolai Rubinstein on Christmas Eve 1874 and received for his pains dismissive criticism. In defence of Rubinstein it has to be said that Tchaikovsky did revise the work after this meeting, improving some key passages (not least the opening). Nevertheless, Tchaikovsky was distressed, as he always was, to receive adverse comments, and rather than to Rubinstein he dedicated the work to the German conductor and pianist Hans von Bülow, who gave the first performance in Boston in October 1875.

Meanwhile Tchaikovsky had completed his Third Symphony, in D major, in the summer of that year. Like Beethoven's 'Pastoral' and Schumann's Third, this symphony is in five movements: a slow movement in the middle is preceded by a waltz and followed by an exquisitely orchestrated scherzo; framing these is a symphonic allegro and a boisterous finale. The allegro betrays Tchaikovsky's worries about the proper construction of a sonata form, for, fearing that his normal style of melody was too rich and individual for correct 'development,' he here used themes of the utmost simplicity. The finale is in polka rhythm, for which reason the symphony is often known as the 'Polish.'

Tchaikovsky's next major work was the ballet *Swan Lake*, composed between the summer of 1875 and the spring of 1876. This was one of the very first full-length ballet scores written by a major composer, and apparently Tchaikovsky wrote it before he had heard Delibes's *Coppélia* (1870), which was the only serious predecessor to *Swan Lake*. The success of the latter has to be seen, therefore, as a sign of a natural aptitude. Partly it was a matter of style: movements in symphonic works had already shown Tchaikovsky's fascination with the waltz

(examples have been mentioned in the First Piano Concerto as well as in the Third Symphony). Moreover, many of his songs, smaller piano pieces (such as the illustrative cycle *The Seasons*, 1875-6, consisting of twelve monthly entries in a musical diary) and operatic numbers had demonstrated his delight in creating small sound-pictures of the kind found in *Swan Lake*. But one may detect also another sort of attraction in the world of ballet, more psychological than musical. Ballet offered Tchaikovsky an ideal world, a glamorous paradise in which fears could be dissolved and hopes realized.

With its story of doomed love the ballet *Swan Lake* returned to the emotional atmosphere of *Romeo and Juliet*. The main character is Odette, who has been turned into a swan by Rotbart, though she and her companions return to their human form at night. One night they are chanced upon by Siegfried (no relation to Wagner's hero), who falls in love with Odette and declares he will rescue her. But then at a ball he encounters Odile, the daughter of Rotbart, dressed by her father to resemble Odette. Siegfried, taken in by the disguise, becomes betrothed to Odile, whereupon Odette appears. He realizes his mistake, rushes off to the lake and is forgiven by Odette, but Rotbart conjures up a storm and the lovers are drowned.

The narrative is faithfully followed in the score, but the best parts of the music are the set pieces: the dances for the swans, including a characteristic waltz, and the suite of regional dances interpolated into the final act. For ballet tastes of the 1870s, however, the music was simply too good, and the first production was poorly received. It was not until 1895 that *Swan Lake* was revealed as a masterpiece, given new choreography by Marius Petipa and

Lev Ivanov, the first choreographers respectively of the later ballets *The Sleeping Beauty* and *The Nutcracker*. By then, though, Tchaikovsky was dead.

While working on *Swan Lake* the composer had written his Third String Quartet in E flat minor (1876), an intensely tragic piece dedicated to the memory of his violinist friend Ferdinand Laub. This had been started in Paris, where he had been deeply impressed by a performance of *Carmen* and stimulated to search

for a similarly dramatic subject for himself. One of the possibilities he considered was the tale of Francesca da Rimini and her tragic lover as recounted in Dante's *Inferno*, but on the prompting of his brother Modest he decided to channel his response to this highly charged material into an orchestral piece, the feverishly passionate and noisy symphonic fantasia

Francesca da Rimini. Before composing this, in the autumn of 1876, he visited Bayreuth for the first performance of the complete *Ring*, and there are some Wagnerian echoes in the work. However, he found Wagner's tetralogy much less to his taste than *Carmen*, and the more extreme effects of *Francesca* – the whirling hellfire and the massive climaxes – owe as much to Liszt and Berlioz as they do to Wagner, while the love music is entirely his own.

His next orchestral work, written straight afterwards in December 1876, was quite different, but equally personal. It was the set of *Variations on a Rococo Theme* for cello and orchestra, delightful and suave music that suggests that the eighteenth century, like the ballet stage, was for Tchaikovsky an ideal world into which he could escape. The 'Rococo Theme' is in fact his own, but the graciousness is that of a chocolate-box Mozart, and the work is evidence of an idealizing veneration of that composer which would also infiltrate later compositions – not least, of course, the suite of arrangements that Tchaikovsky published as the fourth of his orchestral suites, with the subtitle 'Mozartiana' (1887).

At about the time of the *Rococo Variations* Tchaikovsky began his curious association with Nadezhda von Meck, an enormously wealthy widow who for fourteen years was his confidante as he was hers. Yet they never spoke with each other: that was her condition,

Above: Portrait of a Family, an anonymous painting that captures the character of a well-to-do Russian home around the middle of the century; the piano takes pride of place. Tchaikovsky wrote many charming salon-pieces and songs for this lucrative market.

Left: Vasily Perov's portrait of the dramatist Alexander Ostrovsky (1823-86). Tchaikovsky's first opera, *The Voyevoda*, is based on one of Ostrovsky's dramas. He also wrote an overture to Ostrovsky's *The Storm*, and some incidental music to the same playwright's *The Snowmaiden* – soon to be the subject of Rimsky-Korsakov's opera.

Right: Madame Nadezhda von Meck (1831-94), the wealthy widow with a love of music. Her association with Tchaikovsky began in 1876, after she was introduced to his music, probably by Nikolai Rubinstein. It continued for fourteen years, during which they corresponded regularly and she supported him with an annuity. But they never met.

though it probably suited Tchaikovsky just as well to have someone to whom he could open himself only in letters. For both of them, the correspondence offered a contact that could be controlled. It was also exceedingly fortunate for posterity that Tchaikovsky's feelings were thus recorded at a critical period in his life, for it was within a few months of the initiation of this correspondence that he took the long-considered decision to marry.

• Tchaikovsky's marriage •

Right: An illustration from the first edition of Pushkin's verse drama *Eugene Onegin*, the inspiration for Tchaikovsky's most famous opera. It shows Tatyana trying to tell her own fortune by the reflection of the moon.

For a full decade his life had had a regular pattern: he composed, taught at the Moscow Conservatory and spent lengthy periods in the West on holiday, visiting fellow composers or seeing new operas. But since the beginning of 1876, at least, he had been looking for release from his homosexual cravings in marriage. Then in the spring of 1877, with his Fourth Symphony and its fateful tragedy already begun, he received a written declaration of love from one Antonina Ivanovna Milyukova. Almost as if art were setting out to imitate life, he thereupon picked up Pushkin's verse novel *Eugene Onegin*, which had been suggested to him as a possible opera subject and in which the drama hinges on a girl's rejected love letter. Fearing to create a similar situation in his own life, and moved no doubt by Antonina's threats of suicide, he agreed to meet her, and very soon to marry her. He then finished the essential work on the symphony (it remained only to be orchestrated), and sketched out, too, a good proportion of *Eugene Onegin*, before marrying Antonina in a private ceremony on 18 July 1877: he had met his wife for the first time only seven weeks before.

According to letters to his brother Modest, Tchaikovsky had told Antonina that theirs

could be only a platonic marriage, but even this degree of proximity to her rapidly grew beyond endurance. By early August he had fled to the estate of his sister Alexandra (Sasha) Davydov at Kamenka in the Ukraine, always a haven for him. There he began to orchestrate the Fourth Symphony and continued his work on *Eugene Onegin*. The start of the Conservatory term in late September brought him back to Moscow and to his wife, but within days he had made a feeble attempt at killing himself and then hurriedly departed for St Petersburg, where a doctor ordered him never to see Antonina again and to take a complete rest. Proceedings for legal separation were set in train by his brother Anatol, who then took the composer off to western Europe to recuperate.

He remained there until the following April, spending long periods at Clarens, not far from Geneva, but also visiting Paris, Italy and Vienna, where he was deeply impressed by Delibes's *Sylvia*. Meanwhile the symphony and the opera were both completed. These were the works that had lived through his marriage with him, and it is not surprising that they should both be intensely autobiographical, the purely orchestral work even more than the opera. That was always true of Tchaikovsky: it was easier for him to put himself into music where there was no other character.

In the tempestuous key of F minor, the symphony is riven throughout by a motto theme heard at the start and repeated in each of the three subsequent movements. This was a new idea, for César Franck's use of a similar technique began only later, and it gave Tchaikovsky the means to weld the four movements of his symphony very definitely into a whole. However, the motto has not just a structural

Но въ темномъ зеркалѣ одна
Дрожитъ печальная луна.

but also an unmistakable psychological function (possibly Tchaikovsky had been struck by the binding effect and the expressive power of Wagner's *leitmotifs*). After composing the work Tchaikovsky wrote down an explanatory program for the benefit of Mme von Meck, and though it would be unwise to place too much weight on this – he himself immediately expostulated to her on the inadequacy of words to render musically expressed feelings – his

description of the motto as representing fate indubitably rings true.

In the first movement it enters again and again to increase the tension and violence of the music, to wrest the protagonist back, in Tchaikovsky's interpretation, from daydreaming to immediate reality. The resulting structure is unusual. Instead of developing his ideas, he gradually transfers them upwards, a minor third at a time. This has the effect of gradually intensifying the feeling of oppression associated with the fate motto, while at the same time it sets the music not on the normal tonic-dominant axis but on the very much less stable frame of a diminished seventh chord (F–A flat–C flat–D–F). Moreover, a large proportion of the movement can be classified as exposition. The recapitulation, taking place after the music has completed its rise through an octave, is too brief and too intense to bring much feeling of completion: instead it leaves the listener in tense expectation of what is to come next.

What in fact comes next is a slow movement of hopeless nostalgia, which Tchaikovsky in his program saw as describing the sweet sadness of recollection. In the scherzo he made a feature of the orchestration: the first part is for pizzicato strings, after which there is a trio for the wind instruments and timpani, and finally in the repeat of the opening section the strings, woodwind and brass answer one another. The finale is simple and boisterous, with a prominent folksong theme, but even here the implacable fate motif rings out, reminding the protagonist of his tragic destiny even as he joins in popular merriment.

In *Eugene Onegin*, on the other hand, Tchaikovsky was projecting his feelings into his characters, and it was Tatyana, the loving heroine, who gained his sympathy much more than Onegin himself. Onegin, after all, is a man who thinks he understands the world; Tchaikovsky had much more in common with Tatyana, who is prepared to parade her feelings and find the world out of step with them. At the same time she is the ideal woman, tender and vulnerable, for whom Antonina would seem to have been a very poor substitute.

The four main characters are introduced in the first scene: the sisters Olga and Tatyana (mezzo and soprano), and two young men, Onegin (baritone) and his friend Lensky (tenor). Tatyana falls in love with Onegin at first sight, and in the next scene she confesses as much to her nurse. In her fateful letter to Onegin, Tchaikovsky's music catches all her nervous excitement and naïve, fresh passion: this letter scene is one of his finest achievements. In the third scene she meets Onegin in the garden, and he politely rejects her.

Where the first act has been generally intimate and sentimental, the second begins with a ball scene in which Tchaikovsky is able to display his skill in writing glittering dances, as he is again in the opening scene of the third and final act: the two scenes are nicely contrasted, the first taking place in the country where Tatyana's name day is being celebrated at her family home, the second in St Petersburg where she is now a great lady, wife of the Prince Gremin. At the second-act ball Onegin is bored, and takes it out on Lensky by openly flirting with Olga. This causes a quarrel that eventually leads to a challenge; next morning the two men meet for a duel and Lensky is shot. The third-act ball finds Onegin again bored, until he recognizes his hostess as Tatyana. The opera's last scene is set in her drawing room, where Onegin has come to declare his love for her at last. She, however, at the climax of a highly emotional dialogue, has the strength to keep faith with her husband, even as she reflects on what happiness she and Onegin might have had together.

Right: Playbill for the first night of the revival of Tchaikovsky's *Eugene Onegin* at the Bolshoi Theater, St Petersburg, in October 1884. It had been performed three years earlier in Moscow, but had not then met with any real success.

Right: Watercolor (1890) by Repin of the duel between Lensky and Eugene Onegin, in which the former is killed. Pushkin, creator of the story, was himself killed in a duel.

Tchaikovsky wrote most of the libretto himself, knowing that this was an opera of a very personal and special kind. He used the words 'lyric scenes' rather than 'opera' to describe its genre, so drawing attention to how much of the work, even in the ball scenes, is concerned with emotional confession in soliloquy and dialogue. There are a few musical themes that direct the emotion, including most notably a pregnant fate motif and a love theme for Tatyana. *Eugene Onegin* is decidedly not grand opera and, appropriately, its first performance was given in the small opera house in Moscow by a cast of students from the Conservatory.

But that was still more than a year ahead when Tchaikovsky completed the opera in February 1878. Continuing his stay in the West, he settled the following month back in Clarens, where he was visited by Joseph Kotek, a cheerful and handsome violinist in his early twenties who brought him much pleasure. They played through Lalo's *Symphonie espagnole* together, and Tchaikovsky was moved to write, within the space of eleven days, a concerto of his own for his young friend – his Violin Concerto in D. The sunny, generous nature of this work reflects the happy episode that gave birth to it.

In April 1878, with the Violin Concerto already scored, Tchaikovsky returned at last to Russia, but not yet to Moscow: instead he went once more to the Davydovs at Kamenka. When he did go back to Moscow, the following September, it was almost at once to resign from his post at the Conservatory. Mme von Meck was now guaranteeing him a comfortable income, and so he had no financial need to teach. But perhaps even more important to his decision was the knowledge that his homosexual inclination was now public. This made it difficult for him to engage in close contact for the moment with anyone outside the family. It also grieved him that that family still included Antonina. At the distance of more than a century it is hard to know what to make of her; only Tchaikovsky's side of the story is known, from which she emerges as an opportunist and an ignoramus (it seems she knew nothing of his music before marrying him). However, it is quite possible that he was not as honest with her as he imagined, and that she, a mature woman of normal sexual appetites, went into the marriage supposing that it would take a normal course. Nevertheless, she seems to have behaved with less than elegance afterwards, causing difficulties over the divorce, and Tchaikovsky was only able to free himself after she had given birth to an illegitimate child in 1881.

• Barren years •

All this brought about a phase of creative depression. During the previous three or four years his music had been fuelled by his sexual guilt, his despair and the emotional catastrophe of his marriage. All that was now past, and his

Above: Another of Repin's paintings, *On a Turf Bench, Krasnoye Village* (1876), evoking the leisurely country atmosphere that forms a background to the central drama of *Eugene Onegin.*

For example, Tchaikovsky now made a first essay in church music, the *Liturgy of St John Chrysostom*, which he set in the summer of 1878 for unaccompanied choir, as the Orthodox ritual demanded. He also followed ecclesiastical custom in keeping to the church modes and to plain chordal harmony. Nevertheless, the work is more admirable than the rambling and empty Piano Sonata in G major, which had been begun in Switzerland and was finished in the same summer at Kamenka. Having developed his own very individual interpretation of sonata design in the Fourth Symphony, he returns here to his feelings of insecurity and to a corresponding academicism. However, from this Ukrainian hiatus there was another set of six songs, op.38, including the attractive 'Don Juan's Serenade,' while there were also orchestral works that seem to have stirred him to more enthusiasm, not least the sequence of three he wrote in 1880, the *Italian Capriccio*, the Serenade in C and the overture *1812*. The first of these is a vivid and joyous impression based on his experiences during yet another winter visit to western Europe in 1879-80.

The Serenade for Strings is something rather different. It is suite-like in form, but the restriction to strings stimulated Tchaikovsky to a compensating verve and splendor in the harmonization. It has four movements, with a waltz and an elegy in the middle, and though all four are based on scale patterns, Tchaikovsky is here as inventive in varying the obvious as he is in discovering new force, richness and delicacy within the orchestral strings. By contrast, *1812* is music for the massive *tutti*, and effective in the genre of battle music which allows little room for subtlety. It was commissioned for the Moscow Exhibition of 1882 and designed to recount the defeat inflicted on Napoleon during his disastrous Russian winter of seventy years before. 'The overture will be very loud and noisy,' Tchaikovsky wrote at the time, 'but I've written it without affection and enthusiasm, and therefore there will probably be no artistic merit in it.'

Top left: Anna Sobeshchanskaya as Odette, the girl turned into a swan by sorcery, in *Swan Lake*.

Top right: A group of her enchanted swan maiden companions from the same early performance.

Above: The first performance of *Swan Lake*, in February 1877. Tchaikovsky's score was not appreciated until the 1895 version by Marius Petipa and Lev Ivanov.

nature was out in the open – he had nothing to hide, nothing to channel into music. For several years he produced nothing of the first importance. *Eugene Onegin* was succeeded by two forgotten operas, *The Maid of Orleans* (1878-9) and *Mazeppa* (1881-3). The symphony, which had become the medium for the most vividly personal testimony in his Fourth, was a genre he neglected, preferring the more controlled and anonymous form of the orchestral suite: there were three of these, in D (1879), in C (1883) and in G (1884), and then in 1887 a fourth, the already mentioned 'Mozartiana.' Masterpieces like the Serenade in C for string orchestra (1880) were comparatively few and far between, and they tended to be of a lighter character or else in quite new genres.

He certainly took more trouble with his Second Piano Concerto, in G major, finished in the same year of 1880. By this time Nikolai Rubinstein had changed his opinion of the First Concerto, and he had also played Tchaikovsky's G major Sonata. It was for him that Tchaikovsky, with similar generosity, wrote his Second Concerto. This time, however, Rubinstein died before he could give the work its first performance and so avoided being associated with a minor work after he had rejected a masterpiece, for the Second Concerto is no equal to the First.

Other compositions of 1880 included more songs, the seven of op.47, and also Tchaikovsky's only set of vocal duets with piano accompaniment, the set of six (op.46). These works, composed between the Second Concerto and the orchestral works of the autumn, were the product of a summer spent as usual at Kamenka. Tchaikovsky had also met, in the spring of 1880, the Grand Duke Konstantin Konstantinovich, who was a great admirer of his music (Tchaikovsky was to return the compliment in 1887 by setting six of the Grand Duke's poems as songs). Nor was this the only sign of royal favor. The new Tsar, Alexander III, was another admirer, and for his coronation in 1883 Tchaikovsky wrote a cantata, *Moscow*, and a *Festival Coronation March*. There was also more ordinary church music. In 1881 Tchaikovsky edited the sacred music of Dimitry Bortnyansky (1751-1825) and also began a Vesper Service, completed the next year and consisting of sonorous harmonizations of seventeen liturgical items. Smaller sacred pieces followed, in deference to the tastes of the Tsar.

Meanwhile Tchaikovsky wrote another opera, which the Tsar welcomed just as eagerly – *Mazeppa*, begun in the summer of 1881 but not completed until May 1883. During this period the only other important work he composed was his Piano Trio in A minor, written in the winter of 1881-2, which he again spent in western Europe. This was conceived partly as a memorial to Nikolai Rubinstein, which accounts for the tone of passionate regret in the first movement, the second (and last) being a long set of variations on a tune Rubinstein loved. It is said that each of the variations was intended to represent some event in Rubinstein's life.

• Success and recognition •

Mazeppa, most of it composed after the Trio, is in some measure a return to the Ukrainian Tchaikovsky of the Second Symphony, for it is set in the Ukraine in the early part of the eighteenth century, and includes picturesque folk elements, notably the vigorous *hopak* in the first act. Of course, the Second Symphony was only a decade old at this point, but Tchaikovsky's development in the interim had been rapid, particularly around the time of his marriage, and he had moved far away from the

ideals of the Balakirev set in St Petersburg. This is not to say that his music was any the less Russian than theirs. The difference, rather, is that between the Russia of Peter the Great and the Russia of Ivan the Terrible, Tchaikovsky was looking towards the elegance of the West, while Musorgsky, Rimsky-Korsakov and the rest were fastening on indigenous elements. It is significant, too, that when Tchaikovsky is most concerned with folk music, as in the Second Symphony or *Mazeppa*, it is with the folk music of the most westerly part of the Russian empire, the Ukraine, whereas Borodin and Rimsky-Korsakov in particular found more stimulus in the music of central Asia.

The action of *Mazeppa* unfolds in three acts. The first is set on the estate of Kochaby (bass), whose daughter Mariya (soprano) is in love with his friend Mazeppa (baritone). Her love is returned, but when Mazeppa asks for Mariya's hand, Kochaby refuses on the grounds of their difference in age. A more suitable swain is on hand in the young Andrei (tenor); Mariya, however, is adamant, and Kochaby resolves to rid himself of the problem by telling the Tsar of Mazeppa's secret plans to align himself with the Swedes against Russia.

Below: Four graduates from the Moscow Conservatory during Tchaikovsky's years as a professor. Seated, left, is the violinist Joseph Kotek, who advised Tchaikovsky on the composition of the Violin Concerto. The composer nicknamed him 'Kotik' (Tom-cat) on account of his high spirits.

Below: Tchaikovsky (right) in Switzerland in the autumn of 1878, recovering from his marriage to Antonina Milyukova. Also seated is brother Modest. The boy is Kolya Konradi, deaf and dumb, to whom Modest was private tutor.

Above: Ivan Kramskoi's portrait (1878) of Elizaveta Lavrovskaya, a celebrated contralto who gave the first performances of several of Tchaikovsky's songs, including 'None but the lonely heart.' She also suggested to him Pushkin's *Eugene Onegin* as material for an opera.

Top right: One of the last photographs of the composer, taken a few months before his death in November 1893.

The Tsar, however, trusting Mazeppa, hands Kochaby over to him, and the second act opens with Kochaby in Mazeppa's dungeon. Mariya and Mazeppa then share the central scene of the act – and of the entire opera – the scene with which Tchaikovsky began the composition (the libretto is his own, after Pushkin once more), which develops from reproof into a rapturous duet. Left alone, Mariya begins to think of her parents, at which point her mother arrives to elicit her help in saving her father. They rush off, but come too late to stop Kochaby's execution.

The final act begins with an orchestral tone-picture of the Battle of Poltava. Mazeppa, his army defeated, fights with Andrei, who dies in Mariya's arms. The conclusion is pathetic, with Mariya, her mind unhinged, singing a lullaby which recalls the very first chorus of the opera.

The first performance of *Mazeppa*, at the Bolshoi on 15 February 1884, came near the start of a year that marked an upswing in the composer's fortunes. In March Tchaikovsky was decorated by the Tsar with the Order of St Vladimir, albeit fourth class, and in October a revival of *Eugene Onegin* in St Petersburg met with great success. There were knocks too; in November he rushed to Switzerland to be at

the bedside of the dying Kotek. But whereas in previous winters he had wandered through western Europe, this time he longed to be back in Russia and to settle, for the first time in his adult life, in a home of his own. In February he duly bought a house at Maidanova, near Klin, within easy reach of Moscow, and he remained in that neighborhood for the rest of his life.

His new feeling of confidence and worth did not immediately result in any great musical change. As already mentioned, the intended symphony of spring 1884 turned into the Third Suite – though the last movement of that suite, the Theme and Variations, is more inventive and supreme than anything else in these works, and has deservedly gained a place as a concert item divorced from its context. Not so the *Concert Fantasia* for piano and orchestra, also composed in 1884 and again in G major, the key of the Second Piano Concerto and Piano Sonata. This is, however, a finer work than either of its predecessors. Also in 1884 there was another set of six songs, op.57.

All these works of 1884 may be regarded as preparations for the renewed creative achievement of the following year. After revising *Vakula the Smith* as *The Slippers* in the early spring, Tchaikovsky set to work at last on a new symphony, though this time one with a program drawn not from his own direct experience but from the reflection of that experience he found in a dramatic poem, Byron's *Manfred*. The idea for this came, as in the case of *Romeo and Juliet*, from Balakirev, with whom Tchaikovsky had resumed contact in 1882 after a period of estrangement. It was an inspired suggestion. Manfred, to a much greater extent than Onegin, gave Tchaikovsky a character with whom he could identify: a man wandering the Alps in brooding melancholy, wracked by the guilt of nameless crimes, a man of aristocratic mien and sensitive soul.

The idea for a 'Manfred' symphony was one that Balakirev had harbored since the 1860s, when the critic Vladimir Stasov had put the proposal to him and he, feeling it was not his subject, had passed the idea on to Berlioz. One can understand Berlioz not wishing to take it on at this late stage in his career when he had already written a 'Byron' symphony, *Harold in Italy*, but the association with Berlioz persisted in Balakirev's mind, and he even pointed out to Tchaikovsky particular Berlioz movements that might serve as models: the Queen Mab scherzo from *Romeo and Juliet* for the scherzo that forms the second movement of 'Manfred'; the pastoral from the *Fantastic Symphony* for the slow movement; and the 'Brigands' Orgy,' the finale of *Harold in Italy* itself, for the first and last movements.

The first movement is long, and much occupied with the gloomy motto theme, which it develops to a final climax of great force and wretchedness: Manfred's agonizings are powerfully set before the listener. The scherzo is in total contrast, and depicts the hero's encounter with an alpine sprite at a waterfall. In the slow movement he tries to lose himself in a pastoral idyll, and in the finale, as in the finale of the Fourth Symphony, it is bacchanalian revelry that contains the promise of escape. Restless music from the first movement, however, keeps returning to remind Manfred of his inconsolable condition.

Even before he finished the orchestration of 'Manfred' Tchaikovsky had started a new opera, *The Sorceress*, though as with *Mazeppa* the composition stretched over a period of almost two years; it was not completed until

May 1887. Apart from a volume of twelve songs written in the late summer of 1886, his op.60, *The Sorceress* was his only composition of this period, and it proved an unhelpful diversion at a time when he had only just rediscovered his musical self in 'Manfred'. Like its immediate predecessors *Mazeppa* and *Vakula the Smith*, *The Sorceress* is a nationalist piece, and like them too, it contains no character with whom he could sympathize, as he had with Tatyana in *Eugene Onegin*.

• Concert tours •

On 31 January 1887, with *The Sorceress* still in progress, Tchaikovsky conducted the first performance of *The Slippers* at the Bolshoi, his first appearance as a conductor for almost a decade. He suffered much mental anguish before the event, as can be imagined, but the performance was well received, and the experience seems to have pleased him more than he had envisaged. At any rate, the following March he conducted a concert of his music, and on 1 November he directed the first performance of *The Sorceress* at the Maryinsky in St Petersburg. After that he set out on his first foreign tour as a conductor, travelling between December 1887 and April 1888, and taking in Leipzig, Hamburg, Berlin, Prague, Paris and London. He met Brahms for the first time, and

Above: Self-caricature by Fyodor Stravinsky, the composer's father, in the role of Mamirov in *The Sorceress*. He was principal bass in the Imperial Opera and also sang in an early production of *The Oprichnik*.

Left: A costume sketch for Puss-in-Boots, one of Charles Perrault's fairytale characters featured in *The Sleeping Beauty*. The story of the ballet itself is based on another tale from Perrault's collection.

Above: Engraving of the scene by a canal from *The Queen of Spades*, in which Hermann betrays to Lisa his gambling mania. The work, once again based on a story by Pushkin, with a libretto by the composer and his brother Modest, was first produced at the Maryinsky Theater, St Petersburg, in 1890.

Top right: Mikhail Medredev as he appeared in the 1891 Moscow production of *The Queen of Spades*.

Brahms's affability seems to have got over his personal shyness and musical antipathy (he had heard Brahms's First Symphony ten years before and disliked it). He also made the acquaintance of Grieg, Dvořák, Gounod, Fauré, Massenet and Widor.

On his return to Russia he spent a holiday in Tbilisi, from where he wrote to Modest of his idea for an opera based on Pushkin's tale *The Queen of Spades*. As yet, however, the subject did not sufficiently move him, and so, as he continued, 'in the course of the summer I shall *definitely write a symphony*.' There was a new house to move into, and a new garden to tend, but he did indeed write the new symphony, his Fifth in E minor, between May and August 1888. Not only that, he also during the same period began a new narrative piece, the fantasy overture *Hamlet*, which he finished in October. Here there is a return to an earlier Shakespeare work, *Romeo and Juliet*, but the love interest was secondary to Tchaikovsky's identification with Hamlet, whom he saw as a character not dissimilar to Manfred.

The Fifth Symphony is also to some extent a program work, with a ground plan similar to that which had served in the Fourth Symphony: again there is a prominent theme which evidently represents the imperative of fate. The difference is that the fate theme is not a rude interruption but underlies all four movements of the symphony, each of them being a reaction to its summons. Being germinal, the theme also has a different character. As first presented it is no insistent fanfare but a quiet, heavy funeral march. After this comes a searching and highly expressive slow movement, followed by a waltz as scherzo. Tchaikovsky's young friend and colleague Sergei Taneyev had criticized his use of ballet styles in the middle movements of the Fourth Symphony, but clearly he saw no need to change his ways, for the rhythms of the ballet waltz had long been a part of his personal language. In any event, it is the finale of this symphony that has attracted criticism, not least from Brahms, who heard Tchaikovsky conduct it during his second tour of Germany in the winter of 1888-9. What has been regularly condemned here is the hollowness and excessive length of the composer's attempt to convert his fate theme into a triumphal quick march.

The completion of the Fifth Symphony and *Hamlet* went hand in hand with the composition of a further group of six songs, to French poems. These were Tchaikovsky's only settings of a foreign language. Then in December 1888 he started work on a full-length ballet, *The Sleeping Beauty*, commissioned by the Imperial Theaters. His conducting tour interrupted the composition, but he carried on with it during a long return journey by sea from Marseilles via Constantinople to Batum, and finished the essential work at home in June 1889. By the following September he had fully orchestrated the ballet, even though he wrote to Mme von Meck that he found the task of instrumentation more difficult than previously, possibly because he was aiming at more brilliant ballet effects. However, as before with *Swan Lake*, the merits of his ballet music were not immediately recognized. He himself was disappointed by the aloof reaction of the Tsar, and the ballet did not become a mainstay of the repertory until its high quality had been demonstrated by Diaghilev's revival in 1921, a whole generation after Tchaikovsky's death.

The Sleeping Beauty tells the story of the familiar fairytale, with suitable choreographic embellishments, during the course of a prologue and three acts. There are big set numbers which Tchaikovsky's music grandly decorates, but the ballet also has a strong narrative line, at least in the first two acts, and the music supplies character and atmosphere, whether it be in the courtly bustle of the first act or the forest nocturne of the second. The third act is more of a showpiece for dancing, consisting as it does in large part of a wedding *divertissement*, but again the music shows great inventiveness in presenting a succession of different fairytale characters who have come to pay their respects.

•The last stage works •

Soon after the first performance of *The Sleeping Beauty*, at the Maryinsky on 15 January 1890, Tchaikovsky left for Florence. That winter there was no conducting tour. Instead he took with him a libretto that his brother Modest had prepared for another composer, Nikolai Klenovsky. Its source was the one Tchaikovsky had mentioned to his brother nearly two years before, Pushkin's *The Queen of Spades*. The Tchaikovskys' version, however (the composer himself had a hand in the libretto after Modest's work had been done), is somewhat distant from the original, for a sophisticated ghost story becomes a big romantic tragedy, and one centered, at last, on a character, Hermann, with whom Tchaikovsky could identify in his yearning for love, his sense of alienation and his compulsion by fate.

Using a musical style emerging from that of the 'Manfred' and Fifth Symphonies, *The*

Left: The tenor Nikolai Figner as the hero Vodemon in *Iolanta*. The one-act opera, first produced at the Maryinsky Theater in December 1892, was another big success for Tchaikovsky.

Queen of Spades similarly shows the inexorable progress of tragic destiny in ruling the life of its central character, except that this time there is no attempted escape into revelry or triumph. Instead the opera rushes to the final point at which Hermann stabs himself, an outcome not to be found in Pushkin. Hermann (tenor) is introduced in the first scene of Act I, where he confesses to his friend Count Tomsky (baritone) that he is in love with a girl whom he fears may think him beneath her. They are joined by Prince Yeletsky, who turns out to be paying suit to the same young lady, Lisa (soprano), and who goes off with her when she appears with her grandmother the Countess (mezzo-soprano). Tomsky then tells Hermann the story of the Countess, how she was a great gambler in her youth and a great beauty too, surrounded by admirers. One of these revealed to her 'the

Above: A scene from *The Sleeping Beauty*. Despite an excellent production with Petipa's choreography at the Maryinsky Theater in 1890, the brilliance of Tchaikovsky's score again went largely unappreciated.

Left: Maria Petipa, daughter of the choreographer, as the Lilac Fairy in *The Sleeping Beauty*.

57

Right: The Bogatyri
(1898) by the Itinerant
artist Viktor Vasnetsov.
These 'valiant knights'
are a reminder of the
powerful strain of
Russian history that
runs through so much of
Tchaikovsky's work,
from his first opera
The Voyevoda, to his
late symphonic ballad of
the same title.
Vasnetsov called himself
'a story-teller, a
musician using the
language of painting.

*Below: A Girl at the
Piano* (1905) by Repin.

secret of three cards' in return for her favors,
and since then she has passed on this secret
to two others; but she has been warned in a
dream that if she tells it a third time she will
die. Hermann broods on this tale. In the second
scene Lisa is discovered with her companions.
She muses on her sense of impending doom;
Hermann enters and declares his love.

The first scene of the second act is set at a
ball, and includes a pastoral masque in rococo
style. Lisa and Hermann meet at the ball, and
she gives him the key to her room. In the second scene he enters the Countess's room and
pleads with her to reveal the three-card secret.
When she will not he threatens her with a pis-
tol, whereupon she falls dead. Lisa enters and
sends him away. In the third act the tragedy
moves swiftly to its climax. Hermann in the
first scene is visited by the ghost of the Countess, who tells him her secret – three, seven,
ace – after instructing him to marry Lisa. The
second scene is that of Lisa's last assignation
with Hermann; preoccupied with the secret, he
rushes off to the gaming tables, and she throws
herself into the canal. The final scene is set in
the gambling house. Hermann has won hugely
on the three and the seven, and now gambles
on the ace against Yeletsky. But the card turned
up is the Queen of Spades. Hermann sees the
Countess's ghost once more and stabs himself.

Consumed by this story of obsession and
suicide, Tchaikovsky sketched the whole opera
during the course of six weeks in Florence and
by June, back home near Moscow, he had completed the work in every detail. It was even
staged within the year, at the Maryinsky on 19
December 1890, when it scored an immediate
success. Meanwhile Tchaikovsky had written a
much more relaxed and happy tribute to his
time in Italy that year, the *Souvenir de Florence*
for string sextet (summer 1890), which has in
common with *The Queen of Spades* only a neo-

classical atmosphere. In the opera this serves to give a sense of the Russia of Catherine the Great, especially in the dances and masque of the ball scene, whereas the chamber work is rather another instance of that hankering after times which Tchaikovsky supposed to have been musically simpler and more natural, a hankering to be found also in the suites and in the Serenade for Strings.

The autumn brought a bitter return to reality. He received a letter from Mme von Meck in which she stated that she was financially unable to continue his allowance, and that therefore their correspondence must come to an end. This hurt him on two counts. First there was the implication that theirs had been a master-servant relationship which could not continue when payment was no longer involved. Second there was the fact, quickly discovered, that Mme von Meck's finances remained sound. It appears that her real reasons for breaking with Tchaikovsky were her feelings of guilt at having neglected her family in his favor, but he had no inkling of this and was profoundly distressed by her action.

Composition, however, went forward on several fronts. The success of *The Queen of Spades* led to another commission from the imperial theaters, for a double bill of opera and ballet eventually fulfilled by *Iolanta* and *The Nutcracker*. Tchaikovsky worked on the latter between February 1891 and April 1892, and on the opera in the middle of that period, during the second half of 1891. There was also another commission, for incidental music for *Hamlet*, which he supplied largely from existing works – a shortened version of the fantasy overture, for instance, furnished a prelude for the play. Then there was the last of his illustrative pieces, the symphonic ballad *The Voyevoda*, finished in October 1891. This is another history of tragic love, based again on Pushkin. The *voyevoda* (warrior knight) of the title returns home to find his wife in the arms of her lover. He orders his servant to shoot his mistress, but the servant mistakes his aim and kills the *voyevoda* instead. Tchaikovsky's music is fierce in its response to familiar themes of love and death being encountered for the last time, and like *The Nutcracker* it is brilliantly scored: the newly invented celesta, a small piano with the hammers striking chimes of metal plates, is used in both. However, the composer turned against the piece after its first performance and destroyed the score; it was reconstructed from the orchestral parts and published only after his death.

The completion of the *Iolanta–Nutcracker* double bill and then the sketching of a new symphony in E flat occupied Tchaikovsky from May to December 1892. This would have been his first symphony in a major key since the 'Polish' of seventeen years before, but it was not to be. Though the symphony was almost completed (it is sometimes referred to as no.7 and has been reconstructed from surviving materials), he was dissatisfied with it and in the next year converted three movements into

works with solo piano. The first movement became the single-movement Piano Concerto no.3, performed and published posthumously; while the andante and finale were completed and orchestrated in their *concertante* form by Taneyev after Tchaikovsky's death.

Iolanta and *The Nutcracker* were first performed at the Maryinsky on 18 December 1892. Once again the reception of a Tchaikovsky ballet was disappointing, though the weak opera, curiously enough, was liked. The link between the two works is that they are both fairytales, *Iolanta* being Andersenesque and *The Nutcracker* having its origins in one of E. T. A. Hoffmann's fantastic stories. *Iolanta*, the story of a blind princess, offered little to appeal to the composer of *The Queen of Spades*, except possibly in the orchestral prelude suggestive of the heroine's blindness and anticipating the Sixth Symphony. *The Nutcracker*, by contrast, is very much a work in its own right, and it is perhaps a pity that the popular orchestral suite, consisting mostly of characteristic dances from the final *divertissement*, has captured attention at the expense of much fine music elsewhere in the score (the use of the celesta, for instance, is not restricted to the 'Dance of the Sugar-Plum Fairy'). The story is simple. Klara, a young girl, is given a nutcracker by her godfather Drosselmeyer for Christmas. At night she dreams that the nutcracker has turned into a handsome prince, who takes her on a journey to the kingdom of sweets, where the Sugar-Plum Fairy stages the *divertissement* in their honor. The music is

Below: Tchaikovsky's dressing table in the house at Klin, to the north-west of Moscow, where he moved in May 1892.

appropriately sugary throughout, but it is done with the exact craftsmanship that can make a toy into a work of art.

· The 'Pathétique' ·

The period of *The Nutcracker* had been another time of travel. Between March and May 1891 Tchaikovsky had made a tour of the United States, again conducting concerts, and there were further tours of western Europe at the beginning of 1892 and in the winter of 1892-3. Returning home in February he began work on a new symphony, having abandoned the one in E flat only two months before. Again there was a program, which seems to have been sketched some time in 1892: 'The ultimate essence of the plan of the symphony is LIFE. First movement – all impulsive passion, confidence, thirst for activity. Must be short. (Finale DEATH – result of collapse.) Second movement – love; third – disappointments; fourth ends dying away (also short).' This scheme was altered either before or during the composition, since the eventual Symphony, no.6 in B minor (the same key as 'Manfred'), has a long finale, but it is interesting that one of the revolutionary innovations of this work – its slow last movement – was projected at this early stage. Hitherto multi-movement works had always ended positively; Tchaikovsky's Sixth Symphony instead drags towards its conclusion, and so presents a pessimistic finish to obviate the doubts raised by the triumphal finale of the Fifth Symphony.

By April 1893 Tchaikovsky had sketched the work in full. He then broke off work for his last set of piano pieces, the *Dix-huit morceaux* (April-May 1893), and his last set of songs, the six of op.73 (May 1893); none of these gives much clue to his state of mind, which is so

nakedly expressed in the symphony. Before he could get back to that work, though, he made a last visit to England, where he conducted his Fourth Symphony for the Royal Philharmonic Society and received the honorary degree of Doctor of Music at Cambridge, along with Saint-Saëns, Boito and Bruch. He returned home, and finished the orchestration of the symphony on the last day of August. On 28 October it had its première, in St Petersburg. The day afterwards Modest suggested the title 'Pathétique' for it: clearly its intensely personal character had not escaped him. It was the only important work Tchaikovsky completed after finishing *The Nutcracker* in April 1892. It stands alone, therefore, in documenting his life – as his music had always done – during the period of more than eighteen months leading up to his suicide on 6 November 1893, just nine days after the première.

Until 1978, when the story of Tchaikovsky's suicide was established, it was widely believed that he died of cholera contracted from drinking unboiled water, but it seems more likely that the cause of death was arsenical poisoning, self-administered. Apparently, a certain Russian aristocrat had written a letter accusing the composer of having a homosexual affair with his nephew, and had given the letter to an old pupil of Tchaikovsky's own law school. The result was what must have been predicted. The ex-pupil called a meeting of law school alumni to debate the matter, and it was decided that Tchaikovsky should save the honor of the school by killing himself.

Even without knowing this story, it is easy to hear the 'Pathétique' Symphony as conceived under the immediate shadow of death. Nor is this due simply to the fact that the finale is slow and long drawn-out. The first movement starts out from similar somberness, boasts some extreme contrasts and achieves a constant quickening of tension by its increasing compression of sections: the exposition is long, as in the corresponding movement of the Fourth Symphony, while the rest is ever more hurried, and at one climactic point a quotation from the Russian Orthodox Requiem is introduced. The

Bottom left: Cover to the first edition of the score of *The Nutcracker.* The ballet is based on E. T. A. Hoffmann's tale *Nutcracker and the Mouse King.*

Below: A scene from the first production of *The Nutcracker* at the Maryinsky Theater, in December 1892, at which it was billed with the one-act opera *Iolanta.*

second movement is another of Tchaikovsky's ballet waltzes, but one that limps to a 5/4 meter. After this comes a scherzo that develops into a large-scale march, full of menace. The middle movements are thus admirably contrasted without either of them having been slow, and so the stage is clear for the finale to fulfill this function. Both its principal themes are based on a falling scale, and the mood throughout is one of drooping melancholy and resignation, not unmixed with bitterness and resentment. For Tchaikovsky himself it was simply the 'most sincere' thing he had written.

It certainly made an impression on later composers. Mahler, whom Tchaikovsky heard conduct *Eugene Onegin* in Hamburg in January 1892, included adagio finales in his Third (1893-6) and Ninth (1908-9) Symphonies, the latter work being quite close to the 'Pathétique' in general form and character. As for the wider influence of Tchaikovsky's music, his last four symphonies (including 'Manfred') provided stimulus and standards for similar works of the next generation of composers in Russia, including Glazunov and indeed Sibelius, who was born and brought up a citizen of the Russian Empire. Tchaikovsky's symphonies were also of clear importance to Shostakovich and, to a lesser degree, Prokofiev (who was, however, his most notable successor as a composer of full-length ballets). Perhaps the greatest tributes to him, though, were paid by Stravinsky, who made him joint dedicatee with Pushkin and Glinka of his opera *Mavra*, arranged music by him to make his ballet *The Fairy's Kiss* and lost no opportunity of praising him. Speaking of *The Fairy's Kiss*, in which a youth is kissed by the fairy and carried off, he also made one of the most just comments on the nature of Tchaikovsky's creativity: 'As my object was to commemorate Tchaikovsky, this subject seemed to me to be particularly appropriate as an allegory, the muse having similarly branded Tchaikovsky with her fatal kiss, and the magic imprint has made itself felt in all the musical creations of this great artist.'

Above: Dancers in *The Nutcracker*'s first St Petersburg performance. The famous 'Dance of the Sugar-Plum Fairy' was inspired by the composer's discovery in Paris of the newly invented celesta. He asked his Moscow publisher, Peter Jurgenson, to order one – 'before Rimsky-Korsakov and Glazunov get wind of it.'

Left: Autograph of part of the first sketch of the Sixth Symphony's second movement – the waltz in 5/4 time. Tchaikovsky wrote: 'O Lord, I thank thee! Today, 24 March, completed preliminary sketch well!!' His brother Modest suggested the title 'Pathétique' for the symphony.

Left: The composer's house at Klin. It was wrecked during the Second World War, but has since been carefully restored and is now a Tchaikovsky museum.

The Russian Ballet

The foundations of the Russian tradition were laid around 1800 by Ivan Valberg (1766-1819) and Charles Didelot (1767-1837), who brought French styles and techniques to the ballet schools of both St Petersburg and Moscow. Didelot's neo-classical pastoral ballets made a complete break with the old style: rich costumes gave way to gauze tunics leaving arms and shoulders bare, while light slippers made dancing on point possible, a technique perfected by the great ballerina Istomina in the 1820s.

In September 1837, two months before Didelot's death, Taglioni made her début in St Petersburg, and for twenty years Russia was enthralled by the international stars of Romantic ballet, although there were also notable native ballerinas to rival them. Marius Petipa (1818-1910) was one of several male dancers who stayed on in Russia as ballet masters, and with his talented pupil Lev Ivanov (1834-1901) he exercised an overwhelming influence until the end of the century. Petipa choreographed with his dancers like a composer writing a symphony, and, above all through his work with Tchaikovsky, he became the true creator of modern classical ballet.

It was from this tradition that the brilliant group of dancers came who joined the company formed by Serge Diaghilev for a Paris season in 1909, later revealing to all Europe not only the technique and imagination of Russian ballet, but also much of the music of the great Russian masters.

The Three Graces (*left*) embodied by Taglioni, Elssler and Cerrito. Marie Taglioni (1804-84), whose five years (1837-42) in St Petersburg changed the history of Russian ballet, is seen in *La Sylphide* – the first Romantic ballet – in which the poetry of her dancing on point transcended virtuosity; Fanny Elssler (1810-84) had great success in both St Petersburg and Moscow in 1848-50 and is seen wearing the Spanish costume in which she danced her celebrated *cachucha* as Florinda in *Le Diable boiteux*; Fanny Cerrito (1817-1909) visited Russia only at the end of her career, in 1855-7, and is seen here as Béatrice in Adam's *La Jolie Fille de Gand*. Gautier, the arbiter of Romantic ballet, admired her natural vivacity and shapely body, but did not put her in the class of Taglioni and Elssler or his beloved Carlotta Grisi.

Right: Pavlova as Giselle. The most famous of all the Romantic ballets was written in 1841 by Théophile Gautier for Carlotta Grisi, the great love of his life; choreography was by Coralli and Jules Perrot (who later settled in Russia). The tragic story of a peasant girl betrayed by a prince, who goes mad and dies, joining the spirits of other brides who have died before their wedding day, was first performed in St Petersburg in 1842. The original Paris production was meticulously copied, and the leading role was taken by Elena Andreyanova, a dancer Taglioni herself had singled out, who combined the dramatic tradition of Russian ballet with the ethereal Romantic style.

F. Tolstoy's design for a neo-classical ballet, 1838, *The Aeolian Harp.*

Left: Costume – in elaborate eighteenth-century style – by N. Benois for *Le Pavillon d'Armide*, based on a story, *Omphale*, by Gautier and with music by Tcherepnin. This was the first big ballet choreographed by Mikhail Fokine, and it opened Diaghilev's first Paris season in 1909 with tremendous success.

Petipa's *Trilby*, (1871) demonstrated his imaginative use of the corps de ballet; but it was also full of the sensational effects demanded by the St Petersburg public, including a gilded cage full of 'birds' – danseuses of the corps de ballet – and a dance of unhatched chicks performed by pupils of the ballet school. Viktor Hartmann's décor for this (*above*) inspired one of Musorgsky's *Pictures at an Exhibition*.

The sensational effect created by the Ballets Russes in Paris was due above all to the unity of the productions – music, choreography, dancing technique and design each reflected a strong Russian tradition, and they were now combined for the first time. The designs shown above are (*left*) by Nicholas Roerich for Fokine's brilliant new version of the Polovtsian dances from Borodin's *Prince Igor* and (*right*) by Léon Bakst for *Narcisse*, another Fokine ballet with music by Tcherepnin.

Above: Mikhail Fokine and Tamara Karsavina in Stravinsky's *Firebird*, given for the first time in Diaghilev's second Paris season in 1910. Fokine (1880-1942) was the choreographic genius of the Ballets Russes in these early years, creating the striking sense of unity by transforming the sumptuous effects of his admired master Petipa. At the same time, their rigorous training gave the Russian dancers tremendous skills.

The poster (*left*) by Jean Cocteau for Diaghilev's 1911 season in Paris featured Karsavina in *Le Spectre de la rose*, a Romantic ballet after Gautier choreographed by Fokine to Weber's *Invitation to the Dance* and designed by Bakst. Tamara Karsavina (1885-1978), who trained at the Imperial Ballet School and made her début in 1902 at the Maryinsky Theater, became the leading ballerina in Diaghilev's troupe.

Vaslav Nijinsky (1889-1950), depicted (*above*) as the Golden Slave in *Sheherazade*, was the sensational star of Diaghilev's Paris seasons, having already appeared at the Maryinsky (at first while still a student) in Fokine's new ballets and in traditional works. Though *Sheherazade* uses only part of Rimsky-Korsakov's symphonic suite of 1897 and the story is changed, it perfectly embodies the decadent exoticism of his score.

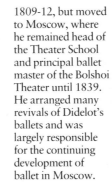

Below: Adam Glushkovsky (1793-1860) in the title-role in *Raoul de Créquis*, or *The Return from the Crusades*, 1819, one of Didelot's pantomine ballets – full-length works in which complex dramatic action is conveyed by mime. Glushkovsky danced in St Petersburg in 1809-12, but moved to Moscow, where he remained head of the Theater School and principal ballet master of the Bolshoi Theater until 1839. He arranged many revivals of Didelot's ballets and was largely responsible for the continuing development of ballet in Moscow.

Above: Charles Didelot (1767-1837) came from Paris to St Petersburg in 1801 and remained in Russia until his death, though absent in France for five years during the Napoleonic Wars. He made brilliant use of the corps de ballet, and his disciple Glushkovsky said of him: 'he replaced all false opulence by the richness of his own fantasy. One could always do without velvet, brocade and gilt in his subject matter: life, interest and grace stood in their stead.'

Above: Evgenia Kolosova (1780-1869) was trained by Valberg, but when he left in 1807 to revive the Moscow Theater School, she became Didelot's leading dancer, and she ran the St Petersburg school during his absence in France. Many of his greatest pantomine ballets, including *Raoul de Créquis* – at the climax of which she rescued her child by impaling a soldier with her husband's standard – were created as vehicles for her outstanding dramatic gifts.

The Napoleonic Wars had created a surge of national feeling in Russia, and both Valberg and Glushkovsky had devised patriotic *divertissements* after the defeat of the French in 1812. Glushkovsky was also the first to turn to the poems of Alexander Pushkin, and his ballet of Pushkin's *Ruslan and Lyudmila*, with music by Scholz, was first performed in Moscow in 1821 (a design for one of the original sets is shown above). Two years later Didelot produced a ballet based on Pushkin's *The Prisoner of the Caucasus*, and he put on a revised version of *Ruslan and Lyudmila* in St Petersburg in 1824. (The Bolshoi Theater there, burnt down in 1811, had reopened in 1818: a ballet performance held at the theater during this period is shown above right.)

Taglioni's arrival in St Petersburg in 1837 opened a new chapter for Russian ballet, introducing the latest Romantic ballets from Paris. Her principal partner was Nikolai Goltz (1800-80), a great favorite of Didelot, who had danced the title-role in *The Prisoner of the Caucasus*, and who partnered Taglioni in over two hundred performances. They are shown (*left*) in *La Sylphide.*

A contemporary wrote: 'Once out of the theater, you forget Taglioni; you remember only the Sylphide, a dream vision which will long continue to obsess you and which will fill your soul like the joyous sounds of Rossini's or Weber's music . . . you are happy, to the highest pitch of ecstasy, and you desire nothing else, until daily life comes to tear you from the voluptuous idleness.'

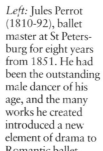

Left: Jules Perrot (1810-92), ballet master at St Petersburg for eight years from 1851. He had been the outstanding male dancer of his age, and the many works he created introduced a new element of drama to Romantic ballet.

Right: Ekaterina Sankovskaya (1816-78), the Moscow ballerina, celebrated as much for her dramatic gifts as for her dancing. In *La Sylphide*, she gave a more emotional performance than Taglioni, and she excelled in the role of Giselle. With her huge tragic eyes, she was the idol of the Moscow audiences.

The Seasons, with music by Glazunov, was one of Petipa's last works, a small-scale ballet produced in St Petersburg in 1900. It was famous for the 'Baccanale,' here (*left*) performed by Petipa's daughter Maria and Pavel Gerdt (1844-1917), for over thirty years principal dancer at the Imperial Theater, who in the 1890s created the leading roles in all the Tchaikovsky ballets of Petipa and Ivanov.

Above: Caricature of Grisi with Lucien Petipa (brother of Marius) in the first Paris production of the oriental fairy ballet *La Péri* in 1843 – reproduced the following year in St Petersburg with Andreyanova in the title-role.

The end of Petipa's era was marked in 1900 by the new production (*right*) of his *Don Quixote* staged in Moscow by Alexander Gorsky (1871-1924). Sets and costumes were a riot of colors, but it was above all the sense of dramatic realism Gorsky introduced that paved a way for the triumphs of Fokine and Diaghilev.

Marius Petipa came to St Petersburg as a dancer in 1847, becoming Perrot's assistant and creating his first ballet in 1855. His first great success was *La Fille du Pharaon* (in which he is shown above), and in all he choreographed some fifty ballets for the Imperial Theaters.

ALEXANDER PORFIRYEVICH BORODIN

JUSTIN CONNOLLY

Alexander Porfiryevich Borodin was born in St Petersburg on 12 November 1833, the illegitimate son of an elderly Georgian prince, Luka Gedianov. His mother, Avdotya Antonova, was highly cultivated and intelligent, besides being a woman of exceptional beauty. She was devoted to her son and showed a strong interest in his education, which took place at home. In accordance with the practice of the time, the boy was registered as the lawful son of one of the prince's serfs, but this accident of birth does not seem to have had any unpleasant consequences for him. His childhood was apparently spent in comfortable surroundings, and during his first six years Alexander's parents shared the same house. He was an attractive child and grew up to be a handsome man whose distinctive appearance showed clear traces of the Georgian ancestry on his father's side.

From his early years Alexander showed himself studious and anxious to please. He learned English, French and German, as well as other subjects, and by the time he was thirteen or fourteen had a small laboratory of his own where he began to explore chemistry, the subject in which he would ultimately become a distinguished professor. At the age of eight he had been fascinated by the music of military bands, and was even able to reproduce at the piano something of what he had heard. It was at this time his mother encouraged him by finding a bandsman to teach him the flute. This was the beginning of a lifelong interest, for even in his earliest compositions Borodin showed a real grasp of idiomatic writing for instruments. Although he never mastered the cello, this was doubtless due to his having been compelled to teach himself. As a pianist he had regular instruction and became a competent player, especially clever at improvisation, which became a valuable aid to composition. Like other members of the Russian school at his time, Balakirev and Musorgsky, he displayed a retentive memory for anything he heard – a necessity in a country where musical life was still in its earliest development, and printed music must have been rare.

During adolescence he began to compose a number of small chamber works to play with friends, but music was necessarily subordinate to his other studies. This state of affairs persisted throughout his life, and in spite of his outstanding qualities as a composer, he remained in the strict sense an amateur of music. Indeed, it is difficult to see how he could have done otherwise; at this time there was no formal structure to the musical profession as it is understood today, and Borodin did not possess independent means, as Glinka had done, which would have enabled him to work solely in music. However, Borodin was also unlike Glinka in that he was never, as the elder man had been, a dilettante. A highly disciplined and serious intelligence, such as Borodin possessed, could not lend itself to amateurism in anything, and he found himself severely taxed by the difficulty of fitting together his busy professional activities in teaching, research and committee work, his personal life (his wife early became an invalid and they had three adopted daughters) and his composition. There can be little doubt that overwork contributed to his death at the age of only fifty-four.

In 1850 he had entered the Medico-Surgical Academy, where he eventually became a student of N. N. Zinin, the grandfather of Russian chemistry. On completion of his studies, in 1856, he was posted to a military hospital as a doctor, serving in this capacity for three years, although he found the experience distressing to his exceptionally sympathetic and sensitive temperament. He also kept up his chemistry studies, so there was little enough time for music, but it was at the hospital that he first made the acquaintance of Musorgsky, when by chance they found themselves on duty together. At this time Musorgsky was a junior officer in a smart Guards regiment, and Borodin remembered him later as having been something of a dandy. They discussed music, and Borodin was keenly interested not only in Musorgsky's own work, but also in his playing of Schumann, a composer previously unknown to him.

In 1858 Borodin published his first paper on chemistry and defended his dissertation for the doctorate of medicine. He had matured into a man whose varied gifts were united in a generous and likeable personality. Although himself of noble descent, Borodin was as critical of aristocratic pretension as he was of the stuffy bureaucracy which flourished under the reactionary autocracy of Tsar Nicholas I. Borodin defined his personal and professional aspirations in terms of science and music, but remained a lively observer of political life and a convinced sympathizer with the progressive cause.

Right: An engraving of Borodin in 1848, when he was fifteen years old. By then he had already learnt several languages, had equipped a small laboratory for chemical experiments, and was composing pieces of music.

Right: An engraving of Borodin in 1848, when he was fifteen years old. By then he had already learnt several languages, had equipped a small laboratory for chemical experiments, and was composing pieces of music.

necessary by Ekaterina's continuing ill-health, and although Borodin had intended to return to Russia, he stayed on in Pisa with her, having been enthusiastically received by two well-known Italian chemists and offered the use of a laboratory where he could continue his experimental work. The summer of 1862 saw the composition of the Piano Quintet in C minor and the *Tarantella* for piano duet. Although these pieces are hardly more adventurous in style than the Mendelssohnian works composed two years earlier in Heidelberg, neither is without interesting features. The second subject of the *Tarantella* has a slight leaning towards the folk idiom of Russia, while in the Quintet there is a more pronounced use of folk-themes. The finale is perhaps the movement in which it is possible for the first time to perceive real signs of the composer that Borodin was soon to become. The theme enters after an introduction, and the intimate relationship between them foreshadows his later practice in the first movement of the Second Symphony and in the moderato of the unfinished Third.

•The First Symphony•

In September 1862 Borodin returned to St Petersburg, to enter upon marriage and professional life. He was appointed reader in chemistry at the Medico-Surgical Academy, and on 29 April 1863 he married Ekaterina. He now renewed his friendship with Musorgsky, and he began work on his First Symphony; indeed much of the opening movement was already in sketch by the end of 1862. He also met Mily Alexeyevich Balakirev, whose influence on his fellow composers was a remarkable phenomenon. His ardent wish to establish a

Right: Ekaterina Protopopova, the young pianist whom Borodin first met while studying at Heidelberg in the spring of 1861. He married her two years later.

In 1857 Borodin traveled abroad for the first time, and in 1859 he again visited Europe, this time as an official delegate of the Academy of Physicians. His teacher Zinin, who hoped Borodin would succeed him, thought that his best preparation for an academic post would be to work at Heidelberg under Robert Bunsen, one of the most distinguished living scientists. During his time at Heidelberg, although he worked hard on his research, Borodin found time to play the cello regularly in chamber music, and he was often in demand as an entertainer at the piano, where he caused general admiration in his circle by playing from memory almost anything requested of him, popular songs and Italian arias being particular favorites. None of his friends knew of his real musical tastes and of his growing discovery of his vocation as a composer. Although reticent to others about his own music, Borodin seems to have composed several large-scale chamber works during his Heidelberg years, the D major Piano Trio and the String Sextet in D minor among them. Neither of these works has survived in a complete form, but both show Borodin striving for a serious and elevated style.

In May 1861 Borodin met a young Russian pianist, Ekaterina Sergeyevna Protopopova, who had come to Heidelberg to seek a cure for incipient tuberculosis. She was a brilliant performer and was interested in playing the most modern music of the day. Through her Borodin became much more closely involved with the music of Chopin and Liszt, and her playing quickened his enthusiasm for Schumann too. Moreover, a personal relationship was developing between them; their common interest in music was its starting point, but within three months Borodin felt sure enough of his feelings to ask Ekaterina to marry him; on 22 August they became engaged. A trip to Italy was made

truly Russian school of composition led him to adopt a positively aggressive, even bullying attitude towards those other composers who came under the influence of his ideas. A restless and perhaps somewhat unbalanced individual, he was always ready to criticize, to praise, to encourage or to berate those who found themselves, not altogether willingly, in the role of disciples. The real significance of Borodin's contact with this remarkable personality was his discovery that there actually were others who shared his ideals in music: they all revered the example of Glinka, whose two operas had captured for the first time in music an authentically Russian feeling.

Borodin heard Balakirev and Musorgsky play a duet version of the finale of Rimsky-Korsakov's First Symphony, and not only was he in immediate sympathy with the music, but he also felt the urge to emulate the achievement of the young naval cadet. Indeed, the chief benefit to the composers of the so-called *moguchaya kuchka* ('mighty handful') of Balakirev's somewhat dogmatic and schoolmasterly interest in their work was that it encouraged discussion and interaction between them. The members of the group certainly needed all the unity they could muster in their struggle to Russianize music and drive out what they saw as harmful western influences, especially those of German music in its weaker, more academic manifestations. The sense that what they wrote was to some extent propaganda for a vital cause, the establishment in Russia of a national consciousness, with a proper regard for all elements of society being able to realize their aspirations, was a real spur to these composers. In a country with no widely organized musical life, they boldly proposed to create the works which they believed would eventually make such an organization inevitable.

Borodin's First Symphony, begun in the stimulating circumstances of his return to Russia in 1862, was finally completed in 1867; a poor performance in 1868 was followed by a much better one in 1869. Both performances were conducted by Balakirev who, having acted the part of midwife during the protracted labor of the symphony's composition, could not resist urging alterations and improvements on its composer. Borodin, for his part, accepted these suggestions in a somewhat ambivalent spirit; conscious of what he owed to Balakirev's enthusiasm, he nonetheless had his own clear ideas as to what to accept and what to reject in the way of advice. He made a good many small changes of his own before the symphony was published in 1882, and he sanctioned further alterations in subsequent performances, largely to please Balakirev.

This E flat major symphony makes use of some aspects of the western tradition so far as overall form is concerned, but in its details it shows some significant departures from usual practice, particularly in its deliberate mixture of styles ranging from folk music to intentional reminiscences of Schumann, and from epic statement to lyrical expansiveness. It is not impossible, given Borodin's type of mind, in which music was so interwoven with other interests – professional, personal and political – that there may be a quite deliberate programmatic structure to the symphony and that the composer saw the work as representing his view of the new world of Russian music and its future.

His biographer, the musicologist and mathematician S.A. Dianin, son of the composer's adopted daughter Liza, suggests that there are a number of unorthodox formal relationships in the symphony to which Borodin seems to want to draw attention. The way in which the introduction gives rise to a main movement whose theme clearly derives from it is in complete contradiction of the usual western practice. The resultant musical image strongly suggests the emergence of something vital and positive from something withdrawn and negative. What could be more natural than to see in this a deliberate analogue to the Russia of Borodin's day, apparently gloomy and hopeless, and yet carrying within it the promise of a more positive future? And there are other unusual features: a phrase heard near the end of the introduction reappears outside the main context in both slow movement and scherzo. Both times it deliberately interrupts the flow of the music, and it may be something like a personal signature, for it does not suggest the kind of motto found in the cyclic compositions of Liszt, but is rather closer to the allusive use of quotation favored by Schumann. The consciously eastern, even oriental style of the slow movement also dramatizes for the listener an attribute of Borodin himself: his exotic ancestry, which he thought of as an influence on his musical personality. In the finale, attention is once again directed to matters of style, for the rhythm and outline of the main theme suggests Schumann so strongly that it is impossible that Borodin could have been unaware of the resemblance.

Top: The Mazurka – a glance at Russian musical entertainment in mid-century.

Above: A sketch of Vladimir Stasov studying a score at the piano. Though primarily an art historian and critic, Stasov strongly supported the work of the 'mighty handful,' as he had labeled them.

Although Borodin had been able to finish the opening movement of the symphony by late 1862, other calls upon his time, both personal and professional, interfered with its progress, and this pattern of interruptions to his creative activity was to continue throughout his life, so that he became accustomed to the idea that real composition would be possible only during the long summer vacation. However, in his First Symphony, Borodin establishes himself for the first time as something more than a gifted amateur composer. None of his previous music can approach the power and conviction of this, his first large-scale work. The First Symphony gives the powerful impression of an individual with something new and important to say. Borodin's natural instinct for instrumental writing, evident from his earliest efforts, here finds an expression commensurate with his new perception of himself as a composer in the grand manner.

• Operatic and vocal music •

In 1867 Borodin spent the summer months on music for a farce by V.A. Krylov called *Bogatyri* (The Valiant Knights). Krylov's idea had originally been that Borodin would write music parodying the current western styles of composition in opera, especially the grand opera of Meyerbeer and Rossini. But Krylov's wish to present the work in the near future at the Moscow Opera meant that Borodin would have needed to give almost a whole year's undivided attention to the project, and in the end he undertook to use existing music by western composers while providing a certain amount of his own. In the event, Borodin wrote a good deal of the music himself, for just under half the score consists either of original music or parodies of the grand opera style, while the remainder uses direct quotation of wittily chosen excerpts appropriate to Krylov's scenario. *Bogatyri* is important as showing Borodin's skill with styles other than his own and as practice for his very different undertaking in his own *Prince Igor* which, though it remained unfinished, certainly benefited from its composer's excursion into stage music, even if it was of such a different kind.

Although the work was a failure when produced, it touched on an issue of great importance to the new Russian School – the use of traditional material taken from folklore. Serov's opera *Rogneda*, which Rimsky-Korsakov described as 'the continual laughing-stock of the Balakirev circle,' was a frigid and pompous attempt at a Russian style of opera, and along with his fragments of Meyerbeer and Offenbach, Borodin had also included several excerpts from Serov's work, as if to show once and for all how Russian opera ought *not* to be written, while the scenario was largely a satire on *Rogneda* itself with its stilted mythological action. For his part, Serov detested the Balakirev group; as critic of *The Voice* he was to write in 1869 about the first performance of Borodin's E flat Symphony: 'A symphony by someone called Borodin gave little satisfaction. Only his friends called for and applauded him with any enthusiasm.'

Opera was very much in the minds of the Balakirev group at this time; Musorgsky was writing *Boris Godunov* and Rimsky-Korsakov had recently embarked on *The Maid of Pskov*, the first of his fifteen operas. Balakirev had suggested to Borodin that he ought to set Mey's

Right: Decembrists' Square, St Petersburg (1870), by the Itinerant artist Vasily Surikov. Behind the equestrian statue of Peter the Great is the recently completed St Isaac's Cathedral. Borodin spent most of his life in the great northern capital, working as a chemist, while much of his composition was done in the country during summer vacations.

historical drama, *The Tsar's Bride*, but no music for this project has survived. However, Borodin was evidently stimulated by all this activity among his friends, for in 1867 and 1868 he wrote five striking and original songs for solo voice with piano accompaniment. Four of them were to his own texts. Perhaps because of his logical and analytical mind, Borodin's power with words is hardly less remarkable than his ability with musical ideas. All his songs, whether to his own words or not, are of exceptional quality, and it is a matter for regret that there are so few, only seventeen altogether. Even Musorgsky, the greatest Russian song-writer, is not his superior, except perhaps in the greater number of songs he actually completed.

These songs for voice and piano do not form a regular set, but each is an expression of a different aspect of Borodin's artistic person-ality. One of the few positive benefits of his necessarily irregular spells of composition was that they imposed a strict discipline upon his creative efforts. It must often have seemed to him that a particular mood must be captured then and there, or lost for ever. Borodin often chose allegory as a means of conveying his deepest thoughts. A reticent and sensitive man, he perhaps found a relatively impersonal diction

Above: The Major's Marriage Proposal (1848) by Pavel Fedotov, a painting that has much of the satirical wit found in Gogol and other contemporary writers and that Borodin himself displayed.

Left: Borodin (second from left) with fellow science students in 1861. Throughout his life, his first duty was always to chemistry and medicine.

71

Far left: Grand Cathedral of the Assumption, Moscow. The liturgy of the Orthodox Church is one of the most specifically Russian musical genres, though Borodin made use of it only towards the end of his life.

Left: Vladimir Stasov in 1873. His scenario, based on an epic poem about the medieval clash between the Russians and the Asiatic Tartars, and the heroic deeds of Prince Igor, was the genesis of Borodin's opera.

awaken. The music of her sleep is extremely bold in its use of dissonance, and this aroused the hostility of the conservatives.

•The Second Symphony and *Prince Igor* •

The first public performance of the E flat Symphony in 1869 had been enough of a success for Borodin to think about writing another. But while he was planning its successor, the B minor Symphony, he began to look about for a suitable subject for an opera. On 20 April 1869 he received from Stasov a scenario based on 'The Lay of Igor's Campaign', a nineteenth-century epic poem reworking medieval material that describes Prince Igor's struggles with the Polovtsians. Borodin immediately began studying the historical sources relating to this epic, and during the summer even managed to write a short aria for Princess Yaroslavna, Igor's wife. But in the autumn he had to abandon music in favor of his chemical work, as he was being put under great pressure by a German rival, F. A. Kekule von Stradonitz, who was working on the same research as he was himself and had accused him, falsely, of having stolen the idea. There was also a certain national prestige involved, for Borodin was a founder-member of the Russian Chemical Society. He therefore felt he had to complete the work as soon as possible and was hurt by the accusations of his musical friends that he was betraying Russian music and was merely making excuses for idleness and procrastination. Partly to still their criticisms, Borodin forced himself to finish three new songs, but he firmly maintained his intention to abandon the *Prince Igor* project as impracticable.

Meanwhile, the fascination it held for him prompted the composition of the first move-

more apt to his purpose than direct statements. Only the music shows how passionately he really felt about his subject matter. There was also another more sinister reason for using allegory – or what the Russians themselves called an 'Aesopian' form of expression. Borodin was a progressive under a reactionary regime, in which every publication had to pass the censor. Rimsky-Korsakov tells us in his memoirs that since at least one of Borodin's songs, the somber and powerful 'Song of the dark forest,' was quite obviously seditious, they resorted to a ruse to get the censor to pass it. Rimsky-Korsakov, whose texts were not politically suspect, never had any trouble with the censor, who always passed his songs without even bothering to read the words. Accordingly, Borodin's song was placed between two songs of Rimsky-Korsakov's, and all three were given the stamp of approval at the same time. This 'Song of the dark forest' speaks of a time in the past when men, angered by the tyranny of their oppressors, assembled in the forest before marching together as a mighty army to the cities, where they destroyed their enemies. The mood of the music is ominous and awe-inspiring, giving a powerful impression of fatal inevitability, and the melody, though freely composed, bears some resemblance to what was later to become the most famous of all Russian folksongs, 'The song of the Volga boatmen.' In another fairy-tale, 'The Sleeping Princess,' a free variation on *Beauty and the Beast*, a princess lies in an enchanted sleep. The music seems to imply that this, too, is a political allegory: the princess is Russia herself, and the knight arrives to waken her but cannot do so. The final words say enigmatically that no one knows when she will

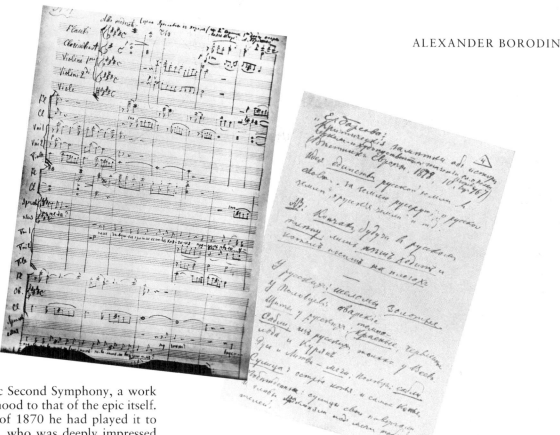

ment of the heroic Second Symphony, a work in a very similar mood to that of the epic itself. By the beginning of 1870 he had played it to Rimsky-Korsakov, who was deeply impressed with its power and conviction. The whole work was complete in a piano version by 1871, but was only orchestrated in 1873-5; it thus overlapped not only with the composition of parts of *Prince Igor*, but also with yet another dramatic project, the fairy opera *Mlada*, a proposed collaboration between Borodin, Cui, Musorgsky and Rimsky-Korsakov. The whole of the fourth act of *Mlada* was to be Borodin's responsibility. For some of the music he raided portions of *Prince Igor*, but much of it was new, and Stasov has testified to Borodin's involvement with the project and to the enthusiasm and speed with which he was working. When the proposed production fell through, Borodin returned to the B minor Symphony. As usual, there was a tremendous amount of chemical work on hand; in 1872 alone he published three learned articles, and in addition he became involved in the establishment of the first medical courses in Russia for women. As a radical and an ardent supporter of women's rights, he welcomed the chance to do something practical in support of his convictions, and he became the lecturer in chemistry for the obstetrics course.

The Second Symphony in B minor, despite the interruptions caused by work on *Mlada* and on *Prince Igor*, does not appear to have suffered any lack of unity, for its heroic and epic manner is closely related to the imaginative world of the two stage works. Borodin himself told Stasov that he regarded the work as illustrating scenes from the heroic past of Russia, the period of the Bogatyri and the manner in which they lived. The composer did not spell out a detailed program for the first movement, which may be taken as embodying the spirit of those ancient times rather than treating of any detailed action. The headlong speed of the scherzo might perhaps suggest the chase, but Borodin tells us nothing explicitly to justify such a view. In a letter to Stasov he says that

the third movement was intended to depict the legendary minstrel Bayan and his instrument, the Russian zither or *gusli*. Bayan tells a story of a struggle resulting in ultimate victory, and the music clearly reflects this. Borodin further describes the finale as a feast in celebration of the victory, and actually specifies in detail which parts of the movement represent the sound of the *gusli*, conversation between the participants, the commemoration of the fallen and festive singing to celebrate the triumph.

It is thus clear from Borodin's own remarks that what can be perfectly well understood in purely musical terms has for him a further analogical meaning, the direct illustration of concrete poetical ideas or actions, and there can be little doubt that the same broad principle applies to all his major instrumental works. The symphonies in E flat and B minor, the string quartets, the symphonic sketch *In the Steppes of Central Asia* and the unfinished Third Symphony all possess a detailed inner structure which corresponds, to a greater or lesser extent, to the poetic 'anatomy' of the images or ideal which inspired them. S. A. Dianin has discovered that Borodin, in choosing themes and formal structures, was shaping them as deliberate musical analogues of particular emotions, experiences and associations. The reason that this is of such interest in relation to Borodin's work is that the structures he creates are musically so satisfying by themselves, without any external frame of reference, that it is something of a surprise to learn of this aspect of his compositional methods.

In 1874 Borodin visited the sites of ancient Russian cities in the province of Vladimir, and this once again aroused his enthusiasm for *Prince Igor*. After corresponding with the ethnographer Mainov about the probable character

Above: Page from the autograph score of *Prince Igor* and some of the composer's production notes for the opera. Borodin was never able to finish the work because of the calls of science, and it was completed by Rimsky-Korsakov and Glazunov. The latter wrote down and orchestrated the overture, having heard Borodin play it on the piano.

of the music of the Polovtsians, he wrote the 'Polovtsian March.' Its images were inspired by a description of a medieval execution ceremony in Japan. At the beginning of 1875 he even found time to work on what was to become his first string quartet. Stasov and Musorgsky strongly disapproved on the grounds of its being irrelevant to the aims of the new Russian School, but Borodin nevertheless went his own way, continuing to admire his colleagues' ideas without abandoning his own position. He realized that he must find somewhere for his annual vacation which would be quiet enough to be conducive to composition. The conditions of Borodin's domestic life continued to be a great strain upon his household; as he said himself, a certain amount of 'spiritual calm' was necessary for creative work, and this he could not enjoy at home. His wife, to whom he remained devoted, was by now a permanent invalid whose insomnia turned night into day for everyone in the house.

The summer of 1875 was spent by Borodin in a borrowed apartment at the Golitsyn Hospital in Moscow, where he worked away until September on *Igor*, on the A major Quartet, and completed the piano arrangement of the B minor Symphony. His friends were delighted with what he had accomplished during the summer and, fired by their admiration, he continued to make strenuous efforts to keep composing despite his other commitments. The 'Chorus of Praise' which concludes the opera was given in St Petersburg with great success, and Borodin felt he had a duty to press on and complete the whole work. As he wrote to a friend, 'The success of the "Chorus of Praise" had a special significance so far as the fate of my opera is concerned. But I ought to point out that on the whole I am a composer in search of oblivion, and I'm always slightly ashamed to

admit that I compose. That's not too difficult to understand. For the others it's a simple matter, a vocation, an end in life; but for me it's a recreation, an idle pastime which provides diversion from my real work, my work as professor and scientist. . . . But now my chorus has been performed, everybody knows that I am writing an opera. There's no getting away from it; now I shall have to finish the opera whether I want to or not.'

Not much is known of Borodin's creative activity in 1876, but the anticipated première of the Second Symphony early in 1877 led to a great deal of extra work, for the scores of the outer movements had been mislaid and Borodin was compelled to reorchestrate them. The first performance was not a success, and Borodin was depressed by attacks on the piece by the conservatives, who were very critical of the heavy scoring for brass and of Borodin's har-

Left: Repin's portrait of Borodin, painted from memory the year after the composer's death.

Above: Louise de Mercy-Argenteau, portrayed by Repin in 1890, the year of her death. She was a Belgian countess who had helped to spread Borodin's musical fame abroad, sponsoring performances of his works and having the words of some of his songs and excerpts from *Prince Igor* translated into French. He dedicated a group of piano pieces to her.

Right: Vasnetsov's dramatic *After Igor's battle with the Polovtsi*, painted in 1880. Prince Igor is defeated by the fierce Tartar tribe and taken prisoner with his son Vladimir. Borodin's opera, the middle two acts of which are set in the Polovtsian camp, hinges on the conflicting claims of love, duty and honor.

monic style, which seemed to them dissonant and uncouth. However, he paid attention to the criticism of the brass writing and thinned it out before the second performance in 1878, when it was a great success.

Rimsky-Korsakov was the member of the *kuchka* to whom Borodin felt closest, both personally and artistically, and his persistent encouragement of the idea that the opera should and could be finished was a great stimulus to the composer. In the summer of 1879 he managed to write more of it than he had done at any time since 1875, and in addition to this work he finally finished the score of the A major Quartet. On his return to St Petersburg the new pieces from *Prince Igor* were received with great interest, though Borodin's duties prevented him from attending a subsequent concert when Prince Galitzky's aria was premièred by the bass singer Fyodor Stravinsky, father of Igor, to considerable acclaim.

Above: Stage design for Act II of the first production of *Prince Igor* at the Maryinsky Theater, St Petersburg, in 1890. This is the camp of the Polovtsi, whose Dances have become Borodin's best-known music.

• The String Quartets •

Borodin's A major Quartet was the first chamber music piece he had written since his student days in Heidelberg. Nothing is known of his reason for doing so; its dedication to Rimsky-Korsakov's wife may have some connection with the fact that both Stasov and Musorgsky had condemned the very idea of such a work, while the Rimsky-Korsakovs, very much disagreeing with what they saw as an extremist view of artistic necessity, took Borodin's side. The quartet, like the symphonies, is in four movements, and on the title-page Borodin draws attention to its being based on a theme from Beethoven. The character of the music is one of constantly changing moods, giving rise to the idea that here, too, there is an underlying narrative basis upon which the events of the piece are built. There are many reminiscences of the folksong 'The sparrow hills' throughout the work and the andante in particular has a shape which fits very accurately the actual text of the folksong so far as its salient features are concerned. The poem is an elegy for a dead hero spoken by an old crow in conversation with an eagle. It is possible that Borodin, as in the Second Symphony, uses the idea of a scenario quite literally in one movement, while exploring in the others images stemming from this central situation. The optimism of the first and third movements contrasts sharply with the somber andante and finale, suggesting perhaps that it is the hero's whole life which is the dominant concern of the work.

Generally speaking, Borodin's quartets belong to a line of descent from Haydn through Mendelssohn and Schumann. Though lively and expressive they have a special suavity and elegance which places them apart from the more obviously dramatic and intense style of the quartets of Beethoven and Schubert. Although better known than the First, the Second Quartet is much shorter and less obviously contrasted in its themes and their treatment. It was completed in August 1881, and all the circumstances, its character and the fact that it was written within two months – a most unusual feat for Borodin – point to its being a celebration of the twentieth year of his marriage to Ekaterina. The ardent and sentimental nature of the music has made it deservedly popular, and while all its themes share this glowing quality, the main tune of the third movement, the nocturne, is as unforgettably tender as the love scene in Berlioz's *Romeo and Juliet*. This tune, since arranged for almost every kind of popular combination, is heard in the quartet on Borodin's own instrument, the cello, and its moving expression of a passionate eroticism is quite unmistakable.

The brilliant and glittering scherzo which precedes the nocturne is also among his supreme achievements and its waltz-like second subject is full of a bitter-sweet charm. The finale, very different thematically from the other movements, recalls the peculiar humor of Borodin's own letters, half-mocking, half-sympathetic. Perhaps it is not too fanciful to imagine him summing up in his own way the contrasting experience of those twenty years: the music's laughing, swiftly changing textures contain no hint of lasting bitterness, which would indeed have been quite contrary to what is known of its composer's personal philosophy.

• Last years •

The final years of Borodin's life, from 1880 onwards, show a pattern of contradictions. On the one hand, his fame was spreading in Europe and his music attracted particular attention in France and Belgium; Liszt's warmly expressed interest and the determination of Borodin's Belgian patroness, the Comtesse de Mercy-Argenteau, led to a dramatic increase in foreign performances of his work. But at home it was a different story. Borodin's standing as a professor involved him in more and more committees, the chaotic disorganization of his home life continued, and by 1884 there were ominous signs that his own health was beginning to fail. His work on *Prince Igor* was now virtually complete in the creative sense, but there remained a vast amount of editorial work to be done, and with a restricted amount of time at his disposal, he felt more drawn towards planning new works than finishing old ones.

The opportunity of a commission to illustrate a tableau in a series to celebrate the accession of a new tsar resulted in his brilliant symphonic sketch *In the Steppes of Central Asia*, still one of his most popular pieces. Though simple in conception, it is carried out with exquisite finesse. The tableau showed Russian soldiers escorting a caravan of camels, and the music is concerned with the contrast of three clearly defined elements, a Russian folk-style tune, the oriental song of the camel drivers and the monotonous tread of the camels themselves, plodding across the empty sands. As elsewhere in his work, Borodin shows a brilliant gift for discovering memorable musical equivalents for realistic phenomena. The place where the highly individual themes of the soldiers and the drivers appear in perfect counterpoint is completely convincing and natural. Taneyev, himself a distinguished theorist, asked Borodin how he had achieved this minor miracle of the composer's art and Borodin, the chemist, had admitted that he composed them together before separating them out for their solo appearances elsewhere in the music. The restraint and economy of this little piece is the achievement of a great composer, whether or not he was an amateur; few professionals could have done so much with so little.

Apart from a few more songs and the Second Quartet of 1881, the main new project of these years was the Third Symphony, which Borodin had long contemplated, though it was never completed, together with a *Miniature Suite* for piano dedicated to his loyal supporter Louise de Mercy-Argenteau. As a result of two visits to Europe in 1885 and 1886, during which he met Liszt for the last time, progress on the symphony was slow, but he had meanwhile taken some important decisions, deciding to make use of ecclesiastical themes he had noted down from the singing of the sect of 'Old Believers.' He continued to work on its composition right through the autumn, despite his official commitments; but he knew that he was seriously ill with heart trouble, and his assistant Dianin had promised Rimsky-Korsakov and Glazunov that he would let them know immediately there was any new music, so that advantage could be taken of Glazunov's phenomenal memory to take it down from Borodin's playing. Borodin's own performance of the projected andante for a friend, Mariya Dobroslavina, has been memorably described by her. 'It was,' she said, 'a set of variations on a song of the Old Believers, as he himself called it. . . . They went in one terrific crescendo . . . with a fanaticism all their own; the final variation struck us with its power and impassioned cry of anguish.'

At this time Borodin showed great energy in working on the symphony, and on 13 February 1887 Dianin heard him playing something extraordinary and impressive in the room next to the laboratory where he was working. 'He thundered away for quite a long time, playing this tremendous music, and then he stopped. A few minutes later he came into the laboratory in a state of excitement and joy; there were tears in his eyes. "Well, Sashenka," he said, "I know that some things I've written are not bad. But this finale . . . What a finale! . . ."' There was to be no opportunity for Glazunov to come and capture this wonderful music. Borodin attended a fancy-dress ball on 27 February; just after it had begun, he collapsed suddenly and died of heart failure within a few seconds.

All that remains of the Third Symphony is the quietly autumnal opening movement and the brilliant scherzo in 5/8 time which Borodin had originally written for string quartet, but intended to incorporate in the symphony. It is likely, given the statements of his friends about the lost music for the work, that Borodin intended the work in some sense as a summing-up of a life, not necessarily his own, but human life as he saw it in general, with its inescapable contradictions; and it is perhaps not without significance that the symphony's tonality of A is the same as that of the First Quartet, which seems to share its preoccupation with a total experience encompassing both joy and grief, life and death.

Given Borodin's understanding of psychology and his talent for illustrating realistic events in musical images, it is the more tragic that *Prince Igor* remained incomplete if not actually unfinished. The original scenario proposed by Stasov in 1869 underwent numerous changes; Borodin always had doubts about the dramatic suitability of the subject, and his method was to prepare material of sufficient quantity and variety to allow a final choice based on contrasts and emphasizing the epic nature of the

Far right: First page of the autograph score of *In the Steppes of Central Asia* – a fine piece of program music, reflecting the Russian peoples' fascination with their Asian territories.

Below right: Title-page, in French, to the first edition of the unfinished Third Symphony, the orchestration of its two movements being completed by Glazunov.

Below: Borodin's ornate tomb in the Alexander Nevsky Cemetery, St Petersburg. Referring to his small and fragmented output, one musical historian has said, 'No musician has ever claimed immortality with so slender an offering.'

whole. He well knew the artistic danger of working in this way, and referred to himself in a letter as 'the unsystematic Bayan,' thus openly recognizing in his method the rhapsodical tendency of the old bards.

In all Borodin's mature work he uses folk-like themes, but without quoting any one folksong in its entirety. His bent is for imaginative variation and transformation of a model, and his undoubted gift for parody is related to this interest. A second aspect of his musical psychology sets him somewhat apart from the majority of composers: he was deeply concerned with the association between musical motifs and extra-musical meanings. Like Schumann, to whom he felt strongly drawn, he never wrote abstract or so-called 'pure' music; his symphonies and quartets were created against a background of associative ideas whose realization in musical terms was none the less quite self-contained. The third im-

portant element in his imaginative make-up was the fact of being a chemist – that is to say, a worker with combinations of material ranging from simple elements to complex structures. It is impossible to ignore this aspect of Borodin's mind, since he himself considered chemistry his life's work, over and above his involvement with music. In fact, from his earliest pieces Borodin shows himself instinctively at home with the literal, combinational aspect of 'com-position,' the art of finding particularly apt means to fit harmonic and melodic shapes together.

Of the 'mighty handful' who set out to provide Russian music with a stable basis for its future development, it is Borodin, the amateur, who remains the most complete artist of the group. Only Musorgsky was his superior in imaginative gift, but Musorgsky's tragic life and premature death demonstrated that the unconscious demands of a restless temperament were such as ultimately to destroy in him the power to carry out fully everything of which he was musically capable. Balakirev, too, suffered an existence blighted by mental problems which interfered with the successful development of his work, whose identity seems somehow blunted and spoiled by his struggle with himself. Here too was a talent potentially of great scope and vitality which was only partly able to justify itself, while Borodin's shy, slightly passive personality did actually manage to reconcile artistic and human necessities in a more satisfactory way. Cui, the least significant, and today the least known of these composers, was probably more important as a critic, while Rimsky-Korsakov, the closest in temperament to Borodin himself, became a notable teacher and the 'grand old man' of Russian music.

MODEST PETROVICH MUSORGSKY

PAUL GRIFFITHS

Opposite: Modest
Musorgsky (1839-81)
in 1865.

Few composers can have made so essential a contribution to western music as Musorgsky in so few works. Of several operas he projected at various times, only *Boris Godunov* was staged while he was alive. He wrote almost nothing for the orchestra, though his single important piano work, *Pictures at an Exhibition*, is well known as a concert piece in the orchestration by Ravel. Otherwise his output consists largely of songs, which the Russian language has served to keep in relative obscurity. Nevertheless, the fierce power of *Boris* and of many of his songs is that of an intense penetration into human characters, a musical realism that is unique.

Modest Petrovich Musorgsky was born in Karevo in the district of Pskov on 21 March 1839; a century later the little village was re-named Musorgsky in his honor. His family had lived in the area since the early seventeenth century as comfortable landowners, though his paternal grandmother had been a serf on the estate until her marriage and it seems he was rather fond of remarking on this 'peasant blood.' He and his brother Filaret, who was three years older, passed their childhood in the family's spacious manor house under the guidance of a nanny through whom, according to his own account, he became acquainted with Russian folk tales. His autobiographical sketch continues with the information that he had piano lessons from his mother and played a concerto by Field to a party at home when he was nine.

By that time he was attending a preparatory school in St Petersburg. His father had taken both boys there in August 1849 with the view that they should proceed, following family tradition, to the Cadet School of the Guards. Modest entered the school in 1852, when he was thirteen, but he kept up his musical interests. He had piano lessons with Anton Herke, a pupil of Henselt, and in his first year at the Cadet School he wrote a *Porte-enseigne polka* for piano, which his father had published. In 1856 he also tried to write an opera after Victor Hugo's *Han d'Islande*, but this never got very far; the same year he left the Cadet School to join a Guards regiment. According to Borodin, he was at this stage a 'very elegant, dapper little officer' who charmed the ladies by playing operatic excerpts at the piano.

The change came in 1857, when he met Dargomyzhsky and began taking composition lessons with Balakirev. Dargomyzhsky was the outstanding Russian composer of this period, while Balakirev, though only twenty when Musorgsky came to him for lessons, assumed the role of tutor to the emerging generation of Russian composers. In 1858 Musorgsky resigned his army commission and devoted himself to music under Balakirev's guidance. He was also starting to compose seriously. In 1857 he wrote a song, 'Where art thou, little star?,' which the following year he orchestrated; there were also two piano sonatas, both lost. In 1858 he composed more songs and two scherzos for piano, one of which, in B flat major, was orchestrated and performed at a public concert in 1860; this was the first time his music came before an audience. Also in 1858 he began an opera on Vladislav Ozerov's tragedy *Oedipus in Athens*, which seems to have got little further than *Han d'Islande*: the only fragment definitely composed was a choral scene which he later adapted for three other operas, *Salammbô*, *Mlada* and *Sorochintsy Fair*.

In the summer of 1859 Musorgsky made a visit to Moscow, which caused him to undergo, as he wrote to Balakirev, 'a sort of rebirth: I have been brought near to everything Russian.' Coming from the classical, westward-looking ambiance of Peter the Great's city, he must have been struck by Moscow's reminders of a deeper Russian past, which perhaps connected with his own memories of the folk tales he had heard as a child, although it had little immediate effect on his music. There is, to be sure, some slight influence of Russian folk music even in his first song, but as yet his style was conditioned by Schumann, watered down to the limitations of the drawing room. In 1859-60 he produced two more songs and piano pieces; in 1860-1 there was an odd stylistic exercise, the *Intermezzo in modo classico* for piano, on a pastiche baroque theme (revised in 1867 and orchestrated).

At this stage he might well have abandoned composition. He was marking time, partly because of lack of application, partly because, it seems, there were no models for the kind of music he wanted to write. Then an outside circumstance did indeed call him away from music. The emancipation of the serfs in March 1861 caused difficulties on the estate and for the next two years Musorgsky spent much of his time back at Karevo. He worked at a symphony in D major, but it came to nothing. The

Top: The Bolshoi Kamenniy (Large Stone) Theater in St Petersburg, built in 1757 and rebuilt during the 1880s to form part of the Conservatory.

Above: The old props room in the Bolshoi Kamenniy Theater.

1865 after the death of his mother. Possibly as a result of that loss he began to drink heavily, and in the autumn of 1865 he had to be taken from the commune to his brother's flat.

He continued to work at *Salammbô* until the summer of the next year, when he abandoned the score after writing more than an hour and a half of music. This was by far his most considerable undertaking so far, but it offers little evidence of the musical realism he was looking for. A good deal of it is in a vein of sumptuous orientalism associated much more with Borodin or Rimsky-Korsakov than with Musorgsky, though the 'Carthaginian Chorus' incorporates what sounds like a Russian folksong. Some moments, however, look straight forward to *Boris Godunov*, and there are parts that were transferred bodily to the later opera.

summer of 1863, however, when he was twenty-four, brought a sudden creative jolt, with a group of songs including 'King Saul,' followed in the autumn by the beginning of work on a new opera, based on Flaubert's *Salammbô*.

This coincided with his return to St Petersburg and his joining a commune in a flat with five other young men of advanced artistic, religious, philosophical and political interests. A recent novel had sparked off a trend for this kind of enterprise, though at the same time Musorgsky had a more orthodox existence as a civil servant, working for the Ministry of Communications. In his music he strove to put into effect the ideas about realism that Dargomyzhsky was grappling with, and that were very much current in Russian intellectual circles generally. One of his first efforts in this direction was the song 'Kalistratushka' (1864), in which a peasant reminisces in music of flexible rhythm and remembers a lullaby his mother sang to him. Similar in tone is the piano diptych *From Memories of Childhood*, which he wrote in April

• Musical realism •

More immediately, *Salammbô* had its echo in a short work for chorus and orchestra, *The Destruction of Sennacherib* (1866-7), which appears to have been conceived alongside a much more important piece, the orchestral *St John's Night on the Bare Mountain* (1867). This piece of musical witchery is Musorgsky's first major work but, like *Boris Godunov* itself, it is better known in a version prepared after the composer's death by Rimsky-Korsakov than in its original form. Indeed, a great deal of Musorgsky's music was posthumously revised by Rimsky-Korsakov and other well-meaning friends who were disturbed by the crudity of his harmony and scoring, and it is only more recently that the composer's own texts have displaced the smoothening efforts of his arrangers. In many cases what Rimsky-Korsakov and others did was apt, or at least understandable; *Boris Godunov* is undeniably a grander opera in the Rimsky-Korsakov version. However, in removing the crudity, any arrangement inevitably also misses the keen edge of Musorgsky's expression, the effect of realism he was intent on discovering, and in the case of *St John's Night on the Bare Mountain* the original score is much the more baldly alarming.

In its original form, this work is a wild orchestral impression of a witches' sabbath on the traditional St John's Night. It seems to have been a distillation from two operatic projects of the late 1850s conceived on demoniac subjects and based on works by Gogol and Baron Mengden, but the eventual composition was completed in a fever of activity. 'I wrote it quickly,' Musorgsky said in a letter at the time, 'straight away in full score without preliminary rough drafts, in twelve days. It seethed inside me, and I worked day and night, hardly knowing what was happening within me.' He did, of course, have examples of the musical macabre in Berlioz and Liszt to work on, but *St John's Night* is full of grotesque effects that are entirely his own and – to him even more importantly, so it would seem – entirely Russian. 'And now I see in my sinful prank,' he continued, 'an independent Russian product, free from German profundity and routine.' So it is. The work is a chilling depiction of the assembly of the witches on their mountain peak, the arrival of Satan and the celebration of a black mass, and though the subject-matter may be horrific in a very naïve way, Musorgsky's music opens up bleak chasms of sonority and harmony that undercut, as he well realized, the ordered continuity of the German tradition. It was, very possibly, a necessary liberation on the way to *Boris Godunov*.

That work was now drawing near, heralded also by quite a flood of songs. Those written in 1865-7 include a number of satires that catch character in quick, sharp strokes. In 'The Ragamuffin' (1867) an urchin shouts insults at an old woman; 'You drunken sot' (1866) is sung by a nagging wife and 'The seminarist' (also 1866) by a trainee priest torn between Latin nouns and a young girl. All three of these songs have words by Musorgsky himself, as also does a less caricatured essay in realism, 'Darling Savishna' (1866), apparently based on a real experience of a village idiot declaring his love. Each of these songs forces itself on the attention as a slice of life translated with the minimum of elaboration into art.

On 10 May 1867 Musorgsky was dismissed from his civil service post, and he went to stay with his brother in the country. It was there that he wrote *St John's Night*, which he finished on 23 June, St John's Eve. In a spirit of enthusiasm generated by the pan-Slavonic Congress he also began another symphonic poem, *Poděbrad of Bohemia*, soon abandoned. Then in the autumn he went back to St Petersburg, where he renewed contact with Dargomyzhsky, deep at work on *The Stone Guest*. He himself, with his new realistic acuity, began to explore the world of childhood, and two songs that

resulted, 'Eremushka's lullaby' and 'With nurse' (both 1868) he dedicated 'to the great teacher of musical truth, A. S. Dargomyzhsky.' 'With nurse' is a particularly vivid example of musical realism, heightening the natural pitch contours of speech and following spoken rhythm exactly, while the accompaniment does nothing to get in the way of the 'musical truth' but only provides atmosphere and punctuation. From this song Musorgsky developed a cycle, *The Nursery*, with the addition of four more numbers in 1870 and a further two in 1872.

Musorgsky's concern with the authentic transfer of speech into song turned his attention again to opera, and, also in 1868, he embarked on the first act of a setting of Gogol's comedy *The Marriage*. Apparently this was suggested to him by Dargomyzhsky, and he took up the challenge with enthusiasm, completing the act for voices and piano within four weeks. Letters of the period bear witness to his aims. 'Throughout,' he wrote to his friend and colleague César Cui, 'I try as hard as I can to note down clearly those changes in intonation which crop up in ordinary conversation for the most futile causes, on the most insignificant words, changes in which lies the secret of Gogol's humor.'

However, when the completed act of *The Marriage* was played through at Cui's house in October 1868, with Dargomyzhsky and the composer himself among the cast of four, the feeling seems to have been one of both astonishment and concern. Musorgsky's fellows were amazed at the exactness with which he had indeed caught the rhythms and mannerisms of speech, but they had their doubts about whether the opera could also be considered 'musicianly and artistic.' Authenticity appeared to have been bought at the price of harmonic coherence, and Musorgsky was not encouraged to go any further with the project.

Above: Mily Balakirev (1837-1910), composer and torch-bearer for the Russian nationalist composers of the 'mighty handful'.

Left: An early illustration to Gogol's story *Sorochintsy Fair*, a peasant comedy set in the Ukraine (Little Russia). Musorgsky's opera of the same name, like his *Khovanshchina*, was unfinished at his death. Several other composers, including both Lyadov and Tcherepnin, produced finished versions of it.

· *Boris Godunov* ·

He had, in any event, already started work on another opera, *Boris Godunov*. This was begun in the autumn of 1868, and although Musorgsky re-entered the civil service at the beginning of 1869, he continued to work with unusual concentration on his opera and had completed it in full score by the end of 1869. In July 1870, after an unaccountable delay, he submitted *Boris* to the Imperial Theaters, and soon afterwards he began another opera, *Bobyl*. This, though, proceeded no further than a single scene, which with characteristic economy he adapted to the later *Khovanshchina*. Perhaps it got no further because he quickly found himself having to work again on *Boris*, for in February 1871 the opera came back rejected.

There may have been various reasons for this. In the first place, Pushkin's play, on which Musorgsky based his libretto, was considered politically dangerous in its depiction of revolt against an anointed tsar. There were also musical

difficulties. In its initial version of seven scenes *Boris Godunov* had no important female role, no ballet and nothing resembling an aria. It was composed, rather, of quick dialogue, choruses and self-searching monologues (for Boris himself), and in orchestral and expressive color it was generally gloomy.

It opens at the Novodevichy Monastery, where the Russian people are ordered to beg Boris Godunov to take the crown, then ordered to acclaim him as tsar. Next, Boris appears in his coronation procession. In Scene 3, Pimen, an old monk, tells the novice Grigory the story of the murder of the young Tsarevich Dmitry, a crime he ascribes to Boris. Grigory notes with interest that Dmitry would have been his own age had he lived. The next scene is set at an inn on the Lithuanian border; Grigory is on the run in the company of two itinerant monks. The police arrive in search of him, but he escapes. In Scene 5, Boris greets his children and surveys with his son a map of his domains. Prince Shuisky tells him of an uprising led by Grigory claiming to be the Tsarevich, and as the clock

Below: A Courtyard in Moscow (1878), by Vasily Polenov, another member of the Itinerant School. The ancient Russian capital, so different in character from cosmopolitan St Petersburg, made a deep impression on Musorgsky when he first visited it in 1859, and awakened his interest in Russian history.

Above: On the Balcony, 1851, by F. Slaviansky. His own comfortable childhood at this time was recalled by Musorgsky in the piano pieces *From Memories of Childhood* (1865) and in the more strikingly original song-cycle *The Nursery.*

Right: The composer in 1873, aged thirty-four, still well groomed despite his heavy drinking.

portrayed as murderers and usurpers, though the historical evidence is conflicting.

Musorgsky's second (1871-2) version of the story seems to have been provisionally accepted by the Imperial Theaters, and on 17 February 1873 the inn scene and the Polish act were staged at a benefit performance in the Maryinsky Theater in St Petersburg. Presumably these extracts were chosen as being the opera's least eccentric scenes; they were certainly not representative. But if the aim was to fan public enthusiasm for the work, it succeeded, and a year later, on 8 February 1874, *Boris Godunov* was performed for the first time. It was still not quite complete, but it pleased the audience and remained in the repertory until 1882, the year after Musorgsky's death.

Possibly its disappearance at that stage was occasioned by a feeling, even among Musorgsky's closest friends, that he was not well represented by the opera as it stood. The orchestration appeared bald even at such moments as the coronation scene, where brilliance seemed to be called for. Still more regrettable was the harmonic awkwardness of much of the music: its dissonances and bareness. Moreover, the fact that Musorgsky had himself prepared two versions of the score seemed to give licence to others to adapt it. Rimsky-Korsakov therefore set about the task of putting *Boris* to rights, and it was his version, published in 1896, that went around the world when the opera became an international success after being produced in Paris by Diaghilev in 1908, with Fyodor Chaliapin in the central role from 1898 onwards. In 1940 a new version was prepared by Shostakovich, though this did not displace the Rimsky-Korsakov edition outside Russia. It was not until 1975 that a reliable edition (by David Lloyd Jones) of Musorgsky's own *Boris* was published, so encouraging a return to the

strikes he is wracked by guilt over Dmitry's death. In the next scene, a simpleton accuses Boris of the Tsarevich's murder. Finally, Pimen tells of a miracle worked by Dmitry's relics. Boris dies in further agonies of guilt.

By July 1872 Musorgsky had greatly amplified the work to make an opera in a prologue and four acts, retaining most of his original material, though with changes and cuts to satisfy the censor. To make good the deficiencies that had been observed in the first version, he introduced an entirely new third act, which takes place in Poland, where Grigory has come to win a bride, the Princess Marina Mniszek, and so 'love interest' is brought into the opera, together with a lighter westernized coloring. He also wrote a new final scene to follow the death of Boris, in which the simpleton's lament over Russia is introduced; it is set in the Kromy Forest, where a rabble gathers to march on Moscow under the false Dmitry. The new scenes were drawn, like the seven of the 1868-9 version, from Pushkin's play, which follows chronicled accounts about as faithfully as Shakespeare's histories. There is a parallel in some respects between Boris and Richard III, in that both are

· Khovanshchina ·

Right: Boris Godunov, Tsar of Russia from 1598 to 1605. He was suspected of murdering the young heir-apparent to the throne, in order to gain the crown for himself. Musorgsky's opera is based on Pushkin's historical drama *Boris Godunov* and Nikolai Karamzin's *History of the Russian State.*

Above: Title-page of the first edition of the full score of *Boris Godunov.*

original score that had not been heard since the St Petersburg performances of 1874-82.

Certainly the Musorgsky text is to be preferred to those of later revisers, however well-intentioned, for what seems cold and bare in his scoring is deliberately so, expressive of the Russian people's miseries and Boris's emptiness of spirit, while the harmonic style is also apt for an opera which achieves no resolution, which is concerned rather to uncover ugliness, meanness and violence. The subject is clearly one that appealed powerfully to Musorgsky, touching as it did on many of the things that moved him most deeply: the magnificence of the Muscovite past, the riches of Russia's folk traditions (there are folksongs all through, but especially in the inn scene and the scene with Boris's children), the tragic vigor of the Russian people. It also gave him a variety of scenes in which to test out the realistic style he had recently attempted in *The Marriage* and the songs of 1866-8.

Indeed, the variety of the scenes gives the opera a markedly heterogeneous character. The prologue and the final scene are big choral tableaux, static and monumental in the case of the former, boisterous and dynamic in that of the latter. In the first act there is a complete contrast between the long historical narrative of Pimen, where the music becomes heightened speech, and the inn scene, which is filled with self-contained songs. The major scenes involving Boris – the second act and the first scene of the fourth – show a more intense style used in the closer depiction of character, and Boris's great bass monologues are Musorgsky's most individual contributions to the musical theater. As for the chorus, the Russian people do, in fact, play a role as one of the characters – arguably the main one – for the opera ends with them and the simpleton's lament for their country, while their contributions are always central to the drama and not in any sense subsidiary.

While he was completing the second version of the opera, from the autumn of 1871 onwards, Musorgsky was living in an apartment with Rimsky-Korsakov, who was at work on a historical opera of his own, *The Maid of Pskov,* treating events shortly before those of *Boris Godunov.* Both composers were then involved in a collaborative venture mooted in the spring of 1872, an opera-ballet, *Mlada,* whose four acts were to be written by four different composers: the others were Borodin and Cui, with whom Musorgsky, Rimsky-Korsakov and their common mentor Balakirev had been grouped by Vladimir Stasov as the 'mighty handful,' united in their pursuit of a powerfully nationalist art in opposition to the westward-looking music of the Moscow composers led by Anton Rubinstein.

Mlada was to have been a fantastic opera set among the pagan Baltic Slavs of the ninth century, and Musorgsky's part in it was to work with Rimsky-Korsakov on the second and third acts, while Cui took care of the first and Borodin the last. He sketched out a market scene, using some music already used in the abortive *Oedipus* and *Salammbô,* and he made a new version of *St John's Night on the Bare Mountain* for a vision of infernal deities and hellish rites at the end of the third act. The fact that he borrowed so much for *Mlada* suggests that he had little enthusiasm for it, and indeed he seems to have been relieved when its collapse left him free to concentrate on a new opera that was already beginning to form in his mind, *Khovanshchina.*

The idea for this had come from his friend Stasov; it was to be a portrait of the period of instability that had preceded the reign of Peter the Great, just as *Boris Godunov* had dealt with a similar time of turmoil. Unfortunately, Musorgsky was not at all given to repeating himself. Having solved the problem of a dramatically realistic depiction of historical events in *Boris Godunov,* he found that he was left with little scope for new ideas for *Khovanshchina.* He worked on it spasmodically until August 1880, but when he died seven months later it was not finished, and it was again left to Rimsky-Korsakov to produce a version for the stage. The Rimsky-Korsakov text, first given by an amateur company in St Petersburg on 21 February 1886, is the one habitually used when the opera is revived, though there have been other tinkerings with the score, notably by Stravinsky and Ravel for a presentation by Diaghilev in 1913; for this Stravinsky actually composed the final chorus on the basis of Musorgsky's themes.

The title *Khovanshchina* may be translated as 'The Khovansky Business,' for Prince Ivan Khovansky was the dominant figure in Russian history at this period, though not so dominant in the opera, which opens, like *Boris Godunov,* with a choral scene set in Moscow. This introduces the Streltsy, a band of ill-disciplined musketeers, mostly Old Believers – dissident

adherents of a traditional form of Russian Orthodox religion; the opera hinges as much on religious controversy as on political conflict. The Streltsy describe their sorry state in a Russia torn by internal dispute between Khovansky and the Regent Sophia. Khovansky orders them to guard the city, and then his son Andrei arrives in pursuit of a Protestant girl, Emma. Dosifey, leader of the Old Believers, rebukes the prince and asks Marfa, one of his followers and formerly Andrei's mistress, to conduct Emma back to her home.

The second act takes place at the house of Prince Golitsin, counsellor and lover of the Regent Sophia. He represents forward-looking Russia as much as the Khovanskys stand for the old feudal order and Dosifey for the mystical devotion of ancient Muscovy. In this act all three of them are involved in political discussion; Marfa is also there to tell Golitsin his fortune (she foresees disaster). In the third act she sings of her continuing love for Andrei, and Dosifey tries to comfort her. Then the Streltsy reappear, and word is brought that Sophia's troops are about to arrive. In the first scene of the fourth act, Khovansky is murdered. There is then a jump in time of seven years, during which Peter has ousted his half-sister Sophia and assumed the throne. Dosifey sees the end coming for the Old Believers and invites his flock to prepare for death together. In the last act, of which Musorgsky left only sketches, they set fire to themselves.

The music of *Khovanshchina* is slower and

steadier than *that of Boris Godunov*. The harmony is less irregular, and the intense realism associated with the clock and death scenes in *Boris* is absent. There is, after all, no big central character to warrant them, though something of Boris's aura is perpetuated in the bass role of Dosifey, and to a lesser degree in the other leading bass role of Khovansky. Similarly, characterization is not so sharp as in the earlier opera. Golitsin (tenor) cannot match the viciousness of Shuisky, though the contralto role of Marfa is more powerfully projected than that of Marina. Even to make such comparisons, however, is fruitless when so little of the music

Above: Autograph score for piano and voice of part of Act I, Scene 2 – An inn on the Lithuanian border, from the 1872 revised version of *Boris Godunov*.

Below: Decor for the coronation scene in the first full production of *Boris Godunov* at the Maryinsky Theater in 1874.

was brought to any definitive conclusion by the composer.

The reason for this was not simply an unwillingness to go over the same ground twice. There was also the difficulty Musorgsky experienced in shaping the historical material, for in this case there was no Pushkin play to provide a dramatic synthesis that he could adapt. Instead he worked directly from the original sources and seems to have attempted to include too much. Perhaps even more importantly, he was suffering from personal difficulties that came to a climax in the summer of 1873, just when work on *Khovanshchina* was starting to make progress. Alcoholism seems always to have lurked in the background of his life; it now claimed him. Also, there was a resurgence of the spiritual and moral crisis of his adolescence. He never married and would appear not to have had any significant sexual liaison; his existence was, rather, monastic in a peculiarly Russian way. He enacted the role of the 'holy fool,' suffering for God in this world, and there is evidence from his letters that he saw himself in a distinctly Dostoevskyan light, certainly from the period of *Khovanshchina* onwards.

• Works of 1874-5 •

In 1874, however, Musorgsky completed two major works, *Pictures at an Exhibition* and the song cycle *Sunless*. The former was suggested by a visit to the memorial exhibition of work by his friend, the painter Viktor Hartmann, who had died the year before. Hartmann was

evidently a versatile artist and his posthumous gift to his colleague was a wide variety of subjects for musical treatment: watercolors, stage designs and architectural sketches. No doubt this variety was one of the things that attracted Musorgsky to the project, quite apart from the wish to honor his friend.

The work is a suite bound by an introductory passage, headed 'Promenade,' which depicts the visitor pacing the gallery and which comes back at intervals throughout. There are ten 'pictures' on display. The first, 'Gnomus,' shows a gnome running on crooked legs; the Hartmann sketch is said to have been a design for nutcrackers, but it is the image, not the purpose, that Musorgsky translates into music. Then comes 'Il vecchio castello,' a misty vision of an ancient castle with a troubadour seen more clearly in the foreground. 'Tuileries' is a scherzo based on a scene in the Parisian park, and 'Bydlo' evokes a lumbering Polish oxcart. 'Ballet of unhatched fledglings' is a piece of bizarre musical fantasy based on a ballet, contrasting with the incisive characterization of 'Two Polish Jews, rich and poor,' the former confident, the latter whining. The seventh piece, 'Limoges,' is another bustling French scene,

Left: Repin's portrait of Musorgsky, which has become the universal image of the composer, though it was painted after he had been admitted to hospital with alcoholic epilepsy and only three weeks before his death.

Below: Design for Kiev City Gate, Main Façade by Viktor Hartmann. Musorgsky's visit to a memorial exhibition of his friend's drawings and paintings resulted in *Pictures at an Exhibition*. This drawing inspired the piece called 'The Heroes' Gate at Kiev,' which brings the work to a triumphant close.

this time picturing a market, and the eighth, 'Catacombes,' is a macabre visit to subterranean tombs. 'The hut on fowls' legs' is another ballet sketch as odd as its title, and Musorgsky adds to the scene the Russian witch Baba-Yaga flying in a mortar. Finally 'The Heroes' Gate at Kiev' is a march of massive chords in the style of Muscovite solemnity used for the coronation scene in *Boris Godunov*.

Sunless is a much more personal work, even though it was composed not to Musorgsky's own words but to poems by Count Arseny Golenishchev-Kutuzov, with whom he was sharing an apartment at the time. Possibly he found it easier to express himself through words given to him by another, his own literary gift being for the presentation of alien characters. Certainly *Sunless* is a cycle of six songs all ranging within the same orbit of a sensitive pessimism that sounds peculiarly Musorgsky's own, musically in its marriage of realistic declamation with lyrical melody and personally in its honesty of tone.

The productive year of 1874, the year of the first performance of *Boris Godunov*, also saw the start of another operatic project, even though *Khovanshchina* was far from finished. The new work was to be, like *The Marriage*, a comedy after Gogol, *Sorochintsy Fair*. It was, however, set aside early in 1875 in favor of a second cycle of Golenishchev-Kutuzov songs, *Songs and Dances of Death*, of which three numbers were written in 1875 and the fourth in 1877. By contrast with the poems of *Sunless*, which are lyrics of subjective emotion, those of this second cycle are narratives with strong descriptive images: a dying child being nursed by his mother; Death serenading a sick girl as her lover; Death dancing a *trepak* with a lost drunkard; Death riding over a moonlit battlefield to claim his own. These were all images to which Musorgsky could respond forcefully

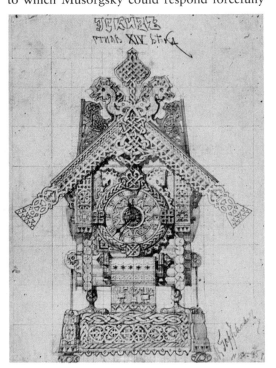

with objectivity intensified, it would seem, by his own awareness of death, and the cycle bears comparison with some of the late piano pieces of Liszt, written at around the same time. And though there is no question here of mutual influence, Musorgsky was in fact an ardent admirer of Liszt as a composer who had released himself from the shackles of German symphonic thought to give a freer expression to his own artistic ideas. He could not, though, be persuaded by Stasov to pay a visit to Liszt at Weimar in 1873. Indeed, he never left Russia.

A few months after the composition of the *Songs and Dances of Death*, Golenishchev-Kutuzov got married and went to live in the country. Musorgsky found lodgings in the home of a retired naval officer, Paul Naumov, and his sister Mariya, to whom he dedicated a song, 'The Sphinx' (1875), in satirical defence of her honor. Another close friend at this time was the operatic bass Osip Petrov, who had taken the role of the vagabond monk Varlaam in the first performance of *Boris Godunov*. Musorgsky became much occupied with the preparations for the celebration of Petrov's golden jubilee as a singer in May 1876, and this stimulated a return to work on *Sorochintsy Fair*, which he had planned for Petrov. For the moment he worked on the two operas together, the comedy *Sorochintsy Fair* and the historical tragedy *Khovanshchina*, but in 1877 he abandoned the latter in favor of the former. He was, in any event, making little headway. Five songs he wrote in 1877, to poems by Alexei Tolstoy, are negligible, serving only to illustrate the remarkable swings in Musorgsky's art between the total mastery he could achieve when the subject gripped him, as it did in the *Songs and Dances of Death*, and the complete mediocrity of which he was capable when not so roused. Similarly insignificant is *Jesus Navin* (1874-7), for contralto and bass soloists with chorus and piano, which is based on the story of Joshua and musically based on material from his abandoned opera *Salammbô*.

Above: Hartmann's *Catacombes*, showing the artist himself, with a friend and a guide, in the Paris catacombs.

Left: The hut on fowls' legs. A clock in Russian style. Musorgsky's treatment of this Hartmann picture depicts Baba-Yaga herself, the terrifying witch of Russian legend, in the form of an infernal dance.

• Decline and death •

The death of his friend Petrov on 14 March 1878 was a double blow, personal and artistic, enough to cause another interruption in work on the opera that had been intended for him. But though this turned out to be a blank year creatively, it brought some improvement in the conditions of Musorgsky's life. Since his re-entry into government service in January 1869 he had been working in the forestry department, which brought him little satisfaction, but in the summer of 1878 he was transferred, thanks to the efforts of Stasov and Balakirev, to a post in the Revision Commission of Government Control. For all the Byzantine sound of its title, this department proved a happier environment for the composer, since it was headed by a folksong enthusiast who was exceedingly indulgent to him. He even made it possible for Musorgsky to take three months' leave of absence in the autumn of 1879 for a concert tour of the Ukraine, the Crimea and towns along the Don and Volga rivers, which he made as the accompanist of an old friend, Darya Leonova. Their programs included some of Musorgsky's songs and improvised transcriptions of scenes from his operas, including the coronation from *Boris*, a march from *Khovanshchina* and the *St John's Night* music, now billed as 'a musical picture from a new comic opera, *Sorochintsy Fair.*' Musorgsky also played a 'grand musical picture,' *Storm on the Black Sea*, which he never wrote down, though two other travel impressions for piano were published as *On the southern shore of the Crimea* in 1880. Like other piano pieces of the same year, they are unimportant.

Indeed, nothing Musorgsky wrote after the *Songs and Dances of Death* shows him at his best. Of the later songs, his setting of Mephistopheles's 'Song of the Flea' from Goethe's *Faust* is a popular comic-satanic piece for bass singers; it was composed in 1879 and was the last song he wrote. But it is a small harvest for a period of four years. Nor is there much evidence that Musorgsky was making any headway with *Khovanshchina* and *Sorochintsy Fair* during this period. The fact that in 1877 he interested himself in yet another operatic project – *Pugachovshchina*, on another period of disruption in Russian history – suggests that he was desperately looking about, rather than that he was confident of bringing these projects to completion. More and more of his life was being absorbed by drinking and hysteria, and at the end of 1879 he lost his post with the Revision Commission.

However, he had never been short of friends confident in his genius, and arrangements were made for him to receive allowances conditional on the completion of *Khovanshchina* and *Sorochintsy Fair*. Leonova also lent assistance by asking him to help her in establishing a school of singing, where his duties would include accompanying, teaching theory and composing practice material; three *vocalises* for female trio and four folksong arrangements for male quartet were written in 1880 for this purpose. The summer of the same year, his last summer, he spent at Leonova's house at Oranienbaum (where just two years later Stravinsky was to be born). There he planned a new orchestral work, a suite on oriental themes, besides doing some work on the two operas.

Writing to Stasov he spoke as if he were full of creative ideas. In January 1880 he had declared: 'My motto, "Dare! Forward towards new shores!" remains unchanged. . . . The time for writing at leisure is past: to give one's whole self to the people . . . that is what is needed now in art.' In August, from Oranienbaum, he wrote: 'I've finished the market scene in *The Fair*. *Khovanshchina* too is advancing. But the scoring – ye gods! – time!' It is doubtful, though, whether lack of time was the real problem. Both of these operas had been in hand for several years, a much longer period than had been needed for the entire composition of *Boris Godunov*. Yet both were left far from complete, *Sorochintsy Fair* even more so than *Khovanshchina*.

There is, indeed, too little of *Sorochintsy Fair* to make anything like an authentic version of what the opera might have been, and though the work was completed by Anatol Lyadov (first production at the Moscow Free Theater on 21 October 1913) and a different version by Nikolai Tcherepnin (first production at the Monte Carlo Opera on 17 March 1923), any completion must be regarded as highly speculative. As with *Khovanshchina*, Musorgsky orchestrated very little of the music he completed, though he did leave the introduction in full score with the heading 'A Hot Day in Little Russia' – Little Russia being the alternative name for the Ukraine, where *Sorochintsy Fair* is set, and whose folk music it draws on for much of its melodic material.

Musorgsky drafted the scenario in 1877 and

Above: Photograph in the form of a medallion of Chaliapin as Boris Godunov in 1896, after Rimsky-Korsakov had extensively revised the opera.

Left: The composer (*right*) in 1880 with Paul Naumov, with whom he lodged while working on both *Khovanshchina* and *Sorochintsy Fair*.

composed much of Act I in vocal score and a good deal of Act II, but practically nothing of Act III, and after the summer spent at Oranienbaum no more appears to have been done. On 15 February 1881 Musorgsky made his last appearance in public when Rimsky-Korsakov conducted a performance of *The Destruction of Sennacherib* and he acknowledged the applause. Eight days later he arrived at Leonova's house in 'a state of great nervous excitement,' as she recalled; 'he said that he was done for, helpless, and that nothing remained for him but to beg in the streets.' She calmed him, but that evening he suffered a fit of alcoholic epilepsy, followed by three more fits the next day. On 26 February he was taken by his friends to Nikolayevsky Military Hospital. He died on 28 March and was buried two days later in the Alexander Nevsky Cemetery in St Petersburg, near to the tombs of Glinka and Dostoevsky.

The subsequent fortunes of Musorgsky's music have already been indicated – how nearly all of it, including even songs that had been published in his original versions, suffered tidying at the hands of Rimsky-Korsakov and others. However, they cannot be blamed who only wanted to make his music acceptable to the musicians and audiences of their time. Rimsky-Korsakov, in particular, was well aware that his solutions were only temporary, and that there might come a time when the original version of the music would be preferred. The problem for the late nineteenth century was that Musorgsky's brand of realism involved stretching music beyond the boundaries of convention, for convention was the very enemy of a composer who wanted to express himself with immediate, unrepeatable truth, never allowing past achievements to supply him with ready made techniques. Inevitably, therefore, the appreciation of his music as he wrote it had to wait for a time after the breakdown of the old tonal tradition and, significantly, it was the composers who took the lead in that revolution who were among the first to recognize Musorgsky's power and originality. Debussy, who acquired the published and undoctored vocal score of *Boris Godunov* when he visited Russia in the 1880s, was much influenced by its natural declamation in his own opera *Pelléas et Mélisande* and in his songs; he also borrowed a phrase from one of the *Sunless* songs to provide the background music of *Nuages*. Stravinsky, curiously, did exactly the same in his opera *The Nightingale*, and though he often declared Tchaikovsky to be his most important Russian predecessor, the bells of *Boris Godunov*, and its incisive musical speech had their echoes in his music right to the end.

NIKOLAI ANDREYEVICH RIMSKY-KORSAKOV

ROY WILKINSON

Opposite: Nikolai Rimsky-Korsakov (1844-1908), portrayed by Valentin Serov.

Nikolai Andreyevich Rimsky-Korsakov was born on 18 March 1844 in Tikhvin in the Novgorod district. His father Andrei was the illegitimate son of a general (though the general regularized the situation) and the grandson of an admiral. His mother was illegitimate too – the daughter of a wealthy landowner; she was Andrei's second wife, the first being the Princess Meschersky, and she gave Andrei his first son – Voin – in 1822 and his second – Nikolai – twenty-two years later.

Nikolai grew up in a world of amateur music. Both his parents played the piano and his Uncle Peter, who lived with them, had a passionate interest in folk music. These homely influences left their mark and Rimsky-Korsakov's memoirs refer to the early signs of his musical ability. He wrote that before he was two he could distinguish all the tunes his mother sang to him; by three or four he was good at beating time on a drum in accompaniment to his father's piano playing, following all the sudden changes of tempo and rhythm; he also began picking out tunes and harmonies himself, and once he had learnt the names of the notes he would stand in an adjacent room and call them out as the notes were played.

But music was only part of his life. As adolescence approached, he became increasingly interested in joining the navy, due no doubt to the influence of his elder brother Voin, himself in the navy, and of his distinguished uncle the Admiral Nikolai Rimsky-Korsakov, with whom he used to stay in the imperial splendors of St Petersburg. And in July 1856 he entered the College of Naval Cadets there. At the same time, piano lessons continued, though what interest he had in the instrument was in the access it gave him to opera. His growing love of opera was fuelled by friends of his brother's family called Golovin. They introduced him to the repertoire of the St Petersburg opera and his memoirs refer to the impact on him of Donizetti's *Lucia di Lammermoor*, Meyerbeer's *Robert le Diable* and especially of Glinka's *A Life for the Tsar* and *Ruslan and Lyudmila*. Glinka became something of an idol for him, and Rimsky-Korsakov avidly arranged excerpts of Glinka's music for piano duet, violin and piano and other combinations: 'I went twice to the publisher's shop and asked to see the orchestral score of *A Life for the Tsar*. I only half understood it, but the Italian names of the

instruments, the terms, clefs and transposing instruments all exercised on me a certain mysterious charm.'

The year 1859 was an important one for him musically. He changed piano teachers, his new one, Théodore Canille, having a large influence on his musical education. The change also coincided with his first enthusiasm for instrumental music: this was the result of a series of symphony concerts at the Bolshoi Theater, at which he was introduced among other things to Beethoven's symphonies. Canille's influence was replaced in December 1861, when he introduced his pupil to Balakirev, Cui and Musorgsky. Rimsky-Korsakov was dazzled by them, especially by Balakirev. Although only a few years older than Rimsky-Korsakov, they were all musicians with reputations as composers and he idolized them. Balakirev was shown some of the work Rimsky-Korsakov had been doing for Canille and he recognized the talent it revealed. Balakirev gave him encouragement and help. One of these works was a sketch for a symphony and he urged Rimsky-Korsakov to continue it; indeed the first movement was soon finished and two others, a scherzo and finale, followed early in 1862.

In January 1862 Voin was appointed director of the Naval College where Rimsky-Korsakov was a cadet, and when their father died, in February, their mother moved to St Petersburg to live with Voin. In April, Rimsky-Korsakov finished his studies and was posted to his first ship, the clipper *Almaz*. In the circumstances it is understandable that he was unenthusiastic about continuing in the navy. He was deeply involved in the musical scene in St Petersburg, which he was going to have to leave behind for three years or so.

Their first port of call was Gravesend and during the four months he was there he managed to complete the slow movement of the symphony, its main theme based on a folk tune Balakirev had sent him. Rimsky-Korsakov in turn sent Balakirev the completed score. It was the first Russian symphony to be written. From England the *Almaz* was sent to the Baltic for several months, then to New York and the East Coast of America. In 1864 the ship sailed for Rio de Janeiro and then to the Mediterranean, finally returning to Russia in 1865. During this long period of absence, contact with Balakirev had ended, musical thoughts had been suspended, and Rimsky-Korsakov says in his memoirs that he had become an officer-dilettante who liked occasionally playing or listening to music but did not regret that his artistic dreams had disappeared.

In September 1865 he returned to St Petersburg and those dreams began to reawaken. Once more it was due to Balakirev, at whose insistence Rimsky-Korsakov first wrote a trio to add to the scherzo of the symphony and then reorchestrated the whole work. In December 1865 the symphony was given its first performance at the Free School of Music – an institution which Balakirev had set up in St Petersburg during Rimsky-Korsakov's absence.

Rimsky-Korsakov now returned to the old way of life that he had so enjoyed as a naval cadet – a little naval duty each day and a great deal of music, chiefly composition. His musical circle was enlarged by the addition of Dargomyzhsky and Borodin, and by an amateur singer, Sofiya Zotova, who inspired a number of songs. The first was a setting of Heine's 'Lehn' deine Wang' an meine Wang',' followed by further settings of poems by Heine, Lermontov, Pushkin and others. Between 1865 and 1867 he wrote sixteen songs. In 1866, under Balakirev's influence, he composed the *Overture on Three Russian Themes* for orchestra, which was his first truly nationalist work.

In 1867 he began work on a Second Symphony, in B minor; completed a *Fantasia on Serbian Themes* for inclusion in a concert of pan-Slavonic music which Balakirev arranged; and composed another orchestral work, *Sadko*, which he described as a 'musical picture.' This was not only his most successful work so far, but also provided much of the material for his opera of the same title (1894-6).

At the end of the year, Berlioz arrived in St Petersburg at the invitation of Balakirev to conduct a series of concerts for the Russian Music Society. Surprisingly, Rimsky-Korsakov did not meet him, but Berlioz's orchestration was eagerly assimilated and this influence can

be seen in the Second Symphony. This symphony, *Antar*, based on an oriental story by Senkovsky, was finished in September 1868. He was to rewrite it later – first in 1875, then in 1897 and finally in 1903, when he changed its title to a symphonic suite, saying that it might be looked on as a legend or a poem, anything but a symphony.

The Second Symphony now out of the way, Rimsky-Korsakov began to write his first opera. *The Maid of Pskov* was a play by Mey from which he had already used words for one of his early songs. He set to work with great enthusiasm, but after writing a few numbers he was obliged by a chain of events to put it aside. When, in 1869, Dargomyzhsky died, he left Rimsky-Korsakov to score his opera *The Stone Guest*, an indication of the general respect felt by the others in his circle for the latter's powers of orchestration. In the same year he decided to rescore *Sadko*, making an even more brilliant and successful job of it. Another interruption came when Cui asked Rimsky-Korsakov to orchestrate the first chorus of his own opera *William Ratcliff*. So it was 1871 before he resumed work on *The Maid*.

In 1871, Azanchevsky, the new director of the St Petersburg Conservatory, invited Rimsky-Korsakov to become professor of practical composition and instrumentation and to take charge of the orchestral class. This came as a complete surprise to the young composer. It was well known that he was in the navy and had received no formal musical training other than from Canille and Balakirev. He had, however, written many brilliant orchestral pieces whose strikingly modern instrumentation attracted attention. He was also a fervent nationalist, as his music proclaimed, and at the age of twenty-seven was a rapidly rising star.

Rimsky-Korsakov hesitated. His ignorance could easily have been exposed, and what reputation he enjoyed would have suffered. He consulted his friends, but only Balakirev knew the extent of his musical ignorance, and it was only after much heart-searching that he decided to accept the post. So when he began his duties in the autumn, the great St Petersburg Conservatory had a professor of composition and orchestral conductor who was a serving naval officer and whose knowledge of theory, harmony, counterpoint and conducting was as small as, if not smaller than, that of his pupils. He was fortunate and was able to bluff his way through, but he had to work hard to keep ahead of his pupils.

At the end of 1871 he became engaged to Nadezhda Purgold, whom he had met at Dargomyzhsky's house in 1868 and who became part of the regular circle there. She had studied composition and piano at the Conservatory and was an increasing influence on him. Not only was she a fine pianist but she was also a composer in her own right and a person with strong, clear ideas about music. As she was far the better trained, her influence on him can well be understood, and it was she who made the piano arrangements of his works.

Below: Young Rimsky-Korsakov's sketch of Tikhvin – about 150 kilometers east of St Petersburg – the town where he was born.

Opposite bottom: Another of the composer's drawings, this one executed a few years later, when he was a naval cadet.

· The Maid of Pskov ·

In January 1872 Rimsky-Korsakov completed *The Maid of Pskov*, a real achievement, in view of his lack of training. He was influenced in some degree by Musorgsky, with whom he had shared a room during the winter of 1871-2, while he was working on *The Maid* and his friend on *Boris Godunov* – which Rimsky-Korsakov was later to revise and rescore. He was even more influenced by Dargomyzhsky's ideas of operatic realism, having been present at the weekly meetings at which the week's work was sung through and discussed during the period when *The Stone Guest* was being composed. Thus in

revolutionary element in it – it was only eleven years since the emancipation of the serfs, and already social restlessness was growing.

However, its undoubted success failed to satisfy Rimsky-Korsakov. As his own studies of harmony, counterpoint and instrumentation progressed, he became only too aware of the roughness of the work as it stood. In 1876 he began to rewrite the whole opera, adding new material and introducing counterpoint; but this destroyed much of the life of the music, so that he ended up feeling less satisfied with it than with the original. Five years later he started on yet another revision and this final version, later given the new title *Ivan the Terrible*, was finished in 1894.

Below left: Rimsky-Korsakov (front, right) as a midshipman on board the clipper *Almaz*, during his three-year cruise to England, the United States and South America. On the voyage he wrote the slow movement to a youthful symphony.

Below: Rimsky-Korsakov, at the age of fourteen, in his naval cadet uniform.

Rimsky-Korsakov's first opera we find melodic recitative often used in preference to aria, and of course there is a strong folk influence. The story is about the struggle between the inhabitants of the semi-independent city of Pskov and Tsar Ivan the Terrible, a subject that soon produced problems for the composer when he sent the finished score to the censor. There were strong objections on the grounds that no tsar could be represented in opera (a singing tsar was not allowed); nor could Pskov – or any other town – be shown as defending its rights against a tsar. At this point Rimsky-Korsakov was able to make use of his friendship with the navy minister, Krabbe, and after a few words in the right ears and a number of modifications in the libretto, the imperial objections were removed. It was eventually given its first performance at the Maryinsky Theater in January 1873, when it had a tremendous reception, being performed nine more times before the end of the season. Part of its attraction was the

Above: Moonlit view of the Neva and the tip of Vasilyevsky Island, in the heart of St Petersburg, by Alexei Bogolyubov. In the background are the Admiralty building and St Isaac's Cathedral.

In February 1872 Rimsky-Korsakov's version of *The Stone Guest* was performed. It was followed by a commission from the director of the Imperial Theaters for Rimsky-Korsakov, Borodin, Cui and Musorgsky to collaborate in an opera-ballet, *Mlada,* but this was soon put aside.

On 12 July 1872 Rimsky-Korsakov, aged twenty-eight, married Nadezhda, four years younger, and their honeymoon was spent in Switzerland and Italy. During the course of 1873 his friend Krabbe created a special post for him, that of inspector of naval bands, and this freed him from other duties. He visited naval establishments, inspecting the bands, inspecting the instruments, complaining of the music and writing what he felt was suitable music for them to play. He even started to compile a treatise on instrumentation, intending to write exhaustively about all the instruments, though he knew little about any of them. This was never completed, although he worked on it intermittently for the rest of his life.

During the summer of 1873 he decided to compose a symphony – his Third, in C major – which was something of a contrapuntal *tour de force,* incorporating the various technical skills which he was only just starting to learn; this did not augur well. It was finished in time for a performance at a charity concert the following March at which he made his public début as a conductor. Cui described the new symphony as 'the best of all Mr Korsakov's productions, the fruit of ripe thought, happy inspiration and strong talent combined with deep and solid technical knowledge.' There were few who agreed with him, however.

Meanwhile, in September 1873, Nadezhda gave birth to Michael, the first of their seven children, to be followed by Sonya (1875), Andrei (1878), Vladimir (1882), Nadya (1884), Masha (1888) and Slavchik (1889).

• Director of the Free Music School •

It was in writing about a concert organized by Balakirev at the Free Music School in 1867 that Stasov first used the phrase 'mighty handful,' which subsequently became the nickname for Balakirev's group of nationalists. But in the 1870s the fortunes of the Free School reached a low ebb. It was nearly bankrupt and Balakirev himself had taken a job in the goods department of the Warsaw Railway to help his own finances; he had a severe breakdown of health and some of his friends thought he was going mad. He cut himself off from the others in his circle and eventually was asked to resign the directorship of the Free School, for he never appeared there. The post was offered to Rimsky-Korsakov, and he accepted in May 1875.

The next few years saw little of importance being written. He immersed himself in the study of harmony and counterpoint, discovering Palestrina, Bach and other early composers. He worked exercises as though he were a student –

six Fugues for piano, a String Quartet, a String Sextet in A, a Quintet in B flat for piano and wind instruments, and a number of choruses – as well as music in connection with his naval post – a Trombone Concerto, a *Konzertstück* for clarinet and *Variations on a Melody by Glinka* for oboe. As director of the Free School he was responsible for the concerts there, but he tended to frighten audiences by filling the programs with unfamiliar music – by Handel, Bach and Haydn among others, some of whose great works received their first Russian performances at these concerts. His nationalist friends and colleagues feared that perhaps he too was taking leave of his senses. They did not understand that he was educating himself; he may have written an opera and three symphonies, but in his eyes he needed to study the old masters and pursue a course which happened to be more appropriate for students than professors.

Gradually, however, the folk influence began to creep back. He made two collections of folk tunes, one a collection of forty folksongs contributed by a friend of Balakirev, the other of one hundred songs mostly relating to pagan rites and rituals – a subject to which he was to return in his later operas.

When in 1876 Balakirev resumed his musical career, he undertook the preparation of a new edition of all Glinka's operas and asked Rimsky-Korsakov to help him. Clearly the latter's familiarity with these scores was an important factor, in addition to his knowledge of instrumentation and harmony: the project marked a general revival of interest in the contemporary Russian musical scene. In this way Rimsky-Korsakov was weaned from his contrapuntal studies and his study of the classics.

Shortly before their marriage, his wife had written a movement based on one of Gogol's *Evenings on a Farm at Dikanka*, short stories about Ukrainian folklore. Nadezhda had urged him to write an opera on the story called *May Night*, and he now embarked on this. By October 1879 it was all but finished, and on 21 January 1880 it had its première at the Maryinsky Theater. It reflects his love of color, humor and fantasy, a story of village life and rivalry in love, with many comic scenes and a *dénouement* which involves the Queen of the Water Sprites.

In 1879 he also composed a Second String Quartet, this time based on Russian tunes. Its four movements were entitled 'In the fields,' 'At the wedding-eve party,' 'At Khorovod' and 'At the monastery.' However, he was not satisfied with it and it was not publicly performed. He started to write an orchestral piece based on Pushkin's prologue to *Ruslan and Lyudmila*, but soon returned to his *Overture on Russian Themes* (1866), which he completely revised. He also started work on his third opera.

He had come across Ostrovsky's play *The Snowmaiden* in 1874, but at that time had found the fairy legend somehow alien to his ideas. By 1880, however, his ideas had changed and the story captivated him, so that he took only three months to write the short score and

the work was finished in April 1881. Its first performance was on 10 February 1882. In his memoirs he tells how his ideas poured out, the moods and colors of particular movements becoming more and more distinct. The level of inspiration can be seen from the quantity of lyrical music, the melodic ideas, the freshness of the harmonic language, the brightness of color and the instrumental mastery. The composer wrote subsequently: 'When I finished *Snowmaiden* I felt I was a mature musician and as an opera composer I could now stand firmly on my own feet.' Tchaikovsky, who had written incidental music for the play in 1873, commented that he was astonished by the mastery revealed in Rimsky-Korsakov's music.

Although he was hardly aware of Wagner's use of *leitmotif*, Rimsky-Korsakov made certain use of it in *Snowmaiden*, and more than he had done previously. The score also shows a new awareness of the need to plan sequences of keys, to think in chapters rather than paragraphs in the organization of material. Under the influence of Berlioz he gave up using the restricted natural brass instruments and intro-

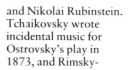

Below: Alexander Ostrovsky reading from *The Snowmaiden* before an audience which includes Tchaikovsky

and Nikolai Rubinstein. Tchaikovsky wrote incidental music for Ostrovsky's play in 1873, and Rimsky-

Korsakov's opera, reputedly the composer's favorite, followed eight years later.

Top: The talented pianist Nadezhda Nikolayevna Rimsky-Korsakov (*née* Purgold).

Above: Scene from the first production (1873) of *The Maid of Pskov* at the Maryinsky Theater. Rimsky-Korsakov's first opera deals with events in the time of Ivan the Terrible and includes a fine bass part for the Tsar himself.

duced chromatic ones, giving his orchestration a new brilliance. The use of blocks of primary colors overlaid with other sonorities became his particular style.

• Works of the 1880s •

Musorgsky died in March 1881, and Rimsky-Korsakov decided to prepare his friend's manuscripts for publication, a huge task which took him two years, during which this and his other activities kept him from original composition, though while rearranging Musorgsky, he also made the second version of *The Maid of Pskov*.

Meanwhile, he was reconsidering his post at the Free School of Music. However useful the concerts were as a platform for his own compositions, and indeed for any that interested him, the running of the school was increasingly

troublesome. Balakirev, now fully recovered in health, was constantly interfering and causing much irritation, so Rimsky-Korsakov decided to resign and hand the directorship back to Balakirev.

However, in 1883 he accepted a new appointment. Balakirev had been made Superintendent of the Imperial Chapel, and he invited Rimsky-Korsakov to be his assistant, a post which he held until 1894. During this period the two composers greatly improved the choir's performances and developed a musical education for the choristers which included theory and instrumental instruction.

In 1884 Rimsky-Korsakov's connections with the navy came to an end, for a change of navy minister led to economies being made, among them the abolition of the composer's post as inspector of naval bands.

For the next few years Rimsky-Korsakov composed little. There was an initial burst of enthusiasm for his duties at the Imperial Chapel and much of his church music dates from this period, which otherwise produced only the one-movement Piano Concerto, based on a Russian tune (1883), a number of songs (1882-3) and a movement for string quartet (1886). However, an important new factor in his life was his friendship with Mitrofan Belyayev, a wealthy merchant devoted to music, especially chamber music. A group of musicians would meet each Friday at Belyayev's house, playing string quartets, trying out ideas, discussing, criticizing. It was clearly a stimulus to young composers, since Belyayev also paid for the publication of their music and eventually started up his own publishing business as well as financing concerts. When Belyayev died in 1903, Rimsky-Korsakov, Glazunov and Lyadov were jointly appointed to administer the large legacy that he bequeathed to Russian music to finance the publishing company, concerts, a Glinka Prize, chamber music prizes and a fund for needy musicians.

In 1885 Tchaikovsky offered the directorship of the Moscow Conservatory to Rimsky-Korsakov, but he refused it. Two years later, in 1887, Borodin died and Rimsky-Korsakov took it upon himself to complete and orchestrate *Prince Igor*, helped by his pupil Glazunov.

During that summer he also looked at some ideas he had jotted down earlier for a violin fantasia on Spanish themes, intended as the pair to the *Fantasia on two Russian Themes* which he had written a few months before. This became the *Spanish Capriccio*, which was given a rapturous première in December 1887 at one of the Russian Symphony Concerts

Left: Vasnetsov's stage design for the palace of Tsar Berendey, the setting for Act II of *Snowmaiden*. The story of the opera is an allegorical fairytale about the seasonal change from winter (the Snowmaiden) to spring, such a dramatic event in the Russian year.

Right: Some of Viktor Vasnetsov's peasant costume designs for *Snowmaiden*, first staged at the Maryinsky Theater in 1882.

sponsored by Belyayev. Even the orchestral brilliance of *Snowmaiden* paled in comparison with that of the *Capriccio*, which, as the composer pointed out, was intended as a virtuoso study in orchestration. Two more big orchestral works followed in 1888 – *Sheherazade* and the *Russian Easter Festival Overture*. Both are highly popular, but *Sheherazade* is the more famous. In taking a story from the *Arabian Nights*, Rimsky-Korsakov displayed again his interest in the exotic.

These three orchestral works marked the climax of a period in which he declared that he had attained 'a considerable degree of virtuosity . . . without the influence of Wagner.' But he could not escape Wagner, for in March 1889 a touring German company performed *The Ring* in St Petersburg. Rimsky-Korsakov attended the rehearsals and followed the music with the score; the result may be heard in his next work, *Mlada*.

Mlada had originally been a composite piece commissioned nearly twenty years earlier. He now returned to the music which he had written at that time and decided to take it up again. Even though he interrupted the work to conduct in Paris and to holiday with his wife in Switzerland and Austria, the draft of the opera was finished in August. Because he had decided to use a Wagner-sized orchestra, the full score took longer than usual to complete. Another conducting visit, to Brussels, caused him to break off work again, and when he returned he found Nadezhda seriously ill with diphtheria. She eventually recovered, but his mother became ill during August and died a month later, and at the end of the year his youngest child Slavchik died too. It is surprising that in these circumstances *Mlada* was finished at all, but by September 1890 it was ready. Its first performance came two years later, on 1 November 1892, but in spite of its success on that occasion, its subsequent neglect matched his own low opinion of it; he felt that it was far inferior to *Snowmaiden*.

• New operas •

The years between 1890 and 1894 were not only musically unproductive; they were a time of self-questioning, illness and increasing depression. He resigned the conductorship of the Russian Symphony Concerts and talked also of giving up his post at the Imperial Chapel (which he did in 1894). He stopped attending the Friday sessions at Belyayev's house and increasingly isolated himself. Even the summer move to the country, where so much useful work was usually done, failed to stimulate him, and after a long illness his daughter Masha died. His own health was also giving cause for concern.

It was Tchaikovsky's death in October 1893 that shook him out of his depression. He decided to honor his friend's memory by conducting a memorial concert given in December by the Russian Symphony Concert Society and

another in Odessa in January. When he returned to St Petersburg the depression had lifted. He immediately started work on a new opera, based on another of Gogol's stories, *Christmas Eve* (which Tchaikovsky himself had set as *Vakula the Smith*), and such was his enthusiasm that within a few weeks he had rewritten the libretto and scored the introduction (there was no formal overture as there had been in his earlier operas).

Christmas Eve was his fourth opera, but it shows little progress on *May Night* (which must be regarded as his first, since the first to have been written was completely revised in 1891-2). It has the same types of rustic Russian characters, the same kind of scenario and much the same writing for voices and orchestra. If the music shows more skill, it is also less lyrical and more artificially contrived. Even Rimsky-Korsakov began to have doubts about it: ' . . . there's nothing lyrical left in me. . . . I'm no longer good for anything. . . .' But by the end

Above: A prize-winning painting (1892), by Nathaniel Sichel, of *Fatima*, the Prophet Muhammad's daughter who became enshrined in Islamic legend. Such exotic images helped to excite the interest of the Russian nationalist composers in Asiatic and oriental subjects. Rimsky-Korsakov's orchestral masterpiece *Sheherazade* was one of the finest fruits of this interest.

of 1894 it was finished and, after problems with the censor over the inclusion of a character who was clearly identifiable as Catherine the Great, it went into rehearsal at the Maryinsky Theater. The troubles with the censor were resolved only because of the good relations Rimsky-Korsakov had with a minister, but this was not the end of the matter. Two members of the Imperial Family who were present at a preview of the opera were furious at what they saw as the impersonation of Catherine the Great. As Rimsky-Korsakov had found with *The Maid*, tsars and tsaritsas could be represented in plays but not in opera. The result of the Grand Ducal complaints was the Tsar's refusal to allow the opera to be performed as it stood. A solution was found – absurd it may have been, but it satisfied propriety: the part of the Tsaritsa was sung by a baritone! So the first performance took place in December 1895, although the composer refused to attend in protest at Imperial interference.

Even while Rimsky-Korsakov was working on *Christmas Eve*, he had ideas for yet another opera – *Sadko*. As so often happened, the preliminary score was completed while the family was at their summer holiday home, and by September 1895 most of the work was finished. Again he wrote his own libretto. Then, having more or less completed it, he was persuaded to add to it by a new friend and admirer, Vladimir Belsky, who spent the summer of 1895 on a neighboring estate and saw much of the composer. Rimsky-Korsakov was not happy with the final result, thinking it too long. However, the work was finished in 1896 and submitted to the director of the Imperial Theaters for approval. Perhaps not surprisingly after the fracas over *Christmas Eve*, the authorities were suspicious. The play-through of the score to Vsevolozhsky, the director, did not go well, and when he

reported that this new opera was in the same mold as the earlier ones, the Tsar refused his permission for it to be included in the next season's list. Rimsky-Korsakov was furious.

Fortunately, a private sponsor came to the rescue. Savva Mamontov was a wealthy patron of the arts who had some years earlier financed the Private Russian Opera, whose famous singers included Chaliapin. This was the company which had put on the new version of *The Maid of Pskov* a few months earlier, and in the summer of 1897 the score of *Sadko* was sent for approval and was accepted, the first performance taking place on 7 January 1898.

Sadko has good claims to be considered Rimsky-Korsakov's best opera, with the most consistently high standard of music. It is episodic, like many Russian operas – he himself described it as a succession of scenes or tableaux set to music – which suited him perfectly, for it was by now clear that sustained dramatic writing of the conventional operatic sort was not his forte. He drew heavily on the music he had used in the orchestral suite of 1867. His brilliance in musical illustration is nowhere better, and his evocative language is an effective mixture of chromatic and more conventional harmony, the former associated with the fantastic element and the latter with the real world.

So prolific were his ideas at this time that, while working on *Sadko*, he wrote part of the libretto and some music for a one-act opera, *The Barber of Baghdad*, but this was never finished, although it provided music for *The Golden Cockerel* ten years later. The winter of 1895-6 was devoted to the revision of Musorgsky's *Boris Godunov*. Just as he had previously rewritten and rescored *Khovanshchina* and Borodin's *Prince Igor*, so Rimsky-Korsakov now

Left: César Cui, the son of a French army officer, and one of the 'mighty handful.' He wrote ten operas, many songs and instrumental works, but he is best remembered today for the assistance and encouragement that he gave to Rimsky-Korsakov and other members of the group.

devoted himself to the massive task of rewriting and reorchestrating *Boris*.

The following year, with *Sadko* completed, he entered a period which can best be described as one of experiment. First he turned to songwriting. He had already composed some thirty songs, mostly between 1865 and 1870, but in 1897 he wrote forty. They show a new type of vocal part, which he described in his memoirs:

Above: Sketch by Repin of Rimsky-Korsakov directing a concert in 1882 at the Exhibition of Russian Arts in Moscow.

'I worked out the accompaniments after the melodies were finished whereas before, with a few exceptions, the melodies had been conceived more or less instrumentally.' The new songs were certainly more like Glinka in their lyricism and much less declamatory than the earlier ones, though the accompaniments tend to be less picturesque. Although perhaps none of Rimsky-Korsakov's songs matches the lyrical quality of his best operatic music, 'Southern night' and 'Spring Night' are outstanding examples of Russian solo song.

His experimenting turned to opera also. Of the three works he wrote in 1897 and 1898, the first, *Mozart and Salieri*, based on a tragedy by Pushkin, was an unexpected reversion to Dargomyzhsky's principle of 'dramatic truth' and recitative. It was produced by Mamontov's Private Russian Opera Company in December 1898 with two other operas, the final version of *The Maid* and the one-act *Vera Sheloga*, written earlier in the year. *Vera Sheloga* was based on a story by Mey and for this the composer used the music of the discarded prologue of the final version of *The Maid*. From this period, too, comes a cantata, *Switezianka*, a

Far left: Repin's impression of the bustling Nevsky Prospekt, St Petersburg, in 1887.

Left: Rimsky-Korsakov in 1885, the year in which he was offered the directorship of the Moscow Conservatory. He turned the offer down, preferring to stay in St Petersburg.

Left: A moment from an early performance of *May Night*. Among the singers is the bass Fyodor Stravinsky (second from left). The scenario of Rimsky-Korsakov's opera, like that of Musorgsky's *Sorochintsy Fair* and Tchaikovsky's *Vakula the Smith*, is taken from Gogol's collection of short stories of Ukrainian folklore and legend.

101

Above: Nadezhda Zabela-Vrubel as the swan-princess in *The Legend of Tsar Saltan*, based on the fairytale by Pushkin about a magic island. The painting was executed in 1900 by the singer's husband, Mikhail Vrubel, who also designed the sets for Rimsky-Korsakov's opera.

Right: Title-page to the 1895 edition of the score of *Christmas Eve*, based on the same Gogol short story as Tchaikovsky's *Vakula the Smith.*

and mighty hero Prince Guidon Saltanovich and of the beautiful Swan Princess. This is a fairy story, and both its libretto (by Belsky) and its music showed that Rimsky-Korsakov had returned to nationalist opera. Most of its composition took place as usual during the summer, and it received its first performance in Moscow in November 1900 at the Private Russian Opera, though by then Mamontov had been imprisoned for fraud and the company was being run by its own members.

The story of the opera has a Cinderella element, Militrissa being the beautiful young girl who is made to do all the work by her two 'ugly sisters.' The great Tsar Saltan overhears her admit that if she married him she would wish to give him a son who would become a great hero, and when the Tsar sees her he falls in love with her and marries her. Their first child, a boy, is born while the Tsar is away fighting and the Tsaritsa's message with the good news is intercepted by her sisters, who change it to read that the new child is a deformed girl. The Tsar, angry and disappointed, sends orders for his wife and daughter to be put into a barrel and thrown into the sea. However, the barrel is washed on to the desert island of Bujan and young Guidon escapes from it and kills a hawk which is attacking a swan. The swan thanks Guidon, revealing that the hawk was a wicked magician and the swan herself a princess. The hawk's death breaks the magician's spells and a fabulous city rises from the sea. In gratitude its citizens make Guidon their king.

Later Guidon wants to visit the country of his birth, so he summons the swan, whose magic powers turn him into a bumble-bee, and in that disguise he visits the Tsar's court. The Tsar, learning of the wonders of the Kingdom of Bujan, determines to visit the island and meet

trio for piano, violin and cello, a string quartet in G and the final version of his Second Symphony which was given the new name, *Antar*, and described as a symphonic suite.

A further opera, *The Tsar's Bride*, followed in 1898. An adaptation by Tyumenev of yet another of Mey's works, it was finished in eight months and given its first performance in Moscow in November 1899. Here the composer continued his new 'vocal' method of composition and introduced ensembles in the manner of nineteenth-century Italian opera. But Russian opera was always strong in crowd scenes and weaker in the formal elements of aria and ensemble, and this sortie into the world of Italian opera was unconvincing.

Rimsky-Korsakov wrote another opera in 1899, but this time he returned to the safer world of Russian folklore. He was attracted by Byron's *Heaven and Earth* and by the *Odyssey* (this eventually turned out as a choral prologue *From Homer*), but he finally chose Pushkin's *Legend of Tsar Saltan, of his son the famous*

the brave King, of whom he has heard so much. The bumble-bee returns to Bujan and becomes the King again. Guidon has heard of a beautiful princess and asks the swan about her, where-upon the bird reassumes her natural form – that of the beautiful Princess herself. When Tsar Saltan arrives, the Swan-Princess tells him that Guidon is his son. With the arrival of Mili-trissa, his happiness is complete.

A suite of music from the opera, which dis-plays all Rimsky-Korsakov's orchestral bril-liance, is made up of 'The Tsar's departure and farewell' (when he leaves for the wars), 'The Tsaritsa in a barrel at sea,' 'The flight of the bumble-bee' (one of Rimsky-Korsakov's best known pieces) and 'March.'

• Russia's leading composer •

In 1900 Rimsky-Korsakov was the leading Russian composer, the most prolific of the 'nationalists' and a revered professor at the St Petersburg Conservatory. Earlier that year he had chosen another of Mey's works for an opera, *Servilia*, a story about ancient Rome, and once again he attempted to write an opera without Russian influence. The music was composed in 1900 during a summer holiday in southern Germany, where he and Nadezhda were visiting their student son Andrei. It was ready by May 1901.

The Imperial Theaters had recently experi-enced a change of director, the new one being Prince Volkonsky, who lost little time in asking Rimsky-Korsakov for a ballet. Though nothing came of this, the way was prepared for a re-sumption of operas by the country's principal composer in its main opera house. The first to be presented was *Sadko*, in February 1901, and *Servilia* was given its first performance at the Maryinsky in October 1902.

During 1902-3 Rimsky-Korsakov worked on several schemes. One which foundered was the story from the *Odyssey – Nausicaa –* which he had been considering for some time. Work was also started on the libretto by Tyumenev for a Polish opera, *Pan Voyevoda*, but even this was put aside in favor of the one-act opera *Kashchey the Immortal*, based on a libretto by Petrovsky which Rimsky-Korsakov did not like and rewrote himself. Musically it is unusual because, although it is a Russian story, it is not treated in his normal 'Russian' style; instead it is distinctly Wagnerian, with much chromati-cism and dissonance. It was completed during 1901-2 and received its first performance on Christmas Day 1902.

In the summer of 1902 Rimsky-Korsakov went to stay in Heidelberg, visiting Andrei, who introduced him to a fellow student there – Igor Stravinsky. Most of the music for *Pan Voyevoda* was written there, and at the same time he worked on a complete rescoring of *The Stone Guest*.

The Polish opera *Pan Voyevoda* was a trib-ute to Chopin. It had little fantasy and much

Right: I. F. Tyumenev, who collaborated with Rimsky-Korsakov on the libretti of both *The Tsar's Bride* and *Pan Voyevoda.*

Below: Title-page by Ivan Bilibin to the score of *The Golden Cockerel*, Rimsky-Korsakov's last opera, based once more on a fairytale by Pushkin. The work again fell foul of the censor, as King Dodon, (seen in the center of the design), who goes off to war in rusty armor, was identified with Tsar Nicholas II, recently humiliated by Russia's defeat in the war with Japan. The magnificent décor for the opera was also by Bilibin.

drama – not a promising recipe for Rimsky-Korsakov. Indeed, it turned out to be an indifferent work, as undramatic as *Servilia* and similarly influenced in technique by Wagner. It was first performed at the Conservatory on 16 October 1904.

It was not until he wrote *Kitezh* that he reverted to his Russian style. With it he returned to the standard of *Sadko*, and it contains some of his best music, brilliantly evocative and highly colored. Its subject involves a mixture of orthodox Christianity and pantheism, with much rather vague symbolism. The libretto was by Belsky. Rimsky-Korsakov started work on it in 1903 and completed the score the following year. Its first performance was at the Maryinsky Theater on 20 February 1907, and it was ecstatically received.

Much had happened, though, between its composition and its first performance. Revolutionary unrest resulting from the disastrous war with Japan began to make itself felt in St Petersburg. Students at the Conservatory were involved. Rimsky-Korsakov shared their views, even giving his support to the idea of a change of constitution at the Conservatory and an end to the power of the *dilettanti*, as he called them, who formed its governing body, and who were all members of the Imperial Russian Music Society. The council responded by dismissing Rimsky-Korsakov and temporarily closing the Conservatory. The composer was treated like a martyr and letters of support poured in from all over the country. He resigned from the Russian Music Society; Glazunov and others resigned from the Conservatory, as did several members of the council. A few days later the second half

of a concert of Rimsky-Korsakov's music turned into a political demonstration, and the police had to be called to clear the hall. This led to a ban on the performance of all his music and the cancellation of other concerts. It was not until the end of the year that the Conservatory reopened with Rimsky-Korsakov and others reinstated and the expelled students readmitted.

The winter of 1905-6 was very unsettled. There were more upheavals at the Conservatory, with Glazunov in conflict with the council. In the summer the Rimsky-Korsakovs holidayed in Europe, and while he was in Italy the composer completed his memoirs, published with the title *Chronicle of my Musical Life*.

In September he returned to St Petersburg, and although he had only recently expressed fears that he was running out of ideas, he was shortly back at work on yet another opera. This time he used a libretto by Belsky based on Pushkin's satirical fairy story *The Golden Cockerel*. Work continued through the winter but was interrupted in May 1907 for a visit to Paris, where Diaghilev had persuaded him to take part in a series of concerts of Russian music which included excerpts from his operas. In June he returned to St Petersburg and resumed work on *The Golden Cockerel*, which was finished by September. It was inevitable that there would be problems with the censor, for the story included a stupid tsar, and in any case Tsar Nicholas II was aware of Rimsky-Korsakov's role in the troubles of 1905. It is hardly sur-

Below: Three of the singers from the first production (1898) of *Sadko* at the Solodovnikov Theater, Moscow. The tenor A. V. Sekar-Rozhansky appeared as Sadko (*center*), the Novgorod merchant who marries the sea-princess Volkhova; while Chaliapin played the Viking merchant (*left*), whose song, extolling the tough and rugged character of his homeland, is one of the best-known bass arias in Russian opera; the sea-princess (*right*) was sung by Zabela-Vrubel. She was Rimsky-Korsakov's favorite lyric soprano, and he composed the music to several roles with her in mind.

prising that the work was banned, and the first performance took place only after his death, in Moscow on 7 October 1909.

Vague as *Kitezh* is in its symbolism, *The Golden Cockerel* is even vaguer. Ernest Newman commented that one of its charms is the fact that not only are we unsure what it means, but we are unsure that it means anything at all. It is pure fantasy and satire, with fabulous virtu-

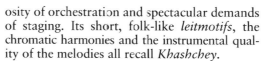

osity of orchestration and spectacular demands of staging. Its short, folk-like *leitmotifs*, the chromatic harmonies and the instrumental quality of the melodies all recall *Khashchey*.

On 23 April 1908 Rimsky-Korsakov had a severe attack of angina pectoris. He suffered another massive attack on 18 June from which he did not recover fully, and another on the 21st killed him. After a service at the Conservatory, he was buried two days later in the cemetery of the Novodevichy Monastery in St Petersburg.

Rimsky-Korsakov was the most energetic and versatile of the Russian nationalists, with a large and varied output of unequal quality. His most important works are the operas, though the orchestral works *Sheherazade* and *Spanish Capriccio* are probably more widely known and more frequently performed. The operas, unlike those of Verdi and Wagner, show no evolution of style, no crescendo of achievement. The most characteristic are those based on the fairytale world of fantasy and humor, where his orchestral skills and vivid imagination enabled him to paint brilliant pictures in sound.

His musical language is a mixture of diatonic and chromatic, the former associated with the 'real' world in his operas and the latter with the fantasy world. It increasingly reflected late nineteenth-century expressiveness, with strong overtones of Wagner and a powerful Russian accent through folksong and national idioms. He also used the whole-tone scale (borrowed from Liszt) as well as unusual metric schemes (7/4 and 11/4). Rimsky-Korsakov's fabulous orchestral skills show at their best in descriptive scenes of village life, landscapes or atmosphere, and of course *Sheherazade*, the *Spanish Capriccio* and the *Russian Festival Overture* are justly popular for their rich colors, exotic effects and lyrical melodies.

As a teacher he had enormous influence on the younger Russian composers – Stravinsky, Prokofiev, Glazunov, Lyadov, Grechaninov among others. Even Debussy, Ravel and other French composers learned much from his use of the orchestra, in the mastery of which he has few rivals in the history of music.

Left: Rimsky-Korsakov in 1900. The inscription on the photograph reads, 'To my dear beloved and admired old friend Kruglikov.' Semyon Kruglikov was a music critic who supported the composer and helped with the first production of *Sadko.*

Below: Chaliapin as Ivan the Terrible, mourning the death of his daughter Olga, in the 1896 revival of *The Maid of Pskov* in Moscow.

A Nordic Romantic Nationalist: Edvard Grieg

All over Europe in the years after 1840 there was an awakening of national consciousness. Inspired by Liszt, musicians looked for native traditions, often discovering them in the rhythms of popular dances and the melodies of folksongs.

Edvard Hagerup Grieg was born in 1843 in Bergen on the west coast of Norway, and his musical talent, encouraged by his family, was first recognized by the violinist Ole Bull. He studied in Leipzig and in Copenhagen – where his friend Rikard Nordraak encouraged his nationalist ideas – and fell under the spell of Liszt and Wagner. Then in 1867 he moved to Norway's capital Christiania (Oslo) as conductor of the orchestra. However, cultural life in Norway was so restricted that the choice lay between self-exile – the path taken by Ibsen – or a creative life cut off from the European mainstream. Grieg chose the latter way and never learned to command large musical forces or forms, though he dreamed of finding a dramatic text that would 'kindle his musical soul' and enable him to write a great national opera. But it was in more intimate works that his natural lyricism could be best expressed and that he could use the melodies and dance rhythms – the *springar*, *gangar* and *halling* – of the Norwegian mountains and valleys.

Grieg's songs (an early collected edition is shown left) occupy a special place in his oeuvre, not least because so many were written for his cousin Nina Hagerup, whom he married in 1867. In his earliest songs he set works by the German Romantic poets, but later he set native Norwegian poems by Ibsen and the young Bergen poets Johan Poulsen and A. O. Vinje, as well as many by Bjørnson, which formed the basis of some of his finest and most deeply felt compositions.

The scenery and peasant life of Norway inspired both Grieg – in such works as *Fra fjeld og fjord*, op.44 – and the artist Adolph Tidemand (1814-76), whose *Bridal Journey on Hardanger Fjord* (painted in 1848 in collaboration with H. Gude) is shown above. Grieg himself lived from 1877 to 1884 on Hardanger Fjord, and on Sundays he would often invite over the peasants and play *hallings* for them to dance to and then play them his own compositions.

Left: Bjørnstjerne Bjørnson (1831-1910), the poet closest to Grieg, whose warmth and generosity of heart was able to remove all the composer's inhibitions. Grieg wrote incidental music for his historical drama *Sigurd Jorsalfar*, and they planned to write a Viking opera together, *Olav Trygvason*, but the text was unfinished and Grieg set only a few fragments.

Ole Bull, the 'flaxen-haired Paganini' of Norway, seen (*below*) with his violin, which had an almost level bridge and a flat fingerboard and, like the *hardingfele*, was richly decorated. Born in Bergen, Bull was largely self-taught, but at nineteen he became embroiled in politics and had to leave Norway; he studied with Spohr in Kassel and then, fearing that the German's cold academic style might destroy his own natural gifts, he went on to Paris, where he heard the playing of Vieuxtemps – and Paganini. From 1842 he started on the triumphant tours in Europe and America which he continued almost until his death. Like Thomas Tellefsen (1823-74), who studied with and was befriended by Chopin in Paris, Bull inspired Grieg more by his example than his music, although all three used the rhythms of Norwegian rustic dances in their works.

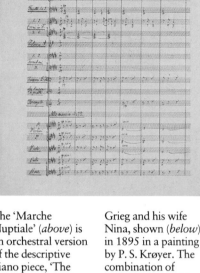

In the folklore of Telemark, in southern Norway, the *Fossegrim*, a fiddler inhabiting mills and waterfalls, puts a spell on all who hear him play; Ole Bull was said to have learned to play the violin from a *Fossegrim*. In Ernst Josephsen's painting (*above*) of 1884 the sprite's music is seen to unleash the untamed wanton forces of nature. Grieg's younger contemporary Johan Halvorsen (1864-1935) included the traditional *hardingfele* in his 1905 suite *Fossegrimen*.

The Swedish artist Anders Zorn's etching *Old Ballad* (*below*) evokes the folk stories of nature spirits which were still preserved in Scandinavian oral tradition. Grieg used these in his *Den Bergtekne*, op.32 (for baritone, string orchestra and horns), based on a ballad that tells of a wanderer in the mountains led astray by elves and fated never again to find his way home; while his *Ballade*, op.24, of 1874-5 is a set of variations on a plaintive Norwegian theme.

OLE BULL.

The 'Marche Nuptiale' (*above*) is an orchestral version of the descriptive piano piece, 'The Wedding Procession Passes By,' the second of Grieg's *Humoresques – Scenes of Popular Life*, op.19. Weddings were the greatest celebrations in a Norwegian village, and the procession was always led by a player of the *hardingfele*; Grieg depicted this again in his 'Wedding Day at Troldhaugen,' op.65 no.6.

Grieg and his wife Nina, shown (*below*) in 1895 in a painting by P. S. Krøyer. The combination of diffidence and self-esteem in Grieg's character required constant support and encouragement, and Nina never failed him. It was for her that he wrote his songs, and on their concert tours it was she who sang them, until her voice began to lose its power around 1898. Even then she performed them for their friends with a perfection of nuance and phrasing.

In 1876 Grieg went with a group of leading Norwegian musicians on a visit to Bayreuth and Leipzig (where the photograph, right, was taken). Grieg hoped to create a 'Norwegian drama with Norwegian music . . . profound and great like a Wagnerian drama.' When he composed, Wagner's scores were always at his side, and there are frequent Wagnerian reminiscences in his works.

Below: Set showing the interior of Aase's house in the 1902 revival of *Peer Gynt* with Grieg's music in Christiania (Oslo). Furniture, rugs and the house itself are based on traditional Norwegian styles.

The sea troll (*below*), seen a drawing of 1887 by T. Kittelsen, was one of the many monsters of Norse legend to survive in Norwegian folklore. Henrik Ibsen (*left*) began the symbolic action of his verse drama *Peer Gynt* (1867) with the hero's killing of a forest troll, an act which enables him to hear secret voices as he embarks on his fabulous adventures.

Grieg first met Ibsen in 1865-6 in Rome, the composer full of youthful enthusiasm for his native land, the writer already disillusioned with the philistinism of his compatriots. Then, in 1874, Grieg was invited by Ibsen to compose incidental music for his verse-drama *Peer Gynt*, written in Italy seven years earlier. Grieg retired to the country to undertake this arduous task, for the philosophical undercurrent of the play was foreign to his more simple nature. Nevertheless, the production in Christiania in 1876 was a great success, and it was revived in 1892 and 1902 in productions by Bjørn Bjørnson, son of the poet, who in the first of these himself played Peer (*left*), while the part of Solveig was taken by Johanne Dybwad (*above*). Grieg later incorporated some of the twenty-two orchestral fragments into two suites.

In 1896 *Peer Gynt* was put on in Paris at the Théâtre de l'Oeuvre with Grieg's incidental music. The program (*above*) was designed by Edvard Munch – who, like Ibsen, found the atmosphere of Norway restricting and for many years worked abroad. It reflects the underlying theme of the play: youthful aspirations that, with experience, turn to disillusion and despair, embodied in the roles of Solveig, who remains true to the faithless Peer, and his mother Aase.

Despite his training in Leipzig, Grieg's music is far closer to that of his French contemporaries Saint-Saëns and Fauré than to Brahms and the German school. His first concert in Paris, at which his Piano Concerto and the two *Peer Gynt* Suites were played, was put on by Edouard Colonne in 1889, and on his return in 1894 he dedicated to Colonne the score of his song 'Le Cygne' (*right*), a setting of Ibsen.

In 1885, after nearly a year of traveling in Holland, Germany and Italy, the Griegs settled at Troldhaugen on the banks of a small fjord near Bergen. As always, he had a small hut (*above*) in the grounds of the house, where he composed, and he continued to divide his time between work here and an arduous round of concert tours.

Above: Grieg in the mountains in 1902, the year of his *Slaater* (Norwegian peasant dances), op.72.

Below: In spite of severe tuberculosis, Grieg continued both his concert tours and his composition to the end. He died on 4 September 1907 as he was about to leave for England to take part in a festival at Leeds.

In his Paris concert in 1894 Grieg included his Piano Concerto (played by Raoul Pugno), as well as the *Holberg Suite* and a selection of songs. Although this was a great success, Grieg took a public stand against the anti-semitism generated by the Dreyfus affair, and on his return in 1903 he had a noisy reception at a concert (*left*) which again included many of his best-known works. However, it was favorably reviewed by Fauré, though dismissed in a savage criticism by Debussy.

Grieg's *Slaater* were based on pieces collected by Johan Halvorsen in the valleys of Telemark, and three were based on performances by the *hardingfele* player Myllargutten (*above*). Grieg took pains to reproduce the characteristic double- and triple-stopping and the sound of the sympathetic strings.

At one of Grieg's concerts in the year before his death, in Amsterdam, the soloist was the great Catalan cellist Pau Casals (*above*), who performed the Cello Sonata in A minor, op.36, which Grieg had written in 1883.

CÉSAR FRANCK

ROY WILKINSON

An unsuccessful piano virtuoso; a composer, the majority of whose works are, even today, scarcely heard of let alone performed, whose music was most often the subject of scathing contemporary critical comment and public rejection, whose first mature work was not composed until he was fifty-seven and whose first popularly acclaimed one not until he was sixty-eight – these descriptions hardly seem applicable to a composer who is generally considered to be responsible for changing the course of French music.

César Franck was born in Liège on 10 December 1822. His father, Nicolas-Joseph, came from Gemmenich, a small town near Aachen, while his mother was of German stock and at the time of her marriage was living in Aachen itself. With a gesture which is perhaps indicative of Nicolas-Joseph's hopes for the future of his family, but which hardly seems suitable for the child of a minor bank official, he grandly named his son César-Auguste-Jean-Guillaume-Hubert, adding Franck de Liège later for concert publicity.

From the start, Nicolas-Joseph appears to have been determined that César and his elder brother Joseph would be virtuoso peformers, child prodigies like Mozart and his sister. His own role would be similar to that of Leopold Mozart, escorting the children round the salons and concert halls of Europe, shaping their careers and ensuring fame and fortune for the family. Joseph, born two years before César, was not as gifted as his brother, but he was a good enough violinist to be included in his father's plans for the public recitals to be given by his two sons, a duo which lasted until 1846. So, with these intentions in mind, Nicolas-Joseph sent the two boys to the Royal Liège Conservatory. César's superiority was soon apparent, and during his time there he was awarded several prizes.

In 1835, when César Franck was thirteen and still at the Liège Conservatory, Nicolas-Joseph organized a recital tour of Belgium, in the course of which the boy performed to King Leopold I. If Nicolas-Joseph expected this to lead to great things he must have been sadly disappointed, for whereas the young Mozart had been unrivaled as a clavier player and improviser, the young Franck had to contend with many established and astonishing pianists, as well as artists on other instruments. This was the age of the virtuoso, a cult dominated by Liszt on the piano and Paganini on the violin; Nicolas-Joseph misjudged things by assuming that his son could rival such figures, for Franck must inevitably have been measured against people like Thalberg, Moscheles, Marmontel, Kalkbrenner and others. Franck's personality was no help either. The quiet, introverted son of a bank clerk lacked the charm and confidence which would have helped him – indeed which were essential – to win the hearts of the sophisticated audiences.

The family moved to the French capital in 1835. Franck had piano lessons with Zimmermann, a leading piano professor, and studied composition with another famous teacher, the Czech Antoine Reicha. Reicha undoubtedly had a great influence on Franck's attitude to form and the classics during the one year he taught him – he died in 1836.

Nicolas-Joseph continued to arrange recitals for his reluctantly obedient son – they were, after all, the main purpose of the family's move to Paris – but few other than critics attended them, and their published views increasingly reflected their impatience with someone whom they regarded as both pretentious and inadequate.

In view of his early years on the concert platform, it is hardly surprising that Franck's first compositions are mainly of a flamboyant nature, or that they are virtuoso pieces, usually *fantaisies* on operatic themes, a genre very popular with audiences. These first works were written when he was only twelve years old – *Variations Brillantes on themes from Gustave III*, *Variations on themes from Pré-aux-Clercs*, a *Grande sonate* (1835), a concerto and a rondo – and all were unpublished; the following year, 1836, saw the second *Grande sonate* and a *Fantaisie*. In 1842 he wrote the *Eglogue* and in 1843 a *Grande caprice*, op.5, and *Souvenir d'Aix-la-Chapelle*, op.7.

• Student years in Paris •

Nicolas-Joseph's most important decision was that his son should enter the Paris Conservatoire, which was far more prestigious than the Liège establishment. For this French citizenship was required, so Nicolas-Joseph went through the requirements of residence, and in October 1837 César Franck became a student there.

Below: Aristide Cavaillé-Coll (1811-99) at his desk. The celebrated organ builder played an important role in the renaissance of French organ music after 1850.

The release from recitals and tours must have been very welcome. Certainly he was happy in the conservative academic establishment; he reveled in harmony and counterpoint and won prizes for piano, organ and fugue as well as receiving a Special Grand Prix d'Honneur not only for the fluency of his sightreading of a test piece but also for its transposition into a different key.

The *Trois trios concertants*, op.1, for piano, violin and cello were composed while Franck was still a student at the Paris Conservatoire and were dedicated to King Leopold I of the Belgians. They are surprising in their originality, and with them Franck staked his claim to be the originator of French chamber music in the classical sense; they certainly show the influence of Beethoven and other classical composers on the young student. The first trio is by far the best and most significant, for in its assured use of cyclic form – the use of themes common to, and developed in, all the movements – it gives Franck a claim as its originator in the nineteenth century. Vincent d'Indy later wrote: 'It marks an epoch in the history of musical form, reducing to practice tendencies dimly perceived by Schumann and Liszt but which they were unable fully to realize, and more especially by reason of its thoroughly French character it may be considered as the starting point of that splendid outburst of instrumental composition which took place at the end of the last century.' This is quite a comment about a work written by an eighteen-year-old student. However, the Trios were swamped by the operatic mania of the period and passed totally unnoticed, and it was not until the founding in 1871 of the Société Nationale de Musique that Franck and others had the incentive to write what they wanted.

All was going well; probably for the first time for years Franck was really happy, preferring his studies to the old life and enjoying his successes. In his fifth year he began to prepare for the Prix de Rome, the composition prize which not only conferred immense prestige on the winner but also gave the opportunity of three years' study in Rome with residence at the Villa Medici.

At this point Nicolas-Joseph stepped in. His son had already completed four years at the Conservatoire and there seemed to be no end to it all; in his opinion, the time had come for Franck's studies to end and his career as a virtuoso to be resumed. In April 1842, therefore, when Franck was nearly twenty, the family abruptly moved back to Liège.

Even though Franck had played a concerto by Hummel at a concert of the Société des Concerts du Conservatoire when he was only sixteen (for which he had been awarded a prize), he had not set the Conservatoire ablaze with his piano playing, so it should have been clear to his father that Franck was unlikely to astound the outside world. Predictably, therefore, Franck's resumed piano career was just as unsuccessful as it had been before, and in less than two years the family was back in Paris.

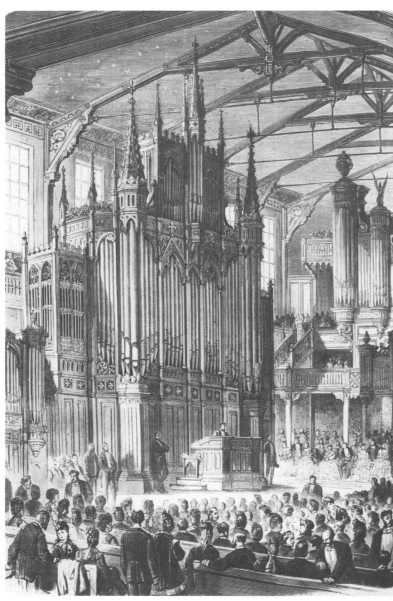

Above: Cavaillé-Coll's organ in the opulent Trocadéro Palace. The picture shows orchestra, choir and organ at a concert during the Paris Universal Exhibition of 1878, for which the Trocadéro was built.

Opposite: The amazing showroom attached to Cavaillé-Coll's organ works. The main model on display is a splendid example of Gothic Revival taste.

Right: Print after the well-known painting by Jean Rongier, of Franck in the organ loft at the church of Ste Clotilde. The instrument, Franck's 'orchestra,' incorporated many of Cavaillé-Coll's most important innovations.

It is interesting to consider what effect these moves must have had on the family. The elder son, Joseph, was in temperament much more like his father; César, the chief cause of these domestic upheavals, was of less stern stuff, and the mild way in which he accepted his father's organization of his life reveals the extent of parental domination as well as the weakness of his own personality. His lack of ambition, his lack of belief in himself, his unparalleled slow musical development and the quantity of immature compositions must all be attributed to the stifling influence of his father.

As far as composition is concerned, Franck had written much by 1844 when, aged twenty-two, he returned with his family to Paris. Apart from the numerous display pieces for piano, the *Trois trios concertants*, his unorchestrated opera *Stradella* and several vocal works, it was piano writing that dominated his output in these early days. However, his return to Paris heralded yet more rebuffs and unsuccessful recitals – the last being in June 1846 – and saw the start of his career as a teacher.

• Teacher and organist •

Franck started teaching to provide an income for the family. The workload his father imposed on him was enormous, the traveling time between pupils being carefully worked out so that Franck could fit more in; he even taught on Sundays. This tedious and exhausting round continued for the next twenty-five years, right up to his appointment in 1872 to a professorship at the Paris Conservatoire. Nevertheless, time was somehow found for composition. The first of his choral works was *Ruth*, started in 1843 and completed two years later, described as an *Eglogue biblique*, for soloists, choir and orchestra. In fifteen sections, the biblical selections being made by Alexandre Guillemin, it is very adventurous in its size. This work was performed to a specially invited audience of musical celebrities, including Liszt, Meyerbeer, Moscheles and Halévy, but the hostile reception by critics and public at the first public performance was a great discouragement to Franck.

A more significant work, because it showed original thought resulting in the creation of a new form, was his symphonic poem *Ce qu'on entend sur la montagne* of 1846, on a subject which Liszt also used for his first symphonic poem. Liszt is always credited with being the inventor of the symphonic poem – a Romantic concept and a mixture of large-scale orchestral writing and program music which reflected many nineteenth-century composers' unease with the established framework of traditional forms – and although Franck's work predates Liszt's by three years, it is known that the latter was working on his first symphonic poem ten years or so earlier. Nevertheless, it is very interesting that Franck wrote such a work at all, for there was little other than piano music and the *Trois trios* preceding it.

The year of revolution in Paris, 1848, saw a revolution in the Franck household too. In spite of the hostile opposition of his father, Franck married Félicité Desmousseaux, the daughter of two popular members of the Comédie Française. She had been one of his piano pupils, and visits to their lively household must have been a welcome relief in his dreary weekly round of teaching. After an argument with Nicolas-Joseph – whose opposition was predictably due more to the loss of his son's income than to fears for César's happiness – Franck took what for him was an extraordinarily self-assertive step and moved to the Desmousseaux house to live. On 22 February 1848 he married Félicité.

Freed from his father's dominating control, Franck settled down to the role of teacher and organist of Notre-Dame de Lorette, the church in which he had married. Domestic bliss and religious convictions must have sustained him through this long period in the musical wilderness, a period in which he was better known for his organ improvising than for anything else. Certainly there was little evidence of ambition or motivation, and it was four years before his next large-scale work was finished, the three-act opera, *Le Valet de ferme* (1851-3), composed mainly after the end of each day's teaching.

There is little doubt that he wrote it at the suggestion of the Desmousseaux family, and it was a typical *opéra-comique* subject with a libretto by two experienced writers, Roger and Vaëz. Franck, however, seemed to have no feeling for the words and to be totally lacking in dramatic sense. Doubtless he should not have contemplated setting the trivial story of an eighteenth-century Irish farm laborer who has an affair with his employer's wife. Even though Liszt supported it sufficiently to try to secure its performance at the Opéra, it was not accepted.

Both musically and dramatically *Le Valet de ferme* was considered a disaster. It was never produced, and indeed the whole project was a *fiasco-banal* with little dramatic interest, a terrible libretto and uninspired music. This new

Above: Notre Dame de Paris painted by Johan-Barthold Jongkind in 1854 – a familiar sight to the composer, who spent virtually the whole of his working life in the city.

failure gave Franck further cause to doubt his own abilities, for failure with opera, the dominating feature of French music for most of the century, made success as a composer impossible.

After the rebuff of *Le Valet de ferme*, Franck suffered a nervous breakdown. He withdrew for the next few years to the secure world of the Church, centering his professional life on the organ loft of St Jean-St François du Marais, where he had been appointed in 1851. The years 1853-8 found him at a very low point in his career. He composed nothing. He gave up some of his teaching in Paris to allow time for visits to Orléans, where he taught and gave a few recitals. During this time, however, Franck became increasingly friendly with the organ-builder Aristide Cavaillé-Coll. His first Paris organ was at Notre-Dame de Lorette, and he had built the organ at St Jean-St François du Marais, as well as that in the new church of Ste Clotilde, to which Franck moved in 1858. This instrument was considered to be the best organ of the time, and we know that Franck was thrilled by its new resources – the solo stops such as the clarinet and flute and particularly the revolutionary couplers, which still further widened the tonal resources by making it possible to add the sounds on one manual to those of another. Franck understandably referred to the instrument at Ste Clotilde as 'my orchestra.'

In the year of his appointment to the new church Franck wrote the *Andantino*, followed in 1859 by *Trois antiennes*. In 1860 he started work on the *Six pièces*, which were completed in 1862. These are his first significant organ compositions and, some would argue, the first significant ones of the century. The movements are: 'Fantaisie in C' – dedicated to Charret, organist of La Trinité; 'Grande pièce symphonique'; 'Prélude, fugue et variation' – dedicated to the pianist and composer Alkan; 'Pastorale' – dedicated to Cavaillé-Coll; 'Prière' – dedicated to Franck's teacher, Benoist; and 'Final' – dedicated to the famous organist Lefébure-Wély. The titles alone suggest a different approach from the sonatas, toccatas and preludes and fugues of earlier organ music; they are more orchestral in conception and more in the nature of character pieces. The 'Grande pièce symphonique' also heralds the organ symphonies of Franck's pupil Vierne, and of Widor, his successor at the Conservatoire.

During this period he also composed the *Messe solennelle* for bass and organ, which has been described as 'timidly respectable,' and between 1860 and 1872 he worked on another Mass, for three voices – soprano, tenor and bass – accompanied by organ, harp, cello and double bass. From the same years are the *Trois motets* (1856-8), an *Ave Maria* for soprano, tenor and bass (1863) and a short oratorio, *La Tour de Babel* (1863). It was not only the *Messe solennelle* that was timidly respectable: all these works show the same pious dullness and lack of imagination. Franck lacked sensitivity to words, and this produced uninspired, undramatic music and caused one disaster after another.

In 1869 he started work on his oratorio *Les Béatitudes*. It was based on the biblical Sermon on the Mount and consisted of a prologue and the eight beatitudes. The concept is an interesting one and Franck took ten years over it;

the result is a work of colossal proportions. Its first performance was in his own home in February 1879 and, even though the second and seventh sections were omitted, its length was such that the audience began to leave long before the end and only a few friends stayed the course. Like his other sacred works, it was a dismal failure. It was monotonous in form; there was a general lack of contrast within the work, partly the result of its cyclic form, partly the essentially undramatic writing; the musical ideas were frequently mundane, especially his music for Satan. The third and eighth sections were included in the concert of Franck's music organized in his honor by his pupils in 1887, but even that occasion was disastrous. Nevertheless, Franck looked on it to the end of his life as his greatest achievement.

• Professor at the Conservatoire •

Franck remained in Paris throughout the upheavals of the Franco-Prussian War and the Commune of 1870-1. Then in 1872 he was invited to succeed his old organ teacher Benoist as professor of organ at the Conservatoire – by no means an expected appointment considering Franck's past failures and present obscurity. He was in his fiftieth year. This was his first important official post and the first recognition of him by the French musical establishment, even though it was his organ playing rather than his composition which the appointment acknowledged.

The Franco-Prussian War, the Commune and the establishment of the Republic in 1871 mark a turning-point in both society and the arts in Paris. The main musical development of this period was the foundation in that same year of the Société Nationale de Musique by Saint-Saëns, Franck, Fauré, Duparc and others. It was a reaction to the frivolous world of the glittering Second Empire, a world in which instrumental music was held in low esteem, and the purposes of the Societé were to encourage French composers to write instrumental works, especially

Above: Stained-glass window in the Paris church of Ste Clotilde, where Franck was organist for more than thirty years.

Left: L'Angélus (1857-9) by Jean-François Millet. Franck took up his appointment at Ste Clotilde in 1858, and the organ music he wrote from this time, as well as his oratorios, were composed in the pious spirit of Millet's painting.

• New departures •

It is generally accepted that the Piano Quintet of 1878-9 is Franck's first truly important work. It is surprising that it was written with such assurance, for his only previous chamber music had been the *Trois trios* written some forty years earlier. First performed in Paris on 17 January 1880, the Quintet is supposed to have been inspired by his feelings for one of his young pupils, Augusta Holmès; whether or not that is true, the dramatic, emotional intensity of the music makes it a plausible theory. Such passionately expressive writing was a shock to those used for so many years to Franck's rather shapeless chromatic wanderings – especially people who remembered the pious music of *Redemption* and *Les Béatitudes*. Saint-Saëns, the pianist at the first performance of the Quintet, disapproved of it so much that he rudely walked off the platform at the end, leaving behind the score which Franck had presented to him. Even Liszt, who was certainly not noted for puritanism, was apparently shocked by the work's passionate outburst. At the time it was considered more erotic than emotional. The language of the Quintet is highly chromatic, with constant modulation, enharmonic key changes and chromatic melodic lines keeping the music at a high fever pitch. The forms of the movements all show original thought, with cyclic form used throughout. The importance of Franck's cyclic idea, with its recurring themes which are transformed in melodic detail, rhythm, harmony and mood, is that it made possible not only a feeling of unity in a long, multi-movement work, but also the development of musical ideas, the attainment of which was always one of the Romantic composers' main problems.

Franck's next work was *Le Chasseur maudit* (1882), based on an eighteenth-century ballad by Bürger about a villainous nobleman who decided to go hunting rather than attend Mass, ignoring church bells, damaging crops and upsetting the feelings of the faithful; he is damned and his soul is hunted eternally by demons. Very different indeed from *Les Eolides*, it is equally effective in a grand late-Romantic way; first there is the excitement of the hunt, during which church bells mingle with hunting calls, then the curse, pronounced by trombones, and the work ends with the frenzied chase by the demons. The music calls to mind Saint-Saëns's *Danse macabre* and Dukas's *L'Apprenti sorcier*, and the orchestral writing seems to include the influence of Berlioz, Meyerbeer and Liszt in its sonority and effectiveness.

Three years later Franck wrote another symphonic poem, *Les Djinns*, based on a poem from Victor Hugo's *Les Orientales*. It broke new ground, being the first work of this type to introduce the piano as an obbligato instrument. The idea apparently came to him after a request for a short concertante piano piece made by one of the leading pianists of the day, Mlle Caroline Montigny-Remaury; Franck obliged

Left: Ste Cécile, one of the designs for the decoration of the new Paris Opéra of 1875. Opera was the real measure of public success in the musical world of Paris, but Franck had little sympathy for the form, and all of his four operas were failures.

chamber music, and to promote concerts of French compositions.

Franck's many pupils benefited from the Societé's growing influence, as indeed did all composers who were sympathetic to its principles, but Franck himself continued to compose mainly church music. In 1871-2 he wrote another religious work, *Redemption*, a *poème-symphonie* for soprano, chorus and orchestra to words by Edward Blau. It is in three sections – an introduction and long choral episode portraying man's origins, followed by an orchestral section representing the strength and happiness found in the Christian faith, which leads to a final section representing redemption through penitence and prayer. Like so many of his sacred works, it shows his preoccupation with the conflict of good and evil; but its general level of inspiration and achievement is inferior to *Les Béatitudes*.

Franck's return to instrumental music dates from 1876, when he completed the symphonic poem *Les Eolides*, mostly written during a holiday that year in the south of France. Based on a poem by Leconte de Lisle, it is about a race of fairies called the Aeolids who live in the mountains and fly down to the valleys from time to time. With its gossamer-like texture, Franck's score captures the lightness and delicacy of the fairies to perfection, belying here his reputation for heavy-handedness and lack of imagination. Inevitable comparisons with Mendelssohn's *A Midsummer Night's Dream* are made, but in its atmosphere and technique it also looks ahead to the impressionism of Debussy.

In 1878 Franck wrote his next important organ work, the *Trois pièces*, which were commissioned for a recital by Alexandre Guilmant on the organ of the new Trocadéro Palace, built for the Universal Exhibition. However, these three pieces – *Fantaisie*, *Cantabile* and the famous *Pièce héroïque* – are not as good as the 1862 *Six pièces*, either in ideas or construction. The following year saw not only the completion of the *Béatitudes* but also the Piano Quintet.

Left: Members of the jury scrutinizing an examination piece at a musical competition in 1878 at the Palais de Luxembourg. Franck is standing in the main group, fourth from the right. Saint-Saëns sits at the piano, and on the right of the group stands Ambroise Thomas, director of the Paris Conservatoire.

with this work, in which the piano is much more of an orchestral instrument than it is in the *Variations symphoniques*. This too, as with so many of his religious works, is about the conflict of good and evil, darkness and light, and the eventual conquest of evil by the power of prayer and faith. It is in a type of sonata form with the customary two main themes in conflict with each other, the orchestra representing evil and the piano's calming arpeggios symbolizing the tranquillity of faith. *Les Djinns* was completed in 1884 and first performed the following year.

In 1865 Franck had written an isolated piece for piano – *Les Plaintes d'une poupée* in the same vein as Schumann's *Kinderscenen* and Debussy's later *Children's Corner* suite, but it was not until 1884 that the first of his important piano works was written. This was the *Prélude, choral et fugue* – not only technically more demanding than the earlier piece, but musically far more substantial and satisfying. It started life as a prelude and fugue, inspired by the one in B minor from Book 1 of Bach's *Forty-eight*, but as he worked on it, Franck obviously felt the need for a slow middle section; so he expanded it into a large-scale work, grand, noble, romantically intense and full of chromaticism. The usual Franck characteristics are present in its themes – it is difficult to think of these shifting chromatic lines as melodies in the accepted sense of the word. Cyclic form is used, giving some unity to this long work. The technical demands are vast; the writing seems to require an extra pair of hands – some would say feet, pointing out in the low octaves the influence of the pedal part of an organ work. It is Franck's most popular piece of solo piano music, separated only by a trifling piece – the *Danse lente* of 1885 – from his last work for solo

piano, the *Prélude, aria et final* of 1886-7. This is similar to the 1884 composition and again is a large-scale work with themes common to all the movements, sonorous, very chromatic and technically very searching.

These two big piano works, so clearly rooted in the past, appear less concerned with display than with musical considerations, and in their solemnity seem closer to Brahms than Liszt; they certainly bear no resemblance to French music of the time, and their size, breadth and style generally put them in sharp relief to the subsequent piano music of Debussy and Ravel.

L'OUVREUSE DU CIRQUE D'ÉTÉ

Accords perdus

H. SIMONIS EMPIS, ÉDITEUR

Left: Caricature of Franck teaching at the Conservatoire, where he was appointed professor of organ in 1872. Among his pupils is Vincent d'Indy, seated at the right-hand side of the desk.

Franck's last choral works were *Rebecca* (a *scène biblique* written in 1880-1), a setting of Psalm 150 composed in 1888 and, in the same year, *Hymne*, for male voices, *Six duos* for equal voices and *Premier sourire de mai* for female voices.

His third opera, *Hulda* (1882-5), was again the result of external persuasion, this time that of his own family, conscious of the need for Franck's success in the operatic field. He chose an unpromising story about medieval Norwegians with a libretto by Grandmougin based on a play by Bjørnson. The heroine, Hulda, meets a predictably ghastly end in a terrible story which, though much more dramatic and bloodthirsty than *Le Valet de ferme*, is simply not the stuff of opera. The director of the Opéra refused to accept the score.

Franck's last opera was never completed. *Ghiselle*, with a libretto by Augustine-Thierry set in the Merovingian court of Neustria, was started in 1889 and had to be completed by his pupils for its first performance in Monte Carlo in 1896.

However, he did achieve real success with his Sonata in A minor for violin and piano, composed in 1886. It was written for the famous violinist Eugène Ysaye, to whom it was dedicated and presented as a wedding present, and for the pianist Mme Bordes-Pène. There is no doubt that Ysaye's frequent performances of it helped to make it the most widely known of Franck's works. After the intensity of the Piano Quintet, the first movement – *allegretto* – of the Violin Sonata is serene and poetic; its opening theme provides the germinal idea, the cyclic element, of the whole work. Intensity is introduced in the second movement – marked *allegro*

Above: Eros and Psyche, a study by the outstanding academic artist A. W. Bouguereau, painted in 1889, the year after Franck had completed his ambitious symphonic poem for chorus and orchestra on the same theme, *Psyché*.

Left: Cover of the first edition of the symphonic poem *Le Chasseur maudit* (1882), Franck's most picturesque orchestral work.

passionato – which is followed by a most unusual movement – *quasi una fantasia* – improvisatory and enigmatic. The finale is a canon, simple, perfectly natural and unforced, and one of Franck's most tuneful and satisfying movements, displaying a superb poise and balance between piano and violin.

• Late orchestral works •

A year earlier, in 1885, Franck had partnered the piano with the orchestra in his *Variations symphoniques*, written for the pianist Louis Diemer, who had also played in *Les Djinns* at its first performance the same year. The new work shows again – as in the two big piano works of 1884 and 1887 – how Franck liked to combine different forms within one big movement, for it is a combination of a symphonic work, a piano concerto and a set of variations, influenced without doubt by Schumann's *Etudes symphoniques*. This choice of form allowed Franck a very free rein because of its looseness, although in the best tradition of sonata form there are two contrasting themes, the first terse and dramatic, the second expressively lyrical. The work opens dramatically with the first theme played on the strings, the piano replying with a gentle motif of its own, not unlike the dialogue between orchestra and piano in the slow movement of Beethoven's Fourth Piano Concerto. Soon pizzicato strings announce the second theme, and this leads to a free cadenza in which the piano develops the opening motif. If the work is looked on as being symphonic in form, then this first section is the exposition, but instead of a development there is a set of six variations of the second theme; finally there is a brilliant concluding section, of huge proportions and based chiefly on the first theme. In this work, as in the other piano works of these last years, Franck makes considerable demands on the soloist's virtuosity, with the usual enormous stretches and powerful octave writing. The popularity of the work is understandable, however, for it has attractive themes, is lyrical, and the final section is particularly brilliant and exciting.

Franck's last orchestral work was his famous Symphony in D minor, started in 1886, finished two years later and given its first performance on 17 February 1889 under the auspices of the Société des Concerts du Conservatoire. It had a very mixed reception. On the one hand was Debussy: 'Franck's symphony is amazing. I should prefer less of a four-square structure but what smart ideas!' – an opinion shared by many. On the other was the view of Gounod: 'It is an affirmation of incompetence pushed to dogmatic lengths.'

In fact there have always been many reservations about the work, part of the problem being what is expected of anything called a symphony. Types of theme, thematic development, the use of keys, any structural weakness or looseness, the appearance of anything approaching emotionalism – all are scrutinized with tremendous care.

Although Franck's musical training had been a classical one, which finally broke through, as we have seen, in many of his last works, he was strongly influenced by Liszt and Wagner as well, and no late nineteenth-century composer could fail to use the richly expressive musical language which had developed in the second half of the century; expressiveness and emotion were natural. In Franck's case, extreme chromaticism was the basis of his language and he expressed his ideas in the symphony with Romantic fervor. Most listeners enjoy the lyricism, excitement and emotional power of this work, with its moods ranging from blazing triumph to gentle poetry; they are not particularly worried by the lack of thematic contrast, nor by the restricted working out of ideas in the development section of the first movement, and are not at all concerned by the assertion that it is not really a symphony at all!

In 1887-8 Franck composed his last symphonic poem, *Psyché*, for chorus and orchestra – an unusual combination in this medium. The myth tells how Psyche, at first asleep, is carried away by the zephyrs to the Gardens of Eros, where she is taken by Eros. Voices warn her not to look back on him (echoes of Orpheus and Eurydice), but she ignores them and in punishment is sent to earth. In Franck's version of the story she has to wait there until the gods forgive her and she is then reunited with her lover. The work is in three sections. The first consists of 'Le sommeil de Psyché,' slow-moving and sensuous, and 'Psyché enlevée par les zéphyrs' – a scherzando movement with a theme borrowed from *Les Eolides*. Part two consists of 'Les jardins d'Eros' and the love scene 'Psyché

Right: The Baptism of Clovis by Joseph Blanc, one of the paintings executed, from 1877, to decorate the Panthéon in Paris with subjects that combined piety and patriotism. That the distinctive French tradition of religious music was able to flourish and develop in the late nineteenth century was due in great part to the compositions and influence of Franck.

et Eros'. Part three begins with 'Le châtiment (souffrances et plaintes de Psyché),' with its implications of sin and guilt, and finally 'L'apothéose.' Throughout, the music is rich and voluptuous, enhanced rather than weakened by Franck's chromatic writing and Wagnerian harmony – he even refers in the love scene to Wagner's *Tristan und Isolde*! As in *Les Eolides*, Franck often points forward to impressionism in his atmospheric sonorities, and the sensuous scoring and exquisite woodwind writing are entirely appropriate.

•The final years•

Right: Autograph of the last page of the piano and vocal score of Franck's last opera, *Ghiselle*, started in 1889, but left unfinished at his death.

Below: One of the last photographs of Franck (seated, at center) on a visit to Tournai in 1890. Eugène Ysaye stands, cigarette in hand, to the right of the composer.

Public recognition in the composer's last years had been very slow to materialize. In 1880 he was passed over for one of the advanced composition chairs at the Conservatoire, but perhaps in compensation he was given a laurel wreath for his pupils' many successes. In 1885 he was made Chevalier of the Legion of Honor, but it was as an organ professor rather than as a composer that he was rewarded. He was elected an Officier de l'Académie and became president of the Société Nationale. In January 1887 a special concert in his honor was arranged by his pupils; the program included the *Variations symphoniques*, *Le Chasseur maudit*, Part two of *Ruth*, the ballet music from *Hulda* and two of the *Béatitudes*. It was a disaster! Pasdeloup, once a most distinguished conductor, was not up to the occasion and, with an inadequately rehearsed orchestra, the performance of the *Variations symphoniques* broke down. Franck, who conducted the second half, had never been much good as a conductor; the orchestra was barely able to sightread the difficult keys of the *Béatitudes* and did little justice to it.

Franck's readiness to allow himself to be persuaded to work in forms in which he had previously failed is some indication of his inability to realize his shortcomings. It is extraordinary that he kept returning to oratorio and opera

GHISELLE, dernière page du manuscrit de CÉSAR FRANCK

when each one was damned by the critics. He had little success as a song-writer either, his insensitivity to words preventing him from achieving much in this sphere. He wrote some eighteen songs, the earliest in 1843, the last in 1888, but when compared with Fauré and Duparc he had little to offer. 'Robin Gray' (1842-3) and 'Souvenance' (1842-3) from his early years and 'Nocturne' (1884) and 'La Procession' (1888) from his last period are probably the best known.

While some would affirm that the Violin Sonata is Franck's greatest work, others would give pride of place to the String Quartet in D major. It was written in 1889 and given its first performance on 19 April 1890 at a concert of the Société Nationale. It received a tremendous ovation, with the audience on its feet calling for the composer – the only time in his life that Franck experienced such a reception. The work is again cyclic and shows to what extent Franck was at home in the medium of chamber music. The first movement is a complex one, described as a sonata-form movement within a *Lied*. The second is a buoyant, rhythmic scherzo-like foil to the third movement, a noble larghetto; this is followed by a sonata-form finale, a movement which recalls in turn the themes of the earlier ones. In its orchestral sonorities, the Quartet shows a new development in chamber music writing; in its influence on later composers, including Debussy and Ravel, it is of the greatest significance.

For his last works Franck returned to his own instrument, the organ. *L'Organiste*, fifty-nine pieces for liturgical use, was finished in 1890, and in the same year he composed the outstanding *Trois chorals*, written mostly in Nemours during the summer of the same year. His stated intention was to write some chorales as Bach

had done, though with a different approach. The first, in E major, consists of a set of variations on the chorale theme; the second is in B minor, the theme appearing first on the pedals so that there is some feeling of a passacaglia about the work; the third is the very popular A minor *Choral* with its dramatic, declamatory opening, its characteristically Franck adagio, restlessly chromatic, and the final brilliant ending for full organ. These three noble pieces show an originality of approach and consistent high level of inspiration which are unique in his organ music and which places them among his finest instrumental music.

In May 1890 Franck was knocked down by a horse omnibus. He was able to continue on his way to a private performance of the *Variations symphoniques*, and he did not bother to have proper medical attention after the accident; unfortunately, the damage was more serious than he knew. Although during the summer months he improved and resumed his teaching and composing, by the autumn his condition again worsened and pleurisy developed. He died on 8 November 1890.

Opinions about the quality and significance of Franck's music rapidly improved after his death, and in 1904 a monument to the composer by Lenoir was unveiled in the square of Ste Clotilde in the presence of a much more representative official gathering than had attended his funeral.

In spite of his chiefly unsuccessful career and the large amount of cloying, sentimental music he wrote, Franck's influence on French music at the end of the century was enormous. This was not through his chromatic language, nor the rather stereotyped turns of his melodies, phrases, harmonies and rhythms, nor even through the undeniably important development of cyclic form. He is important because his work prepared the way for modern French chamber

music, because he re-established instrumental music, giving it a distinctly French accent, because he showed how Romantic language and ideas could be reconciled with a classical framework, and because he influenced a whole generation of composers. These include Saint-Saëns, Dukas, Chabrier – who delivered the funeral oration at his burial service – and Widor, as well as the many pupils he taught privately or at the Conservatoire, among them Boëllmann, Chausson, Duparc, Lekeu, Ropartz, Vierne and d'Indy, each of whom devoted so much energy to spreading Franck's musical gospel.

Left: The Irish composer Augusta Holmès (1847-1903), featured in a popular Paris magazine of 1889. She was one of Franck's pupils and is believed to have inspired the passionate, and in many ways untypical, music of the Piano Quintet in F minor. It has also been suggested that Saint-Saëns's distaste for this work was caused by his own feelings for a woman who also numbered Wagner and Mallarmé among her admirers. Her own compositions include the opera *La Montagne noire*, 1895.

À C. Saint-Saëns
souvenir de son passage en Égypte
F. Rowe 1903

CAMILLE SAINT-SAËNS

RONALD CRICHTON

Camille Saint-Saëns died in his middle eighties in 1921, a national monument, not invariably regarded by his juniors with the affection and admiration such a figure deserved, but active and industrious to the end. His life and his career were so long that it is irresistible to compare the musical world he left with the one into which he came. When Saint-Saëns died, Berg was finishing *Wozzeck*, Schoenberg was working out the twelve-note method, Stravinsky was on the verge of his neo-classical period.

In 1835, when Saint-Saëns was born in Paris (about two weeks after Bellini's death not far away), Beethoven and Schubert had been gone for less than ten years, Mendelssohn, Chopin, Schumann and Liszt were about twenty-five, Verdi and Wagner slightly younger. The Paris Saint-Saëns knew in his young days was a brilliant city where foreign talent, mainly Italian, was acclaimed and assimilated, where Italian opera, French *opéra comique* and instrumental virtuosity (however meretricious) were enthroned. The more reflective forms of music were largely confined to private circles. Rossini, as the leading composer of operas, had abdicated in favor of Meyerbeer (*Guillaume Tell* was produced in 1829, *Les Huguenots* in 1836, both in Paris). Habeneck, who conducted with his bow from a first-violin part but was a serious champion of Beethoven's symphonies, was conductor at the Opéra. Cherubini, a musician of elevated accomplishment but a dour man, was in charge of the Conservatoire. He died in 1842, six years before Saint-Saëns, by then in his teens, entered that establishment as a pupil.

The pupil was precocious. When he was ten, he made his début as pianist at the Salle Pleyel, performing among other things concertos by Mozart and Beethoven. Cherubini's successor at the Conservatoire was Auber (who was to live to an even greater age than Saint-Saëns). Auber appointed Halévy, whose opera *La Juive* had been produced in the year of Saint-Saëns's birth, as teacher of composition. Saint-Saëns joined his class. Halévy was still busy writing operas, less successfully than before. He was a kindly man but not a zealous teacher. In his absences from the classroom, Saint-Saëns went to the library and laid the foundations of his wide musical knowledge. He loved the old Conservatoire building in the rue Bergère, 'that ridiculous and venerable mansion, for a long time already too cramped for the students from every part of

the world who crammed into it.' Some sixty years later he recalled with affection the little courtyard 'where the desperate cries of sopranos and tenors, the rumbling of pianos, the pealings of trumpets and trombones, the clarinet arpeggios, would combine to form that ultra-polyphony which up-to-the-minute composers strive for in vain.' Though Saint-Saëns did not win the Prix de Rome, he was awarded a Conservatoire *premier prix* in 1851. His time at the Conservatoire seems to have been reasonably happy and useful. He never taught there in later life, but for four years from 1861 held a position at a rival establishment, the Ecole Niedermeyer, a school for the training of church musicians, where his pupils included Messager and Fauré, who was to become a close and valued friend, virtually a substitute son.

Saint-Saëns's father, a civil servant, died within weeks of Camille's birth. The child was reared by his devoted and subsequently possessive mother, Clémence Françoise Collin, and the mother's aunt, Charlotte Masson. The great-aunt died in 1872. The mother's place in her son's affections may have seemed threatened by his impulsive marriage (which she did not welcome) in 1875 to Marie Laure Truffot. The marriage did not work and was soon darkened by tragedy. Three years later the elder of the couple's two infant sons fell from a window and was killed. After six weeks the younger son died through illness. In 1881 Saint-Saëns, on holiday with his wife, suddenly left her, for good. She attended her former husband's state funeral in 1921 and lived on until 1950.

Saint-Saëns's mother's close hold on his affections may have had a psychological inhibiting effect on his music, but did not impede his career as performer. When she died in 1888 (aged seventy-nine) he was disorientated. The family apartment in the rue Monsieur le Prince was abandoned. Though Paris remained his center, he became a wanderer, with pet dogs and a manservant, traveling widely as pianist, organist and occasionally conductor of his own works, also traveling for health and pleasure – for though the sickly-looking youth had grown into a tough, wiry man, he could not stand the Parisian winter and took willing refuge in sunnier climates, for preference Egypt or Algiers, where he died.

His career as composer and performer followed smoothly after his Conservatoire days.

Right: Drawing of the composer, when he was about four years old.

The Société Sainte-Cécile, founded by the Belgian violinist François Seghers, performed the young composer's choral *Ode* to the patron saint of music in 1852. The following year saw the first performance of the symphony published as no.1 in E flat. The immense and varied output of symphonies, symphonic poems, concertos and concerted works, chamber music, oratorios and other choral music, songs, piano music and occasional pieces, some of it ephemeral, much unjustly forgotten, rolled on for another seventy years. In only one important field, that of opera (vitally important in Paris), was Saint-Saëns's hold insecure and virtually limited to the one, long-delayed success of *Samson et Dalila*.

In 1853 he became organist in quick succession to the churches of St Sévérin and St Merri (near the present Centre Pompidou). In 1857 he was promoted to the Madeleine, where his improvisations became famous and where, after Saint-Saëns had given a brilliant rendering of Liszt's *St Francis Preaching to the Birds*, Liszt declared him the greatest organist in the world. As a pianist he was evidently an eager, vivacious performer, a fine technician with an exact, objective approach and a complete lack of virtuoso airs and graces. That the coldness of his playing was only apparent is suggested by his intense devotion, from his earliest days, to Mozart, whose piano concerto in B flat (K.450) he had played on the occasion of his debut. In those days Mozart concertos were not in every pianist's repertory, let alone their memory.

Like most French composers of his time, he supplemented his earnings with journalism. Few of them (apart from the always exceptional Berlioz) wrote such fluent, clear, readable, sensible articles as Saint-Saëns. In their reprinted form, notably in the collections *Harmonie et mélodie* (1885), *Portraits et souvenirs* (1899) and *Ecole buissonnière* (1913), they remain a mine of information as well as a source of pleasure.

•Modernist and conservative •

Liszt, whom Saint-Saëns venerated as man, pianist and, especially, as composer, retired from public life in middle age, wreathed in mists of notoriety and music of the future – which, to an extent not generally realized for another century or so, he continued to write in near-solitude. Saint-Saëns, who lived longer, never abjured public life. But he, too, for many years was tarred with the modernist brush. Describing how as a Conservatoire student he used (against the rules, even for composition pupils) to insinuate himself into orchestral rehearsals, he remarked how he would 'bring back to the classroom odors of Beethoven and Mozart which fairly stank of heresy. It was then, before I had written anything, that I acquired the reputation for being a dangerous composer that will be with me all my life. . . .'

He was wrong there. The man who understood Liszt so well, who was instrumental in founding the Société Nationale de Musique in 1871 – at the time a splendid act of defiance – ceased to be regarded as a progressive force some time before the end of the century. In May 1907 the eminent writer on music Romain Rolland described in his journal a concert at the Sorbonne in Paris at which Saint-Saëns played his *Africa* fantasy. While noting that this 'man of over seventy has the fingers of a virtuoso of twenty' and that 'he is the object of triumphal ovations,' Rolland also noted that he appealed at that time to academics rather than to musicians: 'It's odd that one can talk for hours, among musicians, of French music without even thinking of pronouncing the name of Saint-Saëns.'

Saint-Saëns understood and championed two of the most flamboyant Romantics, Berlioz and

Right: Title-page to Camille's first composition, dated 15 May 1841, and proudly quoting his age as 'five and a half.' As a child prodigy, Saint-Saëns rivalled Mozart and Mendelssohn.

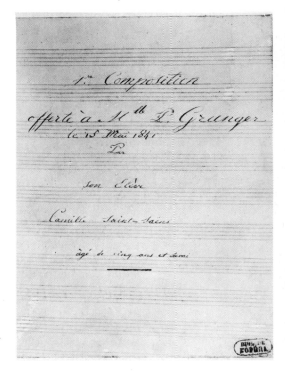

Liszt. His music shows their influence, in the orchestral delicacy and subtlety he learnt from Berlioz and, on the formal side, in the telescoping of movements and thematic transformation he learnt from Liszt. But though his orchestral works and concertos would not have been what they were without those two composers, in their musical temper they are nearer the baroque and *galant* periods. Saint-Saëns confessed that he wrote music as naturally as an apple tree produces apples. As far as his own music was concerned, he distrusted emotion (although he admired emotional music by other

composers). His musical invention was not deep, but it was fertile: he accepted what came, rather too readily. He was a workmanlike composer who, whatever the quality of the material he was working, scorned a shoddy finish. He had the gift of lightness in both senses. He could write excellent 'light music' and he preserved lightness of texture – airiness, luminosity, transparency – in his serious music. At the same time, much of his music shows a strange kind of physical energy – not heavy but light-footed.

For a man who had done so much for the music of his country and for music within his country to have been, during the last two or three decades of his life, cold-shouldered, misprized or ignored by many younger colleagues must have been galling indeed. Writing of the centenary celebrations in Paris in 1935 Reynaldo Hahn, a younger colleague whose admiration remained constant (and who was as impenitent a musical conservative as Saint-Saëns himself), pinpointed this question of ignorance, remarking sarcastically that 'the marvelous post-war musical younger generation, the phalanx that sprang from the great Erik Satie' not only pre-

Left: Saint-Saëns in 1858, aged twenty-three, by which time he had been awarded a *premier prix* at the Paris Conservatoire, had written a choral ode and a symphony, and had been appointed organist at the fashionable Madeleine church.

Left: Drawing of the ten-year-old Saint-Saëns making his first public appearance at the Salle Pleyel, Paris, in May 1846, when he played concertos by Mozart and Beethoven.

tended to be but actually was ignorant of Saint-Saëns and his work.

The music of Saint-Saëns needs to be seen against the background of French, and especially Parisian, musical life in the middle of the nineteenth century. There was a lingering prejudice against serious instrumental music. 'The real public,' wrote Saint-Saëns many years later, 'that is the *bon bourgeois*, recognized no music outside the opera and French *opéra comique*. . . . There was a universal cult, a positive idolatry, of "melody" or, more exactly, of the tune which could be picked up at once and easily remembered. . . . Outside this large group there existed a small circle of professional and amateur musicians who really cared for and cultivated music for its own sake, secret worshippers of Haydn, Mozart, Beethoven and occasionally Bach and Handel.'

If the taste of the public (and of many professionals) was backward, there was much good singing and some good playing (including orchestral playing) to encourage and justify Saint-Saëns's high finish and absolute clarity. The standard was not always so high across the Rhine. Saint-Saëns is said to have been astonished by the poor intonation of the chorus at the Weimar première of *Samson*. It may seem unfair to compare the efforts of a small provincial capital (even with Liszt in charge at the opera) with Paris, but it is certainly strange if the *Samson* choruses proved difficult a quarter of a century after *Tannhäuser* and *Lohengrin*. One can see how the possibilities of good execution coupled with the public's limited appreciation of instrumental music might logically result in the mentally and emotionally undemanding, beautifully written music Saint-Saëns provided in, for example, his symphonies and concertos. Nevertheless, his skill led in time to charges of facility, a quality suspect to those who do not possess it, unless the music in question is old enough.

•Opera•

Saint-Saëns failed to establish himself as a successful opera composer, although he wrote thirteen operas, including *Frédégonde*, which he finished when it was left incomplete by Ernest Guiraud (who had worked so hard on other men's operas such as *Carmen* and *Les Contes d'Hoffmann* after the death of their composers). Yet of these only *Samson et Dalila* triumphed, belatedly. *Samson* was conceived (in the first place as an oratorio) in the late 1860s, but there were no takers. The ostensible reason was the biblical subject, but Fauré was no doubt right when he diagnosed fear of 'symphonism,' plus the fact that the popularity of oratorio (and the oratorio feeling was carried over into the eventual opera) was less widespread in France than in the British Isles or Germany. It was Liszt who encouraged Saint-Saëns to persevere, promising a production at Weimar, but the Franco-Prussian War delayed plans until 1877. Even then, it was not until more enterprising managements had given the work at Rouen and at the Théâtre de l'Eden in Paris that the doors of the Opéra were finally opened to *Samson* – in 1892! By that time, although the general public was to remain faithful, the rising tide of Wagnerism was ready to sweep fashionable Parisian taste away down the new current, and when *Samson* became generally available, the adroit balancing of sweetness (the feline, ambivalent sweetness of Dalila's music) and sobriety (Samson and the Israelites) with outwardly conventional but cunningly employed spectacular elements was not what the snobs wanted.

Right: Posters for three of Saint-Saëns's operas: *Henry VIII* (1883), *Ascanio* (1890) and the *opéra comique Phryné* (1893).

Saint-Saëns resented his inability to conquer the operatic citadel, still essential for Parisian fame. Massenet, a lesser musician who could not hold a candle to Saint-Saëns in other areas of music, possessed and successfully exploited precisely that theatrical flair which Saint-Saëns lacked. Yet Reynaldo Hahn, a shrewd judge and, what is more, a pupil and friend of Massenet as well as an admirer of Saint-Saëns, insisted that the latter was indeed an 'homme de théâtre,' one moreover of a superior brand. Perhaps a distinction needs to be made between the kind of animal instinct possessed by some opera composers, Massenet among them, and the intelligence, sensibility and powers of observation of an all-rounder such as Saint-Saëns. The latter was no stranger to the world of the theater. As a boy he had been taken to hear *Don Giovanni* with Grisi, Mario and Lablache. On a less exalted level, the short study of the composer by his friend and librettist (for the comic opera *Phryné*) Augé de Lassus records a later family visit to the Opéra-Comique to hear Adolphe Adam's *Le Sourd*: the young Saint-Saëns was so taken with the version of 'Sur le pont d'Avignon' which the score contains that he danced on the Pont des Arts on the way home and kept the house in the rue Monsieur le Prince awake half the night playing, singing and embroidering on the number 'Si vous connaissiez Joséphine.' Just as Rossini sometimes appears unbidden in Viennese classics of half a century earlier, so opera, both serious and comic, is in the air in much of Saint-Saëns's music. He was a connoisseur of fine singing but was aware of singers' foibles. One of his party tricks was an imitation of Mme Miolan-Carvalho, prima donna wife to the baritone and impresario Léon Carvalho and the first Marguerite in Gounod's *Faust*, singing the jewel song in that opera a quarter-tone sharp throughout.

Among Saint-Saëns's historical grand operas Hahn reserved special praise for *Henry VIII* and

Right: Costume design for the title-role in the original production of *Henry VIII.*

Below: Stage set by Philippe Chaperon for the first production of *Phryné*, which Saint-Saëns composed to a libretto by Augé de Lassus.

Ascanio. These are written in four and in five acts. Ferdinand Lemaire, the librettist of *Samson et Dalila*, astutely compressed his action into three acts, but *Samson* shares with the other two one typical feature of the time – ballet music in period or exotic style, ancient Philistine (influenced no doubt by the Arab café music Saint-Saëns had heard on his trips abroad) in *Samson* and a medley of styles for the *divertissements* in *Henry VIII* and *Ascanio.*

The liking for old forms (and especially dance forms) reflected not only in the operas but also in the orchestral and chamber music (for example the Septet), is one aspect of Saint-Saëns's

interest in and fondness for the past. His passion for Gluck he shared with Berlioz. To Bach and Handel he added his compatriot Rameau, becoming the general editor of the complete edition of the latter's works undertaken by Durand of Paris.

Interest in the past was balanced by interest in the present, which for the period of Saint-Saëns's middle life meant first and foremost Wagner. Saint-Saëns first met Wagner in Paris at the time of the *Tannhäuser* fiasco (1861) in that city. Later he impressed him with his ability to play his (Wagner's) scores by heart with unusual skill and accuracy. His playing was, not unexpectedly, of more concern to Wagner than his music. When considering Saint-Saëns's cool appraisal of the Wagner movement as a whole, it is as well to remember that he had wider and deeper knowledge of Wagner's music than most of the more single-minded admirers or detractors. He refused to be scandalized like many conventional musicians or puffed along on a gale of rhetoric like the less well-balanced literary men.

•The symphonies•

Saint-Saëns completed five symphonies, of which three were numbered – the other two were published only quite recently. The Symphony in A, written about 1850, published in 1974, is a graceful, Haydnesque work whose *larghetto* slow movement has a *minore* section (marked thus) and a decorated reprise of the *maggiore*. The ebullient finale (*allegro molto*) races to a *presto* end. The so-called Symphony no.1 in E flat, op.2, was completed in 1853 and performed anonymously at the Société Sainte-Cécile. Saint-Saëns had the pleasure of hearing the work warmly praised by both Berlioz and Gounod, neither of whom realized that he was the composer. It is indeed an accomplished score for a young man not yet eighteen, with a delightful march-scherzo for a second movement mingling reflections of Mendelssohn with a main theme that is an early example of the physical quality mentioned earlier (a staid, half-humorous measure, this one) and a slow third movement suggesting a young admirer's ardent tribute to the love scene in the 'Roméo et Juliette' Symphony of Berlioz.

Next, in chronological order, comes another unnumbered symphony, in F, subtitled 'Urbs Roma,' written in 1856, published in 1974. Like the A major Symphony, but unlike its immediate predecessor in E flat, this one has a slow introduction. The scherzo, a rapid movement in common time, comes second. As with the A major finale, there is a racing, faster-and-faster end. The slow movement is a plaintive minor-key march, the finale a set of variations (one of them in 5/4 – a rare excursion by this composer into unconventional meter) on a gracious *poco allegretto* theme in triple time.

The movement ends softly, brushed away into nothing by sweeping upward scales for strings and woodwind.

The Symphony no.2 in A minor, op.55, was introduced to the public in 1860 by Jules Pasdeloup, one of the handful of conductors who fought musical stagnation in Paris. It opens with an introduction, *allegro marcato*, with a prominent violin solo; then, the main theme of the first movement proper has, for Saint-Saëns, an unusually Brahmsian contour. The *adagio* which follows is a kind of slowed-down scherzo, an intimate intermezzo of melancholy, Schumannesque charm. The real scherzo, following immediately, has Beethovenian cross-accents. The *prestissimo* finale rushes past with the gusto

Above: Saint-Saëns, pictured in middle age, at about the time he helped to found the Société Nationale de Musique, to promote the composition and performance of French instrumental music – a challenge to the opera-dominated French musical scene.

Right: Autograph of a page from the piano and vocal score of *La Princesse jaune*, Saint-Saëns's first opera, dating from 1872.

Right: Cats' Concert (1868). Saint-Saëns made his own witty comments on animal life in his popular *Carnaval des animaux* for two pianos and orchestra; but he would not allow publication of the work in his own lifetime in case it harmed his reputation as a serious composer.

of Haydn relaxing at Eszterháza. Just before the end comes a strange, haunting recall of the slow movement.

These early symphonies belong to the class of what might be called high-quality pleasure music, related to the *divertimento* and therefore suspect to solemn persons as 'light music,' but also related to such distinguished exemplars as Haydn's 'London' symphonies and the Second, Fourth and Eighth of Beethoven.

The next and last of the Saint-Saëns symphonies, no.3 in C minor, op.78, belongs to the larger world, takes its place there with panache and, in the finale at least, with plenty of noise. No.3 kept a place in the repertory even when most of Saint-Saëns's serious music was in the trough of reaction. It was written for the Philharmonic Society of London and first performed, under the composer's direction, at St James's Hall in 1886. The scheme of two large movements each in two main sections, paying token homage to the conventional four-movement layout but linking the whole with thematic cross-reference and transformation (Saint-Saëns also used the scheme in his First Violin Sonata and Fourth Piano Concerto), is suitable for a work planned as a thank-offering to Liszt. Since the musician to whom Saint-Saëns owed so much for practical help and encouragement as well as for the example of his music died that year, the published score bears a dedication to his memory. The organ is heard in two of the sections: discreetly in the *poco adagio* second half of the first movement (the key of D flat sounding effectively remote from the tonic); indiscreetly, some may think, in the uninhibited irruptions into the second half of the second movement, the finale proper. This finale is not for the squeamish, for those troubled by the sound of full organ letting rip in a reverberant French Gothic cathedral, or by any show of public enthusiasm of which they do not feel part.

• Orchestral works •

Liszt, whose innovatory symphonic poems are described in one of the essays in *Harmonie et mélodie*, is an even stronger presence in the four compositions in this genre by Saint-Saëns. Of these, the once ubiquitous *Danse macabre* of 1874, which caused a disturbance at its first performance the following year, has worn the least well. More serious and elaborate explorations of the supernatural in the music of Berlioz, of Liszt himself and of later Romantics, are now familiar. The *Danse macabre* had its modest origins in a song whose words describe with matter-of-fact humor a nocturnal dance of skeletons scattered by cockcrow. Here, the transparent texture – solo violin with E string tuned a semitone down, goblin tunes – is a disadvantage. The unreligious Saint-Saëns had little gift for the supernatural. This evocation of the infernal powers is on a miniature, decorative scale. In *La Jeunesse d'Hercule*, op.50

(1877), the young demi-god's indecision, faced with the diverging paths of vice and virtue, is represented by wavering violins in thirds, of delicious, tonally ambiguous airiness. The ensuing conflict between virtuous academic procedures and a bacchanal with faint echoes of *Tannhäuser* is clearly rather than forcefully presented.

Phaéton, op.39 (1875) is an excellent piece, to be cherished for the skill with which Saint-Saëns sets the chariot of the Sun and its overweening driver on their fatal course through the skies, the headlong rhythm light enough to convey hooves and wheels on air, not on the ground. A gruffly assertive theme on the brass sounds like a chip blown backward out of time from the 'burlesque' movement of Mahler's Ninth Symphony. Saint-Saëns perceived that the real subject of the tone-poem was not Jove's thunderbolt but Phaéton's pride and folly. Although he clearly depicts the rumbles of rising godly anger, he plays down the catastrophe.

Le Rouet d'Omphale, op.31 (1872), shows a different side of Hercules, this time in thrall to the Lydian queen whom he surprises at her spinning-wheel. Omphale is unmoved by his

Above: The blinded Samson destroying the temple – the dramatic climax to Saint-Saëns's opera *Samson et Dalila*, first performed at Weimar in 1877 under the patronage of Liszt. The Paris Opéra production was delayed until 1892.

tales of heroic deeds and cozens him to spin for her. The situation lends itself to simple A-B-A treatment, with the groans of the humiliated demi-god and delicate hint of Omphale's mocking laughter as a contrasting middle section. Once again, lightness is all and, as Tovey wrote of *Phaéton*, 'the sense of movement remains delightfully easy.'

Among other orchestral music there are examples of the exotic vein much exploited in the second half of the nineteenth century, when nationalism in music and the new facilities for travel provided by the age of steam worked hand in hand – *Suite algérienne*, *Une Nuit à Lisbonne*, *Jota aragonesa*, *Africa* fantasy (piano and orchestra), *Havanaise* and *Caprice andalou* (both for violin and orchestra). Saint-Saëns was only incidentally a nationalist, but he loved travel in the sun and was happy to describe his less intimate experiences in musical terms. The once popular *Suite algérienne* is for the most part program music, evoking the arrival of a steamer at Algiers, native dancing in a café, an evening at Blidah. The finale, however, is a cocky 'Marche militaire française,' an example of art overtaken and rendered temporarily inexpedient by politics. Saint-Saëns's musical travel-writing has the zest of Rameau portraying imaginary Incas and Persians with the advantage of first-hand knowledge. Even the march, with its confident swagger, has something of the eighteenth century – though not Rameau so much as Handel.

•The concertos•

There remain for discussion, before passing on to the concertos, the chamber and choral music. The former includes two piano trios, two sonatas each for violin and cello with piano, two string quartets (late works) and three woodwind sonatas (even later). Works for other combinations include the piquant Septet, op.65, for trumpet, strings and piano, and the familiar *Carnival of the Animals*, usually associated with large halls, but chamber music none the less. The First Violin Sonata in D minor, op.75, has the four-in-two movement structure mentioned earlier. It also has the literary distinction of containing the model for the 'petite phrase' of the Vinteuil sonata in Proust's novel, not so much a 'little phrase' as an eight-measure subject assiduously treated. The *Variations on a Theme of Beethoven* for two pianos, op.35, show how well Saint-Saëns understood the gracious, playful, yet potentially explosive side of Beethoven.

Of solo piano music there is, for so eminent a performer, less than might be expected: three sets of *Etudes*, one for the left hand only, one of the two-hand sets including the exuberant show-piece called 'Etude en forme de valse'; numerous pieces in dance forms; a suite; no sonata. There is a sprinkling of works for organ and harmonium. Of the hundred or so songs the majority (except perhaps the *Mélodies persanes*) are forgotten. Choral music includes an early

Mass, a Christmas Oratorio, a Requiem, the oratorio *Le Déluge* and a quantity of smaller pieces both sacred and secular.

More perhaps than any other group of his works, it is the concertos that exhibit the merits and defects of Saint-Saëns as a composer. Martin Cooper summed them up: 'Saint-Saëns had the neat, dry mind of an eighteenth-century "philosopher," a sensuous lover of beauty, a chameleon-like sense of style and a dazzling technical skill. He was also a good musical scholar, even something of an antiquary.' And further: 'His music achieves all that can be achieved by the intelligent use of traditional forms in the hands of a polished, witty member of a very highly civilized community, who is also poor in distinct personal qualities and, by an unhappy

Above: Ramses's Harem, panel of a triptych painted by J. J. A. Lecomte-de-Nouy in 1886. Saint-Saëns's travels in North Africa and Egypt lent some authenticity to his own compositions in the popular exotic vein, which included the *Suite algérienne* and the *Africa* fantasy.

Right: Whistler's *Study in Black*, 1884, a portrait of Pablo de Sarasate. Saint-Saëns wrote two of his Violin Concertos (no.1, 1859, and no.3, 1880) for the Spanish violinist as well as the celebrated *Introduction and Rondo Capriccioso* (1863). Among other works written for Sarasate are Lalo's *Symphonie espagnole* (1875) and Max Bruch's Second Concerto and *Scottish Fantasy*, while he himself composed many brilliant pieces for his instrument.

Below: Gustave Moreau's painting of a bacchante with the head of Orpheus, 1865.

conjunction of natural temperament and circumstance, small-hearted.' Some doubts may be allowed concerning the smallness of the heart. Truer, perhaps, to say that Saint-Saëns did not put much of his heart into his music. Ravel's description of his own G major Piano Concerto as 'a concerto in the most exact sense of the term, written in the spirit of the concertos of Mozart and Saint-Saëns' is perceptive as well as provocative.

Of the five Piano Concertos, the First, in D, op.17 (1858), is a link with the virtuoso concertos of the early Romantic period. There is a suggestion in the horn-calls of the opening and later of the high-stepping world of Weber's *Konzertstück*, and in the expressive, recitative-like phrases of the slow movement of the related world of Spohr's Violin Concerto no.8 ('In modo di scena cantata'). Although the concerto is a little too leisurely for its own good, it is a charmer.

The most popular of the five is the Second, in G minor, op.22 (1868), with neo-baroque flourishes in the *andante sostenuto* opening movement ingeniously combining with Romantic influences, a Mendelssohnian scherzo with an impudent second theme whose precise degree of impudence is not always exactly caught by pianists, and a headlong *presto* finale not unlike the corresponding movement in the Second Symphony.

The Third Concerto, in E flat (op.29), was written immediately after the Second but not performed until 1875. As in no.2, the piano opens not with a cadenza but with arpeggio washes suggesting water-games, against which, as in Ravel's Concerto for the Left Hand, fragments of melody emerge out of the haze. It is typical of Saint-Saëns that the melody itself, once fully revealed, should prove to be serviceable but less interesting than the decoration, yet the movement has several points of interest. The *andante* starts with a hushed, mysterious passage lifting the key by a semitone to E major. When the main theme of this movement is heard a second time, it is laid out for the pianist's fingers as in Fauré at his most lyrically contrapuntal. The finale is a rumbustious polka-gallop, a rondo with a tune built on ascending sixths like friendly kicks.

The Third and Fourth Concertos are the most considerable of the set. The Fourth, in C minor, op.44 (1875), has two big movements each divided into two parts. Since themes are treated cyclically, it is fitting that there should be (in the opening theme and some of the subsequent variations, though not in the chorale that emerges in the second part of the movement) some suggestion of Franck. The second movement sets off with a scherzo treating the variation theme more like Brahms than Franck. There is a 6/8 tune, cousin to the one in the scherzo in the G minor Concerto, in which commentators have heard a likeness to 'The man who broke the bank at Monte Carlo.' Music-hall vulgarity is one ingredient in the make-up of this great eclectic, but this more probably derives from Beethoven in 'unbuttoned' mood than from presage of Satie and Les Six. After first hearing the Third Symphony Gounod is said to have observed, 'There goes the French Beethoven' – a remark which, as Gounod conceivably realized, could be understood in more than one way. It is surely to the credit of Saint-Saëns that the extent to which he had absorbed Beethoven shows more convincingly when he is relaxed than when he is consciously 'writing big.' In the finale of the Fourth Concerto the chorale tune, shedding any lingering vestige of sanctimoniousness, is thundered out.

The Fifth Concerto, in F, op.103 (1896), is later and lighter, a holiday-piece from Luxor, played for the first time by the composer at the fiftieth anniversary concert of his Salle Pleyel début (once again he played Mozart's K.450). Occasional whiffs of academicism invade the peaceful lappings of the first movement, though not for long. The andante contains a Nubian song, noted down on the composer's shirt-cuffs, after which the cruise-boat appears to sail a long way east, far enough away from the Nile of *Aida* for the passengers to hear gamelan music. In the finale the ship's engines chug merrily and there are sounds of jollity on board.

Of the two Cello Concertos, the Second seems to have sunk into oblivion. The First, in A minor,

Above: Cover design by Eugène Grasset for the magazine *L'Illustration.*

Below: A Portuguese cartoon of Saint-Saëns. One of his picturesque orchestral pieces is entitled *Une Nuit à Lisbonne.*

op.33 (1872), is a work on whose deft mastery even those who normally disparage this composer's music will agree. The single movement is ingeniously laid out with exposition and development separated by an inset dance movement from a substantial recapitulation-finale, which introduces some new material. The mood is Schumannesque, ardent but written with a degree of clarity that eluded Schumann when he was handling an orchestra. A leading cellist of our day once asked her eminent conductor-husband, 'Why do you never conduct the only concerto in which I know that every note I play will be heard?' Saint-Saëns realized that the cello's capacity for soulful singing may, in a concerto, be nullified by comparable soulfulness in the orchestra. His double woodwind, horns and trumpets (no trombones) and strings are used with a restraint that is anything but dull. The elegiac note at which the cello excels is strongly in evidence in the inset *allegretto con moto*, a subdued, deliberately antiquated minuet with the most delicate and discreet of accompaniments.

Otherwise, and until some cellist rehabilitates the much later Second Concerto, in D minor, op.119 (1902), cellists must be content with two Sonatas and with the *Allegro appassionato*, op.43 (1875), with piano, of which there also exists a version with orchestra.

Small-scale works for solo instruments and orchestra abound. Pianists, apart from the *Africa* fantasy, have a *Rapsodie d'Auvergne* and a *Wedding Cake Caprice*; there are pieces for flute,

Reduzida á fórma pittoresca, a composição de Saint-Saens intitulada *As Noites de Madrid* dá este resultado.

Pelo mesmo processo a peça que se intitula *As Noites de Lisboa* produz isto.

Above: Ticket for the first performance of the opera *L'Ancêtre*, again with libretto by Augé de Lassus, at the Opéra Comique in 1911.

Right: Fauré's amusing caricature of Saint-Saëns. Fauré was one of his pupils at the Ecole Niedermeyer, and later one of his closest associates and friends.

Beethoven, Madame!" he would cry, "Not on Beethoven!" and he would spear his strawberries with his toothpick. My grandfather cut up his meat with the same gesture he would employ presently to attack a phrase with his sporting bow. Yes, this chamber music was not for listening to, not for giving pleasure, but for performing, for sizing up, for shaking the head over. It was a form of sport, like so many others – fencing, canoeing, boxing. . . . Gréber was the cellist. Every time my grandmother tiptoed across the far end of the room, knitting in hand, he rose to salute her while continuing to play, bowing into the void.' Even allowing for poetic licence, the passage indicates that chamber music, in private circles in Paris and in however bizarre a manner, had gained some foothold during the nineteenth century.

The Third Concerto, op.61 (1880), in B minor, has a conventional three-movement layout. The opening *allegro non troppo* makes much use of the accented four-note figure at the

horn and harp; but the violin comes off best with, among other things, the still popular, once inescapable, *Introduction and Rondo Capriccioso*, the elegant, beautifully turned *Havanaise*, and a *Caprice andalou*, ancestors of Ravel's musical excursions across the Spanish border.

The Hispanic flavor in the violin music of Saint-Saëns is usually a tribute to the famous virtuoso Pablo de Sarasate (1844-1908), who called one day on the composer, 'young and fresh as the spring' and, 'as if it were the easiest thing in the world,' asked him for a concerto. In fact Saint-Saëns had just written one, published later as no.2, but he preferred to start again with what is now known as no.1, in A, op.20 (1859), a one-movement work subtitled (not by the composer) 'Konzertstück' – an *allegro* in 6/4 with an *andante espressivo* middle section in D. He also wrote for Sarasate the *Introduction and Rondo Capriccioso* and dedicated to him the Third Violin Concerto. For the assiduity and the excellence with which the violinist played these works across the world, Saint-Saëns remained deeply grateful.

Sarasate was celebrated for brilliant technique, faultless intonation, sweet, vibrant tone and 'a certain lack of emotional involvement.' Some years after Whistler had painted the slim young man with large, inquiring eyes gazing impatiently at the painter, fingers itching to start playing, Sarasate was observed by the child Jean Cocteau, who saw him, and in his *Portraits-souvenir* described him, 'with his big moustache and grey mane,' as 'a lion dressed as a lion-tamer.' The violinist led a string quartet (which included their host among the players) that used to foregather at Cocteau's grandparents' home in Paris for informal concerts. Sarasate himself drove his colleagues there in a four-wheeler: 'On arrival, the exhausted horse was unharnessed and given a soup of warm burgundy and carrots, and the musicians went in to luncheon. Sivori [one of the quartet] was a dwarf. At the luncheon-table my grandmother used to seat him on a pile of scores. "Not on

beginning of the soloist's initial theme – there is no introductory *tutti*. In the *andantino quasi allegretto* the violin sings and decorates an indolent melody over a swaying barcarolle accompaniment, most delicately orchestrated. The finale leads off with a rhapsodic, accompanied cadenza. The lively, curvetting main movement is rich in themes. At times the orchestra suggests Italian opera of an earlier period, and there is an unexpected hint of *Lohengrin*. The solo writing, spun seemingly out of the entrails of the violin, is brilliantly grateful throughout the concerto. Only a churl would demand profundity as well. As Saint-Saëns himself wrote in a generously objective memorial article occasioned by the death of Massenet (reprinted in *Ecole buissonnière*): 'He is superficial, they say; he is not profound. . . . That is true: he is not profound, and that is not important at all. Just as in my Father's house there are many mansions, so there are many in the house of Apollo. Art is immense.'

MUSIC IN THE ERA OF THE EMPEROR FRANZ JOSEPH

HEINZ BECKER

Opposite: A court ball in Vienna in 1900 in the presence of the Emperor Franz Joseph (far right). Brahms, Bruckner and Johann Strauss the Younger had all died in the past four years, while Gustav Mahler was now director of the Opera and conductor of the Vienna Philharmonic Orchestra.

Vienna is more than a mere city – it is the city of music. The names of Haydn, Mozart and Beethoven are closely bound up with the concept of the 'Viennese Classical' period, though none of these three giants of composition was born there. Even more closely connected with it, however, is a kind of music: the waltz. No other city in the world bears a name so indissolubly linked with one particular musical form. Vienna alone has this privilege. Taken at its deepest level of significance, the Viennese waltz is the embodiment of a purely local attitude towards everyday experience, an attitude permeated by its own peculiar way of life and imperial splendor, infused with the tolerance generated by a rich ethnic mix. What is enchanting in the Viennese waltz is something more than the magic of a city. It distills a rich mixture of assorted national attitudes. A whole social spectrum is within it. The prince in his palace responds to the Viennese waltz just as readily as the man in the street.

Franz Joseph's reign (1848-1916) saw Austria's decline as a leading European power, but the splendor of the waltz endured. The state may have withered into impotence, but the music flowed on unchecked. The radical difference between the Viennese waltz and earlier categories of music based on dance forms, indeed the source of its peculiarly telling power of expression, arises above all from its professional quality, seen at its clearest in the works of Johann Strauss the Younger. He used harmonic modes far removed from the traditional approach and closely related to the fully developed compositional methods of the concert hall. Strauss succeeded in raising the art of entertainment to a professional level without robbing it of its approachability. In the hands of Joseph Lanner the *Ländler* still belonged to a primitive and amateur folk art, but the five-part Viennese waltz, evolved by Lanner, developed by the elder Johann Strauss and brought to perfection by his son Johann Strauss II, successfully asserted itself in the world of professional music-making. In addition, this excursion into a hitherto unexplored world of artistic entertainment achieved worldwide recognition, in terms of symphonic and chamber music composition, more rapidly than any other musical form had done until then. Johann Strauss father and son were the first composers in the history of dance music to have secured a place for it in the concert hall and to have provided a conceptual basis for what we now know as the concert waltz.

The era of Franz Joseph cannot properly be described without a glance at Viennese popular music. The specifically Viennese idiom, which is so vividly apparent in the works of Johann Strauss, Gustav Mahler and Anton Bruckner, as well as in Brahms and, above all, Richard Strauss, is deeply rooted in folksong and dance, in the world of the *Ländler* – all ultimately deriving from the primitive origin of popular song. The translation of this fund of folk art into an urban idiom inevitably led to the Viennese waltz, as Lanner and Strauss soon discovered. At the same time, Johann Strauss conducted his orchestra, violin pressed to his side, wearing a smart officer's uniform with military ribbon across his chest, a hint at the intimate fusion of military dash and drill on the one hand with a lightfooted dance step on the other. This connection between folklore, military music and the ballroom was already evident in the open-air concerts by military bands which had become firmly established during the first half of the eighteenth century. It was finally embodied in the rapid flowering of the Viennese operetta, whose last great exponent, Franz Lehár, was originally a military bandsman. Then, there is a specifically Hungarian ingredient in typical Viennese music, and this merges indissolubly with the Alpine idiom. It is no accident that Tzigane orchestras have always chosen to wear hussar uniforms: here too the connection between military smartness, rhythmic verve and folklore tradition is obvious for all to see.

In 1877 Johann Schrammel (1850-93), a former bandsman, founded a trio with his brother Josef and the guitarist Anton Strohmayer. A clarinet was added in 1886, and the group soon achieved fame as the 'Schrammel Quartet.' These musicians modelled themselves on the Hungarian Czardas groups, but replaced the cimbalom with the guitar, and in 1893 Schrammel substituted the piano accordion for the clarinet. In the small world of the cosy local wine shops these musicians succeeded in keeping alive the Viennese folk dance idiom, while at the same time introducing compositions of their own. As a result, *Schrammelmusik* provides a musical background which for the tourist conjures up the Old Vienna of imperial days to a much greater extent than any so-called concert performance.

The year 1848, which saw revolutions break out all over Europe, turned out to be one of destiny for Austria, and especially Vienna. The accession of the Emperor Franz Joseph on 2 December, preceded by the fall of the hated Prince Metternich, did not by itself bring about any immediate political change, but it made a contribution to domestic peace. The young, clever, open-minded new Emperor tried to temper the absolutist stance of the traditional, court-bound state system, and he achieved a remarkable degree of popularity among his subjects as the years went by, though, like Johann Strauss the Elder, he was to experience a generation conflict with his own son. During the closing decades of his life he even won real affection from the ordinary citizens in his capacity as 'the Great Lonely One,' the patriarch who stood for the good old days amid ever-growing urbanization, sweeping technological development and industrialization, all against a *fin-de-siècle* background.

The upheavals of 1848 produced a large crop of poetry, songs and musical compositions in which the revolutionary spirit was freely apparent. Even Johann Strauss wrote a *Freiheitslieder-Walzer* (Songs of Freedom Waltz) in his *Barrikadenlieder* (Songs of the Barricades), op.52, and a *Burschenlieder-Walzer* (Student Songs Waltz), op.55. However, despite the excitement, politics soon sank again into the background as far as the public was concerned, partly because of a series of military misfortunes. The Hapsburg Empire was decaying for all to see, and the monarchy alone carried on the old tradition into the twentieth century, the threadbare symbol of an ostensibly unshakable order of things.

•The new professionals •

During the years that political systems had been crumbling, the cultural picture had become less diffuse and began to assume a clearly defined shape. Operatic and concert activities became established and well organized, and the status of musicians was improved – even including provision for their old age.

The foundation of suitable educational institutions was closely connected with the trend towards a professional approach to music and the establishment of an organized system of musical education. The first moves in this direction came from noble and wealthy patrons who were concerned with improving standards of performance. The measures they introduced ushered in the last phase of purely amateur music-making and the upper-class dilettante approach. The school of singing founded in 1817 by the Gesellschaft der Musikfreunde (Society of the Friends of Music) developed two years later into a school for violinists, and in 1821 it began to offer a comprehensive musical education. Georg Hellmesberger and Joseph Joachim, who were to become such outstanding violinists, both graduated from this institution.

Within a short time, associations for the promotion of similar activities were founded in all the larger Austrian cities with the support of the nobility and of wealthy citizens – in Graz (1815), Innsbruck (1817), Linz (1821), Klagenfurt (1828) and the Mozarteum in Salzburg (1841).

The trend towards professionalism among musicians contributed to a levelling of class differences between them. The growing practice of concert-going now enabled the performing musician to establish his image and make himself familiar to the public, so that a sort of artistic stardom developed as the nineteenth century wore on. Virtuoso players, such as Liszt and Paganini, or prima donnas, such as Jenny Lind, aroused more public interest than princes and duchesses, and their playing enabled the public to develop a far greater appreciation of artistic technique, for they offered levels of performance to which upper-class dilettantes could never aspire. This led to a silent revolution, hardly felt at the time, but all the more enduring for that reason. The stars of the stage and the concert hall began to compete for public recognition with the nobility on a plane where they were invincible, that of assessable performance. This budding, still covert, rivalry certainly did not go unnoticed. When Johann Strauss was playing in Breslau (Wroclaw) during the late 1840s to tremendous applause, a local monarchist critic issued stern warnings against acclaiming this musician in the Silesian press as the waltz 'king.' Such carping, irrelevant though it might now appear, indicates the extent of the tension which built up during the period preceding 1848.

Social life was changing. The mood of good fellowship in which Schubert's art was nurtured cooled off perceptibly. The inclination to look for friends faded. Fear spread. 'Everything is falling silent around me,' wrote Karoline Pichler in 1828, 'one suppresses one's ideas because one does not know who may be listening and reporting. And many people, men

Opposite: Johann Strauss the Elder (left) and Joseph Lanner. Strauss joined Lanner's ensemble as a viola player in 1819, and together they were the real creators of the Viennese waltz.

Below: A Viennese mechanical fairground orchestra. Players around the German innkeeper include: an Austrian (flute) with his dog, a devil (pipes), a Frenchman (clarinet), two Italian comedians, an Englishwoman (violin), a monkey (conductor), and an American (double bass).

Far right: Johann Strauss the Younger leading his orchestra in the Volksgarten in 1851, two years after the death of his father – who had watched his son's growing success with a mixture of pride and jealousy, while they led rival orchestras.

Below: The Schrammel Quartet, violinists Johann and Josef Schrammel, clarinettist Georg Dänzer and guitarist Anton Strohmayer. Their music was part of a living popular tradition, and they played it in taverns and wine-houses, but its quality won them the patronage of the nobility as well as the admiration of the great Wagnerian conductor Hans Richter.

especially, avoid mixed company, stay at home, go to the theater or play cards. . . .' And yet in this police state riddled with informers Metternich proved unable to halt progress, or even to direct it. The best he could do was slow it down a little. Indeed, one could well argue that the heavy stage, book and press censorship he imposed – occasionally with grotesque results – did much to foster resistance to the state and therefore to bring on the revolution. Censorship was not confined to Austria, but it was here that the censors were most crude and aggressive in applying Metternich's directives, so that a number of writers were forced to resort to pseudonyms or allow their works to be published anonymously abroad.

Weber's *Der Freischütz* could only be performed in Vienna on 3 November 1821 without the bullet-casting scene and the appearance of Samiel. Entire scenes were deleted from Meyerbeer's *Robert le Diable* when it was performed at the Vienna Hofoper (Court Opera) on 22 June 1833. As to *Les Huguenots*, the plot of which is essentially concerned with the dreadful St Bartholomew's Eve massacre, it was only cleared for staging in Catholic Vienna in 1839 with a radically altered libretto, removing all reference to religious strife, under the title of *Die Ghibellinen in Pisa*.

The transition from salon music to the commercial concert may also be interpreted as the removal of art which mainly involves personal and private relationships to the anonymity of the concert hall. The deaths of Beethoven (1827) and Schubert (1828) marked not only the end of the Viennese Classical period but also that of Vienna's pre-eminence in the field of music. Until 1862, when Brahms appeared on the scene, Vienna lost its European primacy in terms of true creativity. During this time not a single name of lasting importance in serious music can be quoted.

The effervescent brilliance and variety of Viennese musical life during the first half of the

Above: The Emperor Franz Joseph in 1854, soon after his accession in the wake of the 1848 revolutions.

Brahms and Bruckner are constantly compared, although there is nothing in common between either their personal attitudes or their emotional make-up. Bruckner, a countryman born and bred, fought hard for recognition. Brahms the city dweller, on the contrary, sought to withdraw. The full power of his artistic personality bursts forth from Brahms's work, while Bruckner sought to cover up the deficiencies of his temperament by imparting a monumental quality to his output. Mimicry is a word that might apply to aspects of Bruckner's work, but never to that of Brahms, who was, for better or worse, an eccentric. There are no bridges linking the music of Brahms to that of Bruckner, nor indeed to that of Wagner. Bruckner never fully shed a rustic quality that Brahms never managed to acquire, despite his veneration for the folksong. And it was precisely when Brahms tackled church music that his determination to reject any trace of dogma became most obvious.

Isolated as he was, Bruckner dreamed of the great world outside and moved towards the symphony as an aim, not as a starting point. The comparison with Wagner had already struck his contemporaries, and this was not the least among the reasons for the critic Hanslick's hostility. The latter quite clearly sensed that Bruckner was flirting with conceptual elements in his music, even though he did not go so far as to write program symphonies. It was actually his imagery, the tangible and realistic aspect of his music, the waltzes, the *Ländlers* and the comic streak in his scherzos, a sense of humor of Alpine proportions, which ultimately set him apart from Wagner.

• Concerts and critics •

The Gesellschaft der Musikfreunde founded in 1812 at the instigation of Fanny von Arnstein and the Philharmonic Concerts set up in 1842 by Otto Nicolai were the foundations on which public concert-going in Vienna rested and developed during the nineteenth century. Very soon, smaller associations and choral societies came into existence, and during the course of the century the various musical institutions differed from each other more by the kind of interest that the public took in them than by their standards of artistic performance. These were, in any case, covered by the prevalent practice of an individual holding a number of different posts. Thus, to crown their careers, both Joseph Hellmesberger the Elder and Johann Herbeck achieved the position of Hofkapellmeister, a post uniquely prized in professional terms, but lacking prestige in the public's eyes. It was as an opera director or concert conductor that reputation and popularity were to be achieved rather than by being a Hofkapellmeister. When Hans Richter was appointed Hofkapellmeister in 1893 – a position he occupied until 1900 – his musical reputation had been well established since 1875 as the conductor of the Philharmonic Concerts and a distinguished

nineteenth century contrasts strangely with the decades of creative impotence after Beethoven and Schubert had gone, broken only by the exuberant productive drive of Lanner and the Strausses. Well into the second half of the nineteenth century Vienna relied on musical imports far more than on its own creative output. Two names sum up the creative aspect of Viennese musical life during the second half of the century: Johannes Brahms and Anton Bruckner. Both were conspicuously outsiders and both got into trouble with their environment, each in his own way. Though Brahms at the start regarded Vienna with scepticism, it soon became for him the 'sacred city of musicians.' But, as in Bruckner's case, difficulties initially bedevilled his determination to assert himself as a composer. Both composers resolved their problems through their ability as performers, one as an organist, the other as a pianist. Brahms found his circle of friends mainly among academics. He repeatedly left the city to achieve recognition as a composer elsewhere. He clearly remained north German in his personal affinities. His enthusiasm for the German Emperor and his political attitudes were Prussian rather than Austrian by nature. Yet he became ever more deeply immersed in the emotional atmosphere of Vienna, with its overlapping cultural strata and innumerable cross-currents. Twenty years later, he had himself become a holy figure in this sacred city of musicians.

director at the Hofoper. The attraction of court appointments was by now fading. Moreover, in Vienna as elsewhere it was increasingly accepted that the opera orchestra also played at the Philharmonic Concerts, so that both institutions were virtually identical in terms of performers. The concerts of the Gesellschaft der Musikfreunde also tended to call on the musical resources of the same orchestra; the differences appeared in the choice of programs: The Philharmonic Concerts offered the more weighty repertoire, while the others made greater concessions to popular taste.

After 1848 the Gesellschaft der Musikfreunde found itself in financial difficulties, and in 1850 some thought was even given to dissolving it. However, Joseph Hellmesberger took the direction of the society's concerts firmly in hand and transformed the orchestra into a fully professional body. This was ultimately yet another consequence of the revolution and of the realization that amateur music-making had finally come to an end. The new building of the Gesellschaft der Musikfreunde was inaugurated in 1870 with a program which included works by Bach, Haydn, Mozart, Beethoven and Schubert; the conductor was Herbeck. A daring innovation was the introduction into the programs of works for choir and orchestra – Beethoven's Ninth Symphony and *Missa Solemnis*, Haydn's *Creation* and Brahms's *German Requiem*. These made it possible for choral societies, which

Above: Outside the coffee-house in the fashionable Volksgarten in 1898. Concerts were given here from its opening in 1823 by Lanner, Johann Strauss father and son and, later, Eduard Strauss.

Above: The 'Waltz King,' Johann Strauss II, portrayed in 1887 at the height of his fame, with all his decorations.

139

Right: The Berlin Philharmonic Orchestra, which had been founded in 1882, conducted by Hans von Bülow during his time as their chief conductor (1887-92). The scale and technical demands of music written in the second half of the century, particularly that of Wagner and his followers, led to the development of the great symphony orchestras in Europe and America and to the growing importance and fame of the great orchestral conductors.

invariably consisted of amateurs, to take part, and this in turn guaranteed the purchase of a certain number of tickets by a circle of interested friends and relations, thus putting the undertaking on a solid commercial basis. Between 1872 and 1875 Brahms directed these concerts; but, unfortunately, he found that the public, to put it mildly, failed to share his own dedication to baroque music.

As the patronage of the nobility, which in earlier days had sustained musical life, dwindled away, so too did tolerance in the assessment of artistic performance. After 1848, a modern press began to be established, which included a staff of professional critics, and standards of appreciation rose as a result. Eduard Hanslick, who had been working as a journalist since 1846, became the music critic of the *Wiener Zeitung* in 1848 and went over to the *Neue Freie Presse* in 1864. A brilliant critic, he commented on the musical life of Vienna with occasional flashes of biting irony; and yet, despite all the mistaken judgments that are remembered against him nowadays, it is thanks to this intolerant opponent of the 'New German School' centered on Wagner and Liszt that music criticism in Vienna not only achieved a respectable level, but by its high standard also succeeded in shaping opinion abroad. As much a philosopher of music as a critic, Hanslick provided for half a century a yardstick of operatic and concert-hall life in Vienna which enabled those responsible for music to measure the needs and demands of their time. After 1902, his successor Julius Korngold retained a similar hold on musical opinion.

The Philharmonic Concerts had their origin in the Künstlerverein (artists' union) which was founded in 1833 by Franz Lachner, musical director at the Kärntnertor Theater, to promote public concerts and was made up of members of his orchestra. Although only four concerts took place initially, a start had been made, and the idea was carried on by a group of enthusiasts and supporters after 1834, when Lachner left

Vienna. In 1842 Otto Nicolai not only developed the project further but also drew upon musicians belonging to the Hofoper, the declared object being to promote classical music. Although Nicolai succeeded in organizing only a modest total of eleven concerts by 1847, this very fact underlines the significance of the achievement. The performance of all the Beethoven symphonies and of the last three Mozart symphonies during the early years of Nicolai's activity also demonstrate his conscious allegiance to the Viennese tradition. Karl Eckert resumed the organization of these concerts in 1854, but they only became a permanent feature in 1860. Later conductors were Otto Dessoff for fifteen years (1860-75) and Hans Richter for twenty-three (1875-98). The promotion of the classical masters remained the main objective; Anton Bruckner was only admitted to the program in 1883, and Richard Strauss's *Don Juan* was first heard in 1892.

However, a sentence in Eduard Hanslick's obituary (September 1849) of the elder Johann Strauss, whom he held in high regard, shows that the people of Vienna were not dependent for their musical life on official establishments alone: 'Among the public institutions which regularly made instrumental performances available up to 1849 it is only fair to name Strauss's orchestra immediately after the Philharmonic Concerts. A much better performance of good instrumental works could be heard in excellent open-air performances than in many stuffy concerts billing famous names.'

The Singakademie, which Brahms occasionally conducted during 1862-3 — with little success — was established in 1858, but it failed to achieve the reputation of the Singverein of the Gesellschaft der Musikfreunde founded in the same year. However, the Wiener Männergesangverein, founded in 1843, became much the most influential choral society, an association in which the more convivial kind of music-making found its expression. Men's choirs had originated in Germany, and Metternich regarded

Above: Three leading conductors of the age (top to bottom): Arthur Nikisch (1855-1922), originally a violinist in the Vienna Philharmonic, who played under Liszt, Verdi, Brahms and Bruckner, and later a great interpreter of late Romantic music; Hans Richter (1843-1916), from 1875 director of the Hofoper and conductor of the Philharmonic Concerts; and Hans von Bülow (1830-94), the first of the great virtuoso conductors.

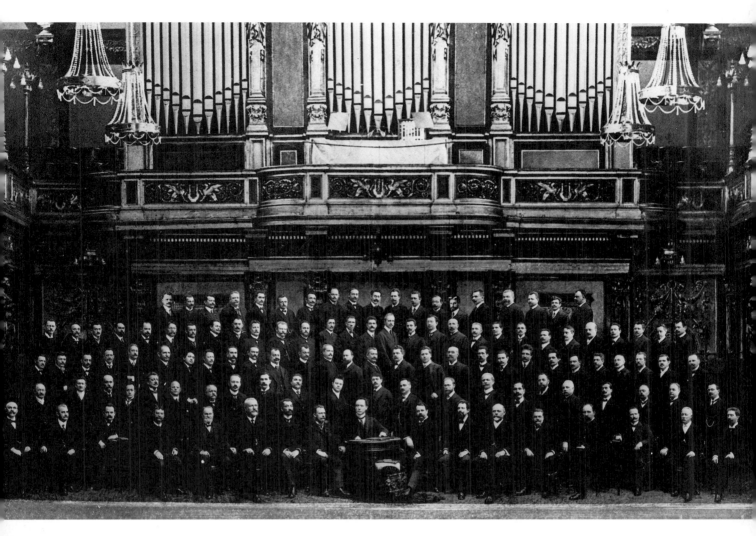

Above: The Vienna Philharmonic Orchestra, conducted by Felix Weingartner (1863-1942) assembled in the great concert hall of the Musikverein in 1910.

their proliferation with the deepest misgivings: 'Abate this poison from Germany for me,' he instructed Sedlnitzky, the Police Prefect of Vienna. Metternich's distrust was not unjustified. The political forces at work in male voice choirs have so far not been acknowledged, let alone given the importance due to them. The emergence of these amateur societies points up the unbridgable – and ever widening – gap between professional and lay musical performance. The fact that no fewer than twenty-one men's choral societies existed in Vienna in 1869 indicates the growing need for such associations of amateurs.

• Opera and the stage •

If 1848 and the fall of the tyrant Metternich led not only to political change but also to a reversal in Austrian political thought, the loss of Lombardy in 1859 (after the battle of Solferino) and of Venice in 1866 (after Königgrätz) brought about far-reaching alterations in the perception of the surrounding world and a cultural reorientation. The connection with Lombardy and Venice had kept Italian cultural influences flowing into Vienna and even conferred official approval upon them. Vienna had been a northern cultural outpost of Italy for centuries, and Italian influence had maintained itself there longer than anywhere else in Europe. During the first half of the nineteenth century, Italian opera retained its pre-eminence in Vienna with Rossini, Bellini and Donizetti, although it had long since lost ground elsewhere in Europe and, in particular, had run into active opposition in Germany.

Weber's German opera *Euryanthe*, which had been specially written for the Kärntnertor Theater, achieved more success with the critics than the public, and this sealed the fate of any further promotion of German opera for the time being. Among all the German musical directors of this 'Italian' period in Vienna, only Konradin Kreutzer and Otto Nicolai made lasting names for themselves as operatic composers.

As the commercialization of culture grew and middle-class requirements became more clearly defined, the city's three major stages began to compete with each other, both for profit and artistic achievement: the Court Theater by the Kärntnertor, the Theater an der Wien and the Theater in the Josefstadt. Farces and popular entertainments were the main concern of the Leopoldstadt Theater with the smallest stage of all, the chief home of the masters of the Viennese *Singspiel* – Wenzel Müller and Ferdinand Kauer. But commercial interests and cultural aspirations never clashed irreconcilably. Theater and opera, as well as – increasingly – the

Right: Lady at a Spinet, 1871, by Hans Makart (1840-84), an unusually intimate masterpiece from the artist whose sensuous handling of paint and generally voluptuous subject-matter made him the painter par excellence of the *Gründerjahre*, the years of Vienna's economic prosperity.

Emperor Franz Joseph the mood was still very relaxed, and the second half of the nineteenth century was not a time of passion nor a period of headlong haste, but rather one of outward orderliness, regardless of growing ethnic tensions. The bourgeoisie found its own place and let officials and nobles operate each within their own sphere while it made the most of its opportunities. Nobody reached out for the unattainable, but whatever was within reach was doggedly pursued. Life in Austria involved a sense of security, a feeling of the self-evidence of things, of durability and continuity. What, one might well ask, could be more conducive to the development of culture, art and music?

On 25 May 1869, the new Opera on the Ringstrasse opened with a brilliant new production of Mozart's *Don Giovanni*, deliberately harking back to the flowering of the Viennese Classical period. Now all could see what Vienna owed to Mozart's genius. The new showpiece on the Ringstrasse put opera at the very center of Viennese musical life. It was clear that the concert hall had slipped into second place.

The other theaters also continued to provide opera. The Theater an der Wien attempted to outdo the rather staid and Italian dominated Hofoper by a skillful choice of repertoire and especially by putting on attractive premières. Similarly, the Josefstadt Theater also managed to leave its imprint on the city's operatic life by concentrating on non-Italian works. Thus in 1833 a censored version of Meyerbeer's universal success *Robert le Diable* and Halévy's *La Juive* were first presented to a Viennese audience here, rather than at the Hofoper, while in 1847 the director of the Theater an der Wien brought off a veritable triumph of public acclaim with Meyerbeer's *Vielka*, thanks to Jenny Lind, a prima donna who had all Vienna at her feet. Wagner's *Tannhäuser* was introduced to Vienna at the Josefstadt Theater's summer theater, the Thalia Theater, and it was only after its unexpected success here in 1857 that those directing the Hofoper pricked up their ears. Faithful friends had smoothed the path for Wagner's entry into Vienna. Eventually, as a result of unrelenting preparatory work by Karl Eckert and Heinrich Esser, *Lohengrin* was given a brilliant first performance at the Vienna Hofoper. *Tannhäuser* and *Der fliegende Holländer* followed. Wagner himself arrived in Vienna in May 1861 to an unprecedented triumphal reception and was extravagant in his praise of Vienna's musical resources. But when the attempt to stage *Tristan und Isolde* during the 1861-2 season failed miserably after seventy-seven rehearsals, he left Vienna in a rage, which he vented in 1862 by a diatribe against the Viennese operatic establishment.

Die Meistersinger was the first new work on the program of the new Hofoper on the Ringstrasse, now under the direction of Johann Herbeck, a conductor as musically gifted as he was greedy for power. The public rejected Wagner's opera. Fighting raged in the stalls as well as on the stage. Wagner fired off indignant telegrams and refused to allow *Die Walküre* and *Tristan*

operetta, probably the most financially rewarding form of stage performance, came to dominate the outlook of the Viennese middle class during the second half of the nineteenth century and therefore ruled the cultural scene. This change of attitude can surely be attributed to a new middle-class mentality which, outwardly, matched surprisingly closely the nobility's traditional need for ostentation.

The growing power of the monied middle class was most clearly exemplified in the Ringstrasse, a magnificent boulevard 4 kilometers long and 57 meters wide. Modern government buildings, museums, a new university, the stock exchange and the new Burgtheater all arose in the immediate vicinity of many aristocratic palaces, as well as the new opera house – the 'Ringstrassenoper' as it was later called.

The Austro-Hungarian Dual Monarchy came into being in 1867. Two years earlier Vienna saw its first horse-drawn tram. Under the judicious rather than domineering rule of the

to be staged. In 1875 the direction of the Hof-oper passed from Herbeck to Franz Jauner, who until then had been director of the Carl Theater, and Jauner, an artist as well as a businessman, succeeded in placating Wagner. He invited him to conduct *Die Meistersinger* and, by engaging Hans Richter as a regular conductor, secured the services not only of someone close to Wagner, but also of an artist of world caliber. Jauner had a lucky touch. He succeeded in bringing Verdi to Vienna to conduct *Aida* and the Requiem in June 1875, and on 23 October of the same year he staged Bizet's *Carmen* – as yet unsuccessful – with specially commissioned recitatives supplied by Ernest Guiraud, thus at once making a world favorite of the work and enriching the operatic repertoire with a major composition. On 2 November 1875 Wagner arrived in Vienna and *Lohengrin* was given its special first performance for the benefit of the Hofoper Chorus on 2 March 1876. Wagner was very keen to make use of Vienna's musical resources, and when Hans Richter went to Bayreuth with an advance of 20,000 marks to buy the performing rights of the *Ring*, Wagner, after some initial hesitation, agreed to the deal. *Die Walküre* received its first performance in 1877, *Rheingold* and *Siegfried* followed in 1878, on 24 January and 9 November respectively, and the cycle was completed with the première of *Götterdämmerung* on 14 February 1879. Vienna had now firmly established its link with modern music drama.

Above: The organ in the main concert hall of the Vienna Musikverein building, designed by the Danish architect Theophil Hansen to contain not only concert halls but also the Gesellschaft der Musikfreunde and its Conservatory. The concert hall was opened on 6 January 1870, and its rich acoustics made it the perfect place for the Philharmonic Concerts, which have been held there ever since.

Left: An early painting by Gustav Klimt – soon to become a leading light of the Viennese Secession school – showing the fashionable audience in the old Burgtheater shortly before it finally closed in 1888.

The ideological basis of Wagner's work, however, projected it into the very middle of an area of intense and agonizing debate. Whoever sided with Wagner was expected to stand up for his beliefs. No less a figure than Hugo Wolf, who earned his living as the music critic of the *Wiener Salonblatt* and had become an ardent admirer of Wagner ever since hearing *Lohengrin*, publicly complained that insufficient respect was being paid to his new idol: 'What is one to say when not a single Wagner opera is on the program for a whole month, while Meyerbeer is staged three times a week? Is it Palestine we live in, or a German city?' One may well wonder at this new note – it reeked of anti-semitism.

• The *Gründerjahre* •

There is no denying that Wagner's writings and – to a lesser extent – his music aggravated the tension surrounding anti-semitism, more particularly in Vienna, where the composer had fallen out at an early stage with Eduard Hanslick, the most influential of the music critics. Jewish businessmen, owing to their greater experience of finance, also led the field during the strong economic boom of the 'promoters' years' in Vienna, the *Gründerjahre*. These new circumstances were there for all to see. The country might be part of a traditional empire, but the new spirit of enterprise set fresh standards with its emphasis on achievement and initiative. Accident of birth, from which the nobility derived its claim to social standing, paled beside the claims of personal achievement. Fresh forces were at work. Vienna grew into a world capital and became cosmopolitan in its outlook. Between 1840 and 1890 its population more than doubled to reach a total of 818,000 inhabitants. Liberalization made real progress, although suffrage was still restricted to the property-owning classes. One way or another, the initiative was passing into the hands of the bourgeoisie. Beethoven had still been able to rely on the support of the nobility and took its demands into account. By the end of the century, the princely families who still resided in their palaces in the center of the city were withdrawing from public life. Their patronage, once jealous enough, was now degenerating into unconcern. The Emperor took not the slightest interest in music, the theater or literature. His world was that of the military, and even this was more a matter of show, colorful rather than heroic.

Towards the middle of the century, the vacuum left by the nobility as it surrendered its leading position in promoting culture was filled largely by the increasingly wealthy Jewish middle class. This social group had always been anxious to fulfill the ambitions of the rising bourgeoisie in the fields of art, music, theater and education. Now, attendance at concerts and theaters, as well as at art exhibitions, was more and more recruited from its ranks. Any new venture in Vienna had to rely on the support of this new estate, the nobility of wealth. Indeed, there was

more to it than that: Jews began to figure in creative activities as the nineteenth century wore on. Meyerbeer and Mendelssohn exemplify this trend in Prussia. In Vienna, names such as Karl Goldmark, Gustav Mahler, Arnold Schoenberg and Anton Webern are characteristic of the cultural scene at the *fin de siècle*, while reference to such international personalities as Oscar Straus, Leo Fall and Emmerich Kálmán makes it clear that the Viennese operetta also knew no frontiers.

The leading literary talent of the period was drawn from the same source: one need only mention the names of Hugo von Hofmannsthal, Arthur Schnitzler or Richard Beer-Hofmann. In another field, Max Reinhardt succeeded in making Vienna the starting point for a new era in the theater, which was just as much a Viennese phenomenon as the 'New Music' founded by Arnold Schoenberg. Moreover, the fresh impetus derived from the creative potential of this Jewish middle class led to a new self-awareness. In the 1890s Theodor Herzl, features editor of the *Neue Freie Presse*, began to dream of a truly Jewish state in Palestine and to recruit followers among like-minded co-religionists.

But the worship of Wagner created a set of tensions in Vienna at this time which was made up of far more complex elements than the primitive labels of pro- and anti-semitism would suggest. Gustav Mahler, who described his Jewish origin as the 'obstacle of obstacles' in terms of his professional career, accepted conversion to Christianity as a last resort to enable him to take up the post of director at the Hofoper. At the same time, it was he who throughout his decade at the Opera set the prevailing standards for the interpretation of Wagner ever since his memorable production of *Lohengrin* on 11 May 1897.

Richard Strauss's *Don Juan* and Mahler's First Symphony, both first performed in 1889, completed the transition to 'modern music' and put an end to links with the past. The last decade of the century was a watershed, not only politically, with the retirement of Bismarck from the world stage in 1890, but also because of the

Above: Artists of the Secession in their gallery – shown (*far right*) in a print by its architect Josef Olbrich – at the exhibition there of Max Klinger's bust of Beethoven in 1902. Gustav Klimt is enthroned on the left.

Below: The Hofoper on the Ringstrasse in the late 1890s, at the time when Mahler took over as musical director.

Above: Silhouette of a recitalist in the Bösendorfer Saal in 1898. The hall, opened by the Vienna piano-maker in 1872, was the scene of many famous recitals by Rubinstein, Liszt, Hellmesberger and other virtuosi, and it was the first center of the Wagner cult in Vienna.

deaths of Bruckner in 1896, Brahms in 1897 and Johann Strauss II in 1899. Richard Wagner, regarded by contemporaries as the antithesis of Brahms, had already died in 1883. But more than a change of generation was involved: a deep transformation was taking place. Brahms's statement that he constantly felt Beethoven standing over him like a giant, makes it plain that he was well aware of the weight of tradition behind him, which he felt he had to overcome. During the nineteenth century – and this is a special feature of it – musical works of art came to acquire a recognized lasting value for the first time. Bach had to be rediscovered before he could be enshrined. Beethoven was the first composer whose entire work retained its standing undiminished after the creator's death. This was not even true of Haydn, whom Schumann described as 'decked in a powdered wig,' or of Mozart, who, in nineteenth-century terms, hardly existed as a symphonic composer. It would be no exaggeration to say that Beethoven provided a common standard. That even goes, in a negative sense, for Bruckner and Mahler, in that they both sought to react against him.

Wagner's concept of the music drama in a sense only transferred to the stage the debate initiated by Liszt's advocacy of the symphonic poem – the suggestion that the idea singled out for representation is more significant than the music, in other words more important than the means employed to interpret it. Hanslick used his authority as a critic to bring the debate to Vienna. He made the city the main forum for a discussion of what should be the philosophy for the music of the future, and the question as to

what constitutes the major form of composition was at the very center of the controversy. Wagner, who had written no symphony in proper form, announced the demise of the symphony in his essay *Oper und Drama*. Brahms, when he reached Vienna in 1862, reluctantly became involved in this open war of words. His drawn-out misgivings up to 1876 concerning his First Symphony can be explained, at least in part, by this involvement.

Bruckner stands well apart in this company due to his massively monumental quality. It is perfectly understandable that he should have irritated his contemporaries. Brahms's quip about 'gigantic symphonic serpents' is of course typical of the failure of one creative spirit to enter into the mind of another and understand it. But this very lack of understanding on the part of Brahms plainly indicates that Bruckner was undermining rather than strengthening traditional, specifically symphonic values. If Brahms's symphonic output can be described, somewhat tenuously, in terms of an approach derived from chamber music, Bruckner must be seen in a dramatic relationship to the stage. The sweeping background tremolo passages, the animated tonal plane, the extravagant gesturing, the broad and enveloping thematic pattern which rejects smallness but fails to achieve greatness, all these can be matched within the parameters of the theater.

• The new century •

Vienna had now become a world capital. Gas and electricity services were brought under municipal control, measures were introduced for the care of the elderly, and the electrification of the tramway network was undertaken. In the Prater fun fair the Ferris wheel became a sort of symbol of the city, signifying pleasure. Hans

Makart, who died in 1884, had imposed his decorative and monumental pictorial style on Vienna. Now it was the turn of Gustav Klimt and Oskar Kokoschka to give a new orientation to painting. Meanwhile, starting in 1905, a new industrial area was to be created on the opposite bank of the Danube, and in the course of a mere ten years – between 1890 and 1900 – the population had doubled. It reached a total of 1,727,000, and by 1910 the two million mark was attained.

The intense progress of industrialization led to the creation of working-class areas in the city and thus to the physical concentration of this new population. The electoral reform implemented in 1907 brought the conflict of interests between the nobility, the middle class and workers into the open, while the ethnic struggle grew more intense despite – or perhaps precisely because of – liberalization. Bosnia and Herzegovina were annexed in 1908, thereby sowing one of the seeds of the First World War. The twentieth century had arrived and the era of Franz Joseph was drawing to its close. Outwardly, the old imperial world had long since faded away, but people continued to act out their false sense of order and stability. Under the surface, antiquated moral concepts were still opposing the ferment of new forces and new ideas. Out of sight, the rivalry between old and young, yesterday and today, continued to grow.

On 23 January 1901 Richard Strauss, with an orchestra from Munich, gave his first concert as a visitor and performed some of his own works, *Ein Heldenleben* among them. Mahler, who approved of Strauss as a champion of the modern movement, offered to stage his opera *Feuersnot*. The work met with wholesale disapproval. A drastic fall in box office receipts forced Mahler to take the opera off after only three performances, but he still remained loyal to Strauss, four years his junior. When he saw the piano score of *Salome* in 1905, he realized that this work pointed the way to the future for musical drama and hastened to stage it, with tremendous enthusiasm. He had, however, not reckoned with censorship in Catholic Vienna, which still cast its shadow over the new century. The performance of *Salome* was banned, ultimately because biblical personages were involved in activities which, as the censor, Emil Jettel von Ettenach, wrote, 'belong to the field of sexual pathology.' He deliberately stressed the inappropriateness of the work 'for our Court stage,' thus cleverly indicating how toleration might be further extended. Vienna, therefore, encountered *Salome* not at the Hofoper but at the Volkstheater on 25 May 1907. The more

Right: The Wind's Bride, Oskar Kokoschka's self-portrait (1914) with Alma Mahler, with whom he lived for several stormy years after the composer's death. The expressionist force of the painting finds a parallel in the work of the 'Second Vienna School,' particularly the music of Schoenberg and Alban Berg.

Below right: Schoenberg acknowledges his debt to Gustav Mahler in his own painting of the composer's funeral in 1911.

conventional of those at Court held aloof, and once again a lesser rival scooped the Court stage. Mahler had done everything possible to turn the Hofoper into Europe's leading operatic establishment, but this demanded first and foremost modern works and modern ideas, not merely a careful choice of repertoire. He had directed the Hofoper since 1897 and had succeeded, largely through his skillful choice of collaborators, in establishing a leading position for Viennese opera throughout the world. He had an outstanding and powerful talent at his disposal in Alfred Roller, the chief stage manager, with whose help he achieved stylistically trend-setting productions of Wagner's works. Wagner's music dramas had by now become both standard and touchstone for the quality of all operatic directors. As an interpreter, Mahler was moved by a sense of mission comparable to that of Wagner, and he carried out his task with uncompromising fidelity. Fidelity of interpretation – a fundamental principle of twentieth-century production – can be traced back to Mahler. He conjured up what in fact lies at the heart of operatic production: fascination. Mahler's impact in Vienna propelled opera everywhere into the new century.

One of the Hofoper's greatest moments came on 8 April 1911 with the first night of *Der Rosenkavalier.* Alfred Roller's staging became a byword all over the world and was adopted by many opera houses abroad. Richard Strauss, who since 1906 had been collaborating closely with Hofmannsthal, Vienna's leading literary light, now himself became intimately involved with the city. In *Der Rosenkavalier* composer

Below: Burning down of the newly built Czech National Theater in 1881. It had opened on 11 June that year with the first performance of Smetana's *Libuše* and was rebuilt to open its doors again with the same opera in November 1883.

senting the première of his new opera, *Die Frau ohne Schatten*, on 10 October 1919, the only première granted to Vienna by Strauss apart from the second version of *Ariadne* in 1916.

•Czech composers•

and author presented the operatic stage with the consummation of Viennese operetta. The Viennese waltz achieved its full cultural recognition with the quotation from the *Dynamiden-Walzer* by Joseph Strauss, now transposed into the fluorescent harmonies of the twentieth century. Gustav Mahler died on 18 May 1911, failing to witness either his protégé's triumph in Vienna or his declaration of allegiance to the city. Strauss and Vienna: *nomen est omen.*

A Richard Strauss Week was organized in Vienna in April 1918. At this time, Strauss was already being considered for the post of co-director of the Opera. The cultural authorities tactfully and gently worked for an agreement with Cardinal Piffl in order to remove the difficulties concerning *Salome* and thereby create the common ground needed for negotiations with Strauss. The Hofoper raised its curtain on *Salome* on 14 October 1918, literally during the last days of its existence. On 10 November, Franz Schalk, a native of Vienna, who had been Hans Richter's successor as conductor at the Hofoper in 1900-4, took over direction of the house. Two days later, the 'German Austrian Republic' was proclaimed. Franz Joseph, the lonely old Emperor, had already been carried to his grave two years earlier. The splendor of the Habsburg crown was extinguished for ever, the great empire had crumbled.

Cultural life, however, remained virtually untouched by the political cataclysm. On 1 December 1919, Richard Strauss assumed the joint direction with Schalk of what had now become the Staatsoper, which the authorities hoped would with his help again assume its leading position. Strauss was the leading operatic composer of his time, acclaimed by Schalk as an artist 'whose name shines far into the spiritual world,' and he returned the compliment by pre-

The collapse of 1918 involved more than the end of Austria's dominating position in the interplay of political power in Europe: it also led to the foundation of a new political entity – the Czechoslovak Republic – on 28 October 1918. This event was the political outcome of a lengthy process of change which developed under the shadow of the Imperial Austrian Eagle's wings in Bohemia and Moravia during the nineteenth century. The ancient imperial city of Prague had become increasingly removed from the policy-making process. Political factors were therefore not the least important among those which caused Prague to develop into a cultural capital in its own right. In this case, physical factors also led to the growth of a large economic potential and the influx of a – mainly Czech – labor force as a result of increasing industrialization. The German-Austrian variety of liberalism and a new cultural orientation involving a marked emphasis on national consciousness now produced a sense of national identity in Bohemia and Moravia, just as they had earlier done in Italy and Hungary, in Russia and Poland. Since the start of the nineteenth century the study of the Czech language had been the principal cultural and political concern of nationally-minded circles. A conflict between the German- and Slavonic-speaking elements of the population was therefore inevitable. Rivalries developed during the second half of the century, which the authorities sought to alleviate through 'ethnic parity' arrangements. But these failed to arrest the gradual shift of political power.

In 1861 Prague elected its first Czech local government majority. The following year saw the foundation of the Provisional Theater, explicitly devoted to promoting Czech opera, and on 30 May 1866 it staged the triumphant première of *The Bartered Bride* by Bedřich Smetana, a work that came to be regarded as the epitome

Top: View of Prague in 1850, looking across the river Vltava from the castle ramparts towards the old town. The Charles Bridge is on the right.

Above: Zdeněk Fibich, composer, dramatist, teacher, critic and one of Smetana's most devoted pupils.

of Czech opera. Smetana worked as conductor in this theater from 1866 until 1874. His opera *Dalibor* was chosen for the gala performance on the day the foundation stone of the new Czech National Theater was laid, 16 May 1868, although it attracted criticism from Smetana's opponents because of its alleged Wagnerian tendencies. But even this dispute was not a matter of purely aesthetic considerations, as was the debate between the Brahms and Wagner factions in Vienna. It was tinged with politics. Smetana made no bones about the fact that he followed the musical precepts of Liszt, whom he described as his 'unattainable model' and who was no ardent proponent of the German spirit. However, as a supporter of the 'New Germans,' Liszt was included among the 'non-Czechs' in this dispute. That was enough to damn him.

In Czech musical history Smetana occupies a position comparable to that of Glinka in Russia. Smetana himself quite objectively recognized this when he said that it was he who had created the Czech national musical style. Antonin Dvořák, whose work was no less emphatically national than that of Smetana, entered this evolution at a later stage and had a much more international outlook than the latter, if only in his marked preference for the rather more formal aspects of Brahms's music. Moreover, Dvořák was in a direct line of descent from the Viennese Classical composers. Therefore, despite the pronounced national style which they share, these two artists clashed just like the supporters of Wagner and those of Brahms in Vienna.

During the eighteenth century German princes and bishops had recruited many musicians from Bohemia, the music school of Europe, for their private orchestras, because through their native musical talent these instrumentalists supplied the counterpart to Italian singers. After 1850, however, this performing potential was increasingly directed into the mainstream of local music owing to the growth of a national consciousness. The remarkable and spontaneous creative originality of Smetana, Dvořák, Fibich and, finally, Janáček would be unthinkable without the tradition of Bohemian musicianship, which ultimately had also underpinned the fine flowering of the Viennese Classical period. Up to the end of the First World War and the foundation of the Czechoslovak Republic in 1919, the cultural life of Prague was still marked by a close blending of German and Czech elements. However, two parallel but distinct lines of cultural development took increasingly clear shape there during the last decades of the nineteenth century: the Provisional Theater was supplemented in 1881 by the Czech National Theater, in a sense a symbol of the nation's rebirth – it was burned down the same year, but reopened on 18 November 1883 with Smetana's *Libuše* – while, at the same time, the German Theater-Verein, founded in 1883, built the New German Theater, which opened on 5 January 1888 with Wagner's *Meistersinger*, the work that exemplified the German spirit at that moment. Such a choice of repertoire in itself led to reciprocal segregation and intensified ethnic tensions rather than the reverse. The Technical High School split as early as 1869, and the University followed in 1882. At the turn of the century Germans in Prague felt isolated, as though living on an island. They formed a social stratum but were no longer part of the nation as a whole. Rapid industrialization, accompanied by a dramatic increase in the proportion of Czechs in the population of Prague, radically altered the former balance. In 1911, when the director of the New German Theater offered the post of senior conductor to a Viennese, Alexander von Zemlinsky, the latter came to a city in which less than a tenth of the population spoke German. Moreover, a large part of this German-speaking element was of Jewish origin. Given such fragmentation, the German community increasingly felt that their homeland was no better than a ghetto in which their life trickled away without hope of a future. While Czech art found its strength with the help of Smetana and Dvořák in national consciousness and the awakening of political feeling, the Germans experienced a sense of decay, a mood of universal alienation and anguish.

•The musical world •

A stylistic era in music is not defined solely by the flowering of outstanding individual talents. It acquires its impetus and character from a host of musicians who weave the close pattern of their cultural landscape in the shadow of their great contemporaries. Those most frequently

Left: Gypsy violinist drawn in 1878 by Mikuláš Aleš. Besides his cycle of paintings, *Our Native Land*, Aleš did hundreds of drawings evoking aspects of Czech culture, including the illustration of many folksongs.

relegated to the background are the teachers who have stimulated such contemporaries, often simply by forcing them to argue. If it had not been for Eduard Marxsen, as well as Eduard Reményi, Brahms might well not have achieved such artistic eminence. As to Bruckner, he would not have found his way to his musical point of departure without Simon Sechter and Otto Kitzler. Often enough, musicians who were

held in high regard in their time only managed to achieve really universal recognition by a few works, sometimes by only a single one which set them apart from their fellow artists. Max Bruch's name lives on only in his Violin Concerto, and would otherwise be forgotten like that of many other no less serious and gifted artists. Franz Schmidt, who achieved high official recognition as head of the Vienna Musik-Akademie (1925-7) and rector of the Technical High School for Music and Visual Arts (1927-31) made a name for himself as one of Bruckner's heirs, especially as a composer for the organ; but he only survives now in public memory through the symphonic intermezzo from his opera *Notre Dame* (1914).

The work of Hugo Wolf demands an entirely separate approach. Wolf took part in the musical life of Vienna without substantially influencing it. Yet he left behind him a body of compositions that continue to live and have a place all of their own in the *fin-de-siècle* scene. He was a strangely unquiet musician and his songs convey disturbance as well as an intoxicating sense of spontaneity. This sporadic output of a wealth of song touched with genius undoubtedly owed much of its origin to morbid psychological factors. It nevertheless flows from a powerfully imaginative emotional response, expressed with outstanding originality. Wolf applied equal intensity to a corrosive criticism of the surrounding world and to the judgment of his own work, leading him rigorously to reject from it anything he considered worthless.

His admiration for Wagner, which bordered on infatuation, disturbed his judgment where

Left: Out of the many more conservative contemporaries of Brahms, Max Bruch (1838-1920) is one of the very few whose music is still played, though he is remembered only for his First Concerto and *Scottish Fantasy* for violin, while his operas, symphonies, choral works and chamber music are forgotten. He enjoyed great success in his lifetime, although even then his music was felt to be somewhat sentimental, and he was admired more for his craftsmanship than for any profound or original musical thought.

Left: Max Reger (1873-1916), seen here at his desk in a painting by Franz Nölken. Reger's prolific output, dismissed in the past as heavy and academic, is now being reappraised. Deeply influenced by Brahms (who saw him as a torchbearer of German music) and by the German organ tradition, he was also close to Busoni and Richard Strauss, and in the transparent textures of his later music and the absence of late-Romantic gesture, he looks forward to twentieth-century neo-classicism.

works of a different sort were concerned. As a music critic 'the wild Wolf' displayed a lack of insight rather than any authoritative guidance. His harsh sallies against Brahms reflect on him rather than on his victim. As a composer Wolf combined in a self-contradictory way lyrical talent with a bent for dramatic development. He made only one attempt at composing stage music with *Der Corregidor* (1896), first performed in Mannheim, which, although famous, is seldom performed. Work of enduring quality was produced by Wolf only in the field of the *Lied*. Here, with his unmistakably idiosyncratic, wholly personal tonal idiom he succeeded in imparting fresh direction to the German song. Inspired by Wagner's theories of music drama, Wolf shaped the song into a miniature symphonic poem, in which the piano accompaniment weaves a characteristic tapestry that the vocal line interprets by its independent poetic statement. Wolf drives the functional use of harmony to its uttermost limit, regardless of program implications. Although he took his bearings from Wagner, his musical idiom is in some mysterious way penetrated by the breath of the Mediterranean. Wolf very much formed part of the Vienna of his time, even though as a creative artist he hardly impinged on its official musical life. He was yet another great solitary artist, one among the esoteric creators who shut themselves away and chose isolation from the surrounding world. This is uniquely important: it was precisely Hugo Wolf who, by his style of vocal composition, provided the link between late Romanticism and the modern world.

• The new wave •

A characteristic feature of modernism after the turn of the century is its lack of coherence, the dissolution of features which had in the past at once signalled and cemented a period. Any attempt to provide a comprehensive account of the untidy coexistence of Gustav Mahler, Arnold Schoenberg, Richard Strauss, Hans Pfitzner, Max Reger and Franz Schreker is fraught with greater difficulties than a similar attempt to summarize the era of Brahms, Bruckner and Wagner. The Viennese critic Hermann Bahr used the concept of 'Modernism' as the absolute opposite of everything covered by the *fin-de-siècle* label: not an end, not a breakdown, not decadence, but a new start, an awakening, a healing. In terms of art, *Jugendstil* implies not only a youthful form of artistic expression, but also the art of the young generation who have turned away from old, decaying traditionalism, and it therefore signifies a generation conflict of unprecedented dimensions.

Vienna grew during this time into a cultural capital of worldwide renown. The Viennese Secession was founded in 1897, a close-knit band of young artists outside the official artistic establishment, with Gustav Klimt as their spiritual leader, and they developed the ideas underlying the *Jugendstil*, formulating and

publicizing the protest of the younger generation against the traditionalists of the *Gründerzeit*. Hermann Bahr gathered around him the group of *Jung-Wiener* writers, who included Hofmannsthal, Schnitzler, Beer-Hofmann and Andrian, while in music Mahler, Zemlinsky, Schoenberg and Webern rebelled against outdated naturalism by radically rejecting it. Music as the representatives of the new Viennese School conceived it relied on the idea of concentration, of turning inwards, and this repudiation of the outside world in turn implied that the constraints imposed by objective reality were unimportant, or even intolerable. The sense of an audience was lost, and by abdicating public recognition the artist chose his own private ghetto. As a result, both Schoenberg and Webern took music beyond its natural boundaries in the system of atonal construction which they developed. By confining themselves to what was strictly and absolutely essential, they ignored certain fundamental musical factors, such as the principle of repetition. But the threatened revolution failed to materialize. The 'young generation' split asunder. They were not at one with each other, even though they were conscious as a group of being different from their contemporaries.

Above: Hugo Wolf (1860-1903), the outstanding composer of *Lieder* after Schubert, but frustrated in his ambition to write a great opera: *Der Corregidor* (1896), based on Alarcón's *Three-cornered Hat*, in which a number of his songs appear in orchestral versions, has never found a permanent place in the repertory.

Two of the masters of Viennese operetta: (*below*) Emmerich Kálmán, composer of *Die Czárdásfürstin*; and (*bottom*) Franz Lehár, with Mizzi Günther, the first 'Merry Widow,' and her Danilo, Louis Treumann.

Like Schoenberg, who eventually moved from Vienna to Berlin, the Austrian composer Franz Schreker worked in Vienna until the age of forty-two and was then appointed director of the Berlin Musikhochschule in 1920, taking over the master class at the Prussian Academy of Arts in 1932. Schreker, who taught Alois Hába and Ernst Křenek, had scored a worldwide success in 1912 with his first opera *Der ferne Klang* (The Distant Sound), and he ranked for a long time with Richard Strauss as a leading modern opera composer, a successor to Wagner who had opened a new way into the future by combining earlier stylistic elements from grand opera with symbolist features. He tended to write sensuous music which relied more on attractive sound than on structure.

Hans Pfitzner's polemical essay *Futuristengefahr* (Danger of Futurism), published in 1917, was directed against Busoni's proposal for a new aesthetic of audio art. Pfitzner saw himself as following and carrying on the work of Schumann, Brahms and – unlikely though this may seem – Wagner. Like Schoenberg, he too set out to bridge the gap separating Brahms from Wagner and to gloss over the conflict that divided them. It is typical of Pfitzner's indiscriminate attitude to musical categories that he was able to transcribe his C minor Quartet, op.36 (1925), as a symphony without substantial changes – a feature which links him with Brahms. The preoccupation with self displayed by modern composers is already present, albeit covertly, in the autobiographical features of Brahms's output – in Richard Strauss's case, it stands out undisguised and tends to dominate his work – and in Pfitzner its positive effects are demonstrated in his opera *Palestrina*, which could never have been achieved without deep reflection upon the process of artistic creation, about which Pfitzner expressed astonishingly aggressive opinions in his pamphlets. Pfitzner not only championed the value of absolute music, he polemicized on its behalf.

Instead of achieving recognition, Max Reger, who died in 1916 at the age of forty-three, was plainly misunderstood. He was denounced for his dissonances, condemned on account of his 'demented modulation,' his 'bestial brutality,' and was accused of a 'nameless discrepancy between wish and fulfillment.' At a time when music was becoming increasingly intellectual he represented the opposite extreme: the uncritical creator, the musician who communicates impulsively and directly. Reger's output covered a wide spectrum, but did not include either opera or – significantly enough – symphony, both of which he longed to compose, but he never realized his ambition. The Sinfonietta, op.90, is on a small scale and must be regarded as chamber music in its proportions as well as its conception. Its classical mood contrasts with the earlier, sweeping symphonic fragment dating from 1902 which was to have become a 'large-scale' work in Mahler's definition, but was never completed.

All these musicians both embodied the spirit of their time and contributed to its expression. They formed the links in a long chain, each indissolubly attached to the next. Wagner, Bruckner or Brahms and Mahler, Schoenberg, Strauss, Pfitzner and Reger, all of them, through their contacts with their contemporaries, formulated the expression of their age. But the line of descent had split: Pfitzner roundly called for a counterattack on atonal modernism; Strauss turned away from it after *Elektra* and in 1909 refused to perform Schoenberg's Four Orchestral Pieces, op.16. In *Rosenkavalier*, he actually set up the Viennese waltz in opposition to modernism almost as an article of faith. As for Max Reger, by 1910 he was already asking, in connection with Schoenberg's Three Piano Pieces, whether the latter's compositions could in any sense 'still be described as music.' The modern movement not only split but dissolved. When all was said and done, it turned out not to be the torch-lit march forward of a close-knit band of fighters but the sulky and solitary pilgrimage of individuals intent on resignation, if that is the correct interpretation of Schoenberg's saying, 'Recognition is to be achieved only after death.'

• Operetta •

The vacuum that was left on the musical scene was filled by a new kind of music, directed towards the public rather than away from it – operetta, an artistic form that was fundamentally and essentially a product of Vienna. Not only

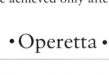

did it grow out of the rich ethnic mix provided by the Danube monarchy, but it could never have come into being and acquired a separate identity anywhere else. Like the Viennese waltz – which it incorporates – the Viennese operetta stands for the era of the Emperor Franz Joseph. Local color, period style, the way of the monarchy and the customs of the middle class are all wonderfully and uniquely blended in it. At the same time, the tradition of the Viennese *Singspiel* blends with the urbanity of Offenbach's French operettas, thus enabling the Viennese operetta to radiate a feeling of universality which crosses frontiers and ensures a worldwide response to it. And yet, it remains essentially Viennese, deeply rooted, unmistakably a picture in sound of a Ruritania on the Danube. That is the fundamental difference between the Viennese operetta and the earlier operettas of Offenbach. These merely reflect the spirit of Paris with its mixture of chic and frivolity, but they do not convey France as a whole in its rich variety.

Johann Strauss the Younger, on the other hand, reached out beyond the specifically Viennese and added a Hungarian element, which was most clearly apparent in *Der Zigeunerbaron* (The Gypsy Baron) of 1885. As for 5 April 1874, that was a date in world history: the première of *Die Fledermaus*. At first it was no more than a moderate success, but it took off in Vienna after a triumphant production in Berlin. *Die Fledermaus* became world famous and with it the operetta obtained its title of nobility. Nor was Johann Strauss the only operetta composer in Vienna. Franz von Suppé, who was the real founder of the genre in 1860, and Karl Michael Ziehrer scored one success after another. What the 'House on the Ringstrasse,' the Viennese Hofoper, failed to give the world in terms of an original Viennese creative contribution to the operatic repertoire was richly made up for in the local operetta theaters.

Until 1883 Franz von Suppé produced a new work every year. Karl Millöcker scored a worldwide success with *Der Bettelstudent* (The Beggar Student) in 1882. Emmerich Kálmán moved from Hungary to Vienna in 1908, and while fighting raged on the Isonzo in 1915 the population of Vienna swayed to the strains of *Die Czárdásfürstin* (The Czardas Princess). Other names became equally famous, notably Franz Lehár and Leo Fall.

Operetta carried the charm of the city on the Danube right around the world, to become a universal ambassador for Vienna. It could never have performed this task of popularizing Vienna as the city of music if mass appeal had not been a basic ingredient in all operetta, which is essentially the expression of an urban attitude to life and demands the vast audiences available in large cities. It not only satisfies a universal longing for a time that never was, but also meets a deep seated need for the spectacular. What Holy Week processions and military parades provide for other reasons and in different circumstances is captured by operetta in the small world of the stage. The splendor of parades

vanished from the streets after 1918 but lived on in the tinsel world of the operetta.

The Habsburg monarchy collapsed, but the city of music survived. That which had actually created the specific quality of Vienna could not be destroyed by political upheavals. Music during the era of the Emperor Franz Joseph was as variegated and multifarious as it was united by its common origin, as stylistically at one as it was emotionally at loggerheads. Time has blurred the outlines; what once seemed rough and abrupt is now softened by distance.

The era of the Emperor Franz Joseph was not only that of the Viennese operetta but also that of the 'Vienna School,' not only of Johannes Brahms but also of Richard Wagner. A wide spectrum of expression covered the field between the poles of folksong and esotericism. If one were to look for a characteristic feature of this period, it would be the unravelling of earlier developments, the growth of divergence and the conspicuous lack of unity. Looking back from the distance of nearly a century, it has to be admitted that the outlines have not perceptibly hardened, that the gaps and breaches are as obvious now as they were then. Schoenberg's move into atonality and serialism has not produced a new, viable form of music, despite many followers and advocates. Music is as fragmented today as ever it was then.

Two tributes to the Viennese waltz: (*below*) *Carnival Greeting* (1898), by the Secessionist artist Koloman Moser; and (*bottom*) Otto Böhler's silhouette of Johann Strauss the Younger 'conducting the *Beautiful Blue Danube* in heaven.'

153

RICHARD WAGNER

ROBERT ANDERSON

Wagner spent his forty-second birthday in London, which had become an 'inferno' because of the Philharmonic Concerts he had to conduct, the 'band of vagabond Jews' who were the London critics, the chilling correctness of English society, and the fogs that meant spring never came. Three weeks later, on 11 June 1855, Queen Victoria heard his seventh concert, admired the *Tannhäuser* overture as 'quite overpowering, so grand, & in parts wild, striking and descriptive,' spoke to him, and then noted in her diary: 'He is short, very quiet, wears spectacles & has a very finely developed forehead, a hooked nose & projecting chin.' There was no doubt about the brow and chin. Behind the one had developed schemes no known definition of opera could contain; the other was obstinately, wilfully, heedlessly, splendidly and apparently hopelessly carving its way through the varied traditions of European music and the strong currents of contemporary thought.

But only to Victoria did he seem 'quiet.' Many were overwhelmed by his restless energy, interminable talking, bubbling humor, his compulsion towards excess. In the summer of 1869 the French writer Catulle Mendès visited him in Switzerland. Wagner roamed about the room, shifting chairs, losing snuff-box and spectacles, never still or seated, his black 'Meistersinger' cap looking like a bedraggled cock's comb, and the flow of talk relentless. What was the driving force behind the magnetic power and prodigious achievement? In his *Communication to my Friends* of 1851 Wagner speaks of the youngest Norn with her gift that might make each child a genius but is usually rejected: namely a mind that spurns contentment and must always seek to create the new. 'Perhaps,' says Wagner, 'she gave it to me;' hence his reckless plunging into art and life, those sure instructors, who yet taught him without system.

The essential fact in Wagner's career was the theater, that magic other world he had known since boyhood. In his youth it seemed as if the spoken drama, under the spell of Shakespeare, might claim him. Then Beethoven overwhelmed him, and Wagner needed the technique to surround his plays with music. Opera was the natural result. But Wagner knew from the first that he must write his own libretti and that he alone could adequately express at all levels the dramatic ideas he wanted to stage. Wagner did not advance at an equal pace as dramatist and

musician. Until *Lohengrin*, perhaps, the dramatist led. By *Tristan* the musician was in masterly control, and the two skills were complementary. Wagner's mature plans were mostly laid before his thirty-sixth birthday; he had thirty-five more years in which to fulfill them. After *Tannhäuser* (1845) over fifteen years passed before Wagner was actually to hear any of his new operas; and even by 1847 the subjects he had chosen expressed his personal loneliness. Hence a third career, as propagandist for theater plans and views on everything beneath the sun.

As Wagner explained: 'I am so hard to accommodate in this world that a thousand misunderstandings are likely to take place.' Since he considered the theater conditions in Dresden unbearable, he revolted and joined the barricades in 1849. Because the newly emancipated Jews seemed to have all the material power that impeded him, Wagner attacked them virulently and beyond reason. His evolving views on opera had to be explained at every step; but it was merely baffling to expound the basis of the future *Ring* when the public knew only *Lohengrin*. So misunderstandings and explanations multiplied, while Wagner's music miraculously matured at the calm center of the storm.

Working out his music required special conditions. The harsh world must be shut out by soft colors and rich fabrics festooned about the walls and windows of his study. For his last opera, *Parsifal*, he needed also a haze of perfumes and essences. A plot might be sketched on a mountain top, an article planned at a café table; but his music was a thing apart, to be conjured only when the scene was rightly set. His muse had luxurious tastes. Colossal debts were the result, and periodically he had to uproot himself and flee the fury of creditors. In his life's cause he suffered almost to martyrdom; nor did it lessen the sufferings to know many of them were self-induced; and it was small comfort to his friends, of whom he demanded unquestioning loyalty, that he was equally demanding of himself.

• Early years •

Richard Wagner was born on 22 May 1813 in Leipzig, with Napoleon's wars nearby. His father was probably Carl Friedrich Wagner,

police actuary and theater-lover, who died the following November. Wagner himself sometimes thought his true father was Ludwig Geyer, soon to join the family in August 1814 as stepfather. Geyer was a playwright, singer, actor and painter. His early death in September 1821 meant that Richard's somewhat chaotic upbringing was the responsibility of his eccentric mother, born Johanna Rosine Pätz. She was religious, and fearful that her whole large family might take to the theater. As the youngest boy, Richard was a lively child but sickly and avid for feminine sympathy.

His paternal Uncle Adolf greatly stimulated Richard's literary tastes, though as a scholar he preferred the study to the stage. At school, Richard started Greek and Latin and absorbed the world of myths and heroes. He translated some of the *Odyssey*, but throughout his life his wide reading depended mostly on the translations available. He spoke French well except when feeling too German to do so; he claimed to speak English only in the dialect of North Wales. The Shakespeare he ardently admired from boyhood was for practical purposes a German Shakespeare. A poem on the death of a schoolfellow was chosen for publication, and at thirteen he launched on a tragedy that was eventually burned because of his sisters' mirth. In 1828, having already read the *Tannhäuser* saga, he completed *Leubald und Adelaide*, a Shakespearean bloodbath whose heroine was named after Beethoven's song.

Leubald was a turning-point for the young Wagner. Under the inspiration of Beethoven's *Egmont* he now wanted incidental music too. He had struggled at the piano in order to play Weber's *Freischütz* overture, but knew nothing about composition. Sheer willpower and curiosity gave him the skill he needed. But it would be wrong to underestimate his musical training. At eighteen, when he was already *studiosus*

musicae at Leipzig University, deeply involved in the more colorful aspects of student life, and had already heard some of his orchestral music performed, he took a course in counterpoint under Theodor Weinlig. The course ended when Weinlig, one of Bach's successors at St Thomas's Church, declared he could teach him no more and would take no fee because of Wagner's outstanding progress.

Through Weinlig's influence Wagner's op.1 was published, a correct and energetic piano sonata of no great character. His Symphony in C was performed at the Gewandhaus in Leipzig when Wagner was nineteen; there were good reviews in the *Harmonicon* of London and by Heinrich Laube in Leipzig. Laube then gave him a political libretto for a Polish opera to be called *Kosciuszko*. But Wagner had clear plans of his own for a first opera, *Die Feen* (The Fairies), completed early in 1834. The medieval fairy world Wagner envisaged in this work has many pre-echoes of his maturity, and contrasts strongly with his next opera, *Das Liebesverbot* (The Ban on Love). This was based on Shakespeare's *Measure for Measure* and was written in reaction to German complexity. Wagner was temporarily entranced by the melodic directness of Bellini, and *Das Liebesverbot* is his tribute to a sensual life uninhibited by hypocrisy. Of *Die Feen* only extracts were performed in Wagner's lifetime; in Magdeburg the first and only performance of *Das Liebesverbot* was a fiasco. In later years Wagner despised *Das Liebesverbot*, except for the vivid orchestration and the Dresden Amen he was to use again in *Tannhäuser* and *Parsifal*.

Between 1833 and 1839 Wagner was a conductor in provincial towns, learning about opera the hardest and most effective way, and finding that he was incapable of living within his means. In 1836 he had married Minna Planer, an attractive actress of sympathetic nature, modest gifts and little education, whose only child Natalie, the illegitimate offspring of a Saxon officer, was always known as Minna's sister. Wagner's next operatic project was designed to extricate him from the German theatrical life he had come to despise and to place him triumphant in the Paris Opéra. *Rienzi* was conceived in the summer of 1837 when Minna had been unfaithful and his domestic and professional lives seemed equally drab. The five enormous acts of *Rienzi*, devoted to the heroic tale of the last Roman tribune, who had sprung from 'the marriage of an innkeeper and a washerwoman' (Gibbon's words), were inspired by the splendid effects of Spontini and the glittering successes of Auber, Halévy and Meyerbeer. The opera abounds in prayers, hymns, processions, martial clamor, situations of extreme despair and elation. Wagner encompasses them with a vigor that exhausts almost before it convinces. Yet the libretto is effective and Wagner shows easy mastery of a genre he had not previously attempted. Wagner would not admit *Rienzi* to the canon of his mature works; it remains a tribute to his lifelong pursuit of the impossible.

Wagner's flight from Riga, his last provincial

appointment, makes a classic escape story. It was the summer of 1839; his creditors ensured that he and his wife had no passport. They had to rush the frontier under cover of darkness after vigil in a smugglers' den, somehow eluding the Cossack guards. With their Newfoundland dog, Robber, there followed an eventful journey in a carriage that overturned, perhaps causing permanent injury to Minna; and a voyage from Pillau to London took three weeks instead of eight days because of mountainous seas. The echoing walls of a Norwegian fjord, where they fled for refuge, deeply impressed Wagner, as did Shakespeare's statue in Westminster Abbey and a debate on slavery in the House of Lords with a contribution from the Duke of Wellington. An introduction to Meyerbeer, the current potentate of Parisian opera who happened then to be in Boulogne, seemed a good omen for the success of *Rienzi*.

Meyerbeer was indeed impressed by what he saw of the work, the libretto plus most of Acts I and II. Letters of recommendation were readily given, but musical Paris was not so easily taken. Wagner was so poor that he needed instant recognition. As he himself wrote, poverty was a crime in Paris; since all Germans were poor, they were necessarily criminals. His name was pronounced Vagner to rhyme with *gagner*; but little was gained. Money came in from his brother-in-law Avenarius, from richer relatives in Germany, from a Leipzig merchant, from pawning and selling Minna's wardrobe, from Wagner's activities as critic and hack arranger. Yet before the completion of *Rienzi* in November 1840 he was probably for some weeks in a debtors' prison. It was a testing time for the marriage, with Minna coping admirably amid terrible privations, and a testing time also for Wagner, whose resource and vitality somehow kept his hopes alive. He grew a beard to symbolize withdrawal from the world.

Rienzi was not mounted at the Opéra, and the Théâtre de la Renaissance went bankrupt

Right: Title from an early nineteenth-century edition of Shakespeare's plays. Wagner always loved Shakespeare and wrote a verse tragedy, *Leubald*, which he described as a mixture of *Hamlet*, *King Lear*, *Macbeth* and *Richard III*. *Measure for Measure*, a play whose liberal sexual morality appealed to the Romantics, was the source for Wagner's second surviving opera, *Das Liebesverbot* (1836).

Right below: The style of French grand opera associated with Scribe and Meyerbeer was the dominant fashion of the 1830s. Their works, such as *Robert le Diable* (1831), seen here, are, typically, historical dramas with sensational plots and lavish scenic effects. Wagner clearly had this idiom in mind when he wrote *Rienzi*.

Bottom: Moritz von Schwind's drawing of the Wolf's Glen in Weber's *Der Freischütz* (1821). The work had a decisive effect on the development of German opera, especially in its exploitation of supernatural effects and its use of folklore. Wagner was infatuated with this music in his youth and maintained a lifelong affection for it.

after accepting *Das Liebesverbot*. Wagner wrote vaudeville music, songs he vainly hoped might be taken up for drawing-room performance; embarked on a treatise for the cornet, an instrument he did not understand; arranged for various combinations popular successes such as Donizetti's *La Favorita* or Halévy's *La Juive*; and practised journalism. Wagner's Paris writings, after the manner of E. T. A. Hoffmann and Heine, have a nice blend of irony and imagination, an ease of style he seldom recaptured. There are accounts of performances at the Opéra, where he could rarely afford to go, of such virtuosi as Liszt and the aging tenor, Rubini; short stories based on personal agonies in Paris, and a skillful telling of a supposed visit to Beethoven, in which the deaf composer expresses his own aims by means of Wagner's theories.

• Der fliegende Holländer •

Paris strengthened in Wagner a longing for Germany. Beethoven's Ninth Symphony at the Conservatoire under Habeneck had been a revelation and may have inspired the first version of his *Faust* overture. Weber's *Der Freischütz* at the Opéra, with recitatives by Berlioz and interpolated ballet based on the *Invitation to the Dance* made Wagner question the very basis of grand opera in Paris. His friends were German, and he immersed himself in German history. His studies resulted in the sketch for an opera to be called *Die Sarazenin* (The Saracen Woman). If completed, it would have further pursued the grand operatic path of *Rienzi*; but Wagner set it aside. Indeed before leaving Paris in April 1842, he was already acquainted with the legends that were to be combined for *Tannhäuser*, and with the Lohengrin epic.

Paris was also responsible for the working out of *Der fliegende Holländer* (The Flying Dutchman). This tale of the cursed sea-captain, fated to sail till crack of doom, may have interested Wagner even before his Riga days. Certainly he was influenced by a Heine story that based the salvation of the Dutchman on redemption by a woman. For Wagner the Dutchman had aspects of Odysseus and the Wandering Jew; moreover he came to symbolize the wretchedness of the composer's own wanderings and buffetings, his own remoteness from reality. Equally important to Wagner was the significance of Senta, the devoted heroine who unhesitatingly risks all for her obsession with the Dutchman. In Wagner's original drafts the heroine's name was Minna, and the scene the Scottish coast. But only in his second wife Cosima did

Above: Sketch for *Die Feen*, Wagner's first surviving opera, completed in 1834. It was the composer's intention to write in the fantastic tradition of Weber and Marschner, and the fairytale libretto was based on Gozzi's play *La Donna Serpente* (1762). The opera was not performed until 1888, five years after Wagner's death.

Right: The Court Theater at Dresden, built by Gottfried Semper in 1838-41. Wagner was Kapellmeister there before his flight from Dresden in 1849, when both he and Semper were charged with revolutionary activities. Semper was later to influence the designs for Wagner's own opera house at Bayreuth.

he at last find a partner dedicated to him, as her father Liszt remarked, with the selflessness of Senta. For profound psychological reasons, then, *Der fliegende Holländer* was not just an opera libretto: it was a passionate statement of a problem based on Wagner's own experience.

And the score, in spite of imperfections, with passages that look forward and others that look back, reflects this conviction. The ocean surges through the music, much of which develops from the sailors' exchanges heard by Wagner in the Norwegian fjord. Only the stark Dutchman theme stands apart, owing something, as Wagner's sketches suggest, to the first movement of

Beethoven's Ninth Symphony. The composition of *Der fliegende Holländer*, in July and August 1841, took just seven weeks; in this work Wagner felt he had been musician and poet equally. Gozzi, Shakespeare and E. Bulwer Lytton had provided the matter for Wagner's earlier operas; Wagner had now gone straight to a legend, compressed it, and made a libretto of somber power. Already, as at the Dutchman's first entry, Wagner had learnt how to rivet attention with music that went to the heart of the matter; his concern now was with the innermost sensibilities of his characters. The full score was completed on 19 November, exactly a year after *Rienzi*, which was already accepted for performance in Dresden. Through the good offices of Meyerbeer, *Der fliegende Holländer* was taken up in Berlin before Wagner left Paris, and the young composer, not yet twenty-nine, seemed on the road to possible success.

For the production of *Rienzi* at Dresden, Wagner had staunch allies. Ferdinand Heine, responsible for the costumes, had been a friend of his stepfather; the stage manager and chorus master, Wilhelm Fischer, was stimulated by the splendid opportunities Wagner had given him. More important still, the tenor Joseph Tichatschek was enamored of the name part, with its

flashing armor, horseback scenes and stirring rhetoric; and Wilhelmine Schröder-Devrient, who was the leading dramatic singer of her day, was ideal for the travesty role of Adriano, had long recognized Wagner's gifts and was pleased to encourage them. Success was assured for the première on 20 October 1842 when Wagner, behind the scenes, 'cried and laughed in one breath, embraced everybody he came across.' Only the length of the work was a problem: he was horrified by the timing even at the end of Act III; by curtain-down in Act V, how to cut *Rienzi* was a main worry.

His triumph meant that *Der fliegende Holländer* was also performed first at Dresden, on 2 January 1843. The dark nature of the work, with its interior monologues and Nordic coloring, caused bewilderment and made no such impression as *Rienzi* had done. At Dresden there had been deaths in the musical establishment and Wagner was an obvious choice for one of the vacancies. With grave doubts about the demands of an official appointment, Wagner accepted through consideration for Minna and the pleas of Weber's widow, who thought highly of her husband's young champion (*Euryanthe*, Weber's Romantic opera, had been Wagner's test piece for the job).

Above left: Scene from Act III of *Rienzi*, set in fourteenth-century Rome, from an early performance in which Henriette Kriete sang Adriano and Joseph Tichatschek Rienzi. Meyerbeer's support had helped make possible the première in Dresden on 20 October 1842.

Above: Tichatschek and Wilhelmine Schröder-Devrient in the première of *Tannhäuser* (Dresden, 19 October 1845). Despite a spectacular production, it did not share the success of *Rienzi*, in part because of an erratic performance by the overweight Schröder-Devrient. Wagner had probably first heard her in Leipzig in 1829 as Leonore in *Fidelio*, and he later gave her leading parts in three operas.

Richard Wagner
ehemal. Kapellmeister und politischer Flüchtling aus Dresden.

Die Nr. 140 der „Leipziger Zeitung" vom 20. Mai 1849 brachte folgenden Original-

Steckbrief.

Der unten etwas näher bezeichnete Königl. Capellmeister

Richard Wagner von hier
ist wegen wesentlicher Theilnahme an der in hiesiger Stadt stattgefundenen aufrührerischen Bewegung zur Untersuchung zu ziehen, zur Zeit aber nicht zu erlangen gewesen. Es werden daher alle Polizeibehörden auf denselben aufmerksam gemacht und ersucht, Wagnern im Betretungsfalle zu verhaften und davon uns schleunigst Nachricht zu ertheilen.

Dresden, den 16. Mai 1849.
Die Stadt-Polizei-Deputation.
von Oppell.

Wagner ist 37—38 Jahre alt, mittler Statur, hat braunes Haar und trägt eine Brille.

Top: Destruction of the old opera house in the May 1849 revolution in Dresden, when the King of Saxony suspended the constitution and dissolved Parliament.

Above: Portrait of Wagner with the text of the warrant for his arrest, describing him as 'a politically dangerous individual.'

• *Tannhäuser* and *Lohengrin* •

Wagner had made an initial prose sketch for *Tannhäuser* before *Rienzi* rehearsals began. If *Der fliegende Holländer* demonstrated the composer's skill in extracting the pith of a single legend, *Tannhäuser* showed him welding together separate legends. Venus, the ancient goddess of love, had taken refuge when Christianity came, so the tale went, in a German mountain called the Horselberg. The other story concerns the thirteenth-century court of the Landgrave of Thuringia, and a singing contest involving notable musicians of the day, among whom Tannhäuser owed his inspiration to the magician Klingsor (potent Wagnerian name). Wagner's sources were varied; the romantic ambivalence of his Tannhäuser, vacillating between delight in Venus's sensuality and the ennobling love of Elisabeth, is his own distillation. In the end it is not the Pope who saves Tannhäuser but the human devotion of Elisabeth, enriched to understanding through suffering.

Tannhäuser, Wagner thought, was 'German from top to toe;' and the work owed its meaning and originality to the advance in Wagner's own understanding of life. Yet *Tannhäuser* was always something of a problem to him and even at the end of his life he was debating further revision. The first performance on 19 October 1845 was no more than a *succès d'estime*, and Wagner was oppressed by the misunderstanding of his aims. Even after the first night he shortened the introduction to Act III. In the summer of 1847 he revised the end of the work, producing a third version twelve years later by lengthening the song of the shepherd boy. The bacchanale was revised for Paris in 1861, and for Vienna in 1872 the overture was spliced with it; this made a total of five versions. Despite Wagner's doubts, the splendor of *Tannhäuser*

always rested on the strength of its dramatic dialogues, on the dissolving of traditional operatic divisions, on the breaking down of set musical numbers, and on the searching Wagnerian drama in the narration of Tannhäuser's pilgrimage to Rome.

Wagner used his Dresden salary not only to furnish himself comfortably, but also to build up an imposing library reflecting his interests. Already he was familiar with the Tristan legend, and in the summer of 1845 he went for five weeks to Marienbad in company with Minna, his dog and his parrot. He immersed himself in Wolfram von Eschenbach, a medieval 'minstrel' Wagner had used as the hero's friend and foil in *Tannhäuser*; his studies were pursued near a 'brook in company with Titurel and Parcival,' two characters in the final opera. He perused also the anonymous Lohengrin epic and read about Hans Sachs and the rules of the Mastersingers in a history of German literature by Gervinus. Wagner was at Marienbad for relaxation, to take the waters and to obey doctor's orders about a respite from work. But by the end of the holiday he had completed a prose sketch not only for *Lohengrin* but for *Die Meistersinger von Nürnberg*, conceived as a pendant satyr-play (in the ancient Athenian manner) to the tragic *Tannhäuser* and set aside for almost twenty years till his humor should be ripened beyond the 'irony' he felt at the time.

The story of Lohengrin, the ideal knightly champion of the Grail, nourished by mysterious forces from a higher world and brought into conflict with clashing human wills, seemed to Wagner the essence of tragedy and a situation central to his own life. The drama was concentrated in the soul of Elsa. Her purity had conjured Lohengrin from Monsalvat, where the Holy Grail, Christ's cup of the Last Supper, was guarded. But as suspect for her brother Godfrey's disappearance she needed the security Lohengrin could never give. She became an easy victim of the pagan Ortrud and asked of Lohengrin the fatal question about his identity which spelled their permanent separation. It was the allegory of betrayed ideals that was to haunt Wagner for much of his creative life. Wagner as musician now had the mastery to create the Grail world, enshrined in the radiant arch of the prelude to Act I, and the tortuous schemings of Ortrud and Frederick at the start of Act II. Music for Wagner was a force of 'love'; it was his supreme achievement that he could convincingly encompass evil too.

Wagner composed Act III of *Lohengrin* first, Act II last. His steady maturing at the task is evident from the contrast between the simplicity of the bridal chorus and the magnificent music drama in the encounters between Frederick and Ortrud, and Ortrud and Elsa, that are the crux of Act II. For the rest of Wagner's life, *Lohengrin* was his most popular work. Indeed the ingredients for operatic success were all there: a frequent use of the chorus, which gave much of the texture a massive excitement to offset the ethereal music associated with the Grail; a quartet of solo parts finely characterized; and underpinning the whole an orchestral score of inexhaustible vitality and richness that brought a whole new range of sounds to the theater pit.

Lohengrin was completed in April 1848; Wagner did not hear a complete stage performance until May 1861. The reasons for this were complex. Wagner's position as court employee in the Dresden theater was becoming increasingly irksome. His ideals were at the mercy of officials who did not understand them; a constantly changing repertoire meant he rarely achieved the standards he was after; his schemes for reform were merely shelved; and his debts, swelled prodigiously by impractical plans for publishing his scores, were now a matter of public scandal. He was allowed on generous terms a loan from the theater pension fund, on whose behalf in 1846 he had directed an epoch-making performance of Beethoven's Ninth Symphony. When during February 1848 revolution broke out in Paris (Wagner was conducting Flotow's *Martha* when he heard the news), he was himself ready for drastic measures.

It was mainly his love of the theater that made a revolutionary of Wagner. To reform the theater and turn it into an agency, as Carlyle would have it, 'for refining the hearts and minds of men,' demanded the overthrow of present social and political conditions. But the Dresden monarchy was to be spared. Indeed the king must speak out, declare Saxony a free state, and become the first republican. These were some of the thoughts behind a speech of Wagner's in June 1848 in which he castigated court officials, undermined his own position, and made the postponement of a *Lohengrin* staging inevitable. The rest of Wagner's time in Dresden was concerned with hammering his ideas into artistic form. He oscillated between history and myth, and his first subject was the Holy Roman Emperor Frederick I: known as 'Barbarossa' (Redbeard), he was supposed to sit sleeping inside a mountain until he should be summoned forth again by the needs of his people. This was to be a spoken play in five acts, of which only the first two were fully sketched.

• Politics and theories •

The 'Barbarossa' subject was detailed and intricate, but Wagner came to realize that his genius lay more with the general than with the particular. A Dresden colleague, Eduard Devrient, put it unkindly: 'Wagner was too much given to fantastic abstractions to possess any real historical sense.' Wagner turned the 'abstractions' to his own ends in his next subject, the 'true man' Siegfried. Now he was in the domain of myth, deep in the study of religion and saga, which he saw as 'products of the people's insight into the nature of things and men.' A hero such as Siegfried showed the spirit of the people expressing its essence to itself. Wagner theorized on the matter in *Die Wibelungen*, a fanciful treatise which precisely expressed Devrient's view of him. But he followed it with a complete prose sketch of the material for his mightiest work, *Der Ring des Nibelungen* (The Ring of the Nibelung), and by the end of the year he gave a reading of *Siegfrieds Tod* (The Death of Siegfried), essentially the future *Götterdämmerung* (Twilight of the Gods). Already the theme was knocked and shaped into the lean alliterative verse that was to give such resonance to the completed *Ring*.

Though convinced that only in 1848, a time he called the springtime of the people and recognized as the true foundation of German political unity, could he have conceived the *Ring*, Wagner was not yet ready seriously to embark on the project. The cancellation of *Lohengrin* at the end of 1848 emphasized his isolation as an artist and effectively severed his links with Dresden. At the outset of 1849, his restless mind reverted to history, but of a special sort. He immersed himself in the gospels, and the result was another five-act scenario entitled *Jesus von Nazareth*. Wagner's interest was centered on the son of man rather than the son of God. His setting is a Judaea in which Barabbas organizes a revolt against the Romans, and Judas Iscariot hopes this may further his master's political aims. Wagner's Jesus brushes aside the house of David: through Adam he sprang direct from God; therefore all men were his brothers. Wagner later wondered whether to make the play into an opera for Paris.

At the beginning of May 1849 Dresden was ripe for revolution. The king revoked the constitution, dissolved the parliamentary chambers, called for Prussian armed assistance, and fled his capital. Karl Marx expressed satisfaction: at Dresden 'they found an able and cool-headed commander in the Russian refugee Mikhail Bakunin.' Wagner was both horrified and attracted by Bakunin: 'everything about him was

Above: Minna Planer. Wagner met Minna in 1834 and they were married two years later. An actress and the mother of an illegitimate child, she was sympathetic by nature, and Wagner relied on her support in times of hardship. However, she later proved ill-equipped to understand his artistic ambitions.

Left: Senta and Erik, with the Dutchman's portrait on the wall; costume designs by Franz Seitz for the production of *Der fliegende Holländer* that took place soon after Wagner's arrival in Munich in 1864.

Der fliegende Holländer.

Right: Page from the score of 'Träume,' one of the *Wesendonck Lieder*.

Below: Title-page of the poem for *Lohengrin*. Wagner was introduced to medieval German literature by the philosopher Lehrs on his first trip to Paris. He later used the anonymous epic *Lohengrin* as a basis for his opera, begun in Marienbad in 1845.

Bottom: Set for an early *Lohengrin* production.

colossal, and he was full of a primitive exuberance and strength.' Bakunin quickly saw that 'Wagner was just a dreamer.' Nonetheless, despite later attempts to play down his part in the Dresden uprising, Wagner seems to have been busy distributing seditious leaflets to the troops, keeping an eye on the barricades, acting as lookout on a church tower. When the situation became hopeless, he left Dresden in Bakunin's company, chattering impulsively about war and similar matters too confused for comprehension.

By a series of chances Bakunin was seized, condemned to death and later to life imprisonment; Wagner escaped to Weimar, imagining he need only lie low for six months to be pardoned, but quickly had to face reality in the form of a warrant for his arrest. Weimar was the musical stronghold of Franz Liszt – the greatest pianist of the day, and on the way to becoming a great composer. Friendship between the two men had gradually ripened; Liszt was at the time mounting *Tannhäuser*. Wagner attended a rehearsal before the warrant drove him out of Germany a few days after his thirty-sixth birthday. By a convenient fiction, Liszt provided funds from future receipts on *Lohengrin* performances and Wagner made for his first exile in Switzerland.

According to Wagner it was his integrity as an artist that made him 'an out-and-out revolutionary, a destroyer of the old by the creation of the new.' The first of his Swiss treatises, *Art and Revolution* (1849), pinpointed the necessity for revolt. In ancient Athens it had been the function of the theater to express in myth the consciousness of a whole people; this art could afford to be conservative. Rome had provided

only vicious spectacle in its amphitheaters, while Christianity had altogether rejected this world to emphasize heaven and hell. Industrial society and commerce now dominated art, and the theater had become their toy. So revolution must overthrow society, and art might again be whole.

In *The Art Work of the Future* Wagner's revolution is less political. Again his starting point is Greek drama, where poetry, music and dance had worked together to produce supreme art. With much special pleading, Wagner argues that all three elements have since gone their separate ways, to the impoverishment of the drama. In isolation they have developed as far as they can and the future must evoke once more a fusion of the arts devoted to the highest ideals. A community of artists must call this fusion into being for an audience distinguished by its 'true, naked human nature.'

This did not imply that 'a romance of Goethe should be read while a Beethoven symphony was played in a picture gallery amid rows of statues.' To illustrate his meaning Wagner appended to *The Art Work of the Future* a poetic version of the legend of Wieland the Smith, a Nordic tale of aspiration, in which the crippled hero forges himself wings with which to rejoin his swan bride. Armed with plans for making Wieland into an opera, Wagner went back to Paris in February 1850 at the insistence of Minna and Liszt. He now had offers of financial support from Frau Julie Ritter, a Dresden admirer, and from the Taylor-Laussot family in Bordeaux. Frustrated by his lack of progress in Paris, Wagner accepted an invitation to Bordeaux. Jessie Laussot, the young wife of a French wine merchant, was pianist enough to be able to play Beethoven's 'Hammerklavier' Sonata, although Wagner was less enamored of her 'sharp, shrill

Above: Mathilde Wesendonck, painted by C. Dorner. Wagner met the silk merchant Otto Wesendonck and his wife in Zürich in 1852. Wagner and Minna were given a cottage on their estate, during which time Wagner fell passionately in love with Mathilde, a relationship which provided inspiration for *Tristan und Isolde*. Minna attempted to excuse Wagner's infatuation – 'I cannot help regretting the all too naïve innocence of this good man' – and squarely blamed the corrupting influence of Mathilde. Wagner's *Wesendonck Lieder*, settings of some of Mathilde's poems, served as sketches for *Tristan*, while the poems themselves contain veiled references to secret sympathies which they shared.

apology for the future direction of the *Ring* called *Opera and Drama*. Wagner's criticism of opera was essentially that the forms of music had interfered with dramatic truth. Modern plays were too much given to narrative and were using the same realistic material as the novel; this constituted a betrayal of drama's finest ideals, which could still be found in myth. And for this purpose German myth was as serviceable as Greek. Wagner argued that just as myth took over at the boundaries of history, or feeling at the boundaries of reason, so music must intervene when language could do no more. Music and words could most fruitfully interact if the words themselves emphasized their roots and their own music through alliteration. Wagner was now proud not so much of his achievements as of what he understood through them. His confused prose has been much criticized, but he had now reasoned himself into readiness for the *Ring*.

•The start of the *Ring* •

Siegfrieds Tod of 1848 had a basic structural problem: how, within one opera, could Wagner encompass the diverse worlds of gods and men? How could he sufficiently explain the significance of Siegfried's death for Wotan's rule of law and the stability of the gods' castle, Valhalla? Narrative and imparting of facts had always been difficult for opera; Wagner's main method had been flashback information cunningly placed within the dramatic structure. *Siegfrieds Tod* had lengthy explanation from the Norns at the beginning of the work; from a group of warrior maidens, the Valkyries, visiting Brünnhilde's rock; from the sinister Hagen's extended dream about his father, the dwarf Alberich; and from the autobiography of the dying Siegfried. Wagner knew this was too much of a good thing. It may have been as early as 1849 that he noted the theme of the Valkyries; in spite of spasmodic urges to start the music, Wagner held back.

A solution seemed to come in the spring of 1851. Liszt was urging the completion of *Siegfrieds Tod* for Weimar, but Wagner produced a counter-plan. He would write a work, *Der junge Siegfried*, to pave the way for *Siegfrieds Tod*. A legend about the boy too stupid to learn fear could be applied to the young Siegfried himself, who would need maximum fearlessness to slay the dragon Fafner, to capture the treasure of the Nibelung dwarf Alberich, and to release the Valkyrie Brünnhilde from within a wall of fire. Three weeks in June sufficed for the writing of the poem, which is closely similar to the present *Siegfried*. But Wagner had made one important shift of emphasis since 1848. *Siegfrieds Tod* ends with the hero triumphantly led to Valhalla by Brünnhilde; the guilt of the gods, who had compromised their own laws, was removed by his death. In *Der junge Siegfried* the earth goddess Erda foresees the end of the gods, and Wotan himself wills it. Wagner wished to make

voice.' But the relationship developed and they contemplated eloping to Greece or Turkey via Malta. Wagner offered Minna half of his income; Jessie's husband, Eugène, threatened to put a bullet through Wagner's head; her mother withdrew the offer of money.

The Laussot adventure put Wagner's marriage under intolerable pressure; it also released in him a strain of rancor that was never far below the surface, and he wrote his bitter essay *Jewishness in Music*. His pent-up loathing for the superficial brilliance of Meyerbeer and the comfortable urbanity of Mendelssohn spilled over into a malicious attack on Jewish influence on contemporary society. Wagner wondered 'whether the downfall of our culture can be arrested by a violent ejection of the destructive foreign element'; others were quick to think so. That summer, on 28 August 1850, Liszt conducted – in Wagner's enforced absence – the first performance of *Lohengrin*, at Weimar. Wagner himself began the composition of the Norns' scene in *Siegfrieds Tod* and continued with twenty lines of the following Siegfried-Brünnhilde duet, with the idea that the completed work should follow *Lohengrin* at Weimar. But he was uneasy about his sketches and temporarily abandoned them.

The last quarter of 1850 was devoted to more theorizing, a densely reasoned, densely worded

Right: Wagner left his marital problems behind for the solitude of the Palazzo Giustiniani in Venice, where he continued the composition of *Tristan*. There he discovered what he described in a letter as 'the profound art of silence in sound.'

Above: Franz Liszt. Wagner met Liszt twice on his first visit to Paris, while he was deeply in debt and Liszt was making a fortune as a piano virtuoso. This caused some resentment on Wagner's part, but a friendship developed, largely because of Liszt's generous championing of Wagner's music. Liszt settled into a position of influence in Weimar and managed to secure the première of *Lohengrin* there in 1850, which he himself conducted.

Right: A letter from Liszt to Wagner, promising the still-exiled composer a respectable performance of his *Lohengrin*. Unfortunately, however, the production was marred by inadequate facilities and a tiny orchestra of less than forty players. In the letter Liszt writes, 'Je trouve votre oeuvre sublime.'

a prompt start on *Der junge Siegfried*, but throughout the summer he hesitated.

The bold mountain scenery of Switzerland, a land of towering peaks and unfathomable lakes, was a delight to the composer. With a superb head for heights, he emerged buoyant from many a perilous expedition, inspired by the vast silences, musing on the somber haunts of ancient gods. And gradually, against this setting, the audacious scheme took shape. The birthplace of the *Ring*, a four-evening opera, was an establishment where Wagner had settled down for the autumn in abject misery at a course of cold baths which he was convinced would cure his nervous disorders. During the first three weeks of November he wrote prose sketches of the introductory *Rheingold* and *Die Walküre*, the second opera in the tetralogy. Halfway through the task, he outlined to a Dresden friend ideas about a possible performance in a specially erected theater on the banks of the Rhine. The piece was to be given once; the score would then, in company with most things at the end of the *Ring*, be consigned to the flames.

During 1852 Wagner conducted concerts and operas in Zürich, culminating in stage performances of *Der fliegende Holländer*, for which he thinned out the orchestration. Encouraged also by steady demand for *Tannhäuser*, he wrote a pamphlet about its proper mounting. But the year's main task was the *Ring* poem. *Die Walküre*, a text that seemed to sum up the sadness of the world, with its star-crossed twin lovers Siegmund and Sieglinde, the breaking of Wotan's will through the force of his own law, and Brünnhilde's loss of immortality, was complete by the early summer. At the beginning of November Wagner finished *Das Rheingold*, a stark statement of how power excludes love: the scene of elemental strife between the primordial nature spirits of the Rhine, the Nibelung dwarfs toiling cunningly for gain, the brawny giants duped to swell the power of the gods, and the gods themselves sealing their own fate through an unscrupulous search for increased might and security.

Early in 1853 Wagner had the poem lavishly printed; Liszt's reaction to the titanic scheme was to recommend the consolations of religion

and faith. In May Wagner was forty; there was a small festival in Zürich to mark the occasion, giving Wagner his first opportunity to conduct excerpts from *Lohengrin*. One of the guarantors was a rich silk merchant, Otto Wesendonck; Wagner laid the festival 'at the feet of *one* beautiful woman,' Wesendonck's wife. It was probably she who wrote the congratulatory poem; she also received from Wagner a polka and a sonata movement for piano. But it was not till 5 September that the music of the *Ring* was released in Wagner as he lay sick and half-sleeping at La Spezia on the Mediterranean: 'The rush and roar soon took musical shape within my brain as the chord of E flat.' And so it was to be, the *Rheingold* prelude at the depths of the river maintaining the chord long enough to indicate the scale of the work to follow.

Wagner's reluctance to start the *Ring* had been concerned mainly with problems of musical structure. Musical form had always depended on balancing the familiar and the new. The sonata style of instrumental music, for instance, with its basic ideas of exposition, development and recapitulation, had the ability to span large expanses of time. Opera had taken full advantage of this fact. The danger, as Wagner saw it, was that a rigid structural scheme could falsify dramatic truth, holding up the action to round off a musical shape, or unnaturally hastening the story in the patter of recitative. The conventions of opera demanded a credulity in the audience that affronted the composer. Could opera really be taken seriously? Wagner was determined that it should be.

To underpin the progress of his new drama, Wagner associated with each character, symbol or idea a typical theme or rhythm. With these materials, all of them highly charged and easily recognizable, the texture of his music achieved coherence. These *leitmotifs* made the thematic blueprint of his music. By their means Wagner could weave through voice and orchestra a symphonic pattern of infinite variety, or maintain over long stretches an almost improvisatory freedom. The motifs themselves become familiar, their combination and succession is varied and ever new as dictated by the action. Wagner had used *leitmotifs* earlier in his career, but never so systematically. In *Lohengrin* there are six main motifs, while *Das Rheingold* has approximately twenty-six, with several minor ones as well. In *Rheingold*, motifs are used some three hundred times, seldom abbreviated and with all the emphasis demanded by clarity of exposition. In *Götterdämmerung* their occurrences are legion, and they appear so topped and tailed it is only the familiarity of three evenings' listening that makes their meaning clear. Wagner the allusive symphonist is perfectly matched with the dramatist.

There were minor and major interruptions to the composition of the *Ring*. Before finally settling down, Wagner was in Paris to hear some late Beethoven quartets and dine with the three Liszt children, including the fifteen-year-old Cosima. At the end of February 1855, with the scoring of Act I of *Walküre* underway, Wagner had contracted to conduct eight concerts in London. There he found society grounded more in the Old Testament than in the New, with the Englishman needing only the right clothes on his back and the right book in his hand to imagine himself in personal communion with God. Wagner endured there like a Passover lamb. For a year after returning from England he had appalling skin trouble which demanded a cure in the summer of 1856. By the end of June 1857 composition had advanced to cover most of Act II of *Siegfried*. But at this point, with the hero stretched beneath a lime tree, Wagner 'bade him farewell with heartfelt tears.' Halfway through the following month Wagner repented of his decision, resumed work, and on 9 August completed Act II with a playful flourish of birdsong.

Wagner knew that in the *Ring* he was making unprecedented demands. The orchestration alone was more than daunting, with quadruple woodwind and a family of not-yet-invented 'Wagner tubas,' to say nothing of the need for eight horns and six harps. The staging, too, posed formidable problems, with its gradual mist-swirled transitions from the depths of the Rhine to a mountain pasture, down again to the sulphurous vaults of Nibelheim and back – let alone the rainbow bridge which was to materialize from the hammer-blow of the thundergod and support his colleagues to Valhalla. Such were the requirements of *Rheingold* alone. For the moment performance seemed out of the question. Other factors contributed to Wagner's discouragement over the *Ring*. Since September 1854 he had recognized in the philosopher Schopenhauer a seminal extension of his own thought. Schopenhauer marvelously anticipated Wotan's 'negation of the will to live;' and Wagner went on to remodel the end of the *Ring* poem yet again, couching Brünnhilde's final words in terms that yearned only for a Nordic nirvana.

• *Tristan und Isolde* •

As Wagner's revolutionary optimism turned gradually to a creative resignation, he became possessed by the idea of a Tristan opera. His feelings for Mathilde Wesendonck were deepening and largely reciprocated. With Minna as his wife, Mathilde became his muse. But Mathilde was happily married and content with her family; she was not the woman to countenance the double divorce envisaged by Wagner when feeling impetuous and unresigned. The emotional tangle, offering him no happy solution, encouraged Wagner to devise a monument to the complete love he had never known. He was back again in the medieval world of *Tannhäuser* and *Lohengrin*, fortified by his Dresden studies, and wondering whether the mortally wounded Tristan might not be visited by Parsifal in his search for the Grail. In December the plan for *Tristan und Isolde* in all its concentration had become clear; as an offering to Mathilde he jotted down ideas for the love duet in Act II. The scale of the work seemed right for a quick popular success.

At the end of April 1857 Wagner and Minna moved into 'Asyl,' a cottage provided by the Wesendoncks near a mansion they were building on the 'Green hill' outside Zürich. Emotional tension between the families increased. Wagner had made sketches for a Buddhist opera, *Die Sieger* (The Victors), faithful to the eastern implications of Schopenhauer's thought. He began to see his financial helplessness in a new light, thinking equably of Buddhist monks 'who beg for alms, not since they need them, but to confer on bestowers the merit of giving.' There had also been preliminary sketches for *Parsifal*, and Wagner's loyalty to the *Ring* was at risk. On his birthday he wrote to Hans von Bülow, a young friend and protégé since Dresden days: 'The desire to continue and to finish my Nibelungs is, today, nil;' and when he started the

Above: Cosima Liszt-von Bülow. The youngest of Liszt's daughters by the Countess d'Agoult, Cosima got to know Wagner through his friendship with her father and with her husband, the conductor Hans von Bülow. Despite an initial dislike of Wagner, she began an affair with him in 1864, and bore his child while still married to von Bülow, who showed an extraordinary tolerance.

Above: Model of the
Act II set from
Chaperon's designs for
Tannhäuser at the Paris
Opéra. Wagner had
arrived in Paris in 1859
to give a series of
concerts, and he later
supervised this
production, which was
ordered by Napoleon III
on the recommendation
of the wife of the
Austrian ambassador,
Princess Pauline
Metternich.

orchestral sketch of Act II of *Siegfried* on 18
June, he noted over the score '*Tristan* firmly
decided.' By then a request had come from the
Emperor of Brazil for an Italian opera to be
done in Rio de Janeiro; *Tristan* could now be
'Italo-Brazilian.'

'Asyl' was full of visitors during the summer
of 1857. Among the last were Hans and Cosima
von Bülow, newly married and on their honeymoon. Wagner climbed up a pear tree through
pleasure at their presence; Bülow, pianist and
conductor of distinction, derived only a 'sense
of blessing and refreshment' from the company
'of this glorious, unique man;' Cosima, child of
Liszt and the Countess Marie d'Agoult, was
initially repelled by Wagner's manners, incon-
siderateness and luxurious tastes. But when
selections from *Siegfried* were played to a company including Minna, Mathilde and Cosima,
it was Cosima who wept.

During the Bülows' stay, Wagner spent his
mornings on the *Tristan* poem, with its wealth
of emotion packed into dense short lines, till it
became a protracted hymn to love, death, and
the night. By the end of the year, Act I of *Tristan*, soaked in a new all-pervasive chromaticism
which threatened the whole tonal system of
western music, was ready for Mathilde's inspection; her birthday on 23 December had
been celebrated with a serenade performance
of 'Träume,' a poem of her own composition
which Wagner had set.

The Green hill was now a smouldering vol-
cano, with Minna and Mathilde at loggerheads. There was an eruption in April 1858
when Minna, already a victim of chronic heart
trouble, intercepted a letter from Wagner to
Mathilde enclosed with a pencil sketch for the
Tristan prelude. The letter was largely if rhap-
sodically concerned with Goethe's *Faust*. 'You
worry a black meaning out of everything,' he
complained to the jealous Minna, and she was
dispatched to Brestenberg for a cure. Wagner
later considered the whole affair to have been a
storm in a teacup; but the situation was such
that 'Asyl' had to be abandoned. Minna emit-
ted 'a low wail of lamentation' at the thought;
nevertheless, Wagner departed for Venice on
17 August. 'Asyl' was later offered to Brahms.

The composition sketch of Act II of *Tristan*
had been completed at the cottage, but it was
while surrounded by the decaying splendors of
Venice, an outlived city which seemed to Wagner
'objective, like a work of art,' that his *Tristan*
sufferings reached their peak. He was all but
prostrated by the music's intensity, as he explained to Mathilde: 'The towering fires of life
burned in me with such unutterable heat and
brilliance that they almost scorched and consumed me.' His particular achievement in Act II
was the subtle and gradual transition from the
coursing vitality of Tristan's entry to the close
of the love duet in 'the devoutest, the most con-
secrated desire of death.' Because Venice was

under Austrian rule at the time, the proscribed Wagner was subject to police surveillance. Extradition in February was avoided on health grounds, but in March he returned to Lucerne, where he felt the lakes and mountains had become healing necessities. Act III was completed on 6 August 1859 after much torment over Tristan's protracted delirium. He now felt that in comparison with *Tristan* his works known to the public were 'mere rough sketches.' The achievement of *Tristan* dumbfounded even its creator; he feared he had outstripped the limits of what was endurable on stage.

His gratitude to Mathilde was unbounded: for 'having written *Tristan* I thank you to my deepest soul to all eternity.' He owed almost as much to her husband, Otto, who bought publication rights in *Rheingold* and *Walküre* for 6000 francs apiece (within months Schott had also bought *Rheingold*, and Wagner kept the money from both sources). In the autumn of 1859 Wagner made for Paris, where Minna joined him for their last protracted spell together. He gave three concerts at the beginning of 1860, for which he dovetailed the *Tristan* prelude and Isolde's final 'Liebestod;' and with his enriched harmonic palette he provided a new ending to the overture of *Der fliegende Holländer*. A near-riot at the first orchestral rehearsal taught Wagner how far in *Tristan* he had exceeded the bounds of known music. A lunch for the players restored order. The concerts mustered support but dissipated Wagner's finances, and the *Tristan* score remained unintelligible even to Berlioz.

The success Wagner hoped for in Paris appeared certain when in March 1860 came an imperial order for *Tannhäuser* at the Opéra. Wagner was informed immediately that a ballet would be required in Act II (this was local practice and considered *de rigueur*); his reaction was to remodel the Venusberg music in Act I. For this scene he had envisaged 'a wild and yet seductive chaos of movements' carried to a delirious pitch of frenzy; but the music seemed inadequate. Now, with Isolde's transfiguration behind him, he was at last ready for the voluptuous splendor of Venus's kingdom. He hurled himself with delight into the most sensuous music he had yet written. It seemed almost an irrelevance that in the midst of it he was at last granted a partial amnesty for his share in the 1849 uprising and could take a brief holiday in Germany. More important was the typhus fever which laid him low in the autumn and interrupted rehearsals at the Opéra. On his recovery he was again asked about the ballet in Act II.

The main characteristics of the Paris Opéra, Wagner thought, were 'extreme frigidity and extraordinary accuracy' – not an encouraging mixture, perhaps; nor did it seem appropriate to advertise the new Venusberg scene as 'divertissement par M. Pétipa.' But no expense had been spared, and Bülow was most impressed with the spectacle: 'The mounting defies description – a thing of such marvellous beauty that it has to be seen to be believed.' Ten dogs and four horses appeared in the hunting scene.

Why, then, were the three performances a fiasco such as Paris had rarely witnessed? There was political dislike for the teutonic Princess Metternich who had urged *Tannhäuser* on Emperor Napoleon III; Wagner was considered so controversial as to cause paranoia among his opponents; the distinction between profane and holy love in the opera was rather lost on the Parisians; the wretched fumbling of Dietsch the conductor had lowered morale among the cast; and above all Wagner had enraged the young bloods of the Jockey Club by depriving them of an after-dinner ballet in Act II. It was in vain that the Tannhäuser threw his pilgrim hat at the audience; the opera was howled and hooted from the stage.

The *Tannhäuser* disaster did not unduly ruffle Wagner, whose main concern now was the performance of *Tristan*. Though a Paris benefactress considered *Tristan* 'quite plainly impossible,' it seemed as if the Duke of Baden might stage it at Karlsruhe. He had profound sympathy for Wagner as a man 'who had suffered so much for his patriotic and independent

Below: The Leap from the Rock (1853), by Julius Schnorr von Carolsfeld, father of Ludwig Schnorr, Wagner's first Tristan. Here, in a painting also inspired by medieval myth, the two lovers have been discovered by the huntsman and die in a suicide pact.

opinions,' and urged him to find soloists in Vienna. There, with great emotion, Wagner heard his first *Lohengrin*; and the performance so impressed him that Vienna seemed preferable to Karlsruhe for *Tristan*. There was unstinted goodwill from the conductor Esser, an enthusiastic Isolde in Luise Dustmann and a promising Tristan in Gottfried Ander. The work went into innumerable rehearsals; Ander had increasing vocal troubles and eventually died insane. After languishing in Vienna for two and a half years, *Tristan* was declared unperformable in March 1864. The only comfort for Wagner was some coaching he had given Ludwig and Malwina Schnorr, a husband and wife team, in the summer of 1862; to them *Tristan* seemed performable.

•*Die Meistersinger von Nürnberg* •

Wagner's defence against *Tannhäuser* and *Tristan* problems was to turn to the sketch he had made in 1845 of *Die Meistersinger von Nürnberg*. Again Paris had made him consciously German, though it was Italy, he said, and in particular Titian's *Assumption* that provided the inspiration. He had been invited to join the Wesendoncks in Venice and he found them in perfect harmony the month he celebrated his own silver wedding – though Minna now lived separately in Dresden. Thoughts for the overture to *Die Meistersinger* came to him on the return train journey, and in Vienna he began background research into the medieval guilds that had formed the backbone of sixteenth-century Nuremberg. Again he convinced himself of an imminent popular success; he also convinced the publisher Schott, and got an advance. Two prose drafts refined and amplified the 1845 scheme, and Wagner somehow mustered the poise and humor to prosecute the work while his outer circumstances steadily deteriorated. To write the poem he lodged in Paris on the banks of the Seine, and by the end of January 1862 it was complete. Mathilde exerted a benign influence on the new work too. 'One must oneself have been in paradise,' Wagner wrote to her, 'in order to find one's way at length to the heart of such a subject.' And she was warned to steel herself against the charms of Hans Sachs. The historical cobbler-poet, staunch citizen of Nuremberg and supporter of the Reformation, came increasingly to dominate *Die Meistersinger*. His knowledge of the Mastersingers' rules, his readiness to champion new musical ideas, his wise guidance of the heroine Eva towards a youthful marriage and his generous renunciation of his own claims on her love tapped some of the deepest springs in Wagner's own make-up. But where Wagner the man never quite rid himself of the bitterness his sufferings had induced, Wagner the artist turned all to a benevolent wisdom and ripe maturity that place *Die Meistersinger* on a pinnacle of operatic achievement. Under the kindly operation of its spell, Wagner's hymn to the achievement of 'holy German art' in its last pages sounds no political or hubristic overtones; he had already substantiated his own claim.

The contrast between the febrile yearnings of *Tristan* and the broad-day C major of *Die Meistersinger* is astounding. The German philosopher Nietzsche, who first got to know *Tristan* in 1861 at the age of seventeen, considered it the *ne plus ultra* of Wagner's art. Wagner was well aware that its tenuous, mysterious chromaticism could 'soak through the subtlest pores of sensation to the very marrow of life,' and that in *Tristan* he had thrust music to its outer frontiers. He then demonstrated in *Die Meistersinger* that the stuff of music and the very roots of song might still be found in a traditional diatonic scale. Much of *Die Meistersinger* was described by Wagner as 'Bach continued;' thus in his new work he paid graceful tribute to the Leipzig where he had been born and Bach had worked, to St Thomas's Church where he was confirmed and Bach had been organist, and to the shrewd instruction he had received from Cantor Weinlig. In the burgeoning counterpoint of *Die Meistersinger* Wagner draws together all the strands of his art and life in a splendid affirmation of German genius.

Progress on the work was slow, however. Schott's enthusiasm was cooled by Wagner's financial demands, and for some time the only source of money was conducting concerts. Wagner extracted for performance 'bleeding chunks' from the *Ring* and his music was heard in the concert halls of Vienna, Prague, Moscow and St Petersburg. Sometimes there was profit, more often loss; and any profit disappeared into the furnishings and cellar of a spacious house he took in the Viennese suburb of Penzing. In May 1863 Wagner was fifty. By then the prelude to *Die Meistersinger* had already been performed; the first scene of Act I was fully scored; the address by the goldsmith Pogner on the St John's Day singing contest had been designed as a tribute to Otto Wesendonck; the prelude to Act III had been worked out on the day Wagner wrote to thank a French countess for 1200 thalers; and the mighty climax in Act III of Sachs's hymn to the Reformation was already clear in Wagner's mind.

In February 1862 the composer had moved to Biebrich on the Rhine, hoping for steady work on *Die Meistersinger*. Minna came the same month, ready to arrange the apartment, but not to compromise when gifts and letters arrived from Mathilde. 'It was ten days of hell,' and the last attempt the Wagners made to live together. For most of the following year Wagner searched in some desperation for a woman to share his life. In June, for instance, he wrote to Bülow about the problem: 'I feel more and more strongly that I need some pleasant feminine creature about me. One cannot live on mere defiant solitude. Where can I get what I want without stealing?' On 29 November a solution was found. For two years Wagner had been aware that a special relationship existed between

Wagner's preface to the published *Ring* text seeking a princely backer for the tetralogy had sunk into his consciousness, and now it was his desire to find Wagner and assist. Ludwig's devotion was absolute: 'An earthly being cannot requite a divine spirit. But it can love, it can venerate; you are my first, my only love, and ever will be.' The ecstatic tone of the Ludwig–Wagner correspondence was sometimes a trial to the composer; it also caused his second wife some jealousy. But the days of Wagner's mendicancy were over. Ludwig was sorely tried by Wagner, and came to prefer letters to personal contact, yet did not waver in essential loyalty. He recognized that the composer needed exceptional treatment to give the world all that was in him; this was the tortured Ludwig's glory. He died in 1886, a presumed suicide, apparently insane; his cousin, the Empress of Austria, thought him more lonely than mad.

During the summer of 1864 Wagner basked in the sunshine of the King's warmth, and the Viennese debts melted. There was daily converse on Lake Starnberg, with Ludwig casting himself as feudal king of a medieval people, Wagner assisting as a friend with no appointment, no functions: 'He is the ideal fulfillment of my desires.' And yet there was something

himself and Cosima von Bülow; in Berlin they took a carriage drive together, thus contributing to Wagner's autobiography a sentence that was omitted in the early editions: 'With tears and sobs we sealed our confession to belong to each other alone.'

• Ludwig II of Bavaria •

Much happiness and much misery stemmed from this decision, but for the moment Wagner's finances were a more urgent matter. He was now in the hands of moneylenders exacting appalling interest rates and was faced with utter ruin. Flight from Vienna seemed inevitable at the beginning of 1864; he left on 23 March, giving instructions that his furniture should be disposed of. Otto Wesendonck refused point-blank to take him in, but he found refuge with another Swiss friend, reading in desperation the diaries of Frederick the Great, some George Sand and Walter Scott. He passed through Basle to Stuttgart, where he saw the Jewish baritone Angelo Neumann as Don Giovanni. In Wagner's case it was not an appointment with a statue; it was the eighteen-year old King Ludwig II of Bavaria who summoned him to solvency at ten o'clock in the morning on 3 May. The royal messenger had searched for him in Vienna; Wagner now considered his friends had been foolish in recommending flight.

Ludwig succeeded to the Bavarian throne on 10 March, tall, handsome, homosexual and a Wagnerian. Twice he had commanded special performances of *Lohengrin*; he had read the *Ring* poem on the mountain lake of Hohenschwangau; he had absorbed the prose works;

missing. Wagner too was lonely, and on 29 June Cosima von Bülow arrived with her two daughters. Hans came later, his health deteriorating as steadily as the love of Cosima and Wagner deepened. Liszt visited, admired what he heard of *Die Meistersinger*, disliked the domestic situation and hoped his daughter might yet lead a holy life. In September Wagner wrote to Hans:

Left: Théophile Gautier, poet and critic, who was the first of the French intellectuals to discover Wagner. His daughter Judith later had a short but intense affair with the composer.

RICHARD WAGNER
ET
TANNHAUSER
A PARIS
PAR
CHARLES BAUDELAIRE

PARIS
E. DENTU, ÉDITEUR
LIBRAIRE DE LA SOCIÉTÉ DES GENS DE LETTRES
PALAIS-ROYAL, 15 ET 17, GALERIE D'ORLÉANS
1861

Above: Title-page of the first edition of Baudelaire's essay *Richard Wagner et Tannhauser à Paris* (1861). *Tannhäuser* – which had a disastrous reception in Paris – turned Baudelaire into a dedicated Wagnerite, and he wrote to the composer: 'Throughout your work I found the solemnity of great sounds, of great aspects of nature, the solemnity of great human passions.'

Left: Albert Niemann as Tannhäuser. He was chosen by Wagner to sing the role in Paris (and later was the first Siegmund in *Die Walküre* at Bayreuth). Despite a childish temperament that added to the many problems of *Tannhäuser* at rehearsal, he was renowned for what the soprano Lilli Lehmann was to describe as 'intellect, vocal power and incomparable expression.'

'She needs freedom in the noblest sense of the word.' But the King formed the apex of another triangle and for too long discretion seemed the better part of honor. Wagner began to weave a web of deceit that was to lose him all support in the King's capital, Munich, and would greatly strain the royal friendship.

Wagner began to function again as a musician too. He wrote the *Huldigungsmarsch* for military band, a spacious march in homage to the King. He sketched, in Cosima's company, string quartet themes that found an eventual home in Act III of *Siegfried* and in the *Siegfried Idyll*. He responded to the royal command for completion of the *Ring* by making a fair copy of Act I Scene 2 of *Siegfried*. A new contract transferred to Ludwig rights in the tetralogy previously owned and paid for by Otto Wesendonck and Schott. *Der fliegende Holländer* was performed in Munich under Wagner; it was followed by *Tannhäuser* with Ludwig Schnorr in the name part; on 10 April 1865 Cosima gave birth to Wagner's first daughter, Isolde, and Bülow conducted the first orchestral rehearsal for a command *Tristan*. The *Tristan* première on 10 June was more than Wagner had dared to hope, with Ludwig Schnorr a hero of rare understanding and passionate conviction. Wagner had been moved to the very core of his being. Within three weeks of the last performance Schnorr died from typhus fever with the words: 'Farewell Siegfried. Console my Richard.'

For Ludwig's pleasure and instruction Wagner began his autobiography, *Mein Leben*, soon after the *Tristan* performances. Using the 'annals' he had kept since 1835, he dictated the bizarre and entertaining story to Cosima. His pen was also busy with political treatises in Munich. *What is German?* shows Wagner wrestling gamely with a definition of the undefinable. He castigated the German for his slavery to France: following in the wake of French operas,

a series of revolutions had been 'mounted' in Germany after the French manner. The German, naturally 'inventive, contemplative, artistic,' was now hemmed in between the Junker and the Jew, whose dominance of the present made it no more than a cosmopolitan synagogue. But human culture might be saved through German genius, which was like a principle of life. When Wagner talked politics, Ludwig tended to look at the ceiling and whistle; Nietzsche summed up the matter by roundly asserting that 'the importance which Wagner attaches to art is not German.'

'Now the whole country is looking to see how I shall use my enormous influence over the young King!' Wagner wrote to von Bülow. This was true enough. There was widespread resentment at Wagner's luxurious lifestyle and his dubious domestic arrangements. There exists a vivid description of Wagner in violet mood: with a curtain of violet velvet over the window, he sat in a violet velvet armchair, wearing a violet velvet robe; at the entry of a visitor he slightly raised his violet velvet cap. Cosima was caricatured as having a pass-key to the royal

Above: The Rhine-maidens guarding their gold: its possession determines the events depicted in the *Ring* cycle. This impression by Knut Ekwal of the opening scene of the first Bayreuth *Rheingold* was published in the Leipzig *Illustrirte Zeitung* in 1876.

Left: Heinrich and Teresa Vogl as Siegmund and Sieglinde in the first production of *Die Walküre*, the second opera of the *Ring* cycle, first performed in Munich in 1870. Both *Das Rheingold* and *Die Walküre* were given in Munich on the orders of Ludwig II, but Wagner refused to participate in their production.

treasury; she was pilloried as the 'carrier-pigeon' winging ceaselessly between the von Bülow and Wagner households; and Wagner's friends found access to him difficult because of the 'Delphic Oracle' who interpreted his wishes at second hand. Press attacks were answered by Bülow or Wagner with both insensitivity and lack of judgment.

Court sources may have fed the press with matter hostile to Wagner; but he was his own worst enemy. At the end of November 1865 he

'Walther von Stolzing,' the young knight of *Die Meistersinger*. In June Hans came too and Wagner could triumphantly announce: 'The whole Bülowium is with me.' That same month Bavaria declared war against Prussia and Ludwig was enmeshed in state affairs; on the day war broke out, a Munich paper published a letter penned by Wagner and signed by Ludwig to the effect that Cosima's good name had been scurrilously besmirched: in reality she was a paragon of virtue. By the end of the year Ludwig realized

Right: The house called Tribschen, on Lake Lucerne, was occupied by Wagner from April 1866 to April 1872, the rent being paid by Ludwig II. The channelling of taxpayers' money into subsidizing Wagner's music and lifestyle had led to government pressure on Ludwig to force the composer out of Munich. The King visited Wagner at Tribschen on the composer's fifty-third birthday.

Right: Wagner and Cosima in Vienna in 1872. Cosima had joined Wagner at Tribschen, although they were not married until 1870. A son, Siegfried, had been born to them the year before, and on Cosima's birthday, Christmas Day, 1870, Wagner surprised her with a performance of the *Siegfried Idyll*, played by a group of musicians outside her bedroom door.

made his position in Munich untenable by free use of the King's name in a newspaper article suggesting the removal of those closest to the royal person. This was political interference, and there was danger of a popular uprising against Wagner. Ludwig had no choice but to allow the cabinet secretary to dismiss him. Munich became detestable to Wagner mainly because of the Cosima problem; in February 1866 he wrote to Ludwig: 'My King, my King, that is a vile place: never, *never* will our work prosper there.' He had now to find a new home. He wandered in Switzerland and France, completed the full score of Act I of *Die Meistersinger*, heard that his wife Minna had died in Dresden on 25 January, and on 30 March saw for the first time the spacious villa on Lake Lucerne that was to house his second Swiss exile over the next six years.

The Tribschen period was productive, happy and fraught. The silken threads of his deceit were drawn tighter. Cosima and the three girls moved to Tribschen in May; for Wagner's birthday the King, having threatened abdication when Wagner left Munich, paid a secret visit as

Above: The building of the Festspielhaus at Bayreuth was the culmination of Wagner's life-long desire to escape the conditions of conventional opera houses. Constructed on a plot of land donated by the city and financed by private and public contributions, it was completed in 1876 and was then the largest timber-framed building in the world. Its revolutionary features include the design of the orchestra pit, sophisticated stage machinery and an auditorium that was a radical departure from the usual horseshoe design of opera-house interiors.

Right: Photographs of singers from the first Bayreuth *Ring* of 1876: Eugen Gura (*top left*) as Donner; Amalie Materna (*top right*) as Brünnhilde; Franz Betz (*bottom left*) as Wotan; and Karl Hill (*bottom right*) as Alberich. The young soprano Lilli Lehmann (who took three small parts) later wrote: 'There was a spiritual bond between all concerned. . . . All took delight in unprecedented efforts to surmount the musical and intellectual problems, as a tribute to the Master.'

that he had been duped; he was now wary of Wagner and never received Cosima again.

Bavaria was quickly defeated by Prussia. Wagner, aware of personal complications, headed the orchestral sketch of Act II of *Die Meistersinger*, 'still on the brink, as usual.' The radiant work proceeded steadily, but Wagner remained on the brink. Malwina Schnorr, his first Isolde, had taken up spiritualism and regained contact with her dead husband. The latter now issued alarming instructions: Malwina was to marry Wagner, while her medium was to marry King Ludwig. The main obstacle was Cosima; and Malwina wrote to Wagner: 'I impeach only the infernal spirit that deludes yours: God's chastisement on her guilty head.' The King was given all relevant information by Malwina. Composition of *Die Meistersinger* was finally completed in 1867, on St Richard's day; within a fortnight Cosima bore Wagner's second daughter. 'Je pardonne,' said von Bülow; 'il faut comprendre,' replied Cosima. In October Liszt came to remonstrate with Wagner about Cosima and stayed to be captivated by *Die Meistersinger*; Wagner suggested he should become a director of Catholic church music in Munich. On 24 October Wagner telegraphed to von Bülow that the full score was finished: 'This evening on the stroke of eight the last C was written. . . . I solicit your silent concelebrations. Sachs.' The première was conducted by von Bülow on Midsummer Night 1868, with Wagner and Ludwig in the royal box.

It was a journey to Italy in the autumn of 1868 that clarified Wagner's and Cosima's minds: whatever the cost, they must no longer be separated. 'What did fate want?' Wagner asked in his diary; and he explained all to the King. On 16 November Cosima finally moved into Tribschen. 'God bless the pair,' wrote the young composer Peter Cornelius, 'if they really love each other deeply, and if poor Wagner, in the evening of his life, has at last found the right woman.'

Apart from von Bülow, the most important disciple Wagner ever had was the philosopher Friedrich Nietzsche. As a twelve-year-old boy, Nietzsche had impiously presaged the future by expounding a 'trinity' made up of God the father, God the son and God the devil. Von

Bülow's piano arrangement of *Tristan* had converted him to Wagner, and the two met for the first time in November 1868 at Leipzig when Wagner read from *Mein Leben* about his student days. Nietzsche was appointed to a chair of classical philology in Basle and in May 1869 began a series of twenty-three visits to Tribschen. He was in the house when Wagner's only son, Siegfried, was born; he also overheard final stages in the composition of the opera *Siegfried*. There was laughter and high spirits as the older man and the younger entwined their ideas. Wagner entrusted proofs of *Mein Leben* to Nietzsche and thought of him as a possible tutor for his son. Nietzsche described in his book *The Birth of Tragedy out of the Spirit of Music* how the drama of ancient Greece

found its culmination in Wagner. There was much delight in Tribschen: 'That is the book I have longed for.'

Wagner had striven hard to rouse the German spirit; he sensed that in 1870 he had succeeded, for Prussia declared war against France on 19 July. The French were now 'the putrefaction of the Renaissance,' and Parisian friends visiting Tribschen had much jingoistic salt rubbed into their wounds. Cosima now secured her divorce from von Bülow and became Frau Wagner on 25 August, King Ludwig's birthday. The year 1870 was that of Beethoven's centenary, which Wagner celebrated with an essay linking the achievements of the great composer, Schopenhauer's theory of music as an ideal world independent of this world, and the

resurgence of the German people as proved by the French capitulation at Sedan. But the music's message was the same as that of Christianity: 'our kingdom is not of this world.' Christmas 1870 saw the first performance, on the staircase at Tribschen, of Wagner's affectionate tribute to his new wife and young son, the *Siegfried Idyll*.

• Bayreuth •

For the eventual production of the *Ring*, Ludwig wanted a monumental theater to be built in Munich. Designs were prepared by Gottfried Semper, an architect friend of Wagner's. But there was public hostility to the plan and Ludwig contented himself with ordering performances, in an existing theater, of *Das Rheingold* in 1869 and *Die Walküre* in 1870, despite Wagner's remonstrances. Ludwig's will was not to be gainsaid; nor was Wagner's. If the King insisted on desecrating the first two *Ring* operas, that was enough. Wagner refused to hand over the score of *Siegfried*, denying it was finished, and from March 1870 began preparing plans for a theater of his own. He was attracted to Bayreuth because of its eighteenth-century ducal theater, which had the deepest stage in Germany. A quick inspection showed its unsuitability, however, and that he must build himself. The King began constructing dream castles on the crags and lakes of Bavaria; Wagner formed an association of patrons to finance a festival theater and announced from his birthplace on 12 May 1871 that the *Ring* would be performed in summer 1873.

The choice of Bayreuth had many attractions: it was within Bavaria and might win King Ludwig's support; it was a small town free of artistic cliques and factions; the Wagner performances would be festival events demanding special pilgrimage; it was a town where cultural traditions for the moment slumbered.

Above: Letter from Wagner dated 23 April 1876 to a friend, referring to his correspondence with the Dresden conductor Ernst von Schuch, in which he had demanded compensation of 21,000 Gulden in respect of the early operas that he had sold to Dresden for small sums; in exchange for this he was willing to give them permission to perform *Tristan* and the *Ring*, but his demand was not acceded to.

173

Right: Klingsor's Magic Garden, painted by Max Brückner after the Act II set design by Paul von Joukovsky for the first *Parsifal* at Bayreuth in 1882. The inspiration for the set came from a visit made by Wagner and Joukovsky to a Moorish palace near Ravello, the Palazzo Rufalo. In the visitors' book there an entry on 26 May 1880 reads, 'Klingsor's Magic Garden is found!'

The municipal authorities supported Wagner's scheme from the first and made a gift of land for the theater above the town on the lower slopes of a wooded hill. In a downpour Wagner laid the foundation-stone on his fifty-ninth birthday, 22 May 1872. The King sent a congratulatory telegram, but would not attend because of Wagner's deception over *Siegfried*; Liszt refused because of the deception over Cosima. The day was crowned with performances of the *Kaisermarsch*, dedicated the previous year to the new German Emperor, Wilhelm I, and to Beethoven's Ninth Symphony. The choir and orchestra had assembled from all over Germany, fired by Wagner's vision, enthusiastic to take part in what seemed a historic event.

For the new theater Wagner took hints from the Riga house he had worked in as a young man and adapted ideas he had worked out for Ludwig's projected Munich theater. It had only to be a temporary structure, mainly of wood, with no embellishments, economical to erect; but for the inside Wagner's requirements were exacting: the rows of seats should be tiered and curved as in a Greek theater so that all would have an unimpeded view of the action; the dimensions of the huge stage behind a double proscenium arch should conjure a heroic reality; the orchestra and conductor must be invisible to the audience by being placed in a cavernous structure extending beneath the stage so as to blend the sound to maximum effect; the gaslights of the auditorium should be totally extinguished during performance. The result was to be a theater with superlative acoustics perfectly adapted to the sonorous weight of a Wagnerian orchestra, equipped with every effect that the daring composer might demand.

Wagner the revolutionary could here find full scope.

But how was the theater to come about? For three years Wagner struggled to build up a band of Bayreuth patrons and a network of Wagner societies. Money came in impressively but insufficiently. He conducted concerts for the cause, working tirelessly with both pen and baton to the detriment of his health. The gigantic framework slowly took shape, reaching its highest point in August 1873. To Cosima it seemed like some monstrous Assyrian building perched upon their mount of suffering. Wagner sometimes wished the wind would blow it down. At the beginning of 1874, with the festival indefinitely postponed, the situation appeared hopeless. Ludwig had been approached for help more than once, but his yearning for a Bavarian Versailles or castle of the Grail was plunging him into financial chaos. And yet by the end of January his sorely tried loyalty revived, and a generous subvention made Bayreuth possible. Wagner was properly if abstractly grateful: 'It is only you on whom the German spirit can look with hope.'

There were some preliminary rehearsals for the *Ring* in summer 1874. *Götterdämmerung*, begun in January 1870, was not yet fully scored, but a team of Rhinemaidens went through their scenes to Wagner's satisfaction. *Götterdämmerung* was completed on 21 November, a moment of achievement marred on Wagner's part by jealous anger when Cosima talked about a letter from Liszt instead of noticing that the last double bar had been ruled. Cosima's suffering was atonement for her guilt. Rehearsals the following summer displayed Wagner's superhuman powers of organization and the splendid qualities of the new theater. His energy and wit were irrepressible, he felt an artist among his fellows; Cosima was different – her reserve caused misunderstandings and friction. Hermann Levi, the Munich conductor, wrote to his father, the Chief Rabbi of Giessen: 'What will take place next year in Bayreuth will cause a radical turning-point in our artistic life.' A boost for Bayreuth finances came from Wagner's *Centennial March*, written early in 1876 to commemorate one hundred years of American independence.

Karl Marx wrote scornfully to Engels about 'the foolish festival of the town musician Wagner.' The three *Ring* performances were hardly a Marxian occasion. The Kaiser came, together with the Emperor of Brazil and Ludwig of Bavaria, heading a procession of crowns and coronets which the revolutionary in Wagner found both gratifying and incongruous, but Cosima was in her element. Nietzsche, already a sick man, produced his essay *Richard Wagner in Bayreuth*, a last flowering of admiration long past its peak; headaches caused him to leave the festival, and he drove Wagner away with aphorisms the more spiteful for their evident truth. The performances had not been perfect: the dragon's head from Wandsworth had gone to Beirut by mistake; Erda's entrance had had a pantomime effect; the Rhinemaidens' swimming area in *Götterdämmerung* had seemed more like a pond than a river. But the bounds of opera had been burst as never before; the Wagnerian orchestra had surged and thundered through scene after scene of cosmic significance; the cast had achieved prodigies of endurance and sensitive interpretation; the audience had battled for food and accommodation, departing from the town exhausted but impressed.

The immediate outcome for Wagner was despair at the festival's debt. It was galling that he owed more to the efforts of a Berlin countess than to the German spirit. The Kaiser was prodigal with decorations for the singers, but showed no interest in the deficit. Wagner discharged his own responsibility by a series of concerts at the Royal Albert Hall in London in May 1877, raising £700. More fruitful was a scheme of Angelo Neumann, baritone turned impresario, at Leipzig. Neumann had been bewitched by the *Ring* and laid plans for a traveling Wagner company. To this venture, starting with a Leipzig *Ring* in 1879, Wagner owed increased popularity and income. 'If anything on this earth could astonish me,' Wagner wrote to Neumann, 'it would be you.' Neumann happened to be Jewish.

• *Parsifal* •

Since 1874 Wagner had been installed in Wahnfried, a stately villa built to his own design backing on the grounds of the Bayreuth castle. The library and music room was decorated with heraldic shields of all the towns with Wagner societies; over the entrance was a large decorative panel with Wagnerian scenes featuring Cosima, their son Siegfried and Ludwig Schnorr. Liszt was a frequent visitor: billiards and whist became favorite pastimes; at the bottom of the garden was their future grave. But the Bayreuth climate drove the family repeatedly to Italy, where their final choice was Venice. Increasing heart trouble dogged Wagner; however, in January 1877 he gathered his thoughts for *Parsifal*; in February 1878 he launched the *Bayreuther Blätter*, a journal for Wahnfried's slant on German culture; and by the summer of 1880

Below: Painting by Lenbach of Wagner in reverie at Wahnfried, showing his vision of characters from his operas, including Siegfried, the Rhinemaidens, Lohengrin, Tannhäuser and Venus, and many more.

Opposite: Palazzo Vendramin, Venice, in which Wagner spent the last five months of his life. He had arrived in Venice in poor health, and his condition was aggravated by his decision to conduct a performance of his early Symphony in C to celebrate Cosima's birthday. He died on 13 February 1883, while working at his desk.

Right: Wagner at Wahnfried with family and friends around the time of *Parsifal* in 1882. From left to right they are: (back row) Blandine von Bülow, Cosima's daughter by her first husband; Heinrich von Stein, a Wagner disciple; Cosima and Wagner; the designer Joukovsky; (front row) Isolde and Daniela von Bülow; Eva and Siegfried Wagner. After Wagner's death, Siegfried helped his mother to run the festival at Bayreuth.

Mein Leben was complete as far as the royal rescue in 1864.

During the composition of *Parsifal* Wagner was much concerned with Buddhism, compassion for the animal kingdom, and a very personal brand of Christianity that made Jesus an Aryan: 'That the God of our Saviour should have been identified with the tribal god of Israel, is one of the most terrible confusions in all world history.' It was now proved beyond dispute 'that the idea underlying Christianity has its origin in India;' it also had distinct traces of Schopenhauer and his negation of the will to live. Wagner toyed with vegetarianism and was passionately against vivisection. He had long recognized compassion as the strongest feature of his moral being and the wellspring of his art. Its influence on *Parsifal* was paramount.

It was also at this time that Wagner met Count Gobineau, retired diplomat and author of a book on the inequality of races that much intrigued the composer. He now maintained that great characters would emerge more probably among the pure Germanic races than in the hybrid stocks of Britain and the old Roman dominions. What part did 'blood,' the quality of race, play in this? But what 'hope was there for Germany when a sumptuous synagogue had arisen opposite Hans Sachs's statue in Nuremberg? Might not the rottenness of contemporary civilization bear witness to corrupted blood in its supporters? Who could answer such questions? Certainly not Wagner, as he toiled at his final masterpiece.

With its origins in 1845, *Parsifal* had more than thirty years to mature in Wagner's mind before he wrote the text in early 1877. Around Good Friday 1857 he outlined the drama in Zürich, writing a year later to Mathilde Wesendonck that the 'compassion' he so prized would become clear 'some day from the third act of *Parsifal*;' but he fought shy of the project, feeling that the sufferings of Amfortas, the lapsed and tormented guardian of the Grail, would be more agonizing than even those of Tristan. In the summer of 1865 King Ludwig asked about *Parsifal*, and the first surviving prose sketch was drafted in four days. The essentials of the plot were clear to Wagner, whose mystic name for Ludwig had long been 'Parzival.' Further details were clarified early in 1877, there was a sketch for the Flower Maidens' music and the finished libretto was read to friends in London.

Because for Wagner the Church had lost its vitality, its symbols were more potent in the service of art. But the main characters of *Parsifal* drew not only on Christian tradition. Kundry, dedicated handmaid of the Grail, was also the ravishing seductress seeking to corrupt the knights; in former incarnations (owed to Wagner's Buddhist studies) she laughed at Christ on his *via dolorosa*, destroyed the Baptist as Herodias, and in Act III of *Parsifal* washes the hero's feet as the Mary Magdalene of Wagner's 1849 Jesus play. Amfortas was the fisher-king of pagan tradition, now also servant of the Grail, wounded when yielding to Kundry by the spear that pierced Christ's side, longing in his agony for death, but forced to live by the power of the chalice that

he must daily reveal to the assembled knights. Opera had not previously attempted such psychological complexity, probed the human mind so deeply or attempted such ambivalence.

Wagner knew *Parsifal* would be his last work. It used many of the ideas for his projected Buddhist opera, *Die Sieger*, and it summed up themes which had long occupied him. Parsifal, the pure fool, ignorant of his origins, of his surroundings, of what he sees, is the last of Wagner's characters for whom knowledge comes only through long and bitter experience. But the kiss of Kundry and his weary wanderings give him not just knowledge but the 'compassion' to understand the plight of Amfortas, the power to destroy the necromantic strength of Klingsor, based on a denial of love through castration, and the wisdom to understand how the world of Nature can but rejoice on Good Friday. Nietzsche scorned a Wagner apparently kneeling at the cross in old age.

Yet even Nietzsche was wonderstruck by the *Parsifal* prelude, those isolated blocks of sound

that state the materials of the drama but give no hint of its development. The composition and its scoring took almost five years. Wagner worked at *Parsifal* in ordered surroundings such as he had never enjoyed for a major composition. Whether in Bayreuth, Italy or Sicily, he was supported unstintingly by Cosima. And on 13 January 1882 the fine-grained score was completed in his neat, meticulous hand.

Parsifal was to be conducted by a Jew, Hermann Levi of Munich. Chorus and orchestra were lent by Ludwig, who did not attend the 1882 festival. The design for the hall of the Grail had been suggested by Siena Cathedral,

all his Nuremberg. Nature and the human heart are both his sphere. Each of Wagner's mature works has its characteristic atmosphere, its own harmonic world, its special orchestral color. No composer brooded longer over his works, and Wagner was aware that in richness of invention and inner logic they had no rivals. During the writing of the *Ring* the composer's technique steadily matured, so that the increasing complexity of the drama was matched by his ripening ability to express it. In Act III of *Die Meistersinger*, Hans Sachs disclaims any intention of playing such a role as King Mark, and *Tristan* is briefly quoted. For a moment two worlds are juxtaposed and Wagner's astonishing range is underlined.

Before starting the *Ring*, Wagner convinced himself that in the interests of clarity no two characters should sing simultaneously, the function of the chorus should be transferred to the orchestra, the set pieces of grand opera and indeed the primacy of music itself must be abandoned in the interests of dramatic truth, and

and that for Klingsor's realm by a luxuriant Italian garden. There were problems with the bells of Monsalvat, which were out of tune; also with the transition to the Grail castle in Act III, which was too short. But the sixteen performances were widely acclaimed and made a profit. In spite of exhaustion, Wagner conducted the final pages of the final performance flexibly and with magisterial breadth. A friend expressed doubt to Angelo Neumann whether a man who penned such ethereal sounds could be long for this world. In September Wagner and the family left for Venice; on 13 February 1883 he had his fatal heart attack.

'Damn Wagner, & his bellowings at Fate and Death,' wrote D. H. Lawrence many years later; *The Times* critic J. W. Davison felt that widespread listening to Wagner would necessitate extra hospitals for the deaf; and Hanslick in Vienna condemned Wagnerian art as recognizing only superlatives. But this was Wagner's essence. He knew the natural pace of his music, equating it with the 'andante' normal to every German; he knew the degree of dramatic concentration necessary to match that pace; repeatedly he found the musical phrase which could most economically define this dramatic moment. The result was an art both forceful and direct, of unprecedented power because stripped of all inessentials. He scored for orchestra more sonorously than anyone up to his time; he wrote for the voice with a virtuoso skill that was exacting yet supremely vocal. His models were those available to any composer of the day; his extraordinary development was due to a mental toughness and artistic integrity with few parallels.

There is death and fate in Wagner, but much besides. If all the world's sorrow seems contained in Wotan's farewell to Brünnhilde at the end of *Walküre*, and appalling doom hangs over the spinning of the Norns at the start of *Götterdämmerung*, equally valid are the carefree song of the Rhinemaidens at the outset of the *Ring* and the radiant vitality that penetrates

Above: Wagner's funeral cortège on its way from Bayreuth railway station to Wahnfried, 18 February 1883. The procession was accompanied by a regimental band playing Siegfried's funeral march from *Götterdämmerung*, and Wagner was finally laid to rest in a tomb in his own garden.

so on. Scarcely had his disciples agreed and his enemies violently disagreed when *Tristan und Isolde* proclaimed that the music was the drama, *Die Meistersinger* assembled the five main characters in a quintet, *Götterdämmerung* displayed the elemental power of a male chorus, and *Parsifal* showed that all the limitations imposed by Wagner's treatise, *Opera and Drama*, had been abandoned. It was Wagner's purpose to destroy grand opera as he knew it. Perhaps he succeeded, perhaps not. Certainly it was his achievement to question the fundamentals of his chosen art, to scrutinize its every component, to dismantle it step by step, and to build from first principles a characteristic structure that places him in the front rank of musical dramatists. If the result is not always distinguishable from grand opera, that is because Wagner the revolutionary came more to believe in regeneration. He failed to regenerate the German people; with opera he had notable success.

The Bayreuth Festspielhaus

Despite the many changes in musical styles and in orchestration, the technical requirements of an opera house did not radically change in the century following the opening in 1778 of La Scala, Milan, designed by Giuseppe Piermarini. However, Wagner's quite new way of composing for the voice and his much heavier orchestration required different acoustic properties in an opera house. From as early as the 1860s he had discussed the construction of a special festival theater – even a provisional wooden building – with Gottfried Semper, the architect of the Dresden opera house and an influential and revolutionary theorist. Yet it was not until 1872 that work finally started on a festival theater at Bayreuth in Bavaria, designed by the Leipzig architect Otto Brückwald (who incorporated a number of features from Semper's earlier models) and conforming with Wagner's requirements. Apart from anything else, Wagner was determined that the design of the interior should be governed solely by artistic

considerations, and that it should be the scene for musical rather than social performances; the notion, implicit in the traditional design, that each of the different sectors of society should have its own position in the architectural hierarchy of the opera house was rejected. Wagner had hoped to have his first festival in Bayreuth in 1873, but it was not until three years after that that all was ready. In 1876 the first complete *Ring* cycles (including the first performances of *Siegfried* and *Die Götterdämmerung*) were staged, followed in 1882 in the second festival by *Parsifal*, the opera Wagner wrote especially for Bayreuth.

Right: Auditorium of the Bayreuth Festspielhaus seen from the stage during a performance of *Das Rheingold*. All the seating is in one fan-shaped block, steeply raked, with no side boxes or galleries. A comparison (*far right*) of the ground plan of Bayreuth with that of La Scala, Milan, shows the full extent of the difference (the seating area is shown in violet, the orchestra in purple, the stage in beige, and the backstage areas in brown). Note the almost complete absence at Bayreuth of public rooms for any social purpose. Apart from a few modifications, the Festspielhaus remains very much as Wagner intended: a place of pilgrimage for those who want to hear the operas as the master wanted them to sound.

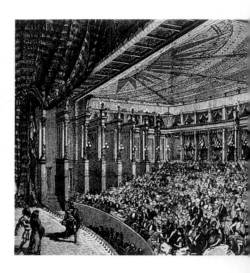

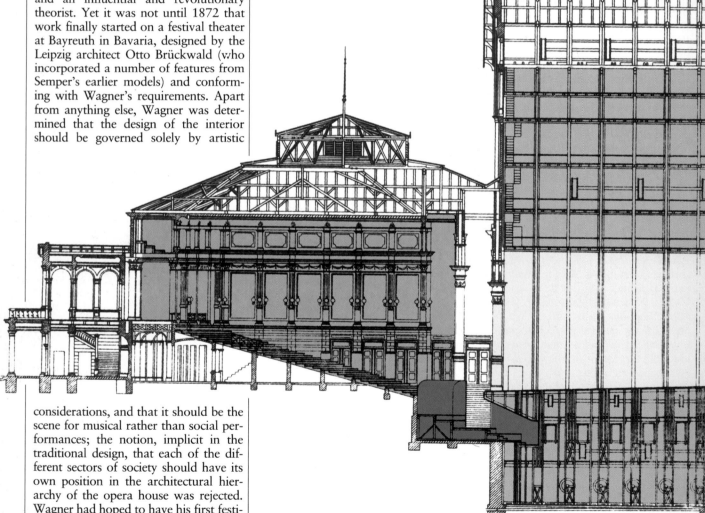

Cross-section of the Bayreuth opera house (*above*) with a comparable cross-section of La Scala, on a smaller scale (*far right*), and a view from the La Scala stage into the auditorium (*bottom right*). The position of the orchestra at Bayreuth is quite revolutionary: the pit is largely covered over (and entirely out of sight of the audience), and part of it extends beneath the stage. This produces a very different quality of sound, and, even with an orchestra of up to 130 pieces, a proper balance is maintained with the voices of the singers. At the same time, the reverberant acoustics of the auditorium ensure that the music

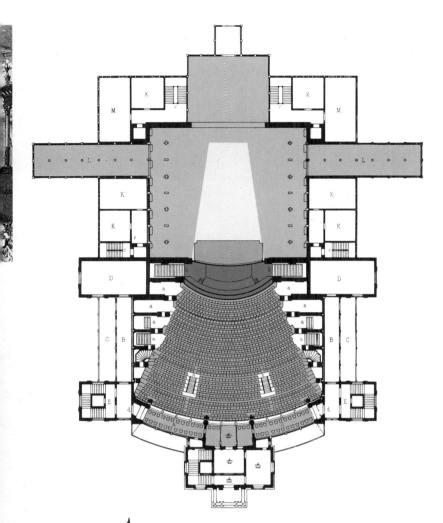

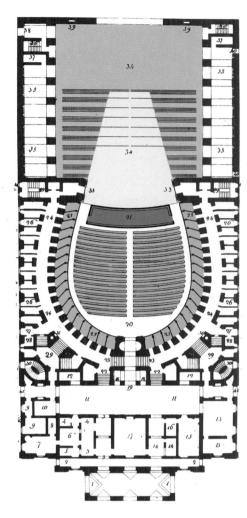

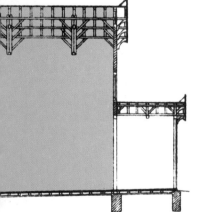

is loud enough in Wagner's great climaxes. A technical comparison of the acoustics of Bayreuth and La Scala shows how each is suited to the music designed to be heard in it. For traditional opera, clear definition both of the different voices and of the words sung is important, and this requires a relatively short reverberation time in the auditorium, though not so dry as to diminish the fullness of tone. The horseshoe-shaped theater with rings of boxes one above another (a plan that goes back at least to 1700) provides this, and the acoustics at La Scala are near ideal – giving a warm, clear, brilliant sound – in spite of its large size. (This is in part because the boxes have quite small openings, effectively reducing the acoustic space.) The box-like auditorium at Bayreuth with its high ceiling has a considerably longer reverberation time (around 1·6 seconds at mid-frequencies when fully occupied, as against around 1·2 seconds at La Scala), giving less definition to the singers' words but a fuller and more thoroughly blended tone.

179

Above: Wagner conducted a fund-raising concert in the baroque court theater at Bayreuth on the occasion of laying the foundation stone of his Festspielhaus on 22 May 1872. The composer had been encouraging the formation of Wagner Societies throughout Germany to help raise interest and funds, but the project was only rescued by a large contribution from his old patron, Ludwig II of Bavaria.

Above right: Gottfried Semper's model for a festival theater for Munich. Wagner's patron King Ludwig agreed in 1864 to erect a large stone theater to meet the composer's needs, and, on Wagner's recommendation, he asked Semper to produce models for this and for a temporary theater to be erected in the Glaspalast. Unfortunately, however. Wagner's unpopularity in

Munich led him to leave the city in 1865, and in his absence the Bavarian politicians dissuaded Ludwig from carrying out his plan. In 1868 the project was abandoned. Semper's theater, which anticipates many of the features of his second Dresden opera house (built following the destruction of the first by fire in 1869), also provided the basic design used by Brückwald at Bayreuth.

Above: Gottfried Semper (*left*) and Wagner. Semper (1803-79) had been a friend of the composer's since the time they both lived in Dresden and had both been driven into exile after taking part in the May uprising

in 1849. Semper, too, was a revolutionary at heart, although his radical architectural rationalism is more evident in his projects than in his completed buildings, where he had to work within contemporary stylistic norms.

Right: The Bayreuth Festspielhaus soon after its completion. Wagner was first attracted to Bayreuth in 1871 because the old Margrave's opera house had a large stage. He found the theater unsuitable but the town ideal for his plans. He persuaded the town council to give the land on which the theater was to be built, and he himself used a gift from King Ludwig to purchase a plot for his own house.

Above: The auditorium at Bayreuth. The resonance is helped by the materials: plaster on brick or wood lath for the walls, plaster on

wood for the ceiling, with the projecting elements that give the seating its fan shape of wood, and a wooden floor. When first planning a festival theater,

Wagner remembered that, as a young man, he had conducted in an 'old, paltry barn of a theater' at Riga which he had very much liked: the seats rose steeply in the

form of an amphi-theater, there was a sunken orchestra, and there was expert handling of lighting. All of these became conspicuous features at Bayreuth.

Right: Photograph of the three Rhine-maidens in the production of *Das Rheingold* that opened the first *Ring* cycle at Bayreuth and (*below*) the machinery used to provide the illusion. In the original production in Munich in 1869, one of the maidens became seasick at rehearsals, so that in the performance they sang from the wings while their places were taken on stage by ballet dancers. Wagner's stage directions – in particular for the *Ring* – required extensive use of special effects at Bayreuth, and his reliance on stage machinery provoked the ridicule of many critics. Eduard Hanslick, one of his most implacable opponents, wrote: 'In Rheingold the arts of decoration, of costume design and of machinery assume an unwarrantable and unprecedented importance. The eye is continually distracted and dazzled by magic scene changes, by supernatural tricks, flying machines, lighting effects and colored smoke. In no other opera has the composer so degraded himself to become the obliging attendant of the machinists and decorators.'

Above: Hans von Wolzogen (1848-1938), who fell under Wagner's spell while a philosophy student in Berlin and was summoned to Bayreuth in 1877 to edit the *Bayreuther Blätter*. He became Wagner's official publicist, writing guides to *leitmotifs* and the sound-symbolism of Wagner's texts and promoting his views on non-musical matters, such as the protection of animals and the status of the Jews in Germany.

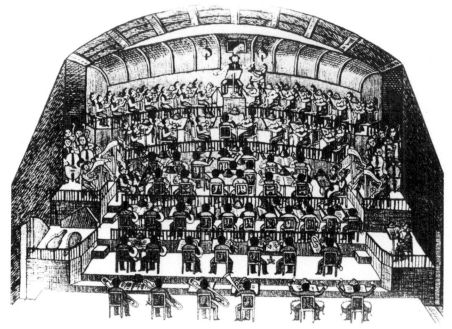

Above: A contemporary illustration of the orchestra in the 'mystical abyss' during rehearsals for *Parsifal*, as seen from the stage. Wagner is giving instructions through the hole in the back to the conductor Hermann Levi. The drawing shows clearly how the conductor and strings are beneath the solid wooden cover that reflects the sound back. *Parsifal* was written with the experience of the Bayreuth acoustics, and Wagner instructed that it should not be performed elsewhere, although this ban was not enforced.

181

JOHANNES BRAHMS

HEINZ BECKER

In October 1853 an article by Robert Schumann appeared in the *Neue Zeitschrift für Musik* in which he introduced to the public a new, unknown musician, 'over whose cradle Heroes and Graces had stood watch.' Schumann had written nothing for this periodical during the past ten years. Yet he now suddenly put pen to paper to herald with due pomp the advent of a young composer of whom nobody had heard until that moment: Johannes Brahms. The restrained, soberly North German subject of this hymn of praise reacted to it with more shock than gratitude: 'The public commendation you lavish upon me will raise expectations towards my achievements so extraordinarily high, that I am not certain how I can justify them to any extent.' In this letter of thanks to Schumann, Brahms touched on the heart of his problem and added with some foreboding: 'This will above all cause me to exercise great caution in choosing items for publication.'

It is known that Brahms destroyed a number of compositions at this time; Schumann's article had shaken his self-confidence rather than bolstered it. The effect on Brahms of meeting the Schumanns in 1853 went so deep that it can confidently be assumed that the enigmatic nature of this artist's character, which has never quite been successfully explained or understood, came into existence at this time.

Brahms was born on 7 May 1833 in Hamburg. His father was a rank and file member of an orchestra and had even earned his living as a street musician when he was young. His mother, who came from a wealthier, middle-class family, was seventeen years older than her husband. She was forty-four when Johannes was born, while his father was not quite twenty-seven, a difference in age which undoubtedly had both psychological and social effects on the boy's upbringing. The striking precociousness and remarkable seriousness of the young Brahms were probably the result of these family circumstances. His later close relationship with Clara Schumann, fourteen years his senior, also points to a mother complex foreshadowed by the situation of his parents. He began to show signs of a marked musical talent at an early age and it seemed perfectly natural to his father that the boy should follow in his footsteps. His only worry was that Johannes showed greater inclination for the less lucrative piano than for any of the more profitable orchestral instruments.

Brahms's first piano teacher was a minor musician named Cossel, in whose house he could also practice, for the Brahms family did not own a piano. By 1843, when he was only ten, the fair-haired boy earned lively applause at a public recital, proof of the progress he had already made. An American talent scout in search of child prodigies tried to book him for a tour in the United States, but his teacher succeeded in foiling this project. When Cossel became aware of his pupil's talent for composition he turned to his own teacher, the well-known composer Eduard Marxsen, who from then on directed the young man's education in musical theory. By now Brahms was taking every opportunity to earn money by playing in ale-houses, cheap places of entertainment and at private performances. This is always deplored as a regrettable misuse of the young musician's artistic talents, without recognizing that it was precisely such an education in elementary music that helped to develop in Brahms a sense of effective sound achieved by the simplest means. His craftsmanship was also sharpened by arranging – and occasionally composing – music for the small coffee-house band at the Alster-pavilion in Hamburg, where his father played.

Eduard Marxsen, at one time the pupil of Beethoven's friend Ignaz Xavier von Seyfried, not only awakened a love for Beethoven in Brahms; he enabled the young man to gain an authentic insight into his compositions. Brahms, however, did not confine himself to the works of Bach and Beethoven but also tackled virtuoso pieces, such as the works of Thalberg and Henri Herz. When Robert and Clara Schumann happened to spend a few harassed days, from 16 to 23 March 1850, in Hamburg in connection with a concert, Brahms seized this fleeting opportunity to have some of his compositions delivered to their hotel room, but with disappointing results: the package was returned unopened. Brahms had chosen a bad moment, but he had picked his target – Robert Schumann.

As for the technical side of composition, Brahms could not have found a better teacher than Marxsen, a solid craftsman with no claim to being a high flier. But Brahms needed no teachers on the creative side, although he himself failed to appreciate this fact. One must bear in mind that the young composer received no regular musical education apart from this private tuition by a modest Hamburg music teacher, to whom he ultimately owed all that he had learned. Obviously the conjunction between this pupil and his teacher was singularly fortunate. Brahms never ceased to value the teacher who had turned him into a professional and reliable pianist. When later in life, in a letter to Elisabeth von Herzogenberg (29 April 1879), he made fun of the Vienna Conservatory, where 'things seemed grisly,' and of the benefits of scholarships, in the award of which he had a say, remarking how 'shameful and irresponsible' it was that 'every year a couple of the talents involved should be so thoroughly and irretrievably ruined,' we can read between the lines unspoken gratitude for his own training, so wholly devoid of any academic approach. Brahms's high regard for his teacher's musical judgment was made plain when he sought out Marxsen's opinion while composing his *German Requiem*. And the dedication of the B flat major Piano Concerto was certainly more than mere well-mannered thanks from a pupil to his former teacher. It was indeed at a later stage, when he had established his standards, that Brahms came to appreciate fully the value of his early education.

The suppression of the Hungarian rising by the Austrians and Russians in 1848 led to the flight of nationalist rebels, many of whom passed through Hamburg on their way to North America, or even settled there. They brought their music with them and continued to produce a series of unaccountably popular successes. It was then that Brahms encountered the Hungarian *czárdás*. The unfamiliar world of irregular Magyar rhythms opened for the first time before the young composer, and he discovered the beauty of Slavonic triple time. The Hungarian violinist Eduard Hoffmann, who called himself Reményi and had been among the rebels, gave concerts in Hamburg in 1850 with Brahms in the audience as an enthusiastic listener. On his return from an American tour in 1852 he persuaded the young musician to join him in a series of concerts. It is not clear whether Reményi was in fact of gypsy origin, as has occasionally been claimed. He clearly was a virtuoso in technical terms but not a particularly polished player. He may indeed have deliberately resorted in his performances to the tzigane mannerisms of his homeland so as to make himself more interesting to his audience. Be that as it may, it is thanks to him that Brahms learnt more or less at first hand the rudiments of playing *alla zingarese*, developed his instinct for improvisation and became more practised in *rubato* work.

Reményi was the kind of easy-going musician who made friends without difficulty, felt at home in every sort of company and quickly established contacts in circles previously quite unknown to him. Brahms, the shy and gauche youth from the sober Hanseatic north of Germany, profited from his connection with this older, more experienced and more worldly musician. It was through him that at Hanover in 1855 Brahms met Joseph Joachim, who immediately recognized his exceptional new talent – the beginning of a lifelong musical friendship. Joachim, a native of Pressburg (now Bratislava), was only two years older than Brahms. He had just left his position as leader of the orchestra at Weimar when Brahms first met him and now held a similar appointment at the royal court of Hanover. Joachim told his mistress that his new friend had 'a quite exceptional talent for composition and a character that could only have developed its absolute purity in the remotest seclusion: limpid as a diamond, soft as snow' – yet another reference both to Brahms's unspoilt nature and to the way in which his native gift was maturing. Joachim directed Brahms's attention both to Franz Liszt in Weimar and to Robert Schumann. There was hardly any need for the latter suggestion because Brahms had long since nursed the ambition to make the acquaintance of the great romantic composer, a wish which became even more intense after he had personally communed with Liszt during six weeks at the Altenburg in Weimar. He came to realize there that his creative instinct pointed in a different direction, one diametrically opposed to that of the 'New Germans,' although he had not previously given this matter any serious thought.

The encounter with a major force of nature on the scale of Franz Liszt, however, helped to clear his mind. In later days he was to describe this extraordinary virtuoso as a swindler, but the appreciation of truth and genuineness requires some experience of falsity. It was in Weimar that Brahms came to terms with himself, and at the same time he now realized the limitations, both as an artist and as a man, of his violin-playing companion. Brahms took leave of Reményi and went on to discuss his musical future with Joachim. The latter became one of the people to whom he turned for advice, one of the most important and best trusted, a friendship that lasted until Brahms's death, despite many storms and estrangements.

Right: Brahms's birthplace in Hamburg – Schlütershof, Speckgang 24 – destroyed during the Second World War. The family lived on the first floor, on the left-hand side.

·The Schumanns·

It was Joachim who arranged his visit to the Schumanns in Düsseldorf, which Brahms with his natural diffidence had once again deferred. Only after a long walking tour along the Rhine did he make up his mind to call on them. The memorable meeting between Brahms and the great musical couple finally took place in Düsseldorf on 30 September 1853. Brahms brought with him his early C major and F sharp minor Piano Sonatas, as well as many other unidentified pieces, which he probably later destroyed.

The meeting with Schumann has been discussed and analyzed often and at length. The composer had founded the *Neue Zeitschrift für Musik* and was a recognized music critic. Yet he had written nothing for the last ten years. Brahms must have made an incredibly deep impression on him, which can only be fully appreciated if it is realized that Schumann, with something akin to exaltation, had for a long time been expecting the 'new Messiah' of music to appear. He asked the young stranger to play to him immediately, then very soon stopped him again and went to fetch his wife with the words: 'Now you will hear music such as you have never heard before.' This is known from Clara Schumann's diary.

What a statement! Indeed what an admission about the nature of his own output! In October 1853, barely a month later, that memorable article about Brahms appeared in Schumann's periodical under the title '*Neue Bahnen*' (New Roads) in which, for all intents and purposes, Schumann enthroned the young artist as the long-awaited Messiah of music. 'We bid him welcome as a doughty fighter.' There could be no doubt about it: this was at once the manifesto of an artistic creed and a fiery call to battle. Schumann was pointing out to the influential 'New German' party their new challenger armed from head to foot. Nothing else could have been intended by this paean of praise for a young musician, none of whose compositions had as yet been printed, whom nobody knew, of whom hardly anyone had even heard. Brahms came to Schumann as a learner expecting advice and help, guidance and artistic instruction. Instead he found he was being sent out to do battle in a war for which he felt utterly unqualified.

This article, often claimed as proof of Robert Schumann's gift of musical prophecy, was in fact no more than a horrifying indication of the pathetic extent to which he had lost his sense of proportion. Of course, Schumann did not fail to identify Brahms's artistic potential to the fullest extent and to describe it. The reference to the piano performance in which Brahms 'unveiled marvelous new areas' and 'turned the piano into an orchestra of alternately lamenting and loudly rejoicing voices' touches deeply on a fundamental tenet of Brahms's musical outlook. His works were conceived with the piano as a starting point but the orchestra as a fulfillment. The specific idiom of the piano, for the mastery of which Brahms has so often been singled out

Eduard Marxsen.

WIEN · K. NEUMANN · J. SCH
L. Rothenthurmstr. 32.

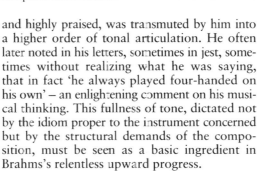

Three of the formative influences on the young Brahms: (*top*) Brahms, standing, and the Hungarian violinist Eduard Reményi, whom he had met in 1849 and made a concert tour with in 1853, ending with a visit to Liszt in Weimar; (*center*) Eduard Marxsen, Brahms's principal teacher in Hamburg; and (*below*) Joseph Joachim, Reményi's teacher, who was won over by Brahms's talent and personality when he heard them play, and who introduced the composer to Schumann.

and highly praised, was transmuted by him into a higher order of tonal articulation. He often later noted in his letters, sometimes in jest, sometimes without realizing what he was saying, that in fact 'he always played four-handed on his own' – an enlightening comment on his musical thinking. This fullness of tone, dictated not by the idiom proper to the instrument concerned but by the structural demands of the composition, must be seen as a basic ingredient in Brahms's relentless upward progress.

Right: Hamburg in Brahms's day. Though he settled in Vienna, the composer retained a deep affection for the great North German port and historic center of the Hanseatic League.

Right: A silverpoint drawing of Brahms, aged twenty, done in Düsseldorf by the French musician, writer and artist J. J. B. Laurens at the request of Robert Schumann. On 30 September 1853 Brahms first met Schumann there, and after playing his C major Sonata (op.1) he was at once received by Robert and Clara as an intimate member of the family.

Indeed, it now looked as though a fast and sharp rise in his prospects lay ahead. His first compositions were published: the three Piano Sonatas – C major, op.1 (1853), F sharp minor, op.2 (1853) and F minor, op.5 (1854) – and the Scherzo in E flat minor, op.4 (1854). The rest remained in manuscript. These works, all composed while he was still in Hamburg (though substantial parts of op.5 originated in Düsseldorf) were Brahms's only published piano sonatas. Thereafter, his piano music consisted entirely of variations, rhapsodies, fantasias, intermezzi, waltzes or – quite simply – 'piano pieces.' The title 'sonata' only recurs in the three Violin Sonatas, op.78 (1879), op.100 (1886) and op.108 (1888); the two Cello Sonatas, op.38 (1865) and op.99 (1886); and the two Clarinet Sonatas, op.120 nos. 1 and 2 (1894). It would appear from this that Brahms no longer took the sonata seriously as a solo form. His interest in the ballad, the rhapsody, the intermezzo – the fourth movement of op.5 is already an intermezzo – or the fantasia may be broadly described as a clear preference for a free formal conception, though by no means for a relinquishing of form. The writing of variations was becoming more important to Brahms than thematic treatment.

Tragedy in the Schumann family next threw Brahms off balance. Robert Schumann fell ill in February 1854 and was taken to a nursing home in Endenich. Clara was then expecting her eighth child, Felix, born on 11 June 1854. Brahms hurried to Düsseldorf to help the family, but Clara saw her husband only once again – just before he died on 29 July 1856. Driven to despair, the widow also got into financial difficulties and was forced at very short notice to prepare to earn her living by public concerts. Meanwhile, Brahms looked after her household and was placed in a somewhat precarious emotional situation by the proximity of this woman whom he admired – in fact, idolized. Brahms immersed himself in Schumann, while sifting through his library and his unpublished writings. At this period of oppressive tension, the young composer emotionally identified himself with Schumann's artistic ideas and intentions, and during the time in which he was very much wrapped up in Schumann's outlook, he produced the *Sixteen Variations in F sharp minor on a Theme of Schumann*, op.9, derived from the latter's *Bunte Blätter*, op.99 no.1, and inscribed by Brahms with an autograph dedication: 'Variations on a Theme by Him – Dedicated to Her,' a work full of enigmatic implications.

Brahms later described the time he spent close to Clara Schumann as his 'Werther period,' a hint at the difficult emotional strains he experienced in the company of this beautiful woman. It was also then that he made the first sketch for the C minor Piano Quartet, completed much later as op.60, which he explained obliquely for the benefit of his friend Hermann Deiters with the words: 'Now try to imagine a man who wants to shoot himself on the spot and for whom there is simply no other way out.' There was also a significant reference to 'the man in the blue coat and yellow waistcoat' – Werther once again – addressed to another friend, the physician Billroth, further evidence of the very close connection between this work and his personal life.

• Brahms in Hamburg •

Soon after Schumann's death Brahms strove to free himself from these personal connections. When Clara went to Berlin to join her mother in September 1857, Brahms returned by way of

Below: Gypsy Dancer by Anselm Feuerbach (1829-80), a close friend of Brahms. It reflects the composer's own delight in Hungarian gypsy music, stimulated by his early association with Reményi.

Detmold to Hamburg where he set up residence. During the last four months of both 1857 and 1858 he taught the piano to a princess at the court of Detmold and acted both as leader of the orchestra and conductor there. He used this opportunity to work with the court orchestra, comprising some forty-five players. Brahms was determined to improve his knowledge of the various instruments. Both the Serenades for Orchestra, in D major, op.11, and A major, op.16, were the result of experimental work with the Detmold Orchestra. The six-movement D major Serenade 'for large orchestra' was originally planned as a nonet, then written for a small orchestra and only transcribed for a large orchestra at its final stage. In the second Serenade Brahms tried out the effect of omitting the violins, which gives the work a markedly experimental character.

In spring 1858 the composer traveled to Berlin to see Clara Schumann again, and an invitation to Göttingen from Julius Otto Grimm led to his meeting Agathe von Siebold, the daughter of a university professor there. Did this encounter help Brahms to heal the scars of his days in Düsseldorf? Was it an attempt to escape old memories? When Clara noticed his growing intimacy with Agathe during a visit to friends in Göttingen she immediately left without a word of farewell. This had a devastating effect on Brahms, and though his friend Grimm tried to persuade him to honor his promise of marriage to Agathe, the composer abruptly broke off the engagement. Again and again throughout his life Brahms reacted in unpredictable ways. As he had never been taught to display his feelings, he was forced to fall back on his music. Agathe was hurt. Clara later reproached him for his conduct as though unaware of the part she had played in it. It took a long time before Agathe faded from Brahms's memory. He produced a lasting memorial to her by his dedication of the G major Sextet, op.36, in 1864. The young girl from Göttingen who had also inspired him to set several songs thus came to share in his own immortality.

Brahms now once more returned to Hamburg, where for a short while he conducted a women's choir, which at times numbered as many as forty voices. He wrote a few minor compositions for the choir and also made some arrangements of folksongs, always great favorites with him.

The origins of the Piano Concerto in D minor, op.15, which Brahms completed in 1858 in Hamburg after many revisions, go back to 1854. Its first performance on 22 January 1859 in Hanover with Brahms himself as the soloist won him some appreciation. The next performance, at Leipzig, where the young musician so warmly applauded by Schumann had been most eagerly awaited, turned into a major fiasco, which Brahms was surprisingly relaxed about, outwardly at least. On the other hand, the performance in Hamburg on 24 March 1860, at which the composer's father played the double bass and the rest of the family sat in fear and trembling in the stalls, proved a considerable

Right: Drawing of domestic music-making by Adolph von Menzel, a chamber music enthusiast and later friend of Brahms.

Above: Wilhelm Hensel's drawing of Clara Schumann in 1846.

success, not only personally but financially. Brahms was now justified in looking forward to a successful career in Hamburg.

In 1860, Brahms involved himself, for the first and last time in his life, in a cultural controversy. In March, together with his friends Joachim, Grimm and Bernhard Scholz, he signed a 'Manifesto' which publicly rejected the artistic tenets of the 'New Germans,' in other words Liszt and his circle. It was an honest but unwise step to take. He was already regarded as a 'comrade-in-arms' of Schumann. Now he was to be numbered among the opposition. He had not merely cold-shouldered the 'Party' but, worse still, rejected them all, even the most influential ones, and so had chosen to tread a lonely and thorny path. When he offered his Piano Concerto, the two Serenades, the *Burial Hymn* and the *Ave Maria* in the summer of 1860 to the publishing firm of Breitkopf & Härtel in Leipzig, the failure of the Piano Concerto had not been forgotten there, and all but the D major Serenade were rejected. Brahms's act of faith as an artist had not gone unnoticed.

The B flat major Sextet, op.18, the *Variations on a Theme of Handel*, op.24, the four-handed *Variations on a Theme of Schumann*, op.23, the early parts of the *Magelone* song-cycle and the *German Requiem*, which he had already planned in Düsseldorf, were all completed in Hamburg. Brahms somewhat warily renewed contact with Schumann's family in connection with the *Variations*, not so much with Clara as with her sixteen-year-old daughter Julie, to whom he dedicated the piece. When he later hinted that he intended to set up house in Vienna, neither the mother nor the daughter grasped that this – in conjunction with the dedication – was meant as a disguised proposal of marriage. Julie eventually married an Italian

count, and that same evening Brahms put his *Alto Rhapsody* into Clara's hands with the remark that this was his betrothal song. . . . The *Rhapsody* contains the solo 'Ach, wer heilet die Schmerzen' (Oh, who can cure the pain). It was only then that Clara perceived its inner meaning.

Brahms used his stay in Hamburg to establish his reputation as a musician and to make contacts. He had high hopes of succeeding the seventy-year-old Friedrich Wilhelm Grund as conductor of the Philharmonic Concerts in his home city, and he was not so unworldly as to ignore the tactics involved in securing such an appointment. He set out to recruit supporters, but to avoid being put forward as a 'local boy' he decided to leave Hamburg for a while. When Clara Schumann had visited him there in 1860 after she had given some concerts in Vienna, she had spoken warmly to him about that city's cultural awareness and the great love for music cherished by the Viennese. She even mentioned her idea of moving to Vienna and opening a school for aspiring pianists. It may have been these very hints which made the metropolis on the Danube so attractive to Brahms. He took part in the Rhine music festival at Cologne in June 1862 and spent a holiday together with Clara in Münster-am-Stein, where he worked on the composition of the Piano Quintet in F minor, op.34, already begun in Hamburg. Then he made up his mind to go to Vienna and establish his artistic reputation there. He left Hamburg on 8 September 1862 and reached the Austrian capital during the second half of that month. Initially, Brahms was only thinking of a short stay and did not yet realize that he had made the decision of a lifetime. He spent only eight months in Vienna on this occasion, but kept on returning until at last he settled there for good. Later, he would set out on long concert tours from Vienna, acting both as conductor and pianist and usually performing his own works, while he regularly spent the summer months – mostly devoted to composition – in his favorite parts of Austria, Switzerland and Germany. He also paid nine visits to Italy.

• Vienna •

In Vienna he at first met friends to whom he had been introduced by Clara or whom he knew from his Hamburg days, thus smoothing his way into the influential artistic circles in the city. His chamber music earned him an exceptionally warm welcome from Julius Epstein and Joseph Hellmesberger, who later helped to popularize many of his compositions. Hellmesberger first played the G minor Piano Quartet, op.25, at sight from the score and then threw his arms round the young musician with the words: 'Here is Beethoven's heir.' Brahms was invited to take part in his concert on 29 November 1862 and this was his debut as a pianist before a Viennese audience. Hellmesberger also performed the new quartet, the *alla zingarese* finale of which brought loud applause. Attempts have occasionally been made in the past to find affinities with Beethoven in the G minor Piano Quartet – probably under the influence of Hellmesberger's remark – in terms of its thematic line and its construction. This comparison is only meaningful in so far as some individual formal aspects are concerned. The same is true of the largely contemporary Piano Quartet in A major, op.26, which Brahms first performed at the second concert on 29 November 1862, and in which attempts have been made to find a direct line of descent from Schubert. Comparisons of this kind are inapplicable: Brahms had already so firmly established his own mode of expression in these works that he needed no support from tradition. The enthralling finale of op.25 alone shows that Brahms had long since discovered the world of Hungarian folk music through Reményi, and had derived more inspiration from it than later critics realized.

Brahms's acquaintance with Otto Dessoff, the director of the Vienna Philharmonic Concerts, was important in terms of his future development because he used both Dessoff's approach to rehearsing an orchestra and his conducting technique as a model. The *Variations on a Theme of Paganini*, op.35, one of the first compositions produced in his newly chosen home, was inspired by his meeting with Carl Tausig, a pupil of Liszt, whose stupendous technique fascinated Brahms. These *Variations*, which were deliberately subtitled 'Studies for the Pianoforte,' may be seen as a contribution to teaching advanced virtuoso work, as well as a personal training aid, in which Brahms incorporated a wide range of piano techniques. In fact, he himself used the variations as finger exercises, yet an attentive ear will occasionally detect his responding (II.4 and II.12) to the sentimental atmosphere of the Viennese coffee house.

Brahms spent the beginning of his time in Vienna in a state of suspense. Even though he made no mention of it, he was anxiously awaiting the decision on the conductor's post in Hamburg. This proved a forlorn hope. Friedrich Wilhelm Grund publicly handed over his baton at a concert on 6 March 1863 – at the end of a Haydn symphony – to Julius Stockhausen, an outstanding singer. This may not have been intended as a demonstrative gesture, but it was interpreted as such, and when Stockhausen performed at a charity concert on 6 May 1863 both as singer and conductor the decision had clearly gone in his favor. Stockhausen had shown less restraint in presenting himself to his future Hamburg audience at the crucial moment and Brahms's fine modest gesture was given no credit – in fact it went unnoticed. The choice made in Hamburg was certainly not bad, but possibly not the best.

When Brahms returned to Hamburg on 1 May to spend his thirtieth birthday with his family, he saw how matters stood and retired to Blankenese to work on his cantata *Rinaldo*, op.50, for tenor, male-voice choir and orchestra on a text by Goethe. It was here during that month

that an invitation reached him to take over the direction of the Vienna Singakademie in succession to Ferdinand Stegmayer, who had died on 6 May. The post may not have been important in itself, but the offer was a matter of satisfaction to Brahms at that time, and Hamburg's loss became Vienna's gain. The die had been cast. Brahms's first journey to Vienna in the early autumn of 1862 proved to have been the start of his firm commitment to the imperial city on the Danube, however often he may have been absent from it. It was also to be – though not as yet apparent – the beginning of Vienna's Second Classical period.

The reserved fair-haired young northerner found his place surprisingly quickly in the Viennese way of life, where the cafés provided a second home for the locals and an air of comfort and conviviality prevailed. Brahms, brought up in a petit bourgeois milieu, took to this environment as to the manner born. Many aspects of this extraordinary mixed world were already familiar to him from time spent with Reményi some years earlier. It bore the marks of fiery Italian melodies, while soft Slavonic melancholy mingled with proud, dashing Hungarian rhythms, and all this was subject to the sense of form imposed by German orderliness. Brahms found his new world here. He entered into it step by step, adopted its features one after the other and fitted them into his own somewhat detached approach. A fortunate – and singular – combination of circumstances thus led Brahms to discover his artistic identity.

Vienna opened up a new universe for him without obliterating the old. He immersed himself deeply in Viennese life, oblivious of the old north German austerity. It is known that in later years he spent entire days in the Prater pleasure garden – his world, the world of ordinary folk. He frequented establishments devoted to refreshment and entertainment, knew

Above: Title-page illustration to Tieck's *Schöne Magelone*, a tale of courtly love containing the sequence of romances set by Brahms as his op.33, his only true song-cycle.

Left: Ludwig Tieck (1773-1853), one of the leaders of the German Romantic movement, who returned to the tradition of the old folk tales.

every Viennese café and was an expert on where to eat cheaply and well. The gaudy traffic of the fairground stalls, the market criers, the saleswomen, the sausage-sellers, the hawkers and, of course, the popular musicians had a powerful attraction for him. He was as much at home in the 'Garden Café,' where the Ladies' Orchestra played, as in the 'Csárdá,' listening all night long to the tziganes. Brahms was never attracted to princely drawing-rooms: high society was not his milieu. When driven into contact with it professionally he knew how to cope with it, but he was equally adept at avoiding it.

First, however, personal matters intervened. His parents' marriage broke up in Hamburg. Brahms did what he could to save the situation, but the unnatural difference of age involved – his father was not yet sixty, his mother well over seventy – created an intractable state of affairs at this stage in their lives. His efforts came to nothing and separation was inevitable. Soon after, in February 1865, Brahms stood beside his mother's grave. This loss was all the more grievous for him because his parents had remained unreconciled. Only a few months later, his father married a widow eighteen years younger than himself, who brought her son with her. Brahms managed to establish a sound relationship with his stepmother. When his father died in 1872, he looked after her and her sickly child.

One of the earliest acquaintances Brahms made after arriving in Vienna in 1862 was the famous Eduard Hanslick, the future doyen of Viennese music criticism. Hanslick had acquired an international reputation with his essay 'Vom Musikalisch-Schönen' (On Beauty in Music), published in 1854, a head-on attack against the 'New German School' around Liszt, in which he formulated a philosophy opposed to that which underlay program music.

Above: Ludwig Knaus's painting of a Viennese *Werkelmann*, or barrel-organist, one of the most common street-musicians in old Vienna.

Right: The Vienna Stadtpark in 1870, showing, at the end of the lake, Hübner's Kursalon, where Eduard Strauss gave 'promenade concerts,' and where Brahms generally took coffee after lunch at 'Zum roten Igel.'

Eduard Hanslick had been teaching the history of music as a visiting professor at the university since 1861. At first he was reticent about Brahms and did not even attend his first concert. But he quickly recognized the unusual talents of the young pianist and in particular his grasp of an incredibly wide historical repertoire with an intimate knowledge of the works of Bach, Handel and the other old masters. Hanslick therefore engaged Brahms, eight years his junior, as musical demonstrator for his lectures in the hall of the old city council attended by the cream of Viennese intellectual society. And so, without planning it, Brahms found himself placed at the very heart of the local cultural élite. In this world, which was so congenial to him, he felt as relaxed as he seemed tense in more official surroundings.

Brahms initially made his name in Vienna as a pianist before he could establish himself as a composer. His work, caught between high spiritual insight and an inclination to favor the easy life, between rapid changes of scale in his range of expression and a resulting neglect of anything modish, earned him the reputation of a puritan. He never aimed at mere elegance of expression but, on the contrary, always tried to be sincere. He was never secretive, but equally never indiscriminately self-revealing. Even Clara Schumann, who knew Brahms better than anyone else had done, was to admit years later that ultimately he had always remained enigmatic as far as she was concerned. He was never predictable. Joachim believed that Brahms had an exceptionally highly developed sense of identity, the distinctive mark of a fully mature – and thus wholly self-sufficient – artistic nature. He had written in 1854 to Gisela von Arnim: 'He is not inclined to compromise his intellectual position in the slightest. Out of contempt for the audience and to suit his own comfort he will not play in public, although he already plays divinely: I have never heard the piano played in a way that satisfied me so completely (with the possible exception of Liszt) – so brightly and clearly, intellectually so cool and mindless of passion. His compositions too make such easy play of the most difficult forms, they are so rich, they drive away all worldly cares without an afterthought. I have never met such talent. He has already gone a long way beyond me.'

Brahms had returned to Vienna as director of the Singakademie. He was therefore expected to promote choral singing, by no means at its best in Vienna at that time. No mixed choral society existed until the mid-1850s, although there were many male-voice choirs, and it is noteworthy that the full version of Handel's *Messiah* was first performed there on 9 November 1862 (conducted by the highly regarded Johann Herbeck at the jubilee of the Gesellschaft der Musikfreunde). Brahms had become familiar with baroque music, partly through his own personal interest in it and partly as a result of his studies in Schumann's library, and he now set out to revive his choir through the old school of choral music. The members of the Singakademie greeted him as a savior, but it soon became obvious that he lacked the quality that is most essential to a conductor: leadership. Brahms was shy in company, awkward at first encounter and inclined only to open up in private. He was therefore hardly qualified to take on the role of a sort of musical lion-tamer, imposing his will on all those around him. He planned the revival of his choir through the performance of ancient choral music, but he also chose unknown works by Schumann and Beethoven for his programs. In order to save money, his second concert included only unaccompanied church music by such composers as Eccard, Schütz, Gabrieli and Rovetta – settings of texts concerned with the world as a vale of tears. The poet Mosenthal sardonically remarked: 'When Brahms for once feels really cheerful, he will sing "The grave is my delight." ' The interest of the members of the choir began to flag perceptibly. Brahms was well aware that this was his fault. He tried to lighten the program by including his own compositions, and ruefully admitted to Joachim: 'I would rather let the public turn against me as a composer than prostitute myself as a conductor and bore it with a long string of choral works.' But when this did not help either, he gave up his post, although he had been reappointed to it. Fate may have been kind to Brahms when it deprived him of the prominent position of conductor in Hamburg, but there was more to it than mere prestige. His livelihood was also involved, since he was dependent on what he could earn.

Although he lived very modestly, Brahms had not been able to subsist on his salary as conductor of the Singakademie and was dependent on additional earnings. Performing as a pianist, later a fairly lucrative activity, did not yield enough as yet. It was therefore very fortunate that Baron von Stockhausen should have asked him to supervise his younger daughter Elisabeth's piano lessons. Elisabeth was then fifteen, very gifted musically, keen to learn and as pretty as a picture. Brahms soon found himself deeply embroiled emotionally and gave up after only a few lessons on a transparent excuse. In 1868 Elisabeth married the young composer Heinrich von Herzogenberg, a pupil

Below: Portrait by Carl Jagemann of Brahms at around the time he first visited Vienna in 1862.

Bottom: Johann Strauss the Younger leading his orchestra at a court ball. Brahms came to know Strauss well, and celebrated his love of the waltz in several of his own compositions.

Above: Brahms's parents, Johann Jakob and Johanna, photographed in 1862. His father was seventeen years younger than his mother, and this age discrepancy led to a separation. The death of his mother in 1865 affected the composer deeply and directly inspired the slow movement of his op.40 Trio for horn, violin and piano.

Right: Four members of the Hamburg Women's Choir, for whom Brahms wrote arrangements and whom he directed as a young man. This photograph was found among his possessions at his death.

of Otto Dessoff. Herzogenberg had been a devotee of Wagner, but he changed his allegiance to Johann Sebastian Bach, principally on the strength of his young wife's highly sophisticated musical taste, and then to Brahms. Although his talent was moderate at best, Herzogenberg ultimately became professor of music at the Hochschule für Musik in Berlin. First, however, he was employed in Leipzig where – again in response to his wife's prompting – he organized a Brahms Week in 1874. As a result, Elisabeth and Brahms met again, and a deep friendship developed between them over the years that followed.

As the wife of a run-of-the-mill musician Elisabeth von Herzogenberg was caught in the difficult situation of enjoying the creative confidence of one of the most famous composers of her time, who remained in close touch with her until her early death in 1892. She inadvertently betrayed her own sober estimate of her husband's ability when she reported on the successful Brahms Week held in Leipzig in 1874 to her friend Bertha Faber, for whose children Brahms had written his famous Lullaby: 'We could do more often with the wing-beat of such a healthy strong genius here, where the half-measure, the decently unremarkable, plays such an important part.' The doubt in the young woman's heart and mind is wholly but involuntarily revealed in these words. She was only able to suppress her feelings because Brahms's intensely human approach smoothed over all differences: 'His fame radiated no aura of infallibility in the Richard Wagner manner,' Elisabeth wrote of him, 'but spread instead an atmosphere of wholesome and gentle warmth from a man who had fulfilled his aim and who, in the best sense, lived and let live.' Brahms's feeling for 'the pretty young thing' went beyond a purely musical interest: he kept a photograph of this 'slender figure of a woman in blue velvet and with golden hair' by him until he died.

• Brahms and Wagner •

Brahms had made the acquaintance of Richard Wagner in 1862. Wagner had arrived in Vienna more or less at the same time as Brahms to direct the rehearsals of *Tristan*, the first performance of which was scheduled for March 1863. This was the famous occasion on which seventy-seven rehearsals were needed to establish that the work could not be staged after all, and Wagner took his revenge in a blistering article about the inadequacy of Viennese operatic resources. Brahms was able to see the score of *Tristan* thanks to Tausig and Cornelius. He also met Wagner, who asked him to play his *Handel Variations* and was greatly impressed. Wagner not only sensed the technical perfection of thematic development in Brahms's style of composition but also the entirely different nature of his conceptual world. Wagner wrote privately to his wife Cosima in 1874: 'Brahms composes as Bach might have composed,' but he kept such approval to himself.

In public Wagner later went so far as to indulge in wholly unjustifiable personal abuse. He could not pillory Brahms for being a Jew, as in the case of Meyerbeer, and therefore picked on the fact that he was a bachelor. In his essay *Über das Dirigieren* (On Conducting) he lampooned Brahms as the 'art eunuch,' the 'guardian of musical chastity.' There are references to the 'essence of hypocrisy,' to 'that abominable sect' and quotations from 'the holy Saint John' whose *Liebeslieder-Walzer* Wagner described as the expression of 'a fervid hankering after "opera."' These public attacks should be seen in the context of Schumann's 'Declaration' and Brahms's manifesto against the 'music of the future.' When Brahms was awarded an honorary doctorate by Breslau (Wrocław) University in 1879 and was described in the diploma as first 'among the contemporary masters of serious music,' Wagner used the occasion for a brutal head-on attack against him in *Über Dichten und Komponieren* (On Writing and Composing). 'This prince of serious music,' so Wagner claimed, would appear 'today in the guise of a street-balladmonger, tomorrow in Handel's Hallelujah wig and some other time as a Jewish *czárdás* fiddler.'

Wagner's polemics invariably turned into personal attacks, while Brahms made the only possible counter-move by not replying. And yet one feels that underneath Wagner's unrestrained abuse there lurks the recognition not just of an equal but of someone greatly superior to him in moral terms. In other words, Brahms found

himself raised on high by his opponent without having in any way contributed to this result. In one respect Wagner was of course right: Brahms had always been inwardly concerned with opera, that most attractive and striking of all musical forms, though he had made no display of this interest. He avoided it all his life and was in no doubt as to why he had done so.

After 1868 Brahms curtailed his traveling as a pianist. His secret hope to return to Hamburg some day as conductor of the Philharmonic Concerts, in spite of all that had happened, had been once more frustrated in 1867. When the succession to Julius Stockhausen came up, he was again passed over, this time in favor of Julius von Bernut, a solid musician with no trace of inspiration, the epitome of the earnest middle-of-the-road performer. Brahms was already a celebrity by then, but they did not even consult him. He was at last offered the post in succession to Bernut in April 1894, three years before he died – but this was little more than an awkward attempt to make up to a man who was by now an honorary freeman of the Hanseatic city of Hamburg. He could not help but refuse the invitation, and nothing else had been expected of him.

Brahms was still extremely keen on a permanent post in 1867, as witness his interest in succeeding Ernst Rudorff at the Cologne Conservatory and his inquiries about the possibility of the position of Hofkapellmeister in Sondershausen when Max Bruch relinquished this in 1870. For Brahms a permanent post carried a decent middle-class image and, as he put it to Klaus Groth, it was a prerequisite for the foundation of a family. As long as he was alone, he could provide for himself by freelance work, and financial straits caused him no concern, but such uncertainties would become unbearable if there were to be a family to look after. In fact, this only applied to his earlier years. As his fame spread, he received so many invitations to take part in concerts that he could travel not merely around Germany, but shuttle among world cities such as Paris, London, St Petersburg, Rome, Milan, Brussels, New York and Boston. Later he would earn so much as to be able to live in comfort while charging a modest fee of 600 marks per concert. He could easily have asked for and obtained far larger sums had he wished to do so, but he found concert work a burden and was glad to avoid it if he could. Everything that might conceivably smack of public show was distasteful to him.

• The *German Requiem* •

The first stirrings of the *German Requiem* hark back to 1854 when Brahms was working on the scherzo of a proposed Symphony in D minor, which he later considered using in his op.15 Piano Concerto. He first abandoned it and then thought of including it in a funeral cantata together with the anthem 'For all flesh withereth as grass.' The idea of the Requiem may have

come to him in Hamburg – the selection of texts from the Bible appears on the back page of the first *Magelone* folio – and his mother's death brought him back to the idea. He completed the third movement up to the fugue in Karlsruhe in April 1866 and set about the organ fugue the following month at Winterthur in Switzerland. The fourth and sixth movements emerged on the Zürichberg during the summer of that year, while the last movement and the coda of the second were added during August in Baden-Baden. The fifth movement was composed later and only completed in Hamburg during May 1868. This sporadic and leisurely approach to the work shows that Brahms only gradually elaborated its general conception and did not work to a preconceived plan.

As a Protestant, Brahms departed in his Requiem from the Catholic concept of a mass for the dead. He was profoundly religious but not liturgically inclined, and this combination of deep faith with a non-denominational approach defined his attitude to divine providence. His rejection of Latin was also a rejection of ritual. The Requiem cannot be put to liturgical use. It was intended from the start as an occasion of solemnity and remembrance, not as an institutionalized service for the dead. 'All the same, a German text is capable of satisfying you just as much as the habitual Latin,' he suggested to Clara Schumann, who was inclined to be sceptical. Brahms always had the Bible by his side, knew his way around it and was well able to find the words he needed. The choice and sequence of the texts outlines his highly personal conception of worldly transience, death and resurrection. Two Beatitudes, 'Blessed are they that mourn' and 'Blessed are the dead,' act as a framework and integrate the composition.

In his very first movement Brahms prepared his audience for the somber moments that were to follow by omitting the violins, as in the A major Serenade, op.16, and doing without the soft sound of the clarinets in the wind section. The introduction of the various sections of the orchestra in succession is a dramatic device familiar to operatic composers. By these various means, Brahms achieved a crepuscular mourning effect that brings home the transience of life. In the second movement, 'For all flesh withereth as grass,' Brahms manages to extract from the dark unison of the vocal treatment and the set pattern of the muted drums the effect of a funeral march, despite the use of triple time. The relentless pounding of the drums imparts to this movement the acerbity of a medieval dance of death. Powerfully supported by the upward surge of the trombones and violins, the choir heralds the coming of consolation: 'But yet . . . .' A sense of awakening and dedication springs from the polyphony.

Brahms shaped the conclusion of the third movement, concerned with hope and justice, into a powerful choral fugue. The even-handed treatment of the voices in the choral polyphony symbolizes faith in the equality of all before the eternal throne. A powerful low D organ pedal-

Above: Eduard Hanslick (1825-1904) in 1862, a photograph he dedicated to Brahms. Hanslick and Brahms became firm friends; but by praising Brahms's art and attacking Wagner's, the celebrated Viennese critic drew Brahms into an area of controversy much against his will.

note solidly anchors this movement to the constancy of faith. Like many less knowledgeable listeners present at the first performance, Hanslick found the movement irritating: 'This pedal had a merciless length of 72 beats of common time (tempo moderato) and is sustained by double-basses (tuned down to D), horns and trombones, as well as a kettledrum ceaselessly beating (not rolling) sextuplets. The composer has failed to calculate correctly the physical effect of this prominent place in the score. First the droning pedal engulfs the interweaving of the voices to render it indistinguishable, then the relentless hammering of the drum on a single note puts the listener into a state of nervous agitation that makes any kind of aesthetic appreciation impossible. I have heard the effect of this pedal note compared with the disquieting sensation experienced when traveling through a very long tunnel.'

Brahms had in fact calculated this passage very carefully, but it went wrong at the first performance and led to chaos. Nowadays this famous pedal is regarded as a distinctive feature of the *German Requiem* as a whole. Brahms seldom ventured out as he did here into an experimental tonal world where every tradition was ignored. In its stark inflexibility the long pedal can be interpreted as an act of faith in justice.

The first performance of these three initial movements at a concert of the Gesellschaft der Musikfreunde on 1 December 1867 under the direction of Johann Herbeck met with an ambivalent response. Even Hanslick found it difficult to make full sense of a message of mourning in such an unaccustomed form, although he perceived the whole magnitude of the work's significance: 'As a superb musical celebration of the dead this composition is suited rather to the church than to a concert hall. The *German Requiem* is a work of exceptional significance and high craftsmanship. It strikes one as being amongst the choicest fruits that the style of

Beethoven's late works has yielded within the field of sacred music.' Hanslick may have felt that such music was out of place in the sober surroundings of the concert hall, yet neither does a church provide an appropriate setting for this composition which throbs with emotion, is rent apart by tremors and then, by contrast, shot through with shafts of light. The *German Requiem* is wholly permeated by dramatic inspiration, so that a theatrical approach colors both of its aspects, the musical offering and the liturgical restraint.

At the age of thirty-four, Brahms had now taken his place as an equal among classical composers with this work that exposed the maturity of his art in its full seriousness and beauty. The performance of the completed work on 10 April 1868 in Bremen Cathedral became an event of far-flung significance. After 1871 the Requiem was often performed throughout Germany to commemorate the casualties of war. It became a sort of accompaniment to occasions of national mourning and made Brahms into a patriotic composer in the public eye. The Requiem had been performed no fewer than eighty-four times by 1876, not only in Germany but in Basle, Zürich, Utrecht, St Petersburg, London and Amsterdam. Brahms had already displayed his patriotic fervor in 1861 with the five songs, op.41, known as *Patriotische Lieder*, and he further stressed his disposition by the *Triumphlied*, op.55, which he composed in 1870-1 to celebrate the victory at Sedan and dedicated to William I on his proclamation as Emperor. Brahms had even at one time toyed with the idea of enlisting as a volunteer. He left for Hamburg in April 1870; moved by enthusiasm provoked by the patriotic war, he could no longer bear to stay in Vienna. From Hamburg he wrote to Hermann Levi: '. . . You were right when you said I must go to Germany just now. I had to share in the jubilation, I could no longer stand it in Vienna . . . Long live Bismarck!' Had it not been

Below: Title-page of the first edition of the *German Requiem*; and (*below right*) autograph of the opening of the fifth movement ('Ihr habt nun Traurigkeit'), which was not, in fact, composed until after the first performance.

for his exceedingly patriotic attitude Brahms could not have composed the *Triumphlied*: its original title was 'Auf den Sieg der deutschen Waffen' (To the Victory of German Arms).

•The *Alto Rhapsody*•

In Germany, in the upsurge of victorious patriotism, the *Triumphlied* was acclaimed as an unparalleled work of art reflecting the proper attitude towards the fatherland, and also as a supreme choral creation. Later on, such views cooled down – a sure indication of its occasional character. In this piece, meticulously composed in a technical sense, Brahms harked back to Handel's 'cathedral style' and wove popular patriotic melodies of the period into the individual movements. A totally different spirit prevails in the Rhapsody for alto, male-voice choir and orchestra, op.53, based on a fragment from Goethe's *Harzreise* (Journey to the Harz Mountains), which Brahms composed in Baden-Baden in September 1869. Brahms first saw the text at the house of his friend Hermann Dieters, a musicologist and student of Beethoven's work, who also showed him an earlier setting of the poem by Johann Friedrich Reichardt. The mysterious youth who had turned his back on the world and become an enemy of mankind, as Goethe envisaged him, became in Brahms's conception the painter Anselm Feuerbach. Feuerbach introduced Brahms to the world of classical antiquity and, like Goethe's prototype, he inclined towards nihilism and contempt for the human race. The *Alto Rhapsody* is closer in conception to *Schicksalslied* (Song of Destiny), op.54, of 1871 than to the Requiem. It is also related to *Nänie* (Elegy), op.82, of 1881 and the *Gesang der Parzen* (Song of the Parcae), op.89, of 1882. In all these compositions Brahms attempted to convey in sound his conception of the classical heritage. He formulated the Rhapsody as a single-voice tragedy in which the dramatic talent that was still latent in the Requiem was now given an undisguised expression.

The work is constructed in three parts. The first consists of a rhapsodic recitative, then follows the aria setting the text 'Ach wer heilet die Schmerzen', and the work concludes with a chorus of reconciliation. By scoring the work without trumpets, trombones, tubas or drums, Brahms again succeeded in imposing his own unmistakable coloring on this composition. The unusual conjunction of a deep female voice with a men's choir has done nothing to popularize this work. And yet it belongs to that very effective part of Brahms's output which so clearly bears witness to his preoccupation with the score of *Tristan*. The agonizing dissonances of the opening and the protracted introduction are both idioms which had been developed by Wagner. Brahms may well have become aware of this himself, since in the final part, when the choir enters, these stylistic elements entirely vanish and give way to a more sober diatonic form of expression. It would be quite wrong to talk of

stylistic incongruity, but there can be no doubt that two worlds of expression are joined together here, two souls, as it were, in a single breast.

Brahms was doubtful – indeed disapproving – where Wagner's style was concerned, but that did not prevent him from studying the works of the master of Bayreuth very carefully. He once remarked that his own music sounded terribly celibate. This ironical statement precisely defines the crux of the difference between his own musical outlook and that of Wagner. Brahms sought to achieve a reverent, chaste form of expression. The plagal idiom at the end of the *Alto Rhapsody*, which is so reminiscent of the concluding Amen in church music, is in complete opposition to the mood at the beginning of the work and equally opposed to the spirit of Wagner. Despite all the ostentatious rhetoric with which the Rhapsody opens, the ecstatic thrusting sequences by which Wagner conveys Isolde's passionate surrender in her *Liebestod* would be quite unthinkable in terms of Brahms's musical perception.

The internationally celebrated prima donna Pauline Viardot-Garcia was engaged for the first performance of the *Alto Rhapsody*, which was given at Jena on 3 March 1870 by the Akademischer Gesangverein under the conductor Ernst Naumann. Viardot had created the role of Fides in Meyerbeer's *Le Prophète*, which the

Above: Interior of Bremen Cathedral, scene of the première of the *German Requiem* on Good Friday, 1868.

Above and right: Fritz Simrock, Brahms's publisher, in 1870; and the composer in 1869 with Julius Stockhausen, conductor of the Philharmonic Concerts in Hamburg in 1863-6, who sang in the première of the Requiem (1868) and joined Brahms on a concert tour at this time.

Above: Theodor Billroth, another member of Brahms's close circle of friends and associates. Billroth was a physician and surgeon and a keen amateur musician. Many of Brahms's chamber and piano works were first performed privately at his home in Vienna.

•The symphonies •

Easy creativity did not come to Brahms naturally. A cautious, carefully measured, slowly maturing method was more in accordance with his character. He delayed the composition of his First Symphony for an unusually long time even though this challenge had fascinated him for many years. 'You can have no conception how it feels to someone like myself always to hear the tread of a giant like this at one's back.' This statement to Hermann Levi accounts for much but not all. Brahms regarded Beethoven as no more and no less than the incarnation of the symphonic spirit. When he chose Beethoven's own key of C minor as that of his First Symphony he was not only carrying on where the latter had left off, but also challenging him. He was doing more than merely writing a first symphony, he was setting out to question tradition. Such an intention demanded careful preparation.

The earliest sketches go back to 1855 during Brahms's stay in Hamburg. The first movement was completed in 1862 (except for the slow introduction). He was not pleased with what he had done and put the symphony aside until the summer of 1874, twelve whole years later. Then with great caution he tried out his orchestration technique once again on a form which he knew well – in the *Haydn Variations*, op.56a. Only then did he finally resume work on the symphony after assessing the orchestral effects achieved by the Variations. Brahms had paid very careful attention to his friend Eduard Hanslick's remarks about the great fugue in the Requiem and his failure to calculate its effect correctly: what is written and what is heard are by no means the same thing. Brahms made considerable progress with the score during the summer months of 1874-6 and managed to complete it during the summer of 1876. Yet just before the first performance, on 4 November 1876 at Karlsruhe with Otto Dessoff as conductor, he felt impelled to shorten the inner movements, a significant indication of the importance he attributed to the outer ones. It was therefore a whole fifteen years before he ventured to put his conception of what a modern symphony should be, in the age of the symphonic poem, before the public. Then Brahms seemed to have overcome his doubts: he took only four months to produce his Second Symphony in D major, op.73. The themes had come to him while he walked near Pörtschach on the Wörthersee. Untypically, the composer seems for once to have been driven by a fast creative urge. The first performance on 30 December 1877 by the Vienna Philharmonic Orchestra under Hans Richter became a real triumph for Brahms. This, in so far as he was concerned, confirmed that the strict symphonic form inherited from the great classical masters still mattered, even in the age of pictorially illustrative music.

Brahms let nearly six years go by before he began to work on his Third Symphony, in F

composer had written specially for her, in Paris in 1849, and she had an exceptional vocal range and outstanding powers of dramatic expression. Later, Amalia Joachim also included the Rhapsody in her repertoire and performed it with great success in a number of cities.

The *Alto Rhapsody* made a deep impression on the composer's circle of friends. Clara Schumann said she had been 'awesomely moved' by the 'marvelous beauty' of the composition. Another friend, the Viennese physician Theodor Billroth, wrote to Brahms after the first performance in Vienna on 21 March 1871: 'You know of my philistine aesthetic doubts about this work for concert purposes; all these have now been put to rest by the deep inwardness of your musical power. . . .'

major, op.90. This was largely completed in Wiesbaden during the summer of 1883 and in it he again made use of older material. Brahms's biographer Max Kalbeck suggests that both the middle movements were derived from the incidental music to Goethe's *Faust* written at the instigation of Franz von Dingelstedt. As this production of *Faust* failed to materialize, Brahms presumably utilized elsewhere what he had prepared for it. It has also been suggested that the *Tragic Overture* derives from this project. All has not been definitely confirmed, but it certainly tallies with Brahms's habit of working available material in with newly created work. It is said that the final movement of the Third Symphony was inspired by the erection of the Niederwald monument near Bingen, high above the Rhine. A ten-meter-tall figure of Germania greeted from its pedestal all who sailed on the river.

In fact this final movement provoked quite different reactions in Joachim; as he told Brahms in a letter of 27 January 1884, it put him in mind of Hero and Leander. As to the composer, he remained silent on the subject. Nonetheless, it should be noted that Brahms even in his own close circle was credited with an illustrative, pictorial conception which would have been more suited to the modern ideas of program symphony composers.

Only a year later, during the summer of 1884, Brahms was already working in the holiday resort of Mürzzuschlag on the composition of his Fourth Symphony, in E minor, op.98. The allegro and andante were completed first, the other two movements, the scherzo – allegro giocoso – and the finale – a monumental passacaglia – followed the next year during the summer of 1885. Hans von Bülow, rehearsing the new work for its first performance on 25 October 1885 under Brahms's direction, was bowled over by the novelty of its symphonic statement. He wrote on 22 October to Hermann Wolff, his concert agent, tersely and to the point: 'Just back from rehearsal. No.4 gigantic, quite original, quite new, most individual. Breathes unparalleled energy from A to Z.'

Brahms wrote four powerful symphonies, yet he was not essentially a symphonic composer, and chamber music held an equal place in his creative output. The emphasis on the outer movements is characteristic of Brahms's cyclic arrangement in the symphonies, although he avoids cheerful conclusions. The last movement of the First Symphony is a grandiose anthem of vast dimensions; its slow introduction finally breaks through into the horns' theme of Nature, modeled by Brahms on an Alpine horn call – symbol of the joy of living and expression of the composer's confidence in his ability to master the symphonic form. The Second Symphony is concerned with the present and conveys a feeling of having been conceived in a festive mood. It contains a hymn of joy in sonata form with a wholly original transformation of the recapitulation through variation. Brahms liked to joke about the deeply 'melancholy' drift of this symphony; he would, so he said, only allow

Right: Agathe von Siebold. Brahms fell in love with her in 1858, but broke off their engagement. He remembered her in his String Sextet, op.36, which contains a theme based on the notes spelling out her name – a device for entwining musical and private life he had surely learnt from Schumann.

it to be published with black borders. Anybody familiar with Brahms will know that this was how he alluded to his cheerful mood.

The Third Symphony swings forcefully into a pastoral F major, but in the final movement culminates in a somber F minor, the reverse of *Per aspera ad astra.* Sadly and despondently it fades away into an irresolute pianissimo. Perhaps precisely for this reason this symphony has come to be regarded as the most typical of Brahms. He opened the final movement with a somber unison. Strong upheavals and sharply syncopated rifts again and again interrupt the

Above: Elisabeth von Herzogenberg, with whom Brahms fell in love, and who after her marriage became, with Clara Schumann, his confidante on musical matters.

Left: Clara and Robert Schumann's daughter Julie. Brahms concealed his love for Julie, and the somber mood of the *Alto Rhapsody* is connected with his disappointment at her marriage to an Italian count.

melodic line. Joachim's suggestion that this symphony reflects the legend of Hero and Leander comes to mind. Might this be the brave swimmer desperately struggling against the unrelenting element surrrounding him? This movement above all has an unquestionable theatrical quality. And then motion suddenly stops – a transition too striking to be explicable in purely musical terms. Progress among the horns and bassoons is suspended, and an entirely new tonal picture unfolds. The wind instruments join in an anthem, the strings supply the background and the conclusion falls away. In the final bars the joyful opening theme is heard again like a whisper, the sad farewell of the unattainable.

Brahms shaped the closing movement of the Fourth Symphony into a strict passacaglia. It is surely no mere coincidence that, given his addiction to formal structure, he should have rounded off his work in the medium of the symphony in strict ostinato form after closing the *Haydn Variations* with a chaconne. This represents his act of faith in craftsmanship. What is astounding, however, is the unobtrusive way in which Brahms handles this classical model. The passacaglia theme recurs more than thirty times yet never unduly obtrudes on the ear. The strictness of the concept is disguised, not highlighted. When Joachim performed the symphony from a manuscript version on 1 February 1886 with the Berlin Philharmonische Gesellschaft, he thought it necessary, for the sake of better understanding, to describe the finale as 'Variations' and to print the theme of the passacaglia in the program so as to provide the listeners with an analytical aid. The final movement is an acknowledgment to J. S. Bach, from whose 150th Cantata this chaconne bass was borrowed.

By 1877, when Brahms released his First Symphony, Wagner's principal works were already known, Musorgsky had seen *Boris Godunov* performed in 1874, and composers such as Bizet, Saint-Saëns and Goldmark, all of them on friendly terms with Brahms, had explored the full refinement of modern orchestration in their scores. However, nothing of the sound effects they used, their deployment of the wind and string instruments, the illustrative impact of the works of Berlioz, Liszt and Wagner, percolated into Brahms's scores. The sensual tone of the cor anglais is as absent from them as the rustling sound of the harp, except for a few rich arpeggios reserved for it in the first part of the Requiem and in some minor works with orchestral accompaniment. Even the racy impact of the percussion is largely excluded from his symphonies and concertos, except for the insistent time-keeping of the timpani. Significantly Brahms jestingly described the *Academic Festival Overture*, in which he employed these instruments, as 'Janissary music.' He consistently aimed at the essential, not the superficial, the substance and not the trimmings.

Despite his pronounced patriotic sentiments, Brahms always disliked loud military bands. He dearly loved the Viennese waltz and nursed

Right: Self-portrait (1867) of Anselm Feuerbach, whose work Brahms admired and whom he came to know when the artist began teaching at the Academy in Vienna in 1873. His nihilistic outlook on the world led Brahms to identify him with the protagonist of Goethe's *Harzreise*, which provided the text for the *Alto Rhapsody*.

a passion for the quivering rhythms of Hungarian music, but he never succeeded in developing a taste for the undifferentiated droning and rhythmic uniformity of military music. The sound of the brasses in his orchestral works never obtrudes into the foreground, and references to military effects are painstakingly avoided. Compared to the classics Brahms widened the tonal range, but extremes are not typical of his style as they are, for example, in Wagner or even more in Richard Strauss. Brahms preferred a middle position and drew from it the full, rich sound so characteristic of his work. He very seldom divided the strings, and when he did so it was not in order to increase the harmonic area but to ensure melodic dynamism by the superimposition of octaves (as, for example, in the last entry of the theme in the third movement of his Third Symphony).

• Conductor of the Gesellschaft concerts •

Brahms persistently looked for a steady professional post at various stages in his life. As far as he was concerned, an appointment meant security. When, towards the end of 1870, the management of the Viennese Gesellschaft Concerts decided to negotiate with him concerning the post of conductor after a series of rapid changes in the job, Brahms showed considerable interest but continued to hesitate until late in 1872, before finally accepting the proposal. His father had died of cancer of the liver in February of that year, there was nothing to attract him back to the north, and so he finally adopted Vienna as his home. He found modest and comfortable quarters at No.4 Karlsgasse, where he remained until the end of his life.

Brahms directed his first concert as the newly appointed conductor of the Gesellschaft Concerts on 10 November 1872. The orchestra was no longer staffed by amateurs as in the past but had been drawn from the best that Vienna could offer – the Hofoper Orchestra. The finest players performed under his baton, and his friend Joseph Hellmesberger acted as leader.

Now, as in the past, Brahms set out to provide a rich fare of older music. Handel and Bach formed the mainstays of the program, while he also used some earlier works to train the choir. Rough patches at the start soon vanished in rehearsal under the impact of his enthusiasm. To the huge delight of the ladies and gentlemen involved, he would reward their work by improvising on the piano after rehearsals, and he enjoyed himself thoroughly doing this. The Viennese public, however, did not give him all the support he hoped for. The demands he was making on the listening habits of a lay audience who were mainly looking for entertainment were too great. Hanslick put it well: 'There is no lack of people in Vienna who appreciate and look for serious beauty in music, but not here – any more than elsewhere – is it the custom to attend concerts solely in order to have oneself buried first in the Protestant and then in the Catholic way.' This was aimed at a concert which included in its program both Bach's Cantata 'Liebster Gott, wann werd ich sterben' (Dearest God, when shall I die) and Cherubini's C minor Requiem.

It was also in 1872 that Brahms's relationship with Hans von Bülow, slight to begin with, ripened into friendship. Bülow had weathered a difficult patch on account of his divorce in 1870 from Cosima Liszt, who had left him for Richard Wagner. This led him to seek Brahms's friendship. Hans von Bülow had until then been an enthusiastic supporter of Wagner and was himself – especially as a conductor – a leading member of the 'New German' movement. He had now experienced the personal trauma of a lifetime and found salvation as a musician in a more stable environment. Brahms's work came

Left: Title-page of the first edition of *Nänie*, op.82, a setting of words by Schiller, based upon the *Naenia* or ritual funeral song of ancient Rome. The work was touchingly dedicated to Feuerbach's stepmother upon the artist's death in 1880. She had had an intensely close relationship with him, and Brahms also knew her well.

Left: Feuerbach's painting *In Spring* (1868), probably inspired by a visit to Clara Schumann in Baden-Baden, where he met the singer Aglaja Orgeni. In another version of the painting the singer bears Clara's features. Feuerbach's muted classicism concealing a deep intensity of feeling has many affinities with Brahms's music.

as a revelation to him. At his first concert in Vienna he played the Scherzo in E flat minor, the *Handel Variations* and two Ballades from op.10. Bülow became a dedicated advocate of Johannes Brahms and remained faithful to him as an artist until his death. 'You know what I think of Brahms,' he gushed to his second wife, 'the greatest, most sublime among all creators of music after Bach and Beethoven.' In other words this was Brahms seen as a classical figure among the Romantics.

Brahms conducted his last performance as head of the Gesellschaft Concerts on 18 April 1875. Outwardly it was administrative snags that drove him to resign his office. He found it difficult to submit to the middle-of-the-road decisions of his management. His forceful artistic personality tolerated no curbs. But these were no more than superficial reasons: he recognized that he lacked charisma and leadership when facing an orchestra. He stood no chance in the era of virtuoso conductors which was then dawning, the age of Hermann Levi, Hans von Bülow, Felix Mottl, Carl Muck and, finally, Gustav Mahler. So he knew very well what he was doing when he resigned the post in 1875. This was also the time at which the forty-two-year-old composer privately decided to remain unmarried. He was now world-famous, with a catalogue of works that included more than sixty items.

The *Haydn Variations*, op.56a, were written at Tutzing in 1873 during Brahms's summer visit to the Starnberger See. Three years earlier the theme of the St Anthony Chorale, which Haydn himself had picked up from an anonymous source, had caught his attention. He was immediately fascinated by it and it stayed in his mind. The actual writing of the Variations during the summer of 1873 was thus no more than a completion, the formulation of a creative act prepared over a long time. It cannot now be established whether the version for two pianos antedates that for a full orchestra, or came into existence simultaneously with it and was directly derived from the score, or whether it

represents a subsequent arrangement written to make private performance easier. Be that as it may, Brahms conducted the Variations at the first concert of the Vienna Philharmonic Orchestra's new season on 2 November 1873 and scored a breathtaking success.

It may have been the irregular pattern of this theme, drawn from the second movement of the first of Haydn's six Divertimenti for wind instruments, which specially caught Brahms's attention. The theme consists of an opening sequence of twice five measures, a middle section of eight measures and a closing part consisting of twice four measures followed by a three-measure ending. Brahms developed eight variations from this theme and a final ostinato movement in the form of a chaconne, itself a closed variation on the ostinato motif. The ostinato consists of parts of the main theme and its bass. This concluding movement, which Brahms actually calls a finale, thus represents a variation in its own right, and by so describing it the composer indicates that what he had provided was no mere set of ultimately interchangeable variations but a strict formal conception. Even the festive intonation of the wind section in the concluding chorale theme acoustically stresses the effect of this figured finale. The ostinato motif occurs no fewer than nineteen times.

Billroth had already pointed in 1874 to the growing popularity of Brahms, and the *Haydn Variations* were an important part of this. They are now, together with the noisy *Academic Festival Overture* (which Brahms wrote as a token of gratitude to Breslau University for conferring an honorary doctorate on him on 11 March 1879, and which incorporates the famous student song 'Gaudeamus Igitur'), among his best loved works.

• Chamber music •

While symphonic composition fitted into a scant ten years of Brahms's life – from 1876 to 1885 – chamber music accompanied him throughout his career. More is involved in this than a method of work: it is a matter of inner inclination. Chamber music was Brahms's proper field because it is essentially introspective. In fact, even if it may be an overstatement, it is certainly no wild exaggeration to claim that the composer's symphonies were shaped in the spirit of chamber music.

The first chamber music work published by Brahms was his Piano Trio in B major, op.8, in 1853. He later revised it, one of the few early works to be so treated. The new 1890 version is in no way superior to the original, which, as Brahms himself noted, is merely 'wilder' in its effect, more agitated and stormy. The later revision only demonstrates the high degree of early maturity which he had achieved in the first version of the work.

It is not by chance that, except for the four clarinet works, wind instruments are conspicu-

Below: The original house sign from Brahms's favorite Viennese restaurant 'Zum roten Igel' (The Red Hedgehog). It stood next door to the old building of the Gesellschaft der Musikfreunde.

Bottom: Another of Brahms's favorite relaxations was playing cards. Here he plays *Skat* with two famous Viennese cronies, Johann Strauss II and the conductor Hans Richter, overlooked, it seems, by portraits of Liszt and Wagner.

ously absent from Brahms's chamber music. This closely tallies with his generally cautious image as a composer. The horn in the E flat major Trio, op.40, represents the exception that proves the rule. One should also bear in mind that Brahms himself allowed the viola as a substitute in the two Clarinet Sonatas, that the A minor Trio, op.114, can be performed with a viola, and that the wind instrument can be replaced by a viola even in the Horn Trio referred to above. These alternatives show how little Brahms was concerned in such cases with the specific idiom of the instrument in question. Only the Clarinet Quintet is clearly conceived as a piece so dominated by that instrument that no alternative would be feasible. Considering how doggedly and intensively Brahms studied the technical opportunities offered by the violin with Joachim's help, and by the clarinet with the help of Richard Mühlfeld in Meiningen, his reserved approach to instruments with which he did not feel perfectly at ease becomes understandable. The horn was the exception in this case; he had played it himself when young – the natural rather than the valved instrument – and so it was that op.40 came to be written for the natural horn.

An attempt to follow the B major Trio with a quartet in 1854 failed, not for the first time. Brahms allowed the sketches to lie fallow for twenty years and worked them over for a Piano Quartet in 1875. For the time being the piano remained his chief medium of expression, but he also kept up his great interest in chamber music for strings. Quietly but persistently he went on learning more about it.

Above: The Hellmesberger Quartet, which championed Brahms with several premières of his chamber works, starting with the powerful Piano Quartet in G minor, op.25 (with Brahms himself at the keyboard), in 1862.

• Chamber music for strings •

The Agathe von Siebold episode in Göttingen brought the composer back to chamber music. His adoption of the sextet after several unsuccessful attempts at quartet writing may be interpreted as an attempt to avoid the unadulterated sound of a four-part string score. This assumption is to some extent supported by the inclusion of a piano in the two adjoining Quartets, op.25 and 26 – both of them in fact string trios to which a piano part had been added as a means of once again enabling Brahms to circumvent the difficulty of composing a piece with four bare string voices. He may well have been inspired to write the Sextet, op.18, by Louis Spohr's work, being well aware that music written for such a set of instruments was liable to be unpopular – and therefore unprofitable in publishing terms. Owing to the number of instrumentalists required, the sextets tended to be unsuitable for music in the home. In fact, this provides an indication that Brahms did not really have domestic use in mind when he was writing chamber music. He made the very highest demands on performers, even in purely technical terms, and was thinking of professionals and the concert hall in his chamber works.

After trying out the Sextet, Joachim wrote to him on 14 October 1860: 'We have played your sextet through twice and propose to perform it in public next Saturday. We liked it exceptionally well, especially the first two movements.' The first performance on 20 October in Hanover proved a great success. The Sextet 'was beautiful beyond my expectations,' wrote Clara Schumann in her diary, 'and those had been great enough in any case.' The second performance at the Leipzig Conservatory confirmed its success and led Brahms to set about the composition of a second sextet in total secrecy. The high proportion of twin works is a striking feature of Brahms's output as a whole, but in this case additional point was imparted to it by the fact that public acclaim had drawn the interest of the publisher Simrock to the young composer.

During Whitsun 1860, in connection with a Schumann Commemorative Festival in Düsseldorf, Brahms made the acquaintance of Fritz Simrock, the publisher's young son, and formed a lifelong friendship with him that went well beyond mere business interests. Young Simrock even attempted after his father's death

Above: Brahms's music room in his Vienna apartment. There is a reproduction of Raphael's *Sistine Madonna* on the wall, a large bust of Beethoven broods above the piano, and below it to the left is a relief portrait of Bismarck. On the table is the percolator in which Brahms meticulously prepared his own coffee every morning for many years.

to tie down the composer to a contract 'for the remainder of his life,' and Brahms was forced to defend his independence with vigor, while preserving friendly relations. Brahms had already used his influence in 1874 to obtain a state stipend for Antonín Dvořák, and the close confidence established between publisher and composer eventually induced him to recommend Dvořák to Simrock, so that his compositions also appeared from then on under this imprint.

All these developments can be traced back to the success of the B flat Sextet, op.18, which was joined in September 1864 by the Sextet in G major, op.36. When Brahms assured Simrock that this Sextet had been written 'in the same cheerful mood' as the B flat major Sextet he did not intend to be taken seriously and meant – as so often in his case – the exact opposite.

Joseph Gänsbacher has stated that it was precisely by means of this work that Brahms intended to set himself free 'from his latest love.' Not only this reference but also measures 163-8 in the opening movement, with the notes A-G-A-H-E (the Christian name of Agathe von Siebold, in which the second violin plays a D to make up for the missing letter 'T') repeated three times, point to Brahms's true intention while composing it. No major formal differences can be detected between these sextets, which follow classical models, but this does not mean that Brahms was going over the same ground. On the contrary, he showed that as far as he was concerned the possibilities of the first-movement sonata form had by no means been exhausted. In the B flat major Sextet he introduces a third principal theme (in F major), and although some commentators have described this as the actual

second subject, the earlier A major theme is stressed so individually that it cannot be denied the place of a subject in its own right. The G major Sextet makes do with the traditional two subjects, although the composer sets out the exposition on more generous lines. The slow movements in both sextets obey the principle of variation, which Brahms, as usual, interpreted in the widest sense, so that he also involved elements of development in the process of thematic transformation. The theme of the slow movement (andante, ma moderato) in op.18 forms the nucleus of a constantly changing re-interpretation of the basic idea, very much in the sense of Schoenberg's 'developing variation.'

By the end of August 1862 Brahms had sent Clara Schumann the first three movements of a string quintet of which she expressed her wholehearted approval. Joachim was also full of praise and only regretted an absence of seductive sound. Brahms put the work into rehearsal, came to the conclusion that Joachim was right and left it unfinished. Another twenty years went by before he picked up this string quintet again. In his first attempt he had used two cellos, but he now resorted to the use of two violas instead. This F major Quintet, op.88, which now counts as his first, was written at high speed during a stay in Bad Ischl early in 1882 with each completed movement cheerfully inscribed 'Spring 1882.' The center of this three-movement composition deserves special attention. In it Brahms fused the slow section and the scherzo passage in the cyclic sonata form. The adagio (which is repeated three times in different versions) encloses a scherzo-like siciliana

Right: Prussian officers quartered in Paris in 1871 (a later painting by Anton von Werner). Though Brahms had by then settled in Vienna, he remained a patriotic German, and celebrated Bismarck's victories in the Franco-Prussian War of 1870-1 with his *Triumphlied* for chorus and orchestra.

which once again recurs in a different form, so that this movement actually represents a five-part variation. The theme of the adagio, incidentally, was taken from an older sarabande study he had written in 1855 during a stay in Hamburg.

Brahms wrote his Second String Quintet in G major, op.111, in Ischl and Vienna in 1890, a whole eight years later. This was not only his last string quintet but also a work by means of which he signalled his intention to withdraw altogether from composition. Yet there is nothing in it of a farewell, or a flight from the world. Max Kalbeck even suggests that the opening of the first movement harked back to sketches which Brahms had prepared for a planned fifth symphony. If there is anything in this suggestion it would be a further indication of how little he was given to observing musical categories when putting his pieces of inspiration into shape. Schoenberg sensed Brahms's inclination to formulate his works outside the strict limits of set categories when he later transcribed the G minor Piano Quartet, op.25, for symphony orchestra and had it performed in Los Angeles in 1938. Schoenberg jokingly referred to this orchestral version as Brahms's 'Fifth' and even publicly defended his position by saying that the piano often blotted out the finer string passages and that for once he wished to hear the lot. Such orchestration involves no sacrilege where Brahms is concerned. There is little doubt about the symphonic sweep of the cello theme in the op.111 Quintet as it clearly asserts itself against the tremolo background of the violins and violas. The work is tightly conceived but full of the joy of life, despite what Joachim described as the 'melancholy, brief adagio' (subjected to the variation principle favored by Brahms). Even without specific refer-

Left: One of a series of sketches of Brahms produced by Willy von Beckerath late in the composer's life. It captures well his down-to-earth, uncharismatic rostrum manner. Brahms himself knew he lacked the personality of a really good conductor.

Above: Hamburg honors its most celebrated son: the certificate, dated 14 June 1889, giving Brahms honorary citizenship, or freedom of the city, an honor he treasured above all others.

ence to the inspired finale in which a Hungarian accent unmistakably asserts itself, the source of the inspiration for this work is not difficult to determine.

Brahms spent twenty years trying to master the composition of pure four-voice string writing and eventually produced the two String Quartets, op.51 nos. 1 and 2 – a pair once again, as was so often his habit. Both works were composed in several stages, included earlier sketches, and were completed during the summer of 1873 at Tutzing on the Starnberger See. This being said, these two works are as unalike as any twins can be. The C minor Quartet, op.51 no.1, seems to hark back to Beethoven's 'Rasumovsky' Quartets, while the A minor, op.51 no.2, tends to reflect Schumann's more amiable, dreamy world of sound. The suggestion that there are reminiscences of Wagner's Erda motif in the dramatically ascending C minor theme at the opening of op.51 no.1 is pure conjecture. A link with Beethoven is nearer the mark, and can be seen in the gentle, exalted A flat major theme of the romanza in the second movement, while the dancing, sunny scherzo with its graceful theme that resolves itself into an animated waltz belongs to the best Viennese tradition.

Brahms thematically incorporated the motto of Joseph Joachim – F-A-E (*Frei aber einsam:* Free but lonely) – into the main theme of the A minor Quartet, which suggests that he originally intended to dedicate it to Joachim. Although it might have been thought that Brahms had achieved release by the composition of his two op.51 Quartets, he nevertheless followed them with one further work of this kind, the B flat major Quartet, op.67, begun in 1876 at Ziegelhausen near Heidelberg and completed in November of the same year in Vienna. To mark, so it would seem, the end of this kind of output the composer shaped the finale of this work into a characteristic set of variations. A song-like theme is interpreted in eight different and inspired ways and intellectually transformed, a work fit to stand beside the *Handel Variations* for piano solo.

• Chamber works for strings and piano •

The three String Quartets are matched by the three Piano Quartets, op.25, 26 and 60. Although closely connected in time, they differ radically in conception. The original idea of the op.60 Quartet, only performed for the first time in 1875 in Vienna, goes back even further than the two Hamburg Quartets op.25 and 26, and may possibly be identical with an earlier quartet which Brahms asked Joachim to try out and then set aside. We know from some of the things he said about it that this work represented a sort of self-portrait into which many autobiographical features had been woven, as well as an account of the moods generated in Brahms by his Werther-like relationship with Clara Schumann. This would indeed explain the composer's protracted hesitation in making his musical confession available to the public at large. The usual gentle features are absent. Dark colors predominate. Agitation, passion, perhaps even despair can be read into this work, but for the rest it remains enigmatic.

The Piano Quintet in F minor, op.34, stands out as an exception in Brahms's chamber music not only by its instrumentation but because of its complicated genesis. It was first sketched out during the summer of 1861 in Hamburg when Brahms still nursed hopes of succeeding Grund as conductor there. He then transcribed it in 1862 as a quintet with two cellos, and it was finally performed as a string quartet with piano accompaniment in 1864 at Lichtenthal near Baden-Baden. When all these changes still failed to satisfy him, Brahms resolutely rewrote the work as a sonata for two pianos and performed it in Vienna with the young virtuoso Tausig on 17 April 1864 at a concert of the Singakademie. Brahms was normally only too willing to jettison anything at all unsuccessful, but he showed remarkable persistence in this case. Even in this form the piece failed to secure public approval, but Clara Schumann who had even been enthusiastic about the original version was insistent: 'Please, dear Johannes, carry on just this once, reshape the work yet again.' Contrary to his usual habit Brahms followed his dear friend's advice. The final result was this piano quintet, and one must agree with the majority verdict that, after such an agonizing creative process, Brahms reached the ultimate summit of his chamber music with this work. He was generally inclined to impart gravity to his last movements and to avoid a cheerful ending, but here the scherzo in the third movement is especially engaging through its unconventional shape and its sparkling fantasy. The entry of the majestic C major theme after the rhythmically strict preparatory introduction opens up the scherzo's subtle range of expression and is among the master's most effective creations. The rhythmic transitional motif is harmonically spun out in the splendid conclusion of the movement.

Right: Sketch by
Ludwig Michalek of the
clarinettist Richard
Mühlfeld, whose playing
inspired several of
Brahms's finest late
chamber works,
including the Trio
(op.114), the sublime
Quintet (op.115) and
the two Sonatas
(op.120).

The B major Piano Trio, op.8, was sketched out during 1853 and completed in January 1854 shortly before Schumann's breakdown. This was Brahms's first published work and the only completed piece he later revised. Nearly thirty years were to elapse before he wrote another trio of this kind. Admittedly the Horn Trio, op.40, first performed in 1865 at the Grosser Saal of the Kasino in Zürich had already been published by 1866, but it does not strictly belong to this group of piano trios. Brahms only began to work on a Piano Trio in C major, op.87, in 1880. A letter to Billroth indicates that once again he was simultaneously working on another twin piece in D flat major. Only the C major Trio, however, was completed at Ischl in June 1882, and the other trio never saw the light of day. Brahms nevertheless provided a companion piece – the C minor Trio, op.101 – produced during 1886 in Thun. The op.87 and 101 Trios are alike in their resolute and vigorous basic approach. Both opening movements are introduced by strong themes infused with energy and drive. Further confirmation of the link between these two works is provided by the thematic correspondence between the motif of the variations in the second movement of op.87 and the scurrying presto theme of the scherzo in the second movement of op.101. Clara Schumann thought that the andante con moto of op.87 with its Lombardic rhythm and restless syncopation had a 'popular' sound. Brahms used this theme as the basis for a spirited set of variations.

The C major andante from op.101 is even more 'popular' in its impact. The relaxed way in which it switches from triple to common time, and particularly the use of triple-time

figures, betrays Bohemian influences, which are concealed by the measured tempo Brahms imposed on them.

• Wind trios and quintets •

The horn and the clarinet, Brahms's first and last loves, lend both the op.40 and op.114 Trios their tonal color. The composer gave the former instrument a privileged – though not predominant – position in his output, a feature he shared with Richard Strauss. The main theme of op.40 occurred to Brahms 'on wooded heights among fir trees,' because he liked to compose in his mind while walking in the countryside. This imparts a sense of inner warmth to the movement quite alien to the fuss of the concert hall. The melancholy adagio mesto in E flat minor, an elegy on his mother's death, embodies 'Dort in der Weiden steht ein Haus' (There stands a house in the meadow), a folksong from the Lower Rhine, which provides the main theme for the closing movement, an allegro con brio, as though Brahms wished to banish all sorrowful thoughts from his mind.

In 1890 Brahms decided to give up composition. He felt that he had done enough. 'With this scrap of paper [a joking reference to the score] you may say goodbye to my notes because it is in any case time to stop,' he wrote in December 1890 to Fritz Simrock in a letter enclosing the score of the G major String Quintet, op.111, which he had chosen to be his last work. But only a few months later, in March 1891 in Meiningen, he met the clarinettist Richard Mühlfeld, whose accomplished tech-

Right: Brahms
photographed in 1893,
at the age of sixty.

nique and exquisite timbre immediately fired him with enthusiasm for the clarinet as a solo instrument.

In a very short time, during June-July 1891, Brahms wrote the Clarinet Trio, op.114, and the Clarinet Quintet, op.115. Both were produced while Brahms was trying to put his affairs in order. Early intimations of death had overcome him, a strange thing in a man only in his sixties. He made his will in May 1891.

There is no trace of experimentation in the Trio, even though this was the first time that Brahms had ever written for the clarinet as a solo instrument. With astonishing assurance he exploited the rich color range of the instrument and its specific tonal attraction. He used its capacity for sustained breath and its rippling

fluency in the adagio cantilena. Brahms pairs the clarinet with the cello in some passages to produce colorful duets of exquisite sound. He does allow for a viola as a substitute for the clarinet, but the part is entirely conceived in the idiom of the latter. High notes are used only with caution and the composer clearly has no liking for the bucolic. Occasionally it is said that Brahms has used 'all the possibilities available to the clarinet,' but this is untenable: he was always selective and never went beyond the limits of his preferred tonal range.

The Clarinet Quintet in B minor, op.115, has sometimes been described – justly – as the peak of Brahms's instrumental music. Hanslick said that it was a work for connoisseurs, but he was wrong: it cannot fail to enchant all lovers of music. Its only earlier rival is Mozart's Clarinet Quintet, and they are at one in their mature mastery of conception. An aura of melancholy tinges Brahms's Quintet, and the power he achieves in it is beyond words. Through the luxuriant, sustained sound of his instrument Mühlfeld conjured up in Brahms's mind a world familiar to him through Vienna, his chosen home – the world of the nostalgic *tárogató* sounding over the Hungarian plain, the *puszta*. It is this strange nostalgic universe that Brahms immortalized here in sound. The dark red glow of the *puszta* breaks through at the end of the first movement. In the middle movement, perhaps the composer's finest ever, a spiritual laughter can be sensed beneath the tears. Brahms achieved a degree of intimacy in this second movement which borders on the sacramental – a musical togetherness. How little is conveyed

by saying that the opening movement obeys the sonata form and that Brahms once again resolves the final movement into a set of variations! The way in which he opens the allegro movement with the voluptuous duo cantilena of the two violins, followed by the clarinet, starting from a dark background and burgeoning softly but strongly into the cantilena, introduces us to a world of its own which Brahms had never before managed to convey with such intensity. The development is dominated by the constant shimmering of the colors which, in the second movement, stream out into the distance, into space and landscape. All the movements are linked by a hidden thematic thread which is not directly apparent. But in the coda, when the second violin openly takes up the initial theme, now transposed down a fifth, the listener becomes aware that Brahms subjected all the movements to a single basic idea and subordinated the work to a single concept. As a result, the entire piece seems to grow like one great variation from a single seed – spiritual freedom asserted by an individualist.

•The concertos •

The history of the solo concerto form is marked by the fact that the most characteristic examples

Left: Herr Lämpel, the teacher, from the original manuscript of *Max und Moritz* (1865), the immortal 'picture story' of two rascals by Wilhelm Busch (1832-1908), an artist and humorist much admired by Brahms.

Below: Title-page of the first piano edition (1892) of a Strauss waltz, dedicated to Brahms, on the occasion of an international musical and theatrical exhibition in Vienna – the Rotunde, built for the 1873 exhibition, is illustrated at the bottom. The title is from Schiller's *Ode to Joy*, notably set in Beethoven's Choral Symphony.

reflect the performing abilities of their interpreters. Brahms wrote four concertos: the D minor Piano Concerto, op.15, in 1854-8; the B flat major Piano Concerto, op.83, in 1878-81; the D major Violin Concerto, op.77, in 1878; and finally the Double Concerto for violin and cello in A minor, op.102, in 1887.

The D minor Concerto had involved Brahms in a spectacular fiasco in 1859 in Leipzig. He sketched out the B flat major Concerto in Vienna in 1878 after his first visit to Italy, completed it during the summer of 1881 in Pressbaum near Vienna and dedicated it to his old Hamburg teacher, Eduard Marxsen, thereby expressing his gratitude for what this sound pedagogue had done to help him master the piano. Billroth remarked that the B flat major and the D minor Concertos were to each other as a grown man is to a boy. Rather unusually, the B flat major Concerto has four movements. It is the longest of its kind composed by Brahms, one of the longest in the whole history of the concerto. In these two concertos Brahms deals in exemplary fashion with the formal alternative of placing the solo introduction at the beginning of the piece or letting it follow the exposition by the orchestra. In the D minor Concerto the solo part only begins after the orchestral opening, while in the B flat major Concerto it starts the movement. In the D minor Concerto Brahms undoubtedly sought to link up with Beethoven but also to break out of the conventional limits by imparting a sense of passionate indignation to the opening. The B flat major Concerto, on the other hand, seems more serene and amiable. Its slow movement in particular, with its cello solo, radiates an exceptional wealth of emotion. The solo part, written by Brahms for his own use, is awkward, being clumsy rather than lying under the hands. His own piano technique was a highly personal affair. Technical perfection apart, his piano scores demand physical strength and a virtuosity equal to the composer's own.

Brahms composed the Violin Concerto in D major at Pörtschach during his summer work in 1878 and dedicated it to his friend Joachim, to whom he owed his intimate understanding of violin technique. The Violin Concerto approximates to the sound of the Second Symphony, that of the violin's own voice. Brahms had originally also given this concerto four movements, but then deleted the two middle ones in the course of revision and composed a new 'poor adagio.' Joachim was himself the soloist at the first performance on 1 January 1879, and he had, as usual, advised Brahms on the violin writing. There is a definite whiff of Hungary in the final movement, inevitably so: that was, after all, where Joachim was from.

The Double Concerto for violin and cello in A minor, op.102, 'the peculiar notion' as Brahms described it, was composed in 1887 in the wonderful surroundings of Lake Thun. 'This concerto is in a sense a work of reconciliation. Joachim and Brahms have spoken to each other again for the first time in years,' wrote Clara Schumann in her diary on 21 September 1887

after the two friends had together rehearsed the concerto in her home with the cellist Robert Hausmann. The collapse of Joachim's marriage in 1884 (in which Brahms with his unyielding sense of justice had uncompromisingly taken sides with Joachim's wife, Amalia Weiss) had led to the rift between them. In 1887, however, when Brahms turned to Joachim for professional advice in order to clear up some points of detail, the violinist eagerly seized this olive branch.

The work was a 'Reconciliation' Concerto not only outwardly but also in substance: after the first figuratively elaborated cello solo the woodwind takes up a theme which has important tasks to perform during the rest of the movement. In fact Brahms was tipping his lifelong associate a friendly wink through this theme, that of Viotti's Twenty-second Violin Concerto in A minor (even the timbre points to this connection). It was one of Joachim's set pieces and they had often played it together when they were young in Hanover, with Brahms – according to Joachim – 'rummaging around the keyboard with sighs of satisfaction.' In this concerto the composer resorted to the technique of the baroque concerto grosso, which he used as a model in scoring the dialogue between the two instruments, while assigning a role of equal importance to the orchestra. His intimate knowledge of ancient music stood him in good stead here, but he also integrated the old formal conception into the contemporary idiom. Brahms was deeply disappointed by the no more than moderate success of the Double Concerto at its first performance on 18 October 1887 at the Gürzenich in Cologne which he himself conducted. To the present day the work remains unaccountably overshadowed by his other great compositions. As we know from Mandyczewski, he had planned – and had probably already sketched out – another double concerto, but this work never saw the light of day.

Top: Brahms taking tea with Adele, the third wife of Johann Strauss the Younger, at Bad Ischl.

Above: Otto Böhler's affectionate caricature of Brahms as a rather eccentric old bachelor, on his way, as indicated, to the 'Red Hedgehog.'

SCHICKSALSLIED

Jhr wandelt droben im Licht
Auf weichem Boden , selige Genien !
Glänzende Götterlüfte
Rühren Euch leicht
Wie die Finger der Künstlerin
Heilige Saiten .

Schicksallos , wie der schlafende
Säugling , athmen die Himmlischen ;
Keusch bewahrt
In bescheidener Knospe
Blühet ewig
Ihnen der Geist ,
Vnd die seligen Augen
Blicken in stiller
Ewiger Klarheit .

Doch uns ist gegeben
Auf keiner Stätte zu ruhn ,
Es schwinden , es fallen
Die leidenden Menschen
Blindlings von einer
Stunde zur andern ,
Wie Wasser von Klippe
Zu Klippe geworfen ,
Jahrlang in's Vngewisse hinab .

FRIEDRICH HÖLDERLIN

Above: Max Klinger's *Brahms-Phantasie* of 1894 concludes with Hölderlin's deeply pessimistic *Schicksalslied* (Song of Destiny), set by Brahms for choir and orchestra in 1868-71 as his op.54. Klinger had known Brahms since 1880 and offered him this set of prints as a belated sixtieth-birthday present. Brahms was 'delighted and moved by the beauty and the deep, serious expression of the pictures,' and he returned the compliment two years later with his dedication to Klinger of his *Vier ernste Gesänge*, op.121.

•Songs and dances•

'The song is now on such a wrong tack that one simply must, come what may, keep at least one ideal firmly in mind: that of the folksong.' This was how Brahms stated his position on the matter to Clara Schumann. The unpretentiousness of the folksong – by no means only the German variety – and its natural, healthy sound acted as a beacon for Brahms throughout his life. This was true even in the realm of instrumental music, where the quality of the folksong finds its expression in the idiom of the dance. It was precisely this 'chaste' aspect of Brahms's output that Richard Wagner set out to lampoon in his public attacks by commenting satirically, even slanderously, on the *Liebeslieder-Walzer* and the Hungarian element in the composer's style. Wagner knew very well that he was touching on a basic feature of Brahms's composition which was beyond his own reach. Brahms's work would make no sort of sense if the world of the waltz and the *czárdás* did not exist. The Viennese and Hungarian idioms, as well as the contribution of Bohemian sound, are so completely amalgamated in his thought and sensibility that their formative effect remains active even when they are not explicitly stressed. It was from this world that Brahms obtained the variable character of his rhythmic patterns, the versatility of his structural combinations, the tendency to use unequal time and the art of extending or shortening selected phrases. The *Hungarian Dances* were largely a matter of arranging existing melodies: only a very few of the tunes are newly invented material, but all of these are in the authentic idiom. Many of them date from Brahms's early days in Hamburg and, as he said himself, hark back to his meeting with Reményi: 'I had heard them at one time along with many others from Reményi and remembered them. . . . I don't know whether I wrote them down by ear or had seen them on the page. . . .' In other words these dances are the direct outcome of musical arrangement applied

to a freely available fund of anonymous melodies. This is also the reason why they have not been awarded opus numbers.

Brahms later arranged some of these *Hungarian Dances* for orchestra. They achieved incredible popularity when he published them in 1874 and this was probably why he added to them (in 1880 in Pörtschach), once again mixing the unidentifiable original with work of his own. Brahms described some of these dances as his own 'inventions,' but it would be more correct to describe them as echoes. However, this second series fails to match the earlier one in freshness and spontaneity. As the composer himself explained: 'I have been at singular pains to imitate the playing of the gypsies in so far as our civilized ears are able to tolerate it,' an undertaking that might be described as the refining of folklore. Something of the same kind applies to the eighteen *Liebeslieder-Walzer*, op.52, part of which Brahms wrote in 1868 at Bad Neuenahr, for piano duet and mixed vocal quartet. The opus number indicated that Brahms – rightly – claimed them as his own compositions, but they are also nevertheless entirely the product of Vienna's environment.

Brahms composed his *Zigeunerlieder* (Gypsy songs), op.103 – again for piano and vocal quartet – during the winter of 1887/8 in Vienna as settings of poems by Hugo Conrat on Hungarian models. A tinge of homesickness colors these songs and gives us a glimpse of the composer's other self through the waltzes, his invariable way of conjuring up some nostalgic memory of youth. How seriously he took these compositions is revealed by his dedication of the sixteen Piano Waltzes, op.39, to no less a personality than Eduard Hanslick. These waltzes, written in 1865, constitute miniature works of art 'in the manner of Schubert' and have little in common with the drawing-room music then in fashion. Hanslick looked up in astonishment when he found the words 'Brahms' and 'Waltzes' side by side on the title page. A subtly written review expressed his gratitude for this offering of refined folklore. Nobody, he suggested, really could credit Brahms, so earnest and taciturn, with such a piece of frivolity and there could therefore be only one answer to the riddle: Vienna itself. Brahms, in fact, had thereby awarded to the Viennese waltz its patent of nobility!

In thirty-five years Brahms published no fewer than thirty-one folios comprising altogether 196 songs, quite apart from many which he later discarded because he considered that they fell short of his critical standards. Apart from a few silent years, Brahms was accompanied by song throughout his life as a composer. External influences are more obvious in his output of songs than in his purely instrumental works, although such connections cannot always be proved with absolute certainty. Nobody would question that the op.14 and op.19 songs owe their origin to his emotional experiences during Agathe's summer in 1858, nor that meeting again with Elisabeth von Herzogenberg found a reflection in his vocal output. Even his infatuation late in life with Hermine Spies was responsible for releasing some of his creative energy.

During Brahms's early days, until about 1860, the number of 'strophic' songs remained roughly equal with that of 'through-composed' songs, in other words those in which the music in the stanzas changes. With op.32 the former category perceptibly diminished in favor of songs subjected to the full treatment of composition or in which the melody changed within the stanza, but from 1873 on this trend was once again reversed.

Brahms's song accompaniments are expressive but not unduly pictorial. Great introductory statements on the piano were alien to his conception of the simplicity of song, and he much preferred to go straight to the heart of the matter. He favored texts that conveyed a mood, and he either avoided or only occasionally bothered with more light-hearted pieces.

Some of his individual settings achieved great popularity, for example 'Die Mainacht' (May night), op.43 no.2, a poem by Ludwig Hölty; 'Feldeinsamkeit' (Alone in a meadow), op.86 no.2, by Hermann Allmers; 'Immer leiser wird mein Schlummer' (Ever quieter becomes my slumber), op.105 no.2, by Hermann Lingg; and above all the lullaby 'Guten Abend, gute Nacht' (Good evening, good night), op.49 no.4, from Scherer's *Deutsche Volkslieder*, which Brahms composed in 1868 for the children of his Viennese friend Bertha Faber and which has now become almost a folksong. He did not always compose his folios of songs consecutively and often put the items together at a later date. He used song composition to fill in gaps between major works, but it should not be inferred from this that he regarded such composition as a lesser activity. The *Fifteen Romances*, op.33, from Ludwig Tieck's *Magelone*, composed in 1861 and 1862 and dedicated to the singer Julius Stockhausen, make up a complete song-cycle. Their publication in 1865 and 1869 by the Rieter-Biedermann firm in Leipzig suddenly made Brahms famous in this field. The songs were composed during a journey to Münster-am-Stein with Clara Schumann and her children. This work is made up of alternating stanzas and was Brahms's only real song-cycle. He demonstrated in it his ability to devise extended introductions and links to the individual stanzas as well as a more elaborate treatment of the stanzas themselves.

A second song sequence, the *Vier ernste Gesänge* (Four Serious Songs), op.121, the texts for which Brahms himself chose from the Bible (principally from Ecclesiastes and the Epistle to the Corinthians), is also closely connected with Clara Schumann. In this sense it links up with the Requiem and may itself be regarded as a commemoration of the dead. In the spring of 1896 Clara Schumann suffered two strokes. The news of her end reached Brahms at Bad Ischl on 21 May and he immediately traveled to Bonn to follow her coffin. The *Vier ernste Gesänge* had already been composed by this time, but it is impossible now to tell whether they had been written under the influence of Clara's illness.

Brahms dedicated the cycle to Max Klinger, thus leaving the issue open. Throughout his life he had all too often known how to conceal his true feelings, had mastered inner surges of emotion and turned away brusquely if he found that outsiders were able to read his mind. He may well have wished to avert posthumous arguments about the work by an innocuous dedication.

The *Vier ernste Gesänge* are among the most exalted music that Brahms ever composed, indeed among the most sublime works of art of all time. Strictly speaking they can no longer be regarded as songs but rather as a non-denominational prayer. They carry a message of humility and faith that reaches out beyond words. Brahms selected the texts to fit his basic conception, formulated the composition almost without ornamentation and thus achieved an unusually strong impact. The *Vier ernste Gesänge* were unprecedented and they remained unique. Brahms had expressed his innermost being in them and it may well be that this was why the first performance on 30 October 1896 in Vienna found little or no response.

When Brahms attended Clara Schumann's funeral he did not know that his own death was not far off. Friends noticed a change in his complexion in June, but he attributed this to jaundice. In fact, however, it was cancer of the liver, the disease which had killed his father. A course of treatment in Karlsbad had no effect. By 26 March 1897 his illness had made rapid progress and he became bedridden. He died only a week later, on 3 April. None of his friends or companions was with him at the time. Only his housekeeper Celestine Truxa, who had looked after him for many years, nursed him through the final moments of his life and closed his eyes.

Thousands accompanied the funeral which took Brahms's body from his home in the Karlsgasse to Vienna's Central Cemetery on 6 April 1897 and laid it to rest beside Beethoven's grave, not far from the Schubert memorial. That day the flags of ships in the harbor of Hamburg flew at half-mast. His north German home town, and with it the entire world, was mourning one of its greatest composers.

Below: Klaus Groth (1819-99), the North German folk poet, whom Brahms first met in his early twenties. During the course of their long friendship, Brahms set fourteen of his poems to music.

Bottom: Brahms's autographed title-page to his 'Wiegenlied' (Lullaby), op.49 no.4, one of the best-loved of all his songs, that was elevated in Germany to folksong status.

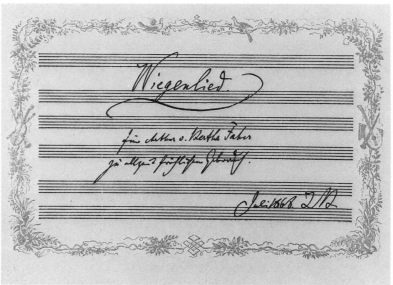

The music critic: Eduard Hanslick

The 'new music' of Wagner, his forbears – Berlioz and Liszt – and his followers – especially Bruckner and Wolf – was attacked nowhere more than in the articles by Eduard Hanslick in Vienna's *Neue Freie Presse*. Hanslick (1825-1904) promoted a formal, classical ideal and rejected music's appeal to the emotions. Among contemporary musicians he found his ideal embodied by Brahms, whose circle in Vienna he joined. Hanslick's public loyalty to Brahms's music was unswerving (although his privately expressed opinions were not always so favorable), while he remained bitterly opposed to what he saw as the perversion of music in the work of Wagner and the Wagnerians. Bruckner suffered cruelly from the attacks of Hanslick and of other Brahmsians, particularly Max Kalbeck (1850-1921), later Brahms's biographer, and Richard Heuberger (1850-1914), composer and Hanslick's successor at the *Neue Freie Presse*. They are shown with Hanslick in Otto Böhler's caricature (*above*) pursuing Bruckner with their pens. Wagner responded with bitter invective to Hanslick's attacks and was at first planning to use his name for the archphilistine, finally named Beckmesser, in *Die Meistersinger*. His supporters, meanwhile, turned their pens on Brahms (who did not himself share Hanslick's unmitigated hostility to Wagner's music), sharply dividing Vienna into two angrily opposed factions.

Hanslick at the height of his power.

Innovation and conservatism have run parallel in Viennese musical life, and many of the best-loved Viennese musicians won real acceptance only after their death. In 1896 a monument to Mozart – once rejected, now almost a symbol of the city – was erected behind the Opera House, and Otto Böhler's silhouette (*above*) shows Brahms (*center*) and other prominent members of Viennese society in front of it.

Accorde (*right*), the first of Max Klinger's *Brahms-Phantasie*, published in 1894. The artist's *fin-de-siècle* symbolism clearly places Brahms in the classical tradition, but at the same time invests music with a mystic power far removed from the formalist aesthetic of Hanslick. Brahms wrote to Joachim: 'though Klinger's fantasy carries him on high and far afield, you will find that the picture, the words and the music unite.'

Page from the finale of Bruckner's Fifth Symphony in the composer's autograph score (1877). The critical campaign against him was crushing: his Third Symphony was first performed that year to an audience that dwindled after each movement, until only ten remained.

Gustav Mahler und die Wiener Hofoper.
Von Ludwig Karpath.

Klimt's evocation of Schubert (*above*) formed part of the decoration of the Parkring mansion of the Viennese industrialist and generous patron Nikolaus Dumba. Schubert's own struggles in an often unappreciative Vienna were now forgotten, and his days remembered with nostalgia as a golden age – evoked here in what Hermann Bahr saw as the 'joyous melancholy' of this 'loveliest picture ever painted by an Austrian.'

Gustav Mahler was appointed director of the Vienna Opera in 1897 with the support of Brahms and Hanslick. In his ten years there he had to contend with all the intrigues of Viennese musical life as he ruthlessly carried out reforms that were to make it a great operatic ensemble. This article (*above*), written in 1903 by Ludwig Karpath in the German paper *Bühne und Welt*, applauds his work in what was later known as the golden decade of the Opera.

The Wagner festivals at Bayreuth, presided over as quasi-religious ceremonials by the composer's widow and son, ensured that the Master's influence remained both powerful and controversial. The caricature by Olaf Gulbransson (*right*) from the Munich paper *Simplicissimus* celebrated Wagner's centenary in June 1913: 'You can't go any higher.' 'The threatened Grail' (*left*), from the same paper a year earlier, shows Cosima Wagner as a Valkyrie supported by her son Siegfried (who had, at least formally, taken over direction of the festivals in 1909) beating off opera directors trying to overcome the composer's ban on all performances of *Parsifal* outside Bayreuth.

Gräfin Monrod.

Böhler's silhouette (*above*) shows 'Hanslick teaching Richard Wagner how he should compose.' Hanslick often used Wagner as the yardstick for all that was bad: reviewing Richard Strauss's *Don Juan* in 1892, he described the composer as a

pupil of the Berlioz-Liszt-Wagner school, complaining that 'the misfortune with most of our young composers is that they think in a foreign language (philosophy, poetry, painting) and only then translate the thought into their native language

(music).' Hanslick's reaction to the current notion of Bruckner as 'the Richard Wagner of the symphony' and Hugo Wolf as 'the Richard Wagner of the song' was that 'each of them makes of his category of art something which it ought *not* to be.'

In the society paper *Wiener Salonblatt* (*above*) from January 1884 to April 1887 the struggling young composer Hugo Wolf wrote a weekly column during the concert and opera season which earned him the nickname 'wild wolf of the Salonblatt' for his attacks on all the new music that

Hanslick held most dear – especially Brahms, who apparently looked forward to the renewed assault each Sunday. At the same time Wolf gave extravagant praise to Berlioz, Liszt, Bruckner and, of course, Wagner, hailing them as the true successors of Gluck, Mozart and Beethoven.

Karikaturen-Winkel.
Dr. Eduard Hanslick.

Figaro 1890 Nr 11.

The caricature (*left*) from the Vienna *Figaro* (1890) shows Hanslick burning incense before the statue of St Johannes Brahms. Brahms had been dragged rather unwillingly into the battle; he would have liked to visit Bayreuth, but dared not for fear of Wagner's disciples. Hanslick, however, could afford to ignore the cartoonists: he had

been professor of musical history and aesthetics at Vienna University since 1856; despite Wagner's popularity in Vienna, there were many who supported Hanslick, both among critics and the more conservative musical public, and he remained for half a century one of the most powerful figures in the Viennese musical world.

Left: Heinrich Porges (1837-1900) was a journalist and music teacher in Munich and one of Wagner's most enthusiastic supporters. In 1863 he became co-editor of the *Neue Zeitschrift für Musik*, in which he championed the music of the 'New German School.'

Two cartoons (*right and opposite*), from Vienna (1883) and Berlin (1876). In one Wagner misinterprets the audience wringing their hands as applause, and in the other he assumes the throne of Wotan at Bayreuth, while Valkyries carry in half-dead subscribers to his festival.

Der Fall Wagner.

Ein Musikanten-Problem.

Von

Friedrich Nietzsche.

LEIPZIG.
Verlag von C. G. Naumann,
1888.

The philosopher Friedrich Nietzsche (1844-1900) (*right*) was as a young man one of Wagner's most ardent supporters, seeing him as the embodiment of the Dionysiac force and the greatest creative genius in Germany; they became friends while Wagner and Cosima were living in Switzerland. Later Nietzsche broke with Wagner, principally because of his own loathing for the Germanic 'Christian' chauvinism and anti-semitism which he saw promoted by the Wagner cult at Bayreuth, and he wrote several powerful – and often very funny – polemics against the composer, including *The Wagner Case* (*left*), published in 1888 (an extract from which is reprinted below left).

From *Der Fall Wagner:* 'The problem of redemption is in itself an honorable problem. Wagner has pondered nothing so deeply as he has redemption: his opera is opera of redemption. With him somebody is always wanting to be redeemed, now a little man, now a little woman – this is his problem. And how richly he varies his *leitmotif*! What rare, what profound modulations! Who but Wagner taught us that innocence would rather redeem interesting sinners (the case in *Tannhäuser*)? Or that even the Wandering Jew is redeemed and settles down if he gets married (the case in *Flying Dutchman*)? Or that depraved old females prefer to be redeemed by chaste youths (Kundry's case)? Or that pretty girls prefer to be redeemed by a knight who is a Wagnerian (the case in *Die Meistersinger*)? Or that married women also like to be redeemed by a knight (Isolde's case)? Or that 'the old God,' after he has compromised himself in every respect, is finally redeemed by a free spirit and immoralist (the case in the *Ring*)? Especially admire this last profound idea! Do you understand it? I guard against understanding it.'
Friedrich Nietzsche

Left: Caricature of Johann Herbeck (1831-77), newly appointed director of the Hofoper, conducting the first Vienna production of *Die Meistersinger* (1870). There was uproar in the audience on the first night, controlled only by the presence of mind of the conductor, who at one point had to sing the part of Hans Sachs from the podium, after the baritone Johann Nepomuk Beck lost his nerve.

Gustav Mahler was conductor of the Vienna Philharmonic Orchestra for three years, from 1898 to 1901. The caricature (*below*) shows him conducting his First Symphony, written eleven years earlier, at a concert in 1900. Again, there was uproar at the performance, with noisy demonstrations and counter-demonstrations. Hanslick wrote after hearing the symphony: 'One of us must be mad, and it is not I.'

ANTON BRUCKNER

CONSTANTIN FLOROS

'Counterpoint is not a matter of genius, merely
the means to an end.'

Bruckner

Every one of the great nineteenth-century composers had a complexion very much of his own,
both as artist and man. Each of them was unmistakably unique. But certainly none was so
out of the ordinary as Anton Bruckner. His
personality remains in many ways enigmatic
right up to the present. His education and his
career as a musician were unusual. And his
output arouses astonishment even now by its
originality and the novelty of its approach.

Bruckner is today regarded by many as the
most important symphonic composer between
Beethoven and Mahler. Yet he was the least
regarded and understood among his fellow
composers during his lifetime. It was not until
his closing years that his significance began to
dawn on his contemporaries, and the full splendor of his achievement was only recognized
after his death. It gradually became clear that
in their day his works had stood in the forefront of the evolution of symphonic writing
and that Bruckner had brought into being a
new, monumental kind of symphony and a
daring contemporary language of sound.

His singularity becomes most clearly apparent when he is compared with Brahms. Brahms's
output was marked by its versatility and embraced every kind of music except for opera.
Bruckner's mature work, on the contrary, almost exclusively concentrated on the symphony,
religious music and a few secular items. Bruckner admired Wagner but wrote neither operas
nor musical dramas, neither songs nor piano
pieces. The String Quartet in C minor of 1862
and the String Quintet in F major of 1879 are
his only contributions to chamber music. He
was a famous organist and much admired as
an improviser yet, paradoxically, he composed
very little for the organ (though his orchestra
now and then comes to sound like a giant-sized
version of this instrument).

One of the most important aesthetic assump-
tions formulated in the nineteenth century was
that life and art should be at one. Many composers – Berlioz, Schumann, Wagner, Liszt,
Tchaikovsky, Mahler and Richard Strauss, for
example – allowed themselves to be stimulated
in their work by personal experiences, literary
and philosophical ideas, as well as visual images.

Many of their works must be seen against an
autobiographical background. How is it then
that Bruckner was described by some of his
pupils as a naïve, clumsy, owlish, even simple-
minded man? Many regarded him as a queer
fellow, an 'odd man out.' On the other hand, in
stark contrast to these descriptions, his symphonic output is regarded as being exceptionally grandiose. There remains, therefore, the
question of whether there was indeed a close
connection between personality and output in
his case or whether the 'world of the mind' was
irrelevant in so far as his work is concerned.

Only carefully conducted research is capable
of clearing away many preconceptions about
Bruckner. A few telling examples may help to
illustrate this. Incontrovertibly, he was a strict
and dogmatic Catholic to an almost unimaginable degree. The long years he spent in the
monastery of St Florian, first as a choirboy and
then as a teacher, left an indelible mark on his
personality. His religious attitude and his piety
became proverbial. Even when he was in Vienna
constant prayer and spiritual exercises formed
an integral part of his daily life. Some idea of
his piety can be gained by glancing at the 'lists
of prayers' in the diary where he recorded every
day how often he had recited the Rosary, the
Pater Noster, Ave Maria and Salve Regina. He
had religious visions and sometimes talked to
his pupil Friedrich Eckstein about the ecstasy
of the Good Friday liturgy and the mystery of
the Maundy Thursday vigil. The ultimate record
of Bruckner's deep religious sense is provided
by the church music of his mature period – the
three masses, the *Te Deum* and the setting of
Psalm 150 – all of them works in which an arch-
Catholic form of piety is manifest. In view of
all this, it is easy enough to understand why so
many saw Bruckner as a mystic, whose religious
world and spiritual experience were reflected in
his symphonies.

Yet no formula fits Bruckner perfectly, least
of all that which ascribes naïveté, simple-mind-
edness or even childishness to him. Bruckner
was certainly anything but a 'man of the world.'
His manners were somewhat clumsy and he
often struck famous artists, as well as his sup-
eriors, as inhibited and brusque. He felt insecure in the great city, having grown up in
village and cloister. But can the word naïveté
really be used in connection with a man who
pursued his professional and artistic aims with

astonishing perseverance and steadiness and whose attitude towards his own output was no less critical than that of Brahms?

To take another example: many nineteenth-century composers, as we know, took an active part in the intellectual, political and social events of their age. Wagner, Liszt, Brahms, Hugo Wolf and Mahler were all well versed in European philosophy and literature. This cannot be said of Bruckner. Yet it is absolutely incorrect to assert – as many of his disciples have done – that he lacked all literary, or even intellectual, interests. It is known for example that he read a number of books – including the very controversial *Life of Jesus* by David Friedrich Strauss – and formed an objective judgment on them. He was so well acquainted with the Bible that he could take issue with many theologians. He was extremely interested in world events and sensational news. He carefully followed information about the Austrian expedition to the North Pole, the history of Mexico and the fate of the Emperor Maximilian, and the meeting of the emperors of Austria, Germany and Russia at Skierniewice in 1884.

Judging by Bruckner's letters and various other reports, he seems to have had a manic-depressive temperament. Periods of deep depression, caused in part by loneliness, alternated in his emotional life with phases of euphoria. It is important to note in this connection that during the summer of 1867 he underwent a nervous breakdown as a result of excessive emotional tension and had to take a cure in a nursing home at Bad Kreuzen. He was suffering from 'total nervous exhaustion and overstrain,' as he wrote to his friend Rudolf Weinwurm. His illness took the form of a 'numbers mania,' which left some traces even after his recovery. A well-known psychologist has recently suggested that Bruckner's main neurosis was a lack of self-esteem. It was indeed easy to make him feel insecure. On the other hand, he was undoubtedly impelled by a strong sense of mission, or he would never have managed to bring into being such a tremendous symphonic output under the circumstances in which he was forced to compose it.

Women played hardly any active part in Bruckner's life, for his relationships with them were always unsuccessful. In old age he kept on falling in love with young girls, proposing marriage to them after a short acquaintance, and being invariably rebuffed. It is often claimed that Bruckner never wanted to marry because he wished to devote himself entirely to his work, but this is not true. Even as late as 6 November 1885 the sixty-one-year-old composer wrote to his patron Moritz von Mayfeld: 'As to my marriage, I have no fiancée up to now – if only I were able to find a suitably dear flame!'

And yet another paradox: Bruckner was very much a late developer as a composer, bearing in mind that Schumann and Brahms had already written their first masterpieces when they were twenty, while Wagner composed his *Flying Dutchman* at the age of twenty-eight. Bruckner, on the other hand, was forty when he com-

Right: Photograph of Bruckner (aged thirty-nine) taken in 1863, the year in which a Linz performance of Wagner's *Tannhäuser* made such a deep impression on him.

Below: The Augustinian monastery school at St Florian, near Linz, where Bruckner served first as a choirboy and then for several years as a teacher and organist.

pleted the D minor Mass, the first work in which he established his own personal style. In order to understand how this belated development came about, it is necessary to be aware of the way in which his training and professional career developed.

• Linz and St Florian •

Bruckner was born on 4 September 1824 in Ansfelden, a village near Linz in Austria. Like Schubert, he came from a family of teachers, and was a teacher himself until he reached the age of thirty-one. He taught as an assistant at Windhaag from 1841 and at Kronstorf from 1843. Between 1845 and 1855 he was employed first as teacher and from 1848 as temporary organist at the St Florian monastery. He diligently studied music in addition to his teaching work, because he was determined to perfect his abilities and knowledge in terms of organ playing and musical theory.

During his long stay at St Florian Bruckner had ample opportunity to become acquainted with religious music from the late Renaissance (Palestrina), the Baroque period (Caldara), and by Classical and the Romantic composers, as well as with secular music by Schubert. His most important works dating from the period between 1843 and 1855 were a Requiem in D minor in 1849 and a Missa Solemnis in B flat minor in 1854. These mainly reflect impressions gleaned from Mozart's Requiem and Haydn's Masses;

it would certainly be an exaggeration to claim any special degree of originality for either of these works of Bruckner's youth.

In 1855 Bruckner was appointed cathedral organist at Linz. His work in this prestigious post satisfied him, for the time being at any rate, but he was unhappy about his inadequate knowledge of musical theory. He got in touch with Simon Sechter, a well-known teacher in Vienna, became his pupil and studied with him for nearly six years. He covered harmony, counterpoint, canon and fugue with such zest that Sechter warned him to watch his health. In November 1861 Bruckner voluntarily took a stiff examination at the Conservatory of the Gesellschaft der Musikfreunde in Vienna and passed it with flying colors. Johann Herbeck, a member of the examination board, remarked: 'It is he who should have been examining us!'

Bruckner learned strict composition technique in all its aspects from Sechter, but was nevertheless well aware that his musical education had until then been fairly one-sided. He did not come into contact with the 'new music' of Wagner, Berlioz and Liszt until 1861. Therefore,

when Otto Kitzler, a practical musician who favored the new approach, came to Linz in 1861, first as a cellist and later as conductor in the City Theater, Bruckner asked whether he might study orchestration and musical form with him. These studies with Kitzler were of crucial importance for Bruckner's development. He came to know the score of Wagner's *Tannhäuser*, and its performance in Linz on 13 February 1863 made such a lasting impression on him that it is no exaggeration to claim that this Wagnerian event released his creative talent. As a result, Bruckner began to feel his way towards a personal style. He became an ardent Wagnerian and retained this allegiance throughout his life. He traveled to Munich in 1865 for a performance of *Tristan und Isolde* and in 1868 performed the final scene of *Die Meistersinger von Nürnberg* in Linz with the Frohsinn choral society, or Liedertafel. He also drew much inspiration from the works of Berlioz and Liszt, to which Ignaz Dorn, another modern-minded musician in Linz, had drawn his attention. Bruckner began to compose instrumental music during his studies under Kitzler – marches, orchestral pieces, an overture and also some symphonies. The F minor Symphony, which he later described as the 'Study Symphony,' was written in 1863. He worked on a Symphony in D minor during 1863-4, which he subsequently described as 'worthless' and designated as 'Number O.' By 1865-6 he had written his First Symphony in C minor, a highly original work which he nicknamed the 'Perky Little Broom' on account of its boldness. Alongside these compositions he also produced several choral works with instrumental accompaniment, such as various anthems and above all the three Masses – in D minor (1864), E minor (1866) and F minor (1868) – which laid the foundation of his fame as a composer of church music.

These works are stylistically notable for the unusual synthesis of the archaic and the modern. Bruckner knew how to put a traditional musical idiom and strict polyphonic techniques at the service of a contemporary 'Neo-romantic' expressive ideal. It is revealing that the E minor Mass, set for an eight-part mixed choir and wind instruments, is more austere in its effect than the other two. It undoubtedly has an affinity with the Renaissance *a capella* style, and the Sanctus is in the manner of Palestrina. On the other hand, in the D minor and F minor Masses, both written for soloists, four-part mixed choir and large orchestra, Bruckner modelled himself on Liszt and on his 'Gran' Mass of 1855 in particular. The setting of the text transcends its traditional framework. It is daring, novel and occasionally dramatic. In the Credo, for instance, Bruckner works with motifs, calls and fanfares which recur with the significance of *leitmotifs*. The strong impact is derived from a combination of pomp and devotion, brilliance and ecstasy, drama and inwardness. And it is also characteristic that Bruckner quoted particular motifs from these Masses in many of his symphonies in order to evoke special associations, especially in the Second, Third and Ninth.

Left: Simon Sechter (1788-1867), the Viennese organist, composer and musical theorist, with whom Bruckner studied composition. Schubert had planned to take lessons from Sechter twenty-seven years previously, just before he died.

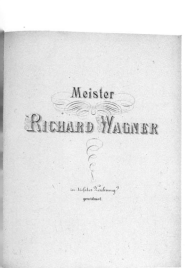

Above: Dedication page of the Third Symphony. Bruckner took the score to Bayreuth to secure Wagner's approval. When Wagner showed him the vault he had prepared for himself at Wahnfried, Bruckner fell to his knees and prayed.

Above: First page of the Third Symphony in D minor, dedicated to Richard Wagner, in Bruckner's autograph score. The quiet opening, characteristic of the composer, gradually builds up to an initial climax.

Below: Wild Boar in the Forest by Friedrich Gauermann (1807-62), the leading Austrian painter of his generation. The hills and forests of old Austria, rather than the cosmopolitan milieu of Vienna, were where Bruckner felt at home.

• Bruckner in Vienna •

His move to Vienna in 1868 was the most important event in Bruckner's life. He was appointed professor of harmony, counterpoint and organ at the Vienna Conservatory on 6 July of that year in succession to his late teacher, Simon Sechter. A little later, on 4 September, he was also named organist-designate at the Imperial Court Chapel, then a purely honorary post. To start with Bruckner lived in straitened circumstances. His income from the Conservatory was very small, and he sometimes had great difficulty keeping body and soul together, so that he was constantly forced to apply for other jobs. He only secured an adequate annual income on his appointment as a member of the court musical establishment in 1878.

In Vienna Bruckner's output was heavily biased towards symphonic writing. Between 1871 and his death in 1896 he produced one symphony after another, more or less without a break, and was often engaged on several simultaneously, writing a new one while revising an earlier work. He wrote relatively little other music: the String Quintet in 1879; the *Te Deum* in 1883; Psalm 150 in 1892; and *Helgoland*, a large work for male-voice choir and orchestra, in 1893. In addition to these he also produced a few minor religious and secular choral works.

Bruckner's vast and fruitful symphonic output during these early years in Vienna was entirely the result of an inner drive, since he received no outside encouragement at all. On the contrary, the Vienna Philharmonic Orchestra at first refused to play his Second Symphony, and

in general Bruckner's symphonies were only sporadically performed in Vienna before 1892. Even as late as 1891 Hugo Wolf complained that Bruckner hardly attracted any notice in Vienna. His opponents all praised Brahms to the skies and were reluctant even to acknowledge him in public as a serious composer. Brahms himself regarded him as a poor demented creature for whom the priests of St Florian bore a heavy responsibility. Throughout the rest of his life Bruckner was the victim of malevolent attacks by influential Viennese critics who repeatedly described his compositions as grotesque, shapeless, overambitious, lacking in musical logic, 'unnatural in expression' and exhibiting slavish admiration for Wagner. In 1886 Gustav Dömpke made the terrible judgment: 'Bruckner writes music like a drunken man!'

The most virulent campaign was conducted by Eduard Hanslick, the burden of whose criticism was that Bruckner had brought Wagner's dramatic style into the realm of the symphony. Hanslick firmly believed that this represented an offence against the highest aesthetic principles, a fatal infringement of the natural boundaries of the symphony. Hanslick's now famous reviews of Bruckner's works make his strong dislike and total lack of understanding of them obvious, but within their limits they are logical enough. A critic dedicated to formalism would necessarily have regarded all Bruckner's symphonies as monstrosities.

The monumental type of symphony developed by Bruckner as part of Beethoven's and Schubert's heritage was outwardly characterized by an enlargement of the individual movements. While the classical sonata form relied on the juxtaposition of two contrasting themes, Bruckner built the outer movements of his symphonies on three extensive thematic complexes, the second of these being conspicuously lyrical in character. He also extended the codas of the movements: the opening subject of a symphony usually returns at the end of the opening movement and again in the finale where it undergoes an 'apotheosis.' Bruckner was a master of the adagio and the finale. No other composer surpasses him in the breadth, grandeur and splendor of the slow movements. And his finales are the equal of the opening movements in their sheer weight and content.

The modern character and boldness of his harmony still provoke admiration even today. Bruckner often modulated in the most unlikely keys, but never lost sight of his ultimate aim. No wonder that many of his contemporaries were simply overwhelmed. Even favorable critics sometimes referred to a 'tonal odyssey of the most adventurous sort.'

The influence of Wagner has generally been seen as paramount and this is obvious in a number of ways: in Bruckner's use of repeated quotations and echoes; in his deployment of the orchestra and in his instrumentation; in his harmony and frequent calls and fanfares; in his predilection for aria and recitative-like elements; in the starkness of his contrasts; and, not least, in a new kind of formal conception which met

with a total lack of understanding among his contemporaries. This conception is dynamic rather than static, and closely resembles the principles of dramatic music. The powerful swell of the climaxes, the overwhelmingly effective crescendos, which in Bruckner's music usually herald a slackening of tension, reflect waves of emotion which rise steeply to a peak and fall away – often very abruptly.

But Bruckner was no slavish follower of Wagner. He had fully mastered the strict technique of baroque form and acquired his approach to symphonic writing from a number of sources: Beethoven, Schubert, Wagner, even the program symphonists – Berlioz and Liszt. The strongest of these influences came from Wagner's Romantic operas and musical dramas, Beethoven's Ninth, Schubert's great C major as well as his 'Unfinished' Symphony, Berlioz's *Harold in Italy* and Liszt's 'Faust' Symphony.

• The early symphonies •

Nobody can deny that the nine symphonies which Bruckner declared 'valid' form a sort of family with many resemblances between its members. Several symphonies have a similar or even identical 'ground plan.' Thus the first themes of the opening movements, for instance, are sweeping and expansive, and are usually supported by a tremolo on the strings. The second themes are often lyrical and *cantabile*, and are contrapuntally set off by a contrasting voice. The third themes frequently start in unison and develop astonishing rhythmic energies. But the suggestion that his symphonic output was 'stereotyped,' or that any symphony by Bruckner is so like another that they could be mistaken for each other is simply not tenable.

Above: Votive painting of 1838, from a pilgrimage church in Upper Bavaria, showing a peasant couple dedicating their horses and cattle to St Leonhard in execution of a vow. The beliefs and customs of Catholic piety, unshaken for centuries, which were an integral part of the rural culture of southern Germany and Austria, were fundamental to the character of Bruckner's life and music.

Bruckner's First Symphony in C minor, written in Linz during 1865-6 and first performed there in 1868, is a work of great boldness and originality. Many of Bruckner's characteristic features are already apparent in it to a marked extent: three well defined themes lending themselves to development underlie the outer movements; powerful waves of sound reaching a climax usually lead to a formal slackening of tension; there is an unmistakable tendency to tight polyphonic writing; and elemental rhythmic bursts of energy develop from the scherzo. On the other hand there are significant differences from the later symphonies. The outer movements are only loosely related to each other in thematic terms. Chorale-like themes are absent. And there are none of those articulating pauses which from the Second Symphony onwards serve to separate the thematic complexes from each other.

Compared to the First Symphony, the Second – completed in Vienna in 1872 – is in many ways more smooth and 'classical' in its effect. Bruckner was striving for greater 'intelligibility' in this work, as the numerous pauses between the various sections immediately indicate. Their purpose is to stress the formal pattern and bridge excessively harsh contrasts, but they unfortunately earned for this work the nickname of the 'Symphony of Pauses.' The Second Symphony is fundamentally important in the evolution of Bruckner's symphonic writing. The dimensions are by now vast: this symphony is twenty minutes longer than the First. The themes merge to form entire complexes. The outer movements are for the first time linked by a common theme. Similarly, chorale-like elements appear for the first time, especially in the adagio. Indeed, epic sweep rather than dramatic animation may be regarded as the basic feature of the Second Symphony.

Compared to the Second Symphony, the Third (completed in 1873 and several times revised) is marked by a number of 'progressive' features. No wonder that Wagner preferred it to the Second when Bruckner offered both to him at Bayreuth in September 1873. The work derived its inspiration from Beethoven, Schubert, Berlioz and Wagner. Bruckner also paid homage to Wagner with numerous quotations from *Die Walküre* and *Tristan* in the first version, some of which were later deleted.

Among Bruckner's early symphonies, it is probably his Third which provides the strongest contrasts. The individual movements differ more sharply from each other than in the Second, and the various themes come across as more plastic and better differentiated. Rugged thematic and dynamic contrasts in close conjunction follow each other more frequently. An impressive example of this is provided in the opening movement at the end of the development. Even the adagio, which displays strong affinities with Bruckner's church music, is not without such effects. Similarly there is tension between the uncannily dynamic scherzo and the *Ländler*-like trio. Such contrasts, however, reach their most extreme dramatic peak in the finale, which

Bruckner himself described as the conjunction of opposites – 'the joy and the sadness of the world' – represented by the contrapuntal interweaving of two figures as ill-assorted as the polka-like strings and the chorale-like wind section in the second subject-group of the finale.

The composer's own program notes relating to the Fourth and Eighth Symphonies, which in the past had usually been either laughed at or ignored, must now be taken seriously. They can contribute to a deeper understanding of the work.

The Fourth – so-called 'Romantic' – Symphony, written in 1874 and radically revised between 1878 and 1881, has always been Bruckner's most popular work. Together with the Seventh, it was the most frequently performed of all the symphonies during his lifetime. Even the first performance on 20 February 1881 in Vienna scored a great success, all the more

remarkable after the resounding failure of the Third.

What caused Bruckner to describe the Fourth as the 'Romantic' and what did he understand by that title? Recent research has suggested that Wagner's *Lohengrin* embodied the essence of Romanticism for Bruckner. This opera conjured up for him conceptions of the miraculous, the mysterious, the religious and the pure, and much of this imaginary world found its way into the Fourth Symphony.

According to a statement by Theodor Helms, Bruckner had elucidated the opening movement of the 'Romantic' Symphony as follows: 'A medieval city – Daybreak – Awakening calls sound from the city's towers – The gates are opened – The knights on noble chargers spring out into the open, the magic of nature engulfs them – Woodland rustling – Birds singing – And so the romantic picture develops further . . .' This 'program' in fact turns out to have been a paraphrase of certain stage directions from two of Wagner's operas – *Lohengrin* and *Siegfried*.

Like the allegretto from Berlioz's symphony *Harold in Italy*, the andante represents a march

Above: The old university in Vienna, where Bruckner became lecturer in harmony and counterpoint after much opposition from Eduard Hanslick, who was himself the professor of aesthetics and music history and was an outspoken critic of Bruckner's music.

of pilgrims by night. The first of the three themes in this movement is elegiac; the second – described by Bruckner as a 'prayer' – is a four-line chorale made up of long notes; while the third theme is a quite differently constructed six-line chorale with a pizzicato accompaniment. Of the two climaxes achieved by the principal theme, the second is far more intense than the first. The scherzo and trio of the first version were replaced by entirely new pieces

Right: Bruckner's 'artistic father,' as he called him, the celebrated Wagnerian conductor Hermann Levi. His rejection of the original draft of the Eighth Symphony in C minor at first shocked Bruckner, but led to a revised and much improved version of the huge work.

Above: The brothers Franz and Joseph Schalk, two of Bruckner's students at Vienna University, who became ardent champions of his music. They organized performances and prepared editions of the symphonies and other works. Franz became principal conductor of the Vienna Hofoper after Hans Richter.

during the revision of 1878. The lightly impressionistic scherzo of the final version is conceived as a hunting piece, which the horn fanfares announce at the start. Bruckner himself described the *Ländler*-like trio as a 'dance tune to accompany a meal on a hunting trip.'

There are no less than three distinct versions of the finale. This movement was so thoroughly reworked during its last revision in 1880 that it completely lost the jaunty character it had in the first version. Not only are new and to some extent dramatic elements introduced in place of the original melodic ideas, but a number of the

original passages acquired a different character through darker coloring. In this final version the movement has become powerfully tense.

The Fifth Symphony, written in 1875-6 and revised during the two years that followed, is often described in the literature on the subject as the 'Symphony of Faith.' This description is more easily understood when it is remembered that chorale-like elements abound in this work and that the finale in fact ends with a grandiose 'chorale' as Bruckner himself described it. Compared with the luminous Fourth, moreover, the Fifth is sterner and more austere in its effect. It is the only one among Bruckner's symphonies which starts with a slow introduction recalling religious music, in which three contrasting figures are stated. These return during the development of the allegro which follows, and in which they are subjected to numerous variations. The second movement, an adagio in D minor, is based on two themes. The first, introduced by the woodwind and supported by pizzicato strings in unison is a 'doleful air.' The fully harmonized second theme, on the contrary, assumes a hymn-like and ecstatic quality. The great climaxes which both themes achieve during the course of this movement are extremely impressive. The adagio and scherzo are closely linked not only by their common key of D minor but also by their themes, since most of the motifs of the first adagio theme return in the scherzo, although the latter also introduces new ideas. The second theme of the scherzo is particularly noteworthy, for Bruckner twines into it contrapuntally a *Ländler*-like melody with figures reminiscent of the Alpine horn. As in Beethoven's Ninth, the finale is preceded by an introduction which quotes passages from the earlier movements, partly by way of recapitulation. A solo clarinet announces the first theme of the finale in the gaps between the quotations, and the movement as a whole represents a highly sophisticated synthesis of sonata and fugal forms. Two of the movement's themes are treated as a double fugue. Bruckner was not exaggerating when he described the Fifth as his 'contrapuntal masterpiece.' A prominent musicologist went even further when he claimed that the conclusion of this symphony is among the most exalted creations of all music – or indeed of the human spirit.

Bruckner composed his String Quintet a few years after the Fifth Symphony. The work was completed in 1879 and composed at the suggestion of Joseph Hellmesberger, the director of the Vienna Conservatory and leader of a famous quartet. Hellmesberger originally did not approve of the second movement, a scherzo, and therefore induced Bruckner to compose an intermezzo instead. Yet at the first Viennese performance of the complete work in 1885 he changed his mind again and opted for the original scherzo. This work, in four movements, incorporates features proper to both symphonic and chamber music, however paradoxical this may sound. Much of the composition is very tightly written and there is no lack of those great surges of sound that are such a feature of

Bruckner's symphonic writing. But the movements as compared to those of the symphonies are more restricted in their scope, and the treatment of the five string instruments is undoubtedly much akin to chamber music. Even Bruckner's opponents were forced to admit that the highly expressive adagio extended 'beyond all similar contemporary instrumental compositions in terms of inventiveness and meaningful combination.'

•The Sixth and Seventh Symphonies•

Ernst Kurth, the distinguished expert on Bruckner, thought that the 'ground color' of the Sixth Symphony in A major, written between 1879 and 1881, seemed to shine forth like a 'radiant light.' Strictly speaking, however, this description fits only the opening movement, whose

Left: Hermann Kaulbach's portrait of the composer, painted in March 1885 while he was in Munich for the performance there of his Seventh Symphony.

Far left: Title-page to the first edition of the Ninth Symphony in D minor, which Bruckner dedicated to God. He died while working on the finale. His sketches for this are quite advanced, and recently a performing version of the movement has been made.

coda does indeed provide a palette of shimmering sounds. The inside movements, by contrast, are less luminous; in fact these are sometimes subdued and dark in coloring. The 'very festive' adagio, for instance, occasionally makes a plaintive sound not far removed from that of a funeral march. And the development of the finale, which begins in the minor keys, makes it plain that the triumphant A major effect of the conclusion cannot be achieved without a painstaking preparation. The motto *per aspera ad astra* was most likely to have been in Bruckner's mind while composing this movement.

The Seventh Symphony in E major (composed between 1881 and 1883) was the first work to bring Bruckner real success and smooth the way to the concert hall for his other symphonies. What is it that imparts such tremendous power of persuasion to this symphony? Its lay-out at first sight hardly seems to differ from that of his earlier symphonies. The opening movement is generous in scope. Both outside movements are based on three thematic complexes. Bruckner's dynamic approach is equally evident here in the great surges of sound. But on closer examination a number of fine distinctions become obvious: the formal articulation is more easy to grasp; the motifs strike deeper; the themes are – as ever in Bruckner's case – strongly contrasted, but they are so fitted together that movement is preserved throughout. Above all, however, the Seventh stands out by its intense luminosity. In this it is comparable with the Fourth (with which it also shares a tendency to sound 'romantic').

The elegiac adagio in C sharp minor has won particular favor among the movements of the Seventh. Its genesis undoubtedly contributed to this. As Bruckner's letters show, the adagio had been fully sketched by 22 January 1883, in anticipation of Wagner's death. When he heard that Wagner had indeed died, Bruckner completed the composition up to the coda. The passage for tubas and horns, apparently written under the immediate impact of the news, was intended by Bruckner as 'mourning music in memory of the Master's passing.' Thematic correlations with the closing movement of the *Te Deum*, only completed in 1884 as part of the second version, indicate that the Christian affirmation of faith, 'Non confundar in aeternum' (Let me never be confounded), equally underlies the adagio, and the way it builds up to a climax is one of the most powerful moments in all symphonic writing. Bruckner first used 'Wagner tubas' in this movement, and was to use them again in the Eighth and Ninth Symphonies.

•The *Te Deum* and the Eighth Symphony •

Right: Hans Makart's design for a memorial church dedicated to St Michael, executed in 1883, the year Bruckner embarked on his setting of the Te Deum.

Below: Three Women in Church (1878-82) by Wilhelm Leibl, who had been the leader of a group of painters in Munich – an expression of the same devout, unquestioning faith that was such an important element in Bruckner's personality.

The *Te Deum*, completed in 1884, is probably Bruckner's best-known religious work. It is written for four soloists, four-part choir and large orchestra, and is divided into three main parts: the grandiose hymn of praise (verses 1-19), the prayer (verses 20-28) and the jubilant conclusion (verse 29). The middle section is once again arranged in matched outer movements: 'Te ego quaesumus' and 'Salvum fac populum tuum' frame the mighty 'Aeterna fac.' Just as in Bruckner's Masses, the *Te Deum* combines splendor with piety, brilliance with enchantment. Numerous thematic links between the various sections lend great unity to the work. The psalmodic passage at the beginning, for instance, returns repeatedly in a variety of versions. The strong impact of the conclusion owes less to the elaborate fugue than to the diatonically firm, powerful, chorale-like idea of

the 'Non confundar in aeternum' which he had used in the adagio of the Seventh Symphony. It is also indicative of Bruckner's spiritual attitude that, as he wrote to Hermann Levi on 10 May 1885, he had dedicated the *Te Deum* to God 'in thanksgiving for so much suffering overcome in Vienna.'

When Bruckner reached the age of sixty, on 4 September 1884, he had already completed the major part of his output – the three Masses, seven of the symphonies and the *Te Deum* – but still had not achieved recognition in Vienna as a composer. His fortunes changed only when the Seventh Symphony was performed in Leipzig on 30 December 1884 by Arthur Nikisch, and in Munich on 10 March 1885 by Hermann Levi. The Munich performance in particular marks a turning-point in the history of Bruckner's reputation. From then on increasing fame abroad came his way. Many conductors began to take an interest in him. He was now able to tell his friends proudly about performances of his works in Germany, Holland, Norway and even the United States. Bruckner could no longer be disregarded in Austria, and honors were showered upon him. In 1886 he was awarded the Knight's Cross of the Order of

Top: The Kustoden-stöckl, or gate-keeper's lodge, at the Belvedere Palace, Vienna, which the Emperor Franz Joseph offered to Bruckner in 1895, when the ailing composer found it difficult to climb the stairs in his old apartment.

Above: A page from Bruckner's notebook recording his devotions for each day. The letters stand for different prayers; the three lines with a stroke through them stand for a rosary. Such entries also reflect the composer's wider obsession with numbers and repetitions.

Franz Joseph and a personal pension from the imperial purse. He was elected to a society for the promotion of musical art in Amsterdam. The Council of Upper Austria voted him an annual recognition grant amounting to 400 Gulden. He was elected an honorary member of the Gesellschaft der Musikfreunde in January 1891. On 7 November of that year his greatest wish of all was fulfilled when the University of Vienna, where he had spent several years lecturing on musical theory, conferred upon him an honorary doctorate. During the ceremony on 11 December, at which this degree was awarded, the rector of the University included in his speech words which have since become famous: 'At the point at which science must come to a stop, the point at which it encounters unsurmountable limits, there begins the realm of art which can express what is denied to the whole of science. And so the rector of the University of Vienna bows before the former assistant teacher from Windhaag.'

In the meantime Bruckner had been working on his Eighth Symphony which he began to sketch out in 1884. He reported its completion to Hermann Levi on 4 September 1887 and sent him the score on 19 September in the hope that he would conduct it in Munich. Levi was disturbed by the vastness of the work and wrote to Joseph Schalk, one of Bruckner's favorite pupils, asking him to break it gently to the master that he lacked the courage to perform the Eighth. He openly confessed that he found the instrumentation 'impossible' and described the finale as 'a closed book' as far as he was concerned. Levi's criticism deeply shocked Bruckner and precipitated a severe psychological crisis. Nevertheless he immediately decided to comply with the authoritative judgment of the great conductor, whom he used to describe as his 'artistic father.' He reworked the Eighth in the course of 1889-90, shortened it, changed a number of passages, completely rewrote several others and so produced a second version.

Bruckner's Eighth Symphony is a grandiose work whether viewed from a structural or a semantic point of view. In a letter of 27 January 1891 to the conductor Felix Weingartner, Bruckner provided fairly extensive program notes for three of the movements. These have attracted no attention until recently, but they are tremendously enlightening. They make it clear, for example, that a dramatic concept underlies the opening movement. Bruckner refers to two passages in particular: he saw the climax of the recapitulation as an 'announcement of death'; and he described the coda as standing for 'resignation' and also as a 'death knell' or a 'death clock.' Both passages are formulated in a rather unusual way. At the climax of the recapitulation the horns and trumpets together intone *fortissimo* the dotted rhythm of the main theme no less than ten times in succession – a passage of elemental power. A general pause then marks an abrupt ending, with three *pianissimo* drum rolls. Then the coda takes up the leading motif of the main theme in dirge-like fashion and fades away quietly.

This is more easily understood when it is realised that Bruckner drew his inspiration for this movement from an aria in Richard Wagner's *Der fliegende Holländer* – the C minor aria of the Dutchman in the first act. The main theme of the symphony bears a striking resemblance to the theme of the aria, the text of which describes the spiritual landscape in which Bruckner's music seeks to find its place. Bruckner refers to 'an announcement of death' and to 'resignation,' while Wagner's text reflects the Flying Dutchman's death-wish as he looks forward to the release that awaits him on 'Judgment Day' and 'the resurrection of the dead.'

The scherzo of the Eighth Symphony, on the other hand, must be interpreted in terms of contemporary history. Bruckner wished this movement to be understood as a portrait of 'Deutscher Michel' (German Michael), a popular traditional lay figure representing the simple-minded ordinary citizen. During the nineteenth century this personage came to symbolize and sum up German political hopes, disappointments and fears: the hopes aroused by the foundation of the German Empire, the disappointment at German political lethargy, and the fear of being worsted in the struggle for domination among the world powers. In the Austro-Hungarian Empire, the character of 'Deutscher Michel' was used as a means of goading the population into political vigilance. Bruckner's contemporaries were well aware of the symbolism involved, and the painter Ferry Bératon in fact portrayed Bruckner as the 'German Michael' in 1892.

Bruckner also provided more detailed indications concerning the finale. He related the main theme of this movement to a world event: the meeting of the Emperor of Austria with the Russian Tsar. There is nothing fanciful about this program indication: the strophically arranged theme, a statement on the brasses in which trumpet fanfares are specially prominent, has the feel of military music. Bruckner designated two other passages in the finale as a 'Death March' and 'Ecstasy.' The third thematic complex is indeed followed by a grandiose march-like section which, in addition, quotes the rhythm of the 'announcement of death' from the opening movement. It cannot therefore be denied that the score of this last movement is full of extra-musical images.

After its first performance in Vienna on 18 December 1892 the Eighth was acclaimed by the majority of the press as 'the crown of the music of our time.' But Eduard Hanslick remained an unyielding opponent of Bruckner and confessed that the symphony as a whole had 'alienated, indeed repelled' him. He went on to express the fear that the future might belong to 'this confused dream-ridden caterwauling.'

Bruckner composed his last religious work, a setting of Psalm 150, in 1892. The praise of the Lord moved him to write a superbly vivid and radiant piece from which darker colors are absent. In baroque manner, the composition falls into a powerful five-part introduction and a skillful fugue, whose monumental effect owes much to the structure of its vigorous theme.

• The last symphony •

Bruckner spent the ten years before his death working on his last symphony, the unfinished Ninth. The work has a special aura, not just because it is his last, but also because he put it about that he would have liked to dedicate it to 'the good Lord.' One's first reaction to this musical torso is astonishment at the novelty and boldness of its tonal structure. Bruckner was reaching out into areas of sound which were only to come into their own later with early expressionist music. The first indications of a new world, on whose threshold this music stood, are unmistakable. The melodic treatment gives special preference to compound intervals, the rich harmony is saturated by Wagnerian chromaticism, and the great surges of sound are characterized by their unusual steepness.

The rich and expressive *misterioso* opening movement is marked by acute contrasts. Bruckner prepared the entry of the powerful main theme superbly by a long-drawn upward swell after a darkly mysterious start. The development and reprise culminate in shattering climaxes, the last of which takes the form of a sharp, long-sustained, unresolved dissonance – an unprecedented mass of sound endowed with staggering power.

The scherzo is the most original of its kind composed by Bruckner. The sound ranges from the soft, virtually impressionistic touches of the woodwind and the strings in a pizzicato dialogue to the massive throb of the *tutti*. The subtle trio, closely bordering on chamber music, has a lightness of touch uncommon in Bruckner's work.

The adagio should above all be interpreted in an autobiographical context. When the com-poser began to outline it in April 1894 he had already been ill for two years. He was suffering from heart and kidney malfunctions, breathlessness and dropsy. His condition would temporarily improve and then relapse again. He was full of intimations of death. Although he was by no means unaware of the growing recognition achieved by his music, he still underwent frequent periods of depression. It is therefore indicative that he wished the elegiac passage on the tuba in the adagio to be understood as a 'Farewell to Life.' The musical quotations contained in the adagio are no less significant. A Miserere phrase from the Gloria of the F minor Mass provides the main formative element for the subsidiary theme. In addition there are quotations from the Benedictus of the F minor Mass, the adagio of the Eighth and the opening movement of the Seventh Symphony. These quotations and other observations indicate that Bruckner embodied in the adagio of the Ninth a gripping artistic expression of his foreboding of death, his religious faith and his hope in God.

Elaborate sketches for the finale of the Ninth have survived and reach as far as the coda. The composer, by now seriously ill, was fated not to complete this movement. He therefore expressed the wish that the *Te Deum* should be performed at the end of the symphony.

Bruckner died at about three in the afternoon of 11 October 1896, after he had worked a little in the morning on the last movement of the Ninth Symphony. On 12 October, Hugo Wolf wrote to his friend Dr Heinrich Potpeschnigg: 'You will probably already have found out from the newspapers that Bruckner has died. The funeral takes place tomorrow. People today have no inkling as yet of the importance of the man whom they will be taking to his final rest tomorrow.'

Below: Bruckner's memorial in Vienna. He had a morbid fascination with death, and his body, at his own request, was placed directly beneath the 'Bruckner Organ' in the crypt of the Stiftskirche of St Florian, the sarcophagus surrounded by the piled-up bones of victims of the seventeenth-century Turkish Wars.

Left: Bruckner seated by his beloved Bösendorfer piano, which he inherited as a young man. This photograph of him was probably taken soon after his move to the lodge in the Belvedere Palace; that is, in the last year of his life.

The Austro-Hungarian Empire

Franz Joseph's Empire embraced peoples of many nations and included all of modern Austria, Hungary and Czechoslovakia, as well as part of Italy, Yugoslavia, Rumania, Poland and Russia. The political history of the Emperor's long reign is dominated by the national aspirations of many groups, and these are reflected in the cultural and musical history.

In 1867 the Hungarians were granted their own constitution, an event that was celebrated symbolically by the coronation of Franz Joseph as King of Hungary on 8 June 1867, and so began the period of the 'Dual Monarchy,' of which the title *kaiserlich und königlich* (imperial and royal) and its familiar abbreviation *k.u.k.* are a constant reminder. But the Czechs in Bohemia bitterly resented Hungary's special status, and for more than ten years, from 1868, they boycotted the Parliament in Vienna, until the 'Young Czech' party showed that obstruction tactics within Parliament itself could be a more effective means of opposition. Meanwhile, the Empire was run by the bureaucracy – Vienna was packed with civil servants – and the status quo was preserved by a policy of 'muddling through.'

In 1873 Vienna's first international exhibition (*above right*), with over a thousand exhibitors and seen by seven million visitors, opened in the Prater on 1 May. Eight days later – on 'black Wednesday' – came the disastrous Stock Market crash, which caused thousands of bankruptcies. Vienna recovered. The city had expanded into a new industrial metropolis linked by railways to the outposts of the Empire, proud of its grand buildings on the new Ringstrasse, yet still – as this painting of 1884 (*below*) shows – an old imperial city surrounded by woods and vineyards sloping down to the Danube.

The undercurrent of tragedy and pessimism beneath the sparkling surface of Viennese life was a part too of the personal life of the Emperor. In 1853 he had escaped an attempt on his life (*right*); his marriage the next year to Elisabeth of Bavaria soon became unhappy; later his only son Rudolph committed suicide; in 1898 his wife was assassinated; finally the assassination of his nephew and heir Franz Ferdinand led to the outbreak of war and the end of the Empire.

The gypsies in the Empire earned a fame far beyond their numbers – there were less than a hundred thousand in Hungary in 1890. They were known as metalworkers and horse-dealers, but above all for their violin playing (the painting below is by Pettenkofen). Almost all the 'Hungarian' color in music from Haydn and Schubert to Liszt and Brahms comes from the gypsy violinists.

Johann Strauss the Younger had already tried the heady mixture of Hungarian *czárdás* and Viennese waltz in Rosalinde's celebrated aria in *Die Fledermaus*; and with his new operetta *Der Zigeunerbaron* (The Gypsy Baron), first performed on the eve of his sixtieth birthday in 1885 (the original poster is shown below), Hungary took Vienna by storm.

From his first year as Emperor until his death in 1916 Franz Joseph took all his official duties with the greatest seriousness: here (*above*) he is shown in his capacity as Hungarian king working at his desk in Budapest. He saw himself as the representative of a divine order, and there could never be any compromise over his position and function as head of the Dual Monarchy.

Right: The Charles Bridge over the Vltava in Prague around 1900. The failure of the Czechs either to achieve a separate status like the Hungarians, or to have their language officially put on a level with German, only intensified their cultural nationalism. Prague, remembering its golden age under Emperor Charles IV five hundred years earlier, before the establishment of the Hapsburg dynasty, was changed in two generations from a German city to one that was almost exclusively Czech.

The silver wedding of Franz Joseph and Elisabeth in 1879 was celebrated by the city of Vienna with a splendid procession in historical costume along the new Ringstrasse. Floats, costumes, trappings were all designed by the society painter Hans Makart, who himself led the procession on a white charger. The painting below is the artist's design for the section of the procession which represented the Imperial and Royal Railways – and displays a wealth of quite unexpected symbolism.

The Emperor's noble Hungarian Bodyguard (*left*) had been founded in the eighteenth century by Maria Theresa, but was disbanded during the revolutions of 1848. After Franz Joseph's coronation as King of Hungary, the Guard was revived, to consist of one hundred distinguished – if rather elderly – Hungarian aristocrats in dashing uniforms.

Right: Empress Elisabeth as Queen of Hungary. When she first went to Budapest with Franz Joseph in 1866, she was entranced by the charm of the Hungarians and by Count Andrássy in particular, and it seems clear that her influence cannot be discounted as a decisive factor in the Hungarians' achievement of their own responsible government in February 1867.

ERZSÉBET CSÁSZÁRNŐ MAGYARORSZÁG KIRÁLY
(AZ 186: " KORONÁZÁS ÖLTONYÉBEN)

The declaration of the Republic in Paris in 1848 sparked off revolutions all over Europe. They were particularly severe in the Austrian Empire, where there had not only been food crises, but where the Italian and Hungarian nationalist movements were becoming increasingly active. By the end of 1849 all resistance had been crushed, but there had been fighting in Vienna itself, in which the students (*right*, building barriers outside the university), who were in the main supporters of Pan-German nationalism, played an active part.

Infuriated by the grant of a constitution to the Hungarians, the Czechs kept up their demands for the old rights and privileges of the kingdom of Bohemia and, in particular, the wider official use of the Czech language. The Bohemian Court Chancellery in Vienna had been disbanded more than a century earlier, and its building (*below left*) now housed the Ministry of the Interior. On 8 June 1900, the Czechs staged a 'concert' in Parliament in Vienna, using toy trumpets and whistles and saucepan lids as improvised percussion, that continued unabated until after midnight, finally degenerating into a brawl as other deputies tried to intervene. The Prime Minister had no alternative but to wake up the Emperor so that he could authorize the immediate closure of the parliamentary session.

Left: Count Julius Andrássy (1823-90). Starting as a supporter of the popular nationalist leader Lajos Kossuth and having followed him into exile, Andrássy returned when an amnesty was granted for the royal wedding and became the Hungarians' chief negotiator with the Emperor for their constitution. He was of excellent family, extremely persuasive, and a man of great personal charm – qualities which enabled him not only to bring the negotiations to a successful outcome but to go on to become Prime Minister of Hungary, Foreign Minister of the Empire and the Empress's confidant.

Right: The imperial and royal patent was much sought after. This advertisement, with its imperial double-headed eagle, appeared on the back cover of the Secessionist magazine *Ver Sacrum* in 1899-1900, designed by Maximilian Lenz, one of the movement's founders.

Left: Karel Kramář (1860-1937), who became the first Prime Minister of Czechoslovakia after the break-up of the Empire in 1918. During the 1890s as a leader of the Young Czechs, he was promoting a closer alignment of the monarchy with Russia rather than Germany, and he was at the forefront of the obstruction concert in Parliament, leading the deputies in the singing of national songs.

One of Vienna's popular traditions was the *Burgmusik* (*above*), played at noon each day for the changing of the Guard. As the band returned to barracks it was always escorted by a crowd of small boys.

The Czech National Theater (*above*), which opened in 1881, was a symbol of the strong renaissance of Czech culture. Its construction – and reconstruction after the disastrous fire in the opening year – was financed almost entirely through popular subscription.

The *Volkssänger* (*left*) were another survival of popular musical traditions in Vienna. They appeared on temporary stages (*Pablatsch'n*) in wine-houses and sang, alone or with a partner, sentimental or comic songs – with words as often as not by Wilhelm Wiesberg and music by J. Sioly – in praise of the easy charm of Vienna, the old *Steffl* (St Stephen's Cathedral), the happy days of Schubert's time, wine and its effects, women and song.

BEDŘICH SMETANA

KURT HONOLKA

Bedřich Smetana is regarded as the creator of an identifiably Czech national music. Czechs still honor him as their first composer of international significance, indeed as their greatest artist ever. They are certainly right in this: it was Smetana who, as composer, pianist, conductor, critic and organizer of cultural life, as well as creative artistic personality, awakened the latent national, intellectual and moral forces at a time when Czechs were once again becoming an integrated nation. Abroad, his fame was overshadowed by that of his younger compatriot Antonín Dvořák, and the only works that have gained real international repute are his immortal comic opera *Prodaná nevěsta* (The Bartered Bride), the symphonic poems *Vltava* and, perhaps, *Z českých luhů a hájů* (From Bohemia's Woods and Fields) and the string quartet *Z mého života* (From my Life). This is far too narrow a selection from a lifetime's rich output consisting of a further seven operas and a multitude of excellent orchestral works, chamber music and works for piano, choir and solo voices.

Smetana's place as founding father of his people's culture is unique. The Czechs owe their first opera, their first string quartet and their first orchestral work of international standing to him. All this came about astonishingly late. No national culture is born overnight, yet the birth of serious music that is specifically Czech in character can almost be dated to a single decade. Smetana's first opera *Braniboři v Čechách* (The Brandenburgers in Bohemia) and *The Bartered Bride* were first performed, one shortly after the other, in 1866. The first of these was still no more than a trial piece, the second a masterpiece which has since found a well-established place in the comic opera repertoire alongside Mozart's *Marriage of Figaro* and Verdi's *Falstaff*, and it remains unrivaled as a popular opera of pronounced national character which, at the same time, achieves the very highest artistic standard.

The late date of this great new national style is all the more surprising when one recalls how richly endowed in musical terms the Czech nation had been since earliest times, with its flourishing folklore and an ancient musical tradition. Masses in the Old Slavonic vernacular were already being sung during the ninth century under the Greater Moravian Empire, while the earliest musical manuscripts available date

from the eleventh century and, during the decades that followed, a school of *Minnesang* developed at the ducal court in Prague under the Přemyslid dynasty, in close parallel with similar manifestations of German culture. The religious chorales of the Hussites (followers of the reformer Jan Hus) in the fifteenth century exerted a later stylistic influence across the border on the German Lutheran chorale, thus making a return for many centuries of fertilization of Czech music by Germany. During the eighteenth century Bohemia and Moravia overflowed with musical talent to such an extent that many who could not find employment at home were forced to emigrate. The princely courts of Germany, as well as Vienna, Paris and the cities of Italy became the adopted homes of 'Bohemian musicians' who were everywhere held in high regard. Johann Stamitz, founder of the 'Mannheim School,' who was a German-speaking Bohemian; Jiří (Georg) Benda, the north-German master of the melodrama; Antonín Rejcha, who called himself Anton or Antoine Reicha; and Carl Czerny, the Czech-born Viennese master of piano studies, were only a few of the celebrated conductors and virtuoso performers scattered across the continent who overflowed from the 'music school of Europe,' as the English musicologist and traveler Charles Burney described Bohemia.

As might be expected, the renewal and rebirth of the Czech nation began with the language. It was German, oddly enough, for so long the instrument of repression, that stimulated newly found Czech self-awareness – the language of Johann Gottfried Herder, who had put 'the gentle Slavs' back on the map and contrasted them favorably with the warlike Germans; and the idealistic and humanist language of Goethe and Schiller, whose works were venerated by the Czechs together with those of Heine. It was Father Josef Dobrovský, the founder of Slavic studies, who directed the nation's attention to the Czech language which had been neglected for so long, and Karel Hynek Mácha created the *Máj* (Month of May) epic under the influence of Byron and the German Romantics, an early monument of Czech poetic diction which is still revered today. At the same time, the historian František Palacký reawakened the Czechs' pride in their great past.

Music had been neglected during this national 'rebirth' (*obrození*). Numerous village choirmasters and organists certainly carried on a musical tradition among this highly talented people, but their approach was extremely conservative. The Viennese classics – Haydn, Mozart and Beethoven – set the tone, and even hesitant attempts to create a Czech *Singspiel* (the most popular of these came from the conductor František Škroup) slavishly followed German models.

• Early life •

Bedřich Smetana was born on 2 March 1824 in Eastern Bohemia in the small town of Litomyšl, some seventy-five miles from Prague as the crow flies. His father, František Smetana (1777-1857) had leased the local landowner's brewery. Such was his delight at the birth of his first son after seven daughters that he had a barrel of free beer set up in front of his house. He was a respected

citizen, industrious, intelligent and companionable. He came from an old family of craftsmen and had worked hard to achieve the moderate degree of prosperity which he had secured for himself. Music was constantly heard in his home, string quartets above all: 'When I reached the age of four my father taught me rhythm. At five I went to school and learned to play the violin and the piano. In my seventh year I played the overture to *La Muette de Portici* at a concert in Leitomischl. ...' Smetana wrote this in his diary – in German – when he was sixteen. Even as a grown man he continued to write in German at all times, even in his love letters, and it was only later in life that he learned to write his native language correctly. This says something about Smetana's open-mindedness, which in no way conflicted with his Czech patriotism,

and more still about the cultural and political situation which prevailed when he was young. It is not particularly significant that Smetana sometimes used Friedrich and at other times Frédéric as a Christian name, and allowed these names to appear in print. What deserves notice is that once he had become a fully fledged and self-confident master he signed himself 'Bedřich.'

The lad grew up with music all around him, and though in no way a child prodigy, he had already written a galop for piano at the age of eight. By that time his family had moved on to Jindřichův Hradec (Neuhaus), where his father leased a more profitable brewery and Bedřich received piano and violin tuition from the choirmaster, František Ikavec. The family moved yet again four years later when his father had a try at becoming a landowner himself on an estate which he had bought at Růžková Lhotice, south of Prague. Bedřich had failed to make the grade at the grammar-school in Neuhaus and was therefore sent first to the grammar-school in the German enclave of Jihlava (Iglau) and then to Německý Brod. Here he made the exciting discovery of a piano score of Weber's *Freischütz*, but he went on to Prague to complete his education. Here the fifteen-year-old boy lived with his aunt in the old city and attended the famous Klementinum grammar-school, whose director, Josef Jungmann, was a pioneer of the Czech revival as the editor of the first Czech dictionary. Smetana heard opera – Donizetti, Marschner and Meyerbeer – for the first time at the German Estates Theater (where half a century before Mozart's *Don Giovanni* had received its première), and he was completely carried away by Liszt's inspired performances at the piano. But he started to play truant from school after being teased about his faulty German accent, and this led to a row with his father, who fetched him home and decided to make a forester of him; he relented, however, and agreed that Bedřich should be given one more chance of finishing school at a grammar-school in Plzeň.

There he lived with a much older cousin, František Josef Smetana, a physics teacher, art-lover and Czech patriot who introduced the boy to local society, which was still predominantly

Left: Wedding photograph of the composer and his second wife, Bettina Ferdinandová, whom he married in 1860.

Below: Page of a letter from the composer, written in German and signed 'Friedr.' rather than 'Bedřich' Smetana, but in which he declares his total commitment to Bohemian art and culture.

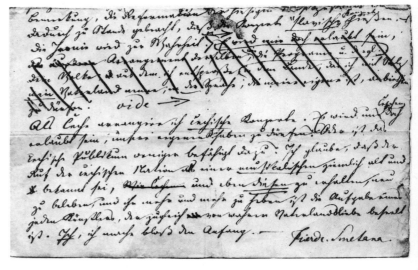

Right: Drawing of 1856 by Josef Mánes, evoking the spirit of Bohemia. Mánes had taken part in the revolutionary activities of 1848-9 and was the leading nationalist spirit among Czech artists.

German-speaking. His brilliant piano playing made him very popular locally, but his tempestuous passion for Kateřina Kolářová, a professional pianist three years his junior and the daughter of a civil servant, elicited no more than a cool response. As far as she was concerned, the young man had to make good first.

He finished school at the age of nineteen, and from that time showed complete single-mindedness. Two years later he wrote: 'With God's help and grace I shall one day be a Liszt in technique and a Mozart in composition.' This he could only achieve in Prague. He eventually wrung consent from a reluctant father and went to eke out a living there by giving piano lessons. The turning-point came when Count Leopold Thun-Hohenstein engaged him for three years as tutor to his children, thereby enabling him to earn enough to cover the tuition fees of the highly regarded musicologist Josef Proksch. This Bohemian-born German, who had been blind since youth, became Smetana's guiding light. Proksch's teaching took Bach and Beethoven as its foundation, but he also brought in contemporary music from Chopin to Liszt, an exceptionally progressive approach in the then predominantly Mozart-oriented musical climate of Prague. But more important still, Proksch's philosophical and ethical conception of music had a profound influence on Smetana: '. . . it is the complete human being who formulates and represents the artistic idea.'

The three and a half years spent by Smetana until 1847 as a tutor in the Count's household and as a pupil of Proksch proved a happy time

for him. He heard Berlioz conducting, became acquainted with the Schumanns, continued to woo Kateřina, who had come to Prague in the meantime, and, since he could not earn enough as a concert pianist, hoped that he might be able to make a living by running a private school of music. In despair, he turned to Franz Liszt, despite the fact that he was not personally acquainted with him. Liszt did help him by finding a German publisher for his op.1, *Six Characteristic Pieces*, a piano cycle with poetic epigraphs in the spirit of Robert Schumann and the first work, after a couple of dozen minor compositions, which Smetana released for publication. He remained bound by gratitude and respect to his benefactor – and later friend – Franz Liszt, as long as he lived.

Smetana opened his modest school of music with fifteen pupils in a backyard on the Old Town Ring during the summer of 1848. Earlier that year, liberally-minded Czechs and Germans had fought together on the barricades in the cause of liberty, and Smetana himself had taken part as a civic guard and had composed freedom marches. But the bloody suppression of the revolution by the imperial troops soon brought about an ever-widening breach between the Germans and Czechs in Bohemia. The two ethnic groups, which had lived in close dependence on each other, even though the Germans had dominated Prague and the larger cities, now began to drift apart.

Smetana was at last able to marry Kateřina Kolářová on 27 August 1849 after a long courtship. A warm-hearted, pretty young woman

Below: Playbill, proudly printed in Czech, for the première of *The Bartered Bride* at the Provisional Theater, Prague, on 30 May 1866. In the uneasy political circumstances, the sparkling opera met with only modest success.

Bottom left: The Czech-born soprano Emmy Destinn as the peasant girl Mařenka, the Bartered Bride. She introduced the role to the Metropolitan Opera in New York in 1909, with Mahler conducting.

Bottom right: Autograph of a page from Act III of the final version of the opera. Much of the best-known music was written for this later revision, which Smetana did not complete until 1870.

and a good companion, she worked as a piano teacher at his new Lehr-Institut im Pianoforte-Spiel (Tutorial Institute for Pianoforte Playing). Smetana was no piano virtuoso, such as his adored Liszt or Thalberg, but more of a poet at the keyboard with a fine sense of shading. Chopin, therefore, as well as Schumann and Liszt, provided the main source of inspiration for his style at the piano. And as Chopin had given artistic vitality to the mazurka, so Smetana ennobled the peasant polka, a dance which had certainly originated in Bohemia or Moravia rather than in Poland.

In 1855, Smetana made his first appearance as a conductor in somewhat difficult circumstances. Yet this was also the occasion for the first performance of his one and only symphony, the 'Slavnostní' (Festive) Symphony in E major composed in honor of the marriage of the young Emperor Franz Joseph, then still the great hope of the liberals. Haydn's famous *Emperor's Hymn* is quoted in three of the four movements. As the official Austrian national anthem, this later became the object of deep hatred among Czechs, and the Symphony as a whole is therefore treated with a good deal of embarrassment by them to the present day.

Four daughters were born to Smetana before 1855, but three of them died at an early age. Smetana marked the death of Bedřiška – the

eldest, and musically very talented – by his Piano Trio in G minor, a deeply felt and fully mature work. It consists of three thematically linked movements and is uncommonly bold in its conception and full of romantic fervor. The presto of the finale converts the sombre G minor key into the major, a musical symbol of life welcomed and suffering overcome. Beethoven's motto *per aspera ad astra* is newly interpreted here in a highly personal musical idiom.

• Years of travel •

All the painstaking work in the music school, which had to move its accommodation more than once, the private lessons, even the regular sessions of piano playing – worth a few Gulden at a time – for the former Emperor Ferdinand, who had been residing at the Hradčin Castle in Prague since his abdication, had failed to give Smetana any real degree of financial security. He therefore decided in the autumn of 1856 to accept an invitation from the distant city of Göteborg in Sweden and try his luck as a musician there. This port and trading center was then dominated by a patrician upper crust of Swedish, German and English merchants who were determined to improve its musical standards. Even Mendelssohn was still regarded there as an obscure modernist. Smetana described local taste as 'antediluvian' and resolutely set about promoting contemporary trends as the conductor of the Göteborg Philharmonic Association and as a very popular piano teacher. He gave performances of overtures by Wagner

and symphonic poems by Liszt in the teeth of conservative resistance.

Smetana had earlier been to Weimar to visit Liszt, whose symphonic poems influenced several orchestral works he composed in Sweden: *Richard III*, based on Shakespeare's tragedy; *Valdštýnův tabor* (Wallenstein's Camp), after the play by Schiller; and *Hakon Jarl*, which evokes a Norwegian prince of pagan times. *Wallenstein's Camp* can be regarded as a disguised four-movement symphony, and march tunes are introduced into the finale as a stylized representation of heroic ideals, a device which Smetana later often used in its fully developed form in his orchestral masterpiece, the *Má Vlast* (My Country) cycle. Indeed, the symphonic poems composed in Sweden are actually important forerunners of *Má Vlast* with their feeling for vivid orchestral color and a free thematic treatment.

Fröjda Benecke, a Swedish lady who belonged by birth to the eminent German Jewish Gumpert family, greatly helped Smetana in his social life in Göteborg and provided him with his main emotional involvement during his stay. But the budding romance ended tamely enough, when Smetana was joined by his wife and daughter. However, Kateřina's lung disease worsened dramatically, and though he tried to take his ailing wife home to Prague in 1859, she died in Dresden on the way.

The composer was deeply shaken by Kateřina's death and traveled restlessly between his native Bohemia, Weimar and Leipzig, where he made the acquaintance of the famous conductor Hans von Bülow. Then, in northern Bohemia, at Obříství, where his brother was a forester,

Above: An outdoor café in Prague, painted by Viktor Barvitius in 1865, during the period of *obrození*, the rebirth of Czech national culture, in the city.

he met and fell passionately in love with Bettina Ferdinandová, sixteen years his junior. She was an estate manager's daughter, well educated, but more gifted in the visual arts than in music. She eventually gave in to Smetana's tempestuous courtship. Yet even after they were married – on 10 July 1860 – she never pretended to love him very deeply. She proved a good mother for Kateřina's daughter Žofie, who was soon joined by her own children, Zdenka and Božena. But she cannot be said to have been a soul-mate who recognized Smetana's genius or provided him with the warm affection he needed in his later illness and isolation.

The couple returned again to Göteborg, but in 1860 when the Vienna 'October Diploma' relaxed the central government's grip on Bohemia after the Hapsburg defeats in Northern Italy, nothing could keep Smetana abroad any longer. He was now bent on reshaping his own and his nation's cultural and political future in his capacity as an established composer. Yet

the first concerts in Prague at which he conducted his own works – *Richard III* and *Wallenstein's Camp* – failed to secure public understanding and support. He was forced to fall back on teaching music and opened his second music school in the Lažanský Palace on the Vltava Quay. In the meantime Czech musical life had begun to flower. New musical associations and choral societies were founded and, above all, the Prozatímní Divadlo (Provisional Theater), the first theater to perform exclusively in Czech. This opened on 1 October 1862 in a modest classical-style building (part of which is now incorporated in the National Theater), and though no more than a stop-gap, it was an epoch-making development for the Czechs. Smetana made great efforts to secure the post of conductor there. He temporarily took over as conductor of the rising Hlahol Choral Society and composed choral works, such as *Česká píseň* (Song of the Czechs), an impressive glorification of the Czech love of singing, *Tři jezdci* (The Three Riders) and *Odrodilec* (The Renegade), the patriotic content of which matched the spirit of the times. Moreover, he organized Czech symphony concerts at which both the German and the new Czech opera orchestras played classical and contemporary works, including *Hakon Jarl* and extracts from his first opera, *The Brandenburgers in Bohemia*, which he was then writing.

• Smetana's early operas •

The young composer was becoming increasingly aware of the importance of opera as a cultural and political factor in Czech music, and for his own future. This sometimes led to sharp differences of opinion within his own camp. The Czechs had split into two political parties in 1863. The 'Old Czechs,' under the leadership of the greatly respected Dr František Ladislav Rieger, mainly looked for support to

Above: Smetana and the members of the Provisional Theater Orchestra.

Top: The Provisional Theater in Prague, where the premières of Smetana's first two operas led to his appointment in 1866 as the theater's chief conductor.

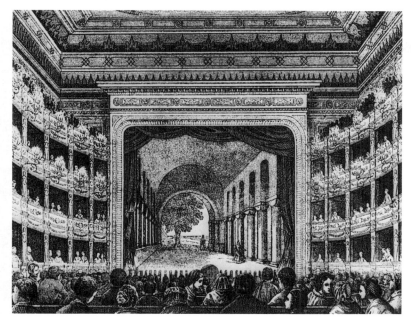

Above: Interior of the New Czech Theater, Prague, which operated from 1876 to 1885. Two of Smetana's later operas, *The Secret* and *The Devil's Wall*, were first produced there. It was also the scene of the hundredth performance of *The Bartered Bride*.

the nobility, clergy and upper middle class, while the more liberal and democratically inclined 'Young Czechs' had journalists and artists on their side. Smetana soon fell out with Rieger on a purely artistic point: 'Old Czech' patriots could conceive of the national opera they longed for only as a sort of potpourri of actual folk tunes. Smetana, on the other hand, uncompromisingly held to the new concept of musical drama put forward by Wagner. This rift with Rieger, then the director of the Provisional Theater, put the post of conductor which he coveted out of Smetana's reach for the time being. The turning-point came when *The Brandenburgers in Bohemia*, which he had composed between the summer of 1862 and the spring of 1863, was performed. He had succeeded in establishing the right to direct the rehearsals himself despite strong resistance, especially on the part of the arch-conservative conductor Jan Nepomuk Maýr. The first night on 5 January 1866 became a historical landmark for the Czech musical theater. This was the first specifically Czech opera in language, subject and musical character of any real substance, and the applause of the Prague audience was no doubt also fired by the patriotic spirit of the work.

In his libretto, the journalist and author Karel Sabina (1813-77) developed an episode of Bohemian history during the thirteenth century into a heroically romantic tale of chivalry: troops from Brandenburg are occupying the country during a conflict over the succession to the Bohemian throne. The three daughters of the Mayor of Prague are abducted and molested by the Czech traitor Tausendmark. In the end they and the whole of Bohemia are freed. 'Arise in vengeance, Thou Lion of Bohemia!' sing the indignant patriots, and Tausendmark is forced to bear the contempt of the foreign enemy as well as that of his compatriots. Even in this first attempt at an opera Smetana followed his Wagner-inspired ideals. He had himself written, as a committed music critic, that operas 'must not be productions in which one only

sings for the sake of singing.' They must be 'raised to the level of drama.' The old type of French or Italian operas with their series of arias or ensembles and sung recitative or spoken dialogue had already been left behind in *The Brandenburgers*. Twenty-eight 'scenes' make up the three acts; the recitative is accompanied by the orchestra throughout; and choral passages take up a good deal of space, as do orchestral interludes.

The director of the Provisional Theater now also accepted Smetana's second opera, which had already been on the stocks for a year. *Prodaná nevěsta* (The Bartered Bride) was given its first performance on 30 May 1866. The career of one of the most carefree, perfect and frequently performed masterpieces in the entire repertory of comic opera began in a thoroughly dismal and depressing atmosphere. The Provisional Theater was only half full, the applause moderate and the critics divided as a result of the mood of this muted first night. Much of this was the result of external circumstances. The war between Austria and Prussia which culminated soon afterwards in the Battle of Königgrätz was casting its shadow. Many inhabitants of Prague, including Smetana himself, fled before the Prussians, who were marching into Bohemia – hardly the best conditions for the success of an uncompromisingly jolly opera. As the noise of war receded into the distance, however, the public of Prague acquired a taste for the work, and Smetana lived to see its hundredth performance, an unheard-of event in those days. But he had by then met with so many disappointments over his other operas that he rather bitterly remarked at the jubilee celebrations: '*The Bartered Bride*, gentlemen, is in fact only an entertainment which I allowed myself at that time. I did not compose it out of ambition, but in a mood of defiance because I had been accused after my *Brandenburgers* of being a Wagnerian and incapable of producing anything conceived in a national, lighter style.' Sabina also minimized his part in what he called 'this operetta,' although he had succeeded in producing one of the best librettos in the entire history of opera. It was indeed thanks to Smetana's own intervention in the scenario that the original one-act farce was turned first of all into a two-act *Singspiel* with spoken dialogue and then, in its fourth and final version, into a fully developed three-act *opera buffa* with sung recitative throughout, in other words the opera we know today. There was a serendipity of sorts about Sabina's libretto: it was entertaining, full of engaging complications and far more natural and relaxed in its language than *The Brandenburgers*. He had combined one of his own stories with a village farce popular at that time based on an age-old theme which reaches back to the *Commedia dell' Arte*: a couple of young lovers succeed in getting their way despite the machinations of their elders. But in this case the general effect is of pristine freshness because the characters in the play are taken from everyday Czech life and brilliantly endowed with a timeless reality thanks to the spontaneity of Smetana's music. The peasant boy and girl, Jeník and Mařenka, love each other, but their parents have already made a different arrangement with Kecal, the marriage-broker. He must therefore be completely out-witted by Jeník. Love triumphs over all ob-stacles but only when coupled with cunning. Jeník, the farmhand, the little man, ultimately has his way with all his powerful and over-bearing opponents. It is an innocent message, brimming with gaiety and catchy tunes, which the Czechs well and truly understood.

'A national style is not created by imitating the melodic impact and rhythm of our folk-songs,' wrote Smetana while he was working on the score of *The Bartered Bride*. This was a pointed attack on the 'potpourri' theory held by the 'Old Czech' conservatives. On the other hand, Wagner's musical drama was equally powerless to inspire the proposed 'operetta.' Where else could inspiration be found? Smetana himself suggested the great source – none other than Mozart. He was in a positively euphoric mood while composing the work. This is, all else apart, reflected in the overture, with its dashing coda, and carries on into the opening chorus, so reminiscent of a Czech folksong and yet, like all Smetana's other folk-like tunes, a product of his own imagination. Jeník and Mařenka, the two lovers, are given specially generous lyrical treatment. Jeník's deep infatu-ation is portrayed in the first duet by engaging runs of sixths, while the lovers' passing mis-understandings provide delightful opportunities for Smetana to display his skill in characteriz-ation, as also in the stuttering arias of the tongue-tied young Vašek and the endless repetitions of the chattering marriage-broker Kecal. The score is full of dashing dance tunes and rich ensembles ranging from duets and trios to choruses, with the A major sextet 'Rozmysli si, Mařenko' (Make your mind up, Mařenka) thrown in as a

bonus. There is not a single weak element among the twenty-one 'scenes,' as Smetana called the parts of the work. The composer had clearly mastered the difficult art of achieving perfec-tion through apparent simplicity, although five more years were to go by before *The Bartered Bride* reached the actual completed form now familiar to us.

• Conductor at the Provisional Theater •

'Nationally speaking, the post of conductor in the Bohemian theater is probably the most important job of all,' as Smetana put it. His success in directing his first two operas raised his stock so high that he was appointed per-manent conductor in the Provisional Theater in September 1866, yet the annual salary of 1400 Gulden a year was so low that it hardly covered the bare necessities of life, a lack of measure between artistic merit and material recognition very characteristic of Smetana's career as a whole. He held the conductor's desk of the Provisional Theater for nine years. His pro-gram policy was to replace the Italian style of *bel canto* opera, which had until then domi-nated the repertoire, by German works – by Gluck, Mozart and Beethoven – and by French operas. The modest resources of the Provisional Theater did not allow his beloved Wagner's works to be staged: its orchestra numbered a mere thirty players, the young Antonín Dvořák among them as a viola player. Smetana unself-ishly promoted the budding development of Czech opera even though, apart from Dvořák, its composers at that time, such as Karel Šebor, Karel Bendl or Vilém Blodek, had only works of minor interest to offer.

Right: Hall in the castle at Vyšehrad, one of the sets for the original production of Smetana's opera *Libuše*, an intensely patriotic work, first performed at the opening of the Prague National Theater in June 1881.

Left: Another of the original sets for *Libuše.*

Below: Playbill for the first performance of *Libuše* on 11 June 1881, given in the presence of Crown-Prince Rudolph and Princess Stephanie. The new National Theater is pictured at the base of the notice.

Smetana was quite unlike the run-of-the-mill conductors of his time. His model was Hans von Bülow, the pioneer of intellectually motivated, progressively inclined conducting and, as the years went by, he was able to persuade more and more singers and orchestral performers to accept his high ideals.

The early years of Smetana's tenure as conductor were perhaps the happiest musical years of his life, but the latter were among the most bitter. They included in particular the total failure of *Dalibor,* his third opera, which he composed with a special degree of dedication. It was intended, as a tragic counterpart to *The Bartered Bride,* to be the first serious and progressive Czech national opera. And it was indeed selected to be first performed on 16 May 1868 in Prague's largest theater of that time, the New Town Theater near the Central Horse Market, on the day when the foundation stone of the Czech National Theater was laid. The première itself was a resounding success, fuelled by the nationalistic fervor generated by the occasion, but the audience soon fell away and only a few more performances followed during Smetana's lifetime. *Dalibor,* now the most popular of all tragic operas among Czechs, had become Smetana's ugly duckling.

He had used a libretto strung together by the German-speaking Bohemian school-inspector Josef Wenzig, which had to be translated into Czech by the lawyer, Ervín Špindler, before it could be set to music. The story was drawn from the history of Bohemia in the fifteenth century. The real Dalibor had been a knight from northern Bohemia executed in 1498 for a breach of the peace. The operatic Dalibor, on the other hand, was a much nobler character who had taken arms to revenge his murdered friend. Milada, his accuser, is so impressed by his chivalrous bearing before the tribunal that she takes his part and makes her way to his cell, disguised as a man. She and Dalibor fall passionately in love with each other, but her attempt to free him fails and she is mortally wounded, while in despair Dalibor throws himself on the swords of his enemies. Many strands culled from the world of opera can be recognized in this libretto, from echoes of *Fidelio* to the pathos of the royal scene in *Lohengrin*, but they fail to knit into an organic whole. The element of folk-music nevertheless harmonizes surprisingly well in Smetana's music with the *leitmotif* technique of Wagnerian music-drama, the most up-to-date approach at that time. The composer's compatriots, however, were conscious only of – to them unwelcome – innovations: no identifiable 'numbers,' such as there had been in *The Bartered Bride* – merely vocal episodes embedded in the continuous symphonic orchestral flow; no ensembles, except for duets and choruses. The theories of the Wagnerian music-drama are very clearly reflected here, but they have been transformed by the composer's own creative approach. Smetana himself bitterly rejected the accusation that he had tried to outdo *Tristan und Isolde*: 'My *Dalibor* is hardly a match for *The Flying Dutchman* . . .' – although this is something of an exaggeration, and *Lohengrin* probably provides a closer comparison. In *Dalibor*, concealed arias still shimmer through the web of symphonically conceived scenes: that of King Vladislav, for instance, or, at the very start, Dalibor's aria as a defendant before the royal tribunal, which any Czech with half an ear for music now hums or whistles, so popular has it become.

Yet, in another sense, *Dalibor* is also very skillfully derived from a single seminal idea on which the entire score is based. This opera, which seems nowadays so simply and engagingly melodious, turns out on closer examination to be an exceedingly complex musical organism. Nearly all the important vocal 'numbers' represent variants of an original basic theme which is first stated in the orchestral overture as the curtain rises: two interlocking rising fourths. Not even Wagner's scores are so monothematically constructed, but Smetana was certainly not led to write in this way by any wish simply to imitate the Wagnerian 'infinite melody,' in other words orchestral symphonic continuity. He had, in fact, explicitly rejected this idea: 'We Czechs are a people who sing and who cannot accept this method.'

• Nationalist controversy •

The rejection of *Dalibor* by the critics and public put Smetana increasingly on the defensive. He was an ardent patriot, but to be labeled a 'Wagnerian' in those days was tantamount to being accused of betraying the nation. Such accusations mainly stemmed from the leading music critic of the 'Old Czech' party, František Pivoda. He had just about managed to welcome *The Bartered Bride*, but *Dalibor* he rejected as

Above: Žofín Academy, Prague, where many of Smetana's chamber and piano works and songs were first performed. It was there that he met Eliška Krásnohorská (*left*), the young Czech poet and singer, who provided him with the librettos for his operas *The Kiss*, *The Secret* and *The Devil's Wall*.

'a lifeless piece of foreign trash,' and from then on he became Smetana's most influential cultural and political opponent. The relationship between them was, on a more modest intellectual level, not unlike that of the Viennese conservative critic Eduard Hanslick to Wagner and Bruckner. Smetana's supporters were led by Otakar Hostinský, a dedicated Wagnerian, now recognized as the founding father of Czech musicology, but a provocative outsider as far as many of his contemporaries were concerned. Smetana, who inclined to democratic principles, belonged to the 'Young Czechs,' who aimed to achieve Czech independence from below, through the people and on liberal principles, while the 'Old Czechs' were working for a greater degree of independence through compromises with the authorities in Vienna.

Smetana took a passionately committed part in these topical controversies, but they never deflected him from his course as an artist. He was overjoyed in 1870 by an opportunity to see first *Rheingold* and *Die Walküre* during a visit to Munich, and then *Tristan*. He went to call on his friend Liszt, who later returned his visit in Prague. But creatively, his independence remained unimpaired: there are, for instance, no traces of any influence from *Tristan* on his national festival opera *Libuše*, although the work was written during just these years, 1869-72. It had, however, no chance of performance after the collapse of *Dalibor*, so Smetana set it aside. It was not until many years later, in 1881, when the Czech National Theater was to be inaugurated with a gala performance that *Libuše* as an opera for special occasions saw the light of day. This is Smetana's least known opera so far as foreign countries are concerned, but the Czechs treat it as a national heirloom. It has never yet been performed outside its own country, although it had been given its thousandth performance in Prague by 1905. It says a great deal about the cultural and political state of affairs in the Bohemian lands, at the time when it was written, that even this specifically patriotic festival piece should have been based on what was originally a German text, once again written by the ethnically German inspector of schools Josef Wenzig and again set in a Czech version by Špindler.

Libuše – or Libussa, as she is called in the original – is the legendary foundress of the city of Prague. A ruling princess of Bohemia, she is vilified as a female ruler in a male-dominated society. She gives in to pressure and, by choosing Přemysl, a local nobleman, as her husband, becomes the founder of the medieval Přemyslid dynasty. Libuše's prophetic vision in the finale of the third act is the highlight of this nationalist opera: 'They will not perish, my dearly loved people of Bohemia, they will arise in splendor from the shadow of the grave!' wrote the German-speaking Wenzig; and these were the words, translated into his national language, that Smetana, the Czech patriot, set to music.

The most Czech in spirit of Smetana's operas is musically the most Wagnerian in style. It reaches out well beyond *Dalibor* by its merging together of scenes treated as integral parts of a continuous process and by the symphonic role awarded to the orchestra. In the earlier work Smetana had developed even the vocal melodies from an original seminal element, while in this case several 'characteristic motives' connected with the individual personages dominate the individual scenes in the form of orchestral structures. The singing develops from the recitative melody, a device which Smetana and his supporters, especially Otakar Hostinský, regarded as particularly progressive. Aria-like numbers, such as Přemysl's 'Lime tree song' or the 'Reapers' chorus,' are inserted very sparingly.

Smetana's salary as a conductor was now at last increased to 2,000 Gulden. He founded an opera school to train future singers. He also countered the unceasing attacks on him by his aesthetic and political enemies in the most noble and creative way possible, by producing a new

opera. *Dvě vdovy* (The Two Widows) is a comic opera, even a *Singspiel* with spoken dialogue in its first version. This was a radical change of course after the tragic *Dalibor* and the moving *Libuše*: it was necessary to make some concessions if he wished to be understood. Yet this was not a mere repetition of *The Bartered Bride*'s successful formula, but something completely different. There had in fact so far been no Czech opera in the 'genteel drawing-room manner,' as the composer himself put it. He commissioned a pretty undistinguished writer, Emanuel Züngel, to turn a French farce by the equally undistinguished playwright Félicien Mallefille into a libretto, and to transfer the rudimentary plot from France to a Bohemian country house. This is inhabited by two widows, one of whom – the unresponsive Anežka – is courted by a young neighboring landowner. In order to bring about a happy ending the good-natured and playful Karolina is forced to pretend that she is jealous so as to break down the barriers of her friend's widowhood. For contrast, Smetana added yet another comic pair of lovers in the revised version of 1877. The gaiety of *The Two Widows* is muted and undoubtedly less effective on the stage than *The Bartered Bride*'s deft comic approach. Yet it is Smetana's most elegant opera by far, with a score which is furthest from Wagner and closest to Mozart, not least in its many brilliant ensembles. Apart from tunes reminiscent of folk music, such as the courting Ladislav's 'Když zavítá máj,' or fiery polkas, the score is marked throughout by a smooth, conversational tone which was new in Czech opera and which the orchestra occasionally supports, thematically. The first night, on 27 March 1874, drew tremendous applause, but the success did not last. The opera-going public had expected another *Bartered Bride* and initially failed to understand the refinements of this aristocratic musical comedy.

• Years of anguish •

Smetana had been working in the meantime on the first two parts of a large-scale symphonic cycle – *Vyšehrad* and *Vltava* – although he was hampered by increasing ill-health. The constant attacks against him as a composer and conductor seriously depressed him, and from July 1874 on he began to feel that his hearing was deserting him. He was afflicted by buzzing in his ears and sought the advice of well-known specialists, to no avail. In October, Beethoven's misfortune struck him down overnight: he had gone completely deaf. A few days later, at the end of the month, he resigned his post as conductor. The Theater Association made some acknowledgment of his services by granting him 1200 Gulden as an annual ex-gratia stipend. But this was in fact no more than an advance, because Smetana had to make all his operas, including future ones, available free, so that it was the theater that had in fact secured the better deal. By now Smetana could hear nothing, not even the en-

Above: Otakar Hostinský, the Prague music critic who stoutly supported Smetana's efforts to apply the concept of Wagnerian music-drama to Czech opera. Arguments on such matters continued between the 'Old Czechs' and the 'New Czechs,' while the Brahms versus Wagner controversy was raging in Vienna.

Right: A bleak winter landscape, painted in 1882 by Mikuláš Aleš. He headed the later Czech national or patriotic school of art, producing works such as the murals in Prague's Old Town Hall.

thusiastic applause of the audience for the first parts of his symphonic cycle glorifying Bohemia, *Má Vlast*, which were first performed on 14 March and 4 April 1875.

Vyšehrad is the name of the oldest historical citadel of Prague, which juts out on a steep crag above the Vltava River. A bard, the legendary singer Lumír, tells of ancient days of chivalry, proud feats and devastating battles. He is represented at the start and finish by festive chords on the harp, between which the 'tales' unfold in free sonata form. *Vltava* portrays the river on which the Bohemian capital stands, in rondo form. Even when Smetana was writing 'program music,' in other words music tied to extra-musical concepts, and creating a form of his own which differed from 'the worn-out old boot,' as he put it, he still kept his musical articulation clear and coherent. The listener does, of course, derive additional advantage from a close acquaintance with the underlying program: if, for instance, he is aware that the two flutes which develop the main theme at the beginning represent the two sources of the Vltava; or that the dramatic cleavage in this theme, shortly before the radiant conclusion, stands for the disturbed waters of the river at its rapids. But the melodic impact and pictorial wealth of this genuine poem in sound can, when all is said and done, be well understood without a knowledge of the program.

The listener accompanies the river as it flows past banks inhabited by people and dreams. He hears a hunt go by. He witnesses a peasant dance with the sound of lively polkas. He follows muted fiddlers into a nocturne populated by elves and water-sprites. And he hears the Vltava

streaming through the golden city of Prague, as the Vyšehrad motif triumphantly tells him, with the orchestra playing at full strength.

Vltava has become Smetana's most popular orchestral composition, renowned throughout the world. It represents a triumph of creative power over illness and the sadness of life: nobody could guess, given its freshness of imagination and splendor of instrumentation that this work was conceived at a time of anguished depression and in total deafness.

Smetana left Prague with his family in the summer of 1876 for a forester's house at Jabkenice, some forty miles north of the city. His daughter Žofie, who lived there with her husband Josef Schwarz, a head forester, made them welcome. Life in town had become unbearable for the composer. He had always been a companionable person in the past, a frequenter of theaters, cafés and drawing rooms. Now despair forced him to seek consolation in nature. The simple single-storey house in the forest, the quiet woods with their mixed species of trees and the lakes in the remote landscape became Smetana's refuge almost until his death. But this was no peaceful idyll. Financial stringency, bringing humiliating arguments over an increase in his stipend, also helped to break up Smetana's marriage. Bettina felt exiled in Jabkenice. She was a good and dutiful mother to her children and also to her stepdaughter, but no more than a cool companion for her husband. And it was well beyond her powers to be a compassionate soul-mate for a suffering genius.

Smetana felt this breach deeply, as several of his works composed at Jabkenice clearly show. The piano suite *Sny* (Dreams), which he com-

Right: A sketch by Smetana's second wife Bettina of the country house at Jabkenice, where the sick composer retired to write some of his late works, including the string quartet in E minor, *From my Life*, in which a recurring single high-pitched note represents the affliction of deafness.

Above: First edition of *From Bohemia's Woods and Fields* – from the group of orchestral pieces inspired by Czech life, history and legend, called collectively *Má Vlast* (My Country).

each of them with an explicit program: the first movement expresses youthful artistic enthusiasm; the polka scherzo of the second, a happy lust for living; the adagio, the joy of first love; and the finale, 'the recognition of the elemental force contained in the nation's music,' until a stark high E rings out above the shivering tremolo in the bass to represent the dramatic onset of his deafness, while the movement ends in an elegiac mood with a sorrowful recall of his former happiness in love. This quartet is another of the world's great masterpieces, as well as one more pioneering effort by Smetana, this time for Czech chamber music.

While working on the String Quartet, the composer experienced the most brilliantly successful first night of his career to date – the première of his comic opera *Hubička* (The Kiss) at the Provisional Theater in Prague on 7 November 1876. Everyone wanted to know whether the master who had now gone deaf was still capable of writing an opera, and discovered how superbly he had managed to do so. Smetana had chosen the twenty-three-year-old authoress Eliška Krásnohorská (1847-1926) as his librettist for the first time. She collaborated with him on three further occasions and proved to be the most adaptable of his writers, even if not the best, as compared with Sabina. She was deeply devoted to the beloved master, but lacked dramatic talent and had no experience whatsoever of the theater.

It is plain from the skimpy plot that the libretto of *The Kiss* is just an unduly protracted anecdote. It is based on the story of the same name by Karolina Světlá, who was regarded as a classic writer on the strength of her realistic novels about Czech village life. The action is elementary. Lukáš, a young peasant and a widower, is wooing Vendulka, a peasant's daughter. She is devoted to him but refuses to give him the kiss he demands before the marriage ceremony because she is superstitious and afraid of disturbing Lukáš's dead wife in her grave. The withholding of this kiss leads to a tempestuous quarrel, but when Lukáš begs forgiveness

pleted in 1875, is full of doleful memories of 'Past Happiness' (the title of one of the pieces) until it ends on a hopeful note in 'A Bohemian Peasant Feast.' The string quartet in E minor, *Z mého života* (From my Life), is an autobiographical work full of retrospective sorrow. The four movements comply outwardly with the classical model of the form, but Smetana also endowed

and foregoes the kiss, he gets it anyway, together with his reconciled bride. Smetana dressed up this village idyll in the most spring-like and spirited music he had written since *The Bartered Bride*, and it is his most mature achievement in the field of comic opera. Songs reminiscent of folk music, such as Vendulka's two cradle songs, or real arias, or the triumphant hymn to nature 'Hlásej, ptáčku' are thematically and symphonically welded together by the orchestra. Smetana was guided by Wagner, but put his reforms at the service of Czech 'folk opera.'

• Last works •

The success of the first night of *The Kiss* stimulated Smetana to further creative effort. Another part of the *Má Vlast* cycle, *Z Českých luhů a hájů* (From Bohemia's Woods and Fields), a glorification of Bohemian nature in the shape of a symphonic poem, was shortly afterwards performed in Prague, once again before an enthusiastic audience. He also wrote an *a capella* work for male-voice choir – *Píseň na moři* (Song of the Sea) – and four polkas. Smetana's health was now deteriorating even further, with noises in his head and attacks of vertigo, to such an extent that he was intermittently unable to work. In spite of this miserable condition, he still found the strength to start on another opera with Krásnohorská, *Tajemství* (The Secret). The plot, a peasant *Romeo and Juliet* story set in a small town in Bohemia, is more complicated than that of *The Kiss*. Two families are so hostile to each other that neither the older gener-

ation of lovers, nor their children, are allowed to come together. A romantic touch and an obscure prophecy, with some treasure-hunting thrown in, come into the story before the loving couples are allowed to fall into each other's arms. Comic and pathetic strands blend in this opera, the gaiety of which seems somewhat muted by comparison with *The Bartered Bride*, but which contains some of Smetana's most accomplished music. He described his own style as 'dualistic,' by which he meant that the pressure exerted by a retrograde public made it necessary to introduce 'agreeable songs' into the forward-looking structure of the symphonically declamatory music. The orchestra, which carries two *leitmotifs* through the score, plays an important role, while the vocal parts – which include finely outlined characterizations – are generally tuneful. The first performance on 18 September 1878 in the New Czech Theater proved to be Smetana's last unclouded stage success. He had finally succeeded in asserting himself, even with the critics who had so often been hostile in the past.

Shortly after the first performance of *The Secret*, Smetana, who had in the meantime seen *Šárka* (later numbered third in the cycle, preceding *From Bohemia's Woods and Fields*) publicly performed, completed the last two parts of *Má Vlast*. The story of *Šárka*, an Amazon who had caused the enemy she loved to be murdered, reaches out into early Czech mythology, while the concluding parts of the cycle combine history and legend with the triumph of the nation. In Smetana's eyes the struggle and defeat of the militant adherents of Jan Hus, the religious and social reformer who was burned as a heretic in 1415, represented the most heroic chapter in the whole of Czech history, and the medieval Hussite anthem 'Kdož jste Boží bojovníci' (Ye who are God's warriors), sacred to all patriotic Czechs, provides the basic element of the *Tábor* tone poem (part 5) – symphonically elaborated. The march theme derived from this becomes in *Blaník* (part 6) the optimistic prophecy of future Czech greatness: the soldiers of God, who

Below: The artist Mikuláš Aleš in lighter mood – one of a series of drawings based on characters from *The Bartered Bride* which he produced to decorate a set of tumblers.

Right: Two of the products of Smetana's collaboration with Eliška Krásnohorská: (*right*) two characters from the first production of *The Secret*; and (*far right*) Marie Sittova singing one of Vendulka's cradle songs in *The Kiss*, which was a great favorite with Prague audiences during the composer's lifetime.

according to legend had concealed themselves in the hill of Blaník, ride forth victorious at the end while the Vyšehrad motive rings out majestically once again, thereby providing a single link for all six movements of the symphonic poem.

The entire *Má Vlast* cycle, though planned as a single entity, had grown together piecemeal over the course of many years. The work was finally given its first performance in 1882. The deaf composer was awarded a reception at once enthusiastic and reverent. It was well deserved, because he had indeed presented the people with something unique, a celebration in sound of myth, history and landscape such as no other nation possesses.

Another, more intimate cycle for piano was completed during the summer of 1877 in the quiet of Jabkenice: the two volumes of *České Tance* (Czech Dances). In contrast to Dvořák's *Slavonic Dances*, written a year earlier, this cycle is entirely confined to Czech models. Rhythmically these pieces are less alluring than those of Dvořák, though more refined in their thematic treatment. Smetana, at any rate, considered them to be his best works.

Two forms relatively neglected by the composer in the past now also received attention: songs with piano accompaniment – the five *Večerní písně* (Evening Songs), settings of poems by Vítězslav Hálek – and instrumental duos – two tuneful works for violin and piano, *Z domoviny* (From my Home), which are reminiscent of the symphonic poem *From Bohemia's Woods and Fields*. He also wrote two pieces for male-voice choir.

The Czech National Theater, for the creation of which Smetana had worked so untiringly throughout his life in Prague, solemnly opened on 11 June 1881 with the composer's festival opera *Libuše*, which had long waited in the wings. Two months later this superb neo-Renaissance building on the Vltava was burned to the ground. It was immediately rebuilt and inaugurated once more in 1883, again with *Libuše*. Ovations and laurel wreaths overwhelmed the composer on both occasions, but spells of the deepest spiritual anguish afflicted him in the meantime, aggravated by physical pain, 'buzzing and rustling in the head,' attacks of vertigo and temporary loss of voice, as well as a feeling of wounding neglect. The theater company fell into arrears with his stipend and Smetana was made to feel a beggar. In addition, he suffered a depressing failure at the first performance of his latest opera, *Čertova stěna* (The Devil's Wall), on 29 October 1882 at the New Czech Theater. Inadequate staging contributed somewhat to the colorless effect of the performance, but it must be admitted that the work was no longer entirely on a level with Smetana's earlier masterpieces.

Little remained in Eliška Krásnohorská's version of 'the humorous libretto, light, witty and comical, without serious situations' which Smetana had thought of; it was just a dull chivalric tale from southern Bohemia featuring two pairs of lovers who can only be united when the tricks of a demon called Rarach have been

Left: One of the last photographs of Smetana, before the onset of his final tragic madness.

set at nought by the innocence and spirit of self-sacrifice of a noble lady in love. Smetana provided Rarach with some of the boldest music he had ever written, with a *leitmotif* reflecting his scintillating Mephistophelian nature in harmonically ambiguous thirds. Apart from the devil, however, the score is somewhat uneven and more dully orchestrated than was Smetana's wont.

The last major work that Smetana managed to produce was his Second String Quartet in D minor, started shortly after *The Devil's Wall*. This was another autobiographical composition, and the somber counterpart to the E minor quartet, which had contained an elegiac backward look at life and love. This work on the other hand deals in its four movements with defiance and the energy of despair, an ungainly work easy neither on the performer nor the listener. It was precisely because of its dissonant crudity that Arnold Schoenberg praised it as a revelation.

Illness now put an end to Smetana's further creative plans. A proposed orchestral cycle called *Pražský karneval* (Prague Carnival) got no further than two incomplete parts. The last sketch for an opera comprises no more than sixty-five pages. Eliška Krásnohorská had suggested *Viola*, based on Shakespeare's *Twelfth Night*, many years earlier, but time had now run out for Smetana. During the first months of 1884 he began to suffer from mental derangement. In April he went mad, with dangerous fits of violence, and had to be removed to the Provincial Lunatic Asylum in Prague. He died there on 12 May 1884. The doctors diagnosed progressive paralysis; his deafness also turned out to have been the result of cerebral disease. Nonetheless, the composer's funeral was a popular demonstration such as Prague had never witnessed before.

ANTONÍN DVOŘÁK

KURT HONOLKA

Antonín Dvořák was the second Czech composer to achieve international rank, and while Smetana holds a special place in the hearts of his countrymen for his pioneering operas and symphonic poems, which played such an important part in the rebirth of the Czech culture, Dvořák's contribution to his country's music includes his specifically Czech symphonies, which are of worldwide significance, his concertos, the enormously popular *Slavonic Dances*, a profusion of string quartets and much other chamber music. Indeed, outside his native country, more of Dvořák's works are performed than of any other Czech composer.

Antonín Dvořák was born on 8 September 1841 at Nelahozeves, a small village on the Vltava some twenty miles to the north of Prague. In those days it was worlds away from urban life, on a level plain with yellow fields of corn and orchards, a peasant country densely dotted with villages, neighborly and cosy. It was inhabited exclusively by Czechs, while the big towns in Bohemia were largely dominated at that time by German patricians.

Antonín was the eldest of nine children, the son of František Dvořák, innkeeper and butcher, and his wife, born Anna Zdeňková. The child inherited his father's Slavonic looks, including the high cheekbones, as well as the Slav gift for music: the butcher liked to make music, as did his brothers, and so the boy's talent was fostered as he joined in the dance music on his fiddle. He was sent to the small town of Zlonice at the age of thirteen to stay with his uncle and learn the butcher's trade, as well as the German language. Studying under the German-speaking village schoolmaster and organist Anton Liehmann, he learned to play the organ, piano and viola, was taught some elementary musical theory and was introduced for the first time to the music of the Viennese classics. After a further year studying music and German in Česká Kamenice, the boy should have returned home to practise his trade, but his musical uncle Zdeněk prevailed upon his father to let Antonín go on to develop his obvious talent in Prague. And so in 1857 the sixteen-year-old boy set out for Prague in a haycart. He was to lodge with relatives while he attended the Organ School.

Prague was then an ancient provincial city where the Jews still lived in their ghetto, German officials and merchants set the social tone, and German was the only language spoken in the upper reaches of society. There was as yet no higher Czech education apart from a single Czech secondary school opened in 1852. But Czech working-class families were coming from the country to settle around the ever-growing number of factories in the suburbs, while the Czech middle class itself was stirred by a wave of increasing national consciousness.

Young Antonín was as little concerned with these patriotic developments as with the fact that all tuition at the Organ School was in German. He simply wanted to become a good musician. As a viola player in the orchestra of the German Cäcilien-Verein he became acquainted with the works of contemporary composers, Liszt and Wagner among them. After two years he was placed second overall when he graduated from the school, but the newly trained organist looked in vain for a job. First he kept himself alive by playing in a café orchestra, then, at the beginning of the 1860s, when the Provisional Theater at last opened on the Vltava Quay as the first Czech-language stage, he came to play first viola in its orchestra. With only thirty-four players it was, as an orchestra, just about as pitiful as the salaries it offered; the annual pay of 348 Gulden did not even cover Dvořák's most modest needs. He was forced for many years to supplement his earnings by giving piano lessons. He could not afford a piano of his own in one little room after another where poverty drove him to live. True, he had had the honor to play the viola at the first performance of Smetana's *Bartered Bride* in 1866. But he had no prospects at all of making his secret dream come true: to be a composer.

• Early compositions •

Dvořák's first works received no notice. Op.1 was a string quintet, op.2 the first of those string quartets which were later to become so brilliant. Schubert and Beethoven stood as godparents at his side and 'Bohudíky' ('Thank God') stands at the end of the First String Quartet, a formula which Dvořák as a devout Catholic was often to inscribe on scores in later years. In 1865 Beethoven's example moved him to write his first symphony, *Zlonické zvony* (The Bells of Zlonice). The cheerful musical naïveté of a cello concerto (with piano accompaniment!)

247

as yet gave no hint of what an accomplished masterpiece he was later to produce in this category. A second symphony, in B flat major, followed in 1865 during the same prolific year. This was another trial work, as was the song cycle *Cypříše* (Cypresses) based on eighteen romantic tear-jerkers by the lyrical poet and novelist Gustav Pfleger-Moravský. They reflect the composer's reaction to his frustrated love for his piano pupil, Josefina Čermáková, who rejected the poor musician in favor of the aristocratic Count Kaunitz. Dvořák followed Mozart's example and consoled himself with her younger sister, Anna, who had also been his pupil and had a fine alto voice. He married her in 1873 and thereby acquired a faithful, loving companion for the remainder of his life.

He had by then already composed three further string quartets for practice purposes, the first of which, in D major, is noteworthy because it makes thematic use in its third movement of the patriotic air 'Hej, Slované' (which the Poles have adopted as their national anthem).

Dvořák's first encounter with Wagner's *Lohengrin* and *Meistersinger* at the Prague German Theater bowled him over, and the example of Smetana, the creator of *The Bartered Bride* and *Dalibor*, encouraged him to turn his hand to opera. It is characteristic both of the guilelessness and the irresistible creative urge of Dvořák as a young man that he should have picked on a play by the German dramatist Theodor Körner, arranged it as best he could and set it in German – in Wagner's own style, moreover. This first opera, named *Alfred*, was also put on the shelf, but that did not discourage the composer from immediately following it by another attempt: *Král a uhlíř* (King and Charcoal-burner), a work with a very strange history. Originally, Dvořák set the story in full Wagnerian orchestral style, but when the conductor – Smetana, as it happened – and the cast found that they could make no sense of it, he completely transformed it into a light-hearted piece full of singable arias. This second version was performed in 1874 at the Provisional Theater, though it met with no enduring success.

Only a little earlier, three of his works had been performed in the concert hall, first the overture to *Král a uhlíř*, conducted by Smetana, then *Hymnus*, or *The Heirs of the White Mountain*, a choral work, and finally an amiable nocturne for string orchestra. *Hymnus* was a triumph, partly due to its national content, since the poem on which it is based, by Vítězslav Hálek, one of the founders of the new national school of poetry, extols loyalty to the 'eternal mother,' the Czech nation. But its success was also to some extent attributable to its grandiose conception, derived from Beethoven, as three hundred singers of the newly founded patriotic Hlahol Choral Society rose from a somber *misterioso* up to the splendid E flat major jubilation.

A year later, in 1874, Smetana conducted the rather Wagnerian Symphony in E flat major – already Dvořák's Third – and this succeeded in disarming the resentment which the young composer, a mere viola player who was only

just becoming known, had harbored for some time against the established and celebrated master. The relationship between these two giants of Czech music did not run smoothly, but jealousy never really obscured their mutual appreciation. It was only their supporters who later poisoned the air.

It was in fact this E flat Symphony which secured for Dvořák – who genuinely needed it in order to survive – a grant of 400 Gulden, awarded in Vienna to promote the development of Czech artists. He had submitted the work to a committee in which Brahms and Eduard Hanslick, the 'Pope' of Viennese musical criticism, had a decisive say, and the prize was awarded to the 'budding talent as a composer' of Antonín Dvořák. This hit the mark. By the mid-1870s, Dvořák's output was bubbling forth with a wealth of compositions, including two more symphonies. His fascination with Wagner was beginning to fade, while Beethoven and Schubert lit the way to the discovery of his own personality. The decision to resign his post in the theater orchestra was part of the same picture. Instead he accepted an appointment as organist at the parish church of St Adalbert shortly after his marriage. At a mere 138 Gulden a year he was paid even less than before, but had very much more time to spare for what he regarded as essential: composition.

The success of *Hymnus* encouraged him to write more vocal music. At that time the writing of a new Czech opera meant everything to a composer; the financial return might only be small, but the wave of national approval made up for it. However, there were still no professional Czech librettists, and so in 1874 he had to make do, once again, for his one act opera *Tvrdí palice* (The Stubborn Lovers), with an amateur script by the lawyer Josef Štolba, who also wrote farces. In sixteen short scenes a cunning and kindly uncle succeeds in bringing together two lovers who, though meant for each other, are thoroughly at cross purposes. The

Below: Dvořák (aged twenty-four) in 1865, when he wrote his first two symphonies, a youthful cello concerto, and his first group of songs.

Bottom: A contemporary view of the castle and church at Nelahozeves, the village by the river Vltava where Dvořák was born.

Above: The sisters Josefina (seated at the keyboard) and Anna Čermáková, two of Dvořák's piano pupils. He first fell in love with Josefina, but later married Anna – a similar situation to that of Mozart and Aloysia and Constanze Weber, but with happier results.

Right: Interior of the church in the North Bohemian town of Česká Kamenice, where the fifteen-year-old Dvořák studied music with the local choirmaster and learned German.

peasant setting in itself militates against high-flown Wagnerian sentiment and in favor of melodic simplicity. It is nevertheless noteworthy that Dvořák favored a supple *arioso* approach and shunned the classical *recitativo secco*, which even the 'progressive' Smetana could still not do without at that time. The first performance, for which the composer had to wait seven years (until 1881), brought him no more than the approval of the music critics.

In the meantime the tragic opera *Vanda* had been performed in 1876 and had totally failed. This episode from medieval Polish history was set in an overblown style pretty indiscriminately derived from a mixture of Smetana, Wagner and Meyerbeer. On the other hand, sparkling, entertaining music in true Dvořák style was squandered on an impossible libretto cobbled together by Otakar Veselý, a twenty-three-year-old medical student, in *Šelma sedlák* (The Cunning Peasant), a three-act comic opera which was well received at its first performance in 1878. *The Marriage of Figaro* and *The Bartered Bride* provided the models for the deplorable libretto. A count in pursuit of local beauties was taken from the former and even the identical names for the two rivals in love, Jeník and Vaclav, from the latter. Dvořák's music, on the other hand, had by now acquired its own character. Here was a masterly young dramatic composer weaving his music against the simple rural background of a jolly folk-opera with its choruses and ensembles, its songlike arias, a heartfelt duet in E flat for the lovers, flowing melody and fiery rhythms. *The Cunning Peasant* in German translation was the first of Dvořák's operas to find its way abroad, to the Berlin Opera in 1879.

Several concert pieces written during the mid-1870s period were even more important in terms of his creative development. Dvořák's only piano concerto – in G minor – is even now regarded by Czechs as a classical repertoire piece. In fact, and closely following Brahms's example, it is really a symphony with piano *obbligato*. The treatment of the solo instrument is so clumsy (Dvořák was no virtuoso at the piano) that it is usually performed in the arrangement made by the piano teacher Vilém Kurz.

Three duets written for friends who were amateur singers provided the starting point for Dvořák's most popular song cycle, *Moravské dvojzpěvy* (Moravian Duets) written over three years and comprising fourteen duets for soprano and alto and four for soprano and tenor with piano accompaniment. Under its German title *Klänge aus Mähren* (Airs from Moravia) it established Dvořák's fame throughout the world, while the twenty-eight *Symphonic Variations on a Czech folksong* (1877) display the composer at the height of his youthful powers, as do the D minor String Quartet (his ninth) and the twelve *Večerní písně* (Evening Songs), settings of poems by Vítězslav Hálek.

It was above all in the *Stabat Mater* (1876) that Dvořák demonstrated the command he had already achieved over the composition of a full-scale oratorio. He was feeling the impact of his small daughter Josefa's death while he sketched out this work. A year and a half later new misfortunes struck the young family when his eleven-month-old daughter Ružena and his eldest child, the three-and-a-half-year-old Otakar, also died. The anguish of a devout Catholic looking to his religion for consolation is powerfully reflected in this vast *Stabat Mater*. Melodic invention and contrapuntal skill are blended here, and it represents, historically speaking, the first great work of lasting value in Czech church music.

• International reputation •

It was Dvořák's friendship with Brahms, beginning in 1877, that was to exert a decisive influence on the younger man's career in the outside world, since Brahms sent his name to the highly regarded publishing house of Simrock in Berlin. Fritz Simrock scored a success with the *Airs from Moravia* and immediately gave a further commission to the Czech composer for what became the *Slovanské Tance* (Slavonic Dances). These were to prove a goldmine for the publisher and a triumphal step towards worldwide fame for the composer. He originally wrote a series of eight piano duets, which he then immediately arranged for orchestra, adding a further eight pieces eight years later. The melodic, rhythmic and tonal invention of the whole set has made it Dvořák's most popular work. The first series was based on Czech models, while the second draws on other Slavonic folk dances, from Poland and Yugoslavia – all transformed by Dvořák into his own unmistakable idiom.

Further works with a pronounced Czech coloring were now composed: the Serenade in D minor for wind instruments, cello and double-bass, a cheerful-sounding piece in spite of the key signature, and the three *Slavonic Rhapsodies* in D major, G minor and A flat minor. But it

was the resounding success of the *Slavonic Dances* that turned Dvořák into a composer in great demand almost overnight. Whatever he wrote was immediately performed, and the most famous conductors of the time, such as Hans Richter, Hans von Bülow and Arthur Nikisch, were most enthusiastic about his orchestral works. This was equally true of Brahms, whose delight at the sparkling fresh imagination of the Czech composer was as constant as the respectful admiration displayed by Dvořák for the mastery and spiritual quality of his protector. This remained one of the most noble and untroubled artistic friendships on record, and was only brought to an end by Brahms's death.

The royalties from the *Slavonic Dances* enabled Dvořák to move from his backyard apartment at No.10 Žitná – or Korntorgasse as it then was – to the more genteel frontage of the same building, where he remained until his death. His daughter Otilie was born there in 1878, and the years that followed were full of good fortune, both at home and in his musical life. This resilient mood is reflected in an abundance of optimistic works written during what has been labeled Dvořák's 'Slavonic period' because of the thread of musical folklore and patriotic idealism which ran through his output at this time. This does not quite apply to his three *Modern Greek Songs*; the very important *Gypsy Melodies* (which are, surprisingly, settings of German-language poems by the Czech author Adolf Heyduk); Psalm 149 – a homage to Handel's greatness; or the E flat major String Quartet, a sunny product of good humor at its best. But it is especially true of amiable pieces such as the *Česka Suita* (Czech Suite) for small orchestra and even more of the major works of this period.

These include the String Sextet in A major, a key which represented happiness and wellbeing in Dvořák's mind, and the Violin Concerto in A minor, which was inspired by the leading violinist of the time, Joseph Joachim, and provides an early example of the composer's characteristic idiom in its fully developed and masterly form. The solo part is symphonically woven into the score on one hand, but it is also conceived with great individual virtuosity, especially in the deeply felt slow movement and the dancing finale. It was, however, the Sixth Symphony in D major which proved most typical of this 'Slavonic period'. This is made plain by the *cantabile* character of the themes and the insertion of a *furiant*, a racy Czech folk dance, into the scherzo. As to the String Quartet in C major, it exemplifies a positively Mozartian speed of composition: though it sounds mature and perfect, it took only a few days to write and the first two movements together were composed within forty-eight hours.

As a result of his reduced commitments, Dvořák undertook the chore of composing, at the request of the theater's director, incidental music for *Josef Kajetán Tyl*, a heart-rending play by Franz Ferdinand Šamberk about the pioneer of the Czech stage, but his opera *Dimitrij* is of much greater importance. Its action starts where Musorgsky's *Boris Godunov* leaves off, and this Slavonic plot typifies the all-embracing Czech pan-Slavic mood prevalent at that time, a style which Dvořák still hoped would finally carry him to the international scene with a truly 'grand opera.' *Dimitrij* was given its first performance in 1882 at the New Czech Theater, modelled on the Bayreuth *Festspielhaus*, but the outstanding success achieved on that first night did not last, and the composer

Above: Mikuláš Aleš's painting of a column of patriotic soldiers during the Hussite wars in the fifteenth century.

Above: Fritz Simrock, who managed one of Germany's largest music publishing companies. Brahms recommended Dvořák to him.

Above: Aleš's idealized portrait of Jan Hus (1372-1415), who led a religious and political uprising in Bohemia, before being tried for heresy and burnt at the stake. The Hussite movement became a powerful symbol of Czech patriotism, and Dvořák composed a *Hussite Overture*, his op.67, in 1883.

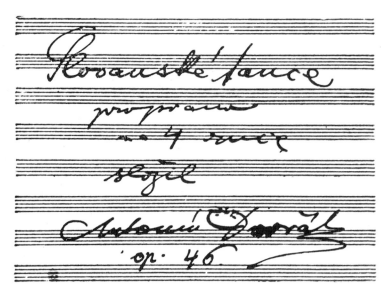

Above: Autograph of the title-page to the first set of *Slavonic Dances*.

Above right: Title-page to Simrock's first edition of the *Slavonic Dances*, a great success which cemented his association with Dvořák.

hopes of breaking through to the world stage remained unfulfilled.

Nevertheless, this work represents one of the most important of Dvořák's operas, alongside *Rusalka* (The Water Sprite) and *The Jacobin*. For the first time the composer had found a usable libretto; Marie Červinková-Riegrová, the daughter of the influential Old Czech politician František Ladislav Rieger, who opposed Dvořák

and rejected Smetana, had skillfully combined Schiller's *Demetrius* fragment with a Czech play and produced a rhymed sequence divided into episodes. This deals with the Russian pretender Dmitry, who collapses when he realizes that he is no more than a tool of Poland and is shot. Dvořák displays in his approach a totally new assurance as a grand opera composer more akin to Verdi than Wagner or Smetana, with solemn double choruses, sweeping finales and *bel canto* arias. But no foreign opera house came forward with a bid for the work, and Dvořák, who had been thrown off balance, tried to achieve recognition by recasting the opera into an – equally unsuccessful – version in the manner of Wagner. It is only recently that the real beauty of this musical drama born of Dvořák's painful endeavors has been uncovered.

In 1884 Dvořák was invited by the London Philharmonic Society to conduct his *Stabat Mater*. He reached the British capital in March with his friend, the pianist Jindřich Kàan. He was overwhelmed by this vast metropolis of a worldwide empire and, even more, as he wrote home, by the gigantic Albert Hall 'where 10,000 people heard the *Stabat Mater*, and 1,050 musicians and singers played and sang – and with that colossal organ on top of it all.' It was completely unheard of for a Czech composer to be asked to conduct one of his own new works in what was then the wealthiest city on earth –

Above: Dvořák in the cap and gown of Doctor of Music, the honorary degree conferred upon him by Cambridge University in 1891, the year in which he also conducted the first performance of his Requiem Mass in Birmingham.

Below: The New Czech Theater, Prague, modelled on the design of Wagner's Festival Theater at Bayreuth. The first performance of Dvořák's grand opera *Dimitrij* took place there in 1882.

such honor had never come Smetana's way — and Dvořák came home in triumph. He was not a virtuoso of the baton, such as von Bülow or Nikisch, so that it had been the composer rather than the conductor who had conquered Britain, not only with the *Stabat Mater* but also with the Sixth Symphony.

The course which Smetana's and Dvořák's lives had taken now offered a strange contrast, with the older composer forced to enter the Prague district mental institution, while the younger master tasted to the full all the good fortune that life had brought him: newly acquired international fame, domestic happiness and a revival of his creative drive exercised in his freshly arranged summer residence. He had had an old sheepfold at Vysoká in Southern Bohemia turned into a simple but very comfortable country house to accommodate both his family and a music room (with a grand piano). An early riser throughout his life, a dedicated nature lover and a pigeon breeder, he would hurry away from the city to spend from spring to autumn there. It was here that most of the works written during the two decades at the peak of his mature talent – apart from those of the American period – were composed.

Meanwhile, he repeatedly traveled to Britain where his reputation grew so great that he came to be described as 'The Bohemian Brahms.' He had already earned this title in 1885 by the first performance in London of his Seventh Symphony in D minor. Although Brahms's Third had provided the model for it, as had Beethoven with his fighting symphonic *per aspera ad astra* approach, one would have to disregard entirely the tunefulness of the song themes, or the introduction by the composer of a typical folk dance – a *furiant* – into the scherzo, in order to deny this symphony its unmistakably Czech character. In the same year, *Svatební košile* (The Specter's Bride), a choral work, had a triumphant performance at the Birmingham Festival. This probably owed more to the massed choir of five hundred singers, which was so typical of English practice at that time, than

to the purely musical merits of this spooky, ballad-like seven-part cantata.

•Sacred works and operas•

Svatá Ludmila (Saint Ludmila), an oratorio first performed in 1886 at a musical festival in Leeds, is of greater significance. After providing the first great Czech church music composition in his *Stabat Mater*, Dvořák now presented the nation with its first outstanding full-length oratorio. Jaroslav Vrchlický, a poet and a classic among Czech writers, had recounted in verse a historical event of the ninth century that lent itself to musical treatment: the conversion to Christianity of the pagan Bohemian princess Ludmila and her betrothal to the recently baptized Duke Bořivoj. It is indicative of the pious Catholic in Dvořák that the patriotic element of the story is almost entirely subordinate to its religious aspect.

Dvořák's self-confidence had been bolstered by his triumphs in England, a successful visit to the Berlin Philharmonic Orchestra and many performances of his *Slavonic Dances* in Germany. He could now dictate the amount of royalties to his publisher Simrock (he got 6,000 Marks for his D minor Symphony instead of the 3,000 he had originally been offered), yet he could tell a compatriot who had written to him in altogether too effusive terms: 'I remain what I have been, a simple Czech musician.' The loving husband and father was delighted by the increase in his family: a second son, Otakar, born in 1885, was followed in 1888 by a daughter, Aloisie. His output bubbled forth more plentifully than it had ever done. On one occasion in 1887, when he was unable to find the manuscript of an earlier piano quintet after rummaging through his trunk, he made up his mind on the spot to write another, also in A major, which became one of his chamber music masterpieces. Its Slav character is particularly evident in the second movement, which he called *Dumka*. This is the name of a Ukrainian folk dance with abrupt changes from quick to slow, from dancetime to a reflective mood. It was also the title given to the op.90 Trio for piano, violin and cello composed three years later. In defiance of the conventional pattern, this is made up of six movements, and it became world-famous as the 'Dumky' Trio. Dvořák was equally determined to 'avoid the accustomed, commonly used and recognized forms' in his Eighth Symphony in G major, written in 1889 and performed the following year in Prague and London to tremendous applause. This is indeed the most unfettered, in a formal sense, among the symphonies of his mature period. In its finale the composer combined the use of variation and sonata form, while this movement and the first are thematically linked, with an intervening scherzo waltz and an adagio full of deep-felt contentment.

Special circumstances led to the composition of further church music. Thus Dvořák's only Mass, in D major, was written for the castle

chapel of a landowner, and therefore originally conceived as straightforward and singable music with organ accompaniment, which was later transcribed for orchestra. The *Te Deum*, commissioned from America in 1892 for the Columbus anniversary celebrations, is more grandiloquent in its effect. It consists of four well-contrasted parts with solos and a generously proportioned finale. It was originally intended that an English language text should be set, as *The American Flag Cantata*, but the text did not arrive in time and the work remained unexceptional.

The Requiem, on the other hand, which was given a brilliantly successful first performance at the Birmingham Choir Festival in 1891, turned out to be a masterpiece of Dvořák's *musica sacra*, a Mass for the dead written in the unclouded fullness of the composer's life – yet another indication of his purely musical creative approach. A theme based on the exalted notes B-A-C-H is subjected to a multitude of variations, while counterpoint and melody are musically reconciled. Thus the 'Quam olim Abrahae' choral fugue is based on a medieval Czech song.

Despite all his successes in the concert hall, the ambition to write opera gave Dvořák no rest. He had for several years refused to consider a new libretto by Marie Červinková-Riegrová, but now decided to set it. This was *Jakobín* (The Jacobin), to which he devoted much time and care. It not only proved a great success at its first performance in the new National Theater in 1889, but also turned out to be one of his best works as a composer of musical drama. For a start, he was very much in his element as far as the subject was concerned. In a small town in Bohemia in the 'good old days' a count and his subjects make up a friendly community, which is only disturbed when a villainous relative throws suspicion of being a militant Jacobin on the count's son. Everything eventually turns out for the best with the help of music, and the character who brings this about is the village choirmaster, Benda – Dvořák's most lifelike and likeable operatic figure and a living memorial to his first teacher in Zlonice, the German Anton Liehmann (the name of his daughter Terynka is used in the opera).

•Visit to America •

While Dvořák was working on *The Jacobin*, Tchaikovsky visited Prague. In return he extended an invitation to Dvořák to visit Russia. This journey to Moscow and St Petersburg in spring 1890 proved a disappointment for the composer, however, and the critics were not well disposed towards him. He bitterly commented: 'Oh thou so-called Slav fellow-feeling, where art thou?' On the other hand he enjoyed his growing fame, imparted to his works in Germany by conductors such as Hans von Bülow and Hans Richter and personally experienced by him as the proud recipient of an

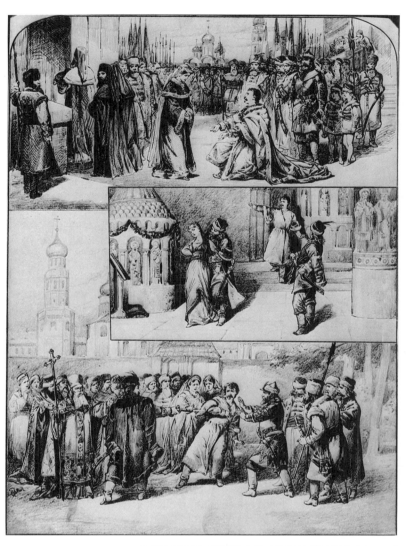

Above: Scenes from the first production of *Dimitrij*. The work is based on events in Russian history closely connected with the story of Musorgsky's *Boris Godunov*. Dvořák's idea was to create a pan-Slavic opera on a grand scale.

Right: Playbill for the first production, at the new Prague National Theater in 1889, of *The Jacobin*. Despite the title, this is a relatively light-hearted opera, set in rural Bohemia and sharing something of the mood of Smetana's *Bartered Bride*.

honorary doctorate from the University of Cambridge. Even his own country now began to honor him. In Vienna, the Emperor awarded him a decoration, conferred in the course of a somewhat stuffy audience. He was elected a member of the Prague Academy and, much more important, appointed a senior professor by the newly-founded School of Composition at the Prague Conservatory, where he taught composition on and off from 1891 until 1901. His pupils there included Josef Suk, who married his daughter Otilie, Oskar Nedbal and Vítězslav Novák.

However, very soon after his appointment Dvořák had to ask for leave of absence. The offer he had received from New York was well-nigh irresistible. Mrs Jeanette Thurber, a millionairess who had founded the New York Conservatory, wanted to lend prestige to her new institution by importing some leading European personality. The Prague Conservatory paid 1,200 Gulden a year, while she offered 30,000. And so the composer crossed the Atlantic in 1892, accompanied by his wife, two of their children and a young assistant, Josef Jan Kovařík, and moved into a house on East 17th Street. He liked the great city from the very start of his stay, and maintained his regular habits, rising early, at six o'clock, giving composition lessons on three days of the week at the nearby school and devoting himself entirely to his family from six in the evening onward. He took practically no interest in concerts or the Metropolitan Opera.

Nostalgia brought him back to Bohemia in the summer, to his much-loved country house at Vysoká and the rest of his family. They were now old enough to accompany him back to America, and a total of eleven, including a maid, spent the summer of 1893 with an American family of Czech origin at Spillville, Iowa. His most popular string quartet, that in F major, was written there. This very accessible 'American' quartet is nevertheless most skillfully constructed, the main themes of all four movements being derived from the same pentatonic nucleus. This inspired piece was sketched out within a mere three days. Dvořák left himself a little more time for the 'Spillville' String Quintet in E flat major, a more ample work but conceived in the same mood of deep contentment. During the return journey the composer visited the Chicago World's Fair on its 'Czech Day' and was quite overcome by the sight of the Niagara Falls. America, and its Indian folk music in particular, fascinated him to such an extent that he did some work on an opera based on Longfellow's Hiawatha.

Dvořák had completed his Ninth Symphony earlier in the summer of 1893. He subtitled it 'Z nového světa' (From the New World) and its first performance at Carnegie Hall on 16 December by the New York Philharmonic Orchestra under Anton Seidl turned it into a triumph which echoed throughout the musical world. It was an event Americans had been looking forward to with special eagerness, because Dvořák himself had advocated a new, specifically American style of music which, according to him,

had to be founded on what he called 'Negro melodies.' This theory had not been adopted by native American composers such as Edward MacDowell, but the Ninth Symphony seemed to be its triumphant vindication. Each movement contains melodic elements that sound 'American,' as, for instance, the first movement's G major theme, which is related to the Negro spiritual 'Swing low, sweet chariot,' but all of them are Dvořák's own inventions.

The sensitive imagination he displayed is all the more surprising in that it was only through his pupils that he obtained a little insight into Negro folklore. As he himself wrote, he had not used 'any Negro or Indian melodies' but merely tried to render their spirit. He once remarked, 'It all is and remains Czech music.' There can in fact be no doubt about this. For instance, there is no mistaking the idealized Bohemian parish festival dance in the trio of the scherzo. Even the most exotically American sounding elements of the 'New World' Symphony were integrated by Dvořák into his own musical idiom, yet America's contribution to his style remains important. This includes a pentatonic approach to melody, the frequent use of a diminished seventh in place of the dominant – a characteristic of Negro folk music – and the very American syncopation which distinguishes the symphony's first movement.

Two further outstanding works were composed on American soil. The Biblické písně (Biblical Songs) cycle represents the summit of Dvořák's compositions for voice and piano. The use of his Czech mother-tongue testifies to his deep personal involvement when he was

Opposite: Josef Mánes's designs for the front and reverse sides of the banner for the Prague Hlahol Choral Society, which often sang under Dvořák's direction. They gave the first performance of one of the works that made his name, the patriotic cantata *The Heirs of the White Mountain* (1872), also known as *Hymnus*, which commemorates the tragic battle in 1620, at the start of the Thirty Years' War, which led to the suppression of all the ancient privileges of the Czechs.

Below: Dvořák (center), Ferdinand Lachner (seated) and Hanuš Wihan, who toured Bohemia and Moravia in 1891 and 1892 giving performances of the composer's 'Dumky' Trio, op.90.

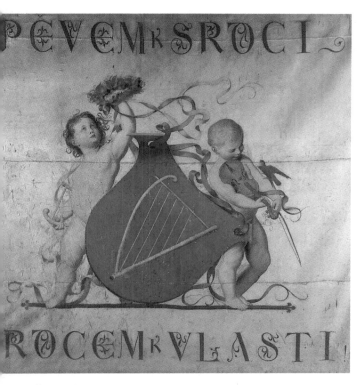

affected by the deaths of his father and of his friends Tchaikovsky and von Bülow. Comparison with Brahms's *Four Serious Songs* is unavoidable, but while pessimism predominates in these, an unshakeable faith lights up Dvořák's somber Biblical landscape.

This song-cycle is seldom heard nowadays in the concert hall, while the Cello Concerto in B minor is a perennial work against which every master of the instrument from Casals to Rostropovich has measured himself ever since. Its idiom is no less 'American' than that of the E minor Symphony, and it surpasses Dvořák's earlier instrumental concertos for violin and piano by its thematic compactness and its richer, highly romantic orchestral color. The solo instrument, which the composer incidentally did not particularly like, is once again symphonically integrated into the score. Although it is never allowed to stand on its own merely for the sake of empty technical effects, it nevertheless announces Dvořak's inspired melodies, which are skillfully elaborated in his characteristic style.

In 1895 the composer once again spent the summer holidays in his home country. In his beloved Vysoká he wrote the eight *Humoresques* for piano, with repeated echoes of his American sketches, of which no.7 in G flat major became a worldwide favorite for amateur pianists. Unconquerable nostalgia drove the composer to curtail his last contractual six months of teaching in New York, and Mrs Thurber in fact continued to owe him several months' salary. Dvořák was back in Prague in April and shortly thereafter resumed his tutorial work at the local Conservatory. He now declared himself 'inexpressibly happy' to be at home, and this mood led to the production of his last two String Quartets – in G major and A flat major. With these works the composer bade farewell to 'pure' music, of which he had produced so much in the past and which he had pioneered among the Czechs. From now on he was to devote himself entirely to works that were poetic or dramatic in character: symphonic poems and opera.

• Late works •

In 1896 tone poems appeared in fairly quick succession: *Vodník* (The Water Goblin), *Polednice* (The Noon Witch), *Zlatý kolovrat* (The Golden Spinning-Wheel) and *Holoubek* (The Wood Dove). These works were all based on Czech fairytales put into ballad form by a collector of folklore, Karel Erben. How did it come about that this famous composer of symphonies

Above: The Decadence of Art in Bohemia, a design for the foyer of the National Theater, Prague, by František Ženíšek, another artist devoted to the cause of Czech nationalism. The allegorical theme is the adulteration of the native culture by foreign domination.

255

Above: The Brooklyn Bridge built in 1883 across New York's East River, much as Dvořák would have known it when he stayed in New York City on his first American visit in 1892.

and chamber music – and Brahms's friend – suddenly turned to the 'New German School' of program music, in other words towards Liszt and Richard Strauss?

He had always been an admirer of Liszt and even Wagner, and he may have come to believe that he could not improve on achievements such as his Ninth Symphony and the Cello Concerto. But he was attracted by the opportunity of casting 'programs' he was given into new musical forms. His least successful attempt was *The Golden Spinning-Wheel*, in which the action-packed plot of the fairytale encouraged too broad an approach. He achieved greater clarity in the shorter ballad-like pieces – *The Water Goblin* is conceived in a free rondo form; *The Noon Witch* in four parts, after the manner of a symphony; and *The Wood Dove* in five parts – works in which Janáček saw a close affinity to folk music and described as 'the most Czech of all Dvořák's works.' By contrast, the passionate *Píseň bohatýrská* (Hero's Song), written the following year, is more akin to the work of Richard Strauss.

Dvořák traveled much less as he grew older. He went to England for the last time in 1896 as a conductor, then to Berlin, and afterwards to Vienna to accompany Brahms's coffin to the cemetery. He was again hard at work teaching young Czech composers at the Conservatory, and he also put his great reputation at the service of the young Czech Philharmonic. When this orchestra, which was later to become so famous, faced the public for the first time, it played works by Dvořák, which he himself conducted.

Ten years had gone by since he had last written an opera. During this period Smetana's *Bartered Bride* had started from Vienna on its triumphal way round the world, Wagner and Verdi were both successful in Prague, and light opera was at the peak of its popularity. Dvořák himself regarded this as 'the most appropriate creative offering for the people,' and he complained ruefully that he was held in high regard only as a symphonic composer, whereas his 'in-

clination was overwhelmingly towards opera.' He therefore jumped at the opportunity offered by the libretto of *Čert a Káča* (The Devil and Kate) suggested to him by F. A. Šubert, the director of the National Theater. *The Devil and Kate* was based on an old Czech folk story which had been adapted in free verse for the stage by Josef Wenig, a twenty-four-year-old teacher. The heroine, Kate, is a rumbustious farm girl so crazy about dancing that she dances right down to Hell with the Devil himself. But once there she plagues him so much that in the end he is delighted to bring her back to her village. The brave shepherd Jirka makes his own contribution to all this and, in a happy ending, gets his Kate.

All this is staged in a most naïve and jolly manner, especially the scenes where Dvořák used a Bohemian village inn to represent Hell. But there is only a handful of catchy arias interspersed with long stretches of recitative based on Czech speech rhythms (in a way much admired by Janáček) and, though the score displays mature craftsmanship, the whole thing does not entirely match the rumbustious mood of a popular fairytale. The success of the first night nevertheless prompted Dvořák to rush into composing another opera with a libretto once again suggested by Šubert.

A young writer, Jaroslav Kvapil, had already offered the libretto of *Rusalka* (The Water Sprite) to the opera composer J. B. Foerster, as well as to Dvořák's son-in-law Josef Suk, but with no success. These rejections are quite understandable, as the libretto lacks dramatic tension and is excessively lyrical. Dvořák, however, proved that this might in fact be an advantage: the fairytale with its inherent poetical quality (expressed, incidentally, in verse of a standard well above the average) and its closeness in style to folklore and nature made him feel at ease and allowed his imagination ample room for musical invention. Rusalka is a water sprite belonging to that species of Ondines and Melusines which has flitted through Europe's fairytale forests and lakes from time immemorial. A prince woos her, but she would lose the power of speech if she left her natural environment for the world of men. A jealous princess turns the prince against her. She returns to the forest but by the time her repentant lover follows her, it is too late: her kiss can only bring death.

The composer's feelings were entirely engaged on the side of nature. The prince and princess are depicted on rather conventional lines, while Rusalka and the creatures that belong to her environment receive the benefit of the most extravagant lyricism generated by any of Dvořák's operas. Rusalka's D flat major aria to the moon and the water goblin's plaintive lament are the outstanding melodic numbers in a score which is full of inspiration throughout. 'I am hugely delighted and pleased that my work should turn out so well!' wrote Dvořák from his cottage at Vysoká, which he called 'Villa Rusalka.' The first performance at the National Theater on 31 March 1901 was Dvořák's greatest success as an operatic composer, and so it remained as far as Czechs were concerned. But decades went by before the outside world came to recognize its lyrical splendor and musical richness.

The 'Czech music-maker' who had achieved worldwide renown was now gathering a growing harvest of honors. Together with Jaroslav Vrchlický, he was appointed by the Emperor to membership of the predominantly aristocratic Upper House of Parliament of the Dual Monarchy in Vienna in 1901, to represent Czech cultural life. He demonstratively took the prescribed oath in Czech, but this first appearance as a parliamentarian also proved to be his last. During that summer, he was elected director of the Prague Conservatory, but he insisted that this also remained a purely representative office – after all, did he not need time for composition? His sixtieth birthday was marked in his native village by solemn Masses, speeches and salutes of guns, at the National Theater by performances of a cycle of his operas, and by concerts throughout the country.

Dvořák hesitated for a long time over a new work after the success scored with *Rusalka*. He was 'unemployed' for some fourteen months, a state of affairs wholly unfamiliar to him throughout his life, and this eventually drove him to take on a libretto which was to prove disastrous. *Armida*, written by the inexhaustibly productive Jaroslav Vrchlický, attracted him because he thought it might pave the way to the international stage, since the subject had already been set to music – by Monteverdi, Lully and Gluck, among others. He was not at all perturbed by the fact that Karel Kovařovic, the highly experienced head of opera at the National Theater, had already turned down this very same libretto. Vrchlický had larded the favorite old love story of Rinaldo, the crusader, and Armida, a pagan girl, with Christian humanist sentiments. It became obvious, however, that by 1900 such a 'magic' opera belonged to a long-outdated genre. The score of *Armida* is far and away the best thing in the work as a whole, but it is hampered by an impossible libretto. Furthermore, the first performance in 1904 at the National Theater was marred by an orchestral and musicians' strike and inadequate stage sets, and it achieved little more than some critical approval.

Dvořák now had the pleasure of welcoming Edvard Grieg during his visit to Prague, and as soon as he had completed *Armida* he chose another, even more unlikely, libretto, based on ancient Czech epics, a vivid illustration of how erratic his judgment could be once a subject impressed him. But *Horymír*, a work cobbled together by his friend, the manufacturer Rudolf Stárek, did not get off the drawing-board.

Dvořák had throughout his life never been ill, but he was now forced to take to his bed with a liver complaint. Seventy-six choral associations gathered from the whole country in the spring of 1904 for the first Czech music festival, with Dvořák's output as its main focus. Sixteen thousand singers intoned the *Saint Ludmila* oratorio. Thousands of listeners celebrated the master of the Ninth Symphony. But he was by now seriously ill and he succumbed to a stroke on 1 May 1904. Tens of thousands lined his funeral route through the streets of Prague. Antonín Dvořák was buried in the cemetery of the former castle of Vyšehrad, the last resting-place of so many great heroes of Czechoslovakia.

Below: Dvořák at the Chicago World's Fair of 1893, where, on 'Czech Day' he conducted a performance of his Eighth Symphony in G major.

Left: Page from Dvořák's sketches for the Ninth Symphony in E minor ('From the New World'), which he composed during his second American tour, and which was first performed by the New York Philharmonic Orchestra to great acclaim in the winter of 1893.

The songs of Hugo Wolf

Hugo Wolf (1860-1903) was the outstanding composer of songs in the second half of the nineteenth century, achieving in miniature and with perfect sensitivity what Richard Wagner had attempted in his music dramas – a vocal line that follows the rhythms and nuances of the words and an instrumental part which reveals and emphasizes every shade of meaning. Wolf also wrote chamber music and some orchestral works and completed a comic opera, *Der Corregidor*. Of his surviving songs, two-thirds – nearly two hundred – were written in a few short bursts of feverish creative energy, the longest lasting barely five months, when Wolf was composing on average more than three songs a week, and sometimes two in a day, generally devoting himself to the work of a single poet. Wolf supported himself by teaching, for a time by criticism – his violently hostile attacks on Hanslick and on Brahms in the *Salonblatt* earned him the nickname of the 'wild Wolf' – and he held a brief appointment as choirmaster at the theater in Salzburg; but in the main he relied on his friends, who remained devoted to him even in the final sad years of his madness.

Wolf first heard Wagner's music in November 1875 and from that moment he was a devoted Wagnerian. Later he was an active member of the Vienna Wagner-Verein, and the first concerts of his music were given under the Society's auspices. This was the initiative of the Society's artistic director Joseph Schalk, who, despite furious opposition from one faction, made Thursday evening concerts of

Wolf's songs a regular occasion. The composer's intense renderings of these in his thin voice were unforgettable, but often he would be joined by Ferdinand Jäger, who had sung Parsifal at Bayreuth, and who became one of his staunchest supporters. The painting below celebrates these evenings in the room dominated by a gigantic head of the master, and shows Wolf and Jäger, with Schalk seated beside the composer.

The first great creative burst of Wolf's song writing came in 1888, when between 16 February and 18 May he set forty-three songs by Mörike (*above*). Eduard Mörike (1804-75) was a pastor and school-teacher, many of whose poems record the joys and bitterness of youthful love, while others show a tender feeling for nature or for his religion, and others again are witty and satirical. His poems had been set by

earlier composers, including Schumann and Brahms, but it was Wolf who revealed their deeper meaning and variety. Songs of markedly different character followed day after day, and, as may be seen from letters to his friends, the process of composition seems sometimes to have been almost automatic. Ten more Mörike songs were composed in the autumn, and the collection published the following year.

Paul Heyse (1830-1914) (*below*) was a master of the miniature, both in his poems and his short stories. He translated two sets of poems, published as the *Italian Songbook* and the *Spanish Songbook* (a joint work with Emanuel Geibel) and Wolf set selections from both. In his Spanish songs Wolf introduced local color to the music, but – to Heyse's disappointment – there is no southern accent to his songs based on the light-hearted Italian poems. Whereas in his Mörike and Goethe songs the genius of Wolf's music seems to reveal the poet's thoughts, here it creates new levels of meaning.

Wolf resumed his feverish composing at the end of the summer of 1888: between 14 September and the following 12 February he completed the last ten Mörike songs, made twelve settings of poems by Eichendorff (*above*) and fifty of Goethe's poems. Joseph von Eichendorff (1788-1857) was one of the masters of Romantic longing, the poet of the German forest, and his verses provide the twilit atmosphere of Schumann's *Liederkreis*. Wolf, who had made several earlier settings of his poems, some as far back as 1880, wanted to complement Schumann's work by a set of songs which drew on the humor and irony of the poet, as in the masterpiece *Das Ständchen*.

For several of his earliest songs Wolf set poems by Heinrich Heine (1797-1856) (*above*) – three in December 1876 and several more in late 1878, in the turmoil of his passion for Vally Franck. In his maturity he scarcely ever returned to Heine, but in that winter of 1888 he did return to Goethe. Wolf's Goethe settings are unequalled for the way their music expresses the essence of some of the finest poems in the language.

Wolf's *Italian Songbook* appeared in two parts, twenty-two songs written in autumn 1890 and winter 1891 and twenty-four in spring 1896 in his last, brief sustained period of creativity. Below is the manuscript of 'Der Mond hat eine schwere Klag' erhoben,' one of the most beautiful songs in the collection.

Above: Adolf Menzel's title-page for the *Spanish Songbook*. Wolf's forty-four settings, of both religious and secular songs, were written in two short periods between late October 1889 and April 1890. He later orchestrated several of the songs – two for inclusion in *Der Corregidor* (1895) and two more in 1897 for his planned opera *Manuel Venegas*.

Wolf's last finished songs were three settings of poems by Michelangelo, written in March 1897. The composer had recently been given a Life of the artist and a book of his poems, and he chose to set poems that reflected the mood of human struggle embodied by Michelangelo's *Atlas* (*above*).

Vally Franck (*above*) was Wolf's first great love and inspired his first rush of creative energy in 1878, the year in which they met. Vally was capricious and alarmed by the intensity and seriousness of her 'brown-eyed Ulf;' in spring 1881 she broke off their relationship. Wolf was desperately unhappy, although in later years he always remembered Vally with affection.

Above: The Köchert children. Wolf set Goethe's mocking poem 'Epiphanias' for the three eldest to sing to their mother on her birthday, accompanied by the composer from behind a screen.

To a composer of Wolf's sensitivity, order and quiet were almost essential conditions for composition. In Vienna he moved from one lodging to another, at one time sharing rooms with Gustav Mahler, his fellow student at the Conservatory, and at another with the writer Hermann Bahr. But the greater part of his composing was done away from the city: his friends the Werners allowed him to use their house in Perchtoldsdorf, a few miles from Vienna, during the winter months, and it was here (*right*) or in the little garden house (*above*) that nearly half of his songs were written – most of the *Mörike Lieder*, all the *Spanish Songbook* and the second part of the *Italian Songbook*. Most of his other songs were composed either in the house of his friend Friedrich Eckstein in the Salzkammergut, or in the house in Döbling, near Vienna, owned by his most devoted friends, the Köcherts.

Left: Fragment of Wolf's unfinished incidental music for Kleist's play *Der Prinz von Homburg*, composed in 1884. Wolf identified closely with the tragic Romantic writer – he also wrote a symphonic poem based on Kleist's *Penthesilea* – and when in Berlin visited Kleist's grave.

Melanie Köchert (*above*) became Wolf's piano pupil in 1881, and she and her family became his most loyal friends. Wolf's letters to her reveal much of his inner life as a composer.

Above: Opening of *Der Corregidor.* Wolf worked on his opera (based on Alarcón's *Three-Cornered Hat*) during 1895, and it was first performed in Mannheim the following June. Mahler's reluctance to stage it at the Vienna Opera was a devastating blow.

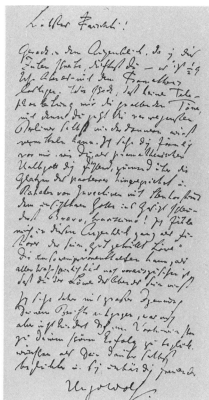

Above: Letter from Wolf to Hugo Faisst, a lawyer and amateur singer, who in 1894 took part in a number of his recitals with Frieda Zerny. It refers to a performance of Wolf's *Prometheus* which Faisst was giving in Berlin.

Below: Wolf with his devoted guardian Johann Scheibner in the Provincial Asylum in Vienna, where he spent the last four years of his life. His condition gradually worsened, and he died in Scheibner's arms on 22 February 1903.

In January 1894 Wolf heard the young soprano Frieda Zerny (*left*) in a concert of his songs. He was strongly attracted to her, and they gave a number of concerts together and planned tours abroad. But it seems that Wolf (seen, above, in 1895) had hoped that his feelings for her would release his creative block; when this was not the case his interest quickly cooled.

Right: Wolf's study in the fourth-floor apartment in Schwindgasse where he lived from July 1896, thanks to the generosity of his friends, especially Hugo Faisst, until the outbreak of his madness in September 1897. Here, Wolf felt for the first time that he had a home of his own, with space for his piano, his books, scores and pictures.

GUSTAV MAHLER

CONSTANTIN FLOROS

'But as far as I am concerned, symphony means using all the technical means available in order to build a world.'

Gustav Mahler

Any reference to an Austrian tradition in nineteenth- and twentieth-century symphonic music usually applies to three artists above all: Franz Schubert, Anton Bruckner and Gustav Mahler. The last two are often mentioned in the same breath anyway, but while there is no doubt that Mahler owed much to Bruckner, they clearly differed a great deal from each other both as men and artists. One common characteristic, however, was a remarkable degree of concentration on a fairly confined creative field. Mahler's entire mature output consists of symphonies and songs. He was a respected opera director and a highly popular conductor, but composed neither operas nor music dramas and, apart from juvenilia, wrote neither piano nor chamber music. His very own creative field was the symphony, and his songs provide a link to it.

Whoever wishes to get to know Mahler's music in depth must first learn to understand his 'spiritual world,' because his personality looms most powerfully behind all his works. Mahler's religious and philosophical thought is inseparable from his overall output. Education, religious feeling, response to the surrounding world, an aesthetic approach and the symphony together provided him with a many-faceted spiritual world which must be taken as a whole.

Mahler was deeply versed in Goethe's works; and Goethe's proposition that the perception of an event and the experience of life were fundamental prerequisites of artistic creation occupied an important place in his thinking. Mahler was a firm believer in 'the parallelism between life and music' and claimed that he had 'never yet written a note . . . which was not absolutely truthful.' Such statements become easier to understand when one realizes that several of his works are autobiographical in their conception. This particularly applies to his first two symphonies, about which he said to his friend Natalie Bauer-Lechner: 'My two symphonies taken together exhaust the tenor of my entire life; what I have set out in them is what I have experienced and undergone, truth and poetry in sound. And if there was anyone really skilled in reading them, the whole of my life would indeed become entirely transparent

for him. In my case creativity and experience are so strongly connected that if my existence henceforth were to flow as quietly as a brook in a meadow I would not – so I believe – ever produce anything worthwhile again.' The Sixth Symphony also contains unmistakable autobiographical features, and Alma Mahler said about it: 'The Sixth is his most personal work of all and a prophetic one too.'

Those of his biographers who knew Mahler personally describe him as a complex character. According to Bruno Walter he had a split personality with 'an intricate inner life.' His temperament is often described as a strange mixture of the demonic and the childlike. Mahler was born a Jew, but it is significant that he wanted to become a Christian. In 1897 in Hamburg, at the age of thirty-seven, he was converted to Catholicism. His wife stressed again and again that he 'believed in Christ' and that he became very heated in conversation with her on the subject. The study of Christ's life and teaching had fascinated him long before he was converted and he had strong leanings towards Catholic mysticism, dogma and eschatology. Yet his attitude to Judaism and Christianity alike is best described as a matter of subtle balance. He undoubtedly bore the scars of his Jewish origin and identified with Ahasuerus, the 'wandering Jew,' whom as a child of eight he had seen in a dream and who had given him his staff. Although he strove throughout his life to become integrated into Christian society, he remained convinced that he was regarded as a pariah, saying: 'I am homeless three times over: as a Bohemian among Austrians, as an Austrian among Germans and as a Jew worldwide . . . One is an intruder everywhere and "wanted" nowhere.'

Mahler's Ahasuerus complex included the characteristically Jewish elements of self-consciousness and a sense of mission. Both Alma Mahler and the stage designer Alfred Roller agreed that Mahler never 'concealed' his Jewish origin but that it gave him 'no pleasure.' However, it did act as 'a spur and a goad to greater and purer achievement.' Mahler explained this to Roller by a simile: 'If a man comes into the world with one arm that is too short, the other arm must learn to work all the harder and may ultimately achieve things which even two healthy arms could not have managed to do' – a perfect example of what modern behaviorist theory calls existential assertion through achievement.

263

Right: Mahler as a child of six, growing up among the German-speaking community in the small town of Iglau in Moravia. His father served on the committee in the local synagogue.

• Early life •

Gustav Mahler was born on 7 July 1860, the son of a tradesman in Kaliště, a village in Bohemia. He spent his childhood and youth in Iglau (Jihlava), the German linguistic enclave in Moravia to which his family had moved by December 1860 and where he attended both primary and secondary schools.

His parents' marriage was far from happy. Mahler said later that they were about as suited to each other as fire and water; his father had been 'stubborness personified' and his mother 'meekness itself.' While his attitude towards his father was reserved, he loved his mother above all. Mahler admitted in a conversation with Sigmund Freud – whom he consulted in Leyden in 1910 – that the quarrels between his parents had badly upset him when he was a child and that the experience of violent contrast between tragic events and everyday banality had fascinated him all his life. This may help to explain the unresolved juxtaposition of the tragic and the trivial in many passages of his music.

The boy's interest in music began very early, and he himself wrote that he had made music and composed from the age of four, even before he could play his scales. He made such progress with the piano that he was able to appear before an audience in Iglau at the age of ten, and he learnt popular and soldiers' songs from the garrison there. His musical talent had been recognized, so he said, from the fact that as a four-year-old he could already sing more than two hundred such songs. Undoubtedly, Mahler's quite exceptional liking for folksong, for military calls and fanfares, and for marches was connected with these childhood musical memories.

When he was fifteen, his father was persuaded to let him study music in Vienna, and he enrolled

at the Conservatory of the Gesellschaft der Musikfreunde there on 20 September 1875. He studied the piano under Julius Epstein, harmony under Robert Fuchs and composition under Franz Krenn, and proved a very good student who completed his studies with a diploma and distinction in 1878. At a competition in composition he secured first prize with a piano quintet.

Although he had not been a good pupil at school – he was regarded as absent-minded and dreamy – Mahler managed to matriculate in Iglau, and he then attended the university. Even during his studies at the Vienna Conservatory, he divided his attention between music and literature, and during the winter term of 1877 he promoted the foundation of a literary club, which many of his friends joined. He wrote much poetry and saw himself principally as a poet-composer, writing the texts for the fairytale opera *Rübezahl* and *Das klagende Lied* (The Song of Sorrow) in 1880, as well as those of a few early songs. He was possessed by a passion for reading throughout his life and often said that reading so many books had radically affected his outlook. His literary and philosophical horizon was astonishingly wide. It began with ancient Greek writers, led on to Shakespeare, to the German mystics (Jakob Boehme, Angelus Silesius), French seventeenth-century writers (Racine, Molière), German classical and Romantic literature, Kant, many German nineteenth-century philosophers, Dostoyevsky and Tolstoy, and finally 'the Moderns,' whose leading representative was Ibsen as far as Mahler was concerned.

The composer whom Mahler revered most of all was Richard Wagner. He numbered him with Shakespeare and Beethoven among 'the most sublime and universal geniuses of modern times,' though it is certainly paradoxical that as a Jew Mahler should not have taken Wagner's anti-Semitism amiss. From the very start he studied Wagner's writings with great sympathy. Wagner's ideas about the religion of art, vegetarianism and the regeneration of mankind specially interested him.

The young Mahler was also strongly influenced by Anton Bruckner, whom he had met during his early years in Vienna and had come to know better as time went on, but without ever becoming his pupil. Mahler had great respect for Bruckner and with Rudolf Krzyzanowski arranged his Third Symphony as a piano duet.

Mahler composed a great deal between 1875 and 1883 – piano music, songs, chamber music and a fairytale play. In addition he started a number of sketches for operas. Unfortunately, little has survived of these juvenilia. Mahler himself destroyed several works and much else has been lost. What has been preserved includes the printed early songs, the fragment of a piano quartet in A minor of 1876, which has only recently been published, and *Das klagende Lied*, a fairytale play for solo voices, choir and large orchestra. This was the first work in which Mahler claimed that he had found his own idiom and which he described as his opus 1.

features: march-like passages, references to fanfares and birdsong, as well as a sense of drama, the use of a backstage orchestra and a sense of dying away at the end.

Right: Caricature of Julius Epstein, Mahler's kindly piano professor at the Conservatory of the Gesellschaft der Musikfreunde in Vienna.

Below: The Royal Municipal Theater at Olomouc, one of a series of provinvial theaters at which Mahler served his apprenticeship as an opera conductor.

•Conductor and composer•

In a sense *Das klagende Lied* played a fateful part in Mahler's life. He had submitted it to a jury of the Vienna Conservatory in the hope of securing the Beethoven Prize, worth 600 Gulden, which would have enabled him to live while he went on composing. But the jury picked another candidate, and he was forced to take up the profession of operatic conductor, which he loathed. He found employment to begin with in the smaller provincial theaters (Bad Hall, Ljubljana, Olomouc), but then went on to work in larger houses: Kassel in 1883, Prague in 1885 and Leipzig in 1886. His reputation as an efficient conductor and an interpreter of genius – even if somewhat idiosyncratic – spread rapidly. In 1888 he became director of the Royal Opera in Budapest. In 1891 the impresario Bernhard Pollini signed him on as conductor at the Stadttheater in Hamburg. After his conversion to Catholicism he was called to the largest existing theater of the day – the Vienna Hofoper – as a conductor. He was very soon appointed director and granted unprecedented powers.

It was as a conductor rather than a composer that Mahler was best known during his lifetime. His international reputation in this sense was based on his exemplary performances of the great works of Mozart, Weber, Wagner and Gluck, on his commitment to contemporary music, on the seriousness of his artistic approach and his perfectionism. He was entirely uncompromising, demanded the utmost from those with whom he worked, struggled against easygoing routine (his stricture 'Tradition is slovenliness' has been widely misunderstood) and championed a conception of opera as a total work of art which foreshadows in an astonishing way present-day ideas about the musical theater.

Mahler's social and professional rise was meteoric. He was just thirty-seven when he achieved the most coveted position – that of artistic director of the Vienna Hofoper. Yet despite all his triumphs as a conductor he remained thoroughly dissatisfied with his profession. He often complained about the slavery of operatic work that left him no free time for composition, to which, throughout his life, he could only devote himself during the summer months – hence the name he gave himself, 'the Summer Composer'. Nevertheless, his widely acclaimed instrumentation and his own unmistakable orchestral sound owed much to his wealth of experience as an executant.

Before discussing Mahler's symphonies one must first mention his songs, as the connection between his symphonic output and his song writing repays close examination. To take only one example, a song by Mahler, 'Das himmlische Leben' (The Heavenly Life), was in a

There are several versions of *Das klagende Lied*. The original one, completed on 1 November 1880, consisted of three parts: 'Waldmärchen' (Forest Fairytale), 'Der Spielmann' (The Minstrel) and 'Hochzeitsstück' (Wedding Piece). The text was written by Mahler himself based on stories and legends told by Bechstein and the Grimm brothers. The influences of Wagner's and Bruckner's music are unmistakably present. And yet the work bears Mahler's stamp, and one can recognize many typical

sense the seed from which the Fourth Symphony was to grow. The music of Mahler's songs provided material for a number of purely instrumental symphonic movements. In addition, Mahler often quoted phrases in his symphonies taken from his songs, while many symphonic passages have a pronounced song-like character – indeed their effect is that of 'songs without words.'

The special nature of Mahler as a song composer becomes particularly clear when one compares him with Hugo Wolf, in so many ways his opposite. The first obvious difference is in their choice of texts. Wolf set poems by Mörike, Eichendorff, Goethe, Heyse and Geibel for choice. Mahler, on the other hand, concentrated, apart from his own poems, on the anthology *Des Knaben Wunderhorn* (Youth's Magic Horn) and the poems of Friedrich Rückert. The popular quality and apparent guilelessness of the *Wunderhorn* texts fascinated him. Of his total of forty-four songs, twenty-four are drawn from this source. Such poetry, as he saw it, differed radically from 'literary poetry' and could more correctly be described as 'nature and life' than art. The most significant part of Wolf's song output was decisively influenced by Wagnerian musical drama; his settings are mostly in the more complex, non-strophic form, draw heavily on Wagnerian recitative and are marked by the application of a bold harmonic technique. Mah-

ler's songs, on the other hand, have very little in common with Wagner's style. They are closely related to folksong, favor strophic setting, mostly keep to a diatonic form and are strikingly sparing of technical devices. Their basic principle is melody, and Mahler achieves great intensity of expression by relatively simple means.

The poems in the famous *Lieder eines fahrenden Gesellen* (Songs of a Wayfarer), com-

Above: The Concert, attributed to Titian. Mahler had a print of this painting in his Hamburg apartment; his young associate, Bruno Walter, saw a striking likeness between the central figure in the painting and the composer.

pleted in Kassel in December 1884, are by Mahler himself. Their 'folk' quality is quite astonishing when one first encounters it. It is worth noting that Mahler drew the first two stanzas of the opening song 'Wenn mein Schatz Hochzeit macht' (When my darling gets married) from *Des Knaben Wunderhorn* and added a stanza of his own. The framework of the cycle, which has an autobiographical flavor, consists – as in Schubert's *Winterreise* – of a story of love rejected; Mahler had been much exercised by his unrequited love for a young actress in Kassel.

•The symphonist •

Monumentality and universality are characteristic of Mahler's approach to symphony. His works include an astonishing variety of movements and expressive features, most of which diverge from the traditional standards of their

kind. Even in purely external ways they obviously belong to a new kind of composition with a number of identifying characteristics. For a start, of his ten symphonies only four – the First, Fourth, Sixth and Ninth – have four movements. Four others have five – the Second, Fifth, Seventh and Tenth – while the Third runs to six movements. It is no less remarkable that two of the four-movement symphonies – the Fourth and Ninth – end with a slow movement. In addition, Mahler based some movements on texts requiring vocalists and choirs, borrowing from his songs for such purposes, and he often contravened the established rules in his use of keys in his movements. At the end of the nineteenth century Mahler was trying to work out

some kind of synthesis between the principles of Beethoven and Wagner. The ideal he pursued during his first creative period was that of the cantata symphony, with Beethoven's Ninth Symphony and its choral finale uppermost in his mind. Four of Mahler's symphonies – the Second, Third, Fourth and Eighth – represent instances of the cantata symphony. Two of these – the Second and Eighth – also have features reminiscent of the oratorio and should be seen as bordering on the Wagnerian 'total work of art' which Mahler so admired. In both these symphonies he pays homage to Wagner's ideas on art, religion and the mystery of redemption as expressed in *Parsifal*.

It is significant that Mahler should have started his symphonic career by composing program symphonies. He regarded his early symphonies in many ways as symphonic poems. Fairly detailed literary and philosophical programs (about the authenticity of which there cannot be the slightest doubt) exist for the first four symphonies. Mahler repeatedly referred to these programs in letters and conversations and freely commented on them. In fact there are program titles for many movements and parts of movements in his autograph scores and sketches. It was only in October 1900 that the composer withdrew from the program-music movement as such and let it be known that henceforth he wished to be performed 'without program.' However, there is no doubt about the confessional character of Mahler's symphonic output. It has been clearly proved that he made the personal, philosophical and religious questions that concerned him the subjects of his symphonies. His programs express the core of his personal beliefs.

He came to consider his first four symphonies as a unified tetralogy, and the First Symphony, completed in 1888, is already a uniquely original work. Many features typical of Mahler are assembled here and sharply defined: grouping movements into sections; borrowing from his song output; idiosyncratic instrumentation; the use of calls and fanfares and the imitation of birdsong; the folkloric coloring of many passages; and – not least – the programmatic conception. The work was first performed in Budapest in 1889 as a 'symphonic poem in two parts.' Mahler provided detailed program notes for the performances in Hamburg in 1893 and in Weimar in 1894. He called the work (originally in five movements) 'Titan,' and its two parts 'Aus den Tagen der Jugend. Blumen-, Frucht- und Dornenstücke' (From the days of youth. Flowers, fruits and thorns) and 'Commedia humana.'

Although he later withdrew the program, as he found it had been misunderstood, it is indispensable for an understanding of the work's autobiographical conception. The opening movement is inscribed in the autograph 'Frühling und kein Ende' (Spring and no ending). The movement begins with a mysterious slow introduction which depicts nature awakening in the forest. The music of the sonata movement that follows is largely drawn from the second of the *Wayfarer* songs, 'Ging heut' morgen übers

Opposite: Music by Gustav Klimt, painted in 1895 for the music room of the patron and industrialist Nikolaus Dumba. The leading Secessionist artist and Mahler became friends in Vienna, and the voluptuous, almost decadent, style of Klimt's paintings has its close counterpart in the composer's music. On the occasion of the great Secession exhibition of Max Klinger's bust of Beethoven in 1902, for which Klimt also painted his Beethoven frieze, the artist persuaded Mahler to arrange a theme from Beethoven's Ninth Symphony for a choir of trombones to be played at the opening.

Left: Title-page to the 1806 edition of *Des Knaben Wunderhorn* (Youth's Magic Horn), the anthology of German folk poetry. The innocent, starry-eyed quality of many of the poems inspired Mahler to set them to music. Features of these songs are also incorporated in his Second, Third and Fourth Symphonies.

Feld' (Over the field I went this morning). The music is bright, colorful and occasionally jaunty, matching the text of a song which expresses a love of life and a sense of unity with nature. Only at the beginning of the development section is there a return to the half-lit mood of the introduction. A rapt sentimental movement, to which Mahler gave the title 'Blumine' (borrowed from the Romantic writer Jean Paul), originally followed the first movement, but was later deleted. The new second movement is a mixture of waltzes and *Ländler* rather than a scherzo, and the original superscription – 'Mit vollen Segeln' (Under full sail) accurately conveys the swinging mood of its outer sections. In the slow movement – 'Totenmarsch in Callots Manier' (Funeral march after the manner of Callot) – Mahler succeeded in producing an astoundingly novel blend of what one might have thought to be incompatible material: the melody of the student canon *Bruder Martin* (*Frère Jacques*) is

lament of the hero.' The finale opens with a shrill dissonance which Mahler interprets as 'the cry of a heart wounded to its uttermost depth.' A semantic analysis of the music has recently revealed that the program title of this movement – 'Dall' Inferno al Paradiso' – was not added afterwards, as Mahler had in fact portrayed both Hell and Heaven by means of thematic allegories derived respectively from Liszt's 'Dante' Symphony and Wagner's *Parsifal*. *Inferno* symbolizes the hellishness of existence, *Paradiso* the conquest of misery and sorrow. However, being a pessimist, Mahler thought that the 'Hero' of his work would achieve victory only in death.

The problem of death and the hereafter in a religious sense exerted a specially strong fascination on Mahler. A dream described by Natalie Bauer-Lechner in March-April 1901 illustrates even more vividly than other such reports how strongly Mahler was haunted by thoughts of death. According to this, Death had appeared

Left: Opening night at the New Theater, Leipzig, in 1868. Mahler worked there between 1886 and 1888 on his way to fame as an opera conductor.

Below: The 'Summer Composer's' little lakeside house at Steinbach am Attersee in the Austrian Salzkammergut, where he worked on his Second and Third Symphonies during the summer holidays from 1893 to 1896.

played over an *ostinato* on muted drums and double basses in the rhythm of a funeral march, interrupted by snatches of gaily commonplace sounds with a Bohemian or Hungarian coloring. The music of the ethereal middle part is taken from the last stanza of the *Wayfarer* song 'Auf der Strasse stand ein Lindenbaum' (A linden tree stood by the roadside). Mahler explained his Funeral March as follows: 'A funeral goes past our hero, and the whole misery, the whole sorrow of the world with its sharp contrasts and its dreadful irony grips him. One should imagine the *Bruder Martin* funeral march being played in a muted way by a really bad band such as so often accompanies funerals. In between and mingling with it one can hear all the crudity, gaiety and banality of the wide world in the strains of a group of Bohemian musicians, and at the same time the deeply anguished

to him in the middle of a large assembly in the person of a big man 'who held himself stiffly in impeccable clothes.' He had pursued Mahler to the farthest corner of the room, finally seized him 'by the arm in an iron grip' and told him: 'You must come with me.'

• The Second and Third Symphonies •

Of all Mahler's works the Second Symphony is the one in which the religious and metaphysical side of his art manifests itself most clearly. In religious terms the subject of this symphony is eschatological. The composer had attempted to answer all the questions round which his thinking revolved – about the meaning of life and death, the ultimate condition of man and the

world – through art, within the program and the poetic text for this symphony. The faith which he thus acknowledged was a belief in immortality formulated in a highly personal way. The text which he himself wrote for the final movement of the symphony culminates in an act of faith: 'I will die so as to live.'

The extremely interesting and illuminating genesis of this symphony demonstrates that Mahler had indeed 'wrestled long' with the material of the work. Its 'seed' was a single-movement symphonic poem called *Totenfeier* (Ceremony for the dead), which had been elaborated in accordance with a detailed program and completed in Prague by 1888. Years were to go by before Mahler had the idea of expanding this composition into a full-scale five-movement symphony. By the summer of 1893 he had completed only the second movement and

the scherzo, which is basically a symphonic setting of the *Wunderhorn* song 'Des Antonius von Padua Fischpredigt' (St Anthony of Padua's sermon to the fish). He based the fourth movement on another text from *Des Knaben Wunderhorn*, the poem 'Urlicht' (Primeval light). This is related to the subject of the *Totenfeier* and puts the primal longing for mystical union with God into poetic form: 'I come from God and wish to return to him! The Good Lord will give me a little light and illumine my way to eternal bliss.'

Mahler discovered the keyword for the finale only after a long search. He wrote to Dr Arthur Seidl that he had 'scoured the whole of world literature including the Bible in order to find the word of release' and had finally been forced to 'put his feelings and thoughts into words of his own.' Clear inspiration had come to him at Hans von Bülow's memorial service in Hamburg: 'The mood in which I sat and thought of the man who had gone to rest fitted in exactly with the spirit of the work that I was carrying within me. And then, from the organ loft, the choir intoned Klopstock's chorale 'Resurrection!' This struck me like a flash of lightning and everything was absolutely clear and distinct before the eyes of my soul!'

The finale of the Second, completed in June 1894, can be described as a splendid picture in sound of the Last Judgment, the Resurrection and eternal life. In the purely instrumental part of the movement, two sections of which are inscribed 'Der Rufer in der Wüste' (He who calls in the wilderness) and 'Der grosse Appell' (The great roll-call), Mahler invested vast resources in order to provide a monumental apocalyptic vision of Judgment Day, while in the vocal part of the movement the chorale is completed by six stanzas written by Mahler himself, which contain a confession of faith in life after death.

The movement opens with a 'Fanfare of Terror' derived from Beethoven, and it is based on a large number of themes and motifs. Among the most important of these are a *Dies Irae* theme, a Resurrection theme and an Eternity theme. A funeral march develops from the *Dies Irae* theme, while the trumpets are set far back to herald the Apocalypse. A cantilena-like chant on the flute and piccolo – 'to be performed like birdsong' and conceived as the 'distant song of a nightingale' expresses 'an echo of life on earth.'

If the program of the Second Symphony can be described as eschatological, that of the Third, completed in 1896, is concerned with cosmology. Something like the story of the creation confronted Mahler as he formulated the work: the idea of life coming forth from 'soulless, lifeless' matter and of evolution to ever higher forms of being: plants, animals, humanity and angels right up to God Himself conceived as Love. In a letter to his friend Fritz Löhr, Mahler described his Third – then in the course of composition – as 'the most original and fertile' of his works. This is how he explained the program idea: '"Was mir die Liebe erzählt" [What love tells me – the title of the sixth movement] is a summing-up of my feelings towards all beings. This does not go without some deeply painful emotional experiences gradually resolved

Left: A photograph of Mahler in 1892. It is dedicated to the singer Richard Pahlen, 'the outstanding interpreter of his songs, in great friendship, Gustav Mahler.'

Above: Klimt's *Farmhouse with Birch Trees* (1900). Painter and composer shared a symbolic conception of nature, which Mahler exemplified in the program of his Third Symphony.

into a blissful state of confidence: "The Joyous Science."' And he added a little later, 'Above all, Eternal Love is at work in us all, weaving away and merging as rays of light do at the focal point.'

During a search for the sources of this symphony's program the present writer came upon a poem by Siegfried Lipiner, a close friend of the composer, published in 1880 under the title of *Genesis* in the form of a cosmogonic dream, a poetic vision of the origin of the world in a large sleeping but speaking cloud. In very pictorial language Lipiner describes how the constellations, worlds, suns and realms of vegetative, animal and human life were generated from this cloud. A comparison of Mahler's explanations with this poem shows that the latter provided the general literary pattern for the work's program, although the composer endowed the poem with a new meaning: Lipiner spoke of love in fairly general terms, but Mahler interpreted the concept of 'Eternal Love' in a religious and ethical context.

Symbolically, the musical formulation of the Third is even more closely governed by the basic program idea than any of Mahler's other symphonies. The six movements which make up the work broadly represent the six chapters of the highly poetic history of creation as Mahler saw it. The opening movement, a structure of colossal dimensions, is set off by the five other shorter movements which make up the second section.

The arrangement of the opening movement is idiosyncratic. A rather irregularly constructed sonata form follows an unusually long introduction rich in thematic features: 'Pan erwacht' (Pan awakes) and 'Der Sommer marschiert ein – Bacchuszug' (Summer marches in – procession of Bacchus), as the thematic groups are described in the autograph. The introduction

mainly derives its character from motifs that are akin to a funeral march or passages of recitative and *arioso*. According to Mahler's own account they stand for 'stiff, lifeless' nature or, as it might be, the lament of life 'in chains.' A chorale-like passage is inscribed in the autograph score with the words 'Pan schläft' (Pan sleeps) – a hidden allusion to Lipiner's poem which begins with the lines: 'Es war, als wär' nur Eine grosse Wolke das ganze All – die Wolke lag und schlief' (It was as though the entire universe was but the vastness of a cloud – a cloud that lay and slept). The sonata section, clearly articulated into exposition, development and recapitulation, mainly relies upon march-like ideas, but also often harks back to the thematic material of the introduction. The exposition adopts the semblance of martial music approaching from a distance, starting quite softly and gradually rising to *fortissimo*. Mahler's title – 'Summer marches in' – suits this well: Summer is here an allegory of life making a triumphal entry.

Mahler thought of several movements of his Third as humoresques. This applies in particular to the second and third movements, inscribed in the autograph score as: 'Was mir die Blumen auf den Wiesen erzählen' (What the flowers in the meadows tell me) and 'Was mir die Tiere im Walde erzählen' (What the animals in the forest tell me). On the other hand, he saw the fourth and sixth movements as profoundly serious. The fourth movement – 'Was mir die Nacht erzählt' (What night tells me) – is based on the 'Midnight song' – 'O Mensch! Gib Acht' (Oh man! Pay heed!) – from Nietzsche's *Also sprach Zarathustra*. Mahler achieved an incredible degree of tenderness and sensitivity in this orchestral song. The fifth movement – 'Was mir die Morgenglocken erzählen' (What the morning bells tell me) – is a sort of *musica cœlestis*, an orchestral song for solo alto voice, with boys' and women's choir, based on the *Wunderhorn* text 'Es sungen drei Engel einen süssen Gesang' (Three angels sang a sweet song).

The finale of the Third Symphony, a slow movement of great expressive power, rests on two contrasting themes: the first, in the major key, resembles an anthem and the second, in the minor, is full of pain. Both these themes work up to superb climaxes and at the culmination the opening movement is quoted. The epigraph of the finale is provided by two lines from *Des Knaben Wunderhorn*: 'Vater, sieh an die Wunden mein! Kein Wesen lass verloren sein.' (Father, look upon these wounds of mine! Let no creature be lost). On 1 July 1896 Mahler commented on the deeper meaning of this music to his friend Anna Bahr-Mildenburg: 'Now do you understand what this is about? It is meant to signpost the summit and highest level from which the world can be seen. I might just as well call this movement "What God Tells Me." In fact, precisely in the sense that God can actually only be perceived as "love." And so my work represents a musical poem which takes in every step of evolution as part of a gradual ascent. It starts at lifeless nature and ascends to the love of God!'

•The Fourth Symphony •

The Fourth Symphony, completed in 1900, is based on a 'philosophical' program. The seed from which the work developed is a song composed in Hamburg in 1892 and described as a humoresque. Mahler set 'Der Himmel hängt voll Geigen' (Heaven is festooned with violins) from *Des Knaben Wunderhorn* and called it 'Das himmlische Leben' (The heavenly life). This poem in five stanzas, which Goethe described as 'Christian cloud-cuckoo land, but not lacking in wit,' portrays a heavenly land of milk-and-honey and ends with praise for the *musica coelestis* (music of heaven): 'No music on earth can be compared to ours.' Mahler constantly found fresh pleasure in this song. He saw it as a singular mixture of 'roguishness' and 'deepest mysticism' and admired its ability to stand 'everything on its head' and throw causality buzsbf gear.

Bearing in mind Mahler's uncommonly strong interest in metaphysical questions it becomes easier to understand why the naïve conception of the world outlined by this poem gave him so much matter for thought. He made up his mind in 1899 to write a '*Symphonische Humoreske*' about the heavenly life. This was the genesis of a four-movement symphony in which the orchestral song provides the finale and the seed from which the work grew in purely musical terms, since Mahler used the thematic material from it in the first three movements of the symphony.

It is quite clear from the composer's own statements that thoughts of 'life after death' guided him in formulating this symphony. Its subject is therefore eschatological, as in the Second Symphony, and Mahler made this entirely plain when he described his approach: 'It is the joyousness of a world superior to our own but unfamiliar and endowed with an awesomely

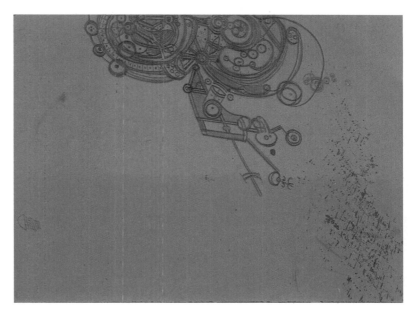

Above: Some of Mahler's doodles on a blotting-paper pad.

disturbing effect in so far as we are concerned. In the last movement the child which already belongs to this world as an infant explains what all this is intended to mean.' A semantic analysis of the score shows that Mahler's poetic vision decisively influenced the musical formulation of the work. Everything in this symphony is conditioned by the program – its overall plan, the arrangement and character of the movements, the thematic outline and the coloring. Thus the ground pattern of the opening movement, which outwardly harks back to classical modes and is rich in nursery melodies – as well as reminiscences of the Viennese classics – springs from a wish to depict an other-worldly gaiety by means of music. Originally Mahler intended to caption this movement 'Die Welt als ewige Jetztzeit' (The world as eternal present). The second movement, a five-part scherzo with two trios, is derived from the idea of the

Left: The Dance of Life (1899-1900), by Edvard Munch. The feverish and morbid character of this Norwegian artist's work has parallels in Mahler's music – not least in the concept of the dance as a symbol for the passage of human life.

Dance of Death. Mahler's own account of this movement is: 'Friend Hein introduces a dance; Death bows the fiddle in a most remarkable way and plays us up to Heaven.' This interpretation is demonstrably correct, as the solo violin part is scored a full tone higher in order to be more shrill in its effect. The curious formulation of the slow third movement needs interpretation in program terms. It is based on two contrasting thematic complexes which are very artfully elaborated in unsymmetrical, mutually stimulating variations. As Mahler saw it, 'festive, blissful repose, earnestly gentle cheerfulness' were the characteristics of this movement, from which painful contrasts were, however, by no means absent, as in 'Reminiscences of life on earth.' The superb E major coda is couched as a vision of paradise: Mahler here allowed the *musica cœlestis* of the finale to ring out in full splendor.

Mahler embarked on an astonishing amount of activity as soon as he had been appointed director of the Vienna Hofoper. He extended the repertory, took many 'novelties' into the program and even dared to stage an unabridged version of Wagner's *Ring*. The audience backed him. The house was sold out night after night.

Right: Alma Schindler, soon after her marriage to Mahler in 1902. She was a good pianist and promising composer, but soon found her talents overlooked by her brilliant husband, a cause for much heart-searching between them.

Above: Woodcut by Carl Moll of the Hohe Warte, Vienna, under snow. It was there, on just such a wintry day, that Mahler and Alma Schindler got engaged. Alma was the stepdaughter of Carl Moll. Her own father, Emil Schindler, was another well-known Viennese painter.

The listeners were often seduced into a reverently festive mood. In 1898 Mahler also took on the direction of the Vienna Philharmonic Orchestra, but this connection lasted barely three years; he was vilified as a 'tyrannical conductor,' was said to demand excessive rehearsal and was accused of having indulged in instrumental 'improvements' in works of symphonic literature – Beethoven, Schubert and Schumann – which had generated much virulent protest.

In November 1901 Mahler made the acquaintance of Alma Maria Schindler, the daughter of a Viennese landscape painter. He immediately fell in love with this young woman – as beautiful as she was intelligent and sensitive, equally talented in literary and musical terms – who had studied composition with Alexander von Zemlinsky. By December he was engaged to her and they were married in March 1902. She bore him two daughters, the elder of whom – Maria Anna – died of diphtheria in 1907. The younger daughter, Anna, later became a well-known sculptress.

Mahler delivered a memorable speech on 20 October 1900 in Munich in connection with a performance of his Second Symphony. This was the occasion on which he took a definite stand against program music and especially against the 'program books' so widespread at that time. Quite logically, he withdrew the programs relevant to his first three symphonies and refused from then on to give any official interpretation of his works.

Three main reasons induced him to take this step. Mahler had, sadly, discovered for himself that the programmatic superscriptions on individual movements led to crude misapprehensions amongst the public at large. A further motive was his fear that his music might be confused with that of the contemporary trend of program work as represented by Richard Strauss. Mahler clearly wished to counteract any possible identification of his symphonic output with the – primarily literary – program music of Strauss, which was also in many ways quite differently formulated. Considerations of musical politics in Vienna also played a part in his decision. When Mahler began to work in the Hofoper in 1897 he was very well aware that the musical life of the capital was dominated by the party of Brahms rather than that of Wagner. Eduard Hanslick, the dreaded 'musical Pope' of Vienna, and the critics surrounding him were bitterly hostile to program music. Mahler took account of this and decided to keep quiet about his programs in future.

• The middle symphonies •

The Fifth, completed in 1902, is the first in a group of three middle symphonies which have a great deal in common. They are all purely instrumental; as opposed to the three *Wunderhorn* symphonies (Second, Third and Fourth), they do without any sung texts, just as they forego any symphonic treatment of existing song material. Although they were to be performed without any program indications, in accordance with Mahler's wishes, all these three symphonies are confessional in character and are based on implicit 'inner' programs which Mahler himself hinted at in conversations.

In the Fifth Symphony, the sequence of movements is unusual. The work opens with a somber funeral march in the minor key and ends with a cheerfully animated rondo finale in D major marked, characteristically, *allegro giocoso*! Does this very stark contrast in itself not point to a new, 'poetic' interpretation of the old motto *per aspera ad astra*? Does it not allow the philosophical concept of the transcendent, the conquest of pain, to shine through? Is not this transcendental idea also the main thought on which Mahler's First and Second Symphonies are based?

The second movement of the Fifth is certainly conceived as a vision of Hell. Mahler compared the scherzo to a 'whirling dance' and 'the tail of a comet.' 'Romantic and mystical considerations,' he added, were not involved – 'only the expression of unparalleled power.' On the other hand, Mahler saw the adagietto as his 'declaration of love' to Alma.

The Sixth, the so-called 'Tragic' Symphony, was composed during the summer months of 1903 and 1904 at Maiernigg on the Wörthersee. It is the only one of Mahler's symphonies which ends neither 'triumphantly' nor 'radiantly,' but in a distinctly somber way. The general impression produced on a listener by the work as a whole is exemplified by the coda of the finale; the passage inscribed *'schwer'* (heavy) – scored for trombones and bass tuba with a drum roll – has a marked requiem-like character. It is also significant that Mahler wrote a hammer into this movement, which is heard (in the first version) on three occasions.

Alma Mahler confirmed in her reminiscences that the Sixth was based on an autobiographical conception. The 'great, sweeping' theme of the opening movement (she was referring to the secondary theme), for instance, was intended as a portrait of Alma. The scherzo was supposed to portray 'the arhythmic play of the two small children as they run toddling through the sand.' In the finale Mahler described 'himself and his downfall or, as he later put it, that of his hero.' Mahler's literal explanation was of 'The hero who suffers three blows from fate, the third of which fells him like a tree.'

'The Sixth,' according to Alma, 'was his most personal work and a prophetic one, moreover. In the *Kindertotenlieder* [Songs of the dead children], just as in the Sixth, he set his life to music by anticipation. He too was to receive three blows from fate and the third did fell him. Yet he had then been cheerful, aware of the greatness of his work, and his branches burgeoned and blossomed.'

It is impossible to understand the deeper meaning of these statements correctly without some knowledge of Mahler's spiritual world. According to Richard Specht, Mahler was 'a complete determinist'; he was convinced that during periods of inspiration 'the creative artist was lifted onto a higher, anticipatory level of his existence, and already foreshadowed in his output the experience that everyday life would inevitably bring.' It is only in the context of this belief that it is possible to make sense of Alma's statement that Mahler was completely shattered and 'lost control of himself' after the dress rehearsal for the first performance of the Sixth in Essen in 1906. None of his works, according to Alma, had touched him so closely.

Above: Charcoal drawing by Emil Orlik of Mahler wielding the baton in 1902.

Left: The building of the giant Ferris wheel in the Prater, Vienna, in 1897 – the year Mahler became musical director of the Vienna Hofoper.

Below: Three silhouette studies by Otto Böhler of Mahler in the opera house orchestra pit.

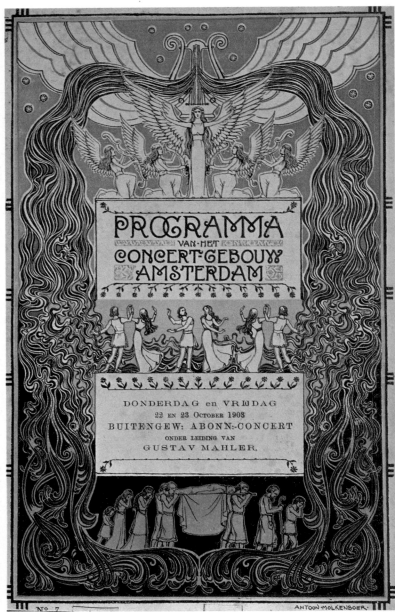

It seems as though Mahler foresaw the tragic events that were to strike his family in 1907.

The Seventh Symphony also came into existence in Maiernigg during the summer months of 1904 and 1905. It is a work in five movements, which include two wildly Romantic 'night-music' movements, the march-like first of which contains a 'bird concert,' while the second – an *andante amoroso* – has the character of a serenade. There is the sharpest contrast imaginable between the outer movements of the Seventh. The symphony opens with a B minor introduction in the form of a funeral march and ends in a magnificently radiant rondo finale in C major! There can be no doubt that the polarity between night and day, nature and spirit provides the basic idea for this work.

In parallel with these three middle symphonies Mahler set ten songs by Friedrich Rückert, a poet to whom he was particularly drawn. He chose five from the more than four hundred *Kindertotenlieder* which Rückert had written upon the death of his two children, set them

Above: Program cover, in art nouveau style, for a concert conducted by Mahler at the Concertgebouw in Amsterdam in 1903. He directed some of the best performances of his own music here, thanks to the support of the chief conductor, Willem Mengelberg.

Left: Portrait by Franz Matsch of Anna Bahr-Mildenburg as Isolde in Mahler's 1903 Vienna Opera production of Wagner's *Tristan und Isolde.* The costume was designed by Alfred Roller, the Secessionist artist whom Mahler secured as director of set and costume design at the Hofoper.

between 1901 and 1904 and made them into a cycle. These settings differ stylistically from the *Wunderhorn* songs in many respects, and their partly polyphonic structure points ahead to the style of *Das Lied von der Erde*. The *Kindertoten-lieder* are probably unsurpassed as an expression of sorrow, although it should be stressed that Rückert's mourning – as well as Mahler's – is deeply embedded in a firm religious conviction. Of the five further Rückert songs set by Mahler the most important are probably 'Ich bin der Welt abhanden gekommen' (I have been lost to the world) and 'Um Mitternacht' (At midnight). The emotional and spiritual implications of the first are central to Mahler's outlook – remoteness and alienation from the world. Mahler himself commented on the restrained treatment of this song that here was sensation rising to the lips, but not going beyond them. 'Um Mitternacht' has a special position in this group in that it dispenses with strings and is orchestrated solely for wind and harp. The basically somber mood of the song eventually lifts and the expression of religious confidence which the poem ultimately attains finds its musical equivalent in a turn towards an ecstatic anthem. Finally 'Liebst du um Schönheit' (Lovest thou for beauty) was composed by Mahler for Alma in 1902.

• Mahler's last works •

The Eighth Symphony – the 'Symphony of a Thousand' – is also dedicated to Alma. It is a gigantic work for large orchestra, eight vocal soloists, a boys' choir and two mixed choirs. Mahler himself regarded it as his *magnum opus*. 'I have just completed my Eighth,' he wrote to the Dutch conductor Willem Mengelberg, whom he so admired. 'It is the greatest I have ever produced. And it is so original in content and form that one cannot write anything about it. Just imagine that the universe begins to sound and resound. There are no longer human voices but planets and suns which are circling.' And later he said: 'All my earlier symphonies are merely preludes to this. The other works still contain the whole subjectively tragic approach – this one is a great dispenser of joy.' The guideline of the Eighth is the idea of 'everlasting love,' by which he meant *agape* or *caritas*. The first part of the work is based on the medieval Latin hymn for Pentecost, 'Veni creator spiritus.' The second is taken from the final scene of Goethe's *Faust*, Part II. Mahler succeeded in welding these apparently unrelated texts by musical means, and his settings reveal the most intimate spiritual relationships between the two parts.

The year 1907 proved fateful for Mahler. His elder daughter, Maria Anna, died of diphtheria on 5 July. Shortly afterwards he was diagnosed as suffering from a heart ailment. These events sapped his strength just when he was coming under pressure from powerful intrigues. He retired from directing the Hofoper, then left for New York where he first acted as visiting conductor at the Metropolitan Opera and later as director of the newly founded Philharmonic Society. Here he was able to perform Bruckner's symphonies and some of his own works. During the summers he traveled regularly to Austria and spent his holidays composing as he had been used to do. This is how the *Lied von der Erde*, the Ninth Symphony and the unfinished Tenth came into existence.

Mahler wrote to Bruno Walter in the autumn of 1908 that the *Lied von der Erde* was the

Left: Autograph sketch for part of the fifth song ('Der Trunkene im Frühling') from *Das Lied von der Erde*, Mahler's last orchestral song-cycle, based on German translations of old Chinese poems.

'most personal thing' that he had yet done. That this statement can also be applied to the Ninth and to the Tenth Symphonies (which he was composing when he died) becomes clear when it is realized that both these works have close affinities with the *Lied von der Erde* and that all three were written at a time of severe personal crisis and existential anxiety.

The letters which Mahler wrote between 1908 and 1910 to Bruno Walter show that he frequently suffered from depression and a state of anxiety. Metaphysical problems were more than ever uppermost in his mind. It is therefore hardly surprising that thoughts of death and leave-taking should have provided the spiritual and emotional medium from which these last works grew. Mahler's annotations in the draft score of the Ninth and in sketches for the Tenth show

tion as a whole; the bringing together of the most diverse musical forms; a taste for sharp contrasts in the coupling of simplicity and demonic impulse, of archaic references and overwhelming expressiveness. The order of the movements is also unusual, though not unique: two slow movements frame two animated ones, an arrangement similar to that of Tchaikovsky's 'Pathétique' (1893), to which Mahler's Ninth owes a great deal.

The first movement of the Ninth, an *andante comodo* in D major (this key notation refers only to the main theme) is already marked by sharp contrasts. Broadly speaking, the course of this movement, constructed in a free sonata form, can be described as a repeated alternation between song-like passages and others which are 'impassioned' or filled with the highest tension.

Below: Mahler rehearsing his Eighth Symphony ('Symphony of a Thousand') in the Ausstellungshalle, Munich, where the first performance took place in September 1910.

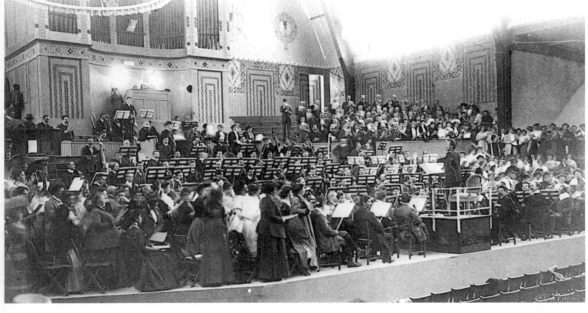

Below: Cover of the 1924 facsimile edition of the unfinished Tenth Symphony. In 1960 the English scholar Deryck Cooke discovered more of Mahler's sketches for the work and produced a completed version.

Above: Bruno Walter, who conducted the first performances of *Das Lied von der Erde* (Munich, 1911) and the Ninth (Vienna, 1912) after Mahler's death.

that retrospect, nostalgia, and leave-taking provide the central themes not only for *Das Lied von der Erde* but also for the last symphonies. Thus the following marginal notes appear on the draft score of the opening movement of the Ninth: 'O youth! You have vanished! O love! You have been wafted away' and 'Farewell! Farewell!' Similarly, a page from a sketch for the Tenth: 'Farewell, my touch upon the strings.'

Mahler had sketched out the Ninth Symphony during the summer of 1909. He described it in a letter to Bruno Walter as 'a very fortunate increase to my small family.' At the same time he commented on it: 'Something is said in it which I have had on the tip of my tongue for quite a time – perhaps (taken as a whole) to be set by the side of the Fourth.' He took the 'completely illegible' score to New York in order to polish the composition and finish the instrumentation. On 1 April 1910 he informed Bruno Walter from New York that the 'clean score' of the work was now ready.

Mahler's Ninth Symphony is a work of unmistakable originality. Several features profoundly characteristic of the composer are strongly represented in it: the fantastic nature of the concep-

The contrasts embedded in the exposition reach a dramatic flashpoint in the somewhat over-extended development. At several places in this movement Mahler added indications above the score which should be seen not merely as 'performing instructions' but often also as conveying a program indication. Thus at the climax of the movement the trombones and the tuba intone the syncopated main rhythm of the andante in triple *forte* and 'with the utmost power.' Soon after this occurs a passage marked 'like a ponderous cortège,' in which individual 'sighing' figures on the wind instruments, complemented by calls on the muted trumpets, intervene in the *ostinato* rhythms of the drums and basses. The place marked *misterioso* deserves very special notice in the recapitulation: it is a passage instrumented as chamber music in a linear setting, outstandingly beautiful and modern.

The second movement takes the place of a scherzo and is conceived as a fantasy about a dance scene. Mahler brought together the most varied types of dances here, as he had done in the second movement of the Fourth Symphony. The 'main movement' is conceived as an 'easy *Ländler*.' Two waltz figures appear in the first trio, while the second trio turns out to be a 'slow *Ländler*'! (Each part of the movement has its own tempo.) The impetus of the movement is provided by the multiplicity of contrasting features. The 'main movement' ('a little gawkish and very robust') is reminiscent of peasant dances; the violins are instructed to play 'clumsily and like fiddles' at this point. One of the two types of waltzes (in E major and D major) is more clearly marked by its melody, the other (in E flat major) by its rhythm. The latter is distinguished above all by the penetrating accompaniment of the grace-note quarter note. The melody of the 'slow *Ländler*,' on the other hand, has a singable, rocking and swinging quality. It is hard to imagine a greater contrast than that between the rather 'coarsely' instrumented E flat major waltz and the romantically dreamy 'slow *Ländler*.' In this partly down-to-earth and partly demonic movement the contrapuntal interweaving of melodies and motifs is also typical of Mahler.

The third movement, an A minor burlesque, is also made up of violently contrasting elements. In formal terms the movement provides a skillful rondo-like structure on the following pattern: main theme – fugato I – secondary theme – main theme – fugato II – secondary theme – fugato III – episode in D major – compressed recapitulation of the main theme – coda. The 'very defiant' main theme is formulated as a march and is reminiscent of the expressionist music of Arnold Schoenberg's atonal period. The melody of the secondary theme, which is built up in stanzas, sounds like a popular song from the beginning of the century. The fugati, which are – in part – shrilly instrumented, anticipate the linear style of the 1920s in the strictness of their polyphonic treatment. The most interesting element of all, however, is the inset D major episode. It opens on a cymbal stroke and a violin and flute tremolo on a triple leger note of A, and acts like a foreign element in the movement as a whole. Its dynamic, timbre and tone confer on it an ethereal, dreamlike and unreal character.

The finale of the Ninth Symphony, a grandiose D flat major adagio, is also composed on the idea of contrast. The movement is based on two thematic groups which take over from each other after the manner of Bruckner. The first of these displays the double-beat motif of the burlesque as a structural element and represents a highly expressive, richly harmonized and mellow theme for the strings. The second thematic complex, a passage in the minor key instrumented as chamber music and performed *piano* throughout, is in some places well-nigh schematic in its effect. The adagio finishes with a coda which fades out *morendo* like *Das Lied von der Erde*.

Mahler conducted his 'Symphony of a Thousand' in Munich on 12 September 1910, a first performance which proved to be a triumphant

success. He returned to the United States in November that year but was no longer up to the demands of his work in America. Illness forced him to break off his concerts in New York in February 1911. He returned to Vienna via Paris and died there on 18 May 1911, shortly after midnight. *Das Lied von der Erde* and the Ninth Symphony were first performed by Bruno Walter after his death.

During his lifetime Mahler had been the target of controversy and obloquy as a composer. He was often labeled as an eclectic or a blind follower of Bruckner, yet he greatly influenced Arnold Schoenberg, Alban Berg, Anton Webern, Sergei Prokofiev and Dmitri Shostakovich. Mahler rounded off the nineteenth-century symphonic tradition and at the same time paved the way for the 'New Music.' However, his immense artistic and historical importance was only recognized after the Second World War. Many contemporary composers owe a great deal to him, while the large number of recordings of his works has contributed greatly to making him one of the most popular symphonic composers.

Top: Sigmund Freud, the Viennese psychiatrist and founder of psycho-analysis. In 1910 Mahler consulted him about personal problems and doubts concerning both his work and his marriage. The meeting took place, not in Vienna, but during a four-hour walk the two men took through the Dutch town of Leyden (*above*).

RICHARD STRAUSS

HEINZ BECKER

Richard Strauss was born on 11 June 1864 in Munich, the son of a court musician, into a conservative and backward world. His father, Franz Strauss, a horn player in the Munich Court Orchestra, introduced him to music early in life, and the child grew up in a musical environment more or less in play, just like his beloved model, Mozart. Strauss was no mere child prodigy and, on the contrary, displayed in later life a robust, blunt, highly realistic character which he probably inherited from his mother, Josephine Pschorr, a daughter of a famous family of brewers. This combination of an artistic nature with a business-like, down-to-earth approach was to provide the composer with his start when he later set out to win worldwide acclaim.

Strauss was by no means self-taught, even though he never attended a school of music. He had his first piano lesson at the age of four and tried his hand at composition when he was six, sometimes even writing music in his school exercise books. The first operas he saw were Weber's *Freischütz* and Mozart's *Magic Flute*. Mozart's last opera brought the proximity of Vienna home to the young musician when he was still a child. It is not by chance that *Der Rosenkavalier* – Strauss's most successful opera – is saturated throughout with the spirit of Mozart's own period and internally linked by the waltz, Vienna's symbol in sound. Broad Bavarian robustness and Viennese charm contrast but can be combined. When one thinks of Baron Ochs von Lerchenau in *Der Rosenkavalier*, one might regard him as the portrait of a four-square Bavarian in Vienna, which is by no means irrelevant, in view of the fact that the composer was more given to self-portraiture than most.

Strauss proved a good and studious schoolboy whose incidental activity – composing music – in no way cramped the remainder of his education. His striking attempts at composition induced his parents to arrange tuition in musical theory and instrumentation for him. He mastered this technical framework with astonishing ease, while his talent now came to the fore. As a twelve-year-old he composed his Festival March in E flat for large orchestra, which he dedicated to his 'dear uncle Georg Pschorr.' This work was published by Joseph Aibl and proudly opens the roll of Strauss's works as op.1. In 1881 Hermann Levi publicly performed his four-movement Symphony in D minor. Strauss's way ahead seemed clearly marked. When Sophocles' *Elektra* was read at his school, he composed a chorus for it which was performed by the pupils. Other works followed, including a string quartet, some piano pieces, a suite for wind instruments and a piano sonata. In 1882 Strauss matriculated with good marks and took up a university course in philosophy, history of art and aesthetics, but only for a short time. In that year he also first visited Bayreuth with his father.

As a musician Strauss had matured at a very early stage. He was later to admit about his performance at the piano that he had never achieved impeccable technique, that 'gymnastic practice' had given him little or no pleasure and that he preferred to sight-read. He had usually accompanied songs without closely following the score and indulged instead in fanciful improvisations. This admission reveals a real musician, driven to compose because he needs to transform and vary the subject-matter.

Franz Strauss had brought up his son not only to love the classics, but also to harbor a relentless distaste for Wagner's work. However, young Richard's own study of Wagner's scores actually fired him with enthusiasm and deeply influenced his musical perception. The nineteen-year-old's first meeting with Hans von Bülow, at that time senior conductor of the famous Court Orchestra at Meiningen, was later described by Strauss as 'the decisive moment' in his artistic life. Bülow not only took the op.7 Serenade into his repertoire and introduced Strauss to Wagner's inner circle, but he also sensed, with prophetic insight, the extraordinary quality of this young musician and secured the position of assistant conductor at Meiningen for him as soon as he reached the age of twenty-one. In so far as Strauss was concerned this appointment under Bülow represented at once a great honor and something of a risk, since he could not exactly boast of any great experience as a conductor. Only determination and steely self-discipline enabled him to weather early difficulties.

It was at Meiningen, at a concert, that Strauss first met Brahms, treated as an enemy by Wagner even though Brahms never reciprocated this hostility. He was well disposed towards young Strauss, whose enthusiasm for Wagner he indulgently dismissed, and drew his attention to Schubert's dances when he discovered that the young musician enjoyed constructing complicated sequences of musical ideas. Strauss later said that it was from Brahms that he had learned not to despise a 'popular melody.'

When Hans von Bülow resigned his position in Meiningen on 1 November 1885, Strauss remained in charge as the sole conductor of the orchestra and was therefore able to acquire experience without constraints. He could in fact have secured the position of chief conductor, but he received an offer from Munich to work as third conductor of the Court Opera there. And opera called him! On 31 March 1886 Strauss gave up his post at Meiningen, thus ending the period of his apprenticeship. The experience he had gathered there in his typically determined way and the acquaintances he had made were to prove most valuable. Among the latter Strauss himself singled out his friendship with Alexander Ritter, the leader of the orchestra, thirty years his senior and dedicated heart and soul to Wagner's ideology and outlook.

Even though Strauss did not realize it, these encounters with Brahms and Ritter brought him to a crossroads: Brahms, conservative and cautious, bent on carrying on the classical heritage, and Ritter, progressive and revolutionary. It was Ritter who won him over, even though Strauss had been brought up in the classical tradition, and he now became Wagner's ardent disciple – irrevocably dedicated to the 'New German School,' in other words to autobiographical expressionism in music. The choice Strauss had to make in Meiningen – between the paths represented by the views of Brahms and of Ritter – was one that none of his contemporaries could escape. Strauss followed his temperament and quite naturally took the path of expressionism. Opera now clearly lay ahead, but had he finally made it his aim? Here we find

yet another aspect of his art which he could never suppress, which distinguished him from Wagner and which set him on a course very much of his own – his roots in folk art. This was what Brahms had revealed to him.

•The road to Munich •

Strauss's beginnings were in pure music. There are fewer than fifteen opus numbers before his first symphonic poem *Aus Italien* (From Italy), first performed on 2 March 1887, almost all of them instrumental compositions: for solo piano; chamber music with piano; orchestra; wind instruments; and string quartet. The only exceptions were *Acht Lieder* (Eight Songs), op.10, settings of texts by Hermann Gilm; the choral work

Left: Strauss's Munich birthplace, 2 Altheimer Eck, fronting the Pschorr family brewery.

Below, left and right: Two pictures of six-year-old Richard, taking part in a children's fancy dress orchestra at carnival time. In the left-hand photograph he is seated, left; and in the other picture he stands at right in the back row.

Wandrers Sturmlied (Wanderer's Storm Song), op.14; and the set of songs for voice and piano, op.15. Pure music still dominated Strauss's imagination. *Burleske*, for instance, a scherzo for piano and orchestra, a youthfully rapturous, whirling concert piece, which foreshadows *Till Eulenspiegel* without rising to anything like its emotional level, already demonstrates his mastery in writing for the orchestra. Strauss composed the work in Meiningen for Bülow, who indignantly turned it down as being 'unfit for the piano, and too ambitious.' Eugen d'Albert gave it its first performance in 1890 at a festival at Eisenach. This work is now seldom performed, but it provides clear pointers to Strauss's future development. Towards the end of the work, and entirely without warning, Strauss introduces a waltz – which is hard to account for in formal terms but in which the composer's future waltz technique is already exemplified in its fully perfected form. This passage bears Strauss's unmistakable signature: an apparently familiar melodic development leads to an elegant – even esoteric – turn of expression, thereby opening up an entirely different universe, the existence of which had been completely unsuspected only a few measures earlier. Anyone who had harbored doubts about the talent of the young musician must have found a few measures sufficient to convince him of the extraordinarily powerful inspiration at his command. Strauss's temperament is clearly expressed in the rapid switching from high-spirited to introspective, even melancholy, passages. Anyone who has appreciated the sparklingly humorous mood of the *Burleske* will not have failed to notice how every now and then, almost without warning, a shadow passes over the glittering and luminous orchestra, often just for an instant, but long enough to sense the fears behind the clown's make-up, a creature's lonely misery disguised as tomfoolery.

Strauss's output is marked from its very start by an addiction to disguise, the fun of dressing-up. This is also expressed in his bent for concealed allusions and cryptic quotations. He developed the knack of bending his musical material by some little trick without apparent effort so that its course is diverted into a wholly different range of expression through some harmonic, rhythmic or dynamic variation. Beethoven was in the habit of working over his themes; Strauss put his into fancy dress.

The young conductor used the time left before taking over his new post in Munich on 1 August 1886 for a journey to Italy, paid for by his father. He traveled blissfully about this country which had always fascinated him: to Verona, Bologna, Rome, Naples, Florence. And it was precisely here, in Italy, at the very fountainhead of music, that Strauss demonstrated his marked capacity for highly personal views when he summed up an evening at Verdi's *Aida* with the dismissive remark: 'Awful! Red Indian music!' And he later wrote in a letter: 'I'm sure I shall never be converted to Italian music – it's simply trash.'

The journey to Italy bore musical fruit, as Strauss tersely put it, 'in an Italian suite,' meaning thereby the Symphonic Fantasia *Aus Italien*. Strauss used the classical four-movement form but gave each movement a title: 'In the Campagna,' 'Among the Ruins of Rome,' 'On the Shore of Sorrento' and 'Neapolitan Street Life.' The future composer of program music was making his position clear. Strauss selected his program references on the strength of musical considerations and therefore subordinated external factors to his own inwardly predetermined musical conception. The first performance of this Fantasia on 2 March 1887 had a very mixed reception and caused 'a great uproar.' This left Strauss unmoved; he had been noticed, and that was all he wanted, because it counted for more than an amiable lack of interest. As he himself put it: 'Nobody has yet become a great artist without being considered insane by his fellow beings.' He dedicated the work to Hans von Bülow, who accepted this tribute, 'adorned by local opposition,' with, so he said, 'enthusiasm.'

His Munich period also produced a few songs, the famous 'Serenade' among them, and the Violin Sonata, op.18, which marks the start of his maturity as a composer of chamber music.

• The symphonic decade •

Strauss's 'symphonic decade' began in 1889. During the ten years that followed, he wrote virtually his entire symphonic output – the *Symphonia domestica*, as a family portrait in sound, lies outside this closed cycle, while the *Alpensinfonie* ('Alpine' Symphony) of 1915 can be regarded as something of a throwback. Strauss described five of his works as symphonic poems: *Don Juan*, *Macbeth*, *Tod und Verklärung* (Death and Transfiguration), *Also sprach Zarathustra* (Thus spake Zarathustra) and *Ein Heldenleben* (A Hero's Life). The titles of three others indicate their formal structure: the Symphonic Fantasia – *Aus Italien*; a Rondeau – *Till Eulenspiegel*; and Fantastic Variations – *Don Quixote*. It is only the last two works that are actually called symphonies – *Symphonia domestica* and *Alpensinfonie*.

Macbeth and *Don Juan* were completed in Munich. *Macbeth* had to be reworked (in 1889-90) and proved a failure, but Strauss scored a great success with *Don Juan*. The work's motto – 'Up and away for conquests ever new while youth's fiery fancies still are on the wing' – can also be applied to Strauss himself. What he had experienced and what he had observed are inextricably entwined in his output.

In classical composition a work usually began with a statement of the main theme, but this approach always posed a problem for Strauss. He did in fact open *Don Juan* with the classically formulated youthful theme pertaining to his hero. But he drove this theme forward with such vigor, thrusting ahead again and again, ascending so steeply through the whole scale of sound that one's breath is taken away. It was an unprecedented opening at that time, and a sweepingly successful breakthrough for Strauss.

Above: Pair of photographs of Strauss in 1889, tall and slim, conducting at the old Court Theater in Weimar, where Liszt had presided for so long. It was there, in the same year, that Strauss conducted the first performance of his *Don Juan*. Like many conductors, Strauss's rostrum manner changed over the years from flamboyant to very quiet and restrained.

Strauss always made the opening a question of access to the heart of the matter. How else could one conceive of music which involves turbulence, the tempestuously unbridled and the whole dimension of the unpredictable? For Strauss, Don Juan was a hero of antiquity, immeasurable, but as beautiful as Apollo. The composer thereby achieved that enigmatic character which is a feature of his personal style. The affinity with Wagner is unmistakable. The chromatic touches of *Tannhäuser* on the violins flit through the score, and in the triumphal conclusion the variations on the hero's theme move ever closer to the *Waberlohe* motive; but only closer, and no further. The work belongs to Strauss.

The work's program is borrowed from a poem by Lenau, but Strauss did not follow closely either its sequence or its formal development. He merely picked on a few stanzas which gave him the key words he needed: desire – fulfillment – attempt – cooling. Strauss would surely have been able to work out, without resorting to Lenau's verse, the development of the hero's theme, which recurs as a rondo and is later replaced by a second theme – a theme on the horn often described as Don Juan's pride – interspersed with softer, more elegiac secondary themes. But he might well not have achieved the pictorial impact of these themes. A carefully prepared, broadly textured discord opens the way for the B major theme on the violin. It appears like a beam of light from the wavering darkness of the background: the noble lady has entered. With questioning phrases – the wordless language of looks – the theme evokes the expectant participants. The horn, Don Juan's personal instrument – the symbol of the hunter in every sense of the word – opens the dialogue. The violins drop their reticence, take up the theme and blush, a dialogue which comes to a climax in quivering triplets, an expression of orgiastic ecstasy. The horn is symbolically contrasted with different instruments representing other loves: the violin, the viola, the cello (G minor), with the oboe (G major) representing chastity. Although all these themes are related to the Don Juan opening theme in formal terms, it is only the oboe theme which secures a mirror-image response. It forestalls the tempestuously

W. HÖFFERT · HOF-PHOTOGRAPH

proud horn by its metrically rhythmic development, and the horn then comes to the fore again in a jubilant recall of an experience which has turned into sound. In fact, the entire dialogue is full of retrospective glances, and when at the end the dissonant trumpet punches through the *piano* chord it seems as though the weary hero gladly, and with lowered guard, surrenders to the point of the sword, 'all passion spent.'

Strauss himself conducted the first performance of *Don Juan* on 11 November 1889 at Weimar. It was a brilliant success for the young master, bringing him not only glory but influence, more important to him than mere fame. In Vienna, Hugo Wolf wrote sarcastically, though he had not heard the work: 'The instrumentation, so I am led to believe, must surpass in refinement anything previously committed in that sphere. . . .' Strauss owed to Hans von Bronsart, a friend of Bülow, an opportunity to extend his activities even further as assistant conductor in Weimar from 1 October 1888. Weimar was a Wagnerian stronghold and lines of communication from it led directly to Bayreuth.

As soon as he had completed the score of *Don Juan*, Strauss, perhaps inspired by Liszt's *Tasso*, set about writing his *Tod und Verklärung*, op.24, a symphonic poem first performed at Eisenach on 21 June 1890. The title was the composer's own invention and so was the underlying idea: the tormented decay and physical dissolution of the hero who, at the very moment of death, sees the most beautiful moments of his life file past him once again, portrayed in sound. With this work Strauss introduced music into the realm of psychology by providing a precise description of a clinically terminal case. In Vienna Hanslick wrote after he had heard the

Strauss's wife, Pauline de Ahna, in two operatic roles, in the year of their marriage: (*right*) as Elizabeth in *Tannhaüser*, which Strauss conducted at Bayreuth; (*bottom*) in a scene from his own early opera *Guntram*, produced at Weimar. It was during rehearsals for this that they became engaged, after stormy incidents in which she had thrown the score at him, and the orchestra had threatened to walk out.

Below: Title-page to the *Vier Lieder*, op.27, which Strauss dedicated to Pauline as a wedding present in 1894. The group includes 'Morgen' (Morning), one of his best-known songs.

work that there was only one final step to be taken as far as this music was concerned: to portray a dimly lit sickroom on the stage.

Hanslick very perceptively recognized the symphonic composer's special talent for musical drama. Strauss had indeed been wrestling with the stage for a long time, and he had started to compose an opera while still in Munich, which he took with him to Weimar. He was also followed there by a pupil from Munich – Pauline de Ahna. Strauss supervised her formation as a singer and resolutely promoted her career. He not only gave her the lead in *Guntram*, his first opera, but made her his lifelong companion. *Guntram* was wholly Wagnerian. It achieved no more than critical approval at its first night on 10 May 1894. Pauline de Ahna's performance was given an ovation, but the work itself was soon forgotten. On the other hand, Strauss the symphonist became a universal topic of conversation. He instinctively understood that his next move must be to conquer the stage by way of the orchestra, since Wagner had made opera into an orchestral genre.

On 10 September 1894, while still in Weimar, Strauss led Pauline de Ahna to the altar and dedicated the four op.27 songs to her as a wedding present, including 'Heimliche Aufforderung' (Secret invitation), which was later to become so famous. Three weeks afterwards, on 1 October 1894, he returned to Munich to resume his duties at the Court Opera.

The following years, until 1898, were crammed with unremitting concert work and travel – to Hungary, Moscow (in 1896), Amsterdam, Madrid, Brussels and London. Strauss undertook an astounding amount of work. He accepted the direction of the Akademiekonzerte in Munich and, in addition, conducted the Berlin Philharmonic Orchestra for two years starting in the 1894-5 winter season. He also conducted for the first time at Bayreuth in 1894 with *Tannhäuser* on the program and Pauline de Ahna-Strauss singing the part of Elizabeth.

• The symphonic poem developed •

Strauss was led to the subject of Till Eulenspiegel by Cyrill Kister's unsuccessful opera *Eulenspiegel*. Till exemplifies the enterprising and cunning trickster settling accounts with the backward and blinkered ways of the philistine. But the work can also be understood as the natural reaction of an artist who, despite the creative dedication that *Tod und Verklärung* demanded of him, has not lost his delight in comedy. *Till Eulenspiegels lustige Streiche* (Till Eulenspiegel's Merry Pranks), op.28, is based on two main themes in rondo form. These sweep through the whole piece in a great variety of moods and guises right up to the final catastrophe of Till's hanging. In *Till* Strauss somewhat toned down one of his basic principles of composition, which he had used in *Don Juan* and in *Tod und Verklärung* to great psychological effect: that of not stating themes, but rather of suggesting and developing them. Here, when the main theme is brought in towards the

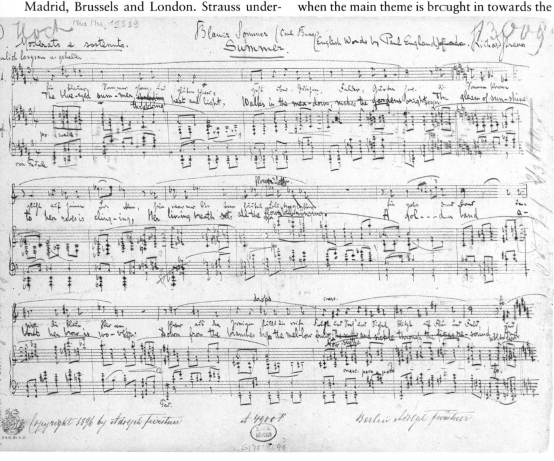

Left: Autograph of the song 'Blauer Sommer' (Blue summer) – with an English translation of the words written in – belonging to another group of *Vier Lieder*, op.31, published in 1896.

end of the work, it appears in the form of a hymn incorporating the many transformations of the Till motive introduced on the horn at the start of the work, but which only now achieves its full form, sixteen measures long.

When Strauss removed the motley having clowned his way through *Till* and wrapped Nietzsche's philosopher's cloak around him, he was less concerned with the solution of existential problems than with a determination to explore as yet undisclosed reaches of sound. The detailed, painstaking reflection of the action in *Till* with its proliferation of points of reference was replaced in his *Zarathustra* by a broad structure consisting of eight major sections identified by epigraphs in the score: 'Of the Afterworldsmen'; 'Of the Great Longing'; 'Of Joys and Passions'; 'The Funeral Song'; 'Of Science'; 'The Convalescent'; 'The Dance Song'; 'The Sleepwalker's Song.' These identifications do not describe a clear cut program. On the contrary, Strauss offers reflections in sound on Nietzsche's *Zarathustra*, not as a mere sequence but as a coherently formulated entity. The hymn 'Most Free of all the Free' has been reset to a quite unphilosophical-sounding piece of mood music. For 'Science,' Strauss chose a theme which includes all twelve chromatic semitones and therefore symbolizes – with a touch of irony – the all-embracing claims of academics.

He set out his highly personal expression of what the dance is about in the inebriated shout of joy of 'The Dance Song.' As to the opening of the work, the composer conceived what probably still is the vastest opening ever invented in musical terms, describing the rising of the sun's radiant disk. One might note, however, that a touch of motley remains, as the original subtitle reveals: 'Symphonic optimism in *fin-de-siècle* form dedicated to the twentieth century.'

By comparison with earlier symphonies, it also becomes increasingly obvious that the formal framework is extended and that the anecdotal tone is gradually replaced by more deeply searching lines of thought. In *Zarathustra* Strauss gave up extensive illustrative detail in favor of a broader formal picture, but the situation was reversed in his *Don Quixote*, first performed on 8 March 1898 in Cologne. The subtitle of the work, 'Fantastic Variations on a Subject of Chivalric Nature,' obscures the fact that a twin subject is involved. As in *Don Juan*, two basic themes underlie the conception, but here it is the contrast between the character of the knight and that of his servant Sancho Panza. Their two themes are elaborated in strikingly dramatic contrast. They are not only differentiated in character but contrasted in tonal coloring: Strauss gave the knight's quirky melody to the solo cello, and the cheeky theme of the relaxed

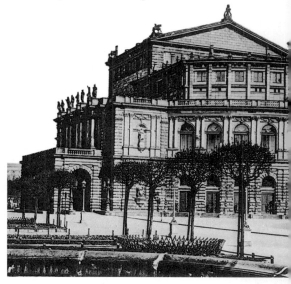

Above: The Hoftheater, Munich, where Strauss worked as a conductor in 1886-8 and again in 1894-7. His father, Franz Joseph, had for many years played principal horn in the Court Orchestra.

Right: Strauss with the Berlin Philharmonic Orchestra in the early years of this century. He was their principal conductor for a short time, from 1894.

Sancho Panza first to the bass clarinet and tenor tuba and later to the viola. In this way the two principal actors in the drama are characterized not only by their *leitmotifs* but also by changes in tone color. Strauss transcended the historical and social context of the story by translating its content into timeless human terms, and he achieved perfect control of the orchestra, using every color shading that came to hand.

In all his symphonic works, not excluding the operas, there is a marked tendency to link the *concertante* element with the symphonic approach and to bring single instruments from the orchestra to the fore in solo roles. In *Ein Heldenleben* this produces a regular concertino for solo violin, and in a similar way in chamber music episodes contribute to an all-embracing sound picture, blurring the boundaries between one musical genre and another.

Strauss's second period of activity in Munich, his home city, failed to satisfy him and ended in disappointment. His reputation was now so great that he could have expected to succeed to the post of chief conductor. So when he heard that the Opera was trying to secure the services of Felix Weingartner in succession to Hermann Levi, he quickly made up his mind to go to Berlin. Here he was received with open arms and given equal standing with the court conductor Carl Muck, with an annual salary of 20,000 Marks. It was a decision he never regretted, and he later wrote: 'I experienced nothing but pleasure there, receiving much sympathy and hospitality. Fifteen years of symphony concerts with the Royal Orchestra were unadulterated hours of the finest artistic work. My associations with the Berlin State Opera have outlasted all my other appointments (in Vienna).'

The young family moved into its first home in Berlin at Knesebeckstrasse 30, in Charlottenburg. The composer's only son Franz had been born in Munich on 12 April 1897.

· Berlin ·

Strauss was already known to Berlin audiences, as he had conducted the Philharmonic Concerts while still living in Munich, and this made it easier for him to accept the new post in the Prussian capital. Substantial parts of *Ein Heldenleben* had been written before he moved. The finished score is dated: 'Berlin-Charlottenburg, 27 December 1898,' and the first performance took place on 3 March 1899 at Frankfurt-am-Main with the local City Orchestra conducted by the composer. This brought Strauss's 'symphonic decade' to an end. Many of his works contain a measure of autobiography, a tendency most strikingly expressed in his habit of quoting from his own works. *Ein Heldenleben*, however, goes even further. It provides a complete self-portrait, sketching out in telling strokes both the composer's artistic activity and his married home life. Strauss imposed no predetermined program on the work. Instead he conformed to classical lines and used the program to provide

an accurate sequence of meaningfully linked but disparate elements, thereby avoiding the use of the standard model of symphonic poem. The various sections thus fit effortlessly into the formal pattern of movements of a cyclic symphonic poem: the hero (exposition and statement of theme); the opponents (quasi-scherzo); the woman in his life (long movement of *concertante* character); the hero's works of peace (quotations from his output, and quasi-reprise); flight from the world and conclusion (apotheosis-like coda). Only the battle scene – a passage of military music – does not fit into the conventional pattern of the symphonic poem and breaks up the structure of the work. But Strauss may well have had in mind that Beethoven also inserted a symphonic military intermezzo at the hero's arrival in the last movement of his Ninth Symphony, an intercalation which has never been convincingly accounted for. With his 'Battaglia,' Strauss provided a well conceived heroic contrast to the extended violin movement in G flat major portraying his temperamental wife Pauline, of whom he had said: 'She is very complicated; a little perverse, a little coquettish, changing from one minute to the next. . . .' The march-past of themes from earlier works may be regarded as a summing-up and a personal farewell to symphonic music. For Strauss, it never was form set in motion by sound, as Hanslick conceived of it, but a direct means of expression. Seen in this way, his symphonic output provides a coherent prologue to Strauss's real world, that of the opera. He used the symphonic poems to develop his instrumental framework and master the orchestral idiom of the stage.

'The aria must be given justice,' the motto which Strauss chose in 1941 for the score of *Capriccio*, is not just the afterthought of a dramatic composer. On the contrary, it represents a maxim which Strauss had obeyed in his symphonic poems and which he used again and again to make clear how much the lay-out of a composition is governed by purely musical considerations or even by audio-psychological factors. Strauss's finely developed artistic instinct told him – and this is indeed a measure of his personal greatness as a composer – when it was time to open the symphonic floodgates and when the hour had struck to resolve thematic problems and dramatic entanglements. It was at such times that he displayed a well-nigh Latin ability to spin out a cantilena in long melodic arches. These immersions in pleasing harmonies after the harshest complexes of modern sound, the interweaving of progressive and traditional elements, the balance between experimental and conventional musical effects are features basic to Strauss's output as a whole, not just his operas.

Strauss was well aware that he had reached the limit of instrumental expression in his symphonic poems, at any rate as far as his own time was concerned. When he read the Flemish legend *Das erloschene Feuer von Audenarde* (The Dead Fire of Oudenaarde), he thought of 'writing a small intermezzo *against* the theater, for personal reasons and as a little revenge upon

Above: The Dresden Opera House, scene of the premières of *Salome* (1905) and of eight other Strauss operas. The building, designed by Gottfried Semper, who also produced plans for a Festival Theater for Wagner, was destroyed in the Second World War.

the dear home town where thirty years ago the great Richard I [that is, Wagner] and now also the small Richard III [that is, Strauss; there being no 'II' as Hans von Bülow once put it] had such – not very pleasant – experiences.' He commissioned a libretto from the well-known writer Ernst von Wolzogen, explaining: 'The spiteful girl must finally sacrifice her virginity to the young magician at the pressing request of the town council and citizens in order to keep the town's fires burning. . . .' When it was finished, this was as merry as it was robust and rumbustious, depicted with strong colors that did not simply suggest these events, but which were quite explicit and told the whole story in vivid detail. As for Strauss, he let rip his love for quotations and borrowed so much from Wagner and from his own works that the whole thing turned into a huge romp. Strauss was without a shadow of doubt deliberately bordering on musical cabaret.

But court society was not yet frank enough to accept such facts of nature. Although the first performance of *Feuersnot* (Fire Famine) on 21 November 1901 was well received in Dresden, in Berlin it was taken off after its seventh performance at the request of the Empress, and Strauss was asked to submit his resignation. As a result, he determined never again to make a work available to Berlin for its première – and he kept his promise. Thus the composition which was intended as an indictment of Munich also had bad consequences for Berlin.

By the turn of the century Strauss had become a composer with a worldwide reputation, even though his great stage successes were yet to come. Such fame also had its commercial aspect, and in 1898 Strauss, together with Friedrich Rösch and Hans Sommer, set up the Genossenschaft deutscher Tonsetzer (Fellowship of German Composers) to campaign for composers' royalties for performances of their works, thus assuming organizational as well as spiritual leadership of the German composers of his day.

• Salome •

Fame brings its obligations, and Strauss had to travel a great deal over and above the demands of his duties in Berlin. In 1902 he made an extended tour with the Berlin Tonkünstler Orchestra; in 1903 he received an honorary doctorate from the Philosophy Faculty of Heidelberg University; and the following year, at the end of February, the Strauss couple set out on a tour of the United States. This turned into a tremendous success for them both: '21 concerts with some 20 orchestras disposed of in four weeks, traveling day and night on top of that, with banquets and the devil only knows what else,' Strauss scribbled to Max von Schillings.

Strauss had tucked a new work into his luggage when he set off for his American tour, the *Symphonia domestica*, op.53, 'dedicated to my dear wife and our boy.' If *Ein Heldenleben* is a musical portrait of the young married couple,

Strauss used the *Symphonia domestica* to depict the young family, now as happy parents. He told the New York press in 1904, before the first performance: 'My next symphonic poem will represent a day in the life of my family. It will be partly lyrical and partly humorous – a triple fugue will reunite papa, mama and the baby.'

This single-movement sinfonia is divided into four sections, which, as in all Strauss's works, conform in arrangement, form and development with purely musical principles. The criticism that the familiar, intimate subject is incompatible with the deployment of a large orchestra is not without some justification. This may have unfairly harmed the reputation of this inspired piece of music; after all, such a comment could not have been made if the composer had not given away the subject. Strauss, however, stood up for his artistic principles and made no bones about the fact that, for him, 'the person must be seen to take part in the action.' At the last

Left: Title-page to the first edition of Strauss's tone-poem *Also sprach Zarathustra* (1896), inspired by Friedrich Nietzsche's great philosophical poem.

Below: The classic 1837 German language edition (reprinted in the 1890s) of Cervantes' *Don Quixote*, with an introduction by Heinrich Heine. Strauss's *Don Quixote* of 1897 is subtitled 'Fantastic Variations on a Subject of Chivalric Nature' and includes important solo parts for cello and viola, representing Don Quixote and Sancho Panza respectively.

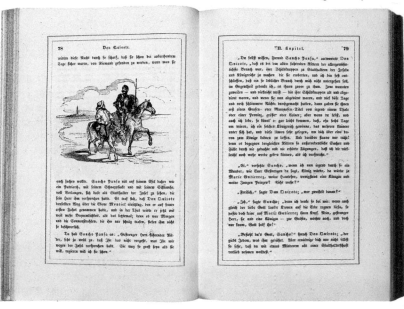

Above: Lithograph (1935) by Oskar Laske illustrating the antics of the folk hero Till Eulenspiegel. Strauss's vivid and rumbustious rendering of his adventures – *Till Eulenspiegels lustige Streiche* (1895) – is his most popular orchestral work.

sexual psychology, touched on perversion and revealed the dualism of the human ego. The intensity with which the composer succeeded in describing psychological borderline cases is astounding. He applied Wagner's *leitmotif* and orchestration techniques but followed his own – quite unmistakably personal – use of melodic line in the vocal writing. His orchestral range is generally pitched higher than Wagner's, and he gave it even greater freedom. For Strauss the orchestra was an equal partner on the stage, not just a means of accompaniment but a direct participant in the action. His stage works, especially *Salome* and *Elektra*, can be described as orchestral operas with even more justification than those of Wagner; his symphonic interludes assumed hitherto unparalleled formal proportions, and he now made full use of the framework he had acquired during the composition of his symphonic poems. It would hardly be an exaggeration to say that these one-act operas are like extra-dimensional symphonic poems – in which the program can actually be seen as it develops – so that Hanslick's suggestion in connection with *Death and Transfiguration* had, in effect, been carried out.

This idea is certainly fulfilled in 'Salome's Dance' – no ballet interlude, even though it represents the most self-contained part of the score. It is known that Strauss rewrote this dance. The stage direction in the libretto says no more than 'Salome dances the dance of the seven veils.' The task of rounding off the text-linked musical exposition by a resolution of the dramatic crux, also using musical means, and of translating into instrumental language the emotional transformation which overwhelms Salome in the course of this ardent *notturno*, must have proved particularly attractive to the master of the symphonic poem. And he made it into a summing-up of the action so far. The significance of the individual motifs and themes can literally be traced in the preceding vocal scenes. Through her dance Salome secures compliance with her wish for the head of Jochanaan. She is not just an obedient daughter of her mother, the intriguer who had suggested this revolting idea. She follows her own compulsive instincts quite independently, full of her own sultry fantasies. Strauss used the moment of suspense before Jochanaan's execution to portray expectancy in musical terms. The unbearable silence, sustained by the unusual effect of bass strings pinched between finger and thumb, culminates in two pauses, after which the orchestra tears into a screaming diminished seventh and an ugly discord as the executioner's axe falls. The exultant horror of the child-woman turns into the seduction motif, the music sinks back into the sensual arousal of the young girl who now feasts her eyes on Jochanaan's head on the salver: 'Ah, you would not let me kiss your mouth, Jochanaan!' Now that nothing can any longer prevent the fulfillment of her desire she delays its accomplishment, as though to intensify it. As the torches go out, the lips of the king's daughter and the dead prophet meet. In this necromantic ceremony the girl's sinful desire is

concert he conducted in New York the work secured 'a colossal, enthusiastic success.' Strauss wrote to his parents that the symphony 'sounded splendid' but had 'proved very difficult.'

The psychology of artistic creativity is a complicated matter, and the fact that Strauss simultaneously tackled two compositions as diametrically opposed in character as his *Symphonia domestica* and the opera *Salome* is a good illustration of this. He was clearly able to devote himself at one and the same time to two compositions which were poles apart in spirit.

He had spent two years setting to music the text of Oscar Wilde's *Salome* in an exceptionally good translation by Hedwig Lachmann. In this case, the translator deserves mention as well as the poet, since she managed to convey Wilde's subtle language in an authentic German equivalent and helped the composer to catch the temper of this archaic world by using an almost biblical idiom. Strauss, however, was not faithful to her actual text, but shortened it considerably, although he also added to it occasionally by transposing, inserting or repeating words – in other words by subjecting the text entirely to his musical requirements.

Salome represents an exception in the main body of Strauss's output; for the first and only time he broke with the traditional tonal scheme and used bi-tonality as a means of character portrayal. He reached out into the sphere of

transmuted into mindless love. The tetrarch's sentence of death remains as unreal to her as Narraboth's earlier suicide. She had been surprised by the wordlessness of the prophet's suffering and had waited in vain for his dying cry. Now she finds her own mute and unyielding *Liebestod* under the soldiers' shields.

In accordance with his promise, Strauss offered the score to Dresden rather than Berlin. Its study faced the singers with unprecedented difficulties. During the previous century singers had become accustomed to parts written to fit their voices. Strauss, however, demanded – to a greater extent even than Wagner – that the performers should adapt to their parts. Rehearsals turned into singing lessons. Marie Wittich, who had been chosen to sing the title-role, felt that too much was expected of her in every respect. She found it impossible to identify with the part in moral terms, and she also knew that her figure was quite unsuitable. This is in fact one of the main reasons why it is often difficult to stage this opera convincingly. The title-role of *Salome* demands an experienced singer with a great sense of music and excellent musical training, endowed moreover with an oriental beauty's face and a young girl's figure so as to enable her to give a credible performance of the Dance of the Seven Veils (although this difficulty is often overcome by using a dancer to double in the part).

The triumph of the première of *Salome* on 9 December 1905 threw all Strauss's earlier successes into the shade. The pick of the critics was present in the auditorium. A few rough edges apart, everybody recognized a watershed in modern opera; a new way forward had opened here beyond Wagner. But the difficulties of making such a work part of any normal repertoire were also clear to all. As for Berlin, that imperial and puritanical city, *Salome* was permitted to be performed there only after Emperor Wilhelm II had been reassured that the coming of the Magi was forecast at the end of the opera by the rising of the morning star! *Salome* won much recognition for the composer, including the Cross of the French Legion of Honor, and it was also a financial success, so that he was able to build himself a villa in Garmisch.

• *Elektra* •

Early in 1906, Strauss attended a performance of Hugo von Hofmannsthal's *Elektra* directed by Max Reinhardt in Berlin, and he immediately recognized this play as a suitable subject for opera. He was, however, overwhelmed by doubt as to whether he had enough strength left to cope with material so similar to that of *Salome*. On 7 March 1906 Hofmannsthal wrote to the composer to ask how he felt about tackling *Elektra*, and this started a working correspondence between them, which became as wide-ranging as it was significant.

The collaboration between these two kindred spirits, which was to last until Hofmannsthal's

tragic death in 1929, is recorded in the letters they exchanged. These provide unique documentation of the process of artistic creativity in general, and a collaboration between librettist and composer in particular. Six operas were to emerge from their relationship. One may be pretty certain on the strength of these documents that Strauss would hardly have achieved such maturity as a composer for the stage – something which is now taken for granted – had it not been for Hofmannsthal's guidance. The latter was able to impose intellectual discipline on the wayward composer again and again, and he often felt obliged to explain the implications of his plays in his letters. He had assessed the strengths and weaknesses of his composer very early in their joint creative activity, as a letter to Harry Graf Kessler shows: 'Strauss is such a splendidly unrefined person. He has a fearful inclination towards triviality and junk. Whatever he wants from me by way of small changes, additions and so on always goes in that direction.'

In later years, Strauss himself confessed to his 'talent for kitsch,' but Hofmannsthal's assessment fails to reflect the whole truth. It was, for instance, only Strauss's request for a change in the Orestes scene in *Elektra* which imparted a musical dimension to the tragedy at that point and made it into an opera. Once again, it was the symphonist in Strauss who sensed the right moment for the melody to blossom forth and conjure up emotion.

Elektra, like *Salome*, was again exceptional in Strauss's operatic output, in that it presented him with a ready-made text – the difference in this case being that the author was still alive and could reshape his play in accordance with the composer's wishes. This led to an unusual situation in the history of libretto writing. Hofmannsthal had written the play with the spoken theater in mind and had made no allowances for it to be set to music – which creates very different circumstances. For one thing, the timing of the action is altered with the addition of music; for another, emotions can be expressed much

more directly, more economically and yet with greater intensity by musical means in places where a poet would otherwise have to elaborate his text.

On 11 March 1906 Strauss told Hofmannsthal in reply to an enquiry dated 7 March that he had 'already put the play together quite prettily for home consumption.' But some doubts remained, and it was only the poet's counterarguments and prodding which finally pushed him into getting down to work. Among the ancillary characters of the stage play only the cook perished under the composer's blue pencil. He mainly attacked the longer monologues, as he had done in *Salome*, but, in this work, he substantially shortened the text of the title-role. Even Strauss had to pay some attention to the physical endurance of his singers.

However, the composer's textual additions are even more interesting than his cuts, because they reveal his intentions as a musical dramatist so clearly. In his play, Hofmannsthal never refers to Agamemnon by name until the recognition scene between his two children, Orestes and Elektra. All through her great opening monologue Elektra refers to him only as 'my father,' and his name is never spoken in the dialogues between Elektra and her sister Chrysothemis or her mother Klytemnestra. Strauss, on the other hand, introduces the name directly into the action. The explosive orchestral exclamation with which the tragedy begins and ends is prosodically modelled on the sound of 'Agamemnon,' and Strauss could not afford to wait until the recognition scene before he disclosed the meaning of this motif – which acts as a *leitmotif* – to the listener. He therefore interrupted Elektra's monologue right at the start and twice inserted 'Agamemnon' – an existential cry, full of despair, with which the daughter, shrouded in darkness, conjures up her father at a spectral meeting. The listener is now able to attach a meaning to the opening

musical motif and recognize that Agamemnon, an invisible but ever-present agent, manipulates the characters in the drama and forces them to act.

The most important change that the composer asked the author to make was in the recognition scene between Elektra and Orestes. In Hofmannsthal's original stage version Elektra's cry – 'Orestes!' – is immediately followed by her brother's feverishly anxious reaction: 'If anyone in the house has heard you, he now holds my life in his hands.' In other words, Hofmannsthal drives on the action, and the emotions of the brother and sister are not highlighted. Orestes moves to embrace his sister but she, wholly obsessed by the object of her vengeance, pushes him away: 'No, you shall not touch me! Stand away, I am ashamed before you. I do not know how you can look at me!' Strauss felt that such a reaction by the sister, immediately after she had recognized the man she had thought dead, was too direct and abrupt. As a musician, his perception differed from the author's. He thought that in circumstances of such extreme stress, emotions could not just be buried, and

Above: Strauss, pictured with his wife Pauline and their son Franz in Berlin, about the year 1904.

that it would be more human and artistically convincing to give the black-mantled Elektra her voice at that moment and let her react as a woman and a sister. What Strauss needed from a musical consideration at this point – the actual climax of the opera – was a meditative instant of suspense, so as to allow the emotional response of the brother and sister to be heard. 'The aria must be given justice.'

At the moment of recognition Elektra experiences the miracle of her transformation; she is no longer an avenger, but a sister with her brother beside her, overwhelmed by the happiness of their reunion. The greatest bliss is mute! Strauss resolved Elektra's emotion by a symphonic interlude based on the Orestes motif and the motifs of recognition and of Agamemnon's children. But the composer needed textual links in order to return from this mood to the more sober mood of the dialogue, and these were not available. He therefore turned to Hofmannsthal on 22 June 1908: 'I need . . . a great moment of repose after Elektra's first cry of "Orestes!" I will insert a tender and tremulous orchestral interlude while Elektra contemplates her Orestes, who has been returned to her: I can let her repeat the words "Orestes, Orestes, Orestes!" in a stammer several times as she does so, but the only other words there that fit are "Nobody is stirring! Oh let me see your eyes!" Couldn't you fit in a couple of fine verses in this mood for me at this point, until I then switch (when Orestes wants to embrace her tenderly) to the sombre mood which starts with the words "No, you shall not touch me . . . !"'

For musical reasons, Strauss does not want to allow Elektra's inner emotion at this point to escape from him. Before she tenderly repeats her brother's name after her first outcry, the Orestes motif quivers through the orchestra in a long sequence and prepares the change of mood.

The continuity of action in this one-act opera is provided by the orchestral interludes, which Strauss uses in place of arias. In traditional opera, Elektra would have been given an extended aria in the appropriate mood at the point when she had recognized her brother; no prima donna of the old school would have given up such a chance of effective display. But Strauss denied the singer this opportunity and transferred the emotion to the orchestra, to pure music, the impact of which requires no explanation. In this way the composer can heighten the effect by directing the surge of emotions inwards while silence prevails on the stage. When Hofmannsthal finally heard the music, he admitted that his poetry had been enhanced by it, but he nevertheless retained an instinctive dislike, fully justified from his point of view, of symphonic interludes during which the poet's words were silenced.

Elektra also became a worldwide success, although its first performance on 25 January 1909, once again in Dresden under the expert baton of Schuch, received a merely favorable reception from the critics and no more. At the start, *Elektra* had to compete with *Salome*, which was acclaimed wherever it was heard.

• *Der Rosenkavalier* and *Ariadne auf Naxos* •

Immediately after this first night, Hofmannsthal and Strauss turned to *Der Rosenkavalier* (The Cavalier of the Rose), and its libretto started to take shape as a result of intensive collaboration. Strauss began to compose even before their joint work on the libretto had been completed. He had at last found his comedy! The period was that of the Empress Maria Theresa, or – more accurately – that of Mozart.

The step from *Elektra* to *Der Rosenkavalier* has sometimes been described as retrogressive in terms of Strauss's development. This is far from true: it is precisely in *Der Rosenkavalier* that the composer's unfailing touch in choosing his musical resources and the use to which he puts them can be most clearly seen. The Vienna of Maria Theresa demanded a completely different range of sound from that which was required by the Atridian harshness of the Elektra story. Strauss set out to discover a more airy, lighter and transparent tonality, helped along by the winging impetus of the Viennese waltz, anachronistic though that may be. The mood of the waltz is well calculated to establish a local atmosphere, and Strauss skillfully adapted Joseph Strauss's *Dynamiden-Walzer*, adding a slightly

Above: A voluptuous portrayal of Salome dancing before John the Baptist's head, painted by the Munich artist Franz von Stuck in 1906. It was Max Reinhardt's Berlin staging of Wilde's play that first roused Strauss's interest.

Right: Alfred Roller's stage design for the first production, at Dresden in 1909, of *Elektra* – the work that started the long and fruitful collaboration between Strauss and Hugo von Hofmannsthal.

Below: Cover design by Lovis Corinth for the piano score of Strauss's *Elektra*, based on Hofmannsthal's new translation of Sophocles's tragedy. Once again, it was Reinhardt's staging of the play that first attracted Strauss to the subject.

morbid, *fin-de-siècle* touch of color, to provide *Der Rosenkavalier* with its background.

Hugo Riemann, the patriarch of German musicology, angrily attacked Richard Strauss in his musical dictionary, published in 1916, saying that it had only too obviously been he who had promoted 'the undisguised pursuit of sensation at any price, so contrary to serious art,' and his reputation could increasingly be seen as that of 'a giant with feet of clay.' This provides a clear illustration of the fact that the German school still failed to recognize the existence of conceptions of musical drama that differed from those laid down by Wagner. Strauss had gradually liberated himself from Wagner's grasp and had come not only to recognize but also to accept the old values of traditional opera. That was all that had happened. The Italian aria inserted in the first act of *Rosenkavalier*, the simultaneous duets, and above all the final scene, are in their very simplicity confessions of faith in opera, in song and in the deployment of the human voice. Unquestionably, Strauss also underwent an inner conversion to the modern approach at this time. In 1909 he admitted to Arnold Schoenberg that he would not risk 'presenting to an ultra-conservative Berlin audience' his Four Pieces for Orchestra, op.16; but the 'Moderns,' of whom Strauss was at that time considered the leader, had already begun to split by 1910. Strauss went his own way as a musician, and it must be admitted that, seen from the closing years of the twentieth century, he was the last German opera composer who – despite *Wozzeck* and *Lulu* – was still capable of producing really viable repertory works.

If one were to say that construction was the essence of Schoenberg's music one might, by contrast, claim that improvisation is at the center of Strauss's. Construction implies that which is calculated, determined, fixed, irremovable. Just the opposite is true of Strauss: everything is transformed, disrupted, disguised and variable. Strauss's motifs are constantly dressed in different new clothes. They are not even firmly linked to a particular work, but may reappear without warning in another composition, differently arranged, differently interpreted, only slightly altered. For the final scene of *Rosenkavalier* Strauss invented one of his finest trios, in which, by paraphrasing popular taste, he came close to triviality; but even though he teetered on the brink, he did not tip over into it. Strauss was well able to judge the margin of safety. The 'folk' music is translated into elegance, and the comic touch fades away with the sadness of parting. If Strauss knew how to plumb the psychological depths of Salome and Elektra, he was also a past master at conveying the emotional ripples in the mood of the Marschallin – a young woman, now past thirty, who finds her fleeting hopes overshadowed by intimations that she will soon have to renounce them. The Marschallin, not the Rosenkavalier, is really the leading figure of the opera.

Elektra's orchestra of a hundred and twenty players is reduced to eighty for *Rosenkavalier*. But this does not imply any reduction of scale: *Rosenkavalier* is also designed for a large, well-equipped orchestra. Yet one constantly finds passages in this score in which Strauss set out to produce chamber music effects and was working with only part of his sound arsenal. The large number of players is used to secure a broad range of colors, rather than a massed effect.

On the other hand, Strauss imposed a 'conceptual' cut on the size of the orchestra for *Ariadne auf Naxos*. This opera is scored for a small orchestra consisting of a mere thirty-seven players: two flutes, two oboes, two clarinets, two bassoons, two horns, trumpet, trombone, two harps, celeste, piano, harmonium, tympani, three percussionists, six violins, four violas, four cellos, two double basses. The conjunction of piano and harmonium occasionally allows the coloring of a Paris café orchestra to shimmer – but no more than shimmer – through the score. Despite all these reductions, Strauss still kept a broad range of color at his disposal. In fact, one of the most admirable things about *Ariadne* is the way in which the composer achieved the effect of a large orchestra with a mere three dozen players, an astonishing technical feat. Strauss chiefly concentrated on lightness and transparency of sound in the interests of the intelligibility of the words, though without surrendering the dominant position of the music.

In order to obtain a well-balanced gradation of sound from his orchestra, he now adopted the practice of separating the individual sections and instruments by means of dynamic instructions, and matching them against each other at different levels of sound. In his instructions to conductors for *Salome* and *Elektra*

he had already asked that these large orchestral scores should be handled like chamber music.

Ariadne was Strauss's second incursion into Greek mythology, but while *Elektra* reflects the somber quality of ancient legend, he imparted a luminous Hellenistic mood to *Ariadne*. In this way the opera is linked with both *Elektra* and *Rosenkavalier*; the psychological investigation of Ariadne's inner personality shows her to be a continuation of the Marschallin, and thus a further portrait of Strauss's wife Pauline, whom he used as a model of femininity. In terms of its content, *Ariadne* deals with one of the basic problems of operatic aesthetic theory and demonstrates the percipient yet masterly way in which the composer reflected the historical opportunities offered by opera as a whole. It was with this work that Strauss made his act of faith in opera and showed that the Wagnerian dramatic concept had been overtaken. Strauss had discovered baroque opera, and he drew no dividing line between the Italian *opera seria* and the French *tragédie lyrique*. While *Ariadne* was first conceived in its 1912 version as an appendage to Molière's *Bourgeois gentilhomme*, it was transformed in the final version of 1916 into a little opera in its own right, and the whole work is rebuilt into an ironically formulated lesson in historical operatic aesthetics. The point is emphasized not only by the retrospective references to baroque opera, with its succession of arias joined by recitative, but also by the juxtaposition of the lofty genre – the 'heroic' style – with the light-hearted comic opera – the statement of the 'human' approach. And so Strauss used closed musical forms, both in the shape of the dramatic aria and for seductive coloratura fireworks, and he made use of recitative, as well as the ironically sobering effect of a spoken part – the major-domo. He was constantly aiming for a humorous effect and therefore fitted these divergent stylistic elements together in such a way that the burlesque and the serious elements

Top: Strauss, seated center, photographed after the première of *Der Rosenkavalier* with some of his close colleagues: seated (right), Ernst von Schuch, who conducted the premières of *Feuersnot*, *Salome* and *Elektra* as well as *Rosenkavalier*; standing (third from left), Max Reinhardt, (center) Hugo von Hofmannsthal, (third from right) Alfred Roller.

Above: The soprano Anna Bahr-Mildenburg as Klytemnestra in the 1910 Covent Garden première of *Elektra*.

are fused into a truly tragi-comic Gallic jest. And Strauss nevertheless remained true to his reputation; even here, he knew how to conjure up a flowering *cantabile* passage that touches the emotions in accordance with the motto: 'Music is a sacred art.' When Hofmannsthal later heard this music (on 16 April 1918) he admitted to himself that Strauss had 'gone entirely his own way' in this work.

• *Die Frau ohne Schatten* •

At the end of May 1912 Strauss, who had already allotted an important place to the dance in *Salome* and *Elektra*, and had reserved passages in the score of *Ariadne* for pantomime and the spirit of the dance, now branched out into ballet. Hofmannsthal had devised, in collaboration with Harry Kessler, the scenario for a ballet about the attempted seduction of Joseph by Potiphar's wife. Strauss immediately seized upon this work with the intention of representing 'dance as drama, and dance as – dance.' But he got into difficulties, as he always did when he was forced to depict something spiritual or ecclesiastical without any chance of introducing irony. Just as Jochanaan, with his rather undifferentiated diatonic treatment, seems conspicuously anemic in comparison with Salome, so the character of Joseph, portrayed in similar, rather colorless diatonic terms, also gave Strauss trouble in composition: 'The chaste Joseph is not my sort of character,' he complained on 11 September 1912 to his librettist: 'whatever irritates me I find it difficult to provide music for. Ah well, maybe there still is in some atavistic recess of my appendix a pious tune that will do for the good Joseph!'

Pious tunes were certainly not Strauss's *forte*. It is not surprising that church music is consistently absent from his otherwise wide-ranging output of works. It was only when Hofmannsthal described Joseph to him as a child genius sprung from a mountain tribe, more like a noble, untamed colt than a devout seminarian,

that Strauss managed to go on with the composition, even though the appropriate archaic and pastoral tone still eluded him. The *Josephs Legende* was loudly acclaimed at its first performance in Paris on 14 May 1914, but it remained a marginal work, even though choreographers have often praised the specifically danceable quality of the music.

Strauss defined his own prophecy that the future belonged to the chamber orchestra with *Die Frau ohne Schatten* (The Woman without a Shadow), first thoughts of which reach back to 1911, and which he completed in June 1917. He went back to an orchestra comparable to that of *Elektra*, even though the conception of this work is very different from that of the earlier one-act opera. It runs to three acts and represents an attempt to write in the grand manner, though in a twentieth-century spirit. It was later described as 'the twentieth century's *Magic Flute*' because of a similar baffling interplay of realism and symbolism, down-to-earth and fairytale features, which together make up a work difficult to penetrate and deliberately obscure in some of its aspects. Hofmannsthal not only used *The Magic Flute*, but also drew on Goethe's *Faust*. The nurse, the evil seductress practicing her wiles, stands for Mephistopheles. There is also a reference to the very end of *Faust* in the 'Chorus of those yet unborn.' The subject of acquiring children through seduction and magic is derived from the world of fairytales. Both the Empress and the dyer's wife atone for their guilt by their acceptance of fate.

The detailed exchange of letters between Hofmannsthal and Strauss, which was supplemented by face-to-face discussions, embodies infinitely subtle gradations in the development of a symbiotic relationship between poetry and music. Strauss was again contrasting two worlds, those of the imperial couple and of the two dyers, the earthbound, claustrophobic environment of the manual workers as opposed to the magical esoteric world of the rulers, by means of graduated tonal values and shadings of color. This provides the most vivid and clear-cut example of the struggle for mastery between words and music in the collaboration between poet and musician. In *Die Frau ohne Schatten* Hofmannsthal assumed a more deliberately independent attitude towards the composer than he had done in the earlier, jointly conceived operas. Then he had reacted as a librettist, even though he believed he was a special kind of librettist endowed with poetic fire. Now, however, he affirmed his claim as a poet. The music must contribute, it must carry the poetry but not disrupt it or even overlay it. Hofmannsthal was certainly aware that despite their joint triumphs he was still consistently relegated to second place, as no more than the l brettist, and that it was Strauss – and not he – who was being acclaimed as the creator of *Rosenkavalier* and *Ariadne*. The situation in which he was caught was most clearly illustrated by *Elektra*, which increasingly lost its place in the repertory as a play to the more persuasive power of the operatic version. Despite all the mutual expressions

Top: Playbill for the première, at Dresden on 26 January 1911, of *Der Rosenkavalier* – from the first night on, the best loved of Strauss's operas.

Above: A contemporary French cartoon showing Salome delivering Strauss's head on a platter, with a rose stuck between his teeth – a comment on the operas *Salome* and *Der Rosenkavalier*, apparently worlds apart in style and mood.

Left: Strauss and Hofmannsthal; a photograph probably taken in 1912.

Right: Two of Alfred Roller's costume designs for the first production of *Der Rosenkavalier*: (*right*) the Marschallin, and (*far right*) Baron Ochs von Lerchenau.

of good fellowship, this touch of muted, but not always well concealed, rivalry runs through the correspondence. In a letter of 22 April 1914 Hofmannsthal mentioned, as though in passing, the 'hitherto unknown' Franz Schmidt. He went on to say that 'the peculiar thing for me about Schmidt's opera was that I understood almost everything in the – otherwise absurd – text as soon as I heard it, and yet this was no thin melodramatic music . . . and – I can't help it – it made a very pleasant impression on me . . . What I am trying to convey, in a thoroughly unqualified manner, is that possibilities simply must sometimes exist to put the word in first place, and that I would feel much had been gained if, on this occasion, that was something which you saw your way to doing.'

This was not merely a veiled criticism of Strauss's tendency to give his scores too thick an orchestral texture, but a cautious attempt to improve the position of the textual element within the framework of the composition as a whole. In a letter about *Arabella*, on 22 December 1927, the poet suggested in passing, but in all seriousness, that, as Strauss saw it, 'the symphonist . . . is constantly at war with the dramatist.' He then bluntly added, 'I find the excess of music-making with the curtain down

an abomination.' Bearing in mind his strong objection to extensive musical interludes, this remark might equally well apply to music-making with the curtain raised.

In *Die Frau ohne Schatten* Hofmannsthal sought to stage a fairytale, while Strauss still hankered after a musician's opera. Hofmannsthal, he felt, was pushing him to the limit of his musical powers of expression. He had boasted that he could compose anything – literally anything – but now got into difficulties trying to give musical form to a shadow. How can this be done? The motif Strauss invented is by no means descriptive, and so the shadow appears more as a lighting effect from above, while failing to darken the stage from the orchestra pit below. Hofmannsthal identified the characters by treating them as symbols and classifying them in categories: only Barak, the dyer, is allowed a name of his own; all the rest are simply set types – Emperor and Empress, dyer's wife, nurse, brothers. The latter complement the *tutti* as representatives of imperfection and are important because they make it possible to fit ensembles into the texture of the monologues and dialogues.

Hofmannsthal took great trouble to integrate the ensemble passages, with seamless transitions, into the flow of the dialogue, a feature which distinguishes this great opera from the traditional 'grand opera,' in which transitions occur as brutal changes of direction or surprise effects. Strauss used every opportunity offered by the full range of vocal articulation, from dramatically fluent song, bizarrely angular melodic declamation, words spoken to music, *arioso* culminating in musical flourishes, to the well-shaped aria and duet. He once said that he intended to give audible form to the difference between the two levels on which the action develops – the real and the illusory – by varying the composition of the orchestra, though he did not actually carry out this idea here. Instead, he relied on his well-tried practice of stylistic differentiation. But he did also identify characters for the listener's benefit by *concertante* use of individual instruments (for example, the solo violin represents the Empress), a principle that fully accords with the traditional practice of grand opera.

In his music for *Die Frau ohne Schatten* Strauss was again able to conjure up the bold strokes of *Elektra*, and he wrote a score which combines the solid strength of the *Elektra* score with the shimmering color of that of *Salome*, so that for many experts today this mature achievement of the fifty-five-year-old Richard Strauss is the spiritual climax of his whole creative work. *Die Frau ohne Schatten*, his 'child of sorrow,' as Strauss later described it, which absorbed his

artistic energies during the fearful years of the First World War, did not receive its first performance until after the war was over, on 10 October 1919 at the Vienna Staatsoper. It was a huge success, but the première in Dresden, which followed less than two weeks later, was badly hampered by the vocal inadequacy of the dyer's wife. Strauss realized that he had created a work that was hard to cast and extremely difficult to stage, and that could only be produced successfully in the world's greatest opera houses. From this aspect too, *Die Frau ohne Schatten* has all the characteristics of a great opera.

In the hundred-day interval between the completion of the second and third acts of *Die Frau ohne Schatten* Strauss scored his *Alpensinfonie*, although the earliest sketches for the work go back to 1911. He added this to his already oppressive workload and completed the piece during the winter of 1914-15. In fact – or so he thought – he had long since discarded the symphonic poem from his musical range. Yet it is precisely this score which displays the complex way in which the most varied – indeed divergent – lines of thought overlie each other in his creative approach. In the *Alpensinfonie* Strauss relived his first meeting with the mountains, and this belated return to earlier musical concepts demonstrates the compulsion which forced him at some point or other to express his creative experiences in music.

• Between the wars •

By 1910 Strauss had given up his administrative duties at the Berlin Opera, but he retained his work as a conductor because it provided a major part of his income. In March 1918 he directed the seven hundredth concert of the Berlin Hofkapelle. He also temporarily took over a composition class at the Berlin Akademie der Künste. On 1 December 1919 he became co-director with Franz Schalk of the Vienna Hofoper, now the Staatsoper. In October 1918 the authorities had finally succeeded, 'after a tricky correspondence with Archbishop Piffl,' in ensuring that *Salome*, a success worldwide – but banned by Austrian censorship – could at last be performed at the Hofoper, one month before the declaration of the Austrian Republic.

Strauss was soon forced to put aside his plans to revive interesting early operas from Gluck onwards, because the investment in money, time and effort was thought to be too great. Although he set up house in Vienna, he preferred his home in Garmisch, and his activities as a guest conductor elsewhere led to increasing tension with Schalk. After five years he found an excuse to resign from the Staatsoper, and it was entirely due to his equable disposition that this Viennese intermezzo did not end in a huge row. A Strauss Week was organized in Vienna in 1924 to celebrate his sixtieth birthday, and he repaid the complement with the première on 9 May of his ebullient ballet *Schlagobers* (Whipped Cream), which he had completed in Garmisch

Below: One of Léon Bakst's costume designs for Strauss's ballet *Josephs Legende*, written to a scenario by Hofmannsthal. The work, choreographed by Fokine for Diaghilev's Ballets Russes, was based on the Old Testament, but set in Renaissance Venice. The composer conducted the first performance at the Paris Opéra just three months before the outbreak of the First World War.

In other words, it was not so much the auto-biographical aspect which was in the forefront of his mind as the testing-out of a specific problem involving operatic aesthetics. The work is full of musical quotations, and Strauss can hardly have expected the ordinary opera-goer to be capable of deciphering such an abundance of thematic cross-references. It is therefore this opera above all which proves that he composed first and foremost for his own sake and was standing himself the greatest treat by this wealth of thematic allusions. The first performance, on 4 November 1924 in Dresden, was another tumultuous success, which, let it be said, was probably mainly due to the personal allusions, since the leading character had been made up to look like Richard Strauss.

Despite his experimentation, Strauss proved unable to achieve any very clear cut style in his next opera, *Die ägyptische Helena* (Helen in Egypt), which explores the personal problems arising from the reunion of Helen and Menelaus after the fall of Troy. Hofmannsthal analyzed the fascinating questions involved in a separately published introduction, but, despite its considerable literary merit, this work fails to connect at all convincingly with either *Elektra* or *Ariadne*. Strauss himself sensed that in his search for a new, original style he had failed to create a specifically Greek atmosphere. He remarked tersely after the first performance: 'There's little to say about the music: it is, I'm afraid, melodious and mellifluous. . . .'

The composer was as usual pressing the author for new material even before he had rounded off the score of *Helena*. Strauss constantly needed to keep up the flow, to be able to think ahead, so as to keep up his 'fingering exercises' as he jokingly put it. Hofmannsthal thought of working out something typically Viennese, getting away from Greek mythology and going once again for a slice of 'here and now' – not a palace of classical antiquity, but a little hotel in Vienna. He used his own story

as early as 1921. *Schlagobers* was intended as an act of homage to the Viennese love for sweets and pastries of all kinds. Cocoa, Sugar and Tea Blossom have roles in the ballet, Princess Praliné makes an appearance, and there is, of course, a deliciously lilting Whipped Cream Waltz.

In 1923 Strauss completed his 'marriage' opera *Intermezzo*, which he had already mentioned in a letter to Hofmannsthal in 1918. Hermann Bahr was to have written the libretto, but the subject-matter as Strauss presented it was so personal that the composer eventually agreed with Bahr that only he himself could write it. The opera is about a misunderstanding which had come near to wrecking Strauss's own marriage. The main characters are the composer and his wife. Strauss, a very acute observer, set his own everyday marriage and professional life on the stage, not omitting even his beloved card game, *Skat* – the whole thing, of course, well laced with irony. Equally important for the composer was his experimental treatment of the relationship between words and music, a fundamental problem of composition to which he later gave full treatment in *Capriccio*. He had already created, in the first act of *Ariadne*, a style of singing in which straight prose alternated with both *secco* and *accompagnato* recitative, a style which he extended and explored further in *Intermezzo*. The title of this opera is therefore ambiguous on several levels, and it is perhaps best interpreted as a reference to Strauss's process of composition – an experimental intermediate area which he preferred to veil in irony. Strauss also developed even more extensively than before the use of symphonic interludes to cover moments of contemplative repose. There are no fewer than twelve of these in the course of only two acts, and changes of scenery were in fact also bridged by such instrumental inserts. Strauss justified this in a remarkable introduction to the opera with the statement that the dialogue had never been so important to him before as now and that he had therefore allowed himself rather few opportunities to develop 'the so-called *cantilena*.'

Above: Strauss in Vichy in 1935, during a summer festival of the International Society of Composers. He conducted a memorial performance of Dukas's *Sorcerer's Apprentice*, which displeased the Nazis, since Dukas was half-Jewish.

Below: Scene from the first performance, in Vienna in 1924, of the ballet *Schlagobers* (Whipped Cream), set in a Viennese cake shop.

entitled *Lucidor* and the scenario of *Der Fiaker als Graf* (The Cabby as Count) to spin an atmospheric plot about the daughter of a count who has come down in the world and is trying to restore his former fortunes by gambling. He sends his last remaining piece of capital, the portrait of his beautiful daughter Arabella, to a former comrade-in-arms in Croatia. Mandryka, the son of his friend, is so taken by the charm of the picture that he travels to Vienna to meet the original. After a lightly handled plot, the two young people are united. This piece owes much of its effect to understatement, and in it Hofmannsthal managed to debunk social pretensions and depict the tawdry elegance of Vienna in the *Gründerzeit*. He had already tackled the problem of two ill-matched sisters in *Elektra*, and this situation is given a further twist in *Arabella* by the jealousy of the younger 'modest rival' at the success of her older, more mature and more level-headed sister.

Here was the account of an everyday episode full of Viennese local color. It reaches deeper only when it strips bare the emotional responses of the characters, and Hofmannsthal even succeeded in linking up with the local pantomime tradition by dressing up Zdenka, the younger sister, as a boy. This was comedy skirting the brink, comedy as a lyrical display. Strauss wired total approval as soon as the completed version of Act I reached him, but Hofmannsthal was never to see this telegram. Just after the funeral of his son, who had committed suicide, the poet was felled by a stroke. An intimate collaboration which had lasted twenty-three years had come to an abrupt and unexpected end. For Strauss Hofmannsthal was irreplaceable.

Fortunately, he had completed the libretto three days before he died. But what was now missing was the written exchange of views established by so many years of joint work and Strauss's off-the-cuff comments as he worked on the score. For the first time since he had begun working with Hofmannsthal, Strauss had to be content with the material before him without any chance of altering it.

In the long dialogue passages Strauss kept to his own *parlando* conversational tone. But he also constantly dipped into his treasury of *cantabile* ideas and used either original folk tunes or imitated their sound to establish a Croatian mood. Three worlds of sound are thus set side by side: the hotel's sleazy environment; the unsophisticated, solid atmosphere of the cabbies' ball, with its coloratura fireworks; and pure, unspoilt naturalness personified by Mandryka. Strauss complied with Hofmannsthal's wish for shorter symphonic interludes, but returned all the more gladly to the closed forms of classical opera. The orchestra, however, remained the leading partner for Strauss, though voice and orchestra, text and music remain in balance.

The première of *Arabella* on 1 July 1933 at the Dresden State Opera brought Strauss his last great worldwide success. *Arabella* is a work parallel to *Rosenkavalier* and, like it, represents a homage to imperial Vienna. Both are snapshots that capture the city's atmosphere at different

Three of the singers in the first production, at Dresden in 1933, of *Arabella*: (*left*) Viorica Ursuleac in the title-role and Martin Kremer as Matteo; (*above*) Margit Bokor as Zdenka, Arabella's sister. All were singers at the Dresden State Opera and sang in a number of Strauss's works of this period. Ursuleac was married to Clemens Krauss, who conducted the première of *Arabella*, and the couple were close friends of the composer.

moments of its history. *Arabella* is not only Strauss's last real repertory opera but can also be described as the very last repertory work in the history of opera which still retains something of the old spirit of traditional gala works.

The year 1933 saw Hitler seize power in Germany. Richard Strauss at sixty-nine was too old to grasp the full significance of this event. In any case, he was no longer fighting for position. He now headed the community of living German composers and was conscious of his responsibility as a patriarch. Just as he had acted in support of composers' royalties from publishers, he now felt it was his duty to offer his services to the cause of German musicians. He thought it perfectly logical that he should be called on to become chairman of the *Reichsmusikkammer*. What, in fact, is an established composer to do in a totalitarian society, if he wishes to go on working rather than keep silent? Besides, Strauss was too old, he had struck too many roots at home to be able to start a new life in a far-away land.

The new rulers certainly set out to use Strauss for their own publicity purposes. His seventieth birthday was celebrated in Dresden with a gala performance of *Rosenkavalier*. The award of the honorary citizenship of Dresden and the grant of honorary membership of the Dresden State Opera struck him as perfectly normal acts of recognition of his worldwide reputation. He should of course have recognized the award of the Eagle Shield of the German Reich as the writing on the wall. Strauss, basically apolitical as an individual, did his best to ignore events or make light of them in his inimitable way.

His relations with the Third Reich changed as he was working on a comedy, *Die schweigsame Frau* (The Silent Woman). The text was by Stefan Zweig, in whom Strauss thought he had discovered a possible replacement for Hofmannsthal. Quite undaunted, and with typical robust Bavarian energy, the composer intervened on behalf of his Jewish author and refused to recognize facts of which Zweig himself had long since been aware. The première of their joint work did take place, and Strauss succeeded, but only by using the full weight of his authority, in ensuring that Zweig's name appeared in the publicity. The Führer, however, demonstratively stayed away from the first night, and the opera disappeared from the repertory for the 'thousand years' which Hitler's régime was meant to endure.

A rash, careless letter to Stefan Zweig, an example of Strauss's infinite naïveté in such matters, was intercepted by the Gestapo and cost him the chairmanship of the *Reichsmusikkammer*. Strauss had fallen from favor, fortunately for him as it turned out, but his worldwide fame forced the authorities to feign support for the composer, so as to enable them to exploit his far-flung travels as a conductor in the interests of the Third Reich's cultural propaganda. The composer quietly put up with this, though not without some inner reservations.

Below: Gustav Klimt's 1907 painting of Danae, the mythological beauty loved by both Jupiter (who visited her as a shower of gold) and King Midas. This was the subject, nearly forty years on, that Strauss and his new librettist, Joseph Gregor, turned into the opera *Die Liebe der Danae.*

• A new librettist •

Strauss chose a Viennese musicologist, Joseph Gregor, a capable, well-read collaborator, but hardly a close partner, as the librettist for his next three operas: *Friedenstag* (Day of Peace), first performed on 24 July 1938; *Daphne*, first performed on 15 October 1938, and *Die Liebe*

der Danae (The Love of Danae), first performed posthumously on 14 August 1952, after it had failed to get beyond its dress rehearsal in 1944. The correspondence between them clearly shows how the intellectual relationship between librettist and composer, to which the audience had become accustomed in Hofmannsthal's time, had now been completely reversed. The mentor, stimulator and moving spirit was now Strauss, though it becomes clear from his correspondence with Gregor how much of his understanding of the stage Strauss owed to Hofmannsthal.

Hofmannsthal had once said to him: 'Let us produce mythological operas – they are the truest of all forms!' *Daphne*, written in 1936-7, actually carries on the lesson of *Ariadne*, the metamorphosis of the maiden who is loved by a god. Using Plutarch's version of the myth – in which Apollo has a rival for Daphne's love, Leukippos, whom he kills out of jealousy – Gregor gives the work an erotic dimension by making Daphne lament her chastity over Leukippos' dead body, regretting that she did not save her friend's life by yielding to the god. The myth has been humanized. Strauss later subtitled this opera a 'bucolic tragedy,' thus hinting at its ambiguous character.

Strauss knew how to guide his librettist so as to achieve a clear, transparent framework, which would also provide situations to inspire his music. His main concern in this work was with the statement of a basic problem implicit in the myth, the embodiment of nature in man. He therefore rejected all irrelevant side issues. Never before had he expressed his dramatic conception of a lyrical conclusion as clearly as in *Daphne*. All the characters who were needed to explain the earthly significance of the plot and give meaning to the emotional conflicts involved are in the end eliminated from the action. Only pure nature remains: the tree (the laurel into which Daphne has been transformed), the image of eternal life and eternal art, symbol of growth and decay, touched by the God of Light without whom life is unthinkable.

In this work Strauss combined the limpidity of *Ariadne* with the compact texture of a one-act drama. There are no distracting breaks, just smooth transitions and a single mood. Enchantment can occur only if the magic is not flawed. Despite the affinity with *Ariadne*, Strauss abandoned the chamber music orchestra in this case and worked with triple woodwind and brass, two harps, percussion, sixteen first and second violins, twelve violas, ten cellos, eight double basses, an organ and – on stage – an alpine horn! The *leitmotif* principle is preserved and the individual motifs are designed so as to interpenetrate. Personal and mood motifs can thus be fitted into each other seamlessly. *Daphne* is a paean to nature, pantheism personified in music, music born out of nature. Daphne herself appears as an allegory of the Aeolian harp when she has become unable to articulate verbally and can only vocalize her lament as a singing tree. Strauss achieved this transformation into unreality by the antithesis between F sharp major and F major, a wavering effect similar to that of

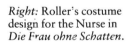

Right and below: Two of Roller's sets for *Die Frau ohne Schatten*: (*right*) the Empress's bedroom; (*below*) the falconer's house in the forest. The complexities of this fairytale work, loaded with symbolism, make it one of the most difficult of all operas to stage effectively.

Right: Roller's costume design for the Nurse in *Die Frau ohne Schatten*.

the silver rose notes in *Rosenkavalier*. In fact, the sound of nature, pictured as an impure sound, is produced here in a highly artificial way, not bitonally, but as the non-functional realization of suspended notes – sounding nature as such.

Transformation proceeds from the roots. It rises from the deep wind section, ripens into a fascinating ramification of colors in the growing tree, the branches of which resolve themselves into Daphne's plaintive sound. Here Strauss was no longer looking for new openings but merely stating what he had already established. *Daphne* is a retrospective score, once again confirming Strauss's familiar theme – transformation – on which so many of his great operas, from *Rosen-kavalier* and *Arabella* to *Ariadne, Die Frau ohne Schatten* and *Danae*, had been such splendid variations. Here Strauss is entirely himself.

'*Capriccio* shall be the end,' Strauss wrote on 15 September 1946 to Clemens Krauss, the great conductor who had at one time been his assistant in Vienna. Krauss prepared the text for this 'conversation piece with music,' which had its first performance at the Munich Staatsoper on 28 October 1942. The problems tackled by the composer were very remote from the questions of the day. He was increasingly cocooned in his own enclosed world of music. The idea of *Capriccio* had originally been suggested to him by Stefan Zweig after reading the libretto of an old opera by Salieri performed in the Orangerie at Schönbrunn in 1786, *Prima la musica e poi le parole* (First the music and then the words). Zweig suggested to Strauss that the fundamental old aesthetic problem of the relative importance of words and sound might be treated on the stage. In the twilight of his life the composer now returned to a question which had preoccupied him throughout its course, especially during his stimulating cooperation with Hugo von Hofmannsthal, a poet who had opposed the dominance of music with both restraint and determination. Now Strauss dismissed the listener in the *Capriccio* tutorial with a twinkle in his eye, by combining words and music in a sonnet which binds them indissolubly into a higher entity. *Capriccio* is a little opera for connoisseurs. Strauss deliberately addressed himself to the educated listener with well-developed taste, accustomed to take up subtle allusions, decipher quotations and correctly place finely shaded points. He swept his way through all the techniques available to an operatic composer, from unaccompanied dialogue, words spoken against the music, *secco* and *accompagnato* recitative, right up to the aria and ensemble. Yet it will not escape anybody's attention that Strauss concealed his true answer in the two-minute orchestral conclusion, a long symphonic afterthought in which his favorite instrument, the horn, is heard once again in a soloist's role: music for him stood above everything, and with this act of faith in it he wrote his private summary of a life that had been devoted to opera.

Below: The Munich National Theater, the old Hoftheater where Strauss had conducted opera since 1886, in ruins at the end of the Second World War. When it was bombed in 1943, Strauss described it as 'the greatest catastrophe of my life.'

•The late concertos •

While his symphonic works occupy a quite specific position in the development of Strauss's ouput (with the exception of the *Alpensinfonie* of 1915), his instrumental concertos provide a kind of framework for it. Between 1881 and 1885 – from the age of seventeen to twenty – the aspiring young composer wrote three Concertos: op.8 for Violin, op.11 for Horn and the *Burleske*, which can be regarded as a piano concerto in one movement. Then came an interval of no less than fifty-seven years before the Second Horn Concerto of 1942. This was followed in 1945 by the Concerto for Oboe and Small Orchestra and in 1947, two years before his death, by Strauss's last instrumental work, the Duet Concertino for Clarinet and Bassoon with string orchestra and harp.

The restrained virtuosity of the Second Horn Concerto marked a return to measured classicism. The beginning of the cadenza for the solo instrument, the harmonic texture with its chords suddenly broken in mid-flight, all bear Strauss's unmistakable signature. The main theme which arches out in a voluptuous E flat major fifth seems to have been derived from the 'Innsbruck Song' and thus bears witness to the composer's liking for rustic simplicity. The orchestra, which has a subordinate role as accompanist to the solo instrument, is pitched somewhat lower than is Strauss's habit, in order to match the horn. There is no trace of inward-looking, dark polyphony, but only gently fragrant relaxation instead. The concluding rondo, in particular, expresses the unconstrained joy of an old man who has given up all idle experimentation.

The Oboe Concerto, written in Switzerland in 1945, soon became popular all over the world. The movements dovetail into each other and are also thematically linked, and in contrast to classical models, the degree of virtuosity increases in the slow movement, in which the cadenza is placed. The concluding *vivace* section, set out as a rondo and influenced by pastoral melodies, clearly seems to point back in its figuration to the model of *Till* – or could these be allusions to *Capriccio*, written at about the same time?

The world was now growing lonelier around Richard Strauss. His native city of Munich was smashed to pieces by enemy aircraft, the house in which he was born destroyed. In a resigned mood, he wrote in a letter: 'I can only wait with faith in God until my blessed namesake and colleague calls me to join him in the heaven of the waltz.' In mid-February 1945 the Dresden Opera House, which had witnessed almost all of Strauss's first performances, was shattered into rubble and ashes. Only a few weeks later, in March, the Vienna Staatsoper was destroyed, another home of art closely connected with the composer's working life. At this time of deepest sorrow and shock, the indefatigable composer again reached for his notebook and recorded his anguish in a symphonic piece written from the heart. 'Trauer um München' (Mourning for Munich) is the title Strauss gave to the sketch with which he began his *Metamorphosen*, a 'Study for 23 Strings,' completed in Garmisch on 12 April 1945, only a few weeks before the final catastrophe. Without the splendid color of the wind sections, it is as though every touch of decoration has been stripped away. Metamorphosis, the transmutation of ideas, runs as a constant thread through the whole of Strauss's symphonic and dramatic output. It forms the real existential center of his creative approach. Strauss used seven themes in this composition, which are well related to each other contrapuntally. The second of them is closely connected with Beethoven's Funeral March from the 'Eroica' Symphony. Strauss at first ignores this connection, but when it obtrudes he relates the entire work to the Funeral March, the theme of which he quotes a few measures before the end, marking the passage in the score with the words 'In Memoriam.' *Metamorphosen* is a lonely meditation on the transience of things. The work, which bears the patina of refined maturity, is a late composition far removed from all the ironies of life and elevated by a sense of ineffable perfection.

• Orchestral technique •

In 1904 Strauss had published a new edition of Berlioz's famous *Manual of Orchestration*, revised in order to incorporate contemporary developments in the evolution of instrumentation technique, and provided with numerous educational notes for students. In 1915 he declared before the first performance of the *Alpensinfonie* that he had 'at last learnt orchestration.' Only a few years later, when he had completed the score of *Die Frau ohne Schatten* in 1917, he again announced that only now had the full range of possibilities provided by the art of orchestration become available to him. As an orchestrator Strauss never reached the end of the road; he kept on learning and trying out new effects.

Strauss had trained his musical perceptions with the aid of the scores of Richard Wagner, who had himself studied the scores of Berlioz and Meyerbeer for the refinements of their instrumental combinations. In his introduction to Berlioz's manual, Strauss recommended the advanced study of string quartet writing as a starting point for the acquisition of orchestral technique, and he laid special stress in this connection on the independent line to be imparted to the inner voices. Although he had condemned heavy orchestration as the death of words properly articulated on the operatic stage, he nevertheless taught that texture was the highest target of achievement for an orchestrator: '. . . It is only truly meaningful polyphonic texture which produces the greatest miracles of orchestral sound. A piece of orchestral writing that includes clumsy, or simply indifferently

Above: Strauss in the last years of his life.

conceived inner and lower voices will almost always have a certain harshness and will never yield the fullness of tone which radiates from a score in the performance of which the second wind players, the second violins, violas, cellos and double basses are equally enabled and inspired to take their share of a well-developed melodic line.'

Strauss used his, hugely enlarged, orchestral range to achieve color contrast rather than a massive sound or the generation of dynamic impact. He only very rarely made use of blocks of *tutti* in which all the instruments available at that point are actually brought in. His orchestral technique is far more concerned with a subtle selection of the tone color range and the unusual and novel use of single voices. Even now the refinements by means of which Strauss brought one instrument out of the shadow of another and then masked it again by yet a third have not been fully deciphered.

The most astonishing fact, however, is that the composer very seldom had to amend the sound he had conceived at his desk after hearing it performed. Any discussion of Strauss's orchestration in the technical literature on the subject usually tends to highlight his descriptive effects: the bleating of sheep or the water dripping from the stricken hero in *Don Quixote*; the effect of translucency and the falcon call in *Die Frau ohne Schatten*; the waterfall in the *Alpensinfonie*; the lighting of the candles in *Der Rosenkavalier*; the banging in the *Skat* game in *Intermezzo*; or the growling of the bear in *Arabella*. Strauss's scores are full of such illustrative cameos. But these are certainly not the things that matter most in his orchestration. He did not compose for the orchestra in the usual sense, but rather composed in orchestral color and used the orchestra as a single instrument, which he tuned as required. Tonal color as Strauss used it is not an overlay, a later application, but an integral part of the conception: it is an essential ingredient of the very process of composition.

Much more important than his external illustrations in sound – which he sometimes overdid out of sheer virtuosity, such as the clashing of instruments in *Don Quixote* or the rustling of the gold dust in *Josephs Legende* – is his ability fully to convey the atmosphere, the symbolic sound, by means of the orchestra at his disposal. There is no fundamental difference between the orchestra used for *Salome* and the rather smaller one of *Rosenkavalier*, but the composer always managed to attain the necessary, totally different-sounding working color. If Strauss is to be celebrated as the greatest orchestrator of his time, it is his ability, which had been beyond the reach of his forerunners, always to secure precisely the required, specific coloring, rather than any illustrative effects, which should be emphasized. He was certainly not afraid of using powerful sounds (in fact, after the première of *Salome* a critic wrote that he might as well in future use one of the new express locomotives), but he knew how to set harmony, sharp dissonance and noisy clashes into meaningful conjunction and use them with economy. He once wrote to Stefan Zweig that he simply would not compose for an orchestra of fewer than fifty players. In other words, the most subtle refinements demand the greatest resources. It was this experience that Strauss applied most carefully in the orchestration of his songs.

• The songs •

Strauss composed nearly two hundred songs. He later transcribed some of them for orchestra so as to be able to perform them with his wife on the many concert tours they undertook together. The period stretching from the 'Christmas Song,' which the six-year-old wrote as his first composition, to the *Vier letzte Lieder* (Four Last Songs), with which the eighty-four-year-old man ended his life as a composer in sorrowful retrospect, is spanned by an output that ranges widely, touching on many areas of expression and reflecting many kinds of mood, the product of his ever versatile genius. For Strauss the song represented a miniature form in which he elaborated and expanded earlier ideas and sometimes provided a background comment. Towards the end of his life he remarked that he now needed the word for inspiration, while the symphonic and purely musical element was a matter for the young.

Many of Strauss's songs were occasional works, in the best meaning of the expression, prompted by some particular event – his marriage, anniversaries, the birth of his son. They always fitted in between other works, and the source of the songs dried up when more important matters were in hand. At the start, his song output represented a counterweight to his orchestral compositions. Well over half of his songs were written before 1901. The work on *Salome* marks a clean break. Strauss wrote the six songs of his op.56 between 1903 and 1906

and then fell silent for twelve years. Only when he was compelled by legal action to honor a contract he had signed fifteen years earlier, in 1903, was his creative spirit released, despite the unfavorable circumstances. Twenty-nine songs followed in quick succession: 1918 might well be described as the 'Year of Song' in Strauss's life as a composer.

Strauss preferred syllabic treatment. He never skimped on detailed work, but he invariably allowed himself to be guided by the basic mood of a song. He worked from the general to the particular, but always preserved the mood. It was connection rather than contrast which marked his output. Strauss regarded a song as a small world in its own right, quite different from the operatic aria. An aria does not stand on its own, and the tension which runs through it integrates it into the work as a whole; a song, on the other hand, represents the complete achievement. If the effect aimed at has been missed at the start, the entire small work of art is disfigured. An unsuccessful aria means, at worst, but a scar on the body. Starting from this consideration, Strauss paid particular attention to the opening of a song; the work as a whole must reveal itself in essence in the very first measures of the piano introduction. He succeeded in producing several real 'hits' as part of his song output, including 'Traum durch die Dämmerung (Dream through the twilight), 'Ständchen' (Serenade) and 'Heimliche Aufforderung' (Secret invitation).

Below: Autograph score of *Metamorphosen*, a work for twenty-three solo strings, composed during the last weeks of the Second World War.

Left: Kokoschka's painting of Gstaad, 1967-8. The violently revolutionary character of the music of Strauss and the Expressionist painting of his younger contemporary Oskar Kokoschka before the First World War gave way in their later careers to a much more mellow style. Strauss's sumptuous *Four Last Songs* of 1948 – written at a time when Pierre Boulez, schooled by Messiaen in the tradition of Webern and the serialists, was producing his first compositions – look back to the lyric tradition of the late nineteenth century.

Above: Death mask of the eighty-five-year-old composer.

The 'Year of Song' was inaugurated by a cycle of a special kind, *Krämerspiegel* (Tradesman's Mirror), a devastating satire on music publishers. Strauss knew how to defend himself with his own weapons. When he was compelled by a court order to write a set of songs for Bote und Bock, he commissioned appropriate texts from the satirist and critic Alfred Kerr, thereby discharging his legal obligation – though not in the spirit intended by the publishers, who were furious and sought to ban the performance of the songs! This was the other side of Strauss, the lyricist – a jester with his cap and bells.

After 1918 the flow of songs stopped again. Apart from three Orchestral Hymns set to texts by Hölderlin, op.71, it did not resume until the five *Gesänge des Orients* (Songs of the Orient), op.77, of 1928. These were followed in 1929 by four *Gesänge nach Goethe-Texten* and in 1933 by three more songs, published as op.88, on texts by Goethe and Weinheber. But this black year brought his song writing to an end – the *Four Last Songs* belong to a different era, as a postscript, a memory. The eighty-four-year-old composer wrote his own apotheosis with these works for soprano and orchestra, which are a reminiscence of his own music-making with his wife. Once more he looked back on their life together, setting 'Frühling' (Spring), 'September,' 'Beim Schlafengehen' (As we go to sleep) by Hermann Hesse and 'Abendrot' (Sunset) by Eichendorff. Despite the restrained but jubilant mood of the first song, the cycle is touched with the sorrowful frost of late autumn. His faculties as acute as ever, Strauss reacted with great sensitivity to the stimulus of the poems' lyrical mood. The three Hesse songs are very tenderly linked by the appearance in the closing measures of a solo horn – his father's instrument, his own favorite, the instrument with which he sent the tempestuous Don Juan forth into life and with which he bade farewell to the operatic stage in the moonlight music of *Capriccio*. Strauss conveyed the 'closing of the eyes that had grown weary' in 'September' by means of exquisitely modulated phrasing. His masterly skill in melodic development is revealed by the spun-out violin solo with which the soul seems to float away in 'As we go to sleep,' not to mention the optimistic lift so sensitively treated at the end of this song.

What tremendous descending curves Strauss could still command, like those with which he introduced Eichendorff's 'Sunset' – 'the mature art of the beginning'! At the words in the poem 'We are weary of straying – could this be death?' Strauss wrote down, as he was reading, the main theme from *Tod und Verklärung*. Not resignation but happy, contented leave-taking flows from the moving harmony of this theme, as it rises from the last words of the song with which the composer recalls his youth, when he wrote so many of his finest songs for the clear soprano of his beloved wife. He did not round off the ending in the manner of a hymn, but instead humbly yielded to the friendly trilling of two larks who soar dreamily into the scented twilight in a *diminuendo* conclusion – the composer kept to his artistic credo even as he bade farewell.

Strauss died at ten minutes past two on the afternoon of 8 September 1949 in his villa at Garmisch. His wife, Pauline de Ahna, followed him the year after, on 13 May 1950.

Albert, Eugen d' (* Glasgow, 10 Apr. 1864; † Riga, Latvia, 3 Mar. 1932). German composer and pianist. D'Albert's origins were Italian, and he never felt himself to be British, but rather German, despite his birth and period of study in England. It was Liszt who foresaw his development as a brilliant pianist. In addition to music for his own instrument – including two concertos – d'Albert also composed a violin concerto, string quartets, songs, and several operas, of which *Tiefland* (1903), a rare example of German verism, is alone remembered.

Arensky, Anton Stepanovich (* Novgorod, 12 July 1861; † Terioki, Finland, 25 Feb. 1906). Russian composer, pianist and conductor. Arensky studied with Rimsky-Korsakov and at the age of twenty-one was appointed professor at the Moscow Conservatory, while he also established himself as a conductor. From 1894 to 1901 he was in charge of music at the Imperial Chapel in St Petersburg. In addition to three operas, a ballet and a cantata, *The Fountain of Bakhchisaray*, to words by Pushkin, Arensky composed two symphonies, a violin concerto and a *Fantasia on a Russian Folksong* with solo piano. His chamber music includes a piano quintet and a piano trio, while the second movement of his Second String Quartet – a set of variations on a children's song by Tchaikovsky – has proved to be his most enduring work, particularly in the version for string orchestra. He also wrote piano music and many songs.

Arensky's music shows the strong influence of Tchaikovsky – like him, Arensky remained aloof from musical nationalism, and although he used folk tunes, these never wholly penetrated his style.

Balakirev, Mily Alexeyevich (* Nizhni-Novgorod, 2 Jan. 1837; † St Petersburg, 29 May 1910). Russian composer. Although he showed exceptional musical promise, at the age of sixteen Balakirev enrolled as a student of mathematics at the University of Kazan, where he supplemented his limited finances by private teaching. He had acquired a reputation as an excellent pianist,

---

and by the age of eighteen had composed songs, piano music and a piano concerto. He then decided on a career in music, moving to St Petersburg, where he met Glinka, who became his mentor.

After Glinka's death in 1857, and despite the onset of a lifelong illness, Balakirev became a leading force in Russian music, dominating for a time a group of composers – Cui, Musorgsky, Borodin and Rimsky-Korsakov – who became known as the 'mighty handful.' In 1862 he took an active part in founding the Free School of Music in St Petersburg, in opposition to the Conservatory there, which was the stronghold of the pro-German group of composers and critics and had opened in the same year with Anton Rubinstein as its director. Balakirev succeeded Rubinstein as conductor of the Russian Musical Society in 1867 and became director of the Free School of Music the following year, although political intrigue combined with his egotistical behavior and militant stance on Russian music led him to relinquish the first post. In 1881 he was reappointed to the Free School, replacing Rimsky-Korsakov, with whom he directed music at the Imperial Chapel.

Granted a pension in 1894, Balakirev was able to devote himself to composition. His orchestral work includes two symphonies, two suites, and two piano concertos, but his major achievement lies in his piano pieces and songs. He also collected and edited many folksongs for publication and was a strong force in the rise of Russian musical nationalism.

Bendl, Karel (* Prague, 16 Apr. 1838; † Prague, 20 Sept. 1897). Czech composer and conductor. Like many Czech musicians, Bendl gained experience abroad, chiefly as an operatic conductor in Brussels and Amsterdam, but he returned to his homeland when the Czech national revival stimulated local artistic activity. His compositions – operas, songs

instrumental works and a ballet – draw on national subject-matter. In his opera *Svanda the Bagpiper*, Bendl's melodic gifts emerged in so original and distinguished a fashion that he must be regarded as one of the most important contributors to the repertory of Czech vocal music.

Bizet, Georges (* Paris, 25 Oct. 1838; † Bougival, nr. Paris, 3 June 1875). French composer. *See Volume II.*

Boëllmann, Léon (* Ensisheim, Haut-Rhin, 25 Sept. 1862; † Paris, 11 Oct. 1897). French organist and composer. Boëllmann studied with Gigout in Paris and became an accomplished organist, taking up various posts in the French capital, where he also acquired a reputation as a fine teacher and outspoken critic. He composed numerous sacred pieces, but his best-known composition is the *Suite gothique* for organ, while his *Variations symphoniques* for cello and orchestra have also remained in the repertoire.

Bordes, Charles (* Vouvray-sur-Loire, 12 May 1863; † Toulon, 8 Nov. 1909). French composer, choirmaster and musicologist. Bordes studied with Marmontel and Franck and from 1890 was director of music at the church of St Gervais in Paris, where he founded a notable choir. In 1889 he was commissioned by the

---

government to collect Basque folk music, and he later devoted much time to reviving music of the Renaissance and Baroque periods. He was a co-founder of the Schola Cantorum, also establishing a branch in Montpellier. Bordes composed an opera, church and choral music, but is principally remembered for his songs.

Borodin, Alexander Porfiryevich (* St Petersburg, 12 Nov. 1833; † St Petersburg, 27 Feb. 1887). Russian composer. *See pp.67-77.*

Brahms, Johannes (* Hamburg, 7 May 1833; † Vienna, 3 Apr. 1897). German composer. *See pp.183-209.*

Bruch, Max (* Cologne, 6 Jan. 1838; † Friedenau, nr. Berlin, 20 Oct. 1920). German composer. It was from his mother that Bruch inherited his musical gifts; she was an established singer and music-teacher who ensured that her son received sound musical instruction. He took lessons from Hiller and Reinecke, and by the age of fifteen had composed some seventy works, all of which he eventually discarded. His published op.1 is a comic opera to a text by Goethe, composed at the age of twenty.

Bruch traveled extensively in his native Germany, was director of the Liverpool Philharmonic Society in England between 1880 and 1883 and until 1890 of the orchestra at Breslau (Wrocław). From 1891 to 1910 he was director of composition at the Königliche Hochschule in Berlin. As a conductor, he had frequent opportunities of introducing his own music, the choral works being particularly well received in Germany, while in England and elsewhere it was the first of his three violin concertos – in G minor – his *Scottish Fantasy* for violin and orchestra and *Kol Nidrei* for cello and orchestra which achieved lasting popularity. Stimulus for the violin works came from Joseph Joachim.

Bruch's three symphonies, chamber music (with the occasional exception of some of the trios for clarinet, viola and piano), piano music, songs and vocal works with orchestra are

rarely heard today, although in recent years the concerto for clarinet and viola has enjoyed a revival, while his shorter pieces for violin and orchestra are also occasionally heard. Bruch lived well into the twentieth century but had little interest in modern musical developments.

Bruckner, Anton (* Ansfelden, nr. Linz, 4 Sept. 1824; † Vienna, 11 Oct. 1896). Austrian composer. *See pp.215-225.*

Bull, Ole (* Bergen, 5 Feb. 1810; † Lysøen, nr. Bergen, 17 Aug. 1880). Norwegian violinist and composer. Bull was one of the greatest violinists of the century, and of paramount significance for Norwegian music. After failing the entrance examination to university, he turned to music as a career, studying the violin technique of Paganini and taking up theory and composition as well. He made a series of tours abroad, including five to North America, playing his own music, written in popular national idiom. This did much to put Norway on the musical map, especially through his promotion of its folk music.

Busoni, Ferruccio (* Empoli, nr. Florence, 1 Apr. 1866; † Berlin, 27 July 1924). *See Volume IV.*

Chabrier, Emmanuel (* Ambert, Puy-de-Dôme, 18 Jan. 1841; † Paris, 13 Sep. 1894). French composer and pianist. Chabrier showed a prodigious ability as a pianist at a very young age but was persuaded by his parents to take a law degree and follow a career outside music. It was not until 1880, after hearing Wagner's *Tristan und Isolde* in Munich, that he resigned from his government post to devote himself full-time to music.

Meanwhile, he had continued to study composition and pursued an interest in painting and poetry (his friendship with Verlaine led to two unfinished operatic projects). His gifts as a pianist gave him entry to the Paris salons where he formed friendships with Fauré, Duparc, Chausson and d'Indy, becoming one of the leading French Wagnerians.

Wagner's influence, particularly in Chabrier's use of the *leitmotif*, is clearly evident in his opera *Gwendoline* (1886), while his only other completed opera, *Le Roi malgré lui*, successfully produced at the Opéra Comique in 1887, displays his flair for comic characterization and elegant melodic style. Only his *España* rhapsody of 1883 is frequently played today.

Chabrier had a strong influence on many of his younger contemporaries, including Fauré, Debussy, Satie, Ravel and the composers of Les Six.

Chausson, Ernest (* Paris, 20 Jan. 1855; † Limay, nr. Mantes, Yvelines, 10 June 1899). French composer. Chausson did not devote himself to composition until he was twenty-one, having previously studied law.

His first teacher at the Paris Conservatoire, which he entered in 1879, was Massenet, but he soon transferred his allegiance to Franck, with whom he studied for three years and who remained a dominating influence on his music. Private means enabled him to concentrate on composition, but because of his self-critical attitude, the number of his completed works is small. At the time of his death, as the result of a bicycle accident, he was working on a string quartet, and there are signs that his musical personality was reaching maturity. Wagner exerted a potent influence on his music, which is characterized by rich chromatic harmony and sensuous melody; Debussy, whom he helped and befriended in the younger composer's early days, also gave him encouragement and advice.

Chausson's compositions include two choral works with orchestra and some sacred music, as well as thirty or so songs, written at intervals throughout his brief creative life, which contain some of his most attractive music. His opera *Le Roi Arthus*, to his own libretto, preoccupied him during the last years of his life, but despite his determination to shake off the Wagnerian influence, the opera remains heavily indebted to *Tristan und Isolde*. His B flat Symphony also cost him much effort and soul-searching, and though redolent of Franck it has

an impressive breadth and richness of scoring. His most successful orchestral composition is, however, undoubtedly the *Poème* for violin (1896). Chausson also wrote four instrumental works – a piano trio, a piano quartet, the incomplete string quartet and the Concerto in D for piano, violin and string quartet, op.21, of 1891 – as well as a handful of piano pieces.

Cornelius, Peter (* Mainz, 24 Dec. 1824; † Mainz, 26 Oct. 1874). German composer and poet. *See Volume II.*

Cui, César Antonovich (* Vilnius, Lithuania, 18 Jan. 1835; † Petrograd, 26 Mar. 1918). Russian composer and critic. Cui was the Russian offspring of a French officer who settled in Poland after Napoleon's defeat in 1812. Despite his obvious musical talents, he graduated in St Petersburg as a military engineer. After meeting Balakirev in 1856, he devoted himself to music, determined to further the cause of Russian music and becoming a member of the 'mighty handful,' while continuing his career as a writer on military matters. From the age of thirty he acquired a reputation as a music critic, strongly attacking the taste for Italian opera prevalent in Russia at the time. His works for the stage were hailed by his own circle as landmarks in the history of Russian opera; none of his nine operas, however, embodied the theories that he preached in his journalism, for his light, lyrical style and use of texts of French origin betrayed the influence of his French background.

For all his trenchant attacks on the conservative state of music in Russia, Cui's own music remained just that. His most attractive work is to be found among his numerous short piano pieces and songs.

Dargomyzhsky, Alexander Sergeyevich (* Troitskoye, Tula district, 14 Feb. 1813; † St Petersburg, 17 Jan. 1869). Russian composer. With Glinka, Dargomyzhsky established a tradition of national opera based on folksong and seeking dramatic truth rather than fanciful,

decorative entertainment. He was born into a rich landed family and as a child showed talent on both violin and piano, but he then entered government service and treated music as an amateur pursuit. His songs and piano playing earned him admiration in the fashionable salons, but it was only in 1833, when he met Glinka, that he decided to devote his life to music. He had no formal lessons in composition, but was able to study the exercise books on harmony that Glinka had completed for his teacher Dehn in Berlin.

Dargomyzhsky was not a prolific composer. His chief works consist of six operas, two of which were left incomplete, three orchestral fantasies and nearly one hundred songs, many of them of great beauty. It was Glinka's friendship and influence that inspired him to write his first opera, *Esmeralda*, based on Victor Hugo's *Notre-Dame de Paris*, but the music was composed in the outmoded tradition of French grand opera. In 1843 he resigned from the civil service and, after traveling abroad, he began to study Russian folksong. This bore fruit in his third opera, *Rusalka* (1855), to a libretto by Pushkin, which introduced his novel approach to melodic recitative, through which he managed to convey a remarkable range of emotional expression. This was taken to its extreme in his *magnum opus, The Stone Guest*, based on Pushkin's version of the Don Juan legend, which was completed after his death by Cui and Rimsky-Korsakov and which exerted a profound influence on the course of Russian opera.

Delibes, Léo (* St-Germain-du-Val, Sarthe, 21 Feb. 1836; † Paris, 16 Jan. 1891). French composer. After studying at the Paris Conservatoire, Delibes worked as organist at various churches in the French capital and as accompanist at the Théâtre Lyrique, and it was with music for the theatre that he made his reputation. After writing a succession of operettas for Offenbach's Bouffes-Parisiens, at the age of twenty-eight Delibes joined the staff of the Opéra, also working for a time as inspector of music in schools. The ballet *La Source* (1866), which he wrote in collaboration with Minkus, led to the commissioning of a 'Pas des Fleurs' for a ballet by his former teacher Adam; this in turn gave rise to his first great ballet, *Coppélia* (1870), which was followed six years later by *Sylvia*.

Delibes also wrote operas, the most successful of which were *Le Roi l'a dit* (1873) and *Lakmé* (1883). His incidental music – a set of dances 'dans le style ancien' – for Hugo's play *Le Roi s'amuse* is still popular today.

Draeseke, Felix (* Coburg, 7 Oct. 1835; † Dresden, 26 Feb. 1913). German composer and teacher. Draeseke studied at the Leipzig Conservatory under Julius Rietz, who later took him on as a private pupil. He developed fast as a composer, his orchestral works from the start showing the influence of Liszt, and by 1856 performances of his first symphony were being given. In the following year he met Liszt and allied himself with the 'New German School.' Soon afterwards he composed his first symphonic poems, which with his Piano Sonata, op.6, and some of his smaller piano pieces are his most interesting compositions.

Dubois, Théodore (* Rosnay, Marne, 24 Aug. 1837; † Paris, 11 June 1924). French composer, teacher and organist. Dubois studied at the Paris Conservatoire under Thomas and Benoist (organ), and from 1855 to 1861 he held organ posts in Paris. In 1861 he won the Prix de Rome. Between 1863 and 1877 he was choirmaster first at Ste Clotilde, where Franck was organist, then at the Madeleine, where he himself was appointed to the organist's post. From 1871 to 1905 he was also on the staff of the Conservatoire,

first as professor of harmony, then of composition, finally as its director. His involvement in 'l'affaire Ravel' in 1905, in which the brilliant young composer was excluded from the final round of the Prix de Rome competition, precipitated his resignation.

Dubois was an industrious composer, particularly of music for the stage, writing successful ballets (following the example of Delibes) and light opera. He also composed a substantial quantity of orchestral, religious and chamber music.

Dubois's most important and enduring contribution is probably his theoretical teaching material, which was much used in French conservatoires. As a performer and composer of organ music, he may be regarded as one of the founders of the nineteenth-century French organ school, which developed as a direct result of the new 'orchestral' organs built by Aristide Cavaillé-Coll and through the influence of Franck.

Duparc, Henri (* Paris, 21 Jan. 1848; † Mont-de-Marsan, Landes, 12 Feb. 1933). French composer. A handful of songs forms the basis of Duparc's reputation; a perfectionist as far as his own work was concerned, he destroyed manuscripts of several early compositions, and apart from the songs only a symphonic poem, *Lénore*, an orchestral nocturne and a group of five *Feuilles volantes* for piano survive. The songs cover a period from his twentieth to his thirty-sixth year; thereafter he became a recluse, living in Switzerland and composing no further music.

Musical talent did not manifest itself until Duparc started piano lessons as a young man with César Franck, with whom he also studied composition. Sensitive to the influences of the German *Lied*, of Wagner, and of Franck himself, Duparc, with his sensuously chromatic style, brought to the song a profound expressiveness and 'penetrating nostalgia' which ensure him a lasting place in recital programs. His songs (some of which he later orchestrated) include settings of poems by Baudelaire, Leconte de Lisle, Gautier, Sully-Prudhomme, Lahor and Goethe.

Dvořák, Antonín (* Nelahozeves, Bohemia, 8 Sept. 1841; † Prague, 1 May 1904). Czech composer. See pp.247-257.

Erkel, Ferenc (* Gyula, 7 Nov. 1810; † Budapest, 15 June 1893). Hungarian composer, pianist and conductor. The most important of a large family of musicians, Ferenc Erkel received his first musical instruction from his father. By the time he was twelve, his talent as a pianist was recognized and he was sent to Pozsony (Bratislava) to continue his studies under Károly Turányi.

In 1827 he became music master to the household of Count Kálmán Csáky for a period of seven years; this was followed by several other short-lived positions before his appointment as musical director of the National Theater in Pest, after which he devoted himself to becoming the first composer of true Hungarian opera.

In 1840 the first of Erkel's ten operas, *Bátori Mária*, established him in the forefront of Hungarian composers. His next, *Hunyadi László* (1844), brought him even greater success, since its music reflected the prevailing sense of national fervor and generated the most passionate response from his audiences. Shortly afterwards, his *Hymnusz* became the Hungarian national anthem, making him a national hero.

Erkel composed a further eight operas, of which *Bánk bán* (first performed 1861) and *Brankovics György* (1868-72) are the most important, the music of the latter presaging several works of the twentieth century. His music is still performed in Hungary, and his endeavor undoubtedly made possible the achievement of later Hungarian nationalist composers.

Fibich, Zdeněk (* Všebořice, Bohemia, 21 Dec. 1850; † Prague, 15 Oct. 1900). After Smetana and Dvořák, Fibich was the most prominent Czech composer of the second half of the nineteenth century. For a short time he held posts as conductor at the Prague Provisional Theater and at the Russian Orthodox Church there, but at the age of thirty he chose the freedom of an independent composer's life. He was much more imbued with the ideals of the German Romantics than

either Smetana or Dvořák and had little enthusiasm for the Czech national music school. His compositions, which include three symphonies as well as symphonic poems, operas, melodramas and chamber works, lack the strong rhythms of folk music and are characterized by a gently lyrical melodic approach. Most remarkable are *Moods, impressions and reminiscences*, a collection of 376 piano pieces which make up a musical diary of his passionate love for a young pupil.

Foster, Stephen Collins (* Lawrenceville, Pittsburgh, 4 July 1826; † New York, 13 Jan. 1864). American composer of popular and minstrel songs. A self-taught musician, Foster worked as a bookkeeper for his brother until he was able to launch himself as a successful professional songwriter. An agreement with the Christy Minstrels in 1850 gave them exclusive rights to the first performance of every song he wrote. The next year saw his most successful song, 'Old Folks at Home,' and others achieved such popularity that they soon became almost folksongs. Despite his success, Foster died in poverty.

Franck, César Auguste (* Liège, 10 Dec. 1822; † Paris, 8 Nov. 1890). Franco-Belgian composer and teacher. See pp.111-121.

Franz, Robert (* Halle, 28 June 1815; † Halle, 24 Oct. 1892). German organist and composer. Against the wishes of his parents, Franz studied music from the age of twenty. He subsequently worked as a teacher and organist in Halle, but by the age of fifty-two had become almost totally deaf and was forced to resign his posts. Through the generous support of Liszt, Joachim and others, a fund was established which saved him from penury. He was able to continue working on the editing and arranging of the music of Bach and on his own songs, and his reputation as a song-writer spread throughout Germany.

Apart from some religious choral pieces, the bulk of his work consists of some 44 sets of songs (over 250 in all), which prolong the tradition of Beethoven,

Schubert and Schumann. Many are settings of poems by Heine which echo the strophic, folksong idiom of the texts, so that their range, though Romantically expressive and lyrical, remains somewhat limited.

Fuchs, Robert (* Frauenthal, Styria, 15 Feb. 1847; † Vienna, 19 Feb. 1927). Austrian composer, teacher, organist and conductor. Court organist in Vienna, Fuchs left an impressive number of compositions of the most varied kinds, including two operas. However, his real importance lies in his teaching as Professor of Theory at the Vienna Conservatory, where Wolf, Mahler, Schreker and Zemlinsky were among his pupils.

Gade, Niels (* Copenhagen, 22 Feb. 1817; † Copenhagen, 21 Dec. 1890). Danish composer, conductor, violinist, educator and administrator. A figure of great importance in the history of his country's music, Gade combined in his compositions the first signs of nationalism in Scandinavian music with the best influences of Mendelssohn and Schumann, gained from his time working in Germany, first as assistant to Mendelssohn at the Leipzig Gewandhaus and later as its principal conductor.

On the death of Mendelssohn in 1847, Gade assumed the directorship of the Gewandhaus but returned to Denmark the following year. In 1850 he was appointed conductor of the Copenhagen Musical Society, which he raised to a new level of excellence, introducing the works of his contemporaries – Schumann, Berlioz, Liszt and Wagner among

them – to Danish audiences. Gade continued to compose to the last year of his life. Eight symphonies in all, several overtures and marches, a large corpus of choral music, and chamber and instrumental works make up his output. A late string quartet in D is outstanding and, with the best of his symphonies and piano music, deserves to be more widely known.

Gevaert, François-Auguste (* Huysse, nr. Oudenaarde, 31 July 1828; † Brussels, 24 Dec. 1908). Belgian musicologist, teacher and composer. Gevaert showed exceptional promise in his youth, at the age of nineteen winning two competitions, the second of which was the Belgian Prix de Rome. Two years later, he left Belgium, visiting France, Spain, Italy and Germany before settling in Paris. There most of the stage works which established his reputation were produced, and at the age of thirty-nine he was made director of the Paris Opéra.

In 1870 he returned to Belgium, becoming director of the Brussels Conservatoire and devoting much of his time to scholarly research into vocal music of the seventeenth and eighteenth centuries. He also published books on orchestration, harmony, and general musical theory.

His most successful stage works were *Georgette, ou le Moulin de Fontenoy* and *Le Billet de Marguerite*. His Requiem represents his most important contribution to sacred music.

Glazunov, Alexander Konstantinovich (* St Petersburg, 10 Aug. 1865; † Paris, 21 Mar. 1936). Russian composer. Glazunov's precocious talents were noticed by Balakirev, and he was encouraged to take lessons with Rimsky-Korsakov, whose star pupil he became. At the age of seventeen, his first symphony, performed by both Balakirev and Rimsky-Korsakov, attracted the attention of the music publisher Belyayev, and of Liszt, who conducted it in Weimar. By the age of twenty, Glazunov had composed a dozen or so major works, and his fame spread rapidly through Europe. Until he

was forty he was a tireless and prolific composer. his music showing affinities with the nationalist school. although his somewhat conservative style precludes any pronounced Russian idiom. He collected examples of folk music from Russia, Hungary, Spain and the East, and his early music was frequently colored with orientalism, although Liszt, Tchaikovsky, Rimsky-Korsakov and Borodin were the main influences on his work as a whole.

The majority of his compositions, which include eight symphonies, two piano concertos, a *Concerto-ballata* for cello, various orchestral suites and numerous chamber works, are instrumental, with only a few songs and piano pieces. He was also a skilled orchestrator, completing and orchestrating some of Borodin's *Prince Igor* and orchestrating a number of pieces by Arensky, Chopin, Liszt, Schumann, Tchaikovsky and others. Three of his compositions have remained very popular – the ballet music for *Raymonda* and *The Seasons* and his A minor Violin Concerto, written in 1904.

Glazunov had a long and influential teaching career, becoming a professor at the St Petersburg Conservatory in 1899 and six years later its director. His increasing tendency towards a more abstract, less programmatic style did not prevent the post-Revolution Russian government from conferring on him the title of 'People's Artist of the Republic'; however, he composed relatively little after 1917, and he left Russia in 1928, dying in Paris.

Glinka, Mikhail Ivanovich (* Novospasskoye [now Glinka], nr. Smolensk, 1 June 1804; † Berlin, 15 Feb. 1857). Russian composer. After an unconventional education, Glinka resisted family pressure to enter the foreign service and became a musical dilettante in St Petersburg. There he associated with Pushkin and other writers, and in the rich cultural life of the city he found the models for his earliest works, although the elements he used were French, German and Italian

and there is little evidence of the nationalistic features which were later to win him the title of father of the nineteenth-century Russian nationalist school.

In 1830, Glinka left Russia for Italy, where he was to stay for three years, meeting Bellini and Donizetti. On his way back he undertook five months of formal tuition with Siegfried Dehn in Berlin – the only systematic study of composition he made.

Glinka's first opera *Ivan Susanin* (the title of which was changed to *A Life for the Tsar* for its first performance in 1836, after the Tsar had shown interest in the work) was received rapturously, and in 1837 Glinka was appointed director of the Imperial Chapel. His second opera, *Ruslan and Lyudmila*, completed in 1842, by which time Glinka had resigned his post and been involved in considerable matrimonial and amorous upheavals, was received coolly, and he set out for Paris, where he was befriended by Berlioz, in June 1844, moving to Spain in May 1845. Time spent in Warsaw in 1848 and 1849 brought him under the influence of Chopin's music, and there was a further stay in Paris in 1853-4.

As he grew older, Glinka's compositional powers failed. In May 1856 he set off to study again with Dehn in Berlin, but died there a few months later.

Godard, Benjamin (* Paris, 18 Aug. 1849; † Cannes, 10 Jan. 1895). French composer and violinist. Godard entered the Paris Conservatoire at the age of fourteen, studying with Vieuxtemps, and began his career as a composer with chamber works, piano pieces and songs. From 1887 he was himself a professor at the Conservatoire. Godard's compositions include operas, the most successful of which was *La Vivandière* (1895, with orchestration completed by Paul Vidal), though it is by the 'Berceuse' from *Jocelyn* (1888) that he is best remembered. He also wrote orchestral music – including several programmatic symphonies, two violin concertos and two piano concertos – and chamber music – including string quartets and five sonatas for violin and piano.

Goetz, Hermann (* Königsberg [Kaliningrad], 7 Dec. 1840; † Hottingen, nr. Zürich, 3 Dec. 1876). German composer and pianist. Although he showed an early aptitude for music, Goetz did not study it seriously until he was seventeen. From 1860 to 1862, he studied composition and piano at the Stern Conservatory in Berlin with Ulrich and von Bülow, who became his lifelong friend and supporter.

Goetz started performing in public at eighteen and succeeded Theodor Kirchner as organist at Winterthur. His first opera, *The Taming of the Shrew* (1872), was a major success throughout Germany, while his Symphony in F, op.9, was once considered the finest work in the form since Beethoven. Other noteworthy compositions include the Piano Concerto in B flat, the Violin Concerto in G, and several chamber works, most notably the Piano Trio in G minor, the Piano Quartet in E, and the Piano Quintet (with double bass) in C minor.

Goldmark, Karl (* Keszthely, 18 May 1830; † Vienna, 2 Jan. 1915). Hungarian composer. Despite lack of money, and, consequently, any thorough musical training, Goldmark was admitted to the Vienna Conservatory at the age of seventeen to study violin and composition. He later studied for two years in Budapest, returning to Vienna at the age of thirty and establishing himself as a teacher of piano and a composer of some repute, concerts of his own works in Vienna and Budapest attracting a good deal of attention.

Wagner and Mendelssohn were the chief influences on Goldmark's work. His best-known compositions are his 'Rustic Wedding' Symphony and Violin Concerto in A minor, although it was his operas, and in particular the first, *The Queen of Sheba*, which were most successful in his lifetime. Other works include a number of choral pieces and chamber music.

Gottschalk, Louis Moreau (* New Orleans, 8 May, 1829; † Tijuca, Brazil, 18 Dec. 1869). American composer and pianist. The first American composer of any importance, Gottschalk made his name as a virtuoso pianist, composing almost all his music for his own instrument. The son of a successful businessman, he went to the best local teachers and when barely in his teens was sent to Paris to study seriously. He was refused even an interview at the Conservatoire, the belief being that an American could not be musical, and instead studied privately under Hallé and Maleden, with Saint-Saëns and Bizet as fellow pupils. He did, however, make influential friends in Paris and was soon accepted and helped by both Berlioz and Chopin. Gottschalk became a favorite of the French salons, particularly for his playing of his own compositions in a Creole style, noteworthy for their novel melody and rhythm.

His compositions include operas, symphonies and works for piano and orchestra, but the majority are virtuoso piano pieces – many of a rare vulgarity, especially when he emulated the European style. However, he was unquestionably the first American composer of importance, and his American- and Creole-inspired works are of genuine worth.

Gounod, Charles (* Paris, 18 June 1818; † Saint-Cloud, nr. Paris, 18 Oct. 1893). *See Volume II.*

Grieg, Edvard (* Bergen, 15 June 1843; † Bergen, 4 Sept. 1907). Norwegian composer, pianist and conductor. *See pp.106-9.*

Guilmant, Alexandre (* Boulogne-sur-Mer, 12 Mar. 1837; † Meudon, nr. Paris, 29 Mar. 1911). French organist, composer and editor. The son of an organist, Guilmant is regarded as one of the fathers of the modern French organ school. He rapidly acquired mastery of the instrument and a reputation as performer and teacher. In 1871 he became organist of the Trinité church in Paris, a post he held for the next thirty years. He undertook extensive and highly successful tours of Europe and the United States, and his influence spread still further when he became professor of organ at the

Schola Cantorum, which he had co-founded with Charles Bordes and Vincent d'Indy in 1894. Two years later he took over from Widor as professor of organ at the Conservatoire.

Guilmant composed a large amount of organ music and some sacred music, as well as editing organ music by earlier, neglected French and foreign composers.

Guiraud, Ernest (* New Orleans, 23 June 1837; † Paris, 6 May 1892). French composer. Guiraud settled in Paris in his youth, studying at the Conservatoire, where, in 1859, he won the Prix de Rome. He subsequently became professor of harmony and accompaniment (1876) and then professor of composition (1880).

He is best remembered for his work on Bizet's *Carmen*, for which he composed recitatives, and on Offenbach's *Tales of Hoffmann*, the orchestration of which he completed for its première in 1881, but he was also the author of an important book on orchestration and was the teacher of Dukas and Debussy.

Guiraud wrote several operas, as well as the ballet *Gretna Green*, orchestral suites and a caprice for violin and orchestra.

Halvorsen, Johan (* Drammen, 15 Mar. 1864; † Oslo, 4 Dec. 1935). Norwegian violinist and composer. Halvorsen studied at the Stockholm Conservatory, and then in Leipzig, Berlin and Liège. He was appointed conductor of the theater at Bergen in 1892, and of the National Theater in Christiania in 1899, a post he retained until 1929. His own compositions follow the Romantic national tradition of Grieg and Svendsen, but Halvorsen brought to them his own distinctive flair for brilliant orchestration.

Hartmann, Johann Peter (* Copenhagen, 14 May 1805; † Copenhagen, 10 Mar. 1900). Danish composer and organist. The son of an organist and grandson of a distinguished German court musician, Hartmann received his early musical training from his father, becoming organist and teacher in Copenhagen while still a young man. He also graduated in law, combining government work with an active career as organist, composer, conductor and teacher.

Hartmann was a prolific composer in all genres, but his main achievements were in the theater. His opera *The Raven* (libretto by Hans Christian Andersen) attracted praise from Schumann, while *Little Christine*, another collaboration with Andersen, is generally regarded as his most successful composition. He provided incidental music for some sixteen plays, and his music for Bournonville's ballets resulted in a long and celebrated partnership. Also popular were his many biblical and national songs and choral pieces.

Drawing on the wealth of Scandinavian mythology, Hartmann became an influential and popular figure, regarded by many – including Grieg – as the father of Scandinavian music. He also became joint director with Gade (who became his son-in-law) of the new Conservatory in Copenhagen.

Henselt, Adolf von (* Schwabach, nr. Nuremberg, 9 May 1814; † Warmbrunn [Cieplice Sl. Zdroj], Silesia, 10 Oct. 1889). *See Volume II.*

Humperdinck, Engelbert (* Siegburg, nr. Bonn, 1 Sept. 1854; † Neustrelitz, Mecklenburg, 27 Sept. 1921). German composer and teacher. Humperdinck first studied composition in Cologne with Hiller, then in Munich with Lachner and Rheinberger. In 1880, while in Italy, he met Wagner, with whom he worked at Bayreuth during the next two years. He then held various teaching posts, first in Barcelona, then in Cologne, Frankfurt and Berlin, and for a time was music critic of the *Frankfurter Zeitung*.

Humperdinck's opera *Hänsel und Gretel*, which received its first performance under the baton of Richard Strauss in 1893, was immediately successful and has retained its international popularity. None of the six operas he composed subsequently achieved any lasting success, nor have his choral works (among them two ballades for chorus and orchestra), his vocal music (five songs for voice and orchestra, and a song cycle *Junge Lieder*), his orchestral pieces (*Humoreske* and *Die Maurische Rhapsodie*) or the String Quartet found a lasting place in the repertory. Humperdinck also wrote a quantity of incidental music for the theater, principally for productions by Max Reinhardt of Shakespeare's plays.

Indy, Vincent d' (* Paris, 27 Mar. 1851; † Paris, 2 Dec. 1931). French composer, teacher and writer on music. D'Indy's early talent for music was encouraged by piano and harmony lessons, and at the age of twenty he came into contact with César Franck, whose composition classes he attended, while also studying the organ and embarking on a career as a conductor in the provinces. Franck's sense of form and use of cyclic techniques were to exercise a decisive influence on his style, and, with Duparc and Chausson, he became one of the 'bande à Franck,' being active in the foundation of the Société Nationale de Musique – whose motto was 'Ars Gallica.' A tour of Germany, followed by a visit to Bayreuth, made a profound

impression on him, and his subsequent career may be summarized as an attempt to reconcile French and German musical philosophies.

D'Indy divided his energy between composition and administration, in addition to conducting and becoming head of the Schola Cantorum, of which he was also a co-founder. His art is at its most refined in his chamber music – which includes three string quartets, a string sextet, a piano quintet, and the *Chansons et danses* for wind – as well as in certain works on a larger scale, such as the symphonic variations *Istar*, the popular 'Symphony on a French Mountain Theme' and the operas *Fervaal* and *L'Etranger*.

He continued to compose well into the twentieth century, and of these works the orchestral *Jour d'été à la montagne* (1905) and the *Diptyque méditerranéen* (1925-6) are among several in which d'Indy responded to the innovations of Debussy and his followers.

Ippolitov-Ivanov, Mikhail Mikhailovich (* Gatchina, nr. St Petersburg, 19 Nov. 1859; † Moscow, 28 Jan. 1935). Russian composer, teacher and conductor. Ippolitov-Ivanov studied under Rimsky-Korsakov at the St Petersburg Conservatory, later becoming director of the Music School and Opera at Tbilisi. He was associated with the Moscow Conservatory from 1893 until his death, as professor, and, for a time, as director. After the Revolution he became director and conductor at the Opera in Moscow, writing music which satisfied the country's new leaders. In 1924 and 1925 he was asked to supervise the reorganization of the Conservatory at Tbilisi.

Throughout his career Ippolitov-Ivanov was an energetic and influential teacher, administrator and conductor, as well as a prolific composer. Musically he adhered to a conservative, Russian-Romantic style, influenced not only by Tchaikovsky and Rimsky-Korsakov, but also by folk music, especially that of Georgia. Among his most successful works are the *Caucasian Sketches*, *Iveriya* and

Armenian Rhapsody for orchestra, while the catalogue of his compositions also includes several tone-poems on Russian subjects, a symphony, six operas, two string quartets, a piano quintet, songs and a quantity of liturgical and choral music.

Jensen, Adolph (* Königsberg [Kaliningrad], 12 Jan. 1837; † Baden-Baden, 23 Jan. 1879). German composer. Jensen was a child prodigy, who had composed sonatas, overtures, chamber music and songs by the time he was fifteen. Before his twentieth birthday, he was earning his living as a piano teacher in Russia and, shortly afterwards, began traveling around Europe in search of an appointment, which he did not find until 1866, when Tausig made him a professor of piano at his piano school in Berlin.

Jensen was a fluent composer, whose main source of influence was Schumann, particularly in his many collections of miniature piano pieces. His most successful works include a Piano Sonata in F sharp minor and the seven pieces called *Erotikon*, op.44, as well as some fine songs.

Joachim, Joseph (* Kittsee [Köpcsény], nr. Bratislava, 28 June 1831; † Berlin, 15 Aug. 1907). Austro-Hungarian violinist, composer, conductor and teacher. Joachim studied under Serwaczyński from the age of six, and at the age of eight was sent to Vienna to complete his studies. Following a triumphant public début in 1843 in Leipzig, Mendelssohn took an interest in his career and was instrumental in his visiting London, where he performed in 1844. In 1850, as Konzertmeister under Liszt of the Grand Duke's orchestra at Weimar, he came into brief contact with the 'New German' circle, but he later shifted his allegiance to Brahms. In 1852 he was appointed solo violinist and conductor to the King of Hanover, and he became director of the Music School in that city. In 1868 he moved to Berlin as director of the newly founded High School for Practical Music.

Joachim was prized not only as a soloist, but also as a chamber music player – founding the Joachim String Quartet, one of

the first regular chamber groups, in 1869. Their interpretations of Beethoven's late string quartets were regarded as a landmark.

As a composer, Joachim wrote some twenty works, which are characterized by a marked seriousness of approach, the best known being the 'Hungarian' Concerto for violin, op.11.

Kàan, Jindřich z Albestů (* Ternopol, Galicia [now Ukraine], 29 May 1852; † Roudná, Tábor district, Bohemia, 7 Mar. 1926). Czech teacher, administrator, pianist and composer. Kàan accompanied Dvořák to London in 1884, took over a piano professorship at the Prague Conservatory in 1889, and became its director in 1907. As well as being a pianist of note, he was also a composer of operas and instrumental works. His *Bajaja* was the first great Czech ballet.

Kalinnikov, Vasily Sergeyevich (* Voina, Oryol district, 13 Jan. 1866; † Yalta, Crimea, 11 Jan. 1901). Russian composer. Kalinnikov's early years in Moscow were dogged by poverty, and he earned his living as a violinist and bassoonist in various Moscow theaters. In 1892, on Tchaikovsky's recommendation, he was appointed assistant Opera conductor, but the illness which was to bring about his early death forced him to resign.

Kalinnikov's aim as a composer was to create a national idiom. He was an accomplished craftsman, with a gift for vigorous, colorful scoring and charming, lyrical melody. His First Symphony, completed in 1895, was enthusiastically received and was followed two years later by a Second. His other works include a suite, overtures and a symphonic poem for orchestra; incidental music; an opera, *In 1812*, which shows the influence of Musorgsky; piano music; choruses and church music; songs; and two Miniatures for string quartet and obbligato double-bass.

Kjerulf, Halfdan (* Christiania [Oslo], 17 Sept. 1815; † Christiania, 11 Aug. 1868). Norwegian composer and piano teacher. Kjerulf came late to the serious study of music, qualifying initially in law. In 1840, following the death of his father, he turned to piano-teaching and journalism in order to support his family, also undertaking conducting engagements. A state grant enabled him to visit Copenhagen, where he met Gade and Hartmann, and then Leipzig, where he had lessons with E. F. Richter. At the age of thirty-six he returned to Norway, acquiring, despite poor health, a national reputation as conductor, piano-teacher and composer. Among his particular achievements were the foundation of a choral tradition – he composed some 30 pieces for

male-voice choir – and the organization of Norway's first symphony concerts (1857-9).

Although his earliest compositions date from 1841, it was not until 1853, when Lindeman published his first collection of Norwegian folk tunes, that folk melody and rhythm consciously became the foundation of his style. In 1861 he published 'Twenty-five Selected Norwegian Folk Dances' for piano, and another forty-five appeared over the next few years. The lyrical, chromatic style of his original piano pieces and 200 songs had an unmistakable influence on the music of Grieg.

Klenovsky, Nikolai Semionovich (* Odessa, 1857; † Petrograd, 6 July 1915). Russian conductor and composer. Most of Klenovsky's compositions remain unpublished and unplayed, although both Glazunov and Tchaikovsky, who taught him at the Moscow Conservatory, thought highly of his work, which consisted chiefly of music for the theater, including ballets, orchestral music and cantatas. He was active as a conductor, both in the Conservatory concerts (1883-93) and at the Imperial Theatre, and he took part in the première of Tchaikovsky's *Eugene Onegin*. From 1902 to 1906 he was assistant director at the Imperial Chapel in St Petersburg. Klenovsky also collected and edited an amount of Russian folk music.

Lalo, Edouard (* Lille, 27 Jan. 1823; † Paris, 22 Apr. 1892). French composer of Spanish

descent. On announcing to his father, a veteran of the Grande Armée, that he intended to make his career in music, Lalo was forced to leave home at the age of sixteen, moving to Paris where he entered Habeneck's class at the Conservatoire and earned his living through engagements as an violinist. He was slow to develop as a composer, and by the time he was forty had written only a handful of songs and four chamber works. His first significant work was the opera *Fiesque* (1866), which won a prize at the Théâtre Lyrique but was not performed. In 1871 he participated in the foundation of the Société Nationale de Musique, and the music for which he is best known now – the *Symphonie espagnole* for violin and orchestra and the Cello Concerto – came from his most prolific period in the early 1870s. Works of importance that followed include the ballet *Namouna* (1882), the orchestral *Rapsodie norvégienne* (1881), the Symphony in G minor (1886) and the opera *Le Roi d'Ys*. Although the score of the opera was completed in 1880, it was not until 1888 that it received its première at the Opéra Comique, but then it scored a huge success.

Lalo did much to revive chamber and orchestral music at a time when France was dominated by opera, and his own work is given a particularly French flavor by its clarity of sound, its rich orchestral color and its melodic vitality.

Lanner, Joseph (* Vienna, 12 Apr. 1801; † Oberdöbling, nr. Vienna, 14 Apr. 1843). Austrian dance composer and violinist.

Lanner was the creator of the 'concert waltz,' a development of the simple dance form into a five-part pattern with introduction and coda. He formed his own group in 1818 and in 1829 became director of dance music at the Imperial Court, where his *Hofball-Tänze*, *Schönbrunner* and galops sent the Viennese into a waltzing ecstasy.

Johann Strauss the Elder played in Lanner's group before leaving to form his own orchestra.

Lecocq, Charles (* Paris, 3 June 1832; † Paris, 24 Oct. 1918). *See Volume II*

Lehár, Franz (* Komárom, Hungary, 30 Apr. 1870; † Bad Ischl, 24 Oct. 1948). Austro-Hungarian composer. The son of a military bandmaster, Lehár seemed set to follow his father's career despite studies as a violinist at the Prague Conservatory, but thanks to Dvořák's encouragement, he decided to devote himself to composition. *Wiener Frauen* (1902) was the first of some thirty operettas – including his most celebrated stage work, *Die lustige Witwe* (The Merry Widow, 1905), as well as *The Land of Smiles* and *The Count of Luxembourg* – which established him as the successor to Johann Strauss and the leading operetta composer of the twentieth century.

Lekeu, Guillaume (* Heusy, nr. Verviers, 20 Jan. 1870; † Angers, 21 Jan. 1894). Belgian composer. Lekeu began composing at the age of fourteen and in 1889 became a pupil of César Franck, continuing his studies with d'Indy after Franck's death in 1890. Wagner (whose music he heard at Bayreuth) and Franck exerted a powerful influence on his compositions, which express the passionate, introspective and yearning moods characteristic of much *fin-de-siècle* music.

Despite his early death, Lekeu produced a quantity of music. One of his most successful works was the Sonata for violin and piano, written on cyclic principles, while his *Fantaisie sur deux airs populaires angevins*, in which the idiom of folksong lightens the normally intense style of his writing, was extremely popular for a time. Lekeu's choral music includes the cantata *Andromède*, and his chamber music two piano trios and two works completed by d'Indy after his death – the Piano Quartet and the Sonata for cello and piano.

Liszt, Franz (**Ferenc**) (* Doborján [Raiding], 22 Oct. 1811; † Bayreuth, 31 July 1886). Hungarian composer and pianist. *See pp.23-41.*

Litolff, Henry (* London, 6 Feb. 1818; † Bois-Colombes, nr. Paris, 6 Aug. 1891). French composer, music publisher and pianist. Litolff was a pupil of Moscheles from the age of twelve, and a year later made his public début in London. He left England when he was seventeen, and after a spell in

Paris embarked on a series of concert tours. When he finally settled, it was to become a music publisher, first in Brunswick for nine years, and then, for the rest of his life, in Paris.

Although Litolff is known to most people solely through the huge popularity of one movement of a four-movement work, the scherzo from his Concerto Symphonique no.4 for piano and orchestra, his compositions embraced most forms, including seven operas, an oratorio, concertante works, chamber music and solo piano works.

His best music is to be found in those works with piano – the later Concertos Symphoniques, the Piano Trio in D minor and the smaller solo pieces.

Lyadov, Anatol Konstantinovich (* St Petersburg, 11 May 1855; † Polinovka, Novgorod district, 28 Aug. 1914). Russian composer, conductor and teacher. The son of a professional musician, Lyadov studied with Rimsky-Korsakov at the St Petersburg Conservatory, later joining the staff as a professor of harmony and composition and also teaching at the Imperial Chapel. Much of his energy went into teaching, and he completed no large-scale compositions.

As a pianist, Lyadov wrote for his instrument particularly well, with Chopin the strongest influence on his style. He also wrote a number of songs, including three charming sets for children, and collected Russian folk songs, editing over one hundred for publication. His orchestral tone-poems on Russian legends – *Baba Yaga*, The Enchanted Lake and *Kikimora* – have proved his most enduring works in the concert hall.

Lyapunov, Sergei Mikhailovich (* Yaroslavl, 30 Nov. 1859; † Paris, 11 Nov. 1924). Russian composer, pianist and conductor. Between 1878 and 1883 Lyapunov received lessons from both Tchaikovsky and Taneyev at the Moscow Conservatory, and soon after graduating he became assistant director at the Imperial Chapel in St Petersburg, later accepting a professorship at the Conservatory there. He was one of a group of composers who succeeded the 'mighty handful' as supporters of Balakirev, and the influence of older Russian composers permeates much of his work, especially his piano music, whose chief model, however, was Liszt. Another strong influence was that of Russian folk music, Lyapunov arranging a number of folksongs for publication in 1897. His style finds its most successful expression in his shorter piano pieces and songs, which reflect his nationalist beliefs and awareness of the Russian landscape. His more ambitious orchestral compositions include two symphonies, two piano concertos, a violin concerto, and tone-poems, while his vocal music includes quartets for male voices.

Lyapunov collaborated with Balakirev on editing the complete works of Glinka, and from 1905 to 1911 he was associated with the Free School of Music. After the Revolution he moved to Paris, where he directed a music school for Russian exiles.

MacDowell, Edward (* New York, 18 Dec. 1861; † New York, 23 Jan. 1908). American composer, pianist and teacher. MacDowell received his musical education in Europe, first in Paris and then in Germany with Louis Ehlert and Joachim Raff. After working as a piano teacher at the Darmstadt Conservatory, he returned to New York in 1888 to become the first professor of music at Columbia University. MacDowell, who often used Indian and Negro themes in his works, is regarded as one of the leading American composers of his time.

Mackenzie, Alexander (* Edinburgh, 22 Aug. 1847; † London, 28 Apr. 1935). Scottish composer and conductor. In his youth, Mackenzie studied the violin and played professionally in Germany, returning to Britain and entering the Royal Academy of Music at the age of fifteen. His subsequent career as violinist, conductor, composer, teacher and administrator developed rapidly, culminating in his appointment as principal of the Royal Academy of Music in 1888, a post he held until 1924. He wrote prolifically in all genres, although program-music was his strong point, most of his orchestral music consisting of dramatic overtures (*Twelfth Night*) and suites (*London Day by Day*). Other works include choral

pieces, several operas, numerous part songs (many to the poetry of Burns), solo songs, piano pieces (including collections of Scottish vocal and dance tunes), and some organ and church music.

Magnard, Albéric (* Paris, 9 June 1865; † Baron-sur-Oise, 3 Sept. 1914). French composer. After obtaining a degree in law, Magnard studied composition with Massenet and Dubois at the Paris Conservatoire and later with d'Indy. His compositions never reached a wide public, and several manuscripts disappeared when the invading German army destroyed his home in 1914.

Despite early Wagnerian influences, in his maturity Magnard adhered resolutely to a profound aversion towards anything other than absolute music, aiming in his compositions at purity of form and musical logic. His best music combines bold, dramatic, rhythmic drive with melodic poise and tenderness, achieving at times that spiritual serenity which he so admired in the late chamber music of Beethoven. Magnard wrote three operas, four symphonies, three sets of songs and some piano music, although it is his chamber music – a quintet for piano and wind, a string quartet, a piano trio and sonatas for violin and for cello – which represents his finest achievement.

Mahler, Gustav (* Kalište, Bohemia, 7 July 1860; † Vienna, 18 May 1911. Austrian composer and conductor. See pp.263-277.

Massenet, Jules (* Montaud, St Etienne, 12 May 1842; † Paris, 13 Aug. 1912). French composer. *See Volume II.*

Medtner, Nikolai Karlovich (* Moscow, 24 Dec. 1879; † London, 13 Nov. 1951). Russian composer and pianist. *See Volume IV.*

Messager, André (* Montluçon, Allier, 30 Dec. 1853; † Paris, 24 Feb. 1929). French composer, conductor, opera director and critic. *See Volume II.*

Millöcker, Karl (* Vienna, 29 Apr. 1842; † Baden, nr. Vienna, 31 Dec. 1899). Austrian composer and conductor. After appointments in Graz and

Budapest, Millöcker was conductor at the Theater an der Wien in Vienna from 1869. He was principally a composer of operettas, including the internationally successful *Der Bettelstudent* (1882).

Mosonyi, Mihály (* Boldo-gasszonyfalva, 4 Sept. 1815; † Pest, 31 Oct. 1870). Hungarian composer, double-bass player, teacher and writer on music. An almost entirely self-taught musician, Mosonyi became, with Erkel, one of the most important figures in the revival of a Hungarian national musical idiom, both through his compositions – which found success once he left behind the German influence of his early works in favor of the expression of his native idioms – and through his regular writings for a Hungarian music magazine.

Mosonyi's most notable works are the *Funeral Music* of 1860, the series of six string quartets, much of the piano music and his second opera, *Szép Ilonka* (1861).

Moszkowski, Moritz (* Breslau [Wroclaw], 23 Aug. 1854; † Paris, 4 Mar. 1925). German composer, pianist and conductor of Polish descent. Moszkowski studied in Germany, where he was later to establish himself as a piano-teacher. He toured frequently abroad as pianist and conductor, his last years being spent in Paris. Although he wrote an opera and a number of large-scale works for orchestra, including concertos for violin and for piano, he was best known during his lifetime for music of a lighter character composed for his own instrument, especially the two books of *Spanish Dances* in versions for solo pianos and for piano duet.

Musorgsky, Modest Petrovich (* Karevo, Pskov district, 21 Mar. 1839; † St Petersburg, 28 Mar. 1881). Russian composer. *See pp.79-89.*

Nápravník, Eduard (* Býšt, nr. Hradec Králové, 24 Aug. 1839; † Petrograd, 10 Nov. 1916). Czech conductor and composer.

Nápravník studied piano, organ and composition before moving in 1861 to St Petersburg, where he worked as a conductor at the court. Within two years he had become

assistant to Lyadov at the Imperial Theaters, becoming chief conductor in 1869. He devoted much of his time to the advancement of Russian opera, and under his direction performances reached new standards of excellence. He conducted the premières of over eighty Russian operas (including Musorgsky's *Boris Godunov*, Dargomyzhsky's *Stone Guest* and works by Rimsky-Korsakov and Tchaikovsky, who dedicated to Nápravník *The Maid of Orleans*. In his own compositions, which include four operas, four symphonies, a piano concerto, a symphonic poem, chamber music, songs and piano music, Nápravník reflects the strong influence of Tchaikovsky and contemporary Russian composers.

Nordraak, Rikard (* Christiania [Oslo], 12 June 1842; † Berlin, 20 Mar. 1866). Norwegian composer. The works completed in Nordraak's short life include piano pieces and incidental music for plays by his cousin B. Bjørnson, who later collaborated with Grieg. Nordraak's influence on his compatriot, whom he befriended in Copenhagen in 1865, was decisive for Grieg's endeavor to create a national musical style.

Paine, John Knowles (* Portland, Maine, 9 Jan. 1839; † Cambridge, Mass., 25 Apr. 1906). American composer and teacher. Paine studied organ, piano, harmony and counterpoint in Maine with a German émigré, Hermann Kotzschmar, and then in Berlin for three years. He returned to Boston in 1861, and as a result of his public lectures on music and series of organ recitals, was appointed to the music faculty at Harvard, where he remained for virtually the rest of his life. His compositions include an opera, oratorios, cantatas and church music, symphonic and chamber works and ceremonial music. His Symphony no.2 in A, op.34, 'In Spring,' which received its première in Cambridge in 1880, was the first native symphony to be published in America.

Parry, Sir Hubert

(* Bournemouth, 27 Feb. 1848;
† Rustington, Sussex, 7 Oct.
1918). English composer, scholar
and teacher. Parry obtained his
Bachelor of Music degree while
still a pupil at Eton, then went to
Oxford, graduating in 1870. Ten
years later the première of his
Piano Concerto in F sharp made
his name known to the public at
large. He joined the staff of the
Royal College of Music when it
opened in 1883, becoming its
director in 1894. In 1900 he
became professor of music at
Oxford. Although relatively little
of his music is heard today – apart
from *Jerusalem* and the anthem *I
was glad* – he was a prolific
composer, writing four
symphonies and producing many
works for British music festivals,
and had a profoundly revitalizing
influence on English musical life.

Pedrell, Felipe (* Tortosa,

19 Feb. 1841; † Barcelona,
19 Aug. 1922). Spanish composer,
teacher and musicologist. Pedrell
derived first-hand knowledge of
Spanish church music as a choirboy
and also learned the guitar, an
instrument whose importance
in the history of Spanish music
he soon came to acknowledge.

His greatest achievement was his
four-volume collection of Spanish
folk music, *Cancionero Musical
Popular Español*, and his research
into this and into the classical
Renaissance period represented,
according to his pupil de Falla,
'the cornerstone of the arch upon
which our modern music rests.'
Other important collections
included old Spanish theater and
organ music, liturgical music by
Victoria, Cabezón, Morales and
others, and an edition of the
complete works of Victoria. His
theories on the formation of a
Spanish musical style were printed
in a manifesto *Por Nuestra
Musica*, published in 1891.
His influence in the renaissance of
Spanish music at the turn of the
century was crucial, since he was
the teacher of Albéniz, Granados
and de Falla. His last pupil,
Roberto Gerhard, paid tribute to
him in two works, one based on
folksongs Pedrell had collected.

As a composer, Pedrell wrote a
number of works for the stage,
but although he attempted to do
for Spanish opera what Wagner
had done in Germany, his operas
have never gained international

success. Pedrell also composed
some religious works – which
include a Requiem, a Mass and a
Te Deum – cantatas, a string
quartet, a little orchestral music
and some songs.

Pfitzner, Hans (* Moscow,

5 May 1869; † Salzburg, 22 May
1949). German composer and
conductor. The son of a
professional violinist, Pfitzner
studied at the Frankfurt
Conservatory from 1886 to 1890.
After holding various teaching
posts, he became much in demand
as a conductor in Germany.

In composition, the German
Romantics, from Schumann to
Wagner, were Pfitzner's models,
and he found a supporter in
Mahler, who conducted the first
performance of his opera *Die
Rose vom Liebesgarten* in 1901.
His earliest compositions include
songs (of which he was to write
more than one hundred), choral
music, incidental music to Ibsen
and his first opera, *Der arme
Heinrich*. His later work included
two symphonies, two cello
concertos and concertos for violin
and for piano, but of greater
significance was his chamber
music, which includes three string
quartets, works for piano and
strings and a sextet for wind,
strings and piano. The choral
work *Von deutscher Seele* sets
texts by the Romantic poet
Eichendorff. His opera *Palestrina*,
a dramatically intense projection
of Pfitzner's own life and artistic
credo through the life and work of
the great sixteenth-century
composer, is his best-known
work. His last opera, *Das Herz*,
appeared in 1931. For all the
complexity of his scores, Pfitzner
was a reactionary, crossing
swords with many progressive
contemporaries, including Busoni.

Raff, Joachim (* Lachen, nr.

Zürich, 24/5 May 1822;
† Frankfurt-am-Main, 25 June
1882). German composer and
teacher. Raff displayed early
musical talent, although lack
of money denied him the
opportunity to study music
seriously until he was over
twenty, by which time he had
become a proficient performer on
the piano, violin and organ. In
1843 he sent his first attempts at
composition to Mendelssohn,
who was impressed and arranged

for their publication. Two years
later, Liszt met Raff in Basle and
was sufficiently impressed by him
to find him a job in Hamburg, and
later, in 1850, to take him on as
an assistant at Weimar. During
these years Raff learned much
from his employer, developing as
a composer in his own right, while
Liszt in turn benefited from Raff's
natural ability as an orchestrator,
as is shown in his symphonic
poems of the period.

Raff gave up his post with Liszt
in 1856, feeling that he was by
now able to support himself by his
own composition. He moved to
Wiesbaden, where he became
much in demand as a piano
teacher, and his first opera, *König
Alfred*, was performed there to
critical acclaim in 1858. By the
following year, Raff was being
wooed by several publishers, and
his rise to fame had begun. He
soon became one of the most
popular composers of his day –
his symphonies, operas and
chamber music were widely
performed; his piano pieces were
to be found in every home; and
his arrangements for brass band
were played throughout
Germany. For the last five years of
his life he was director and
teacher of composition at the
Hoch Conservatory in Frankfurt.

Reger, Max (* Brand, Oberpfalz,

19 Mar. 1873; † Leipzig, 11 May
1916). German composer.
Though he died aged only forty-
three, Reger left a long and
impressive catalogue of works in
every important medium except
opera. His principal teacher was
Hugo Riemann, and he rapidly
acquired mastery not only of the
piano but also of the organ, an
instrument for which he wrote
some of his finest music, while
making an intensive study of the
organ music of Bach and of
nineteenth-century Germany. His
knowledge of the orchestra was
also profound, thanks to his wide
experience as a conductor. From
1907 to 1911 he was professor of
composition and director of music
at Leipzig University.

Despite the enthusiasm aroused
by his keyboard playing, Reger's
compositions met with hostility,
largely as a result of his
idiosyncratic harmonic style (the
perversity of his modulations was
a specific reproach) and complex

counterpoint. However, works
such as the *Fantasia and Fugue on
B-A-C-H*, op.46, and *Variations
and Fugue on an Original Theme*,
op.73, both for organ, are real
masterpieces. His orchestral music
includes concertos for violin and
for piano, a setting of Psalm 100
and the *Symphonic Prologue to a
Tragedy*, as well as a Serenade
and the *Comedy Overture*, the
last two epitomizing the Romantic
lightness of touch found also in
chamber works like the Serenade
in G for flute, violin and viola.

Other chamber music is on a large
scale and counts among Reger's
finest achievements, notably the
Piano Quintet op.64, the String
Quartets op.109 and op.121 and
the fine Clarinet Quintet op.146.
He also composed two piano
quartets, two string trios and a
string sextet, as well as making an
important contribution to the
literature for solo violin and solo
viola, and he wrote more than
250 songs.

Reinecke, Carl (* Altona,

Hamburg, 23 June 1824;
† Leipzig, 10 Mar. 1910). German
composer, teacher, administrator,
pianist and conductor. Son of an
able musician, Reinecke was
taught the violin by his father.
He subsequently changed to the
piano and, though never a
virtuoso performer, earned the
post of professor of piano at
Hiller's Conservatory in Cologne
in 1851. After conducting posts at
Barmen (1854-9) and Breslau
(1859-60) he was appointed
conductor of the Gewandhaus
concerts in Leipzig and became a
very influential teacher at the
Conservatory there for over forty
years.

As a composer, Reinecke was
conscientious and prolific. He was
most influenced by his friendships

with Mendelssohn and Schumann in Leipzig, although he was never officially a pupil of either. Of his compositions, the concertos for piano and for flute have survived through their attractive melodies and skillfull handling of the orchestra. His other works include operas, symphonies and much chamber and instrumental music.

Reubke, Julius (* Hausneindorf, nr. Quedlinburg, 23 Mar. 1834; † Pillnitz, nr. Dresden, 3 June 1858). German composer, pianist and organist. Son of a celebrated organ builder, Reubke was born into a musical environment and showed natural ability while still young. His music teachers were undistinguished until, in 1853, he met and impressed Hans von Bülow, who recommended him to Liszt, from which point he became one of Liszt's most favored pupils.

Apart from a number of small piano pieces and songs, Reubke wrote two compositions of considerable size and value: the Organ Sonata on the 94th Psalm and the Piano Sonata in B flat minor. The Organ Sonata has held its own as a virtuoso recital piece and remains one of the most performed organ works of the nineteenth century. The Piano Sonata is less well-known, but it reveals a harmonic originality which at times foreshadows Mahler and Reger.

Rezniček, Emil von (* Vienna, 4 May 1860; † Berlin, 2 Aug. 1945). Austrian composer and conductor. Rezniček embarked at first on legal studies; however, at the age of twenty-two he abandoned law and enrolled as a student under Reinecke at the Leipzig Conservatory. He gained extensive experience as a conductor in various German theaters before taking up conducting posts at Weimar and then at Mannheim. At the age of forty-two he settled in Berlin, organizing concerts and becoming director of the Komische Oper from 1909 until its closure in 1911. He also traveled to Warsaw and to Russia to fulfill conducting engagements.

As a composer, music for the stage formed the most important part of Rezniček's output, his most successful work being the comic opera *Donna Diana*, produced in Prague in 1894. His other compositions include four symphonies, orchestral suites, a violin concerto, choral and vocal music, three string quartets and some organ music.

Rheinberger, Joseph Gabriel (* Vaduz, Liechtenstein, 17 Mar. 1839; † Munich, 25 Nov. 1901). German composer, teacher, conductor and organist. Rheinberger was precociously musical – by the age of seven he had an appointment as organist at the Vaduz parish church, and a

year later his first composition, a Mass, was performed there. In 1848 he went to study with Philipp Schmutzer at Feldkirch and in 1851 was accepted by the Royal Conservatory in Munich. After graduation, he settled permanently in Munich, where he earned his living as a piano teacher and concluded his composition studies under Franz Lachner. In 1859 he was appointed piano tutor at the Royal Conservatory, and when it was reorganized under Hans von Bülow he became professor of organ and composition.

Despite critical successes in almost every musical form, Rheinberger earned the reputation of being an academic composer. His best music is in his choral compositions and works for organ – the twenty organ sonatas are firmly established in the repertory. Many of the piano pieces and chamber works are also interesting and attractive, but the outstanding masterpiece in a total of over 600 works is the Christmas Cantata, *The Star of Bethlehem*.

Rimsky-Korsakov, Nikolai Andreyevich (* Tikhvin, Novgorod district, 18 Mar. 1844; † St Petersburg, 21 June 1908). Russian composer. *See pp.91-105.*

Rubinstein, Anton Grigoryevich (* Vikhvatinets, Podolsk district, 28 Nov. 1829; † Peterhof, nr. St Petersburg, 20 Nov. 1894). Russian composer, pianist and teacher of German-Jewish descent. Rubinstein received his first piano lessons from his mother, herself an accomplished player. The family moved to Moscow in 1834, where Rubinstein made his public début when he was ten years old, to be followed a year later by a concert tour of Europe during which he received the highest praise from Chopin and Liszt. After a second tour he settled in Berlin in 1844 to study composition with Siegfried Dehn, but on the death of his father in 1846 he was forced to support himself and so went to Vienna to become a teacher himself. This was not a success, and in 1849 he returned to Russia, where he settled for six years in St Petersburg – his first serious period of composition.

After 1854 Rubinstein divided his life between concert tours, composition and teaching, and

achieved triumphant successes in all three fields. He had a legendary reputation as a pianist and amazed audiences with the length and serious content of his recitals, sometimes including up to eight Beethoven sonatas in one program. He also used these tours to launch his own works. In 1862 he founded the St Petersburg Conservatory and became its first director. He remained in charge there until 1867, when he resigned in favor of his brother Nikolai and left Russia for the most triumphant of all his European tours, followed by a tour of the United States in 1872-3. In his 239 days there he gave 215 concerts and recitals from one side of the country to the other.

For a man whose life was occupied in public performance and teaching, Rubinstein's output as a composer was enormous. He left six symphonies, five piano concertos, chamber music, more than 200 songs, fourteen operas, five sacred operas and innumerable piano pieces – many of which, together with some of the piano concertos and symphonies, have remained in the repertory.

Saint-Saëns, Camille (* Paris, 9 Oct. 1835; † Algiers, 16 Dec. 1921). French composer. *See pp.123-133.*

Sarasate, Pablo de (* Pamplona, 10 Mar. 1844; † Biarritz, 20 Sept. 1908). Spanish violinist and composer. Sarasate was probably the greatest violinist of the second half of the nineteenth century. As a child of remarkable gifts, he was sent to the Paris Conservatoire when only twelve, becoming the favorite pupil of Alard and winning every prize available to him. He also briefly studied composition with Reber. By the age of fifteen he had embarked on his career as a violinist, and there were few parts of the civilized world that he did not visit in the next forty years. Contemporary reports of his playing suggest a rare talent – a combination of perfect technique and beauty of tone with innate musicianship. He inspired superlatives in the opinions of fellow musicians and

was the dedicatee of many compositions, including concertos by Lalo and Bruch.

Sarasate's own compositions were exclusively for the violin and consist of transcriptions and fantasies based on Spanish airs and dances and a number of Romances. His *Zigeunerweisen* and *Jota Aragonesa* are still favorites in the repertory today.

Scharwenka, Philipp (* Samter [Szamotuly], nr. Poznań, 16 Feb. 1847; † Bad Nauheim, nr. Frankfurt-am-Main, 16 July 1917). Polish-German composer and teacher. Philipp Scharwenka studied in Berlin then took up teaching appointments, in due course becoming co-director of the Scharwenka Conservatory in Berlin founded by his younger brother Xaver.

His compositions mainly consist of songs and piano pieces, although he also composed some symphonic works on a larger scale as well as two works for chorus and orchestra and one for chorus and piano, while much of his later work consists of chamber music.

Scharwenka, Xaver (* Samter [Szamotuly], nr. Poznań, 6 Jan. 1850; † Berlin, 8 Dec. 1924. Polish-German pianist, composer, and educator. Scharwenka studied music at the New Academy in Berlin, and having made a considerable reputation while still a pupil he stayed on there as a teacher. In 1874 he embarked on a series of concert tours, which became a regular part of his life until 1914 and through which he gained a brilliant reputation in Europe and America. In 1881 he opened his own Conservatory in Berlin and ten years later went to New York in answer to a request to open a branch there.

Scharwenka's first piano concerto appeared in 1876, the style reflecting his own skill as an interpreter of Chopin and his admiration for both the lyrical and virile qualities of Chopin's music.

The rest of his considerable output consists of three further piano concertos, a symphony, an opera, chamber music (all with piano), songs, two piano sonatas and numerous smaller pieces for the instrument as well as an important series of technical exercises.

Schillings, Max von (* Düren, 19 Apr. 1868; † Berlin, 24 July 1933). German composer, conductor and teacher. Schillings was undoubtedly an intellectual composer lacking in spontaneity. He came to music late in life, having studied law, art history, philosophy and literature. Under Strauss's influence he resolved to devote himself entirely to music, undergoing a major conversion while working at the Bayreuth Festival in 1892, when the work of Wagner so impressed him that he became one of his devotees.

Years as a composer, conductor and teacher in Munich followed, where Furtwängler and Robert Heger were among his pupils. He went to Stuttgart to take up a post at the Royal Opera House in 1908 and achieved a great deal during his ten years there. He staged many first performances of new works, among them *Ariadne auf Naxos* by Strauss in 1912 and *Eine florentinische Tragödie* by Zemlinsky in 1917. His own most important composition, the opera *Mona Lisa*, also had its première there in 1915.

In 1919 Schillings went to Berlin as Intendant of the Prussian State Opera, which left him less time for composition. He was appointed President of the Prussian Academy of Arts and, in the year of his death, General Intendant of the State Opera.

Schmidt, Franz (* Pressburg [Bratislava], 22 Dec. 1874; † Perchtoldsdorf, nr. Vienna, 11 Feb. 1939). Austrian composer, pianist and cellist. Schmidt was a cellist in the Hofoper orchestra and leader of the Musikakademie in Vienna before he took over the direction of the Hochschule für Musik und darstellende Kunst. As a composer, his work follows in the tradition of Bruckner, including four symphonies, organ works, chamber music and also two operas, the first of which, *Notre Dame* (1904), includes an interlude which has remained in the repertory. His best-known composition is his oratorio based on the Book of Revelation, *Das Buch mit sieben Siegeln* (1937).

Schreker, Franz (* Monaco, 23 Mar. 1878; † Berlin, 21 Mar. 1934). Austrian composer, dramatist and teacher. *See Volume IV.*

Sechter, Simon (* Friedberg, Bohemia, 11 Oct. 1788; † Vienna, 10 Sept. 1867). Austrian theorist, composer, conductor and organist. *See Volume II.*

Serov, Alexander Nikolayevich (* St Petersburg, 23 Jan. 1820; † St Petersburg, 1 Feb. 1871). Russian composer, critic. At his father's insistence Serov embarked on a legal career, attempting to improve his knowledge of music in his spare time. Frustrated, he turned at the age of thirty-one to music criticism, soon acquiring a reputation with his trenchant style of writing. His belief that the future of music lay outside Russia and his indifference to the formation of a nationalist school of composition, reinforced by a visit to Germany in 1858 where he was most impressed by the music of Wagner, brought him into conflict with many of his contemporaries.

Serov's compositions were strongly influenced by Wagner and Meyerbeer. His opera *Judith* was enthusiastically received in 1863, attracting the attention of Tchaikovsky, and was followed in 1865 by the even more spectacular *Rogneda*. He also wrote a little orchestral and some sacred music.

Sgambati, Giovanni (* Rome, 28 May, 1841; † Rome, 14 Dec. 1914). Italian composer, pianist, conductor and teacher. Sgambati's mother was English, and he was brought up among the colony of foreign artists and intellectuals in Rome. He was an able pianist by the time he was eight, a talent that was developed at the Naples Conservatory under Natalucci. At the age of twenty, he intended to go to Germany to study with Liszt, but was fortunate to meet him in Rome, where the two men struck up a friendship that endured until the elder's death. Wagner also championed his music, helping him to get his works published.

After 1870, Sgambati became a much sought-after teacher and was founder of the celebrated Liceo Musicale in Rome. At about the same time he became more involved in composition and, with the exception of an early overture, his first orchestral works date from this period. His compositions include two symphonies, a piano concerto, two piano quintets and a string quartet, as well as a large quantity of piano music and songs.

His importance in re-establishing an interest in instrumental music in Italy was further increased through the school that he founded.

Sinding, Christian (* Kongsberg, 11 Jan. 1856; † Oslo, 3 Dec. 1941). Norwegian composer. After studies in Germany, Sinding devoted himself entirely to composition. The influence of the late German Romantics is evident in his music, as are rhythms and themes clearly inspired by folk dance elements. His considerable output includes four symphonies, three concertos for violin and one for piano, some 250 songs – the two *Symra* collections, op.28 and op.75, and the *Sange*, op.18, being the most important – an opera, *The Sacred Mountain*, and a large amount of music for piano, including his most famous composition, *The Rustle of Spring*.

Sinding also contributed to the chamber music repertory, the Piano Quintet, op.5, being typical of his vigorous, extrovert style.

Skriabin, Alexander Nikolayevich (* Moscow, 6 Jan. 1872; † Moscow, 27 Apr. 1915). Russian composer and pianist. *See Volume IV.*

Škroup, František Jan (* Osice, nr. Pardubice, 3 June 1801; † Rotterdam, 7 Feb. 1862). Czech theater musician, composer and conductor. Škroup worked at the Estates Theater in Prague from 1827 as second, and then principal conductor, a post that he retained for twenty years. It was here that he arranged the performance of Wagner's *Tannhäuser* in 1854 and acquainted audiences in Prague with further works by the master during a Wagner week in 1856. Škroup also conducted the two concert series in the city, in which he offered both the latest works by

his Czech compatriots and also those of Berlioz. He is remembered today as the composer of the first Czech opera, *Dráteník*, and of the first part of the Czech national anthem (which is taken from one of his musical dramas).

Smetana, Bedřich (* Litomyšl, Bohemia, 2 Mar. 1824; † Prague, 12 May 1884). Czech composer. *See pp.231-245.*

Smyth, Dame Ethel (* London, 22 Apr. 1858; † Woking, Surrey, 9 May 1944). English composer. Smyth joined the Leipzig Conservatory in 1877 and met Brahms, Grieg, Tchaikovsky, Dvořák, Clara Schumann and Joachim, all of whom encouraged her in her compositions. In January 1893 her Mass in D was performed in the Albert Hall, and in 1909 her opera *The Wreckers* was also performed in London. Smyth played a large part in the revival of English music around the turn of the century, and her compositions include orchestral, choral, instrumental and chamber works, as well as further operas, of which *The Boatswain's Mate* (1916) testifies to her ardent support of the suffragette cause.

Stanford, Sir Charles Villiers (* Dublin, 30 Sept. 1852; † London, 29 Mar. 1924). Anglo-Irish composer, teacher and conductor. Stanford's father, a lawyer, permitted his son to take up music on condition that he first go to university, then study music abroad. This meant Cambridge and Leipzig and, later, Berlin. At the age of thirty-five, Stanford was appointed professor of music at Cambridge, having already been appointed professor of composition and orchestral playing at the newly founded Royal College of Music in 1883. He held both posts until his death, and from 1885 to 1902 also conducted the London Bach Choir.

Stanford is regarded as one of those responsible for the revival of English music in the late nineteenth century. He revitalized choral music, and through his teaching of composition influenced many young composers. His own compositions include many substantial works: operas, oratorios, church music and seven symphonies, as well as chamber and piano works and songs.

Strauss, Johann the Elder (* Vienna, 14 Mar. 1804; † Vienna, 25 Sept. 1849). Austrian conductor and composer. Originally a bookbinder, Strauss was a viola player in the orchestras of M. Pamer and then of J. Lanner. After his break with Lanner in 1825, Strauss founded his own ensemble, and in 1831 made his first appearance at a court ball. Between 1833 and 1849 he traveled extensively in Austria, Hungary, Germany, Holland, Belgium, France and England with

considerable success. He wrote almost 150 waltzes, along with galops, quadrilles, polkas and marches, of which the most famous is the *Radetzky-Marsch*, op.228.

Strauss, Johann the Younger
(* Vienna, 25 Oct. 1825; † Vienna, 3 June 1899). Austrian conductor and composer. His father, Johann Strauss the Elder, intended that he should take up banking as a career, but his mother arranged secret music lessons for Johann and his brothers, all of whom eventually followed their father's calling. Johann the Younger made his début as a conductor in 1844 with considerable success. He became reconciled with his father two years later, but they continued to conduct rival orchestras, and Johann the Younger undertook extensive concert tours. On his father's death he amalgamated the orchestras, but in 1853 handed over his baton to his brother Joseph, conducting only during the summer season.

Among the many waltzes by Johann Strauss the Younger are *Accelerationen*, op.234, *Morgen-blätter*, op.279, *An der schönen blauen Donau*, op.314, *Wiener Blut*, op.354, *Rosen aus dem Süden*, op.388, *Frühlingsstimmen*, op.410, and *Kaiser-Walzer*, op.437. He also wrote sixteen operettas, including *Die Fledermaus* (1874) and *Der Zigeunerbaron* (1885).

Strauss, Richard (* Munich, 11 June 1864; † Garmisch, 8 Sept. 1949). German composer. *See pp.279-303.*

Suk, Josef (* Křečovic, 4 Jan. 1874; † Benešov, nr. Prague, 29 May 1935). Czech composer and violinist. *See Volume IV.*

Sullivan, Sir Arthur (* London, 13 May 1842; † London, 22 Nov. 1900). English composer and conductor. After two years at the Royal Academy of Music, Sullivan went to Leipzig for further studies in composition, piano and conducting. His first work to attract wide attention was his incidental music to *The Tempest* (1862), but for some years he lived by teaching and playing the organ, while continuing to compose prolifically. In 1875, the impresario Richard D'Oyly Carte arranged for Sullivan to collaborate with W. S. Gilbert, the result being their first major success, *Trial by Jury*. This was followed by the celebrated series of Gilbert and Sullivan operettas which brought fame and fortune to them both – *The Sorcerer, HMS Pinafore, The Pirates of Penzance, Patience, Iolanthe, The Mikado, Ruddigore, The Yeomen of the Guard* and *The Gondoliers*. Sullivan also composed a number of other stage works, as well as a quantity of liturgical music, part-songs, songs and orchestral music. He was active as a conductor and was made first director of what was eventually to become the Royal College of Music.

Suppé, Franz von (* Spalato, Dalmatia [now Split, Yugoslavia], 18 Apr. 1819; † Vienna, 21 May 1895). Austrian composer and conductor of Belgian origin. While still in his teens Suppé settled in Vienna, where he gained a living as a composer, arranger and conductor. His first success came in 1847 with *Das Mädchen vom Lande*, and he went on to write a succession of light operas, of which the best-known is probably *Zehn Mädchen und kein Mann*. The overtures *Light Cavalry* and *Poet and Peasant* have kept his name alive in the world of light orchestral music.

Svendsen, Johan (* Christiania [Oslo], 30 Sept. 1840; † Copenhagen, 14 June 1911). Norwegian composer, violinist and conductor. Svendsen was the son of a military bandmaster, a position that he was himself to hold by the age of fifteen. As a boy he studied flute, clarinet and violin, and he seemed set for a successful career as a solo violinist when in 1862 paralysis of the hand cut short his career. Svendsen then turned to composition, attending Leipzig Conservatory, where his teachers included David and Reinecke. He returned to public performance as a conductor, becoming one of the most celebrated of his time and traveling widely in Europe.

Although he was not prolific, Svendsen's compositions are of a consistently high standard and

attracted the praise of Grieg, Liszt and Wagner. They include a quartet, quintet and octet for strings, 'Norwegian Rhapsodies' for orchestra, two symphonies, concertos for violin and for cello, some songs and the Romance in G for violin and orchestra.

Taneyev, Sergei Ivanovich
(* Vladimir, 25 Nov. 1856; † Dyudkovo, nr. Moscow, 19 June 1915). Russian composer, pianist and teacher. Taneyev entered the Moscow Conservatory at the age of ten, studying the piano with Nikolai Rubinstein, with whom he gave concerts abroad, and establishing himself during his student career as one of the finest pianists of his time. He also studied composition with Tchaikovsky, who thought highly of his work, and of Taneyev's suggestions and criticisms regarding his own music.

In 1878, Taneyev succeeded Tchaikovsky as professor of composition at the Conservatory, and on the death of Rubinstein he became professor of piano – Skriabin, Glière, Rachmaninov and Lyapunov were among his pupils. In 1885 he was appointed to the post of director, but he resigned four years later in order to devote himself to composition.

Taneyev's music was influenced more by the work of Bach and the Renaissance contrapuntal composers than by Russian nationalism, and his volume on theoretical counterpoint became standard teaching material in Russian conservatories. His works include the operatic trilogy *Oresteia*, four symphonies, some music for piano, a number of songs and several choral pieces. His most lasting contribution,

however, was to chamber music, and it was as a pianist in his own music that he returned to the concert platform during the last ten years of his life, the Quintet, Quartet and Trio with strings being regarded as his most accomplished compositions.

Tausig, Carl (* Warsaw, 4 Nov. 1841; † Leipzig, 17 July 1871). Polish pianist and composer. Carl Tausig was the son of Aloys Tausig (1820-85), a brilliant pianist and composer of piano pieces. He studied under his father until the age of fourteen, when he was taken to Liszt, under whose tuition he soon became one of the great pianists of the age. Although his original compositions are few in number – the only original works he wished to acknowledge at the end of his life being the virtuoso piano studies, *Deux études de concert*, op.1 – he made successful transcriptions of the works of many other composers,

including a once famous version of Bach's organ Toccata and Fugue in D minor, several Strauss waltzes and movements from the late Beethoven string quartets.

Tchaikovsky, Peter Ilyich
(* Kamsko-Votkinsk, Vyatka district, 7 May 1840; † St Petersburg, 6 Nov. 1893). Russian composer. *See pp.43-61.*

Tcherepnin, Nikolai Nikolayevich
(* St Petersburg, 15 May 1873; † Paris, 26 Jun. 1945). Russian conductor and composer. Tcherepnin was a pupil of Rimsky-Korsakov at the St Petersburg Conservatory, where from 1907 he directed the orchestra class. In 1909, he was engaged by Diaghilev to conduct the first season of the Ballets Russes in Paris, and he remained with the company until 1914.

After the Russian Revolution he was appointed director of the Conservatory and conductor of the Opera at Tbilisi, but in 1921 he moved to Paris, where he remained for the rest of his life. He is best known for his ballet scores, but he also completed Musorgsky's score of *Sorochintsy Fair* for its first performance in 1923. His own music was traditional in flavor, with a strong element of Russian nationalism.

Tellefsen, Thomas (* Trondheim, 26 Nov. 1823; † Paris, 6 Oct. 1874). Norwegian composer and pianist. From his earliest years, Tellefsen appears to have had a passion for the music of Chopin. In 1844 he began to study with him in Paris, quickly becoming his master's favorite pupil and receiving on his death the only complete manuscript of his compositions, which he used for his edition of Chopin's works.

Tellefsen's own creative output, mostly for the piano, mirrors that of his great hero, with two piano concertos, sonatas, nocturnes, waltzes and mazurkas. A few late pieces pay homage to his origins in their use of Norwegian folk melodies.

Thalberg, Sigismond (* Geneva, 8 Jan. 1812; † Posillipo, nr. Naples, 27 Apr. 1871). Said to be the illegitimate son of Count Moritz von Dietrichstein, himself a talented amateur musician, Thalberg was given every advantage when he showed early musical ability, his teachers including Hummel, Kalkbrenner, Moscheles and Pixis. His early concert tours were arranged to coincide with the diplomatic trips of the Count, but after 1830 his concert career began in earnest, culminating in a meteoric rise to fame in Paris, where, in the absence of Liszt, he was hailed as the greatest pianist of all. This resulted in the return of Liszt to Paris and the famous contest, staged at a charity event in 1837, of which Liszt emerged as winner. Liszt was, however, an admirer of Thalberg's legato playing, describing him as 'the only artist who can play the violin on the keyboard.' For the next twenty-five years, before retiring to be a wine-grower in Italy, Thalberg was triumphantly successful as a pianist throughout Europe and the Americas, becoming the first of the traveling virtuosos whose fame was world-wide.

Apart from two unsuccessful operas and a piano concerto, trio and sonata, Thalberg's works consist entirely of solo piano fantasies, studies and caprices. His fantasies on Rossini's *Moses* and *The Barber of Seville* and on Donizetti's *Don Pasquale* have gained a regular place in Romantic recital programs.

Thomas, Ambroise (* Metz, 5 Aug. 1811; † Paris, 12 Feb. 1896). French operatic composer. *See Volume II.*

Verstovsky, Alexei Nikolayevich (* Seliverstovo, Tambov district, 1 Mar. 1799; † Moscow, 17 Nov. 1862). Russian composer. *See Volume II.*

Vieuxtemps, Henri (* Verviers, 17 Feb. 1820; † Mustapha, Algeria, 6 June 1881). Belgian violinist and composer. After lessons from his father and from a local violinist, Vieuxtemps's first tour, at the age of seven, led to a meeting with the great Belgian violinist Bériot, who took him on as a pupil for the next four years. During this time, Vieuxtemps made his successful début in Paris.

With the exception of the years 1846-52, when he was court violinist to the Tsar and professor of violin at the St Petersburg Conservatory, Vieuxtemps spent the next forty years of his life traveling. By the time of Paganini's death in 1840, he was ready to assume the role of foremost violinist of his age.

In 1834 Vieuxtemps studied counterpoint for a short time with Sechter in Vienna, and in Paris, the following year, composition with Reicha. His music, written almost exclusively for the violin, shows him to be a fine melodist and able craftsman, and of his seven concertos two remain favorites with violinists: no.4 in D minor, op.31, described by Berlioz as 'a magnificent symphony with solo violin,' and no.5 in A minor, op.37.

Vieuxtemps succeeded Fétis in 1871 as professor of violin at the Brussels Conservatoire, where Ysaye was his pupil.

Wagner, Richard (* Leipzig, 22 May 1813; † Venice, 13 Feb. 1883). German composer. *See pp.155-177.*

Widor, Charles-Marie (* Lyons, 21 Feb. 1844; † Paris 12 Mar. 1937). French organist, composer and teacher. Widor taught composition and the organ, in succession to César Franck, at the Paris Conservatoire, as well as being an active music critic. His music, in particular the ten symphonies, still forms the basis of the repertoire of many organists. Other works include

two orchestral symphonies, concertos for piano and for cello, a symphony for organ and orchestra, a symphonic poem, a Mass, music for the stage, operas, a ballet, and a lyric drama. A substantial list of chamber music compositions includes two piano quintets, a piano quartet and piano trio, sonatas for violin and for cello with piano, and two suites for flute and piano. Widor also composed a number of songs and short piano pieces.

Wieniawski, Henryk (* Lublin, 10 July 1835; † Moscow, 31 Mar. 1880). Polish violinist and composer. Henryk was the most famous of a family of musicians. From the age of six he was sent to study with Stanisław Serwaczyński and at the age of eight entered Clavel's class at the Paris Conservatoire, completing the course by the age of eleven. In 1848 he launched himself on a career as a virtuoso which was to establish him as one of the great violinists of the nineteenth century, notable above all for his amazing technique. In 1860 he took over Vieuxtemps's post as violinist to the Tsar, and in 1872-4 undertook a huge tour in the United States, which included a series of concerts with Anton Rubinstein. In 1875 he succeeded Vieuxtemps as professor of violin at the Brussels Conservatoire.

Although he had little serious education in music, Wieniawski composed with natural ability, and his Violin Concerto in D minor, op.22, is one of the finest Romantic concertos in the repertory.

Wolf, Hugo (* Windischgrätz [now Slovenjgradec, Yugoslavia], 13 Mar. 1860; † Vienna, 22 Feb. 1903). Austrian composer. *See pp.258-261.*

Ysaye, Eugène (* Liège, 16 July 1858; † Brussels, 13 May 1931). Belgian violinist and composer. Ysaye studied the violin from the age of four, first with his father, then at the Liège Conservatoire and in Brussels with Vieuxtemps and Wieniawski. He was the outstanding violinist of his generation, leader of his own quartet and founder of a concert series devoted to contemporary music, and a great teacher. He was also the dedicatee of many works, notably by Lekeu, Franck (Violin Sonata), Chausson and Debussy (String Quartet, *Nocturnes*, and *Pelléas et Mélisande*). His own compositions were principally sonatas, concertos and other pieces for his own instrument, although he also composed an opera at the end of his life.

Zarebski, Juliusz (* Zhitomir, Ukraine, 28 Feb. 1854; † Zhitomir, 15 Sept. 1885). Polish pianist and composer. A remarkable child performer, who played his own works in public at the age of nine, Zarebski is now all but forgotten, and his music is seldom performed. He was a pupil of Liszt in 1875 and followed this with concert tours that brought him great success. As a composer, he emulated the more Polish spirit of Chopin, to which he attempted to add something of the virtuoso elements of Liszt. The results in the piano music are effective in performance, but of little depth. However, the Piano Quintet in G minor, op.34, composed towards the end of his life, is an exceptional work of its kind, quite worthy to stand alongside the pieces in the same form by Schumann and Brahms.

INDEX

317

PICTURE CREDITS

The producers and publishers wish to thank the following institutions, collectors and photographers who have made illustrations available: Akademie der bildenden Künste, Vienna (151); Bayerische Staatsbibliothek, Munich (29, 283); Bibliothèque Inguimbertine, Carpentras (186b); Bibliothèque Nationale (8a, 9ab, 10b, 12ab, 13ab, 21a, 28a, 37a, 46a, 84a, 99, 102b, 103b, 106ac, 107bc, 109bg, 112b, 118b, 120a, 121b, 122, 124ab, 125ab, 126abc, 127b, 128ab, 132b, 133ab, 296a); Bibliothèque de l'Opéra, Paris (26b, 157b); British Library (26a, 34b, 38ab, 157a, 179bc, 194a, 199a, 205b, 218a, 222a, 243b, 251b, 267, 282b, 286ab, 291b); Wilhelm Busch Gesellschaft, Hanover (206a); Camposanto, Pisa (38c); Conservatoire de Musique, Geneva – Mercier (25c); Deutsches Theatermuseum, Munich – Broszat (159a, 172bc, 173bc, 181a); – © Schott-Fürstner Musikverlag, Mainz (29ab, 299abc); Eichendorff Gesellschaft, Würzburg (259a); Focke Museum, Bremen (195); Galleria dell' Accademia, Florence (259e); Galleria Pitti, Florence (266b); Gesellschaft der Musikfreunde, Vienna (207b, 204, 265a); Graphische Sammlung Albertina, Vienna (287); Hamburger Kunsthalle – Kleinhempel (187, 190a, 223a, 227a, 259b); Historisches Museum der Stadt Wien (134, 137abc, 138, 139ab, 143b, 191ab, 196c, 201ab, 210a, 216a, 226bc, 227e, 228b, 229ad, 258ac, 272b, 277a);

Hungarian National Gallery, Budapest – Schiller/Journeyman (28c); Internationale Gustav Mahler Gesellschaft, Vienna (274b); Kunsthalle, Kiel (199b); Kunstmuseum, Basel – Hinz (147a); Ferenc Liszt Academy of Music, Budapest – Schiller/Journeyman (22, 24c); Musée des Arts Décoratifs, Paris – Sully-Jaulmes (132a); Musée Carnavalet, Paris (27b, 31a); Musée du Jeu de Paume, Paris (6); Musée du Louvre (34a, 114, 115b, 131b); Museo Teatrale alla Scala, Milan (154); Museu d'Art Modern, Barcelona (11b); Museum of Art, Carnegie Institute, Pittsburgh, Pa., Museum Purchase 1896 (131a); Museum of Czech Music, Prague – Olga Hilmerová (148bc, 230, 232a, 234abc, 236ab, 237, 238, 239a, 240ab, 241, 243a, 244abc, 245, 246, 248a, 249ab, 252ab, 253ab, 254, 257a); Museum of Fine Arts, Budapest – Szelényi/Journeyman (35c); Museum für Geschichte, Dresden (160a); Museum für Geschichte der Stadt Hamburg (186a); Museum für Geschichte der Stadt Leipzig (159b, 268a); Nasjonalgalleriet, Oslo (106b, 108d, 271b); Nationalgalerie, Berlin (West) – Anders (30a, 202); National Gallery, Prague (149, 233, 235, 242, 250a, 251a, 255ab); Nationalmuseet, Stockholm (107e); Neue Pinakothek, Munich – Blauel (© Galerie Welz, Salzburg – Artothek) (266a); New York Public Library (281ab); Oesterreichische Galerie – Otto (142, 146 – © Galerie Welz, 223b, 270); Oesterreichische

Nationalbibliothek – Musiksammlung (210d, 216b, 218b, 221b, 224b, 276c, 284c, 292a); – Theatersammlung (271a, 274a); Pinacoteca, Bologna (35b); Prins Eugens Waldemarsudde, Stockholm (107a); Max Reger Institut, Bonn (150b); Royal College of Music (40, 41a); Sagrestia Nuova, Florence (39b); San Marco, Florence (39a); Schiller Nationalmuseum, Marbach (258b); Schönheitengalerie, Schloss Nymphenburg (30c); Staatliche Graphische Sammlung, Munich – Deutsche Fotothek (157c); Staats- und Universitätsbibliothek Carl von Ossietzky Brahms Archiv, Hamburg (182, 184, 194b, 196b, 208, 209a, 211c); Stadtarchiv, Munich (276a, 284a); Stadtmuseum, Linz (214); Städtische Galerie im Lenbachhaus, Munich (290); Statens Museum for Kunst, Copenhagen – Hans Petersen (106d); Stiftung Pommern, Kiel (198); Theatermuseum der Universität Köln (291a); Tretyakov Gallery, Moscow (82); Victoria and Albert Museum (218c); Richard Wagner Museum, Bayreuth (27a, 30b, 33, 158a, 160b, 162ab, 163, 164c, 169bc, 170b, 171a, 174, 175, 176, 177b, 180a); Wallfahrtskirche St Leonhard, Siegertsbrunn – Hansmann, 219a; Wiener Philharmoniker (141, 143a); Wiener Staatsoper – Vodicka (262); Wiener Stadt- und Landesbibliothek (206b, 227c, 275); Zentralbibliothek, Zürich (203a); Erich Auerbach (301); Willy von Beckerath Erben, Munich (© 1984) (203b); Prof. Rudolf

Hartmann, Munich (278, 303b); Kurt Hofmann, Hamburg (185abc, 192bc, 193, 196a, 197abc, 205a); Dr Dietrich Mack (164b); André Meyer, Paris (293b); Christian Nebehay, Vienna (222b, 226a); Christopher Raeburn, London (145c); Georg Schäfer, Schweinfurt (167); Frau Alice Strauss, Garmisch-Partenkirchen (280bc, 282ac, 288, 289b, 297ab); Private collection, New York – Otto (147b); Private collection, Switzerland (302); Fine Art Society, London (130); Fischer Fine Art, London (295); Marlborough Fine Art, London (© Cosmopress, Geneva) (303a); Galerie Welz, Salzburg (211a, 298); Agence Presse Novosti (14a, 16a, 17ab, 42, 44a, 48a, 49ab, 53b, 54b, 56b, 59, 60ab, 61ac, 66, 68b, 71b, 73a, 74a, 77ab, 81a, 83b, 85a, 86a, 88, 89bc, 90, 100a); Archiv für Kunst und Geschichte (140abc, 158b, 189a, 209b, 232b, 239b, 248b, 250b, 251c, 256, 257b, 284b); BBC Radio Times Hulton Picture Library (177a); Bildarchiv der Oesterreichischen Nationalbibliothek (37b, 140d, 144, 145a, 148a, 150a, 152ab, 153b, 192a, 200b, 207a, 210bc, 212abc, 217, 220, 221a, 225ab, 228d, 229b, 260d, 261fg, 264, 265b, 268b, 269, 272a, 273bc, 276b, 280a, 292b, 296b); Bildarchiv preussischer Kulturbesitz (188b); Costa (179d); Werner Forman (136, 200a); Giraudon (27b); – CFL (6); – Lauros (8b, 11a, 18a, 118a, 119, 131b, 186b); *Grove's Dictionary of Music and*

Musicians (229e, 293c); Robert Harding Picture Library (166); Illustrat on – Sygma (9c, 45b, 65b, 80a, 112ac, 116, 121a, 128c, 129); Istituto Geografico de Agostini (50b); Elsa Landon (190b, 222b); Mansell Collection (171b); Federico Arborio Mella (180ef); Rainsville Archive (10a, 14b, 15ab, 16b, 18b, 19ab, 20a, 21b, 44b, 45a, 46b, 47ab, 48b, 50a, 51, 52abc, 53a, 54a, 55ab, 57abc, 58ab, 61b, 62a-d, 63a-f, 64a-f, 65ac-f, 68a, 69ab, 70, 71a, 72ab, 73b, 74bc, 75, 81b, 83a, 84b, 85b, 86b, 87ab, 89a, 92, 93abc, 94ab, 95, 96, 97abc, 98ab, 100b, 101abc, 102c, 103a, 104ab, 105abc, 107d, 108abcefg, 109ac-f, 117b, 145b, 153c, 156, 159b, 161b, 164a, 165, 169a, 178ab, 179a, 180bc, 181bcd, 188a, 189b, 211e, 212de, 213a-e, 224a, 227bd, 228ace, 229cf, 255c, 259cdf, 260abce, 261abce, 273a, 293a); Scala (35b, 38c, 39ab, 154, 259e, 266b); Sousse Ohana (20b, 56a, 77c, 80b, 110, 113, 115a, 161a); Süddeutscher Verlag (300); Hans Tasiemka Archive (211bd, 261c); Ullstein Bilderdienst (289a); Roger Viollet (78, 172a, 173a, 180d, 277b); – Harlingue (117a, 120b); Joseph P. Ziolo (82, 162c, 170a, 293b); – Tréla (127a); Robert Bory, *La Vie de Franz Liszt par l'image*, courtesy of *Journal de Genève*, photo Bodleian Library, Oxford (24ab, 25ab, 28b, 31b, 32abc, 35a, 36, 41b).